WASHITA MEMORIES

WASHITA MEMORIES

Eyewitness Views of Custer's Attack
on Black Kettle's Village

compiled and edited by
RICHARD G. HARDORFF

UNIVERSITY OF OKLAHOMA PRESS
Norman

Also by Richard G. Hardorff

The Custer Battle Casualties: Burials, Exhumations, and Reinterments (El Segundo, Calif., 1989)

(comp. and ed.) *Lakota Recollections of the Custer Fight: New Sources of Indian–Military History* (Spokane, Wash., 1991; Lincoln, Nebr., 1997)

Hokahey! A Good Day to Die!: The Indian Casualties of the Custer Fight (Spokane, Wash., 1993; Lincoln, Nebr., 1999)

(comp. and ed.) *Cheyenne Memories of the Custer Fight: A Source Book* (Spokane, Wash., 1995; Lincoln, Nebr., 1998)

(comp. and ed.) *Camp, Custer, and the Little Bighorn: A Collection of Walter Mason Camp's Research Papers on General George A. Custer's Last Fight* (El Segundo, Calif., 1997)

(comp. and ed.) *The Surrender and Death of Crazy Horse: A Source Book about a Tragic Episode in Lakota History* (Spokane, Wash., 1998; Lincoln, Nebr., 2001)

The Custer Battle Casualties, II: The Dead, the Missing, and a Few Survivors (El Segundo, Calif., 1999)

(comp. and ed.) *On the Little Bighorn with Walter Camp: A Collection of W. M. Camp's Letters, Notes, and Opinions on Custer's Last Fight* (El Segundo, Calif., 2002)

(annotated) *Walter M. Camp's Little Bighorn Rosters* (Spokane, Wash., c. 2002)

(comp. and ed.) *Indian Views of the Custer Fight: A Source Book* (Spokane, Wash., 2004; Norman, Okla., 2005)

Library of Congress Cataloging-in-Publication Data

Hardorff, Richard G.
    Washita memories : eyewitness views of Custer's attack on Black Kettle's village / compiled and edited by Richard G. Hardorff.
        p.   cm.
    Includes bibliographical references and index.
    ISBN 0–8061–3759–2 (alk. paper)
    1. Washita Campaign, 1868–1869—Sources.   2. Washita Campaign, 1868–1869—Personal narratives.   3. Custer, George Armstrong, 1839–1876—Sources.   4. Black Kettle, Cheyenne chief, d. 1868—Sources.   I. Title.

E83.869.H37 2006
973.8'1—dc22

                                                                        2006044559

The paper in this book meets the guidelines for permanence and durability of the Committee on Production Guidelines for Book Longevity of the Council on Library Resources. ∞

1 2 3 4 5 6 7 8 9 10

To CASEY
with endearing memories

Contents

List of Maps xi

Preface and Acknowledgments xiii

Introduction 3

1. Indian Depredations in the Department of the Missouri,
   August 10–November 27, 1868 32

2. Clara Blinn, Civilian Captive 41

3. Little Rock, Cheyenne 44

4. Edmund Guerrier, Civilian 50

5. Black Kettle, Cheyenne 54

6. George A. Custer, Seventh Cavalry 58
   Official Report, November 28, 1868 60
   Official Report, December 22, 1868 66
   Letter to K. C. Barker, May 26, 1869 80
   Extract from *My Life on the Plains* (1874) 82

7. Albert Barnitz, Seventh Cavalry 96
   Letter to Jennie Barnitz, December 5, 1868 98
   Lt. Edward S. Godfrey to Jennie Barnitz,
       Letter Extracts 102
   Extract of Journal, November 23–27, 1868 106
   Extract of Narrative Account, 1889 112
   Interview by and Correspondence with
       Walter M. Camp, 1910 116
   Letter to Joseph Thoburn, November 28, 1910 124

8. Edward S. Godfrey, Seventh Cavalry 129
   Interview and Notes by Walter M. Camp, 1917 130
   Extract of Narrative Account, 1928 132
   Excerpt of Critique on Homer Wheeler, *Buffalo Days*, 1926   147
   Letter to Elizabeth B. Custer, December 15, 1918 149

9. Francis M. Gibson, Seventh Cavalry 151

10. Charles Brewster, Seventh Cavalry 157

11. James M. Bell, Seventh Cavalry 162
    Interview by Walter M. Camp, ca. 1910 163
    Correspondence with Walter M. Camp, 1911 167

12. Anonymous Correspondent, *New York Daily Tribune* 171

13. Frederick W. Benteen, Seventh Cavalry 174

14. Winfield Scott Harvey, Seventh Cavalry 180

15. Dennis Lynch, Seventh Cavalry 184

16. John Ryan, Seventh Cavalry 189

17. J. C. Pickens, Seventh Cavalry 199

18. Ben Clark, Seventh Cavalry 202
    New York Sun Interview, May 14, 1899 204
    Kansas City Star Interview, December 4, 1904 215
    Revision of *Star* Interview, October 22, 1910 221
    Interview and Field Notes by Walter M. Camp,
       October 22, 1910 224
    Letter to Frederick S. Barde, May 1, 1903 235

19. DeB. Randolph Keim, *New York Herald* 237
    Extract of Dispatch, December 1, 1868 237
    Extract of Dispatch, December 4, 1868 249
    Extract of Dispatch, December 6, 1868 253
    Extract of Dispatch, December 11, 1868 255

20. Milton Stewart, Nineteenth Kansas Cavalry 264

21. Henry E. Alvord, Tenth Cavalry 267

22. Thomas Murphy, Bureau of Indian Affairs 270

23. Philip H. Sheridan, Department of the Missouri 274
    Official Report, December 3, 1868 275
    Official Report, December 19, 1868 278
    Official Report, January 1, 1869 281

24. James S. Morrison, Agency Employee 282

25. Benjamin H. Grierson, Tenth Cavalry 285

26. William B. Hazen, Southern Indian Military District 288

27. Hugh L. Scott, Seventh Cavalry 291
    Letter to Walter M. Camp, December 4, 1910 292
    Interview Notes by Walter M. Camp, undated 294

28. Homer Heap of Birds, Cheyenne 295

29. Magpie, Cheyenne 301

30. Judson Cunningham, Roger Mills County Recorder 312

31. Stacy Riggs, Cheyenne 317
    Account of Black Kettle's Daughter, as Told to Her Son,
      Stacy Riggs, November 18, 1936 318
    Extract of Letter to *Cheyenne Star,* July 1934 320

32. Moving Behind Woman, Cheyenne 323

33. John L. Sipes Jr., Cheyenne 329

34. Mrs. B. K. Young Bird, Cheyenne 332

35. Mrs. Lone Wolf, Cheyenne 335

36. Red Bird Black, Cheyenne 338

37. George W. Yates, Seventh Cavalry 339

38. Wolf Belly Woman, Cheyenne 341

39. Sarah C. Brooks, White Captive 343

40. Trails the Enemy, Kiowa 345

41. Philip McCusker, Interpreter 349

42. George Bent, Interpreter 353
    Letter to Robert Peck, December 1906 356
    Letter to George Hyde, September 1905 361
    Letters to Joseph B. Thoburn, December 27, 1911, and
      January 9, 1912 365

43. Vincent Colyer, Special Indian Commissioner 367

Appendixes
    A. Military Records of Seventh Cavalry Officers 373
    B. Squadron Formations at the Washita 383
    C. Roster of the Sharpshooters 387

D. Roster of the Band 389
E. Roster of the Osage Scouts 391
F. Cavalry Casualties 393
G. Indian Casualties 397
H. Exhumations and Reburials of Indian Remains 405
I. Genealogical Outline of Black Kettle 427

Bibliography 433

Index 459

Maps

Routes of Seventh Cavalry during the Winter Campaign 62

Route of Seventh Cavalry from Fort Hays to Washita River . . . 83

Route of Elliott's Squadron, drawn by Albert Barnitz 105

Route of the Ambulance Train, drawn by James M. Bell 169

Historical Locations on the Washita Battlefield,
    drawn by Fred S. Barde 216

Washita Battlefield Landmarks, identified by Ben Clark 232

Washita Course in Northwest Corner of Battlefield,
    drawn by Dale Wesner 298

Location of Black Kettle's Village, drawn by Frank Rush 304

Washita Battlefield, drawn by Joseph G. Masters 313

Washita Artifact Locations, after four maps
    drawn by Jim Bruton 409

Washita Battlefield Surveys
    by the Oklahoma Historical Society 418

Summary Map of Artifact Discoveries
    on the Washita Battlefield 420

Preface and Acknowledgments

During the latter half of the nineteenth century, the Cheyenne Indians made a desperate attempt to preserve their buffalo culture from the advance of white civilization. This confrontation resulted in the subjugation of the Cheyennes, who suffered numerous calamities afterward. Their decline commenced in 1830 with the capture and desecration of the Sacred Arrows by the Pawnees. In the following six decades, the power and independence of the Cheyennes were further eroded by cholera epidemics, genocide, the extermination of the buffalo, starvation, the eradication of their political system, and finally the loss of their lands.

This book is a documentary of perhaps the most tragic event during this long decline, the attack on Black Kettle's village in 1868. It presents the combat recollections of officers, soldiers, and scouts on the one hand, and Indian survivors on the other hand. The text also includes the impressions of individuals who visited the battlefield shortly afterward as well as the views of Indian Bureau employees.

The corpus of papers selected for this volume comes from a wide variety of sources and includes official reports, journals, letters, interviews, and newspaper accounts. Each document is preceded by an introduction and annotated with extensive footnotes. Although this proved to be a time-consuming exercise, the benefit derived from these annotations far outweighs any drawbacks. The contextual information adds dimension to the individuals and events mentioned in the documents, enriches the reader's understanding and appreciation of the recorded and oral evidence, and enhances the overall historiographic value of the resulting work.

This volume was made possible through the generous assistance of numerous individuals. The following have been particularly helpful and have earned my enduring gratitude:

John Ahouse, Doheny Memorial Library, University of Southern California, Los Angeles, for his help with the Hamlin Garland Collection.

Ron Barshinger and Cherie Hauptman, Sven Parson Library, Northern Illinois University, for their cheerful assistance with the seemingly endless stream of interlibrary-loan requests.

Steve Black, historian, and Craig Moore, education technician, Washita Battlefield National Historic Site, Cheyenne, Oklahoma, for providing information and various documents.

Mary Ann Blochowiak, editor, *Chronicles of Oklahoma*, for permission to reproduce several articles.

Alan Bogan, The Old Guard Museum, Fort Myer, Virginia, for his assistance with the John H. Page manuscripts.

Jim Bruton of Shamrock, Texas, for permission to publish his artifact maps of the Washita Battlefield and the surrounding land, surveyed by him during the late 1960s and early 1970s. Bruton is to be commended for his foresight to keep detailed maps of his artifact finds. The contextual information contained in his letters to me enhances the value of these survey maps.

Julie C. Cobb, reference assistant, Special Collections, Newberry Library, Chicago, Illinois, for assistance with the Grierson Papers.

Kitty Deernose, museum curator, Little Bighorn Battlefield National Monument, Crow Agency, Montana, for providing documents from the Walter Mason Camp Collection.

Karen Delaney Gifford, library assistant, University of Colorado, Boulder, for providing the George Hunt manuscript.

Dr. Don DeWitt, curator, and Tom Sommer, research assistant, University Libraries, University of Oklahoma, Norman, for their assistance with the Ben Clark and Richard Blinn Collections.

Barbara Dey, Colorado Historical Society, Denver, for her assistance with the George Bent letters.

Sarah Erwin, curator of archival collections, Gilcrease Museum, Tulsa, Oklahoma, for her assistance with the Lt. Heber M. Creel Papers.

Jerome A. Greene, Arvada, Colorado, for providing information from his letters of the Godfrey Collection.

Peter Harrison of Southampton, England, for sharing his extensive knowledge of Cheyenne genealogies.

Judith P. Justus, Perrysburg, Ohio, for providing information on the Blinn and Harrington families.

Bob Knecht, head, Library and Archives Division, Kansas State Historical Society, Topeka, for providing manuscripts and microfilms from several collections.

Bruce Liddic, Syracuse, New York, for the use of his extensive Custer Library and for his many contributions to this publication. Liddic is a well-known Custer authority and the author of a number of books and articles on the subject. Although his evaluation of Custer's conduct at the Washita is decidedly more generous than my own, his scholarly opinions provide a counterview that benefits this study.

Connie Massey, Fort Gibson National Cemetery, Fort Gibson, Oklahoma, and Karen Wagner, Muskogee, Oklahoma, for providing genealogical data on Maj. Joel H. Elliott.

George Miles, curator, Yale Collection of Western America, Beinecke Library, Yale University, New Haven, Connecticut, for his assistance with the Albert Barnitz Papers.

David W. Penney, chief curator, Native American Art, Detroit Institute of Arts, Michigan, for providing information on Little Rock's shield.

Rebecca M. Post, national historic landmark coordinator, National Park Service, Santa Fe, New Mexico, for providing documents from their files.

Bob Rea, sites supervisor, Fort Supply Historic Site, Fort Supply, Oklahoma, for sharing genealogical information from his Ben Clark manuscript.

Don Schwarck, South Lyon, Michigan, for sharing his extensive knowledge of the Burton Historical Collection at the Detroit Public Library.

Dr. Douglas Scott, Great Plains team leader, National Park Service, Midwest Archeological Center, Lincoln, Nebraska, for providing information about the Washita Battlefield surveys and for identifying battlefield artifacts.

Gary Scott, Cheyenne, Oklahoma, for providing information about Washita artifact locations and recoveries and for contacting numerous individuals in the Cheyenne area for historical information. Also, his wife, Jeanette, daughter of the late Betty Wesner, for making several DVDs of the Washita Battlefield landscape, the landmarks in the surrounding terrain, and Sheridan's campsite in the Washita Valley near the Big Bend.

Saundra Taylor, curator of manuscripts, Lilly Library, Indiana University, Bloomington, for providing information from the Walter Camp Manuscripts.

Judy Tracy, Larry Bradshaw, Billy Chalfant, and Sheriff Joe Hay, all of Cheyenne, Oklahoma, who contributed valuable information relevant to this study.

Robert Utley, Georgetown, Texas, for the loan of his microfilm of the Regimental Returns of the Seventh Cavalry and for providing copies of his collection of Barnitz letters and journals.

Kim Walters, head, Braun Research Library, Southwest Museum, Los Angeles, California, for her assistance with the George B. Grinnell diaries and notebooks.

William D. Welge, director; Dr. Mary Jane Warde, Indian historian; and Chad Williams, manuscripts archivist; all of the Archives Division, and also Edward Connie Shoemaker, director, Library Resources Division, Oklahoma Historical Society, Oklahoma City, for providing numerous documents.

Brad Westwood, manuscript curator, Special Collections and Manuscripts, Harold B. Lee Library, Provo, Utah, for his assistance with the Walter M. Camp Collection and the Camp Manuscript.

Janet Whitson, curator, Detroit Public Library, and Don Schwarck for providing documents from the Burton Historical Collection.

I would like to pay special tribute to the late Betty Wesner, widow of Dale Wesner. Mrs. Wesner owned the land of the Washita Battlefield and wanted to preserve the historic ground for future generations. Her vision became a reality in 1997, when the National Park Service purchased the land. Mrs. Wesner's knowledge of the Washita action and its postbattle history is evident in her voluminous correspondence with me. Her enthusiasm for my research was spontaneous, and she participated with unlimited energy. Thriving in her capacity as a fellow researcher, she exhibited a rare ability to discover little-known facts. She would not quit until she got the answer to a question, even if it meant tramping across the battlefield to check topographical details despite her advanced age. She knew everybody in Cheyenne and the surrounding area and had gained the respect of all, including the council members of the Cheyenne Nation. Betty Wesner died suddenly on January 21, 2003. I am deeply indebted to her for her many contributions to this volume.

WASHITA MEMORIES

Introduction

This brief outline chronicles the subjugation of the Southern Cheyennes during the turbulent years between 1820 and 1868.

The Decline of an Indian Nation

By 1820 small groups of Cheyennes had ventured into the country south of the Platte River. They were motivated by intermittent warfare with hostile nations, the migration of friendly neighboring tribes, and their determination to maintain their role as middlemen in intertribal trade. Other factors also came into play, such as easier access to the large herds of wild horses near the Arkansas River and the presence of an abundant food supply. Occasionally, Cheyenne parties traveled as far south as the Red River to raid the large pony herds of the Kiowas and Comanches.

In 1832 the Hair Rope band of Cheyennes visited the stockade of Charles Bent at the Arkansas near present Pueblo, Colorado. Yet it was too far west for them to engage in regular trade. The Indians proposed that they would winter along the Arkansas and trade their robes with Bent if he established a new trading post farther east near the buffalo range.

Bent's new fort was built in 1833 on the north bank of the Arkansas about fifteen miles above the mouth of the Purgatory River. The adobe structure was completed in 1834 by Mexican masons from Taos, who also brought smallpox to the region. That same year several Cheyenne and Arapaho bands moved down from the South Platte and wintered at the Big Timbers, thirty-five miles below the fort. As a result of this migration, the Cheyenne and Arapaho tribes each separated into a northern and a southern division.

The events of the next decade had little effect on the Indians living in the country between the Platte and Arkansas rivers. This Cheyenne and Arapaho country lay between the great overland trails, off the beaten track and thus sheltered for a while from contact with whites and their vices, and was bordered on the west by a formidable mountain range that imposed severe obstacles to those wishing to cross the continent. Nonetheless, in 1845 whites brought measles and whooping cough to the Platte Valley trails. These epidemics swept through the Indian camps on the central plains with disastrous results.

After the Mexican War of 1846–48, the U.S. government took measures to protect the Santa Fe Trail by establishing several forts along the Arkansas. This was followed by the Mormon exodus to Utah in 1847 and the discovery of gold in California in 1849. The now-endless stream of immigrants on the overland trails brought cholera to the southern plains. Conservative estimates suggest that nearly half of the Cheyenne population perished during the ensuing epidemic; one of the victims was William Bent's wife. With the Indian trade in decline, Bent offered his adobe fort for sale to the government for use as a military installation. Unable to obtain a satisfactory price, though, he blew up his fort in August 1849 and moved his stores farther down the Arkansas. Bent relocated near the Big Timbers, where he built a stone fort on the north bank. He leased this compound to the United States in 1860. Originally named Fort Wise, it became Fort Lyon in 1861.

In 1851 the United States established the boundaries of the Southern Cheyenne and Arapaho lands in the Treaty of Fort Laramie. The assigned reserve lay roughly between the North Platte and Arkansas rivers, bordered on the west by the Rocky Mountains and on the east by the Santa Fe Trail crossing of the Arkansas. The Indians accepted this treaty in consideration of annuities. They pledged to remain at peace, to permit immigration along the trails, and to stay within the boundaries of their land. The Indians recognized this treaty despite the Senate's ratification that reduced the annuity term from fifty years to fifteen.

For nearly ten years after the Fort Laramie Treaty, the Cheyennes and Arapahos refrained from hostilities against settlers and immigrants. But occasional clashes between the Indians and the army did take place. In April 1856 troops plundered and burned a Cheyenne village after the occupants refused to give up a stray horse. That same year six Cheyennes were killed in Nebraska without apparent provocation. In retaliation the Cheyennes and Arapahos made several forays on the overland trails.

In 1857 an expedition was organized to chastise the Cheyennes for past depredations committed along the Platte and Arkansas. In July Col. Edwin V. Sumner attacked and defeated the Indians at the Solomon Fork in Kansas. After burning their village, he confiscated their annuities stored at Bent's Fort. The expedition was abandoned upon the outbreak of the Mormon War. During the same year, a small party of Missouri gold seekers discovered gold in the Pike's Peak region of Colorado. Harassed by Indians, the Missourians left the mountains and retuned to the States to organize a large party of miners.

The news of the gold discovery spread like wildfire in 1858 and threw the frontier into wild excitement. Denver City was born in the same year, and in the following spring and summer, as many as one hundred thousand whites crossed the plains for the foothills of Colorado. Several great gold discoveries were made, the richest being on the placers along Cherry Creek near Denver. Against the protestations of the Indians, the whites founded cities, established farms, and opened roads in the Indian lands—all in clear violation of the treaty articles. No real attempt was made by the United States to enforce the agreement. Within a few months the settlers began to demand protection against the Indians, who now found themselves the objects of jealousy and hatred.

In February 1861 the Territory of Colorado was established, and the Cheyennes and Arapahos were induced to sign a treaty at Fort Wise, formerly Bent's Old Fort. The Indians surrendered their rights to most of the lands reserved for them by the Fort Laramie Treaty, including the eastern half of Colorado, a large part of western Kansas, and parts of Nebraska and Wyoming. The new reservation assigned to them consisted of a triangular tract of land bounded on the east and northeast by Sand Creek, Colorado; on the south by the Arkansas and Purgatory rivers; and on the west by a line stretching some ninety miles from the junction of Sand Creek and the Arkansas. The reservation was closed to all white people except government employees and authorized traders. In compensation for this huge cession of land, the United States agreed to pay the sum of thirty thousand dollars annually for the next fifteen years.

Congress passed two pieces of legislation in 1862 that would have drastic consequences for the buffalo country and the nomadic cultures of the Indian tribes. The first was the Homestead Act of 1862, which granted plots of 160 acres to immigrants who settled on the frontier. The second was the Pacific Railroad Act. This law provided additional incentives for westward migration by connecting settlers to market centers. This federal legislation, combined with the efforts of state governments and private land companies, brought into Kansas thousands of settlers, who filed claims on 6 million acres during the rest of the 1860s.

In April 1864 Colorado volunteers attacked a small Cheyenne party at the South Platte. A month later Lt. George S. Eayre shot and killed a prominent Cheyenne chief named Lean Bear without provocation. Being a militia officer, Eayre was under orders of the Colorado authorities "to kill all Indians he came across." That same year a regular-army officer warned Washington that the rogue actions of the Colorado volunteers would lead to an expensive Indian war. The wisdom of this statement was confirmed by the events that followed. In retaliation for the unprovoked aggression, the Cheyennes and Arapahos killed small parties of whites traveling on the overland trails and burned stage stations and isolated farms.

The prospect of an Indian war panicked the population of Denver. After appealing to Washington for help, Gov. John Evans received permission to raise a one-hundred-day regiment of volunteers for home defense. That August some of the Indian leaders made peace overtures and came to Denver for a council with Evans, who refused to come to terms with them. Instead, the governor advised the Indians to surrender to the soldiers, which they did, erecting their lodges at Sand Creek, not far from Fort Lyon. Evans, a former ex-officio superintendent of Colorado Indian Affairs whose duty required him to receive and encourage any and all peace overtures made by Indians, was later severely rebuked by the Indian Bureau for his uncompromising stand.

If Evans had made peace at this time, the War Department might have criticized him for overreacting to the Indian situation and for wasting federal money. Rather than preventing a general Indian war, the governor adhered to his decision that the Third Colorado Regiment was "raised to kill Indians, and they must kill Indians." This policy of genocide was executed at dawn of November 29, 1864, when Col. John M. Chivington and some 900 troops attacked the peaceful Sand Creek village and butchered some 150 men, women, and children. In retaliation for the Sand Creek Massacre, the frontier was set ablaze by the Indians.

In October 1865 the United States held a peace conference with the Indian tribes at the mouth of the Little Arkansas. Only eighty lodges of Cheyennes attended. The terms agreed upon by the Cheyennes and Arapahos specified that they surrender their rights to the reserve at Sand Creek for a new reservation in Kansas and Indian Territory. But the Indians were not to settle upon this new land until the United States had extinguished the titles of the nations who then resided there. This treaty was later ratified by the Senate with the amended clause that "no part of the reservation shall be within the state of Kansas." In effect, the Cheyennes and Arapahos surrendered ownership to all the lands between the Platte River and the southern line of Kansas, though they retained hunting rights in this region.

During the fall of 1866, Lt. Gen. William Sherman, commander of the Military Division of the Missouri, visited Kansas and Colorado during an inspection tour of the western forts. The only troubles he encountered during his travels were steeped in rumors and innuendos. Referring to these, Sherman stated that these were all very mysterious and could only be explained on the supposition that "our people out West are resolved on trouble for the sake of profit resulting from the military occupation."

Indian hostilities on the Kansas frontier erupted again in 1867. That April Maj. Gen. Winfield S. Hancock led an expedition down the Smoky Hill River to impress the Indians with a show of force. Hancock seemed ignorant of Indian matters and proved inept at commanding such an expedition, his belligerent attitude immediately alarming the Indians. Fearing another massacre, the Cheyennes and their allies fled their village at the Pawnee Fork, which was promptly burned by Hancock. In retaliation for this unprovoked act, the Indians attacked the Smoky Hill Road. By this time, engineers had advanced the Kansas Pacific Railroad westward into the Cheyenne buffalo range. The Indians immediately began a series of depredations all along the line, which halted further construction and disrupted all travel for a period of four months.

In October the United States induced the Indians to sign a new accord, the Medicine Lodge Treaty. The agreement set aside two reserves for the Indians. The first lay north of Nebraska, where the Sioux were later relocated. The second lay south of the Arkansas and was known as Indian Territory. This southern reserve was the old lands of the "Five Civilized Tribes," which had been taken from them in 1866 for siding with the Confederacy. By acceptance of this treaty, the Cheyennes and Arapahos were now confined to a small reservation of barren land and brackish water between the Cimarron River and southern border of Kansas.

A war party of Cheyennes raided a Kaw village in southeastern Kansas in June 1868 in retaliation for the death of five Cheyennes slain the previous year. Neither side sustained any casualties, but the incident caused a great deal of excitement among the settlers. The Cheyennes were charged with depredations by the Indian Department, which immediately banned the scheduled issue of arms and ammunition at Fort Larned. This decision was reversed on August 9, unbeknown to a band of militant Cheyennes and Arapahos that slashed through the Saline and Solomon settlements a few days later. In September Kiowas and Comanches attacked Fort Dodge and destroyed a wagon train on the Santa Fe Trail. Farther north, the Cheyennes and Arapahos conducted a number of forays along the Smoky Hill Road and disrupted travel once again.

As a result of the hostilities of 1868, U.S. peace commissioners recommended that the management of the Indians be transferred to the War Department for military action. Maj. Gen. Philip H. Sheridan, the new commander of the Department of the Missouri, planned the subsequent campaign. His policy embraced a concentration of peaceful bands south of the Arkansas and a relentless war against all others. In September Brig. Gen. Alfred Sully was ordered to invade the region south of the Arkansas to engage the hostiles. At the same time, Maj. George A. Forsyth and a party of fifty frontiersmen were to take the field in the western part of Kansas. Neither operation turned out to be successful. Sully conducted his slow-moving expedition from the comfortable seat of an ambulance and was nearly trapped by the Indians at the Canadian River. Forsyth's force was besieged on a small island in the dry bed of the Arikaree Fork and barely escaped annihilation.

In October 1868 Sheridan received approval from the War Department to commence a winter campaign. This offensive called for the concerted operation of three separate columns. One from Fort Bascom, New Mexico, was to descend the Canadian River. The second was to march southeast from Fort Lyon toward the North Canadian. Sheridan's main force was to strike south into Indian Territory from Camp Supply. This third column consisted of army regulars of the Seventh Cavalry and a regiment of volunteers, the Nineteenth Kansas, which was mustered at Topeka and led by former governor Samuel J. Crawford.

Sheridan's strategy was to force the Indians back to their reservations and expose their vulnerability to winter attacks on their villages. The main strike was to be launched from Camp Supply, Lt. Col. George A. Custer leading the Seventh Cavalry and the Nineteenth Kansas. But deep snows and unreliable scouts delayed the arrival of the Kansans. Consequently, Sheridan decided to commence the expedition without the volunteers. Thus, the stage was set for the brutal confrontation at the Washita.

The Destruction of Black Kettle's Village

On November 23, 1868, the Seventh Cavalry left Camp Supply and marched south about fourteen miles in a blinding snowstorm. The men bivouacked in a clump of fallen timbers along Wolf Creek, just north of the present town of Fargo in Ellis County. During the night, the snow continued, soon changing over to sleet and rain. The enlisted men slept in wet clothes on frozen ground that was covered with eighteen inches of snow.[1]

---

[1]Shirk 1959.

The weather cleared the next morning, and the regiment resumed the march toward the southwest. After proceeding sixteen miles, the troops camped in a wooded section along Willow Creek, a few miles east of the present town of Shattuck. During the morning, Custer and his scouts killed a number of buffalos to supply the companies with fresh meat. A Cheyenne war party heard the echoing shots but attributed the gunfire to Cheyenne hunters.[2]

On the November 25 the regiment marched eighteen miles due south through very deep snow. Camp was made late that day in a grove of timber along Commission Creek, about a mile north of the Canadian. The Antelope Hills were plainly visible across the river, distinguished by five large buttes that rose nearly three hundred feet above the landscape.[3]

At dawn a detachment of three companies under Maj. Joel H. Elliott marched west up the Canadian to scout for Indian signs. The morning was excessively cold, and a dense fog shrouded the terrain. The troopers dismounted often and walked short distances to prevent their feet from freezing. Meanwhile, the balance of the regiment and the wagon train crossed the river to the south bank and halted on the flats east of the Antelope Hills.[4]

Three miles upriver Elliott's command discovered an abandoned night camp where Indians had sheltered during the blizzard a few days ago. One mile farther, near the Texas border, a fresh trail, made on the previous afternoon by a war party of some 150 Indians, crossed the Canadian and led southeast toward the Washita. After sending a dispatch to Custer, Elliott pressed on. In the afternoon a courier arrived from Custer with orders for the major to continue his pursuit; the regiment would follow immediately. Shortly after dark Elliott halted his exhausted squadron in a grove of trees along a tributary of the Washita. The balance of the Seventh Cavalry arrived about 9 P.M.[5]

Following a brief halt, the troops resumed the pursuit and struck the Washita about midnight. The regiment followed the

[2]Barnitz 1868a; Grinnell 1956.
[3]Godfrey 1928.
[4]G. A. Custer 1966.
[5]Barnitz 1868a; G. A. Custer 1966.

Indian trail to the east bank and forded numerous tributaries during the night. Several large travois trails leading from the north merged with the warrior trail. Some distance farther down the river the scouts discovered a smoldering campfire in a grove of trees. This telltale evidence revealed that Indian herders had recently vacated the location and that a village was probably not far away.[6]

Shortly after 2 P.M., November 27, the regiment crossed a final tributary and followed the Indian trail to a high ridge over a horseshoe bend of the Washita. After cresting the ridge the scouts proceeded to a knoll some eight hundred yards east. From this location they discovered Black Kettle's village. The cries of an infant and the tinkling of a pony's bell confirmed the Osages' observation. Custer immediately halted his column, which was strung out on the trail. The wagon train, commanded by Lt. James M. Bell and escorted by Capt. Frederick W. Benteen's squadron, was still some two miles to the rear.[7]

The route of Custer's approach to the village can be traced on modern topographical maps with a reasonable degree of accuracy. (See map on p. 232) The travois trail left the Washita near the northwest corner of Section 2, Township 13, Range 24, Roger Mills County. The steep hill ascended by the regiment is situated in the northwest quarter of this section. The knoll from which the Osage scouts discovered the village rises a half-mile to the southeast on the base line of the northeast quarter. The foothills are part of a formation known as the Horseshoe Hills. From Osage Knoll, Custer's command turned south and followed the Indian trail down an easy slope to an ancient pony crossing. This ford crossed the Washita in Section 2 near the east section line, just outside the western boundary of the present Washita Battlefield National Historic Site. Pioneers who settled the land after 1892 identified this ford as Custer's Crossing.[8]

Custer next assembled the officers and formulated a plan for the attack. The regiment was divided into four squadrons, each being assigned a position around the perimeter of the village.

[6]Gibson 1907.
[7]G. A. Custer 1966; Bell [1910].
[8]Clark 1904, 1910b; A. Moore 1968.

Major Elliott was assigned the command of three companies, consisting of Captain Benteen's squadron of H and M Companies, and Capt. Albert Barnitz's G Company. From Osage Knoll, Elliott was to circle through the Horseshoe Hills past the village and occupy a position along the river, east of the encampment. His column moved out about 3 A.M. During this wide detour, Major Elliott and Captain Barnitz climbed a steep conical hill for observation. This height, now known as Barnitz Hill, rises near the center of Section 1, about a half-mile north of the Washita. Along the east line of this same section lays a steep ravine, which runs south from the highlands. This ravine was probably the "deep, narrow canyon" described by Barnitz through which the column descended to the river.[9]

The moon had now disappeared, limiting vision. Benteen's squadron was recalled from the rear and assigned to Elliott's column. So complete was the darkness that Benteen lost his orientation and did not join Elliott until just before dawn. Even the band, under Chief Trumpeter Albert Piedfort, had mistakenly followed Elliott's command but returned just in time to the main column, to which it had been assigned. Shortly before dawn Captain Barnitz crossed to the south bank of the Washita, dismounted his company, and deployed his men in skirmish order across a belt of woods, his right flank resting on the riverbank. His left flank consisted of ten mounted men known for their marksmanship. Benteen's squadron of H and M Companies occupied the north bank and deployed in mounted skirmish order. (These deployments took place near the east section line of the present Washita Battlefield Site.) The three companies of Elliott's command had marched nearly forty-five miles since dawn of November 26.[10]

Capt. William B. Thompson was assigned the second column, which consisted of B and F Companies. His squadron was to countermarch on the trail, recross the stream forded earlier by the regiment, and then turn south. After crossing the Washita, Thompson was to circle east behind the hills to occupy a position south of the village and cooperate with Elliott's column. Thomp-

---

[9]Barnitz 1868a.
[10]Barnitz 1889.

son's squadron moved out about 3 A.M. to make a circuitous march over difficult terrain.[11]

Capt. Edward Myers was given command of the third column, consisting of E and I Companies. Myers was to move his squadron directly south, cross the Washita, and take a position on the south bank. He was instructed to deploy one company, I, in dismounted skirmish order across the woods, while the other company, E, remained mounted on the right flank, outside the fringe of timber. Myers's column moved out one hour before dawn, about 5 A.M. The captain suffered from snow blindness and when his condition worsened after sunrise, he transferred command of E Company to his junior officer, 1st Lt. John M. Johnson.[12]

The main column was commanded by Custer personally and consisted of two squadrons. The left wing, A and D Companies, was commanded by Capt. Louis M. Hamilton. The right wing was commanded by Capt. Robert M. West and was comprised of C and K Companies. In addition to Custer's staff, the column also included a company of sharpshooters under Lt. William W. Cooke, Piedfort's musicians, and the white scouts and Indian guides. This force would follow the Indian trail from the foothills to the village. All columns were to occupy positions close to the encampment without alarming the inhabitants. The synchronized attack was to take place upon the first notes of "Garry Owen," a martial air played by the musicians at Custer's signal.[13]

On the morning of November 27, the air was frosty and biting cold. The moon had reappeared, its light intensified by the snow covering the ground. Landscape pockets and fringes of timber were eerily accentuated by blue shadows formed in the moonlight. Just before dawn the eastern sky was illuminated by the brilliance of a rising morning star. Custer named it "the Star of the Washita," believing that it announced a victory for him. Fog began settling over the valley floor.[14]

At the approach of dawn, Custer formed his column behind the crest of Osage Knoll. Captain West's squadron occupied the right

[11]G. A. Custer 1966; Barnitz 1868a.
[12]G. A. Custer 1966.
[13]Gibson 1907.
[14]G. A. Custer 1966; Clark 1899; Godfrey 1928.

of the line, while Captain Hamilton's squadron deployed on the left. Custer, his couriers, the Osage scouts, and the band occupied the center of the line. The sharpshooters formed in advance of the left flank and were instructed to deploy along the riverbank in dismounted skirmish order. The men of all five companies were ordered to remove their greatcoats and haversacks to achieve greater mobility. Each of the five companies detailed a trooper to guard the five piles of baggage, which were to be loaded on the wagons upon the arrival of Lieutenant Bell's train.[15]

After deployment, Custer's command moved over the crest and followed the Indian trail south toward the river. The distance to the timber was nearly a mile, farther than it appeared in the darkness. The men caught occasional glimpses of tepees, smoke plumes from smoldering fire pits sharply defined against the sky. The first rays of sunlight crept over the eastern hills, glistening off of the hoarfrost on the grass and the leafless trees. The eerie stillness of the morning air was suddenly broken by a single gunshot fired in the village. It was answered immediately by a trumpet signal and the rollicking strains of "Garry Owen." The notes echoed in the hills but ended in discord when the musicians' spittle froze in their instruments. Nevertheless, Custer's two squadrons charged toward the river at about 6:30 A.M.[16]

The Indian village was stretched out along the south bank of the river and covered a distance of a half-mile. Related families had grouped their tepees in small camps on the floodplain bordering the curving stream, the lodges erected at intervals for privacy and sanitary considerations. Black Kettle's camp stood on the west side of the village, a few hundred yards east of the pony crossing. Others were strung out downstream, including Little Rock's camp, whose lodges stood near the eastern perimeter of the village. The south bank of the graveled stream was low, while the north bank was bold and very steep. The streambed was perhaps fifteen feet wide, with a swift current and a knee-high water table. Sheets of ice had formed near the banks where the current was slower. A heavy belt of cottonwoods and oaks fringed both banks, but the north side of the river was a level bottomland with scat-

---

[15]Lynch 1909.
[16]G. A. Custer 1966.

tered timber. Farther back lay the tall-peaked sand hills that formed the outcroppings of the Horseshoe Hills. The floodplain south of the river terminated against a low terrace that rose to a steep wall in the eastern half of the battlefield.[17]

Custer's two squadrons approached the river over a wide front. Underbrush and fallen timbers and a precipitous north bank impeded their crossing. Custer and his staff crossed the stream at the pony ford, which the colonel's horse cleared in one jump. After the companies reformed on the south bank, the left wing under Captain Hamilton advanced through the thick timber toward the lodges bordering the stream. The right wing under Captain West charged over the wooded floodplain toward the south side of the village. The roundup of the pony herds was assigned to Lts. Edward S. Godfrey and Edward Law of K Company. Godfrey charged through the southernmost lodges without encountering any resistance. Custer and his staff ascended the terrace wall south of the village and established a command post on a small knoll overlooking the valley. It was now about 7 A.M.[18]

Black Kettle's camp bore the brunt of the attack. The inhabitants were caught in the crossfire from Hamilton's squadron and the sharpshooters posted on the north bank. The result was disastrous. Black Kettle was hit in his chest and back while urging his pony through the stream. His Ponca wife, seated behind him on the pony, was also hit. Black Kettle died in the icy waters. His wife, Medicine Woman Later, was shot down on the north bank. His second wife, Sioux Woman, was killed near the south bank by a bullet in the back. Nearby lay the mutilated remains of a pregnant woman and the unborn child that had been ripped from her womb. High Bank, a Sioux relative of Black Kettle, was also killed in the camp, along with his wife and one daughter. Cranky Man, also known as Bitter Man or Bad Man, was killed in front of his lodge while firing at Hamilton's soldiers. Most of the survivors of Black Kettle's camp fled downstream under cover of the high banks. Some ran west toward Plum Creek, while the rest fled to the hills south of the village.[19]

---

[17]Ibid.; Barnitz 1889; Magpie 1930; Lynch 1909.

[18]Godfrey 1928; G. A. Custer 1966; Clark 1904.

[19]Magpie 1930; Moving Behind Woman ca. 1937; Hyde 1968; Cometsevah 1999.

Below the village Elliott's companies began to move upstream just before dawn. Benteen's squadron of H and M Companies advanced mounted on the north bank. G Company under Barnitz moved out from its position on the south bank. During the advance, the dismounted skirmishers forded the tortuous stream a number of times. Day was breaking rapidly. Farther upstream the troops came across bunches of ponies feeding on bark and branches gathered in piles by herders. The appearance of the soldiers startled several Indian boys—night herders—who ran toward the camps. Barnitz's company pressed on and had just reached the edge of a shallow ravine when a gunshot rung out in the village. The sounds of "Garry Owen" and the distant cheers of soldiers followed. Benteen's squadron immediately charged upstream and crossed into the village shortly after 6:30 A.M. His squadron was the first to arrive. During the ensuing combat, Benteen killed Blue Horse, a relative of Black Kettle.[20]

At the start of the battle, Captain Barnitz halted his men on the east side of a shallow ravine. This swale carried the drainage from the hills to the south and contained numerous tree stumps. The slope on the west side of the swale was much higher, and in the distance Barnitz could see a cluster of tepees nestled among the trees. Upstream the air resounded with war whoops, yells, and the quick discharge of firearms. Dogs began barking frenziedly, and the cries of infants intermixed with the wailing of women. Refugees began to appear in front of Barnitz's company and were met by a sharp fire. Some of the Indians returned the shots from behind the tree stumps until they either were killed or escaped around the flanks of Barnitz's line.[21]

While waiting for the arrival of Thompson's squadron, Barnitz noticed a large group of Indians fleeing over the sand hills to the south. He immediately detailed Sergeant McDermott and a squad of ten mounted men to head off the refugees. The captain soon decided to accompany this detail to learn more about the whereabouts of Thompson's missing squadron. Somewhere in the sand hills near the eastern edge of the battlefield, Barnitz exchanged fire

---

[20]Barnitz 1889; Benteen 1896.
[21]Barnitz 1889, 1910b.

with one of the refugees and sustained a severe gunshot wound to the abdomen. He turned back toward the village, but after riding a few hundred yards, the pain became unbearable. He lay down behind some boulders on the crest of a hill and was found some time later by two soldiers from McDermott's detail. Indians began to appear but were driven off by the timely arrival of Captain Thompson's B Company at about 8 A.M.[22]

At dawn of November 27, only two columns—those of Custer and Elliott—had reached their positions in time to participate in the opening phase of the attack. The columns of Thompson and Myers arrived late and did not factor into the surprise assault. Leaving the regiment in the hills about 3 A.M., Thompson's squadron countermarched on the trail and crossed the stream at the point where the troops had forded earlier. The column then turned south and after a mile reached the Washita near the mouth of Broken Leg Creek, which enters the Washita from the south and has a level floodplain. Thompson's squadron quite likely ascended Broken Leg. After perhaps a mile the column turned east behind the hills to prevent detection. The line of march possibly followed the route of present Highway 47 for several miles, then turned north toward the village. Thompson's squadron arrived on the bluffs shortly after 7 A.M., too late to cooperate with Elliott's column but just in time to prevent the killing of Captain Barnitz.[23]

Myers's squadron moved out about 5 A.M. The two companies probably descended to the river through the ravine just west of Osage Knoll. The stream was reached in less than a mile, and after crossing to the south bank in the darkness, the men halted in the timber to await the arrival of dawn. Just before daylight, I Company under Lieutenant Brewster deployed on foot across the woods bordering the streambed; Myers and E Company deployed in mounted formation outside the timber on Brewster's right flank. The squadron moved out at dawn and had only advanced a short distance when the strains of "Garry Owen" signaled them to attack. Myers's mounted company responded immediately, galloping across the floodplain and across a small tributary named

---

[22]Barnitz 1868b, 1889, 1910b.
[23]Godfrey 1928; Gibson 1907; Barnitz 1910b.

Plum Creek. Instead of charging straight into the village, E Company veered to the right in hot pursuit of a group of fleeing women and children, who were shot down indiscriminately.[24]

This incident is not mentioned in any of the accounts by military personnel. We would never have known about it if not for the fact that it was mentioned many years later by Ben Clark, Custer's chief of scouts. Clark witnessed the shooting from a distance and asked the colonel whether it was his intention to kill women and children. Custer seemed offended by Clark's meddling, but after a short hesitation he ordered Captain Myers to hold his fire and bring in the survivors. According to Clark, the killing site was "on the high ground southeast of two buttes." This description seems to match the Twin Knolls in the south half of Section 12. These heights are located about three hundred yards due south of the former Betty Wesner residence along Highway 47A. Southeast of the Twin Knolls the land rises, and it is conjectured that Clark may have seen the refugees here. Somewhere nearby Myers's men captured a Mexican who was married to a Cheyenne woman. The man had tried to make his escape with his infant daughter when he was discovered in a ravine by the troops. The child was taken from him, and he was executed on the spot.[25]

Shortly after Elliott's column went into battle, the major left his troops and established a command post on a hill just east of Custer Knoll. Some time before 8 A.M., Elliott noticed a group of Indians fleeing through the woods north of the present town of Cheyenne. These refugees may have been the same Indians with whom Captain Barnitz had his near-fatal encounter. Determined to intercept them, Elliott and his orderlies, along with Sgt. Maj. Walter Kennedy, returned to his command and called for volunteers from Benteen's squadron. By this time Myers had arrived in the village, for five men of his squadron joined Elliott. As the detachment moved out, Elliott hollered to Lt. Owen Hale the prophetic words, "Here goes for a brevet or a coffin."[26]

Two miles below the village, Elliot and seventeen men caught up with a small group of refugees near a small horseshoe bend,

---

[24]G. A. Custer 1966; Barnitz 1868a; Clark 1910b, c.
[25]Clark 1899, 1904, 1910b, c; Magpie 1930.
[26]Clark 1899, 1904, 1910b, c; Godfrey 1928.

situated about a half-mile northwest of the site of Cheyenne. Its streambed is now dry, for the river carved a new channel across the base of the bend during a flood many years ago. In 1868, however, the current here was very swift and ran over a deep bottom that stretched the width of the streambed. A number of refugees had escaped from the village by jumping into the river. They waded downstream through the icy waters and escaped the bullets by staying close to the high banks. When they reached the horseshoe bend, elders alerted them to the danger of drowning, advising them to ascend the bank and run across the tongue of land formed by the curving stream.[27]

The group of Indians that emerged from the riverbed consisted of three warriors, twenty women, and a number of children. When Elliott's soldiers charged on these people, the warriors fought to cover the flight of the noncombatants. These brave men were known as Chief Little Rock and She Wolf, both Cheyennes, and Trails the Enemy, who was a Kiowa. They were armed with bow and arrows, while Little Rock also carried a muzzleloading rifle. During the ensuing skirmish, one of the cavalry horses was shot down by Little Rock, who himself was killed shortly afterward by a gunshot to the forehead. Little Rock's arrows were taken by Trails the Enemy, who with She Wolf, continued to fend off the soldiers. The women and children were able to reach the riverbed below the bend and were joined soon after by the two remaining warriors.[28]

Some distance below the horseshoe bend Elliott's detachment captured two women and several children who were exhausted from running. The women were sisters of Little Rock, one of them a seventeen-year-old girl named White Buffalo Woman, and the children may have been other relatives. Elliott decided to take these noncombatants back to the village as prisoners under guard of a single soldier whose horse had been killed earlier. After proceeding a short distance upstream, the man was jumped by a party of warriors on the west side of Sergeant Major Creek and killed. The rescued women and children were taken to the lower camps.[29]

---

[27]Bent [1906]; Grinnell 1956; Hyde 1968.
[28]Trails the Enemy n.d.; Bent [1906]; Hyde 1968.
[29]Bent [1906]; Grinnell 1956; Hyde 1968.

After the capture of White Buffalo Woman's party, Major Elliott decided to pursue other refugees farther downstream. After crossing Sergeant Major Creek, the detachment continued the pursuit until sighting a large force of warriors coming from the lower villages. The command left the bottomland and turned south toward the heights east of the present town of Cheyenne. Indians now swarmed over the hills farther east. Elliott retreated immediately toward Sergeant Major Creek, where Indians blocked his advance and encircled his command. Faced with wounded men and dying horses, Elliott prepared to make a stand in a grassy swell two hundred yards east of the creek at about 9 A.M. Here the small force was killed to the last man in about the same time it takes "to smoke a pipe four times."[30]

The capture of the pony herds was assigned to Lts. Edward S. Godfrey and Edward Law, who each commanded a platoon of K Company. Upon the signal to attack, Godfrey charged through the south side of the village without encountering any resistance. As his platoon reached the eastern perimeter of the encampment, the lieutenant noticed the arrival of Thompson's squadron on the ridge south of the village. He also caught a glimpse of Myers's "Grey Horse Company," which had come into view farther back. The sun had emerged as a fiery red ball over the eastern horizon. The time was now about 7 A.M.[31]

Near the river Godfrey's platoon came across two fleeing women. One of these was a daughter of Black Kettle. Although she raised her hands as a sign of surrender, Sgt. E. F. Clear shot her to death with his pistol before Godfrey could prevent it. Across the valley the lieutenant noticed other groups of Indians fleeing downstream. Continuing a mile below the village, the soldiers came across bunches of ponies scattered along the south bank. After rounding up the mounts, the platoon started back and was met by Lieutenant Law, who took the herd to the village. Godfrey, however, decided to pursue the Indians he had seen earlier.[32]

After returning to the last-known location of the refugees, Godfrey crossed his platoon to the north bank about 8 A.M. One

[30]Clark 1904; Keim 1869; Bent [1906]; Roman Nose Thunder 1913.
[31]Godfrey 1896, 1917.
[32]Godfrey 1896, 1917, 1928.

mile down the Washita, they discovered a large pony herd in a wooded draw. Instead of rounding up the animals, Godfrey continued after the refugees, who now were mounted. Two miles farther downstream the platoon came in sight of a funeral lodge. Shortly afterward they spotted two Indians in the hills, signaling the approach of the soldiers. A high ridge protruding across the floodplain blocked Godfrey's view of the valley beyond. Halting his platoon, he ascended the ridge and from the crest observed clusters of tepees stretched downstream as far as he could see. Warriors were coming up the valley to engage the soldiers. He immediately ordered his platoon to fall back over the high ground, skirmishing with the Indians most of the way. Sometime after 9 A.M., while halfway back to Black Kettle's village, Godfrey's command heard heavy firing on the opposite side of the stream, the sounds of Elliott's last stand, which died away an hour later.[33]

The village was secured only a few minutes after the attack had begun. A line of troopers soon extended across the valley and formed a ring around the site. While dashing among the lodges, the soldiers "shot everything" and trampled a number of children under the hooves of their excited horses. Many women and children had concealed themselves in their lodges. Custer's interpreter, Rafael Romero, assured them that they would not be harmed. The captives were placed in two large lodges near the center of the village and guarded by men from Benteen's squadron. Near the river the Indians continue to offer fierce resistance to protect their fleeing families. Eventually they were driven off by two platoons fighting dismounted in the timber on the south bank.[34]

While flowing through a sharp bend around the village, the Washita had cut deeply into the north bank during a spring freshet and caved in a section. This mass of dirt had fallen in the river, forming a wall with a cave behind it. The opening was shielded from view by the overhanging turf and tree roots. Seventeen men, women, and children had taken refuge behind this natural breastwork and hid from sight during the heaviest fighting.

---

[33]Godfrey 1917, 1928.
[34]Lynch 1909; Red Bird Black n.d.; *New York Daily Tribune* 1868; G. A. Custer 1966; Magpie 1930.

They were discovered during a lull in the battle but refused to surrender. Sharpshooters poured a hail of bullets into the cave, and the Indians' return fire eventually diminished and finally ceased altogether. In the end a woman arose from behind the breastwork, holding a light-skinned infant. In an act of despair the mother killed her child with a knife and then buried the blade into her own breast. After her death, a trooper needlessly fired a bullet into her head, blowing off part of her skull. The Cheyenne infant was identified as a white captive in Custer's report to further incriminate Black Kettle's people and to furnish justification for the brutal attack.[35]

During the early hours of November 27, Lieutenant Bell received orders to halt his train, which was then several miles in the rear of the troops. He was to advance at the first sound of firing and rejoin the regiment in the village. The train consisted of two wagons and four ambulances. Its cargo included three days of rations, forage, and medical supplies and twenty thousand rounds of Spencer ammunition, which Bell had brought along without authorization. The personnel with the train included the camp police, officers' orderlies, sick men, deserters, teamsters, and Mrs. Courtenay, who was Custer's cook. Because the rear-guard squadron had been reassigned to take part in the attack, Bell thought it prudent to advance his train at the first light of dawn. After following the trail for a half-mile, the train arrived at a tributary, where it crossed with great difficulty. The sudden sound of distant gunfire increased Bell's anxiety, and he hurried his wagons up the steep slope of a towering ridge. Reaching the crest, the train descended the eastern slope and arrived at Custer's deserted bivouac along the bottom of a wooded swale.[36]

Nearby Bell sighted a detail of five troopers with the greatcoats and haversacks of Custer's command. While loading the baggage, Indians began to appear on both flanks. Fearing capture of the ammunition, Bell abandoned half of the coats and sacks and ordered his teamsters to move out immediately. During the headlong rush for the village, the wagons bounced and slid down the

---

[35]Clark 1899, 1904, 1910c; G. A. Custer 1966.
[36]Bell [1910], 1911; Godfrey 1928.

frozen slope while taking fire from the Indians. The excessive friction ignited the tar in the wheel hubs, and by the time the wagons reached the river, the wheels were engulfed in flames. Miraculously, not one of Bell's men was wounded when they arrived in the village about 8 A.M. In 1975 Jim Bruton of Shamrock, Texas, discovered several buttons and a number of imbedded rounds from Spencer carbines and Indian weapons in the northwest quarter of Section 2. These artifacts provide mute evidence about the baggage site and the fire exchange that took place there between the Indians and Bell's troopers.[37]

While proceeding down the south bank of the Washita, Lieutenant Bell discovered a group of forty or fifty women and children fleeing upstream through the brush. He blocked their escape and returned the captives to the village. Earlier Captain Barnitz had prevented the escape of another large group of noncombatants east of the village, driving them back upstream. Barnitz recalled that forty-eight of these refugees were eventually captured and may have been the same group later confronted by Bell. Captain Myers also captured a number of noncombatants on the heights south of the village. If we add all of these to those captured in their lodges, the sum total of prisoners far exceeds the number of fifty-three reported by Custer.[38]

By 10 A.M. Lieutenant Godfrey entered the village with his second herd of captured ponies. He immediately reported to Custer and briefed him about the existence of a second village farther downstream. Mounted Indians began to appear on the ridges a mile east of the battlefield, near Elliott's last stand, which suggests that the major's fight had ended by then. Alarmed about the growing Indian presence, Custer again questioned Godfrey a short time later and pressed him for details. By now the lieutenant had learned that Major Elliott was missing. Recalling the heavy firing he had heard during his sortie, Godfrey suggested that Elliott might be engaged below the village. Custer already knew from Ben Clark that Elliott had gone downstream, but despite this accumulative

---

[37]Bell [1910], 1911; Gibson 1907; Bates 1936; J. Bruton to author, Sept. 29, Oct. 11, 2002.

[38]Bell [1910]; Barnitz 1889; Clark, 1910a; Custer 1868.

information, he rejected Godfrey's suggestion on the basis that Captain Myers had been fighting in that sector all morning and "probably would have reported it."The colonel did act, however, on Godfrey's intelligence regarding the lower villages and interrogated the captives, who confirmed the information.[39]

Indian resistance within the village had been silenced and only a few isolated pockets remained near its outskirts. Custer reformed his regiment to meet the anticipated threat posed by Indians arriving from the lower villages. The timber in the bottomland concealed the strength of his troops, and for a while the Indians hesitated to press the attack. In the meantime the pony herds were collected near the terrace wall inside the troop lines and a field hospital established in the center of the village. Military casualties had been light, consisting of two men killed and fifteen wounded, of whom two would die later. The fate of Elliott's men was not known then.[40]

Custer next ordered the burning of the village and its contents. This task was assigned to the squadron of Capt. Robert West. The lodges were pulled down and all property piled on top. Orders were issued to prohibit looting, though initially the men had been promised the spoils if they did not falter during the attack. The destruction began at Black Kettle's camp and continued downstream with each successive cluster of lodges. Huge bonfires sprang up all over the bottomland. The flames gave off an intense heat that burned underbrush and scorched trees. Ammunition and powder bags exploded in the fires, filling the air with their acid smell. Low clouds of choking black smoke began to settle over the valley, intermixed with the repugnant odor of burning flesh. The destruction of the village was completed about 2 P.M.[41]

While the village was burning, Indians began to mass in large numbers on the hills and slopes north of the battlefield as if to threaten an attack. Small parties of warriors began to test the strength of the troops and pressed their lines with spirit and audacity. The firing soon became general all around the village. To

---

[39]Godfrey 1926, 1928; G. A. Custer 1966.
[40]G. A. Custer 1966.
[41]Ibid.; Custer 1868; Benteen 1869; Clark 1899; Godfrey 1928.

meet this aggression on the north side of the river, Custer ordered Captains Weir and West to form their squadrons along the bank and charge the Indians. Acting in support of each other, the squadrons vigorously executed the maneuver and soon cleared their adversaries from the field.[42]

On the east side of the village, several hundred Indians began to press the advance pickets. To meet this threat, Benteen's squadron was ordered to deploy along the high ground. After the Indian charge was repulsed, Captain Myers's squadron was ordered to disperse the warriors. Myers, still bothered by snow blindness, was unable to fulfill his orders. Custer then directed Benteen to take command of Myers's squadron and execute the order. Benteen deployed the two companies in four platoons, with E Company in the lead, and was able to drive the Indians from the field in great confusion. When the recall was sounded, E Company had gained the ridge west of Sergeant Major Creek and was then within a mile of the kill site of Elliott's men.[43]

Although the Indians were cleared from the field near the village, they continued to reappear at unexpected times at different places. Some owned long-range rifles and were able to send bullets into the village from Barnitz Hill. Annoyed by this sniping, Custer placed the captured women and children in the line of Indian fire, which soon halted. The snipers then shifted west of the troop lines and took a position on a rise within firing range of the village. Lt. Matthew Berry with C Company was ordered to charge the position and subsequently drove off the Indians.[44]

The sounds of combat alarmed the pony herds, and at the outset of the battle, many bunches rushed into the village and were captured. Godfrey had taken two herds totaling some 400 ponies below the village. Captain Benteen and a scout named California Joe, assisted by three enlisted men and two captured women, brought in an additional herd of 300 animals. All were turned over to Captain West, who collected the mounts along the terrace wall. The estimated total was 875 ponies and mules. Since it was not

---

[42]Godfrey 1928; Clark 1904; G. A. Custer 1966.
[43]Ryan 1909; Benteen 1869, n.d.(b).
[44]G. A. Custer 1966; Clark 1910b.

feasible to drive the herd to Camp Supply, Custer decided to destroy the ponies to prevent their recapture by the Indians.[45]

Before the destruction began, however, the officers and the men selected some of the best animals for their own use; Custer himself selected four fine mules. Each of the officers was allowed two ponies, which were picked by their orderlies. Lieutenant Bell selected a number of mules for his wagon teams to replace those that either were worn out or had been killed. Some enlisted men with disabled horses also took ponies, as did the Osage scouts, who each selected a fine string. Lastly, the captured women were told to take two ponies for transportation, which were later given to the Osages as war booty. In all some 225 captured animals were taken to Camp supply. The remaining 650 ponies were to be destroyed.[46]

The unpleasant task of the slaughter was assigned to Captain West. His Company K received instructions to rope the animals and cut their throats. This method required considerable effort as the ponies resented the smell of white men. They became frantic at the approach of the soldiers and fought furiously before they could be subdued. It thus took too much time, and the men, splattered with blood, soon wearied from the physical struggle. Time became an important factor. Supplied with Bell's extra ammunition, Custer decided to shoot the animals and assigned F Company under Captain Yates to assist with the killing. One company took position along the terrace edge above the herd while the second company and the sharpshooters formed a ring around the ponies on the bottom below. Firing volley after volley, it took the troops nearly two hours to destroy the herd, which was completed by about 4 P.M.[47]

Not all of the ponies were killed outright. A number of wounded horses broke away and moaned loudly, sounding just like human beings. They kept running around, snorting and bleeding, until they finally weakened and collapsed from loss of

[45]G. A. Custer 1966, Benteen 1896.
[46]Clark 1899, 1910c; Ryan 1909; Barnitz 1868b.
[47]Godfrey 1928; G. A. Custer 1966; Bell [1910]; Ryan 1909; Benteen 1869; Clark 1899.

blood. They lay on the frozen ground, with eyes wide open in fear and their sides heaving, the steam of their breath clearly defined in the cold air. The killing ground was 150 yards from Custer Hill and covered four acres. The terrace wall and the snow-covered ground below was splattered and smeared with the animals' blood. Two weeks later returning troops found the frozen carcasses of these mortally wounded ponies. The signs on the ground showed that they had been unable to stand up and had eaten all the grass within reach before they died.[48]

During the slaughter of the herds, many Indians remained on the bluffs and continued to pose a threat to the troops. Custer decided to make a feint attack on the lower villages in the hope that this movement would clear the Indians from his front. About 4 P.M. the troops, with colors flying and the band playing, moved rapidly downstream, to the consternation of the Indians. The warriors immediately withdrew and hurried off to warn the lower villages. The regiment continued the advance for several miles after twilight, then countermarched on the trail under cover of darkness. Four days later the jubilant soldiers arrived at Camp Supply and were heralded for a glorious victory. At the Washita grieving Cheyennes tenderly sepulchered their dead on the now-hallowed ground along the stream.[49]

Almost immediately after Custer's return, rumors began to circulate that Major Elliott and his men had been abandoned. At the surface it does appear that Custer had displayed indifference to their fate. On the morning of November 27, Ben Clark told the colonel that Elliott had gone downstream. Not long thereafter Lieutenant Godfrey reported hearing heavy firing two miles below the village. It is hard to believe that Custer was unable (or unwilling) to put the proverbial "two and two" together. This was not the case with Godfrey, who had learned that Elliott was missing and concluded that the major was engaged downstream. Godfrey mentioned this to Custer, who rejected it on the basis that Myers's squadron was deployed east of the village and would have reported

[48]Moving Behind Woman ca. 1937; Riggs 1936; Lone Wolf 1905; Keim 1868; Lynch 1909.

[49]G. A. Custer 1966; Gibson 1907; Godfrey 1928.

any heavy firing on its front. This conversation took place some-time after 10 A.M. Even if a relief force were dispatched immedi-ately, it would have been too late to safe Elliott's command.[50]

More difficult to dismiss is the criticism about Custer's failure to ascertain the fate of Elliott's men and recover their bodies. To justify his actions (or lack thereof), Custer listed a rising concern for the safety of his pack train, his many casualties, the lack of sup-plies for both men and horses, and the superior number of his Indian adversaries—reasons that have been convincingly refuted by historian Milo Quaife. The abandonment of Elliott and his men came "to the dumb amaze of some of his best officers." In their view Custer violated a cavalry principle that required officers "to take any risk to attempt the rescue of a comrade in peril." One senior officer considered Custer's conduct an arrogant display of indifference toward Major Elliott and his missing men.[51]

At Camp Supply Custer was unable to give Sheridan a satisfac-tory account about the missing men. When queried by the gen-eral, Custer expressed the opinion that Elliott's detachment probably was lost and would sooner or later show up. To Sheridan this rather strange suggestion was "a very unsatisfactory view of the matter," especially since the colonel's report listed Elliott's men among the dead instead of the missing. Custer's failure to account for their remains also led to sharp criticism "in many quarters afterward" and firmly established a rift in the regiment between Custer and his senior officers.[52]

The split had originated in 1867, when a majority of the officers took offense at Custer's harsh treatment of the enlisted men. That same year Custer was court-martialed and found guilty of, among other things, excessive cruelty and illegal conduct in the treatment of deserters. He also was found guilty of abandoning two of his men to hostile Indians on the Smoky Hill Trail. The controversy surrounding his abandonment of Elliott's men reopened an old wound in the regiment, aggravated by personality conflicts, petty jealousies, tension between West Pointers and volunteer officers,

---

[50]Keim 1868; Benteen,1868; Clark 1899; Godfrey 1928.
[51]G. A. Custer 1966; C. King [1925]; Godfrey 1928; Benteen 1869.
[52]Sheridan 1888; G. A. Custer 1966; Bell [1910].

and Custer's own favoritism and nepotism. The result was a deep factionalism that embittered the relationships of the officers during their lifetimes and complicated and obscured the facts of history down to the present day.[53]

The military viewed Custer's "glorious victory" as a brilliant success achieved during a fierce battle with Black Kettle's hostile Cheyennes. But the Indian Bureau held a different view and labeled the affair a massacre of innocent Indians. Humanitarians in the East denounced Custer's attack as a "cold-blooded butchery" of women and children. The same diversity in opinions may be found among historians and scholars who have analyzed the engagement. One writer holds the extreme view that certain aspects of the Washita bear an eerie similarity to Vietnam. In his opinion a frustrated army, up against guerilla fighters whose unconventional tactics could not be matched, moved in and destroyed an entire village, the theory being that even small boys might wield weapons against their enemies.[54]

Historian Joseph B. Thoburn expressed a somewhat similar view many years earlier. Thoburn considers the destruction of Black Kettle's village too one-sided to be called a battle. The action, in his view, consisted of a surprise attack by a superior force. The comparatively few warriors who died had fought with the courage of desperation because they were not allowed an alternative. Thoburn reasons that had a superior force of Indians attacked a white settlement containing no more people than in Black Kettle's camp, with like results, the incident would doubtless have been heralded as "a massacre."[55]

Historian Paul Hutton provides an opposing view of the engagement. Although Hutton acknowledges that the fight was one-sided, he does not consider it a massacre because the soldiers were not under orders to kill everyone. He adds that Black Kettle's Cheyennes were not unarmed innocents living under the impression that they were not at war. A number of the warriors had

---

[53]Sheridan 1888; G. A. Custer 1966; Bell [1910]; Utley 1977; Frost 1968; Stewart 1955; Utley 2001.
[54]Jakes 1987.
[55]Thoburn and Wright 1929.

recently fought the soldiers, and Black Kettle himself had been informed at Fort Cobb that there could be no peace until he surrendered to Sheridan.[56]

Hutton's view of the Washita fight has been challenged by historian Stan Hoig. The latter argues that having weapons does not prevent anyone from being massacred and that Black Kettle and his people were given no chance whatsoever to surrender, even though they had tried to do so at Fort Cobb. Hoig reasons further that, orders or not, the troops attacked without warning, offered no opportunity for surrender during the action, and killed people promiscuously. In his view the troops did, in fact, massacre the village, precisely as Webster defines the word: "to kill indiscriminately and mercilessly and in large numbers."[57]

Walter M. Camp, a civil railroad engineer, developed a genuine interest in the Plains Indians during the many years of his historical research. Commenting in 1910 on the struggle between Indians and Euro-Americans, Camp points out that the history of race prejudice among civilized peoples shows that there are individuals who are not far removed from savagery. Elaborating on this, he states that one does not have to hunt up Indians to learn about brutal behavior, for there is no animal as fierce and bloodthirsty as man. In this respect the only difference between the Indian and the civilized man is in method. In Camp's opinion, the Indian was direct in his method, while the civilized man, through policies, used the machinery of war to accomplish the destruction of anyone opposing progress. Camp acknowledges the long-suffering of the Indian race, adding that Black Kettle seems to have been the victim of circumstances, that one cannot help but sympathize with him upon reading the truth.[58]

Historian Gaston Litton holds the opinion that the battle of the Washita could easily have been avoided if the temper of the white military commander had been mixed with more mercy and less martial spirit. Gaston's assessment deserves some merit when

---

[56]Hutton 1985.
[57]Hoig 1993.
[58]Transcripts, Unclassified Miscellaneous, 7:815, Camp Manuscripts, Lilly Library, Indiana University, Bloomington.

compared with Custer's Sweet Water confrontation with the Cheyennes in March 1869, which the colonel resolved by tact and shrewdness instead of the use of arms. Gaston also considers that both Black Kettle and Little Rock, who were friendly to the whites, were deserving of a much kinder destiny than what befell them at the Washita. He concludes that people of his day and age, who are so far removed from the tensions of the frontier unrest and distress, can not rightly judge either of the protagonists in this bitter engagement.[59]

The Cheyennes of today have a strong sense of the injustice done to their people at the Washita. They continue to view the brutal attack as a horrible event in their tribal history. Some have opposed the development of the Washita Battlefield National Historic Site because they feel that the ground is hallowed and should be left undisturbed rather than opened to the public. Most consider the attack a massacre and would like to see the name of the historic site changed to reflect that view.[60]

Many of the Washita survivors refused to talk about what they considered a horrifying event. They concluded that the tragedies of Sand Creek and Washita were best forgotten. This silence, and the loss of elders slain during the attacks, had a severe effect on the Cheyenne people, a factor that is usually overlooked in evaluating the historical event. The death of their elders—keepers of tribal history and traditional information—curtailed the knowledge of their families and original names. This essential point, according to Indian historian Mary Jane Warde, illuminates the long-term ramifications of the action on Cheyenne families and their identity. The Cheyennes express the hope that someday history will reflect their perspective in the interpretation of Custer's attack on Black Kettle's village. The present volume attempts to do just that.[61]

---

[59]Litton 1957.

[60]Francis Beard, Melvin Whitebird, Larry Roman Nose, and Terry Wilson to Mary Jane Warde, Oklahoma Historical Society, 1999, summaries of interviews, attached to letter to the author, Mar. 15, 2000.

[61]Joe Osage and William Sage to Mary Jane Warde, Oklahoma Historical Society, 1999, summaries of interviews, attached to letter to the author, Mar. 15, 2000.

1

Indian Depredations in the Department of the Missouri, August 10–November 27, 1868

The following chronology identifies battles and skirmishes with Indians as reported by troop commanders and civilians in the Department of the Missouri from the raid on the Saline settlements on August 10, 1868, to the retaliatory attack at the Washita on November 27. Examination of records discloses a total of seventy-eight specific acts of Indian aggression, resulting in the deaths of 131 civilians and twelve soldiers, the rape of fifteen women, and the capture of several children. Raiders burned twelve farms, two stage buildings, a ranch, and three wagon trains and captured 735 horses and mules and 931 head of stock. The army's humiliating inability to prevent these attacks caused considerable embarrassment to departmental commander Philip H. Sheridan. Facing political pressure and sharp criticism from special interest groups, Sheridan developed a strategy that included a winter campaign against the hostiles. The battle of the Washita would mark its culmination.

The following list is extracted primarily from Record of Engagements with Hostile Indians within the Military Division of the Missouri, from 1868 to 1882, Lieutenant-General P. H. Sheridan, Commanding *(1882).*

August 10, 1868.

—Saline River, north of Fort Harker, Kansas. A party of 225 Cheyennes, Arapahoes, and Lakotas appears at the advance settlements and, after being hospitably fed by the settlers, they suddenly attack, plundering and burning six houses, and brutally rape four women.

—Cimmarron River, Kansas. Indians attack the advance guard of a column of troops commanded by Lt. Col. Alfred Sully, but are repulsed by a charge during which two Indians are killed. In a separate attack on the rear guard one soldier and eight Indians are killed.

August 12, 1868.
—Southern Kansas. A large force of Indians attacks General Sully's column, but are repulsed after a severe fight lasting several hours during which two soldiers are killed. Twelve Indians are reported killed.
—Solomon River, Kansas. Indians plunder and burn five houses, steal ten head of cattle, murder fifteen settlers, and rape five women. Two of these women are shot and badly wounded.
—Republican River, Kansas. Indians kill two settlers and retreat with two captive children of the Bell family.
—Solomon River, Kansas. Indians again attack the settlers, but are routed by Company H, 7th Cavalry under Capt. Frederick W. Benteen who rescues two women who had been captured and raped by the Indians.
—Near Fort Dodge, Kansas. Cheyennes rob the camp of R. M. Wright.
—Near Cimmarron Crossing, Kansas. Indians capture 132 horses and mules from a Mexican wagon train.

August 13, 1868.
—Southern Kansas. Indians attack General Sully's command and kill one soldier. Troops rout the Indians of whom ten are reported killed.
—At Cranny Creek, on the Republican, Kansas. Indians plunder and burn a house, kill one civilian, and capture and rape one woman.
—Near Fort Zarah, Kansas. Indians capture twenty mules, which are recaptured by the troops who report one Indian killed.

August 18, 1868.
—Pawnee Fork, Kansas. Indians attack a wagon train, and keep it corralled for two days, but are dispersed upon the arrival of

troops from Fort Dodge. Indians attack the same train at night, but are again repulsed with a reported loss of five Indians killed.

August 19, 1868.
—Twin Butte Creek, Kansas. Indians attack a party of wood choppers and kill three civilians, capturing 25 animals.

August 20, 1868.
—Indians attack the Comstock ranch and kill two settlers and mortally wounded another who dies at Fort Wallace the next day.

August 22, 1868.
—Sheridan, Kansas. Indians capture twelve head of stock.

August 23, 1868.
—Near Cheyenne Wells, Colorado. Stagecoach is forced to return to Cheyenne Wells, being chased by Indians for four miles.
—Between Pond Creek and Lake Station, Colorado. Denver stage coach is attacked by Indians, forcing it into Fort Wallace.
—Lake Station, Colorado. Indians kill William McCarty.
—Big Spring, Kansas. A band of 250 Indians forces Capt. Butler, 5th Infantry, to return his wagon train to Big Springs.
—Northern Texas. Eight civilians are killed and 300 head of stock captured.
—Bent's Fort, Colorado. Indians capture fifteen horses and mules and four head of cattle.
—Colorado. Acting Governor Frank Hall telegraphs army officials that Arapahoes are killing settlers and destroying ranches in all directions.
—Near Fort Wallace, Kansas. William Comstock and Sharp Grover, U.S. scouts, are attacked by Cheyennes after leaving the camp of Chief Bull Bear. Comstock is killed, but Grover escaped.

August 24, 1868.
—Bent's Fort, Colorado. Indians attack three stage coaches and
   one wagon train.

August 25, 1868.
—Near Fort Dodge, Kansas. Indians kill a herder.
—Southern Colorado. Acting Governor Hall reports a band of
   two hundred Indians devastating the southern part of the
   state.

August 27, 1868.
—Cheyenne Wells Station, Smoky Hill Road, Colorado. A
   party of thirteen Indians kills a civilian named J. H.
   Woodworth.

August 28, 1868.
—Kiowa Station, Kansas. Indians kill three civilians and capture
   fifty head of stock.

August 29, 1868.
—Near Fort Lyon, Colorado. Indians attack and destroy a train
   of thirteen wagons and kill all the oxen; however, the train's
   escort of twenty-one civilians escapes during the night to
   Fort Lyon.

August 31, 1868.
—Kiowa Creek, Kansas. Indians capture 200 horses and forty
   head of cattle from stage station.

September 1, 1868.
—Lake Station, Colorado. Indians kill a woman and her child
   and capture thirty head of stock from the station.
—Reed Springs, Colorado. Indians kill three civilians.
—Spanish Fort, Texas. Indians kill four civilians, capture fifteen
   horses, rape three women, one of whom is killed along with
   her four children.

September 2, 1868.
—Little Coon Creek, Kansas. A band of forty Indians attack a
   wagon train guarded by a squad of soldiers from Troop A,
   Third Infantry, commanded by Sgt. Dittoe. Three soldiers
   are badly wounded while four Indians are reported killed.

September 3, 1868.
—Colorado City. Indians kill four civilians.
—Hugo Springs, Colorado. A large force of Indians attacks the
   stage station, but are repulsed by the herders.

September 5, 1868.
—Hugo Springs, Colorado. Indians capture five head of stock.
—Willow Springs Station, Colorado. Indians burn station.

September 6 and 7, 1868.
—Colorado. Indians kill twenty-five civilians. The Hon.
   Schuyler Colfax telegraphs that "hostile Indians have been
   striking simultaneously at isolated settlements in Colorado
   for a circuit of over two hundred miles."

September 8, 1868.
—Near Sheridan, Kansas. A band of twenty-five Indians kill
   two civilians.
—Turkey Creek, Kansas. Indians capture seventy-six horses and
   mules from Clark's wagon train.
—Cimmarron Crossing, Kansas. Indians attack a wood train,
   kill two employees and capture seventy-five head of cattle
   during a fight lasting four days, the engagement ending with
   the arrival of Lt. Wallingfort, Seventh Cavalry.
—Near Cimmarron Crossing, Kansas. Five miles west of the
   aforesaid incident, Indians kill fifteen civilians and burn their
   train of ten wagons.

September 9, 1868.
—Between Fort Wallace and Sheridan, Kansas. Indians burn a
   ranch and kill six civilians. This same ranch was burned two
   weeks before by the Indians and had been rebuilt.

September 10, 1868.

—Purgatoire River, Colorado. Indians raid settlements, but are overtaken by a detachment of the Third Infantry under Capt. Penrose who reports four Indians killed and recovers twelve head of stolen stock. Two soldiers are killed.

—Lake Station, Colorado. Indians fire into the stage station.

September 11, 1868.

—Lake Creek, Colorado. Indians capture eighty-one head of cattle belonging to Clarke & Company, hay contractors.

September 11–15, 1868.

—General Alfred Sully's command of Third Infantry and Seventh Cavalry has a series of skirmishes with Indians who kill three soldiers. Twenty-two Indians are reported killed.

September 12, 1868.

—Bent's Old Fort, Colorado. Indians capture eighty-five head of stock belonging to Thompson & McGee.

September 15, 1868.

—Big Sandy, Colorado. A force of one hundred Indians attacks Troop I, Tenth Cavalry, commanded by Capt. Graham. Eleven Indians are reported killed.

September 17, 1868.

—Ellis Station, Kansas. Indians burn station and kill one civilian.

—Saline River, Kansas. Indians again attack the settlements, but are driven off by a detachment of the Seventh Cavalry. Three Indians are reported killed.

—Fort Bascom, New Mexico. Indians kill a herder and capture thirty mules.

September 17–25, 1868.

—Arickaree Fork, Republican River, Colorado. A force of 700 Cheyennes, Arapahoes, and Lakotas attacks a company of fifty scouts commanded by Col. George A. Forsyth. During

a siege lasting eight days, the Indians kill Lt. Frederick H.
Beecher, Surgeon John H. Moore, and four scouts. Nine
Indians are killed.

September 29, 1868.
—Sharp's Creek, Kansas. Indians attack a house and kill Mr.
  Bassett and capture Mrs. Bassett and her newly-born baby.
  They rape Mrs. Bassett, strip her naked, and leave her and
  her infant to perish on the prairie.

October 2, 1868.
—Fort Zarah, Kansas. A band of one hundred Indians attack
  the fort, but are driven off.
—Near Fort Zarah. Same Indians attack a provision train,
  killing one teamster and capture the train's mules.
—Near Fort Zarah. Same Indians attack a ranch and capture 160
  head of stock.
—Between Fort Larned and Fort Dodge, Kansas. Indians attack
  a wagon train and kill three civilians and capture fifty mules.

October 4, 1868.
—Near Fort Dodge, Kansas. Indians attack a wagon train and
  kill two civilians, destroy stores and provisions, and capture
  the stock.
—Asher Creek, Kansas. Indians capture seven head of horses
  and mules at settlements.

October 9, 1868.
—Arkansas, below Fort Lyon. Indians attack a wagon train and
  capture Mrs. Clara Blinn and her infant. Indians also capture
  ninety-nine head of cattle, two mules, and one horse.

October 10, 1868.
—Fort Zarah, Kansas. Indians capture eight horses and mules.

October 12, 1868.
—Near Ellsworth, Kansas. Indians kill one civilian; several
  civilians are reported missing.

October 13, 1868.
—Brown's Creek, Kansas. Indians attack a house.

October 14, 1868.
—Prairie Dog Creek, Kansas. Indians attack a camp of Fifth
	Cavalry and kill one soldier and capture twenty-six horses.

October 15, 1868.
—Fisher and Yocucy Creeks, Kansas. Indians attack a house and
	kill four settlers. One woman is captured.

October 18, 1868.
—Beaver Creek, Kansas. Indians attack three companies of the
	Tenth Cavalry commanded by Capt. L. H. Carpenter. Ten
	Indians are reported killed.

October 23, 1868.
—Fort Zarah, Kansas. Indians kill two civilians. Two Indians are
	reported killed.

October 25–26, 1868.
—Beaver Creek, Kansas. Indians skirmish with a column of the
	Fifth Cavalry commanded by Major E. A. Carr. Thirty
	Indians are reported killed.

October 26, 1868.
—Near Central City, New Mexico. Indians kill three civilians.

October 30, 1868.
—Grinnell Station, Kansas. Indians attack station.

November 7, 1868.
—Coon Creek, Kansas. Indians attack a stage and capture a
	horse.

November 15, 1868.
—Near Fort Harker. Squadron of Seventh Cavalry skirmishes
	with party of Indians and pursues them for ten miles.

November 17, 1868.
—Near Fort Harker. Indians attack a wagon train and capture
   150 mules.

November 18, 1868.
—Near Fort Hayes, Kansas. Indians kill two government scouts
   and capture their horses.

November 19, 1868.
—Little Coon Creek, Kansas. One civilian and five Indians are
   killed.
—Near Fort Dodge, Kansas. One civilian and two Indians are
   killed.
—Near Fort Dodge, Kansas. Indians attack a detachment of
   Tenth Cavalry under Sgt. Wilson. Two Indians are reported
   killed.
—Near Fort Dodge Kansas. Indians attempt to stampede a beef
   contractor's herd, but are pursued by a detachment of the
   Fifth Infantry under Lt. Q. Campbell. Four Indians are
   reported killed.

November 20, 1868.
—Mulberry Creek, south of Fort Dodge, Kansas. Indians kill
   two government scouts named Marshall and Davis.

November 27, 1868.
—Washita River, Indian Territory. Battle of the Washita takes
   place.

2

Clara Blinn,
Civilian Captive

Clara Isabel Harrington was born on October 21, 1847, in Elmore, Ohio, the daughter of William T. Harrington and Harriet Bosley. She married Richard F. Blinn on August 12, 1865, and the following year gave birth to their son, Willie. In the spring of 1868, the extended Harrington family migrated west and settled in Ottawa, Franklin County, Kansas. From there the Richard Blinn family traveled on to Colorado Territory, where Richard formed a partnership with his brother-in-law, John F. Buttles of Fort Lyon, Colorado, to furnish supplies to government outposts.

On October 5, 1868, the Blinns departed from Bogg's Ranch in Colorado with a train of eight wagons and headed east along the Arkansas River to Fort Dodge, Kansas. On the afternoon of October 9, Arapahos jumped the train near the mouth of Sand Creek and captured the supply wagon with Sara and Willie. The remaining wagons were set on fire with flaming arrows. Richard Blinn and the wagon crew of ten men survived the ordeal, though trapped for five days before a volunteer started for Fort Lyon to seek relief for the besieged.

On November 7 Cheyenne Jack, an employee of William Griffinstein's trading post at Fort Cobb, located Clara Blinn in Yellow Bear's Arapaho camp. Cheyenne Jack provided Clara with pencil and paper and carried back her emphatic plea for help. Griffinstein received this message on November 25 and turned it over to Maj. Gen. William B. Hazen, special military agent, who had just arrived at Fort Cobb to take control over the peaceful Indians. Hazen authorized Griffinstein to negotiate the release of the Blinn captives. Tragically, before the merchant could begin negotiations, the battle of the Washita took place. In the aftermath of the human destruction of November 27, 1868,

41

Clara and her infant son suffered violent retaliatory deaths by the Indians.

Clara Isabel Blinn was described by her family as a tiny, beautiful girl with dark hair, a freckled face, and a dimpled chin. She was an inveterate joker who exuded exuberance and a joy for living. Her message, which follows, was published in the Leavenworth Bulletin, *December 22, 1868. It is reproduced in U.S. Senate,* Indian Battle on the Washita River, *40th Congress, 3d session, Senate Executive Document 18.*

Message
November 7, 1868

Saturday, Nov. 7th, 68.

Kind Friend,

Whoever you may be I thank you for your kindness to me and my child. You want me to let you know my wishes. If you could only buy us off the Indians with ponies or anything and let me come and stay with you until I could get word to my friends, they would pay you and I would work and do all I could for you. If it is not too far to their camp and you are not afraid to come I pray that you will try. They tell me as near as I can understand they expect traders to come and they will sell us to them. Can you find out by this man[1] and let me know if it is white men? If it is Mexicans I am afraid they would sell us into slavery in Mexico. If you can do nothing for me write to W. T. Harrington, Ottawa, Franklin Co., Kansas—my father. Tell him we are with the Cheyennes and they say when the white men make peace we can go home. Tell him to write to the Governor of Kansas about it and for them to make peace. Send this to him.

We were taken on the 9th of Oct. on the Arkansas below Fort Lyon. I can't tell whether they killed my husband or not.[2] My

---

[1]The man spoken of was Cheyenne Jack, the emissary sent by William Griffinstein, post trader at Fort Cobb. Rister 1940, 156–57.

[2]Richard F. Blinn survived the attack on his wagon train. He searched for his captured wife and infant son for several months before learning of their deaths in January 1869. After visiting their graves at Fort Arbuckle Cemetery, the grief-stricken man returned to his father's home in Perrysburg, Ohio, where he died of tuberculosis on September 18, 1873. Justus 2000, 19.

name is Clara Blinn. My little boy [is] Willie Blinn who is two years old. Do all you can for me. Write to the Peace Commissioners to make peace this fall. For our sake do all you can and God will bless you. If you can let me hear from you again let me know what you think about it. Write to my father. Send him this.

Goodbye
Mrs. R. F. Binn

3

Little Rock, Cheyenne

Little Rock (Ho-han-i-no-o) was born about 1805 and was a minor council chief of the Wutapiu band of the Southern Cheyennes. A signatory of the Medicine Lodge Treaty in 1867, he fully understood the futility of war with the whites but was powerless to restrain his young men. On several occasions he acted as a mediator between his band and the representatives of the federal government, despite threats made to him and his family by members of the warrior societies. He was present when Black Kettle and the Cheyenne delegation held a conference with Maj. Gen. William B. Hazen at Fort Cobb on November 20, 1868.

Little Rock's ornamented lodge stood at the lower (east) end of Black Kettle's village. During the cavalry attack, he, She Wolf, and Trails the Enemy formed a rear guard to shield the fleeing women and children from the charging soldiers, thought to have been Major Elliott's detachment. Little Rock carried a muzzleloading rifle, powder horn, and a bow and arrows. He sustained a fatal gunshot wound to the forehead while running across the tongue of land in the horseshoe bend below the village. His wife Skunk Woman, his daughter Spring Grass (Meotzi), his sister White Buffalo Woman, another sister, and his elderly mother all survived the battle. Little Rock's mother and daughter were among the captives taken to Camp Supply.

The following interview took place at Fort Lamed, Kansas, on August 19, 1868, at the request of Indian agent Col. Edward W. Wynkoop, who sought to learn the particulars of the Saline and Solomon raid. Little Rock comes across as a troubled man trying to establish peaceful relations between two opposing cultures while dealing with pressures from both. This transcript is from U.S. Senate, Indian Battle on the Washita River, *40th Congress, 3d session, Senate Executive Document 18.*

Interview
August 19, 1868

Report of an Interview between Colonel E. W. Wynkoop,[1] United States Indian agent, and Little Rock, a Cheyenne chief, held at Fort Larned, Kansas, August 19, 1868, in the presence of Lieutenant S. M. Robbins,[2] 7th United States cavalry, John S. Smith,[3] United States interpreter, and James Morrison,[4] scout for Indian agency.

---

[1]Born in Philadelphia in 1836, Edward Wanshear Wynkoop joined the Pike's Peak gold rush in 1859 and was one of the founders of Denver City. He entered the Civil War as a first lieutenant of the Denver Cavalry and in March 1861 accepted a commission in the First Colorado Volunteer Cavalry, being promoted to captain the same year. He was prominent in the defeat of the Confederates at Glorieta Pass, New Mexico, in March 1862, for which he was awarded a commission of major of volunteers. As commander of Fort Lyon in May 1864, he encouraged the peace efforts of the Cheyennes but was suddenly transferred to Fort Riley, Kansas, in November 1864, where he learned of the Sand Creek Massacre. He was ordered to investigate Col. John M. Chivington's conduct at Sand Creek, which led to the condemnation of the latter's brutal action. Wynkoop was brevetted lieutenant colonel in March 1865 and became the commander of the District of the Upper Arkansas the following June. In August he commanded the escort for the peace commissioners who negotiated a new treaty with the Indians at the mouth of the Little Arkansas. But by July 1866 he had become disillusioned over the federal government's failure to keep its promises, and he resigned his military commission to accept an appointment as Indian agent for the Cheyennes and Arapahos. His efforts to keep his charges peaceful were severely hampered by the Hancock expedition of April 1867. Although a new treaty was signed at Medicine Lodge in October 1867, hostilities flared up once again in August 1868, when Indians raided the peaceful settlements in the Saline and Solomon Valleys. Wynkoop immediately demanded the surrender of the ringleaders in an effort to head off a general Indian war. But the military countered with the Sully expedition in September and followed that with the winter offensive that led to the destruction of Black Kettle's village. Two days later Wynkoop submitted his resignation as Indian agent in protest over the military actions. He returned to Philadelphia and went into business with his brother. After the failure of this venture, he went back to the plains in 1874 and searched for gold in the Black Hills. In 1890 Wynkoop became the warden of the New Mexico penitentiary and died soon after in Santa Fe on September 11, 1891. Utley 1977, 282–83; *New York Times,* Dec. 19, 1868.

[2]For information on Samuel M. Robbins, see Appendix A.

[3]Born in Kentucky in 1810, John Simpson Smith came to the northern plains at an early age to engage in trapping. He married a Blackfoot woman and, during the succeeding years, became widely known as Blackfoot Smith. In 1830 he went to Colorado, finding employment with the firm of Bent and St. Vrain. He married Na-to-mah, daughter of Cheyenne chief Yellow Wolf, who gave birth to a son in 1842. Christened Jack Smith, he was murdered at Sand Creek in 1864 by Chivington's order. John Smith was a fluent Cheyenne speaker and was frequently employed as a U.S. translator during numerous treaty negotiations, including at Fort Laramie in 1851, at Fort Wise in 1861, at Little Arkansas in 1865, and at Medicine Lodge in 1867. He selected the site for Camp Supply in 1868 and accompanied a Cheyenne-Arapaho delegation to Washington in

Question by Colonel Wynkoop. Six nights ago I spoke to you in regard to depredations committed on the Saline. I told you to go and find out by whom these depredations were committed, and to bring me straight news. What news do you bring?

Little Rock. I took your advice and went there. I am now here to tell you all I know. This war party of Cheyennes which left the camps of these tribes above the forks of Walnut creek about the 2nd and 3d of August went out against the Pawnees, crossed the Smoky Hill about Fort Hayes, and thence proceeded to the Saline, where there were 10 lodges of Sioux in the Cheyenne camp when this war party left, and about 20 men of them, and 4 Arapahoes, accompanied the party. The Cheyennes numbered about 200; nearly all the young men of the village went; Little Raven's son was one of the four Arapahoes.[5] When the party reached the Saline they turned down the stream, with the exception of about 20, who, being fearful of depredations being committed against the whites by the party going in the direction of the settlement, kept on north towards the Pawnees. The main party continued down the Saline until they came in sight of the settlement; they then camped there. A Cheyenne named Oh-e-ah-mohe-a, brother of White Antelope,[6] who was killed at Sand Creek, and another man named Red Nose, proceeded to the first house; they afterwards returned to the camp and with them a woman captive.

1870. Smith died of pneumonia on June 29, 1871, at Darlington Agency and was buried in the sand hills on the north side of the Canadian near present El Reno. Mooney 1907a, 441; Hoig 1974, 226.

[4]For information on James Morrison, see the introduction to chapter 24.

[5]Little Raven was a principal chief of the Arapahos and was widely known for his intellect and oratory. He married a Kiowa-Apache woman in 1840 and had two sons and a daughter with her. The daughter was named High Singer and was listed on the agency rolls as Anna Little Raven. She was the only one of his three children who was sent East to be educated. Little Raven was a signatory of the Little Arkansas Treaty of 1865 and the Medicine Lodge Treaty of 1867. He died at Cantonment in 1889. Berthrong 1963, 83.

[6]White Antelope was born in 1789 and became one of the most respected leaders of the Southern Cheyennes. A member of the first Cheyenne delegation that visited Washington in 1851, he was a signatory of the amended Fort Laramie Treaty of 1853. Throughout his life he advocated friendly relations with the whites. White Antelope and his wives Sage Woman, Yellow Calf, and Pipe Woman were killed during the Sand Creek Massacre in 1864. His brother Breaks the Marrow Bones instigated the Saline and Solomon raids in August 1868. Schukies 1993, 269–72.

The main party was surprised at this action, and forcibly took possession of her, and returned her to her house. The two Indians had outraged the woman before they brought her to the camp. After the outrage had been committed, the parties left the Saline and went north, towards the settlements of the south fork of the Solomon, where they were kindly received and fed by the white people. They left the settlements on the south fork, and proceeded towards the settlements on the north forks. When in sight of these settlements they came upon a body of armed settlers, who fired upon them; they avoided the party, went round them, and approached a house some distance off. In the vicinity of the house they came upon a white man alone, upon the prairie; Big Head's son[7] rode at him and knocked him down with a club. The Indian who had committed the outrage upon the white woman, known as White Antelope's brother, then fired upon the white man without effect, while the third Indian rode up and killed him. Soon after they killed a white man, and, close by, a woman—all in the same settlement. At the time these people were killed, the party was divided in feeling, the majority being opposed to any outrages being committed; but finding it useless to contend against these outrages being committed, they gave way, and all went in together. They then went to another house in the same settlement, and there killed two men, and took two little girls prisoners [sic]; this on the same day. After committing the last outrage the party turned south, towards the Saline, where they came on a body of mounted troops; the troops immediately charged the Indians, and the pursuit was continued a long time. The Indians having the two children, their horses becoming fatigued, dropped the children without hurting them.[8] Soon after the children were dropped the pursuit ceased; but the Indians continued on up the Saline. A portion of the Indians afterwards returned to look for the children, but were unable to find them. After they had proceeded some distance

---

[7]Big Head was the leader of a Dog Soldier band and uncle of George Bent. He was a signatory of the Little Arkansas Treaty in 1865. His son Porcupine Bear participated in the Saline and Solomon raids.

[8]The two Bell girls were abducted on August 12, 1868, from the family homestead near present Beloit in Mitchell County, Kansas. They were released unharmed on the prairie about thirty miles south of their homestead. White 1969, 335.

up the Saline, the party divided, the majority going north, towards the settlements on the Solomon, but 30 of them started towards their village, supposed to be some distance northwest of Fort Larned. Another small party returned to Black Kettle's village, from which party I got this information. I am fearful that before this time, the party that started north have committed a great many depredations. The other day when I talked to you, you gave me instructions what to do, with a great deal of risk and danger. I have followed out these instructions, and returned to you with what is straight, and which I have just given you. I want you, as my agent, to give me advice as to what to do. I do not wish to be at war with the whites, and there are many of my nation who feel as I do, and who are in no way guilty, and do not wish to be punished for the bad acts of those who are guilty. We are ready and willing to abide by any advice which you may give us.

Question by Colonel Wynkoop. Before I give you any advice, I want to ask you some questions. Do you know the names of the principal men of this party that committed depredations besides White Antelope's brother?

A[nswer.] They were Medicine Arrow's oldest son, named Tall Wolf; Red Nose, who was one of the men who outraged the woman; Big Head's son, named Porcupine Bear; and Sand Hill's brother, known as Bear That Goes Ahead.[9]

Q. By Col. W. You told me your nation wants peace; will you, in accordance with your treaty stipulations, deliver up the men whom you have named as being the leaders of the party who committed the outrages named?

A. By L.R. I think that the only men who ought to suffer and be responsible for these outrages are White Antelope's brother and Red Nose, the men who ravished the woman, and when I return to the Cheyenne camps and assemble the chiefs and headmen, I think those two men will be delivered up to you.

Q. By Col. W. I consider the whole party guilty; but it being impossible to punish all of them, I hold the principal men whom you mention responsible for all. They had no right to be governed and led by two men. If no depredations had been committed after the

---

[9]For information on Medicine Arrow and Sand Hill, see chapter 42.

outrage on the woman, the two men whom you have mention[ed] alone would have been guilty.

A. By L.R. After your explanation, I think your demand for the men is right. I am willing to deliver them up, and will go back to the tribe and use my best endeavors to have them surrendered. I am but one man and cannot answer for the entire nation.

Q. By Col. W. I want you to return to your tribe and tell the chiefs and headmen, when assembled, the demand I now make. Tell them that I think complying with my demand is the only thing that will save their entire nation from a long and destructive war. I want you to return as soon as possible with their answer. I will see that you are safe in going and coming, and your services in this respect will be rewarded. You will be looked upon by the whites as a good man, and one who is a friend of them as well as to his own people; and as the result of your action in this matter, you will be considered by the government as a "great Chief," one in whom in the future they can always put the utmost confidence.

Little Rock. I am here in your service; at the same time I am a Cheyenne, and want to do all I can for the welfare of my nation. If the chiefs and headmen refuse to comply with your demands, I want to know if I can come with my wife and children, (whom I love,) and place myself and them under your protection, and at the same time act as a runner between you and my people?

Colonel Wynkoop. Should my demands not be complied with, you can bring your lodge and family here, and I will protect you.

4

Edmund Guerrier,
Civilian

*Edmund Gasseau Chouteau Le Guerrier was born on January 16, 1840,
in a Cheyenne camp along the Smoky Hill River in western Kansas.
His father, William Guerrier, was an illiterate Frenchman born in St.
Louis in 1812. His mother was Tah-tah-tois-neh, a young woman from
Little Rock's Wutapiu band of Cheyennes. William Guerrier was
employed by William Bent until 1848, then accepted a partnership with
Seth Edmund Ward and became a licensed trader for the region of the
Upper Platte and Arkansas Agency. In 1849 cholera swept the plains,
and Guerrier lost his Cheyenne wife and an infant child. The surviving
son, Edmund, entered a Catholic mission school near present St. Mary's,
Kansas, in 1851 and upon graduation enrolled at St. Louis University.*

*By 1853 William Guerrier, Seth Ward, and a few other partners
operated a trading post along the Platte, seven miles west of Fort
Laramie, along with a ferry and a toll bridge. To facilitate his Indian
trade, William had married a Sioux woman. On February 16, 1857,
while at a trade camp on the Niobrara River near present Lusk,
Wyoming, William dropped a spark from his pipe into an open keg of
powder and was instantly killed by the resulting explosion.*

*With his father's death, Edmund withdrew from St. Louis Univer-
sity and, after trying his hand at a variety of jobs, returned to his
mother's people, who remembered him as Chicken Hawk, son of Tah-
tah-tois-neh. He was at Sand Creek in 1864 when the Chivington
massacre took place and barely escaped. By 1865 Guerrier had married
Julia Bent, the sister of George Bent. Like his brother-in-law, Guerrier
accepted employment with the Interior Department. An interpreter for
Indian agent Jesse H. Leavenworth, he was present at the Little
Arkansas negotiations.*

After working as a trader for David A. Butterfield, a licensed arms dealer to the Indians, Guerrier was hired by the War Department in March 1867. He was assigned as an interpreter to the Seventh Cavalry, part of Maj. Gen. Winfield S. Hancock's command during the futile spring campaign against the Cheyennes. Guerrier played an essential roll in the expedition as a shuttle diplomat, interpreter, and peacemaker, risking his life to carry massages between the whites and the Indians, who remarkably continued to trust him. That October Guerrier was an interpreter during the Medicine Lodge talks. In 1869 he was an interpreter for Maj. Gen. Eugene A. Carr's Fifth Cavalry, then returned to civilian life as a trader at Camp Supply for the firm of Lee and Reynolds. In 1871 and again in 1884, Guerrier was employed by the Interior Department as an interpreter to accompany delegations of Cheyenne leaders to Washington, D.C.

In 1875 the Guerriers settled along the Cimarron River near the present town of Kingfisher, where in 1877 their daughter, Rosa, was born. In 1880 the family moved to Darlington Agency and obtained allotments along the North Canadian River near the present border between Blain and Canadian counties. Their son, William, was born there, but in 1884 tragedy struck when Rosa passed away after a short illness.

Edmund Guerrier was well educated and respected by whites and Indians alike. He had property in Colorado, was a successful rancher, and bred some of the finest racing horses on the reservation. The town of Geary was named after him, albeit with a phonetic spelling. Otherwise, he never attracted much attention, which he undoubtedly preferred. Edmund Guerrier died on February 22, 1921, and was buried next to his daughter at the Guerrier ranch along the Canadian.

On February 9, 1869, Guerrier gave an affidavit to the military regarding the Saline and Solomon atrocities. It corroborates the statement given by Little Rock to Colonel Wynkoop the previous year. Guerrier's willingness to provide a sworn statement was based on the realization that he could face charges of aiding the enemy. The affidavit text is from U.S. House, Difficulties with Indian Tribes, *41st Congress, 2nd session, House Executive Document 240.*

Affidavit
February 2, 1869

Headquarters Dep't of the Missouri, in the Field,
Medicine Bluff Creek, Washita Mountains, February 9, 1869.

Personally appeared before me, Edmund Guerrier, who resides
on the Purgatory River, Colorado Territory, who, being duly
sworn, testifies as follows:

I was with the Cheyenne Indians at the time of the massacre on
the Solomon and Saline Rivers, in Kansas, the early part or middle of last August, and I was living at this time with Little Rock's
band. The war party who started for the Solomon and Saline was
composed of young men of Little Rock's, Black Kettle's,[1] Medicine Arrow's, and Bull Bear's[2] bands, and as near as I can remember, nearly all the different bands of Cheyennes had some of their
young men in this war party, which committed the outrages and
murders on the Solomon and Saline. Red Nose, and The Man
Who Breaks the Marrow Bones, (Ho-eh-a-mo-a-ha,) were the
two leaders in this massacre; the former belonged to the Dog Soldiers, and the latter to Black Kettle's band. As soon as we heard
the news by runners, who came on ahead to Black Kettle, saying
that they had already commenced fighting, we moved from our
camp on Buckner's Fork of the Pawnee near its headwaters, down

---

[1]For information on Black Kettle, see the introduction to chapter 5 and Appendix
I.

[2]Born about 1835, Bull Bear, the recognized leader of the Dog Soldiers, was
described as a man of pleasing and commanding appearance. He was the first signatory
of the Medicine Lodge Treaty in October 1867 despite the inexcusable burning of his
village by Hancock's troops the previous spring. Bull Bear participated at Beecher
Island in 1868 and was present during the Red River War of 1874–75. After his surrender in March 1875, his band settled along the Cimarron River in present Kingfisher
County, Oklahoma. He was the first Cheyenne chief to enroll a son (born in 1867 and
who later took the name Richard A. Davis) at Darlington Agency School in 1876; Bull
Bear's two older sons were Thunder Cloud (Jock Bull Bear) and Foolish Bear, who was
found guilty of killing surveyor E. N. Deming in the spring of 1873. Bull Bear was only
fifty-four years old in 1889, when Fredrick Remington met him in Indian Territory and
noted that he was "a very old man . . . with his many wrinkles, gray hair, and toothless
jaws." Berthrong 1963, 278–79, 400; Franks 1974, 431.

to North Fork, where we met Big Jake's[3] band, and then moved south across the Arkansas River, and when we got to the Cimarron, George Bent[4] and I left them and went to our homes on the Purgatory.

Edmund Guerrier.

Witness: J. Schuyler Crosby,[5]

Bvt. Lieutenant Colonel U.S.A., Aide-de-Camp

---

[3]Born in 1794, Big Jake was known among the Cheyenne people as Little Wolf, the younger brother of Man Above. He was a council chief of the Ridge Men band and was recognized for his friendly relations with the whites. After the establishment of Seger Colony in 1886, Big Jake's band settled along the Washita at Big Jake's Crossing, near present Weatherford, Custer County, where he died later that year. He was succeeded by his son Little Medicine, a former head soldier born in 1834. Named Little Big Jake by whites, he was appointed as the first Cheyenne tribal chief in 1891 upon the allotment of the reservation. He frequently traveled to Washington to seek financial assistance for the tribe but resigned in 1897 following the death of his favorite son. Grinnell n.d.; Grinnell 1971, 21; *Cheyenne Transporter,* Aug. 30, 1884; Page 1915, 56.

[4]For information on George Bent, see the introduction to chapter 42.

[5]Born in New York in 1839, John Schuyler Crosby entered the army as a lieutenant in the First Artillery in August 1861. He was appointed captain in June 1863 and was honorably mustered out in August 1866. In recognition of his gallant and meritorious services, he was awarded brevets of lieutenant colonel in both regular and volunteer grades. He served as aide-de-camp to General Sheridan from March 1869 to July 1870, when he was honorably discharged at his own request. Crosby served as governor of Montana Territory from 1882 to 1884 and died on August 8, 1914, at Newport, Rhode Island, while on a yachting trip.

5

Black Kettle,
Cheyenne

Born about 1797 in the Black Hills of present South Dakota, Black Kettle (Moke-tah-vah-to) was the son of Black Hawk, or Hawk Stretched Out, a Sutai council chief who died young. His mother was a Sutai named Sparrow Hawk Woman, or Little Brown Back Woman. Black Kettle gained prominence as a warrior in 1838 during the great battle against the Kiowas, Comanches, and Apaches on Wolf Creek in western Oklahoma. In 1853 he carried the Sacred Arrows against the Pawnees and later led the first Cheyenne raiding party into Old Mexico. In the autumn of 1854, he was the leader of a war party against the Utes. During the retreat, his young wife was captured and was never heard of again.

In 1855 Black Kettle married into Bear Feathers's Wutapiu band and was elected council chief upon the latter's death. In the winter of 1856–57, he led a raiding party against the Pawnee to recover a herd of stolen ponies, successfully returning with six Pawnee scalps in addition to the stolen stock. In 1857 the Cheyenne leader was present at the Smoky Hill encampment when Col. Edwin V. Sumner led his unconventional saber charge against the Indians.

By 1861 Black Kettle realized that the survival of his people depended on peaceful relations with the whites and agreed to sign the Fort Wise Treaty, the first chief to do so. But his trust was shattered at Sand Creek in 1864 with the genocidal attack against innocent men, women, and children by Chivington's volunteer troops. Black Kettle's wife sustained nine bullet wounds but miraculously survived. In October 1865 government commissioners met with Black Kettle, who spoke sorrowfully of the people who had died because they had trusted him, adding that his "shame was as big as the earth."

Despite the betrayal of his people, Black Kettle continued to pursue peaceful relations with the whites and signed the Treaty of the Little Arkansas, ceding all the lands between the Arkansas and Platte rivers. To compensate the Cheyennes for their sufferings at Sand Creek, each widow and orphan was granted 160 acres of land and each chief received a half-section on the Arkansas reservation. The land provisions were never fulfilled. During a council with Agent Wynkoop in 1866, Black Kettle requested restitution for the six hundred ponies lost at Sand Creek and the return of two Cheyenne children taken captive by Chivington's men. Neither request was honored. Despite threats from the powerful Dog Soldiers, the chief signed the Medicine Lodge Treaty in 1867, by which the Cheyennes agreed to accept a reservation in Indian Territory.

In October 1868 Black Kettle's band hunted buffalo near the Antelope Hills in the western part of present Oklahoma. Acting upon rumors of troop movements against the Cheyennes, Black Kettle and a small delegation traveled to Fort Cobb for a conference with General Hazen. Their request to relocate their people nearer to the agency for protection was denied. Hazen advised them to return to their winter camps and to make peace with the soldiers of General Sheridan. Destiny would not give them that opportunity. On November 27 the bands of Black Kettle and Little Rock were annihilated by Custer's brutal dawn attack. Black Kettle and his wife were among the first to die.

The following speech by Black Kettle was made at Fort Cobb on November 20, 1868. It represents the last recorded words of a man who remained one of the best Indian allies of the whites despite strained relations. The statement is contained in U.S. Senate, Indian Battle on the Washita River, *40th Congress, 3d session, Senate Executive Document 18.*

Speech
November 20, 1868

Record of a conversation held between Colonel and Brevet Major General W. B. Hazen,[1] United States army, on special service, and chiefs of the Cheyenne and Arapaho tribes of Indians, Fort Cobb, Indian Territory, November 20, 1868.

---

[1]For information on Hazen, see the introduction to chapter 26.

Black Kettle, Cheyenne chief. I always feel well while I am among these Indians—the Caddoes, Wichitas, Wacoes, Keechies, etc.—as I know they are all my friends; and I do not feel afraid to go among the white men, because I feel them to be my friends also. The Cheyennes, when south of the Arkansas, did not wish to return to the north side because they feared trouble there, but were continually told that they had better go there, as they would be rewarded for so doing.[2] The Cheyennes do not fight at all this side of the Arkansas; they do not trouble Texas, but north of the Arkansas they are almost always at war. When lately north of the Arkansas, some young Cheyennes were fired upon and then the fight began. I have always done my best to keep my young men quiet, but some will not listen, and since the fighting began I have not been able to keep them all at home. But we all want peace, and I would be glad to move all my people down this way; I could then keep them all quietly near camp. My camp is now on the Washita, 40 miles east of Antelope Hills, and I have there about 180 lodges.

I speak only for my own people; I cannot speak nor control the Cheyennes north of the Arkansas.

. . . .

General Hazen. The Great Father . . . sent [me] here as a peace chief; all here is to be peace; but north of the Arkansas is General Sheridan,[3] the great war chief, and I do not control him; and he has all the soldiers who are fighting the Arapahoes and Cheyennes. Therefore, you must go back to your country, and if the soldiers come to fight, you must remember they are not from me, but from the great war chief, and with him you must make peace. I am glad to see you and glad to hear that you want peace and not war; I cannot stop the war, but will send your talk to the Great Father, and if he sends me orders to treat you like the

---

[2]In 1868 the Arkansas River formed the northern boundary of the Cheyenne-Arapaho reservation as stipulated by the Medicine Lodge Treaty. But in order to obtain provisions of beef, flour, coffee, sugar, and salt, the Cheyennes were forced to cross the Arkansas in April 1868 and travel to Fort Larned or Fort Dodge, where the goods were distributed. The distribution of arms and ammunition on August 9 also took place at Fort Larned, and it is assumed that Black Kettle is making reference to these two occasions in his speech. Berthrong 1963, 301, 305.

[3]For information on Sheridan, see chapter 23.

friendly Indians I will send out to you to come in. But you must not come in again unless I send for you, and you must keep well out beyond the friendly Kiowas and Comanches. I am satisfied that you want peace; that it has not been you, but your bad men, that have made the war, and I will do all I can for you to bring peace; then I will go with you and your agent on to your reservation and care for you there. I hope you understand how and why it is that I cannot make peace with you.

All the chiefs present replied that they did.

Recorded by order of Colonel and Brevet Major General W. B. Hazen.

Correct: Henry E. Alvord,[4]
                                              Captain 10th Cav. A.A.I.G.,
                                              District Indian Territory.

---

[4]For information on Alvord, see the introduction to chapter 21.

6

George A. Custer, Seventh Cavalry

George Armstrong Custer was born on December 5, 1839, in New Rumley, Ohio. After graduation from West Point in 1861, he was commissioned a second lieutenant in the Fifth U.S. Cavalry. His limitless energy, driving ambition, and aggressive attitude earned him a meteoric rise in the volunteer ranks. In 1863, at the age of only twenty-three, Custer was promoted to brigadier general of volunteers and assigned to the Michigan Brigade, which became famous under his leadership. The culmination of his distinguished Civil War career came in 1865, when he was promoted to major general of volunteers and led the Third Cavalry Division from one victory to another. Custer's perceptive faculties, decision of character, dash, and audacity had won him the favor of his superiors and the adulation of the general public, and at the close of the war he was hailed a national hero.

During Reconstruction, Custer commanded a division in the South. He then served in the Department of Texas as chief of cavalry until 1866, when he was mustered out of the volunteer service. In the same year, with Sheridan's help, Custer won appointment as lieutenant colonel of the newly formed Seventh U.S. Cavalry. He participated in the futile Hancock expedition in southwestern Kansas and Indian Territory during the spring of 1867. General Hancock's main accomplishment in this operation was the burning of a vacated Sioux and Cheyenne village, which only escalated the hostilities.

During the summer of 1867, Custer led his regiment on an expedition to the Republican River valley in search of Indians. He soon realized that conventional methods of warfare were no match for the guerrilla tactics of his Indian adversaries. Failing to engage the hos-

tiles, he returned with his regiment to Fort Wallace, then hurriedly departed without permission for cholera-stricken Fort Riley to check on the welfare of his wife. Shortly thereafter he was arrested and court-martialed for leaving his post of duty without authorization, for excessive cruelty and illegal conduct in regards to deserters, for the abandonment of two soldiers attacked by Indians, and for marching his men excessively. Convicted on all counts in November 1867, Custer was sentenced to suspension from the army for one year.

In September 1868 this sentence was remitted at the request of Sheridan. The general had assumed command of the Department of the Missouri and wanted Custer to lead the Seventh Cavalry in a winter campaign against the Cheyennes. This campaign culminated with the Washita attack in November 1868, which established Custer's reputation as an Indian fighter. The following spring he confronted the remainder of the hostile Cheyennes at the Sweetwater in the Texas Panhandle. In stark contrast with his bloody confrontation at the Washita, the colonel gained the release of two white women and the surrender of the tribe without any bloodshed.

Custer served at Fort Hayes and Fort Leavenworth until 1871, when his regiment was ordered to Kentucky. Remaining there until 1873, he and his command then joined Brig. Gen. Stanley's Yellowstone expedition to protect the surveyors of the Northern Pacific Railroad. Afterward the Seventh Cavalry was stationed at Fort Abraham Lincoln in Dakota Territory. In 1874 Custer led his troops on an exploring and mining expedition to the Black Hills, where they discovered gold in the heart of the Sioux reservation. In 1875 the U.S. government attempted to negotiate the sale of the Black Hills, but the Sioux compassionately refused. When some bands refused to comply with a government order to return to the reservation, an punitive expedition was launched in the spring of 1876. The Dakota Column included Custer and the Seventh Cavalry, under the command of Brig. Gen. Alfred Terry. This was to be Custer's last campaign. On June 25 he along with two of his brothers, a brother-in-law, a nephew, and all the men of five troops under his personal command were slain by Sioux and Cheyennes at the Little Bighorn in Montana. The following year the colonel's remains were exhumed from a shallow grave at the battlefield and reinterred with military honors in the post cemetery at West Point.

Custer is adjudged by his contemporaries and biographers as one of the most controversial figures in American history. His admirers find him to be a mixture of unlimited energy and endurance, driving ambition, courage, quick perception, and instant reaction. Yet there was a darker side to him, exposed briefly by his court-martial in 1867. His detractors see him as an immature egotist prone to exaggeration, a reckless glory hunter who showed indifference to the fate of others. Regardless of the flood of adulation on the one hand and the volume of recrimination on the other, today Custer is remembered primarily for his enigmatic death in a disastrous defeat. He wrote a number of articles on his military experiences and was the author of My Life on the Plains, *which in part treats the battle of the Washita.*

The Custer papers gathered below consist of the following four documents: Custer's official report of the Washita battle, dated November 28, 1868; his official report of his return to the battlefield, dated December 22, 1868; a letter to K. C. Barker, president of the Detroit Audubon Club, dated May 26, 1869, in which Custer describes several war trophies taken from the Washita battlefield; and an extract from the Washita chapters in My Life on the Plains.

Official Report
November 28, 1868

Headquarters 7th United States Cavalry,
In the Field, on Washita River,
November 28, 1868.

Major General P. H. Sheridan,
Commanding Department of the Missouri.

General: On the morning of the 26th instant, this command, comprising 11 troops of the 7th Cavalry, struck a trail of an Indian war party, numbering about 100 warriors. The trail was not quite 24 hours old, and was first discovered near the point where the Texas boundary line crosses the Canadian river. The direction was towards the southeast.

The ground being covered by over 12 inches of snow, no difficulty was to be experienced in following the trail. A vigorous pursuit was at once instituted; wagons, tents, and all other impediments to a rapid march were abandoned.

From daylight until nine o'clock at night the pursuit was unchecked; horses and men were then allowed one hour for refreshment, and then at 10 P.M. the march was resumed and continued until 1.30 A.M., when our Osage trailers reported a village within less than a mile from our advance. The column was countermarched and withdrawn to a retired point to prevent discovery.

After reconnoitering, with all the officers of the command, the location of the village, which was situated in a strip of heavy timber, I divided the command into four columns of nearly equal strength; the first consisted of three companies, under Major Elliott, was to attack in the timber from below the village; the second column, under Brevet Lieutenant Colonel Myers, was to move down the Washita and attack in the timber from above; Brevet Lieutenant Colonel Thompson, in command of the third column, was to attack from the crest north of the village;[1] while the fourth column was to charge the village from the crest overlooking it on the west bank of the Washita.

The hour at which the four columns were to charge simultaneously was the first dawn of day, and notwithstanding the fact that two of the columns were compelled to march several miles to reach their positions, three of them made the attack so near together as to appear like one charge—the other column was only a few moments late. There never was a more complete surprise. My men charged the village and reached the lodges before the Indians were aware of our presence. The moment the charge was ordered the band struck up "Garry Owen," and with cheers that strongly reminded me of scenes during the war, every trooper, led by his officer, rushed towards the village.

The Indians were caught napping for once. The warriors rushed from their lodges and posted themselves behind trees, and in the deep ravines, from which they began a most determined defence.

The lodges and all their contents were in our possession within 10 minutes after the charge was ordered, but the real fighting, such

---

[1] Thompson's battalion attacked from the bluffs south of the village.

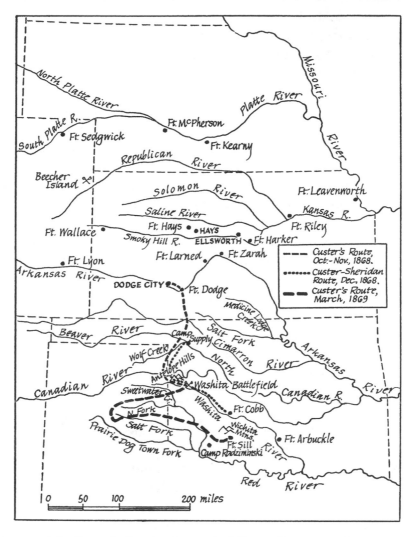

Routes of the Seventh Cavalry during the Winter Campaign of 1868–1869. Reproduced from George A. Custer's *My Life on the Plains.*

as has rarely if ever been equalled in Indian warfare, began when attempting to clear out or kill the warriors posted in ravines or underbrush; charge after charge was made, and most gallantly, too, but the Indians had resolved to sell their lives as dearly as possible. After a desperate conflict of several hours, our efforts were crowned by a most complete and gratifying success. The entire village, numbering 47 lodges of Black Kettle's band of Cheyennes, two lodges of Arapahoes, and two lodges of Sioux—51 lodges in all—under command of their principal chief, Black Kettle, fell into our hands. By actual and careful examination after the battle, the following figures give some of the fruits of our victory: The Indians left on the ground and in our possession the bodies of 103 of their warriors, including Black Kettle himself, whose scalp is now in the possession of our Osage guides. We captured in good condition 875 horses, ponies, and mules, 241 saddles, some of very fine and costly workmanship, 573 buffalo robes, 390 buffalo skins for lodges, 160 untanned robes, 210 axes, 140 hatchets, 35 revolvers, 47 rifles, 535 pounds of powder, 1,050 pounds of lead, 4,000 arrows and arrowheads, 75 spears, 90 bullet moulds, 35 bows and quivers, 12 shields, 300 pounds of bullets, 775 lariats, 940 buckskin saddlebags, 470 blankets, 93 coats, 700 pounds of tobacco. In addition, we captured all their winter supply of buffalo meat, all their meal, flour, and other provisions, and, in fact, everything they possessed, even driving the warriors from the village with little or no clothing.

We destroyed everything of value to the Indians, and have now in our possession, as prisoners of war, 53 squaws and their children. Among the prisoners are the survivors of Black Kettle and the family of Little Rock. We also secured two white children, held captive by the Indians. One white woman who was in their possession was murdered by her captors the moment we attacked. A white boy held captive, about 10 years old, when about to be rescued, was brutally murdered by a squaw, who ripped out his entrails with a knife.[2]

The Kiowas, under Satanta,[3] and Arapahoes, under Little Raven, were encamped six miles below Black Kettle's village; the

---

[2]In actuality, this was a Cheyenne infant who was killed by his mother out of despair. See chapter 18.

[3]Santanta, or White Bear, was perhaps the most influential of the Kiowa chiefs. Born about 1830, he was a great orator, with a splendid physique and a piercing glance, and had a reputation as a notorious raider with a great fondness for whiskey. He became the leader of a Kiowa faction upon the death of Little Mountain in 1865 and was a signatory to the Medicine Lodge Treaty (1867). His involvement in the torture of seven teamsters of the Henry Warren wagon train in 1871 led to his imprisonment in Texas. Released in 1873 but ignoring the conditions of his parole, he participated in the Red River War and was later arrested and returned to the penitentiary in Huntsville. Satanta committed suicide on October 11, 1878, by jumping headfirst out of a second-story window; he was

warriors from these two villages came to attempt the rescue of the Cheyennes. They attacked my command from all sides about noon, hoping to recover the squaws and herd of the Cheyennes.

In their attack they displayed great boldness, and compelled me to use all my force to repel them, but the counter-charges of the cavalry was more than they could stand; by 3 o'clock we drove them in all directions, pursuing them several miles. I then moved my entire command in search of the villages of the Kiowas and Arapahoes, but after a march of eight miles discovered they had taken alarm at the fate of the Cheyenne village, and had fled.[4]

I was then three day's march from where I had left my train of supplies, and knew that wagons could not follow me, as the trail had led me over a section of country so cut up by ravines and other obstructions that cavalry could with difficulty move over it. The supplies carried from the train on the persons of the men were exhausted; my men, from loss of sleep and hard service, were wearied out; my horses were in the same condition for want of forage; I therefore began my return march about 8 P.M., and found my train of supplies at this point, (it only having accomplished 16 miles since I left it.)

In the excitement of the fight, as well as in self-defence, it so happened that some of the squaws and a few of the children were killed and wounded; the latter I have brought with us, and they receive all the medical attention the circumstances of the case permit. Many of the squaws were taken with arms in their hands, and several of my command are known to have been wounded by them.

The desperate character of the combat may be inferred from the fact that, after the battle, the bodies of 38 dead warriors were

---

buried in the prison cemetery. The chief was survived by his wife, two daughters, and two sons. Both daughters married Trails the Enemy, a Kiowa scout at Fort Sill. Santana's youngest son, Mark, mustered in L Company, 7th Cavalry, an Indian scout company, while the oldest son became a member of the Indian Police on the reservation. After a long court fight in 1963, the Texas legislature granted a request by Satanta's grandson, James Auchiah, to exhume his grandfather's remains for reinterment in the post cemetery at Fort Sill. Nye 1969, 127, 255–56.

[4]This was an Arapaho village. It was located on the east side of the Washita near where present Highway 33 crosses the river. Although Custer asserts that he advanced as far as this village, Lt. Edward S. Godfrey contradicts this statement. See the extract from Custer's *Life on the Plains* in this chapter and Godfrey's account in chapter 8.

found in a small ravine near the village in which they had posted themselves.

I now have to report the loss suffered by my command. I regret to mention among the killed Major Joel H. Elliott and Captain Louis M. Hamilton, and 19 enlisted men; the wounded includes three officers and 11 enlisted men—in all, 35. Of the officers, Brevet Lieutenant Colonel Albert Barnitz, captain 7th Cavalry, is seriously, if not mortally, wounded; Brevet Lieutenant Colonel T. W. Custer, and Second Lieutenant T. J. March, 7th Cavalry, are slightly wounded. Brevet Lieutenant Colonel F. W. Benteen had his horse shot under him by a son of Black Kettle, whom he afterwards killed. Colonel Barnitz, before receiving his wound, killed two warriors.

I cannot sufficiently commend the admirable conduct of the officers and men.

This command has marched five days amidst terrible snow storms, and over a rough country covered by more than 12 inches of snow. Officers and men have slept in the snow without tents. The night preceding the attack, officers and men stood at their horses' heads for hours, awaiting the moment of attack; this, too, when the temperature was far below the freezing point. They have endured every privation, and fought with unsurpassed gallantry against a powerful and well-armed foe, and from first to last I have not heard a single murmur; but, on the contrary, the officers and men of the several squadrons and companies seemed to vie with each other in their attention to duty, and their patience and perseverance under difficulties.

Every officer, man, scout, and Indian guide, did their full duty. I only regret the loss of the gallant spirits who fell in the "battle of the Washita." Those whose loss we are called upon to deplore were among our bravest and best.

Respectfully submitted:

G. A. Custer,
Lieutenant Colonel 7th Cavalry, Bvt. Maj. Gen. U.S.A.

Official Report
December 22, 1868

Headq'rs Troops Operating South of the Arkansas,
In the field, Indian Territory, December 22, 1868.

Brevet Lieut. Col. J. Schuyler Crosby,
A.A.A.G., Department of the Missouri.

Colonel: I have the honor to submit the following report of the operations of my command from the 7th instant up to the present date.

Acting under the instructions of the major general commanding the department, who, though not exercising command of the troops, accompanied the expedition, I moved from the supply depot, on Beaver Creek, on the morning of the 7th instant. The expedition was composed of 11 companies of the 7th United States Cavalry, 10 companies of the 19th Kansas Volunteer Cavalry, Colonel S. J. Crawford[5] commanding, a detachment of scouts under Lieutenant Pepoon,[6] 10th Cavalry, and between 20 and 30

---

[5]Samuel Johnson Crawford was a native of Indiana who settled in Kansas in 1859. He received a commission as captain in the Second Kansas Cavalry in May 1861 and was promoted to colonel of the Eighty-Third Colored Infantry in November 1863. Crawford participated in numerous skirmishes and battles west of the Mississippi, including Old Fort Wayne in October 1862, Jenkins' Ferry in April 1864, and Westport and Little Osage in October 1864, and was brevetted brigadier general of volunteers in March 1865 for meritorious service. While still less than thirty years of age, he resigned his commission on November 7, 1864, upon his election as governor of Kansas. Faced with escalating Indian hostilities, Crawford resigned his office on November 4, 1868, to organize and command a volunteer cavalry regiment to protect the settlers on the Kansas frontier. Ordered to participate in a winter offensive against the Indians, his unit was to join the Seventh Cavalry at Camp Supply. But severe weather delayed the Kansas regiment's arrival and prevented its participation in the battle of the Washita. Crawford died on October 21, 1913. Crawford 1911.

[6]Born on June 13, 1834, in Painesville, Ohio, Silas Pepoon served in the First Oregon Cavalry from November 1861 until 1866, when he was honorably discharged at the rank of first lieutenant. In November 1867 he was commissioned a second lieutenant in the Tenth Cavalry, promoted to first lieutenant in May 1872. Lieutenant Pepoon commanded the Indian scouts during most of his services on the southern plains. He was present with the relief force sent to the beleaguered Beecher Island scouts in 1868 and accompanied the Southern Plains expedition following the Washita fight. In 1874 he and his scout force participated in the Red River campaign conducted by General Miles. While facing a court-martial for conduct unbecoming an officer and a gentleman,

whites, Osage, and Kaw Indians, as guides and trailers. I aimed by a new route to strike the Washita below and near to the scene of the late battle between the 7th Cavalry and the combined bands of the Cheyennes, Arapahoes, Kiowas, Sioux, Apaches, and Comanches. On the evening of the 10th my command reached camp on the Washita, six miles below the battleground. A halt of one day was made at this point to rest and graze the animals, and to afford an opportunity of visiting the battlefield, to learn, if possible, the exact fate of Major Elliott and his party of 17 men, who, on the opening of the attack on Black Kettle's village, had pursued a party of flee-ing Indians beyond our lines, and had never returned. So confident was I of their fate, however, that in my official report of the battle I numbered them in my list of killed. With 100 men of the 7th Cav-alry, under command of Captain Yates, I proceeded to the battle-field early on the morning of the 11th. Indians had evidently paid a hurried visit to the scene of the late conflict.

The bodies of nearly all the warriors killed in the fight had been concealed or removed, while those of the squaws and children who had been slain in the excitement and confusion of the first charge, as well as in self-defense, were wrapped in blankets and bound with lariats, preparatory to removal and burial. Many of the Indian dogs were still found in the vicinity lately occupied by the lodges of their owners; they [were] probably subsisting on the bodies of the ponies that had been killed and then covered several acres of ground nearby. As 10 days had elapsed since the battle, and scores of Indian bodies still remained unburied or uncon-cealed, some idea may be had of the precipitate haste with which the Indians had abandoned that section of the country. A thor-ough examination of the immediate battleground failed to dis-cover anything worthy of special report, except that Indian bodies were found that had not previously been reported in my first despatch, and which went to prove what we are all aware of now, that the enemy's loss in killed warriors far exceeded the number (103) first reported by me.

In setting out upon our return to camp, Captain Yates was directed to deploy his men in search of the bodies of Major Elliott

---

Pepoon became increasingly despondent and died of a self-inflicted gunshot wound to the head on October 16, 1874, in his tent near Fort Sill. Jacob 1924, 31.

and his party. After marching a distance of two miles, in the direction of which Major Elliott and his little party were last seen, we suddenly came upon the stark stiff, naked, and horribly mutilated bodies of our dead comrades. No words were needed to tell how desperate the struggle which ensued [must have been] before they were finally overpowered. At a short distance, here and there, from the spot where the bodies lay could be seen the carcasses of some of the horses of the party which had been probably killed early in the fight. Seeing the hopelessness of breaking through the lines which surrounded them, and which undoubtedly numbered more than one hundred to one, Elliott dismounted his men, tied their horses together, and prepared to sell their lives as dearly as possible. It may not be improper to add that in describing as far as possible the details of Elliott's fight, I rely not only upon a critical and personal examination of the ground and attendant circumstances, but am sustained by the statements of Indian chiefs and warriors who witnessed and participated in the fight, and who have since been forced to enter our lines and surrender themselves up under circumstances which will be made to appear in other portions of this report.

The bodies of Elliott and his little band, with but a single exception, were all found lying within a circle not exceeding 20 yards in diameter. We found them exactly as they fell, except that their barbarous foes had stripped and mutilated the bodies in the most savage manner.

All the bodies were carried to camp; the latter we reached after dark. It being the intention to resume the march before daylight the following day, a grave was hastily prepared on a little knoll near our camp, and, with the exception of that of Major Elliott, whose remains were carried with us for interment at Fort Arbuckle, the bodies of the entire party, under the dim light of a few torches held in the hands of sorrowing comrades, were consigned to one common resting place. No funeral note sounded to measure their passage to the grave; no volley was fired to tell us a comrade was receiving the last sad rites of burial, yet not one of the living but felt that the fresh earth had closed over some of their truest and mostly daring soldiers!

Before interment I caused a complete examination of each body to be made by Dr. Lippincott, chief medical officer of the expedition, with directions to report on the character and number of wounds received by each, as well as the mutilations to which they had been subjected. The following extracts are taken from Dr. Lippincott's report:

Major Joel H. Elliott—two bullet holes in head; one in left cheek; right hand cut off; left foot almost cut off; [penis cut off]; deep gash in right groin; deep gashes in calves of both legs; little finger of left hand cut off; and throat cut.

Sergeant-major Walter Kennedy—bullet hole in right temple; head partly cut off; seventeen bullet holes in back; and two in legs.

Corporal Harry Mercer, troop E—bullet hole in right axilla; one in region of heart; three in back; eight arrow wounds in back; right ear cut off; head scalped and skull fractured; deep gashes in both legs; and throat cut.

Corporal Thomas Christie, troop E—bullet hole in head; right foot cut off; bullet hole in abdomen; and throat cut.

Corporal William Carrick, troop H—bullet hole in right parietal bone; both feet cut off; throat cut; left arm broken; [penis cut off].

Private Eugene Clover, troop H—head cut off; arrow wound in right side; both legs terribly mutilated.

Private William Milligan, troop H—bullet hole in left side of head; deep gashes in right leg; [penis cut off]; left arm deeply gashed; head scalped; and throat cut.

Corporal James F. Williams, troop I—bullet hole in back; head and both arms cut off; many and deep gashes in back; [penis cut off].

Private Thomas Downey, troop I—arrow hole in region of stomach; thorax cut open; head cut off; and right shoulder cut by a tomahawk.

Farrier Thomas Fitzpatrick, troop M—scalped; two arrow and several bullet holes in back; throat cut.

Private Ferdinand Lineback, troop M—bullet hole in the left parietal bone; head scalped and arm broken; [penis cut off]; throat cut.

Private John Meyers, troop M—several bullet holes in head; skull extensively fractured; several arrow and bullet holes in back; deep gashes in face; throat cut.

Private Carsten D. J. Meyers, troop M—several bullet holes in head; scalped; 19 bullet holes in body; [penis cut off]; throat cut.

Private Cal. Sharpe, troop M—two bullet holes in right side; throat cut; one bullet hole in left side of head; one arrow hole in left side; [penis cut off]; left arm broken.

Unknown—head cut off; body partially destroyed by wolves.

Unknown—head and right hand cut off; three bullet and nine arrow holes in back; [penis cut off].

Unknown—scalped; skull fractured; 6 bullet and 13 arrow holes in back; three bullet holes in chest.

In addition to the wounds and barbarities reported by Dr. Lippincott, I saw a portion of the stock of a "Lancaster rifle," protruding from the side of one of the men. The stock had been broken off near the barrel, and the butt of it, probably 12 inches in length, had been driven into the man's side a distance of eight inches.

The forest along the banks of the Washita, from the battleground to [a] distance of 12 miles, was found to have been one continuous Indian village, Black Kettle's band being above; then came other hostile tribes, camped in the following order: Arapahoes, under Little Raven; Kiowas, under Satanta and Lone Wolf;[7]

---

[7]Born about 1820, Lone Wolf was a man of great natural ability and dignified bearing known for his diplomatic skills. When aroused, however, he was quick to resort to violence. Lone Wolf became a leading chief of the Kiowas in 1865 upon the death of Little Mountain, the principal leader since 1834. A signatory to the Medicine Lodge Treaty (1867), by 1872 he had become the recognized leader of the Kiowa nation. The next year his son and a nephew were killed during a raid in Mexico. Becoming increasingly hostile toward whites, Lone Wolf participated in the battle of Adobe Walls in June 1874 and avenged the death of his son a month later by killing a Texas Ranger. In 1875 he was imprisoned at Fort Marion in St. Augustine, Florida, for depredations. After his release he returned to the reservation at Anadarko, where he became afflicted with malaria during a severe epidemic in 1879. He died the same year and was buried in an unmarked grave on the north side of Mount Scott. Before his death, Lone Wolf gave his name to his favorite nephew, Namay-Day-Te, as a gift. Young Lone Wolf, as he was thereafter known, lived near present Hobart, Oklahoma, and was eventually converted to Christianity at Rainy Mountain Mission. He visited Washington in 1890 as a member of the Kiowa delegation and was recognized by many as a chief. Nye 1969, 277.

the remaining bands of Cheyennes, Comanches, and Apaches. Nothing could exceed the disorder and haste with which these tribes had fled from their camping grounds. They had abandoned thousands of lodge poles, some of which were still standing as when last used; immense numbers of camp kettles, cooking utensils, coffee-mills, axes, and several hundred buffalo robes were found in the abandoned camps adjacent to that of Black Kettle's village, but which had not been visited before by our troops.

By actual examination and estimate it was computed that over 600 lodges had been standing along the Washita during the battle and within five miles of the battleground, and it was from these villages, and others still lower down the stream, that the immense number of warriors came, who, after my rout and destruction of Black Kettle and his band, surrounded my command and fought until defeated by the 7th Cavalry, about 3 P.M. on the 27th ultimo. It is safe to say that the warriors from these tribes that attempted the relief of Black Kettle and his band outnumbered my force at least three to one. On returning from the battleground to the camp of my command, and when in the deserted camp which, according to the statement of some of my Cheyenne prisoners who were brought along with me, was lately occupied by Satanta with the Kiowas, my men discovered the bodies of a young white woman and child, the former apparently about 23 years of age, and the child probably 18 months old. They were evidently mother and child and had not long been in captivity, as the woman still retained several articles of her wardrobe about her person; among others a pair of cloth gaiters but little worn; everything indicating that she had been but recently captured; and upon our attacking and routing Black Kettle's camp her captors, fearing she might be recaptured by us and her testimony used against them, had deliberately murdered her and her child in cold blood. The woman had received a shot in the forehead, her entire scalp was removed, and her skull horribly crushed. The child also bore numerous marks of violence.[8]

---

[8]The remains were those of Clara Blinn and her infant son, Willie. Dr. Mahlon Bailey of Topeka, attached to the Nineteenth Kansas Volunteer Cavalry, discovered the corpses. H. L. Moore 1900, 35. But see also chapter 20 below.

At daylight the following morning the entire command started on the trail of the Indian villages, nearly all of which had moved down the Washita toward Fort Cobb, where they had reason to believe they would receive protection. The Arapahos and remaining band of Cheyennes left the Washita valley and moved across in the direction of Red river. After following the trail of the Kiowas and other hostile Indians for seven days over an almost impassible country, where it was necessary to keep two or three hundred men almost constantly at work with picks, axes, and spades, before being able to advance with our train, my Osage scouts on the morning of the 17th reported a party of Indians in our front bearing a flag of truce. At the same time a scout came from the same direction stating that he was from Fort Cobb, and delivered to me a despatch which read as follows:

Headquarters Southern Indian District,
Fort Cobb, 9 P.M., December 16, 1868.

To the commanding officer troops in the field:
Indians have just brought in word that our troops to-day reached the Washita, some 20 miles above here. I send this to say that all the camps this side of the point reported to have been reached are friendly, and have not been on the warpath this season. If this reaches you it would be well to communicate at once with Satanta or Black Eagle,[9] chiefs of the Kiowas, near where you are now, who will readily inform you of the position of the Cheyennes and Arapahoes, also of our camp.

Respectfully,

W. B. Hazen, Brevet Major General.

The scout at the same time informed me that a large party of Kiowa warriors under Lone Wolf, Satanta, and other leading chiefs, were within less than a mile of my advance, and notwithstanding the above certificate regarding their friendly character, had seized a scout who accompanied the bearer of the despatch, disarmed him, and held him a prisoner of war.

---

[9]Black Eagle was the moderate leader of a small Kiowa band and a signatory of the Medicine Lodge Treaty (1867).

Taking a small party with me I proceeded beyond our lines to meet the flag of truce. I was met by several of the leading chiefs of the Kiowas, including those above named. Large parties of their warriors could be seen posted in the neighboring ravines and upon the surrounding hill tops. All were painted and plumed for war, and nearly all were armed with one rifle, two revolvers, bow and arrows and lance. Their bows were strung. Their whole appearance and conduct plainly indicated that they had come for war. Their declaration to some of my guides and friendly Indians proved the same thing; and they were only deterred from hostile acts by discovering our strength to be far greater than they had imagined, and our scouts on the alert. Some twenty of the principal chiefs of the Kiowas, Apaches, and Comanches then approached and proposed to accompany us to Fort Cobb, the Kiowas assuring me that their village was already near that point and moving to the post. Yet at the same time these chiefs were giving me these assurances their entire village, with the exception of the war party which accompanied them, was hastening away toward the Wichita mountains with no intention of proceeding to Fort Cobb, and the proposition of the chiefs to accompany my column was intended as a mere ruse to cover the escape of the village. On reaching camp I gave rations to the entire party of chiefs and warriors who accompanied my column, intending to do no act that might be construed as unfriendly. They all promised to proceed to Fort Cobb with us the following day except two or three, who were to rejoin the village and conduct it to the fort, but upon resuming the march the next morning it was found that but three Kiowas and two Apache chiefs remained; the rest had taken their departure.

Before proceeding far the few who remained intimated their intention and desire to proceed to their village and change their ponies as well as to give directions about the movement of the former to Fort Cobb. This they repeated several times along the line of march. I finally permitted the Kiowa chief lowest in rank to set out for his village, with the distinct understanding that it was for the purpose of hastening the march of his people to Fort Cobb. They were then represented as being within less than ten miles of the post. I then placed Lone Wolf and Satanta, the head chiefs of the Kiowas, and the two head chiefs of the Apaches under guard, determined to hold them as hostages for the faithful fulfillment of the promise which they and their people had been under for several months, and which was one of the stipulations of the last treaty made with them.

At the same time I knew it was the intention of the department commander to assemble all the hostile tribes in the vicinity of Fort Cobb, by force if necessary, in order that they might learn the decision of the government regarding past offenses and the treatment they might expect in the future.

The communication received through scouts from Brevet Major General Hazen, United States Army, superintendent of the southern Indian agency, in which it is stated that "All the camps this side of the point reported to have been reached are friendly, and have not been on the war path this season," occasioned no little surprise upon the part of those who knew the hostile character of the Indians referred to.

We had followed day by day the trail of the Kiowas and other tribes leading as directly from the dead bodies of our comrades, slain by them within the past few days, until we overtook them about 40 miles from Fort Cobb.

This of itself was conclusive evidence of the character of the tribes we were dealing with; but, aside from these incontrovertible facts, had we needed additional evidence of the openly hostile conduct of the Kiowas and Comanches, and of their active participation in the late battle of the Washita, we have only to rely on the collected testimony of Black Eagle and other leading chiefs. This testimony is now written and in the hands of the agents of the Indian bureau. It was given voluntarily by the Indian chiefs referred to, and was taken down at the time by Indian agents, not for the army, or with a view of furnishing it to the officers of the army, but simply for the benefit and information of the Indian bureau. This testimony, making due allowance for the concealment of much that would be prejudicial to the interests of the Indians, plainly states that the Kiowas and Comanches took part in the battle of the Washita; that the former constituted a portion of the war party whose trail I followed, and which led my command into Black Kettle's village; and that some of the Kiowas remained in Black Kettle's village until the morning of the battle.

This evidence is all contained in a report made to one Thomas Murphy,[10] superintendent of Indian affairs, by Philip McCaskey [McCusker],[11] United States interpreter for the Kiowas and Comanches. This report is dated Fort Cobb, December 3, while the communication from General Hazen, vouching for the peaceable character of the Kiowas and other tribes, is dated at the same place 13 days later. It cannot be explained by supposing General Hazen ignorant of the information contained in the report, as I obtained a copy of the report from him. It only proves what the Indian bureau regards as "friendly" Indians. In addition to all the above evidence and facts, a personal conversation with Lone Wolf, Satanta, Black Eagle, and other prominent chiefs, convinces me, even had we no other information to rely upon, that a large number of the Kiowas, led by Kicking Bird[12] and other Kiowa chiefs, voluntarily participated in the battle of the Washita, and that they formed a considerable portion of the hundreds who surrounded and killed Major Elliott and his party. The horse ridden by one of my men who was killed in that battle has since been recognized in the hands of a Kiowa.

All this testimony is more than confirmed by the statements of a very intelligent squaw, sister of Black Kettle,[13] who is among my

---

[10]For information on Thomas Murphy, see the introduction to chapter 22.

[11]For information on Philip McCusker, see the introduction to chapter 41.

[12]Custer's statement is not born out by the facts. Kicking Bird (Striking Eagle) was a moderate who favored peace and one of the most distinguished Kiowa leaders in history. His standing in the tribe came from his superior intellect, courage, and force of character, which also gave him considerable influence among whites. He was described as a remarkable man, slight in form, tall, agile, and very graceful. Honorable and friendly, he sought to bring his people in line with the wishes of the Indian agents, having signed the Medicine Lodge Treaty. During the Red River outbreak of 1874, he quickly brought most of his people back to the reservation, though forced by the military the following year to select a number of hostile tribesmen for imprisonment at Fort Marion. One of these convicts supposedly hired a medicine man named Sky Walker to kill the chief by means of witchcraft. Whether a coincidence or not, Kicking Bird was stricken by a sudden and mysterious seizure and died on May 3, 1875. He was buried in an unmarked grave at Fort Sill Cemetery. Battey 1875, 102; Nye 1962, 278–79; Tatum 1970, 223.

[13]This Cheyenne emissary was Mahwissa, also known as Red Hair. She was the daughter of Wood and Magpie Woman, and Custer described her as a middle-aged woman. Upon the colonel's arrival at the hostile camps along the Sweet Water, Red Hair claimed that the Cheyennes had "detained" her. She was temporarily imprisoned at Fort Hayes on April 17, 1869, released with the other Washita prisoners at Camp Supply on June 22. According to the Cheyenne concept of family relationships, Red Hair may actually have been a cousin to Black Kettle since a man's female cousin is also addressed as "sister." G. A. Custer 1874, 170–71; E. B. Custer 1966, 90–91; Burkey 1976, 65.

prisoners, and who, on account of her intelligence and character, I despatched a few days ago as bearer of a message to the hostile Cheyennes. She pointed out to me, when in the vicinity of the battleground, the location of Satanta's village at the time of the battle. She, as well as other[s] of my prisoners, are confident as well as positive that Satanta and his tribe were there, and that they participated in the engagement. It was from her, too, that I learned that it was in Satanta's village that the bodies of the white woman and child were found.[14] I have not intimated to Lone Wolf or Satanta that all this evidence is in our possession, nor do I propose doing so until the last Kiowa has come in.

Soon after reaching this point it became evident that these chiefs were attempting their usual game of duplicity and falsehood. Under the pretence that their village was coming to this point to renew friendly relations with the government, they visited my headquarters and professed the most peaceable intentions. It was only after receiving information that their village was attempting to escape to the mountains, [that] it was deemed necessary to resort to summary measures to compel these refractory chiefs to fulfill their promise.

They were placed under a strong guard the moment we reached this point. Even this failed to produce the desired effect. All evidence went to show that their village was still moving farther off. Then it was that I announced to Lone Wolf and Satanta the decision which had been arrived at regarding them. I gave them until sunrise the following morning to cause their people to come in, or to give satisfactory evidence that they were hastening to come in. If no such evidence appeared, both these chiefs were to be hung at sunrise to the nearest tree. At the same time I afforded them every

---

[14]The remains of Clara Blinn and her infant son were discovered in Yellow Bear's Arapaho camp, which stood on the right bank (east side) of the Washita, some five miles downstream from Black Kettle's village. Sheridan expressed his sympathy to the Blinn family through a letter of condolence and a hem piece cut from Clara's mulberry-colored calico dress. The articles were forwarded to the bereaved family in a beaded, fringed Arapaho pipe bag found in the camp. Since the Arapahos were close allies of the Cheyennes (one of Black Kettle's wives was an Arapaho woman), it is quite likely that the Cheyenne informant concealed the Arapaho involvement in the Blinn slayings and blamed the Kiowas instead. Clark to Barde, May 1, 1903; undated newspaper clipping, in Richard F. Blinn Collection; Haines 1999, 182; Ross 1988, 46–47.

facility to send runners and communicate their desires to their tribe. This produced the desired effect. By sunrise several of the leading Kiowas came to my camp and reported the entire village on the move, hastening to place themselves under our control. At this date I have the satisfaction to report that all the Apaches, nearly all of the Comanches, and the principal chiefs and bands of the Kiowas have come in and placed themselves under our control; not to make a treaty and propose terms of settlement, but begging us to announce the terms upon which they can be allowed to resume peaceful relations with the government. Of the five tribes which were hostile at the opening of the campaign, three are already in our power, being virtually prisoners of war.

The remaining two, the Cheyennes and Arapahoes, were the principal sufferers in the battle of the Washita, and are, no doubt, the most anxious of all to abandon the warpath. They are supposed to be concealed in the mountains, 40 or 50 miles from this point, awaiting the result of the present negotiations with the three tribes now assembled here.

On the 20th instant I sent one of my prisoners (a Cheyenne squaw, sister of Black Kettle,) and a leading Apache chief, as bearers of a message to the Cheyennes and Arapahoes. As in the case of the tribes now here, no promise or inducement has been held out. I have made no pretence to be friendly disposed. Whatever I have asked the tribes to do or accede to has been in the form of a demand.

They have, from the commencement of this campaign, been treated not as independent nations, but as refractory subjects of a common government.

I have reason to believe that within a few days, or weeks at furthest, the two remaining hostile tribes, Cheyennes and Arapahoes, smarting under their heavy losses in the battle of the Washita, will unconditionally come in and place themselves under the control of this command, willing to accede to any terms that may be proposed to them. The tribes now here have discarded the arrogant ideas in the indulgence of which the numerous treaties recently entered into have encouraged them. They now seem to realize that the government, and not a few thieving, treacherous chiefs of predatory bands of savages, backed up and encouraged by unprincipled and designing Indian agents, is the source of all authority.

The chiefs now have repeatedly informed me that they no longer claim the right to propose terms regarding the future course of the government towards them, but are not only ready but anxious to accede to any rule marked down for their control and guidance.

The above, I believe, contains a brief statement of the operations of the command, and the results thereof up to this date. Everything indicates a speedy, satisfactory, and permanent solution of the Indian difficulties so far as the tribes referred to are concerned.

It is not proposed that they be permitted to resume peaceful relations with the government until proper atonement be made for past offenses, and sufficient guarantee for future good conduct be given.

I take pleasure in adding that, although I am in command of the forces composing this expedition the major general commanding the department has accompanied it in person, and all negotiations and official action on my part regarding the Indian question has been in accordance with his previously expressed desire, or has received subsequent approval.

In relation to the battle of the Washita I find, by taking the admissions of the Indians who are now here and who participated in the battle, that the enemy's loss far exceeded that reported by me in my first despatch concerning the fight. I reported 103 warriors left dead in our possession. The Indians admit a loss of 140 killed,[15] besides a heavy loss in wounded. This, with the prisoners

---

[15]There exists considerable controversy about the Indian casualties reported by Custer. In the initial report of November 29, he states that by "actual and careful examination" the bodies of 103 warriors were counted after the battle. Yet a statement by Edward Godfrey makes it clear that the dead Indians were not counted at all but rather were guessed at later. Godfrey goes on to explain that on the second night after the battle, Custer interrogated the company commanders about the number of enemy dead seen in the village, which became the basis for the colonel's guesstimate. According to Benteen, "Custer assembled the officers to inquire of each how many dead Indians *each* had seen; then what each had seen were added. *They all had seen the same dead Indians* [emphasis in original]. (Benteen n.d.(b), 233)" John Poisal and Jack Fitzpatrick, mixed-blood scouts attached to the Seventh Cavalry, provided additional information about this inflated count. Commenting on Custer's official report of the fight, both scouts

we have in our possession, makes the entire loss of the Indians in killed, wounded, and missing not far from 300.

The report of Indians regarding their heavy losses is confirmed by the fact that on the march, and when revisiting the battle ground, we found dead Indians six miles from the scene of the battle,[16] where they had probably crawled and died after receiving their wounds. These of course were not reported in my first despatch. The head chiefs now here admit that the Indians have never suffered so overwhelming a defeat with such terrible losses.

Upon referring to the terms of the treaty defining the limits of the reservations upon which these hostile tribes were to locate themselves, and upon which they were to remain, it is found that the battle of the Washita took place nearly 100 miles outside the limits of the reservation.

Respectfully submitted:

G. A. Custer,
Brevet Major General U.S.A., Commanding Expedition.

---

stated that it was "very much exaggerated" and that there were "not over twenty bucks killed." See chapters 8 and 24 below.

Custer's revised casualty total invites even more skepticism. This new number was based on information obtained from two imprisoned Kiowa chiefs at Fort Cobb who faced death by hanging. In view of their predicament, it seems likely that these men would have said anything to avoid the gallows. But such skepticism is not warranted in the case of the Washita prisoners. The Cheyenne women were allowed to mingle freely with the officers and knew many of them on an intimate basis. They were assured good treatment and had no apparent reason to distort their statements about dead kinsmen. Questioned by Sheridan at Camp Supply, the women reported that the killed consisted of thirteen Cheyenne men, two Sioux, and one Arapaho chief. Subsequent information from independent Cheyenne sources confirmed this number, while the overall dead count was stated as from twenty-nine to thirty-eight people. For those who still express doubts about this low Indian casualty count, consider the battle of the Little Bighorn (1876), where the Sioux and Cheyennes lost only forty people during two days of fighting. For further information on Indian casualties, see Sheridan's report dated December 3, 1868, in chapter 23 and "Composite List of Names" and "Aggregate Totals" in Appendix G below. For Indian casualties at Little Bighorn, see Hardorff 1993.

[16]On the afternoon of the Washita battle, Lieutenant Godfrey and a platoon of K Company left the battlefield in pursuit of Indians fleeing downstream. From a promontory on the west bank several miles northeast of the battlefield, Godfrey noticed a lone lodge set apart some distance from the main village, which was strung farther back along the river. This may have been a funeral lodge. If so, Custer may have mistaken the deceased for a combat casualty. See chapter 8 below.

Letter to K. C. Barker
May 26, 1869

Headquarters 7th U.S. Cavalry
Near Fort Hays, Kansas.
May 26th, 1869.

Hon. K. C. Barker[17]
President of Audubon Club
Detroit, Michigan.

Dear Sir

Permit me to present through you to the worthy club over which you preside the accompanying Indian curiosities, obtained by me during the campaign of last winter. The scalp is that of Little Rock who was killed at the battle of the Washita. He was a very prominent chief of the Cheyennes, second in rank to Black Kettle. The shield is a highly prized implement [*sic*] of Indian warfare, the loss of which is considered a great disgrace. It is constantly worn in battle and is perfect protection against arrows or against balls striking it at an angle. It is made of the hide of a buffalo bull taken from the neck where the skin is the thickest and toughest. A great deal of ceremony, or as the Indians term it "Medecisn," is considered necessary to be observed before the shield is considered as dedicated to war. The shield I send you was captured during the past winter from the Cheyennes, the most warlike and troublesome tribe on the plains as well as the most powerful.[18]

---

[17]The Custer letter is housed in the Burton Historical Collection, Detroit Public Library, Michigan, and is reproduced herein by special permission. An amicable, corpulent man, Kirkland C. Barker served as the mayor of Detroit, Michigan, from 1864 to 1865 and was the owner of the K. C. Barker Tobacco Company. He was known as an avid sportsman and had presented Custer with a litter of Scots staghounds in 1866. While visiting Kansas as a guest of the Custers in October 1869, Barker nearly suffered a fatal accident when he was thrown from his horse during a buffalo chase near Fort Hays. Schwarck 1992, 16, 21.

[18]The owner of the shield was Little Rock. Both the scalp and the shield were part of the holdings of the Audubon Club in Detroit until 1877, when the entire collection was transferred to the Detroit Scientific Association. In 1885 the Scientific Association deeded its natural history collection and "curiosities" to the Library Commission of Detroit. Being temporary custodians, the commission transferred the collection in 1895

The beaded buck skin dress is that of a squaw [and] also a relic of the Washita Nov. 27th, 1868.

The bow and quiver, the latter full of war arrows, was given to me in the Indian Territory last winter by a Kiowa warrior, father of the famous Kiowa Chief Sa-tun-ta whose murderous exploits have rendered his name a terror along the entire western frontier, and who at the time referred to, you may remember, was held a prisoner in my hands as a hostage for good conduct of his tribe. Satunta is the second Chief in rank and influence in his tribe. The present of the bow and quiver full of arrows was made with a view of securing the release of Satunta.

The bow, quiver and arrows are all fine specimens of their kind and it is with great difficulty that an Indian can be induced to part with them. The saddle is a good specimen of the saddle used by the Indians of the plains.

They are manufactured and covered with rawhide by the squaws. The one I sent you was captured at the battle of the Washita. Hoping this collection may prove interesting and acceptiable [*sic*] to the members of the club

I remain
Truly your friend
Signed —— G. A. Custer
Bt. Maj. Gen.
U.S.A.

---

to the Detroit Museum of Art, which in 1919 became the Detroit Institute of Arts. Although the institute affirms the existence of Little Rock's shield in their collection (accession number 76.144), Little Rock's scalp is not, and never has been, part of their holdings, according to the chief curator. Kan and Wierzbowski 1979, 127; David W. Penney to the author, July 22, 1999.

The shield, thought to have been a dream shield, one whose design and painting are revealed to the owner in a vision, is 19 1/2 inches in diameter and has a black background. It is composed of a rawhide core of bison hide and a cover of tanned buckskin stretched over the core. The center contains a thunderbird surrounded by four smaller blue-green birds. Seven white dots at the bottom represent the Pleiades. Trimmed eagle feathers and owl feathers, cornhusks, and bells are attached to the shield at certain points. These painted designs and appended elements were believed to serve as potent devices to strengthen the spiritual protective powers of this shield. Since no combat signs are found on the surface or in the core, it seems likely that Little Rock's shield was held in particular high esteem for the tremendous spiritual protection it afforded the owner. Kan and Wierbowski 1979, 127, 133.

Extract from *My Life on the Plains* (1874)[19]

We had approached near enough to the village now to plainly
catch a view here and there of the tall white lodges as they stood in
irregular order among the trees. From the openings at the top of
some of them we could perceive faint columns of smoke ascending, the occupants no doubt having kept up their feeble fires during the entire night. We had approached so near the village that
from the dead silence which reigned I feared the lodges were
deserted, the Indians having fled before we advanced. I was about
to turn in my saddle and direct the signal for attack to be given—
still anxious as to where the other detachments were—when a single rifle shot rang sharp and clear on the far side of the village
from where we were. Quickly turning to the bandleader, I directed
him to give us "Garry Owen." At once the rollicking notes of that
familiar marching and fighting air sounded forth through the valley, and in a moment were reechoed back from the opposite sides
by the loud and continued cheers of the men of the other detachments, who, true to their orders, were there and in readiness to
pounce upon the Indians the moment the attack began. In this
manner the battle of the Washita commenced. The bugles
sounded the charge, and the entire command dashed rapidly into
the village. The Indians were caught napping; but realizing at
once the dangers of their situation, they quickly overcame their
first surprise and in an instant seized their rifles, bows and arrows,
and sprang behind the nearest trees, while some leaped into the
stream, nearly waist deep, and using the bank as a rifle-pit, began a
vigorous and determined defense. Mingled with the exultant
cheers of my men could be heard the defiant war-whoop of the
warriors, who from the first fought with a desperation and courage
which no race of men could surpass. Actual possession of the village and its lodges was ours within a few moments after the charge
was made, but this was an empty victory unless we could vanquish
the late occupants, who were then pouring in a rapid and well-

---

[19]This is an extract from chapters 15–16 of G. A. Custer 1874. The book was a reprint
of Custer's articles serialized in the *Galaxy* magazine between January 1872 and October 1874. The earliest publication of a Washita installment (chapter 15) appeared in the
Army and Navy Journal, June 21, 1873.

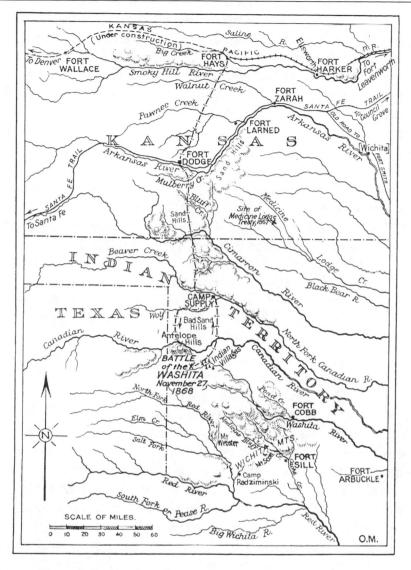

Route of Seventh Cavalry from Fort Hays to Washita River, 1868. Reproduced from Edward S. Godfrey's "Some Reminiscences, Including the Washita Battle," published in the *Cavalry Journal*.

directed fire from their stations behind trees and banks. At the first onset a considerable number of Indians rushed from the village in the direction from which Elliott's party had attacked. Some broke through the lines, while others came in contact with the mounted troopers, and were killed or captured.

Before engaging in the fight, orders had been given to prevent the killing of any but the fighting strength of the village; but in a struggle of this character it is impossible at all times to discriminate, particularly when, in a hand-to-hand conflict, such as the one the troops were then engaged in, the squaws are as dangerous adversaries as the warriors, while Indian boys between ten and fifteen years of age were found as expert and determined in the use of the pistol and bow and arrow as the older warriors. Of these facts we had numerous illustrations. Major Benteen,[20] in leading the attack of his squadron through the timber below the village, encountered an Indian boy, scarcely fourteen years of age; he was well mounted, and was endeavoring to make his way through the lines. The object these Indians had in attempting this movement we were then ignorant of, but soon learned to our sorrow. This boy rode boldly toward the Major, seeming to invite a contest. His youthful bearing, and not being looked upon as a combatant, induced Major Benteen to endeavor to save him by making "peace signs" to him and obtaining his surrender, when he could be placed in a position of safety until the battle was terminated; but the young savage desired and would accept no such friendly concessions. He regarded himself as a warrior, and the son of a warrior, and as such he purposed to do a warrior's part. With revolver in hand he dashed at the Major, who still could not regard him as anything but a harmless lad. Leveling his weapon as he rode, he fired, but either from excitement or the changing positions of both parties, his aim was defective and the shot whistled harmlessly by Major Benteen's head. Another followed in quick succession, but with no better effect. All this time the dusky little chieftain boldly advanced, to lessen the distance between himself and his adversary. A third bullet was sped on its errand, and this time to some purpose, as it passed through the neck of the Major's horse, close to the shoulder. Making a final but ineffectual appeal to him to

---

[20]Benteen held the brevet rank of lieutenant colonel in 1866, when he was commissioned as captain in the Seventh Cavalry. In August 1868 he was brevetted colonel for gallant and meritorious conduct in an engagement with hostile Indians at the Saline River in Kansas. Since it was military protocol to address officers by their brevet rank, it seems rather strange that Custer refers to Benteen as "Major," while later in the same chapter he identifies him as "Colonel." The "error" appears to be intentional and may have resulted from Custer's dislike for Benteen.

surrender, and seeing him still preparing to fire again, the Major was forced in self-defense to level his revolver and despatch him, although as he did so it was with admiration for the plucky spirit exhibited by the lad, and regret often expressed that no other course under the circumstances was left him. Attached to the saddlebow of the young Indian hung a beautifully wrought pair of small moccasins, elaborately ornamented with beads. One of the Major's troopers afterwards secured these and presented them to him. These furnished the link of evidence by which we subsequently ascertained who the young chieftain was—a title which was justly his, both by blood and bearing.[21]

We had gained the centre of the village, and were in the midst of the lodges, while on all sides could be heard the sharp crack of the Indian rifles and the heavy responses from the carbines of the troopers. After disposing of the smaller and scattering parties of warriors, who had attempted a movement down the valley, and in which some were successful, there was but little opportunity left for the successful employment of mounted troops. As the Indians by this time had taken cover behind logs and trees, and under the banks of the stream which flowed through the centre of the village, from which stronghold it was impracticable to dislodge them by the use of mounted men, a large portion of the command was at once ordered to fight on foot, and the men were instructed to take advantage of the trees and other natural means of cover, and fight the Indians in their own style. Cooke's sharpshooters had adopted this method from the first, and with telling effect. Slowly but steadily the Indians were driven from behind the trees, and those who

---

[21]The name of this casualty was Blue Horse. According to Benteen, the young Cheyenne carried two pistol holsters on his belt and was dismounted when he fired "six shots from his pistol," after which Benteen "charged up to him and killed him." Born about 1847, Blue Horse was the son of Cut Lip Bear and Corn Tassel Woman and the brother of Magpie Woman, the wife of George Bent. Corn Tassel Woman and a young son survived the attack and were captured. After the battle the mother recognized a pair of beaded moccasins taken by Benteen's men from her son's saddlebow, which led to his identification. According to Bent, Blue Horse was Black Kettle's nephew and acted as a herder of the chief's pony herd. Although Bent consistently stated that Black Kettle did not have any children, some Cheyenne genealogists maintain that Blue Horse was actually his son. Since Blue Horse's biological father was killed at Sand Creek in 1864, it is possible that Black Kettle had adopted his nephew as his own son. Benteen n.d.(b), 220; Hyde 1968, 253, 317; Peter Harrison to author, Nov. 12, 2001; Halaas and Masich 2004, 259.

escaped the carbine bullets posted themselves with their companions who were already firing from the banks. One party of troopers came upon a squaw endeavoring to make her escape, leading by the hand a little white boy, a prisoner in the hands of the Indians, and who doubtless had been captured by some of their war parties during a raid on the settlements. Who or where his parents were, or whether still alive or murdered by Indians, will never be known, as the squaw, finding herself and prisoner about to be surrounded by the troops, and her escape cut off, determined, with savage malignity, that the triumph of the latter should not embrace the rescue of the white boy. Casting her eyes quickly in all directions, to convince herself that escape was impossible, she drew from beneath her blanket a huge knife and plunged it into the almost naked body of her captive. The next moment retributive justice reached her in the shape of a well-directed bullet from one of the troopers' carbines. Before the men could reach them life was extinct in the bodies of both the squaw and her unknown captive.

The desperation with which the Indians fought may be inferred from the following: Seventeen warriors had posted themselves in a depression in the ground, which enabled them to protect their bodies completely from the fire of our men, and it was only when the Indians raised their heads to fire that the troopers could aim with any prospect of success. All efforts to drive the warriors from this point proved abortive, and resulted in severe loss to our side. They were only vanquished at last by our men securing positions under cover and picking them off by sharpshooting as they exposed themselves to get a shot at the troopers. Finally the last one was despatched in this manner. In a deep ravine near the suburbs of the village the dead bodies of thirty-eight warriors were reported after the fight terminated. Many of the squaws and children had very prudently not attempted to leave the village when we attacked it, but remained concealed inside their lodges. All these escaped injury, although when surrounded by the din and wild excitement of the fight, and in close proximity to the contending parties, their fears overcame some of them, and they gave vent to their despair by singing the death song, a combination of weird-like sounds which were suggestive of anything but musical tones. As soon as we had driven the warriors from the village, and the fighting was pushed to the country outside, I directed "Romeo," the interpreter, to go around to all the lodges and assure the squaws and children remaining in them that they would be unharmed and kindly cared for; at the same time he was to assemble them in the large lodges designated for that purpose, which were standing near the centre of the village. This was quite a delicate mission, as it was difficult to convince the squaws and children that they had anything but death to expect at our hands.

It was perhaps ten o'clock in the forenoon, and the fight was still raging, when to our surprise we saw a small party of Indians collected on a knoll a little over a mile below the village, and in the direction taken by those Indians who had effected an escape through our lines at the commencement of the attack. My surprise was not so great at first, as I imagined that the Indians we saw were those who had contrived to escape, and having procured their ponies from the herd had mounted them and were then anxious spectators of the fight, which they felt themselves too weak in numbers to participate in. In the mean time the herds of ponies belonging to the village, on being alarmed by the firing and shouts of the contestants, had, from a sense of imagined security or custom, rushed into the village, where details of troopers were made to receive them. California Joe, who had been moving about in a promiscuous and independent manner, came galloping into the village, and reported that a large herd of ponies was to be seen near by, and requested authority and some men to bring them in. The men were otherwise employed just then, but he was authorized to collect and drive in the herd if practicable. He departed on his errand, and I had forgotten all about him and the ponies, when in the course of half an hour I saw a herd of nearly three hundred ponies coming on the gallop toward the village, driven by a couple of squaws, who were mounted, and had been concealed near by, no doubt; while bringing up the rear was California Joe, riding his favorable mule, and whirling about his head a long lariat, using it as a whip in urging the herd forward. He had captured the squaws while endeavoring to secure the ponies, and very wisely had employed his captives to assist in driving the herd. By this time the group of Indians already discovered outside our lines had increased until it numbered upwards of a hundred. Examining them through my field glass, I could plainly perceive that they were all mounted warriors; not only that, but they were armed and caparisoned in full war costume, nearly all wearing the bright-colored war-bonnets and floating their lance pennants. Constant accessions to their numbers were to be seen arriving from beyond the hill on which they stood. All this seemed inexplicable. A few Indians might have escaped through our lines when the attack on the village began, but only a few, and even these must have gone with little or nothing in their possession save their rifles and perhaps a blanket. Who could these new parties be, and from whence came they? To solve these troublesome questions I sent for "Romeo," and taking him with me to one of the lodges occupied by the squaws, I interrogated one of the latter as to who were the Indians to be seen assembling on the hill below the village. She informed me, to a surprise on my part almost equal to that of the Indians at our sudden appearance at daylight, that just below the village we then occupied, and which was a part of the Cheyenne tribe, were located in succession the winter villages of all the hostile tribes of the southern plains with which we were at war, including the Arrapahoes, Kiowas, the remaining band of Cheyennes, the Comanches, and a portion of the Apaches; that the nearest village was about two miles distant, and the others stretched along through the timbered valley to the one furthest off, which was not over ten miles.

What was to be done?—for I needed no one to tell me that we were certain to be attacked, and that, too, by greatly superior numbers, just as soon as the Indians below could make their arrangements to do so; and they had probably been busily employed at these arrangements ever since the sound of firing had reached them in the early morning, and been reported from village to village. Fortunately, affairs took a favorable turn in the combat in which we were then engaged, and the firing had almost died away. Only here and there where some warrior still maintained his position was the fight continued. Leaving as few men as possible to look out for these, I hastily collected and reformed my command, and posted them in readiness for the attack which we all felt was soon to be made; for already at different points and in more than one direction we could see more than enough warriors to outnumber us, and we knew they were only waiting the arrival of the chiefs and warriors from the lower villages before making any move against us. In the meanwhile our temporary hospital had been established in the centre of the village, where the wounded were receiving such surgical care as circumstances would permit. Our losses had been severe; indeed we were not then aware how great they had been. Hamilton, who rode at my side as we entered the village, and whose soldierly tones I heard for the last time as he calmly cautioned his squadron, "Now, men, keep cool, fire low, and not too rapidly," was among the first victims of the opening charge, having been shot from his saddle by a bullet from an Indian rifle. He died instantly. His lifeless remains were tenderly carried by some of his troopers to the vicinity of the hospital. Soon afterwards I saw four troopers coming from the front bearing between them, in a blanket, a wounded soldier; galloping to them, I discovered Colonel Barnitz, another troop commander, who was almost in a dying condition, having been shot by a rifle bullet directly through the body in the vicinity of the heart. Of Major Elliott, the officer second in rank, nothing had been seen since the attack at daylight, when he rode with his detachment into the village. He, too, had evidently been killed, but as yet we knew not where or how he had fallen. Two other officers had received wounds, while the casualties among the enlisted men were also large. The sergeant-major of the regiment, who was with me when the first shot was heard, had not been seen since that moment. We were not in as effective condition by far as when the attack was made, yet we were soon to be called upon to contend against a force immensely superior to the one with which we had been engaged during the early hours of the day. The captured herds of ponies were carefully collected inside our lines, and so guarded as to prevent their stampede or recapture by the Indians. Our wounded, and the immense amount of captured property in the way of ponies, lodges, etc., as well as our prisoners, were obstacles in the way of our attempting an offensive movement against the lower villages. To have done this would have compelled us to divide our forces, when it was far from certain that we could muster strength enough united to repel the attacks of the combined tribes. On all sides of us the Indians could now be seen in considerable numbers, so that from being the surrounding party, as we had been in the morning, we now found ourselves surrounded and occupying the position of defenders of the village. Fortunately for us, as the men had been expending a great many rounds, Major Bell, the quartermaster, who with a small escort was endeavoring to reach us with a fresh supply of ammunition, had by constant exertion and hard marching succeeded in doing so, and now appeared on the ground with several thousand rounds of carbine ammunition, a reinforcement greatly needed. He had no sooner arrived safely than the Indians attacked from the direction from which he came. How he had managed to elude their watchful eyes I never could comprehend, unless their attention had been so completely absorbed in watching our movements inside as to prevent them from keeping an eye out to discover what might be transpiring elsewhere.[22]

Issuing a fresh supply of ammunition to those most in want of it, the fight soon began generally at all points of the circle. For such in reality had our line of battle become—a continuous and unbroken circle of which the village was about the centre. Notwithstanding the great superiority in numbers of the Indians, they fought with excessive prudence and a lack of that confident manner which they usually manifest when encountering greatly inferior numbers—a result due, no doubt, to the fate which had overwhelmed our first opponents. Besides, the timber and the configuration of the ground enabled us to keep our men concealed until their services were actually required. It seemed to be the design and wish of our antagonists to draw us away from the village; but in this they were foiled. Seeing that they did not intend to press the attack just then, about two hundred of my men were ordered to pull down the lodges in the village and collect the captured property in huge piles preparatory to burning. This was done in the most effectual manner. When everything had been collected the torch was applied, and all that was left in the village were a few heaps of blackened ashes. Whether enraged at the sight of this destruction or from other cause, the attack soon became general along our entire line, and pressed with so much vigor and audacity that every available trooper was required to aid in meeting these assaults. The Indians would push a party of well mounted warriors close up to our lines in the endeavor to find a weak point through which they might venture, but in every attempt were driven back. I now concluded, as the village was off

---

[22]For Lieutenant Bell's recollections, see the interview by Walter Camp in chapter II.

our hands and our wounded had been collected, that offensive measures might be adopted. To this end several of the squadrons were mounted and ordered to advance and attack the enemy wherever force sufficient was exposed to be a proper object of attack, but at the same time to be cautious as to ambuscades. Colonel Weir, who had succeeded to the command of Hamilton's squadron, Colonels Benteen and Myers with their respective squadrons, all mounted, advanced and engaged the enemy. The Indians resisted every step taken by the troops, while every charge made by the latter was met or followed by a charge from the Indians, who continued to appear in large numbers at unexpected times and places. The squadrons acting in support of each other, and the men in each being kept well in hand, were soon able to force the line held by the Indians to yield at any point assailed. This being followed up promptly, the Indians were driven at every point and forced to abandon the field to us. Yet they would go no further than they were actually driven. It was now about three o'clock in the afternoon. I knew that the officer left in charge of the train and eighty men would push after us, follow our trail, and endeavor to reach us at the earliest practicable moment. From the tops of some of the highest peaks or round hills in the vicinity of the village I knew the Indians could reconnoitre the country for miles in all directions. I feared if we remained as we were then until the following day, the Indians might in this manner discover the approach of our train and detach a sufficient body of warriors to attack and capture it; and its loss to us, aside from that of its guard, would have proven most serious, leaving us in the heart of the enemy's country, in midwinter, totally out of supplies for both men and horses.

. . . .

. . . We felt convinced that we could not, in the presence of so large a body of hostile Indians, hope to make a long march through their country, the latter favorable to the Indian mode of attack by surprise and ambush, and keep with us the immense herd of captured ponies. Such a course would only encourage attack under the circumstances which would almost insure defeat and unnecessary loss to us. We did not need the ponies, while the Indians did. If we retained them they might conclude that one object of our expedition against them was to secure plunder, an object thoroughly consistent with the red man's idea of war. Instead, it was our desire to impress upon his uncultured mind that our every act and purpose had been simply to inflict deserved punishment upon him for the many murders and other depredations committed by him in and around the homes of defenseless settlers on the frontier. Impelled by these motives, I decided neither to attempt to take the ponies with us nor to abandon them to the Indians, but to adopt the only measure left—to kill them. To accomplish this seemingly—like most measures of war—cruel but necessary act, four companies of cavalrymen were detailed dismounted, as a firing party.

. . . .

. . . The firing party was already to proceed with its work, and was only waiting until the squaws should secure a sufficient number of ponies to transport all the prisoners on the march. The troopers had endeavored to catch the ponies, but they were too wild and unaccustomed to white men to permit them to approach. When the squaws entered the herd they had no difficulty in selecting and bridling the requisite number. These being taken off by themselves, the work of destruction began on the remainder, and was continued until nearly eight hundred ponies were thus disposed of. All this rime the Indians who had been fighting us from the outside covered the hills in the distance, deeply interested spectators of this to them strange proceedings. The loss of so many animals of value was a severe blow to the tribe, as nothing so completely impairs the war-making facilities for the Indians of the Plains as the deprivation or disabling of their ponies.

In the description of the opening of the battle . . . , I spoke of the men having removed their overcoats and haversacks when about to charge the village. These had been disposed of carefully on the ground, and one man from each company left to guard them, this number being deemed sufficient, as they would be within rifle-shot of the main command; besides, the enemy as was then supposed would be inside our lines and sufficiently employed in taking care of himself to prevent any meddling on his part with the overcoats and haversacks. This was partly true, but we had not calculated upon Indians appearing in force and surrounding us. When this did occur, however, their first success was in effecting the capture of the overcoats and rations of the men, the guard barely escaping to the villages. This was a most serious loss, as the men were destined to suffer great discomfort from the cold; and their rations being in the haversacks, and it being uncertain when we should rejoin our train, they were compelled to endure both cold and hunger. It was when the Indians discovered our overcoats and galloped to their capture, that one of my staghounds, Blucher, seeing them riding and yelling as if engaged in the chase, dashed from the village and joined the Indians, who no sooner saw him than they shot him through with an arrow. Several months afterwards I discovered his remains on the ground near where the overcoats had been deposited on that eventful morning.

. . . .

Riding in the vicinity of the hospital, I saw a little bugler boy sitting on a bundle of dressed robes, near where the surgeon was dressing and caring for the wounded. His face was completely covered with blood, which was trickling down over his cheek from a wound in his forehead. At first glance I thought a pistol bullet had entered his skull, but on stopping to inquire of him the nature of his injury, he informed me that an Indian had shot him in the head with a steel-pointed arrow. The arrow had struck him just above the eye, and upon encountering the skull had glanced under the covering of the latter, coming out near the ear, giving the appearance of having passed through the head. There the arrow remained until the bugler arrived at the hospital, when he received prompt attention. The arrow being barbed it could not be withdrawn at once, but by cutting off the steel point the surgeon was able to withdraw the wooden shaft without difficulty. The little fellow bore his suffering manfully. I asked him if he saw the Indian who wounded him. Without replying at once, he shoved his hand deep down into his capacious trouser pocket and fished up nothing more nor less than the scalp of the Indian, adding in a nonchalant manner, "If anybody thinks I didn't see him, I want them to take a look at that." He had killed the Indian with his revolver after receiving the arrow wound in his head.

After driving off the Indians who had been attacking us from the outside, so as to prevent them from interfering with our operations in the vicinity of the village, parties were sent here and there to look up the dead and wounded on both sides. In spite of a most thorough search, there were still undiscovered Major Elliott and nineteen enlisted men, including the sergeant-major, for whose absence we were unable to satisfactorily account. Officers and men of the various commands were examined, but nothing was elicited from them except that Major Elliott had been seen about daylight charging with his command into the village. I had previously given him up as killed, but was surprised that so many of the men should be missing, and none of their comrades be able to account for them. All the grounds inside of the advanced lines held by the Indians who attacked us after our capture of the village was closely and carefully examined, in the hope of finding the bodies of some if not all the absentees, but with no success. It was then evident that when the other bands attempted to reinforce our opponents of the early morning, they had closed their lines about us in such manner as to cut off Elliott and nineteen of our men. What had been the fate of this party after leaving the main command? This was a question only to be answered in surmises, and few of these were favorable to the escape of our comrades. At last one of the scouts reported that soon after the attack on the village began he had seen a few warriors escaping, mounted, from the village, through a gap that existed in our line between the commands of Elliott and Thompson, and that Elliott and a small party of troopers were in close pursuit; that a short time after he had heard very sharp firing in the direction taken by the Indians and Elliott's party, but that as the firing had continued for only a few minutes, he had thought nothing more of it until the prolonged absence of our men recalled it to his mind. Parties were sent in the direction indicated by the scout, he accompanying them; but after a search extending nearly two miles, all the parties returned, reporting their efforts to discover some trace of Elliott and his men fruitless. As it was now lacking but an hour of night, we had to make an effort to get rid of the Indians, who still loitered in strong force on the hills, within plain view of our position. Our main desire was to draw them off from the direction in which our train might be approaching, and thus render it secure from attack until under the protection of the entire command, when we could defy any force our enemies could muster against us. The last lodge having been destroyed, and all the ponies except those required for the pursuit having been killed, the command was drawn in and united near the village. Making dispositions to overcome any resistance which might be offered to our advance, by throwing out a strong force of skirmishers, who set out down the valley in the direction where the other villages had been reported, and toward the hills on which were collected the greatest number of Indians. The column moved forward in one body, with colors flying and band playing, while our prisoners, all mounted on captured ponies, were under sufficient guard immediately in rear of the advanced troops. For a few moments after our march began the Indians on the hills remained silent spectators, evidently at a loss at first to comprehend our intentions in thus setting out at that hour of the evening, and directing our course as if another night march was contemplated; and more than all, in the direction of their villages, where all that they possessed was suppose to be. This aroused them to action . . . and [they] began a precipitate movement down the valley in advance of us, fully impressed with the idea no doubt that our purpose was to over-take their flying people and herds and administer the same treatment to them that the occupants of the upper village had received. This was exactly the effect I desired, and our march was conducted with such appearance of determination and rapidity that this conclusion on their part was a natural one. Leaving a few of their warriors to hover along our flanks and watch our progress, the main body of Indians, able to travel much faster than the troops, soon disappeared from our sight in front. We still pushed on in the same direction, and continued our march in this manner until long after dark, by which time we reached the deserted villages, the occupants—at least the non-combatants and herds—having fled in the morning when news of our attack on Black Kettle's village reached them. We had now reached a point several miles below the site of Black Kettle's village, and the darkness was sufficient to cover our movements from the watchful eyes of the Indian scouts, who had dogged our march as long as the light favored them.

Facing the command about, it was at once put in motion to reach our train, not only as a measure of safety and protection to the latter, but as a necessary movement to relieve the wants of the command, particularly that portion whose haversacks and overcoats had fallen into the hands of the Indians early that morning.

7

Albert Barnitz,
Seventh Cavalry

Albert Trorillo Siders Barnitz was a captain in the Seventh Cavalry, commanding G Company of Major Elliott's squadron during the battle of the Washita. Born on March 10, 1835, at Bloody Run, Pennsylvania, Barnitz enlisted in 1861 as a sergeant in G Company of the Second Ohio Volunteer Cavalry. He saw action on the Kansas frontier against William Quantrill's guerrilla and was promoted to second lieutenant in 1862. As a result of regimental reorganization, the young officer was promoted twice in 1863 and became a senior captain.

In the spring of 1863, Barnitz led a daring raid on Confederate transportation lines in Tennessee. This mission was a complete success but proved nearly fatal to Barnitz, whose horse slipped and fell on him, causing severe injuries that included a broken jaw. After convalescence, he was reunited with his regiment in 1864 and served in Virginia, where the Second Ohio had become part of the Army of the Potomac. Barnitz was later awarded a brevet to major for gallantry and meritorious services at Ashland Station, where he was wounded in the thigh while leading his men in a charge on foot.

Barnitz returned to his regiment in the autumn of 1864 and fought with the Third Cavalry Division under Custer in the Shenandoah Valley. In March 1865 he commanded the Second Ohio Cavalry in the absence of senior officers and participated in numerous battles during the war's closing months, earning a brevet to lieutenant colonel for gallantry and meritorious services at the battle of Saylor's Creek. After Lee's surrender, Barnitz and the Second Ohio were transferred to Springfield, Missouri, until September 1865, when they were mustered out of service.

In November 1866 Barnitz received appointment as a captain in the Seventh Cavalry. He joined the regiment at Fort Riley, Kansas, in March 1867 and participated in Hancock's expedition in western Kansas. Afterward Barnitz saw sharp action near Fort Wallace while commanding several companies against a band of two hundred Sioux and Cheyennes on June 26, the first engagement of any magnitude fought by the Seventh Cavalry. Although his command sustained a loss of six men killed and six wounded, Barnitz received the praise from his superiors as well as the eastern newspapers.

In September 1868 the captain participated in Sully's ineffective campaign in the Sand Hills. The Seventh Cavalry then retired to Fort Dodge, Kansas, to prepare for a winter campaign against the Indians, culminating in the battle of the Washita. During the morning of November 27, Barnitz sustained a gunshot wound to the stomach while skirmishing with fleeing Indians. Although he was expected to die, the captain survived his ordeal and was awarded a brevet to colonel for distinguished gallantry. But he never recovered fully and was consequently granted a disability retirement in December 1870. Albert Barnitz died on July 18, 1912, in Asbury Park, New Jersey, from the effects of a growth that formed around the old wound. He was buried at Arlington National Cemetery.

Barnitz read law, dabbled in politics, and enjoyed prose throughout his life. A gifted writer, he was the author of a large volume of poetry, The Mystic Delvings, *published in 1857. His literary talent is also evident in his numerous letters and diaries. Rich in detail, they offer a revealing view of the lonely Kansas frontier and of the officers with whom he served.*

The Barnitz items gathered below consist of the following documents: Barnitz's letter to his wife, Jennie, dated December 5, 1868, in which he describes the attack on Black Kettle's village and his gunshot wound; Lt. Edward S. Godfrey's letter to Jennie of the same date in which he comments on Albert's condition; Barnitz's journal from November 23 to 27, 1868; an extract of a narrative that details the movements of Elliott's squadron on the early morning of November 27; his interview by and correspondence with Walter Camp in 1910; and a letter to Joseph B. Thoburn, dated November 28, 1910, which contains Barnitz's reminiscences.

Letter to Jennie Barnitz
December 5, 1868[1]

> Camp Supply, Ind. Ter.
> Beaver Creek
> Decr. 5th, 1868.

Dearest

The dispatches which have gone forward have doubtless made you very uneasy about me, as you will have heard thereby that in a recent severe engagement with the Indians I was severely wounded. I therefore hasten to allay your fears at this the earliest moment that an opportunity has been afforded me, by letting you know how rapidly I am persevering, and how comfortably I am situated, so that you may not be uneasy about me.

I am wounded through the left side. It is difficult to say that it is a fearful wound from a huge-size rifle ball, and that the Doctors both told me that they did not believe I would recover, or live till morning. Yet I have lived, and though it is nine days since I received my wound I am now considered out of danger.

The battle was fought among the Wichetaw [Wichita] Mountains, on the Wichetaw [Washita] river. We had been following the Indians for several days through deep snow and under great difficulties until at length we found a trail of a large war party, and following this all night came upon a village before dawn and surrounded it before it was light. It was a wild scene and terrible to the Indians. The scenery in the vicinity of the village was wild and picturesque. Tall peaks, some many hundreds of feet high, covered with snow, and on the summits of which the wolves were howling. Timbered streams running in very deep channels and forming intricate labyrinths, crossed and intersected our path.

The ponies were lariated out on the hill side to graze. Some of these kept neighing restlessly, while the tinkling of little bells appraised us of the whereabouts of the centre of the herd.

When the appointed moment had arrived, the Regimental Band struck up "Garry Owen," the squadrons moved forward

---

[1]This and the Godfrey letter following are housed in the Albert Barnitz Papers, Yale University Library, New Haven, Connecticut.

with a rush, and all was activity; the Indians were completely taken by surprise, yet they were instantly up and around. The fighting was severe but I am unable to say how many were killed. The bodies of one hundred and three warriors were found in and around the village, but many more must have been killed whose bodies were carried off by their friends. It was surprising to see how soon, when once the action had commenced, how all the hills were alive with mounted warriors, armed and equipped with their shields, and war bonnets. These, as it was afterwards ascertained, had come from other villages in the valley, having heard the firing.

Shortly after the firing commenced I observed a large body of Indians running off towards the left. I at once dashed in among them, passing through a large drove of squaws and children who were screaming and very much frightened. I came upon the war riors who were ahead and striking out as hard as they could run for their ponies. Riding up close along side the first, I shot him through the heart. He threw up his arms, by the same movement drawing his bow from the scabbard [and] let fly an arrow at me. This was the last act of his existence. I pressed on to the second and shot him in the same manner.

There was yet another close to me. He was armed with a large Lancaster rifle given to him by the peace commission. He took aim, while I was closing upon him and about to fire, but was several times disconcerted by my acting as if I was about to fire upon him myself, until finally I had some doubt if his rifle was loaded. When however I got quite close to him to fire, he returned my fire at the same instant, both shots taking effect. Mine I believe must have passed through his heart, as he threw up his hands frantically and, as I was told by others of my company, died almost immediately.

I rode back toward the village, being now unable to manage my horse, and the pain of my wound being almost unendurable, I dismounted and lay down in such a way that I would not bleed internally. As soon as the fight was nearly decided I was placed upon a buffalo robe and carried down the hills a few hundred yards further, where I was allowed to rest in a place of comparative security until Doctors Lippincott and Renicke arrived. Both men [were] so blind from the effects of snow that they with difficulty could attend to the wounded, and pronounced my case truly hopeless, but made every effort for my comfort for the short time it was supposed I had to live. All the officers gathered about me, as the progress of the fight permitted, and endeavored to cheer me up with their condolences.

In the meantime the Indian village was burned, together with a quantity of stores, supplies, gun powder, etc., and all the ponies that could be gathered together were driven in. Two were selected for each of the squaws, who were captured, and two for each officer; the remainder, some eight or nine hundred, were shot to prevent them falling into the hands of the Indians. We now awaited the arrival of our ambulances, which were toiling towards us through the intricate labyrinths where our horses could hardly proceed by file. When at length these arrived the wounded were loaded in, and we commenced our return march towards this point.

You may judge that my ride for five days was a very tedious one, during the whole time I could not eat one morsel of anything, and for every spoonful of water that I drank I vomited up two. Immediately upon my arrival here General Sheridan came to see me, attended by his chief Medical Officer, and greeted me very kindly, placing me in quite comfortable quarters in the field. His cook has been directed to furnish me with anything I might desire.

Perhaps you would like to know just how I am situated at present. Well, first, as to the bed, it is a small cottage bedstead with two comfortable mattresses. All the officers who possessed such luxuries as feather pillows, have placed them at my disposal, so that I am now very comfortably furnished in that line, and can vary my position at will. I am almost entirely free from pain, and have a good apatite for such small deer as I am permitted to eat. My principal diet consists of beef tea and farina. As to my furniture, my tent contains a comfortable little Sibley stove, an improvised table and a chair or two, and you can perhaps imagine the rest.

. . . I do not expect to see you soon. I do not much anticipate that you intended traveling to Leavenworth until the last of the month, and I do not think it is necessary or best for you to come all the way out here, merely to go back in the dead of winter in a few weeks when we will return to Leavenworth.

The whole command, that is, the 7th Cav., the 19th Kansas Cav. and Genl. Sheridan and staff march southward on Monday morning to make a final closing up of the Indians and I trust they will have short work of it.

Genl. Custer visited me today and stated that as soon as the command had returned from the expedition, the Regiment would move immediately into Leavenworth. He said that he had no doubt that within three weeks I would be on the return march to that point.

Major Inman[2] leaves this depot on Tuesday with a train of wagons for Fort Dodge. He has kindly promised to place his private ambulance at your disposal should you have concluded to come down here with his return train. He says it will be amply guarded, and also that you will have a tent with fire in it every night, and that he will see to it that you are made comfortable on the way. Major Inman is a gentleman in every respect, and I know of no one to whose care I would sooner entrust you in case you have concluded to come out this far. So you will see that it is not impossible for you to come even here. Genl. Sully[3] at Fort Harker will give you any

---

[2]Henry Inman was a popular and energetic quartermaster who received a brevet to lieutenant colonel in February 1869 for his efficient management of Sheridan's logistics during the winter campaign. Born in New York in 1839, Inman enlisted in 1857 as a private in the Ninth Infantry and saw action against the Indians in Oregon and California. He was appointed a second lieutenant in the Seventeenth Infantry in May 1861 and spent most of his service during the Civil War on quartermaster assignments. He emerged from the war with brevet ranks of captain in 1862 and major in November 1866 for meritorious service. Careless and less adept in administrative duties, Inman was continually plagued by problems with his paperwork and accounts, which eventually led to his dismissal in July 1872. Afterward he became a journalist in Kansas, where the town of Inman in McPherson County was named after him. During his later years, he became known as a prolific writer of stories about the Great Plains. Henry Inman died in Topeka, Kansas, on November 13, 1899. J. Murphy 1923, 260.

[3]Alfred Sully was the commander of the Upper Arkansas District in 1868, though reassigned by Sheridan, who preferred Custer to lead the winter campaign. Born in 1821, Sully graduated from West Point in 1841. He fought in the Seminole War and the Mexican War and saw service in California with the Second Infantry, being promoted to captain in 1852. Appointed colonel of the First Minnesota Infantry in March 1862, he was promoted to brigadier general of volunteers the following September for his valorous conduct at Second Manassas. Sully gained further distinction during the Sioux uprising in Minnesota in 1862 and led campaigns against hostile Indians for the next three years. In March 1865 he attained the rank of major general of volunteers and was appointed lieutenant colonel of the Third Infantry in July 1866. But his reputation became tarnished in September 1868, when he led a timid expedition against the Indians south of the Arkansas River. Nevertheless, in December 1873 he became colonel of the Twenty-First Infantry. Sully died on April 7, 1879. Langdon Sully, *No Tears for the General: The Life of Alfred Sully, 1821–1979* (Palo Alto, Calif.: American West, [1974]).

information and assistance in regard to the route and will be glad to do so. I must remain here quietly now to recover. I have no doubt that by the time the regiment returns here I will be so strong that I can accompany the command back to Leavenworth.

And now, dear, I think there will be no trouble about my obtaining a leave of absence for any time that I may desire in the spring. It will be a long time I suppose before I can wear a belt with ease, and in the meantime I can obtain a sick leave which will enable us to attend to the affairs which we have so long contemplated this summer and see our friends once more. It may not be out of the way to say to you in conclusion that Genl. Custer told me today that within a few weeks I would receive a Brevet for the recent engagement. It is pleasant to be remembered kindly.

And now, dear, may all the good angels watch over you until I see you once more.

Your own
tranquil hopeful,
Albert

1st Lt. Edward S. Godfrey[4] to Jennie Barnitz
Letter Extracts

Camp Supply, Ind. Ter.
Decr. 5th, 1868.

My Friend

From our camp on the Washita River I telegraphed you that Col. Barnitz was badly wounded—to be candid [it] was thought at the time to be mortal—yet delicacy impelled me to leave the word "mortally" out; now I am glad I did so. Your husband has every indication of recovering. His color is good, almost as well as before his wound was made. The wound was made by a ball from a Lancaster rifle (supplied by the Interior Dept.) fired by a Cheyenne warrior. The ball entered his left side on a line with the left groin and about four inches above the naval; coming out on the left side of the spine, cutting the top of his pants. The wound

---

[4]For information on Godfrey, see the introduction to chapter 8.

is one that rarely occurs without cutting the intestines, and that was what was at first appeared to be the case. Happily recent indications have shown that not to be and all the surgeons (Drs. Ash [*sic*], Sternberg, Lippincott, Marsh, and Renick)[5] agree that he will recover, though 'twill be some time before he will be [ready] for duty. 'Twas a terrible shock on his system yet his cool and heroic conduct during his affliction has saved his life. After the battle was over the Drs. gave him up and delegated me to inform him. I very reluctantly did it in as delicate terms as possible. He insisted that his case was not hopeless.

I transcribe here the notes I took down. "Tell Mrs. B. that I don't regret the wound so much as I do leaving her. It has been so long since we met, that the expectations of the happiness we would enjoy upon our reunion is more than I can bear. I am glad she is not here to see my suffering as she could do me no good. Tell her not to grieve for me, that I love her."

Then his suffering and emotions became so great that nothing was audible or could be understood. After resting a time he gave me his mother's address [and] also his brother['s]. Then he talked about the possibilities of his recovery if he could only be where he could remain quiet and not be moved. Such a thing was out of the question however, as we had a train of over a hundred wagons, guarded by Lt. Mathey with only 80 men, and should the Indians find him all our supplies would be lost.

Col. [Barnitz] with his troop was under Maj. Elliott [and assigned] to attack the village from the east side. Col. with the troop was posted so as to cover a neck of woods. Moving along a ravine, he took the left of the line mounted and Lt. March the right dismounted. When the attack began the Indians poured out of the village upon Col's flank. Col. killed two Indians, he is sure of, and the third he was aiming at, when he would dodge behind his pony. This continued a short time when both took aim and

---

[5]Capt. Morris Asch was a surgeon on Sheridan's staff, and Capt. George M. Sternberg was chief surgeon of the winter expedition. Sternberg was assisted by the following medical personnel: Capt. Elias J. Marsh (surgeon), assigned to the infantry battalion at Camp Supply; Capt. Henry Lippincott (assistant surgeon), assigned to Custer's command; and William Renick (acting assistant surgeon), a civilian contract surgeon who was also assigned to Custer's column. S. C. Craig 1998, 202–203.

both fired at the same instant and both were wounded. The Indian reached for his scalping knife when he saw the Col. was wounded, but was too weak to carry out his intention of scalping. Col. thinks he has gone to the happy hunting ground. Col. then rode back of the lines and was taken in charge. He described the yell of despair given by the first Indian he shot, the wicked, vindictive and malicious look of the third, when skirmishing for the shot.

I will leave all these things for him to tell you. We are all going to miss his face among the active. Yet am thankful that his case is not as bad as at first supposed. He is now receiving every care and attention that circumstances will admit of. Genl. Sheridan had ordered that whatever may be necessary for him be ordered from his own stores.

I did not forget your injunctions upon me just before you left that if he was taken ill or had anything happen to him to see that he would be cared for—it has been seen to most cheerfully.

. . . .

Decr. 6th, 1868

I went down to see Col. last evening. He was sleeping very nicely and resting comfortably. Botzer[6] and Mullen are waiting on him. You doubtless remember them as very faithful men, and fully devoted to their charge.

Lt. Nowlan[7] has been in waiting for the Col., but I write because I feel it a duty and it may as the Col. said day before yesterday be more home[?] coming from me. Any thing you may want me to do shall be done. You can't ask too much of me. How long he will remain at this point is more than I can tell.

We start tomorrow. Genl. Sheridan and staff, 7th Cav. and Kansas Vols. make up our force.

We are having a heavy "Norther"—strong north wind, snow drifting, and very cold. Many of our men have no overcoats nor

[6]Edward Botzer was born in 1846 in Bremerhaven, Germany, and enlisted in the Seventh Cavalry as a trumpeter in G Company in November 1866. Having just been promoted to acting first sergeant, Botzer was killed by Indians during Reno's retreat at the Little Bighorn on June 25, 1876. Hammer 1995, 31.

[7]Henry James Nowlan was a second lieutenant in the Seventh Cavalry. He was assigned to Camp Supply as post commissary on November 18, 1868, and was not present at Washita.

boots, and other clothing very indifferent. A train of . . . 300 wagons came in yesterday with supplies, but brought no clothing. 'Tis awful to contemplate the suffering that will be on the campaign.

Very Respectfully,
your friend,
Edw. S. Godfrey

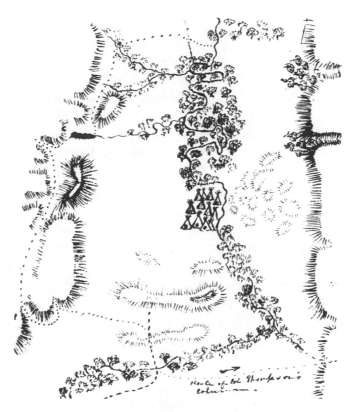

Route of Elliott's Squadron, drawn by Albert Barnitz. The Barnitz map was to accompany an article he had written for the *Atlanta Constitution* in 1889. The drawing shows the location of Custer's bivouac and the routes of Elliott's and Thompson's squadrons on the morning of the Washita battle. The dotted line along the left side of the map depicts the movements of Elliott's column. Note that Barnitz shows the location of Black Kettle's village on the left (north) bank. Most eyewitnesses, however, place the village on the right bank, where a low bottom sheltered the lodges from the north winds. Reproduced courtesy of Yale University Library.

Extract of Journal
November 23–27, 1868[8]

Camp on Middle River.[9] Nov. 23, 1868. The regiment broke camp at "Camp Supply" this morning at the hour designated, 6 A.M., and marched through a blinding snow storm, with the wind in our faces, through the soft snow a foot in depth, to this point, where we arrived about 1:30 P.M. and went into camp. During the march it was impossible to see more than a few hundred yards in any direction on account of the falling snow. Ravines ran off to our left, apparently. Distance marched today was 16 miles, direction S. 30 degrees W. Sandhills as we approached this stream. . . . This has been a *very* disagreeable day. I wore buffalo overshoes and lodge-skin leggings.

Second Camp on Middle River. Nov. 24, 1868, 9 P.M. Snow and occasional sleet and rain all last night. So dark this morning while at stables that I could not distinguish the horses. The driver of "G" Troop train slow, [and] did not commence harnessing until "forward" had sounded. "G" Troop marching on left flank opposite rear of train. Col. Benteen [marched] in rear. The drivers of supply train [did] not awake in time, and had not fed or harnessed mules. "G" Troop remained in camp until all had moved out. Found 8 pairs [of] spurs, nose bags, etc. in camp. Morning very cold. Snow a foot deep. Horse of "K" Troop gave out and I ordered him to be abandoned, which was done. . . . Osages and sharpshooters and Genl. Custer kill numerous buffalo.[10] I go out with Harris and Shebrosky and get steak and ribs. A good many mules are about "played." Teams had to be doubled repeatedly at sandy crossings. High peaks on our right. Sandhills probably. Sandhills on our left,

---

8The journal is located in the Albert Barnitz Papers, Yale University Library. Robert M. Utley who edited the Barnitz papers for his acclaimed publication, *Life in Custer's Cavalry*,. kindly provided the editor a copy. The entries here commence with Custer's departure from Camp Supply. The text has been edited for excessive punctuation, which was the prevalent style when Barnitz made his entries.

9The Middle River was the Wolf River. For a reconstruction of Custer's route, see Rea 1998, 244–61. See also Record of Events for November 1868 (U.S. Army 1868), which contains Barnitz report for the activities of G Company.

10A small party of Cheyennes led by Bear Shield heard the reports of these shots. Rather than investigating their source, they attributed the firing to Cheyenne hunters and, despite the warning of one of their party, continued on their journey to the Washita villages. Grinnell 1956, 301.

all along the stream. Artemisia grows everywhere, stream well timbered, water plentiful and excellent. . . . After marching 16 miles up right bank of Middle River in southwesterly direction went into camp on right bank of stream in woods. . . .

Camp Supply, Ind. Ter. Jan. 7, 1869. I will now attempt to make some notes in my journal from memory. Nov. 25. Command broke camp at the usual hour and marched south all day, through deeper snow than hitherto encountered, over the great "divide" between the "Middle River" and the [South] Canadian. About dusk we crossed a tributary of the Canadian, a stream of considerable size, and after marching about 2 miles further (a distance of perhaps 35 miles during the day), we reached and encamped upon the north bank of the Canadian at a point where there is considerable dead timber—oak, walnut, and coffee-tree principally—very suitable for fuel. This was the first time we had encountered oak and walnut since leaving the vicinity of Fort Riley. Beyond the Canadian at the point where we encamped are some stupendous summits. . . . They can be seen for a distance of 15 or 20 miles, approaching from the north. Had some difficulty to feed the horses in the darkness, so as to ensure each horse getting his allowance of grain (3 lbs!). . . .

On Thursday morning, Nov. 26, reveille was as usual two hours before daylight, and just before daylight we marched, "G," "M," and "H" Troops, marching upstream (westward) under Major Elliott, while the other portion of the regiment, together with the train, under Genl. Custer proceeded downstream with the intention of going into camp about 10 miles below, and awaiting our return. We were to march about 25 miles before rejoining the other portion of the regiment. The morning was excessively cold and a dense fog prevailed. It was necessary to dismount very often and walk in order to prevent our feet from freezing. As the snow was a foot deep with a hard crust which broke beneath out feet, walking was exceedingly difficult and tiresome. After proceeding about two miles I saw a bear track, the first I had seen, and shortly afterwards the Osage Indians who were with us called our attention to a trail resembling a "buffalo path" which was covered with snow, but which had evidently been missed during the prevalence of the snow storm, as the snow in the path was not so deep as elsewhere, whereas it should have been deeper if the path had been made by buffaloes. Besides the path was parallel to the stream, and buffalo paths always lead direct to water, and after having drunk the buffalo scatter out and proceed to grazing. Moreover buffalo do not move about much during a storm, but remain huddled together in sheltered places. From all these considerations it was obvious that we were in close proximity to Indians, or at least that the valley had recently been traversed by a considerable body of them, but whether a war party or a hunting party we could not tell. After proceeding about a mile further we came upon a timbered tributary of the Canadian and, proceeding cautiously up its bank for a short distance, we found where the Indians had encamped during the storm and had cut down cottonwood trees to browse their ponies—all traces of their camp were snowed over, except the broaches of branches which were still standing. We now crossed the stream and returned to the Canadian whither the paths led, and after continuing up the stream for a mile further we came suddenly upon a plain fresh trail which had obviously been made in the afternoon of the day previous by a war party of from one to two hundred Indians. It was known to be a war party from the fact that the Indians had no dogs with them, whereas hunting parties are always accompanied by dogs. The trail led southeast. The command was now formed by fours (it had previously marched by twos on account of the difficulty of breaking a path through the snow), stoppers taken from the muzzles of the carbines, magazines loaded, levers tested to see whether they were frozen fast, as was often the case; and then a couple of couriers (from my troop) were started back to General Custer with intelligence that we had found a trail, and would follow it rapidly until we received further orders; we then pressed forward along the trail, crossed the Canadian (a wide stream with a deep, rapid current in the centre, and filled with floating ice), and entered a strip of timber on the southern bank in which we found a large, broken-down pack mule, which had been abandoned by the Indians.[11] Beyond the stream the trail led up a steep, mountainous ascent, which was in places quite precipitous; so much so that we found it necessary to dismount and lead our horses

---

[11] A narrative account written by Barnitz in the 1880s reveals that "a number of serviceable pack mules and ponies had been left behind" in this abandoned Indian camp. See "Extract of Narrative Account."

for a distance of a mile, or further. Having passed the summit of the ridge we continued to press forward until about 11 o'clock, when coming suddenly upon a ravine in which we found a quantity of dry oak wood (as well as some small green trees, in the top of which was an eagle's nest). We halted for an hour to rest, put out pickets, and built up good comfortable fires. Having rested, we moved on and about 2 or 3 o'clock were joined by a courier from Genl. Custer with orders to continue pursuit, and with intelligence that he (Genl. Custer) would follow us with all the other mounted men of the command and with the ambulances and a few wagons lightly loaded with forage and rations. Just after dark, after having marched a mile or two through the timbered sandhills along a stream or rather dry sandy "arroyo" which is probably a tributary of the Washita, we were overtaken by a courier from General Custer with orders to halt and build fires for the command, as he was going to hurry forward with forage and rations, so that we might feed and get something to eat, when we would continue the pursuit. The wagons having arrived the horses were all fed—receiving full forage for the first time within two or three weeks, and the men were allowed time to make coffee and then we continued pursuit. About midnight we struck the Washita, and the trail now became quite difficult on account of the sinuous character of the stream, which runs in a deep channel, and which we were obliged to cross and recross very often. Shortly after midnight we began to discover traces of "tepee" poles, which entered the trail from the left and followed down in the direction that we were going. The traces of tepee poles at length became quite numerous, always entering our trail from the left, from which it was obvious that a village, traces of which Genl. Custer had found about ten miles below our encampment on the Canadian, was moving in the same direction as the war party which we were following.[12] About 2 or 3 o'clock in the morning, just as I was crossing the Washita for perhaps the 10th or 15th time, Lieut. Moylan, the Adjutant, rode back and stated that Genl.

---

[12]In his narrative account Barnitz states that some time after the resumption of the march, he noticed the tracks of two Indian ponies coming from a rise toward the main trail at great speed, "one [Indian] being mounted on a sleek mule and the other upon a pony." The captain concluded that the Indians had seen the approaching command, and he accordingly informed Custer. Many years later a Cheyenne named Crow Neck

Custer directed that I should halt my command, and, accompanied by Lieut. March, my lieutenant, should report at the head of the column—that the whole valley in front was full of ponies, and that the Indians (from all appearances) were not aware of our approach. A rapid gallop of a few minutes took me to the head of the column where I found the other officers already assembled, or assembling, and as soon as all were collected, Genl. Custer stated that the scouts in advance had reported that the valley in advance was filled with ponies, and that the tinkling of a little bell could be distinctly heard; that he wished us to leave our horses and go quietly with him on foot to the crest of a ridge in front, and carefully study the topography of the country and see what we could make out; he stated that no talking would be done above a low whisper until our return when we would deliberate, and make plans for the attack. So we all crept very quietly and slowly to the top of the ridge, removing our hats or caps as we neared the summit, and I could not help thinking that we very much resembled a pack of wolves, and that if the Indians should discover us they would very likely mistake us for wolves, and so take no notice of us. One thing however was against us. The snow was about a foot deep and the surface was frozen hard, so that when crushed beneath our feet the noise could be heard for a considerable distance. Having gained the crest of the ridge we could see, though not distinctly, the course of the Washita on our right, with what appeared to be tributaries entering from the left and possibly from the right, and the summits of steep bluffs were seen looming up on all sides of the valley, but the herds of ponies, and tepees were not visible although the tinkling of a little bell could be distinctly heard at times, and some of the officers who looked through a night glass were of the opinion that they could discern herds of ponies. Having made our observations, we returned to the point where our horses were left, when the following plan of attack was announced by General Custer.

---

told anthropologist George B. Grinnell that he had been with the party whose trail Custer followed from the Canadian and that he had left a worn-out pony in a wooded grove along the Washita some fifteen miles above Black Kettle's camp. While going back for this pony on the afternoon of November 26, he noticed a long line of moving figures on the hills toward the Canadian and thought they were soldiers, but for inexplicable reasons, Crow Neck failed to alert the village. Grinnell 1956, 301–302.

The command was divided into four columns. The first, Companies G, H and M, under Major Elliott, was to pass around the hills to the left (of the position [occupied] at the time the plan was adopted) and reach the Washita below the village, and then move up the stream to the attack at the proper time. The second, Co's B and F, under Col. Thompson, was to countermarch, recross the stream which had just been crossed, and march, under the cover of the bluffs that skirted the right bank of the stream, to a point opposite the village and there await the signal to charge down upon the village. The third column, E and I, under the command of Col. Myers, was to move directly down the right bank of the stream, keeping within the timber which skirted it, until within view of the village, and there await the signal for attack.

The fourth column, Companies A, D, C, and K, and the Sharp Shooters, under Genl. Custer, was to move directly toward the village from the ridge upon which the officers had crept to make their observations, previous to the announcement of the plan of attack. The attack was to be made at daybreak, and in the meantime each column was to get as close as possible to the village without giving any alarm. If, however, in spite of all precautions, the Indians should discover our advance and endeavor to escape, or fire upon any portion of the command, the attack was to be made at once; otherwise, the signal of attack was to be sounded at daybreak by the band, which was to play on the summit of the ridge from which Genl. Custer's column was to advance, and instantly, at the appointed signal, or at the firing of a gun, the advance was to be made from all directions—all were to go in *with a rush*, and this was particularly enjoined upon all the officers by Genl. Custer, as he fully realized the importance of concentration.

The plan of attack having been announced, the columns were ordered to move at once to their respective positions, as only about an hour remained until daybreak. As Major Elliott's column moved out, a number of dogs belonging to the command followed, and as it was feared that they would alarm the Indians prematurely, some of the men were directed to catch them and strangle (or muzzle) them with lariat ropes, and dispatch them with knives. After the [Elliott] column had marched a few hundred yards toward the bluffs (to the left) we crossed several distinct and well-beaten trails leading toward the point where, from all indications, we had previously concluded that the village must be located, and subsequent events proved our conclusions to be correct. Attempting to ascend the bluffs at one point, Maj. Elliott was fearful that we were too close to the Indian village, and that the Indians would either hear our horses crushing through the snow or else see us outlined against the sky, and so he countermarched the column (no orders were given, except by signs or in a low tone) and ascended the bluffs at a point more remote from the village. We now moved on until we were behind a towering bluff, which rose on our right, about, as we supposed, opposite the point on the stream where the village was located. Here Major Elliott halted the command and requested me to go with him to the summit to make observations; we dismounted, and leaving our horses with an orderly, climbed to the top of the bluff, and lying down on the snow, looked down into the valley below and endeavored to make out the location of the village (which, as we afterwards found, was directly in front of us on the stream below, and no more than half a mile distant), but the night was so dark that we could see nothing except the dark outline of the timber along the stream.[13]

Extract of Narrative Account
1889[14]

As we [Major Elliott and Captain Barnitz] reached the base of the hill after our observation [of the village], judge of our surprise and consternation as we were beset by half a dozen of large fox hounds belonging to the [regimental] band, and their baying

---

[13]At this point the journal abruptly ends. Barnitz was still convalescing at Camp Supply when he began this update. Perhaps he was interrupted at this point by his physician or by visiting friends and never found sufficient reason to finish.

[14]This narrative account is part of the Barnitz Papers, Yale University Library. It consists of some forty-three letter-size pages, written on lined paper and on stationary from the Kimball Hotel in Atlanta, Georgia, and the W. M. Scott & Company (whose real estate office was located next door), and is entitled "The Washita Interview for the Constitution." The stationary has a preprinted date of "188-," and on one of the narrative pages appears "Feb. 21st, 1889" in Barnitz's handwriting, which is assumed to be the date the narrative was written. Robert M. Utley kindly provided the copy transcribed for this publication. The extract starts where the journal leaves off. I have paragraphed the text and deleted excessive punctuation.

might, without doubt, have been heard for miles in the still air, and we now had no longer any hope that our approach was unheralded to the Indians. We found to our surprise that the band, which should have remained with General Custer, was through some misconception of orders, following us, and that Col. Benteen's squadron, which should have accompanied us, had not yet come up. The band was at once sent back and we pressed forward and . . . at length reached the stream below the village, at a ford, the approach to which was much trampled by ponies. We were halted, without crossing, and facing up the stream, dismounted to fight on foot. I however selected ten picked men who were expert shots on horseback, and placed them under charge of Sergeant McDermott on the prolongation of the left flank. As Colonel Benteen's squadron had not arrived, and as it was still an hour or two until dawn, and [as] the whinnying of multitudes of ponies could be heard among the bluffs beyond the stream, Major Elliott and myself crossed over and made a prolonged reconnaissance to ascertain, if possible, if other villages were located in the canyons where the ponies were heard, but our observations only confirmed our belief that the entire village lay above us on the stream.

Having completed our reconnaissance, and [seeing] indications of approaching dawn appearing in the east, and Col. Benteen having at length arrived, I forded the stream with my command and then dismounted, as before, placing the ten mounted men on the left flank, and having the horses of the dismounted men led in column behind us, set forward, with my right resting on the stream. Benteen at the same time moved forward, mounted on the right (left bank) of the stream. As we proceeded, it became necessary for my men to repeatedly ford the crooked stream, the water of which was about knee-deep and cold as ice, but notwithstanding this, they preserved their alignment as though on dress parade, and pressed forward with zeal, for day was breaking rapidly and we were anxious to gain our position at the appointed time.

As we moved forward we soon came to ponies and mules tied beneath cottonwood trees, with piles of branches piled in front of them, and which they were eating with evident relish. An Indian wrapped in a red blanket, presently sprang up from among the animals and ran rapidly in the direction of the camp. Others quickly followed him, until we appeared to have started a numerous covey. Some of my men raised their carbines to fire upon them, but wishing to prevent alarming the camp until the last moment, I forbade them to fire, and we pressed forward with increased speed.

We had just reached the edge of a shallow ravine beyond which we could see the clustered tepees, situated among wide-branching cottonwood trees, when a shot was fired in the village, and instantly we heard the band on the ridge beyond it strike up the familiar air "Gary Owen" and the answering cheers of the men, as Custer and his legion came thundering down the long divide, while nearer at hand on our right came Benteen's squadron, crashing through the frozen snow, as the troops deployed into line at a gallop, and the Indian village rang with unearthly war-whoops, the quick discharge of firearms, the clamorous barking of dogs, the cries of infants and the wailing of women.

As we afterward found out, other villages were situated lower down the stream, and a natural impulse incited the Indians in the village we had surrounded to rush in that direction. As they did so they encountered my line and were either killed, or driven back into the ravine, where some of them for a time made a determined stand. A moment later I discovered a large party running from the village over some sand hills on our left, in the direction of herds of ponies which had attracted the attention of Major Elliott and myself, and I directed the fire of my men upon them for an instant, without apparent effect, and fearing they would escape, I sent Sergeant McDermott with his mounted men to head them off and drive them toward where Col. Thompson's squadron was expected to come down the bluffs and join in the fight; and in order if possible to ascertain where that squadron was, and be able to cooperate with it, and at the same time lay out a few of the Indians myself, I put spurs to my horse and dashed among those nearest my position, but on riding into their midst, I discovered that they were all old squaws, some with papooses astride of their necks, and leading others by the hand, and did not care to waste ammunition on them, though to tell the truth I was not at all sentimental about it, for they were always fiendishly cruel in torturing captives.

I was about to rejoin my command (not seeing anything of Thompson's squadron), and had driven the squaws some distance in that direction, where they were eventually captured, by my men— forty-eight squaws in all—when looking in the direction in which they had been running, I saw the warriors running, and now distinctly outlined against the sky, and dashing forward I soon rode into the rear of them, and quicker than I can tell converted two of them into very good and harmless Indians, though their feathered arrows just singed my neck, and then seeing an Indian aiming at me with a gun, I made a dash for him, with head depressed behind my horse's neck, intending to have him on my right side when I reached him, so as the better to use my revolver; but when I reached him, he wasn't there. He knew too much about war, and preferred to be on the other side of my horse's neck, but instantly turning my horse I made another dash for him, and again he jumped to the left, and was aiming at me as before. I now closed my right leg back of the girth, and carrying my bridle hard to the left, caused my horse to passage, as it is called to the left, so as to close up nearer to the Indian, as I did not wish to take any chances of failing to dispatch him with one shot, for I had need for all the others. I suppose the Indian felt the same way, for he still held his fire, and adroitly avoiding my maneuver, [he] fell back so as to be partially covered by my horse's head, but still on my left side, where he again aimed at me, but still did not fire on the instant, but as I aimed at him threw up a dressed buffalo skin, which he had about him, with the apparent design of causing my horse to jump, and thus disconcert my aim. However, we at length both fired almost simultaneously. He had aimed at my heart, but I had fired just an instant sooner than he did, and my horse bounded slightly when I fired, and this alone saved my life. He stood so near me that the blaze from his gun burnt my overcoat. His ball appears to have struck the lower edge of a rib, and then glancing downward as I was leaning forward at the time, cut the next rib in two, and a piece out of the next rib below, where it was deflected, and passed through my body and out through the muscles near the spine, passing again through my overcoat and cape. You see he was loaded to kill.

. . . As the smoke cleared a little, I was surprised to see him still on his feet. He had dropped the butt of his gun to the ground and stood holding the muzzle with his left hand, and with his right hand thrust beneath his buckskin garments, and was leaning forward with a horrible grimace on his face, as though about to drop his scalping knife and make a rush for me. I thought at the time that was his intention; but perhaps he had placed his hand where my ball had passed through him, and I never knew how it was, but acting on the first supposition, I turned my horse to the left, cocking my revolver as I did so, and leaning on my horse's neck, as though about to fall off, until I had the Indian directly on my right side and very near me, when quickly raising my pistol I fired, and the Indian turned and fell headlong over his gun, just as two of my mounted men reached the spot. I endeavored to speak to them, as they passed me, riding toward the remaining Indians, but could not utter a sound. So I turned about and rode slowly and painfully toward the village. . . .

Interview by Walter M. Camp
May 7, 1910[15]

Barnitz told me May 7, 1910, that he and Hamilton did not charge through the village, but met the Indians as they were running out of it to make their way down the river to the other camps. Says he is not sure whether Hamilton was commanding his company or [was] just accompanying it.[16]

---

[15]The Barnitz interview is contained in the Walter Mason Camp Manuscripts, Indiana University Library, Bloomington; the Barnitz letters are housed in the Walter Camp Collection, Harold B. Lee Library, Provo, Utah; and the Camp letter to Barnitz (copy) is housed in the Walter M. Camp Collection, Little Bighorn Battlefield National Monument, Crow Agency, Montana. The aforesaid documents are reproduced herein by special permission. Walter M. Camp was a dedicated student of the Indian wars of the West. He was the editor of the *Railway Review*, a magazine devoted to railroad affairs, and the author of a textbook, *Notes on Tracks*. His editorial work required him to attend railroad conventions all over the country, which afforded him opportunities to meet and interview hundreds of people connected with historical events. Camp's main interest was the Seventh Cavalry and the battle of the Little Bighorn. His ambition was to write a comprehensive historical work. Before he could accomplish this task, however, Camp suddenly died on August 3, 1925, at Kankakee, Illinois.

[16]Capt. Louis McLane Hamilton commanded a squadron consisting of A Company and D Company. Stationed near Custer just before the attack, Hamilton rode along the front of his line encouraging his men, saying, "Now men, keep cool, fire low, and not too rapidly." G. A. Custer 1869c, 371–72.

Barnitz, with Company G, was in [the] timber, and when the village above them was attacked by sharpshooters and other troops the Indians came running through this timber and the troops just lit into them and piled them up.

Hamilton was killed just ahead of Barnitz. Barnitz and an Indian fired simultaneously at each other and both were shot, Barnitz through the back under the heart. After a while Barnitz rode up to the top of a hill enclosed by a ring of stones and got inside of it and lay down and wrapped his overcoat about him, thinking he would die soon. For this reason he kept his bridle around his arm, thinking that if he died the presence of his horse would attract the presence of the troops.

After a while his horse began to try to snort and try to climb out of the enclosure, dragging Barnitz first to one side and then the other. Presently two G Company men came along and said, "Captain, the Indians are charging down upon us—what shall we do?" It happened fortunately that just at this time Thompson's (?) troop came up. The men were ordered to let their horses loose, throw saddles into [the] enclosure and get in and fight. The Indians, however, seeing these men, rode off, and there was no fight there.

Extracts of Correspondence with Walter M. Camp

Continental Hotel
Mr. W. M. Camp   Philadelphia
7740 Union Ave., Chicago, Ill.   Jan'y 12, 1910

Dear Sir:

. . . .

In my interview with Mr. Denton I give an account of the route followed by Elliott's column,—led by my troop ("G" Troop)—and in the interview I speak of having with Major Elliott ascended a *very steep conical hill,* and lying down, in the snow on the summit, endeavoring to peer down through the darkness and through the concealing timber along the stream into the village, or at least gain some definite idea as to where it was located,—but that it was like looking down into a well;—and we could see absolutely nothing of the village; though we felt sure, from the barking of innumerable

Indian dogs that it was there—just at the base of the hill—and not far beyond it, and on the side opposite that at which our column, Elliott's column, had halted, while Elliott and myself were making—or endeavoring to make our observations. The short snappish barking of the Indian dogs were not easily distinguished from the barking of coyotes, but these letter always ascend an eminence when they indulge in their nocturnal diversions of barking and howling—whereas the dogs referred to remained on the low ground in the village—and from this alone—as there were no other noises to indicate our proximity to the village, we were clearly satisfied that the village was at the exact locality where the dogs were assembled. And this proved to be the fact. Descending the hill with long strides through the deep snow, we rejoined the column, which was halted, as I have said, on the side furthest from the village—*and river,*—and on the left side of the hill—(i.e. the hill was on the right side of our column—and of our line of march.) Having rejoined the column, I say, we pressed on rapidly in the direction we had been marching, and very soon, within a few hundred yards, or less maybe, descended into a deep, narrow canyon, with a level floor-like bottom and precipitous walls of rock on its sides—we descended into this with some difficulty, and by single file—and marched down it for a short distance toward the village, where it appeared to debouch upon the stream—and finally found a spot where we were enabled to climb out of it, in single file, by holding onto the manes of our horses, and so continued our course until we reached the river at a point perhaps 3/4 of a mile below the village—and from which point, after waiting in the cold until daybreak, with the men standing to horse—while Major Elliott and myself made two reconnaissances to the points across the river to determine the whinnying of multitudes of ponies which we found lariated in canyons, where we surmised, at first, that there might be other villages—as indeed there were in the near vicinity, but further down the stream.

But having told the story of the battle quite fully in my interview with Denton, which you will of course see when it gets into print,[17] I will not further digress here—my only object in giving

---

[17]The letter gives the impression that the Denton interview was to be published sometime in 1910. It is possible that he is actually referring to "The Washita Interview

these details is to enable any one who visits the locality to locate the battlefield with certainty by finding the steep conical "sugar loaf" hill, on or near the left bank of the Washita, which we ascended, and just beyond which—that is down the river—eastward, as I suppose, from the hill is the canyon, running directly toward the river and village where the battle occurred.

It appears from a letter written by some one on the staff of the Kansas City Star—and published in that newspaper several years ago—that a great granite boulder, on which are engraved cross sabers, and the words "Seventh Cavalry, November 27, 1868" now marks the site of that memorable battle.

. . . .

Yours truly,
Albert Barnitz, U.S.A.

Col. Albert Barnitz,   Nov. 6, 1910.

    co Adjt. General, U.S.A.,
    Washington, D.C.

Dear Sir:—

I am pleased to be able to tell you that I have visited the site of the battle of the Washita. I was there about two weeks ago, with Ben Clark, who was Gen. Custer's chief of scouts at the battle, and of whom you probably know more than I do.[18]

We found the place unchanged, according to the observations of Mr. Clark. The river (or really the creek) flows in precisely the same channel that it did in 1868, and the same timber remains along the banks of the stream. The country is now thickly settled along the valley, but the identical ground on which the village of Black Kettle stood has not been plowed up, as yet. It is on the farm of Mr. W. T. Bonner, and is just two miles west of the town of Cheyenne, which is the county seat of Roger Mills County, Okla.

---

for the Constitution," which may have lain dormant all these years, or else written at a much later date than previously suggested.

[18]For information on Clark, see chapter 18.

This is a town of 900 people, and it is 26 miles north of the Rock Island R.R., at Sayre, Okla.

Mrs. W. T. Bonner, by the way, has organized a society of ladies, in Cheyenne, whose purpose it is to find means to erect some kind of memorial on the battlefield.[19] She accompanied us over the ground, and as Mr. Clark told of the various incidents of the battle she asked for the names of the survivors, and I gave her your name as one of them, and your address care of the Adjt. General.

I had your letter with me (I refer to the letter in which you described to me the landmarks of the vicinity.) I readily found the "sugar loaf" butte on which you and Maj. Elliott spent some time reconnoitering before daylight the day of the battle. It is a conspicuous landmark and I had no difficulty in pointing it out; in fact it was the first thing that I recognized as we drove toward the battlefield. Mr. Clark verified my designation of this butte. The canyon through which you marched to the river, after leaving this butte, is also still there, being one of the drainage channels from the line of high bluffs (further back).

There are numerous other buttes in different directions from the battlefield that are not so conspicuous as the one above referred to, and I could not just satisfy myself as to the particular one on which you lay down to give up the ghost, after being wounded.

Mr. Clark told me how it came that a stream was named after you some 50 miles from the battlefield. In a previous letter to me you expressed some curiosity to know who did you the honor to attach your name to that part of the country. It happened in this way:

When Gen. Custer and the 7th Cavalry made the second expedition to that part of the country, in early December, 1868, accompanied by Gen. Sheridan, the command struck the Washita about

---

[19]As a result of Mrs. Bonner's efforts, a chapter of the Platonic Club was organized in Cheyenne in 1910, presided over by Mrs. A. G. Gray. Some of its founding members were Mesdames Baird, Bonner, Gray, Gregoire, Jackson, Mitchell, McKinney, and Turner along with Misses Bonner, Greer, McKinney, and Young. The club's ambition was to erect a suitable monument on the Washita battlefield, which finally became a reality in 1932 with a large granite stone donated by Peller Brothers of Granite City, Oklahoma. This monument, engraved "Custers Battle, Nov. 27, 1868," was placed over the grave of an unknown Indian whose remains had been reinterred on the battlefield in 1930. Clippings from *Cheyenne Star*, Oct. 13, 1910, Jan. 18, 1933, in Wesner various. See also Appendix H.

six or seven miles down stream from where the battle was fought. Of course, you were not along on that trip. After taking a look at the battlefield, and burying Maj. Elliott and the men killed with him, Custer marched down the Washita 66 miles, and found that the country was terra incognita, and so Gen. Custer instructed his engineer officer to give names to the tributaries of the Washita as he went along. Maj. Elliott was killed at the mouth of a creek 2 1/2 miles east of Black Kettle's village. This was named "Sergeant Major" creek—I suppose in honor of Sergt. Maj. Kennedy who was killed with Elliott. The engineer kept applying names, and when he got down stream about 50 miles, near the present town of Arapaho, he thought of you, and one stream he named Barnitz creek, and another Seventh Cavalry creek and another Quartermaster's creek, and so on.

The boulder on which "Seventh Cavalry, November 27, 1868," was chiseled and placed on the site of the battlefield was a piece of red sandstone. This was done by Lieut., now Maj. Hugh L. Scott, of the 7th Cavalry, in December, 1890. People have kept knocking off souvenir chunks until it is now reduced to the size of a half bushel. I was able to lift it off the ground and place it on top of a little heap of stones, where it would appear to better advantage.[20] The bones of the captured pony herd that Gen. Custer had shot at the time of the battle are widely distributed about the county as souvenirs of the occasion. Some of the old Cheyenne and Arapahoe warriors who were camping along the creek at the time of the fight are still living on allotments in adjoining counties.

Mr. Clark thought that Lieut. Robbins, C Troop, was the officer serving as engineer on the second expedition to the Washita, and [he is] therefore the officer who named the creeks tributary to that stream. If you can verify this I would be glad to learn the result.

While in that part of the country I secured a county surveyor's map of the county wherein the battle of the Washita was fought,

---

[20]Some time during 1928, Sheriff Jim M. Lester of Roger Mills County moved the deteriorating monument into a corridor of the Cheyenne courthouse for safekeeping. It remained at this location until 1934, when it was transferred to the Cheyenne Star building, where it was exhibited along with the bones of a Washita Indian victim. In 1959 the monument was transferred to the newly opened Black Kettle Museum in Cheyenne. Rucker 1930.

and it is a very good one. If you are going to be in Cleveland this winter I would like to be permitted to call on you there and fight the battle over again. I will very likely be in Cleveland once or twice on other business between now and the end of the year.

Yours truly,
[Walter M. Camp]

Cleveland, O., Nov. 18, 1910.

Mr. W. M. Camp

7740 Union Ave., Chicago, Ill.

My dear sir,

. . . .

Well, as I have said I am much interested in your letter. I suppose you didn't climb the "sugar-loaf butte," as I did, with Major Elliott;—and didn't come down with long strides, as we did, through the deep snow, to be beset, at the foot of the butte, by four loud-voiced foxhounds, which had escaped from the train, parked back on the Canadian River, and followed on our trail, and which by their barking had, as we supposed, given warning to the Indians of our proximity, so that concealment of our movements was therefore unnecessary—though the result proved that the Indians were totally unconscience of our presence until my command had arrived within gunshot of the tepees, as will be disclosed in the interview which I gave to Mr. Denton. . . .

Yours truly,
Albert Barnitz,
U.S.A.

Cleveland, O. Nov. 29, 1910
Mr. W. M. Camp   7740 Union Ave., Chicago, Ill.

My dear sir:

. . . .

Hamilton's squadron, "A," his own, and one other troop, "C," perhaps, charged with Custer and came down through the Indian village, toward my command, which was on the other side of the village on a lower plateau, bordering a swale or rivulet, filled with stumps, behind which Indians secreted themselves, and returned our fire, for a time, after they were repulsed from my front. Hamilton appears to have been on the left of Custer's advancing line, as it approached the village (from the other side of it, as you say, of course—I having *gone around the village* as you are aware, and approached it from the other side—the side opposite that from which General Custer charged). Hamilton was killed near the stream, as I was told, on the left flank of Custer's command, among the trees, or bushes, bordering the stream, and but a few hundred yards in front of the position occupied by my dismounted men. I hope this is now clear to you, and if not, I will further expound the situation when I see you.

I did not ascend any hill or "butte," by the way, to breathe my last, after being killed, but rode back for a few hundred yards toward the village, over a level, or slightly descending plain—while my horse was on his tip-toes, so to speak, snorting, and prancing, as stray shots from the valley came by us, and there was much shooting and yelling down there; until I came unexpectedly to a circle of large boulders, encrusted with frozen snow, and riding into this, trough an opening, dismounted, and taking the reins over my horse's head, passed an arm through them and then placing my hands in the ends of my overcoat sleeves, lay down to die, as I supposed, expecting that some of my men would eventually discover my horse, thus attached (as they did, in fact) . . . and that my fate thus become known. These granite boulders must still lie there, no doubt. . . .

As ever,
Yours, truly,
Albert Barnitz,
U.S.A.

Letter to Joseph Thoburn
November 28, 1910[21]

Mr. Joseph B. Thoburn,
910 West 21st Street
  Oklahoma City, Oklahoma.

Dear Mr. Thoburn:

Your very interesting letter of the 21st inst. came duly to hand, and I will "watch out" for that copy of the December number of Strum's Oklahoma Magazine—which is to contain your account of the circumstances attending the naming of Barnitz, Quartermaster, and Cavalry Creeks. You are undoubtedly right about the date when they were so named, as they would hardly have been named the night after the battle, on which occasion *General Custer did* in the afternoon of the day of the battle, Nov. 27, 1868, march down the valley of the Washita, for about 12 miles, following the fleeing "salvages"—I know this, for I was along, riding luxuriously in an ambulance (!) with the curtains rolled up, so that I might see the painted aboriginees, bedecked with warbonnets, as they made many desperate charges, in efforts to stampede the mules of the ambulance train, but were, on each occasion successfully repulsed by counter charges of the cavalry:—our troopers, on the flanks of the train, riding toward them on each occasion when they attempted a charge, until within a few hundred yards of them, and then at the

---

[21]This letter from Barnitz is housed in the Joseph B. Thoburn Collection, Oklahoma Historical Society, Oklahoma City; it is reproduced here by special permission. Joseph B. Thoburn was a noted historian who spent his entire life chronicling Oklahoma's colorful past. Born in Ohio in 1866, he moved with his parents to Kansas at an early age and later graduated from Kansas A&M College at Manhattan. He moved to Oklahoma City in 1899 and became the secretary of the Oklahoma Chamber of Commerce in 1902. Commissioned in the Oklahoma National Guard that same year, he was also elected to serve on the Board of Directors of the Oklahoma Historical Society. Thoburn became the first secretary of the Oklahoma Territorial Board of Agriculture in 1903, was instrumental in the establishment of Epworth University at Oklahoma City in 1904, and was the author of a textbook on the history of Oklahoma published in 1908. Well known for his pioneering work in the field of Oklahoma archaeology, from 1917 to 1930 he also served the historical society as editor, secretary, and research director at various times and was elected to the Oklahoma Hall of Fame in 1932. Joseph B. Thoburn died on March 2, 1941, and is buried at Rose Hill Cemetery in Oklahoma City. Judge Edgar S. Vaught, "Memorial to Dr. Joseph B. Thoburn," *Chronicles of Oklahoma* 34, no. 3 (1956): 336–37.

command, "Dismount to fight on foot!" springing from their horses, and kneeling down poured a destructive fire into the advancing line of warriors, which speedily caused such of them as were not killed, to wheel about, cover themselves with their shields, and "whup up" for all that they were worth, with their quirts, until out of range of our carbine fire. In more recent years, I have often "by special invitation," fact nevertheless, been to Buffalo Bill's "Wild West Shows," but have never seen any such "cutting up" quite so edifying and interesting to behold!—for, be it remembered, [what] those "salvages" were "up to regardless," with their eagle feathers, and red paint, which they wasted "quite recklessly" on that occasion, in their effort to appear dreadful to the undaunted troopers, who were following the trail of their demoralized and fleeing villages, and had it not been for the diverting antics of those stalwart red men, who were *literally red* on that occasion, there would have been such a dearth of amusement that your present correspondent might have felt lonesome in the seclusion of his ambulance, and possibly grown despondent from reflecting on the discomforting nature of his wound.

Well, we went down stream on that occasion for about 12 miles, and then halted, as though going into camp for the night, fed the mules and horses sparingly a little of the grain which General Custer had providently brought with him in the ambulances, from the Canadian, where he had parked the train, and the men made coffee and fried a little of the bacon which was brought along in the same manner; and then, finding that the Indians had all cleared out from our front, and apparently gone off to condole with their squaws, and find something for themselves and ponies to eat, and a chance to get warm, our mules were silently hooked up, and we started on the back trail, for Camp Supply, and when the Indians found it out, which was not until the following morning probably, we were many miles away, and the Indians were too demoralized to follow. They probably didn't know just what to make of it.

I have thought, sometimes, that Barnitz Creek, or one of the others, may have been, the stream on which we halted to feed that night, and from which we turned back on that occasion,[22] but of

---

[22]Barnitz Creek runs through Custer and Dewey counties and empties into the Washita River near the present town of Clinton.

course I know nothing about the circumstances under which the streams were named. Mr. [Walter M.] Camp writes me another letter dated Nov. 22, in which he says—or was it in a former letter?—that he was told that Lieut. Robbins, 7th Cavalry, was acting as Engineer Officer on the march to Fort Cobb, (detailed to keep the *itinerary* perhaps,) and that he was probably the one who, in obedience to the suggestion of General Custer or Sheridan, named the streams, and [Camp] asks me whether I can verify this.[23] Lieut. Henry Jackson, 7th Cavalry, was detailed as Acting Engineer Officer by Genl. Sully, commanding [the] District of the Upper Arkansas, probably on the expedition, and he made the plan and elevation of the stockade, lunettes, and block houses, intended to be erected, and which were afterward erected at Camp Supply, at the junction of the North Fork of the Canadian (or was it Beaver Creek?) and Wolf Creek. I saw this elevation very creditably and artistically drawn in India ink by Lieut. Jackson, while at Fort Dodge, shortly before we started on the "Expedition," and this drawing may still be preserved among the Records of the District in question, which were in due time boxed up and shipped to the War Department, where they are of course still preserved. You might get a photographed copy perhaps through an application of some member in Congress, and it might be servicable and *very interesting* in illustration of your lectures. Jackson, (Brig. Genl., retired) has recently died. I found him as a lieutenant in command [of] a detachment, part of my troop, when I first joined it, at Fort Harker, Kansas, in winter of 66–7.[24]

---

[23]Camp to Barnitz, Nov. 6, 1910 (above).

[24]Normally assigned to F Company, 1st Lt. Henry Jackson had been on detached service at department headquarters since February 28, 1868, and was not present at Washita. Born in England in 1837, Jackson served in the British army before immigrating to the Unites States. He enlisted in the Federal army in 1863 and served with the Fourteenth Illinois Cavalry and the Fifth U.S. Cavalry during the Civil War, rising in rank from a private to a first lieutenant. Jackson was honorably mustered out in March 1866 and the following July was awarded a commission as a second lieutenant in the newly formed Seventh Cavalry. Promoted to first lieutenant in July 1867, he became a captain in June 1876 to fill one of the many vacancies resulting from the Little Bighorn disaster. Jackson served in the regiment until 1896, when he became major of the Third Cavalry. Henry Jackson retired in May 1901 with the rank of colonel and died at Leavenworth, Kansas, on December 9, 1908.

. . . .

[In 1868] I had a white horse, to be sure, the only one in the regiment of that color, I believe, but I didn't happen to ride him in that fight [at the Washita]; instead, I rode my (supposed) thorobred horse known as "the General," a chestnut-colored horse, as all [of] my troop—"G" Troop—were then mounted on chestnut-colored horses, and as a matter of fact I didn't charge through the village in such heroic style as is represented, and didn't charge through the village at all (!) My fight was all alone, on the upland about three quarters of a mile from the village beyond the sand hills, or what I took to be such, though I may have been mistaken, for the ground was all covered with deep snow and frozen. I rode alone and unattended into a crowd of about 400 warriors, running for their ponies, which I had discovered during the preceding hours of the night, as will appear from the (intended-to-be) syndicated article, if it ever does appear. I rode into that crowd, with intent to prevent as many of them as possible from reaching their ponies. . . .

It was no doubt a little imprudent to ride into that crowd, under the circumstances, but they were going after their ponies, and I did not approve of their becoming mounted, under the circumstances, and so did what I could to prevent it. . . . When I rode out of that crowd, and engaged in a duel with a solitary warrior, armed with a gun, one of the Lancaster muzzle-loading guns with octagonal barrel, and brass-lidded patch box in the stock, carrying a big, round bullet.

He was a brave and sagacious warrior, and no mistake; and in the language of Kipling, I "never got a ha'p'worth change of him!" and if any of his race are left I would be willing to certify that they are right good stock. I surely felt no enmity toward him, personally, nor toward the other Indians, but when they would not keep their treaties, they had to be punished, and it devolved upon the army to administer the punishment.

. . . .

Yours truly,
Albert Barnitz
U.S.A.

P.S. Pardon my trespassing so largely upon your time, but elderly people are disposed to become garrulous, it is said, and you have no idea how much I have omitted to write about, which might be of interest to future generations of Oklahomans, even the Indians, against whom I certainly cherish no animosity, and never did, and I am surely glad that, in recent years, they have ceased to go on the war path, and are now disposed to be good. A.B.

. . . .

8

Edward S. Godfrey,
Seventh Cavalry

Edward Settle Godfrey was a first lieutenant and commanded K Company of Capt. West's squadron at the battle of the Washita. Born in Kalida, Ohio, on October 9, 1843, Godfrey served briefly with the Twenty-First Ohio Infantry during 1861. He won appointment to West Point in 1863 and was commissioned a second lieutenant in the Seventh Cavalry upon his graduation in 1867.

Godfrey served with the Seventh Cavalry for twenty-five years. He participated in the fighting at the Washita in 1868, the Yellowstone expedition of 1873, the Black Hills expedition of 1874, and the battle of the Little Bighorn in 1876 (being appointed a captain the same year due to the many officer deaths). During the Nez Perce campaign of 1877 he was severely wounded while leading his men in action, earning him a Medal of Honor and a brevet to major. Godfrey was present at Wounded Knee in 1890, thus becoming the only officer of the Seventh Cavalry to see action in all the major engagements with the Plains Indians.

Appointed major of the First Cavalry in 1896, the following year he was transferred back to the Seventh Cavalry. Godfrey remained with the regiment until 1901, when he was appointed lieutenant colonel of the Twelfth Cavalry following service in Cuba. That same year he was promoted to colonel of the Ninth Cavalry and commanded the regiment in the Philippines. In 1907 he was appointed brigadier general in command of the Department of the Missouri and later that year retired at Fort Riley, ending a forty-year military career. Edward Godfrey died on April 1, 1932, in Cookstown, New Jersey, and was buried in Arlington National Cemetery.

After the Little Bighorn disaster in 1876, Godfrey became a staunch defender of Custer, and in later years he was a close friend of the general's widow. He was known as a leading authority on the Little Bighorn and wrote a number of articles about his own experiences on the frontier, including the battle of the Washita.

The Godfrey documents below consist of the following: Godfrey's interview by Walter M. Camp on March 3, 1917; an extract of Godfrey's narrative account from 1928; his 1926 critique on the Washita chapter in Col. Homer W. Wheeler's Buffalo Days; *and a letter to Elizabeth B. Custer, dated December 15, 1918, containing some reminiscences.*

Interview by Walter M. Camp
March 3, 1917[1]

At Washita Bell had some ambulances and one wagon to each squadron (five squadrons and a single troop). [The] following were the squadrons and commanders:

Thompson: B and F
Myers: E and I
Elliott and Benteen: H and M   Squadrons
Barnitz: G
West: K and C   with Custer
Hamilton: A and D

Godfrey says [the] sun came up brightly before the fight started. Godfrey was ordered to charge thro village with his platoon of about twenty men, which he did, and got the pony herd. Then he saw large numbers of Indians escaping down [the] north side of [the] Washita and pursued them and came in sight of a village down four or five miles below. [He] says it was a big village and started back and [a] large force of Indians followed us back. On [the] way down [they] had heard heavy firing across [the] river. (This was Elliott.)

Godfrey says when [they] charged thro [the] village [they] fired thro tepees and took no care to prevent hitting women.

---

[1]The original interview is in the Walter Mason Camp Papers, Brigham Young University Library, Provo, Utah; it is reproduced here by special permission.

Dr. Lippincott said Barnitz couldn't live if moved and suggested [that] one troop should be left to take care of him. I went to Custer and volunteered to stay with Barnitz, and Custer said [he] could not do that. So I went to Lippincott and told him, and he then said I should go and tell Barnitz he could die, and as I knew his family, he might want to tell me some things to tell his family. I hesitatingly told Barnitz this. He lay covered up with buffalo robes and he said, ["]Oh, Hell. You think he was my own doctor and tell me that I am going to die. Take these robes off me. I am almost smothered, and warm me up.["] Accordingly I took off the robes and had the men build fires all around him.

[Regarding] Sergeant E. F. Clair (Clear).[2] While we were charging out of the village [we] came across two Indians. I saw they were women and one of these threw up [her] hands and at once I said, "Don't shoot," but just at that instant Clear fired with his pistol and killed her. This was Black Kettle's daughter.[3]

[The] whole command of the advance four companies left [their] overcoats and haversacks in a pile. Bell was to bring these, but Indians attacked him and he had to whip up and drive thro and did not get our overcoats, and Indians got them.[4]

On [the] second night [after the battle,] Custer interrogated the officers as to what Indians they had seen dead in the village, and it was from these reports that the official report of Indians killed was made up. The dead Indians on the field were not counted by the troops then, but guessed at later, as explained.

Field Notes

Godfrey says that Custer's statement in Ten Years on Plains about going to a lower village after destroying Black Kettle's village, and finding it empty or deserted, should not be construed to mean that the command went there. Godfrey says that if scouts

---

[2]Elihu F. Clear was born in 1843 in Randolph County, Indiana, and enlisted in the Seventh Cavalry as a private in January 1867. He was a sharpshooter and was regarded by the officers as one of the best marksmen in the regiment. Clear was fatally shot by Indians during Reno's retreat across the Little Bighorn on June 25, 1876. Hammer 1995, 60.

[3]Black Kettle had as many as seventeen children by four wives, some of whom were slain at either Sand Creek in 1864 or the Washita in 1868. J. H. Moore 1987, 272.

[4]For information on James M. Bell, see the introduction to chapter 11.

went to that village and reported, he never knew it and he doubts if scouts ever went downstream that far that day. Godfrey says he had told Custer of his trip down that way and having seen the village, and that it was a big one, and he also told Custer about hearing the heavy firing (Elliott's fight), but Custer replied that Col. Myers had gone down that way and that the firing was probably Myers's. No one then suspected that the firing had been Elliott's.

Anyhow, when Custer started down the river he kept asking Godfrey where the village was as to the point from which Godfrey had seen it, etc., but Godfrey says the command did not go to the village nor even in sight of it, but turned around and got out of the country before having gone far enough to see the village.

At [the] battle of Washita, Godfrey, with one platoon of his company, of which he was lieutenant, made an advance down the stream, on the north side, pursuing fleeing Indians. He went down about five miles, he thinks, until he came in sight of a large village down there, or of lodges scattered along for a good distance. He then returned on the same side of the stream, and when about half way back to Black Kettle's village, [he] heard firing to his southwest, across the stream, and supposed it was the firing of some other detachment of Custer's command. The firing he heard was, of course, that of the attack on Maj. Elliott who, like Godfrey, had gone down the stream in pursuit of fugitives, but on the other side of it.

Extract of Narrative Account
1928[5]

"November 22nd, 1868—The morning is cold; it snowed all night and is still snowing. Cleared up at noon and got warmer. We took our horses out to graze at noon and let them pick all they can this Sunday. . . . Still it snows. . . ." (From the diary of Blacksmith W. S. Harvey, Troop K, 7th Cavalry, now living at Belle Vernon, Pennsylvania.)

---

[5]This extract is from Godfrey's narrative published in the October 1928 issue of *The Cavalry Journal*, a continuation of his reminiscences printed in the *Journal* of July 1927.

We were grazing the horses in the sand hills on that day when, in the afternoon, orders came to return to camp at once and prepare for [a] thirty days' campaign. It is my recollection that three wagons were assigned to each troop, this for convenience for picket line—one for troop mess, etc., one for officers' mess, extra ammunition, etc., and one for forage. Baggage was limited to necessities.

Finding the Trail

November 23rd—Reveille at 3 o'clock. Snowed all night and still snowing very heavily. The darkness and heavy snowfall made the packing of the wagons very difficult, but at dawn the wagons were assembled in the train and daylight found us on the march, the band playing, "The Girl I Left Behind Me," but there was no woman there to interpret its significance. The snow was falling so heavily that vision was limited to a few rods. All landmarks were invisible and the trails were lost. "We didn't know where we were going, but we were on the way." Then General Custer, with compass in hand, took the lead and became our guide.

As the day wore on the weather became warmer and I have never seen the snowflakes as large or fall so lazily as those that fell that day. Fortunately there was no wind to drift the snow to add to our discomfort. They melted on the clothing so that every living thing was wet to the skin. The snow balled on the feet of our shod animals causing much floundering and adding to the fatigue of travel. About two o'clock we came to Wolf Creek, crossed to the right side of the valley, and continued to march till we came to a clump of fallen timbers and there went into camp with our wagon train far behind. As soon as the horses were unsaddled everyone except the horse holders was gathering fuel for fires. The valley was alive with rabbits and all messes were supplied with rabbit stew. Our rawhide covered saddles were soaked. The unequal drying warped the saddle trees which subsequently caused that bane of cavalry—many sore backs. Snow, eighteen inches "on the level"; distance marched, about fifteen miles.

The snowfall ceased during the night. The sun rose on the 24th with clear skies and with warm weather. The snow melted rapidly. The glare of the bright sunshine caused much discomfort and a number of cases of snow blindness. Some buffalo were killed and many rabbits. Some deer were seen. We camped on Wolf Creek. Distance marched, about 18 miles.

November 25th we marched some distance up Wolf Creek and then turned in a southerly direction toward the Canadian. As we approached the summit of the divide, the peaks of the Antelope Hills loomed up and became our marker for the rest of the day. We made camp late that evening on a small stream about a mile from the Canadian. The day's march had been tedious. The melting snow balled on our shod animals during the long pull to the divide. A number of horses and mules gave out, but were brought in late that night. Wood was very scarce, but usually the quartermaster sergeants would load some wood in the cook wagon when packing and they usually were on the lookout for fuel on the march.

At daybreak, November 26th, Major Elliott, with Troops G, H, and M, some white scouts and Osage trailers, started up the north side of the Canadian to scout for a possible trail of war parties. The remainder of the command and the wagon train marched to the Canadian to cross to the south side. To "California Joe" had been given the task of finding a ford.[6] The river was high and rising, current swift and full of floating snow and slush ice. After much floundering he found a practical ford. The cavalry crossed first and assembled on the plain. Owing to the quicksand bottom, each wagon was double teamed and rushed through without halting. A mounted man preceded each team and other mounted men were alongside to "whoop em up."

While this tedious crossing and parking was going on, General Custer and a number of officers went to the tops of the hills to

---

[6]Born in Kentucky in 1829, Moses E. Milner was given the sobriquet "California Joe" after his return from the California goldfields in 1849. He served in the Union army during the Civil War as a member of Hiram Berdan's First U.S. Sharpshooters. By the fall of 1868, California Joe had drifted into Fort Dodge, Kansas, and was hired by Custer to serve as chief of scouts for the winter expedition. But his fondness for whiskey endangered the expedition and led to his arrest and demotion. In 1870 he prospected for gold in Colorado, and after a short-lived cattle venture in Nevada, he drifted into Wyoming. He was a member of the Jenny expedition in 1875, and upon its return he settled on a homestead near Rapid City. While serving as a scout for General Crook, he was killed on October 29, 1876, in an ambush at Camp Robinson and was buried in the post cemetery. McGillycuddy 1941, 66; Stone 1982, 11–12.

view the country. The highest peak was about three hundred feet above the plain. Suddenly we were enveloped in a cloud of frozen mist. Looking at the sun we were astonished to see it surrounded by three ellipses with rainbow tints, the axes marked by sun dogs, except the lower part of the third or outer ellipse which seemingly was below the horizon, [revealing] eleven sun dogs. This phenomenon was not visible to those on the plain below.

As the last of the wagons had crossed and the rear guard was floundering in crossing, someone of our group on the hills called out, "Hello, here comes somebody." But General Custer had already seen him and had focussed his field glasses on the galloping scout, but he said nothing. It was a tense moment when Jack Corbin rode up and began his report.[7]

Major Elliott had marched up the Canadian about twelve miles when he came to the abandoned camp of a war party of about one hundred and fifty; he had crossed the river and was following the trail which was not over twenty-four hours old, and asked for instructions. Corbin was given a fresh horse to return to Major Elliott with instructions to follow the trail till dark, then halt till the command joined him.

Officers' call was sounded and when assembled we were told the news and ordered to be prepared to move as soon as possible. One wagon was assigned to each squadron (two troops), one to Troop G and the teamsters, and one to headquarters; seven in all, and one ambulance under the quartermaster, Lieutenant James M. Bell.[8] These were to carry light supplies and extra ammunition. I cannot

---

[7]Custer described Jack Corbin as one of the most reliable scouts attached to his command. But he also had a darker side. In 1869 Robert M. Wright hired Corbin at Dodge City as a trail hand for his wagon train bound for Camp Supply. According to Wright, Corbin continually stole whiskey from the cargo and "began the trip drunk and proceeded to break all commonsense rules about firing his gun, sleeping on the night watch, shirking day duty, and generally making a nuisance of himself." In 1870 Corbin posed as a government detective and "confiscated" a mule from a man named Crawford in Butler County, Kansas. A few nights after this incident, someone stole three teams of horses from Crawford's homestead. When Corbin was later seen in Wichita with the stolen mule, Crawford notified the authorities. Corbin was arrested and hanged at Douglass, Kansas, on November 8, 1870. Haywood 1998, 29–30; Stratton 1981, 201.

[8]According to Quartermaster Bell, the train consisted of four ambulances and two wagons and carried a cargo of ammunition and a three days' supply of rations. See chapter 11.

recall of just what the limited supplies consisted. Each trooper was ordered to carry one hundred rounds of ammunition on his person. (They were armed with the Spencer magazine carbine and Colt revolver, paper cartridges and caps.) The main train guarded by about eighty men under the command of the officer of the day was to follow as rapidly as possible. For this guard men with weak horses were selected. Captain Louis M. Hamilton, a grandson of Alexander Hamilton, was officer of the day. He was greatly distressed because this duty fell to him and begged to go along to command his squadron, but was refused unless he could get some officer to exchange with him. Lieutenant E. G. Mathey, who was snow-blind, agreed to take his place.

Soon the regiment was ready to move and we struck in a direction to intercept the trail of Elliott's advance. We pushed along almost without rest till about 9 P.M. before we came to Elliott's halting place. There we had coffee made, care being taken to conceal the fires as much as possible. Horses were unsaddled and fed. At 10 P.M. we were again in the saddle with instructions to make as little noise as possible—no loud talking, no matches were to be lighted. Tobacco users were obliged to console themselves with the quid. Little Beaver,[9] Osage Chief, with one of his warriors, had the lead dismounted as trailers; then followed the other

---

[9]Little Beaver was the patriarch of the Beaver band of the Little Osages and was the second chief of the Osage Nation. He was the recognized leader of the scout contingent attached to Custer's command. Little Beaver was described as a fine-looking man, sixty years old, over six feet tall, straight as an arrow, and muscular, with aquiline features and a thoughtful expression.

The Osage contingent enlisted on October 20, 1868, and consisted of twelve guides and a mixed-blood interpreter named Gessau Chouteau, who was of French and Osage descent. They arrived at Fort Hays on October 29 and were each issued one uniform coat, one pair of mounted trousers, one shirt, one pair of stockings, and one great coat. The Osages left Fort Hays with a supply train on November 1 and arrived at Fort Dodge five days later. To distinguish the Osages from hostile Indians, each was issued one military blouse and one cavalry hat with tassel. Each also received a Model 1866 Springfield breechloading rifle along with sixty rounds of ammunition. Although the enlistment term was for a period of three months, the scouts remained on active duty until March 29, 1869, when they were discharged upon Little Beaver's request. The men were mustered out at Fort Hays in April and returned triumphantly to their villages along the Verdigris River in southeastern Kansas. For the names of the Osage guides, see Appendix E. U.S. House, *Difficulties with Indian Tribes,* 41st Cong., 2nd sess., H. Exec. Doc. 240; Keim 1885, 81; J. A. Greene 2004, 80; G. A. Custer 1868a.

Indian and white scouts with whom General Custer rode to be near the advance. The cavalry followed at a distance of about a half mile. The snow had melted during the day but at night the weather had turned cold and the crunching noise could be heard for a considerable distance.

After a couple of hours' march, the trailers hurried back for the command to halt. General Custer rode up to investigate when Little Beaver informed him that he "smelled smoke." Cautious investigation disclosed the embers of a fire which the guides decided from conditions had been made by the boy herders while grazing the pony herds and from this deduced that the village could not be far distant. The moon had risen and there was little difficulty in following the trail and General Custer rode behind the trailers to watch the developments. On nearing the crest of any rise, the trailer would crawl to the crest to reconnoiter, but seeing Little Beaver exercise greater caution than usual and then shading his eyes from the moon, the General felt there was something unusual. On his return the General asked, "What is it?" and Little Beaver replied, "Heap Injuns down there." Dismounting and advancing with the same caution as the guide, he made his personal investigation, but could only see what appeared to be a herd of animals. Asking why he thought there were Indians down there, Little Beaver replied, "Me heard dog bark." Listening intently they not only heard the bark of a dog, but the tinkling of a bell, indicating a pony herd, and then the cry of an infant.

The Plan of Battle

Satisfied that a village had been located, the General returned to the command, assembled the officers, and, after removing sabres, took us all to the crest where the situation was explained or rather conjectured. The barking of the dogs and the occasional cry of infants located the direction of the village and the tinkling of the bells gave the direction of the herds. Returning and resuming our sabres, the General explained his plans and assigned squadron commanders their duties and places. Major Elliott, with Troops G, H, and M, was to march well to our left and approach the village from the northeast or easterly direction as determined by the

ground, etc. Captain Thompson, with B and F, was to march well
to our right so as to approach from the southeast, connecting with
Elliott. Captain Myers, with E and I, was to move by the right so
as to approach from a southerly direction.. The wagons under
Lieutenant Bell and Captain Benteen's squadron—H and M—
had been halted about two or three miles on the trail to await the
outcome of the investigations.

Just after dismissing the officers and as we were separating,
General Custer called my name. On reporting, he directed me to
take a detail, go back on the trail to where Captain Benteen and
the wagons were, give his compliments to Captain Benteen and
instruct him to join the command, and Lieutenant Bell to hold
the wagons where they were till he heard the attack which would
be about daybreak. "Tell the Adjutant the number of men you
want and he will make the detail. How many do you want?" I
replied, "One orderly." He then said, "Why do you say that? You
can have all you want." I replied that one was all I wanted—"to
take more would increase the chances of accident and delay."

I delivered my messages and returned with Captain Benteen's
squadron. The camp guard remained with the wagons.

Upon the arrival of Captain Benteen's squadron, Major Elliott
proceeded to take position, also Captain Thompson and later
Captain Myers.

Before the first streak of dawn, General Custer's immediate
command as quietly as possible moved into place facing nearly
east, Lieutenant Cooke's sharpshooters in advance of the left dismounted. General Custer and staff were followed by the band
mounted. Captain West's squadron was on the right and Captain
Hamilton's on the left, the standard and guard in the center.
Troop K (West's) was on the right flank and I had command of
the first platoon.

With the dawn we were ordered to remove overcoats and
haversacks, leaving one man of each organization in charge with
orders to load them in the wagons when Lieutenant Bell came up.
Following the General, the command marched over the crest of
the ridge and advanced some distance to another lower ridge.
Waiting till sunrise we began to feel that the village had been
abandoned although the dogs continued their furious barking.

Then "little by little" we advanced. Captain West came to me with orders to charge through the village but not to stop, to continue through and round up the pony herds.

The Battle

With all quiet in the early dawn, Major Elliott's command had reached a concealed position close to the village, but was waiting for the signal from headquarters. The furious barking of the dogs aroused an Indian who came from his lodge, ran to the bank of the Washita, looked about and fired his rifle. I was told that a trooper had raised his head to take aim and was seen by this Indian. With the alarm thus given, the command opened fire. The trumpeters sounded the charge and the band began to play "Garry Owen," but by the time they had played one strain their instruments froze up.

My platoon advanced as rapidly as the brush and fallen timbers would permit until we reached the Washita which I found with steep, high banks. I marched the platoon by the right flank a short distance, found a "pony crossing," reformed on the right bank, galloped through the right of the village without contact with a warrior, and then proceeded to round up the pony herds.

As I passed out of the village, Captain Thompson's and Captain Myers' squadrons came over the high ridge on my right. Both had lost their bearings during their night marching and failed to make contacts for the opening attack.

At the opening of the attack, the warriors rushed to the banks of the stream. Those in front of Custer's command were soon forced to retire in among the tepees, and most of them being closely followed retreated to ravines and behind trees and logs, and in depressions, where they maintained their positions till the last one was killed. A few escaped down the valley. This desperate fighting was carried on mostly by sharpshooters, waiting for a head to show. Seventeen Indians were killed in one depression.

Lieutenant Bell, when he heard the firing, rushed his teams to join the command and while loading the overcoats and haversacks was attacked by a superior force and the greater part of them had to be abandoned. His arrival with the reserve ammunition was a welcome reinforcement.

While the fighting was going on, Major Elliott seeing a group
of dismounted Indians escaping down the valley called for volunteers to make pursuit. Nineteen men, including Regimental
Sergeant Major Kennedy responded.[10] As his detachment moved
away, he turned to Lieutenant Hale, waved his hand and said:
"Here goes for a brevet or a coffin."

After passing through the village, I went in pursuit of pony
herds and found them scattered in groups about a mile below the
village. I deployed my platoon to make the roundup and took a
position for observation. While the roundup was progressing, I
observed a group of dismounted Indians escaping down the opposite side of the valley. Completing the roundup, and starting them
toward the village, I turned the herd over to Lieutenant Law who
had come with the second platoon of the troop and told him to
take them to the village, saying that I would take my platoon and
go in pursuit of the group I had seen escaping down the valley.

Crossing the stream and striking the trail, I followed it till it
came to a wooded draw where there was a large pony herd. Here I
found the group had mounted. Taking the trail which was well up
on the hillside of the valley, and following it about a couple of
miles, I discovered a lone tepee, and soon after two Indians circling their ponies. A high promontory and ridge projected into
the valley and shut off the view of the valley below the lone tepee.
I knew the circling of the warriors meant an alarm and rally, but I
wanted to see what was in the valley beyond them. Just then
Sergeant Conrad, who had been a captain of Ohio volunteers, and
Sergeant Hughes, who had served in the 4th U.S. Cavalry in that
country before the Civil War, came to me and warned me of the
danger of going ahead. I ordered them to halt the platoon and
wait till I could go to the ridge to see what was beyond. Arriving at
and peering over the ridge, I was amazed to find that as far as I
could see down the well wooded, tortuous valley there were

---

[10]Only seventeen men actually responded to Elliott's call for volunteers; for their
names, see Appendix F. The faulty casualty figure of nineteen undoubtedly found its
origin in Custer's official report of November 28, in which he states that his loss consisted of Hamilton, Elliott, and nineteen enlisted men. In his memoirs Custer again
mentions the loss of Elliott and nineteen men, omitting the fact that two of the killed
had died in the village and that their remains were brought along in an ambulance.

tepees—tepees. Not only could I see tepees, but mounted warriors scurrying in our direction. I hurried back to the platoon and returned at the trot till attacked by the hostiles, when I halted, opened fire, drove the hostiles to cover, and then deployed the platoon as skirmishers.

The hillsides were cut by rather deep ravines and I planned to retreat from ridge to ridge. Under the cavalry tactics of 1841, the retreat of skirmishers was by the odd and even numbers, alternating in lines to the rear. I instructed the line in retreat to halt on the next ridge and cover the retreat of the advance line. This was successful for the first and second ridges, but at the third I found [the] men had apparently forgotten their numbers and there was some confusion, so I divided the skirmishers into two groups, each under a sergeant, and thereafter had no trouble.[11]

Finally the hostiles left us and we soon came to the pony herd where the group we had started to pursue had mounted. I had not had a single casualty. During this retreat we heard heavy firing on the opposite side of the valley, but being well up on the side hills we could not see through the trees what was going on. There was a short lull when the firing again became heavy and continued till long after we reached the village, in fact, nearly all day.

In rounding up the pony herd, I found Captain Barnitz' horse, *General*, saddled but [with] no bridle. On reaching the village I turned over the pony herd and at once reported to General Custer what I had done and seen. When I mentioned the "big village," he exclaimed, "What's that?" and put me through a lot of rapid fire questions. At the conclusion I told him about finding Captain Barnitz' horse and asked what had happened. He told me that Captain Barnitz had been severely and probably mortally wounded.

Leaving the General in a "brown study" I went to see my friend and former captain, Barnitz. I found him under a pile of blankets and buffalo robes, suffering and very quiet. I hunted up Captain Lippincott, Assistant Surgeon, and found him with his hands over his eyes suffering intense pain from snow blindness. He was very pessimistic as to Barnitz' recovery and insisted that I tell him that

---

[11]This retreat is discussed in greater detail in Godfrey 1896.

there was no hope unless he could be kept perfectly quiet for several days as he feared the bullet had passed through the bowels. I went back to Captain Barnitz and approached the momentous opinion of the surgeon as bravely as I could and then blurted it out, when he exclaimed, "Oh hell! they think because my extremities are cold I am going to die, but if I could get warm I'm sure I'll be alright. These blankets and robes are so heavy I can hardly breathe." I informed the first sergeant and the men were soon busy gathering fuel and building fires.

In the midst of this, the General sent for me and again questioned me about the big village. At that time many warriors were assembling on the high hills north of the valley overlooking the village and the General kept looking in that direction. At the conclusion of his inquiry, I told him that I heard that Major Elliott had not returned and suggested that possibly the heavy firing I had heard on the opposite side of the valley might have been an attack on Elliott's party. He pondered this a bit and said slowly, "I hardly think so, as Captain Myers has been fighting down there all morning and probably would have reported it."

Mopping Up

I left him and a while later he sent for me again, and, on reporting, told me that he had Romeo,[12] the interpreter, make inquiries

---

[12]Nicknamed "Romeo" by the officers, Rafael Romero was described as a short, heavy-set Mexican with swarthy skin and coarse features, full lips, flat nose, and a low forehead. According to Custer, he spoke several Indian languages and was considered invaluable both as a scout and as an interpreter. Born about 1844, Romero was captured by Comanches during an 1852 raid in Texas and was traded to the Kiowas shortly thereafter. After the outbreak of the Civil War, he enlisted in L Company, Second U.S. Cavalry, and served from 1862 through 1863. In 1864 he was hired as a scout for Chivington's troops and probably was present at the Sand Creek Massacre. Around 1865 he settled among the Arapahos and married one of their women but left after a few years following a shooting incident with Big Mouth's son. Three years later Romero was hired as a scout at Fort Hays and assigned to Custer's command. After Washita he married one of the Cheyenne captives, Coming in Sight Woman, who gave birth to his daughter, Ella. During the 1870s, Romero worked for Indian traders and served as a guide and interpreter for the agency. He accompanied the Kiowa, Comanche, and Cheyenne prisoners to St. Augustine, Florida, in 1875 but was dismissed by a Captain Pratt because he was fluent only in Cheyenne. When Comes in Sight Woman left him about 1880, Romero married a fifteen-year-old Cheyenne girl named Sand Hill Woman, by whom

of the squaw prisoners and they confirmed my report of the lower village. He then ordered me to take Troop K and destroy all property and not allow any looting—but destroy everything.

I allowed the prisoners to get what they wanted. As I watched them, they only went to their own tepees. I began the destruction at the upper end of the village, tearing down tepees and piling several together on the tepee poles, set fire to them. (All tepees were made of tanned buffalo hides.) As the fires made headway, all articles of personal property—buffalo robes, blankets, food, rifles, pistols, bows and arrows, lead and caps, bullet-molds etc.—were thrown in the fires and destroyed. I doubt but that many small curios went into the pockets of men engaged in this work. One man brought to me that which I learned was a bridal gown, a "one piece dress," adorned all over with bead work and elks' teeth on antelope skins as soft as the finest broadcloth. I started to show it to the General and ask to keep it, but as I passed a big fire, I thought, "What's the use, 'orders is orders'" and threw it in the blaze. I have never ceased to regret that destruction. All of the powder found I spilled on the ground and "flashed."

I was present in August, 1868, at Fort Larned, Kansas, when the annuities were issued, promised by the Medicine Lodge Peace Treaties of 1867, and saw the issue of rifles, pistols, powder, caps, lead and bullet molds to these same Cheyennes.

While this destruction was going on, warriors began to assemble on the hill slopes on the left side of the valley facing the village, as if to make an attack. Two squadrons formed near the left bank of the stream and started on the "Charge" when the warriors scattered and fled. Later, a few groups were seen on the hill tops but they made no hostile demonstrations.

As the last of the tepees and property was on fire, the General ordered me to kill all the ponies except those authorized to be

---

he had numerous children. During the 1890s, he was accused of allotment fraud after registering a daughter under both her Christian and Cheyenne name. Labeled by one agent as an "irresponsible, unscrupulous and ignorant Mexican, who drinks to excess," Romero nonetheless served a vital roll as an intermediary between Cheyennes and whites for more than thirty years. He died on July 2, 1902 at Calumet, Oklahoma. G. A. Custer 1874, 161, 255; E. B. Custer 1966, 25, 56; J. H. Page ca. 1895; *Clinton (Okla.) Times*, Feb. 19, 1933; Clark 1910c; Berthrong 1976, 277–78.

used by the prisoners and given to scouts. We tried to rope them and cut their throats, but the ponies were frantic at the approach of a white man and fought viciously. My men were getting very tired so I called for reinforcements and details from other organizations were sent to complete the destruction of about eight hundred ponies. As the last of the ponies were being shot nearly all the hostiles left. This was probably because they could see our prisoners and realized that any shooting they did might endanger them.

Search parties were sent to look for dead and wounded of both our own and the hostiles. A scout having reported that he had seen Major Elliott and party in pursuit of some escapees down the right side of the valley, Captain Myers went down about two miles but found no trace.

The Return March

A while before sunset, as the command was forming to march down the valley, the General sent for me to ride with him to show him the place from which we could see the village below. There was no attempt to conceal our formation or the direction of our march. The command in column of fours, covered by skirmishers, the prisoners in the rear of the advance troops, standard and guidons "to the breeze," the chief trumpeter sounded the advance and we were "on our way," the band playing, "Ain't I Glad to Get Out of the Wilderness." The observing warriors followed our movement till twilight, but made no hostile demonstrations. Then as if they had divined our purpose there was a commotion and they departed down the valley.

When we came in sight of the promontory and ridge from which I had discovered the lower villages, I pointed them out to the General. With the departure of the hostiles our march was slowed down till after dark, when the command was halted, the skirmishers were quietly withdrawn to rejoin their troops, the advance countermarched, joined successively by the organizations in the rear, and we were on our way on our back trail. We marched briskly till long after midnight when we bivouacked till daylight with the exception of one squadron which was detached to hurry on to our supply train, the safety of which caused great anxiety. I was detailed to command the prisoners and special guard.

Aftermath

At daylight the next morning, we were on the march to meet our supply train and encountered it some time that afternoon. We were glad that it was safe, but disappointed that Major Elliott and party had not come in. After supper in the evening, the officers were called together and each one questioned as to the casualties of enemy warriors, locations, etc. Every effort was made to avoid duplications. The total was found to be one hundred and three. General Custer then informed us that he was going to write his report and that couriers would leave that night for Camp Supply and would take mail. I visited Captain Barnitz and wrote a letter and telegram to Mrs. Barnitz that he had been seriously wounded but was improving. California Joe and Jack Corbin started with dispatches and mail after dark.

On November 30th, California Joe, Jack Corbin and another scout, rejoined the command with mail and dispatches including General Sheridan's General Field Order No. 6, which embodies the purport of General Custer's official report. The command was formed as it reached camp on Wolf Creek and this order was read ... [in which Sheridan congratulated Custer and his men].

General Sheridan was informed as to the probable time of our arrival at Camp Supply and received us in review. Before we came in sight of the cantonment, the command was formed for the review of triumph. The Osage trailers, painted and in picturesque tribal garb, were at the head of the column, followed by the white scouts in motley frontier dress; then my prisoners blanketed or in buffalo robes. At a distance in the rear came the band, followed by Lieutenant Cooke's sharpshooters, and the regiment in column of platoons, the wagon train in the rear. As we came in sight of the cantonment, the Osages began chanting their war songs and at intervals firing their guns and uttering war whoops with some exhibitions of horsemanship. California Joe and scouts emulated the Osages' exuberance in Western frontier style. The prisoners were awed and silent till the band began playing "Garry Owen" for the review of the regiment when they awakened to conversation.

This pageant and review rivaled and no doubt was the prototype of the modern Wild West Shows. It was the real thing. We camped on the Beaver and that evening buried Captain Hamilton near the camp with all the formalities and solemnity of the military funeral, the Seventh Cavalry and the Third Infantry present in formation. Hamilton had been an officer in the Third Infantry prior to promotion to the Seventh Cavalry and had been its regimental quartermaster. General Sheridan, General Custer, Colonel Crosby, Captain Beebe,[13] and Lieutenant Cooke, Custer and Joseph Hale[14] (3rd Infantry) were the pall bearers.

We soon learned that the campaign was to be extended through the winter and began preparations. I turned my prisoners over to the garrison. Later they were transferred to Fort Hayes where they were held for some months as hostages for the safety of white captives known to be in the villages of some of the tribes and to compel the tribes to go to their agencies.[15]

----

[13]William M. Beebe Jr. was commissioned as a first lieutenant in the Forty-First Ohio Infantry in June 1862 and was promoted to captain in May 1864. He was brevetted major of volunteers in March 1865 for gallant and meritorious services and in the same month was appointed lieutenant colonel of the 128th U.S. Infantry. Honorably mustered out of the volunteer service in April 1867 with a brevet of major in the regular army for gallant and meritorious services in the battle of Stones River, Beebe became a captain in the Thirty-Eighth Infantry. He was honorably mustered out at his request on January 1, 1871. William Beebe died on October 12, 1896.

[14]Joseph Hale enlisted as a private in the Fifth Massachusetts Infantry in April 1861 and rose swiftly through the ranks to second lieutenant in the Third U.S. Infantry in May 1864. He was promoted to first lieutenant in March 1865 and served as regimental adjutant from May 1872 to March 1885, when he became a captain. Hale died on October 12, 1898.

[15]On December 8, 1868, Major Inman, escorted by units of the Fifth Infantry and the Nineteenth Kansas Cavalry, left Camp Supply with 180 empty wagons, fifty-three captives, and twenty-one sick and nine wounded men of the Seventh Cavalry bound for Fort Dodge. On December 10 a blinding snowstorm struck, causing death and injury to many of the animals. Kindhearted in nature, Inman issued blankets to the captives and also provided extra rations. One of the sick, Pvt. William M. Manes of H Company, died en route. Upon arrival at Fort Dodge four days later, Capt. Andrew Sheridan, Third Infantry, issued orders to send the prisoners under guard to Fort Hays, where they were to be detained in a prison stockade. On April 17, 1869, an additional three Cheyenne males, captured by Custer at the Sweet Water, and a Cheyenne woman were turned over to the commanding officer at Fort Hays for imprisonment. On May 1 the prisoners were issued fifty-eight sets of drawers, flannel shirts, and blankets; fifty

We had the satisfaction that we had punished Black Kettle's band, whose warriors were the confessed perpetrators of the attacks and outrages on the Kansas frontier settlements of August 10th—the originators of the Indian War of 1868.

Excerpt of Critique on Homer Wheeler, *Buffalo Days* 1926[16]

At the Washita Capt. Hamilton was killed while leading his squadron, under Custer's immediate command, as we charged the village. He was the first to fall. Maj. Elliott saw some dismounted Indians escaping over the hill just below the village on the right side of the valley, and calling for volunteers started after them, saying: "Here goes for a brevet or a coffin!" My recollection is that this remark was made to Lieut. Hale.

The orders given to me by my captain were to charge with my platoon through the village and not to stop but to make for the pony herd and drive it back to the village. While rounding up the herd I saw some dismounted Indians escaping down the left side of the valley. I turned the herd over to Lieut. Law, who had followed me with his platoon (the second) and started in pursuit of the Indians. After going a mile or more I found another pony herd and saw that the Indians had mounted. I followed their trail down the valley until I found that there was another village below and

---

flannel sack coats; and eleven pairs of trousers. On May 9 a revolt broke out at the stockade, during which two male Indians were killed. On June 4 a young Arapaho captive was taken under escort to Camp Supply, where he was released into the custody of Little Raven. On June 13 the remainder of the Washita prisoners left Fort Hays under escort of D Company, Seventh Cavalry and were released at Camp Supply on June 22. Carriker 1970, 26–27; "Weekly Report of Sick and Wounded, Dec. 19, 1868," in U.S. Army 1868–69; *New York Times,* Dec. 27, 1868; Burkey 1976, 65, 68–69, 73; E. B. Custer 1966, 110–11.

16This critique of Homer Wheeler's book is found on Reel 9, Elizabeth B. Custer Collection, Little Bighorn Battlefield National Monument, Crow Agency, Montana (microfilm). In it Godfrey addresses the many factual errors contained in the 1925 publication, *Buffalo Days: Forty Years in the Old West, the Personal Recollections of a Cattleman, Indian Fighter, and Army Officer.* This excerpt deals with the battle of the Washita and refutes Wheeler's statement that on November 27, 1868, Major Elliott and Captain Hamilton were together in the party of twenty that was cut off and killed, that friends of these officers charged Custer with having deserted them, and that many Indians followed the returning expedition nearly to Camp Supply.

continued until I could see something of its extent, though the trees along the banks made the view difficult.

We were soon discovered. Several Indians began to circle their horses, and I knew that this action meant an alarm and a rally. I saw that I had to fight my way back. This I did by retreating alternate sections of my platoon until the Indians left me.

I heard heavy firing on the opposite side of the valley. I came to a herd of about two hundred ponies and saw among them Capt. Barnitz's horse. We caught the horse and herded the ponies to the command. I at one reported to Custer, told him of finding the horse and also of discovering the Indian village below. "What's that?" he exclaimed, and then began a rapid fire of questions as to its distance, extent, etc. The General told me that Capt. Barnitz was wounded, and I now went off to find him. He had been my captain when I was a second lieutenant. Soon an orderly came for me to report to the General, and upon doing so I again underwent a rapid fire of questions. In the meantime I had heard of Maj. Elliott's absence and so [I] told the General that possibly the firing I had heard was by the Major's party. He did not think so because Capt. Meyers was down that way and had been fighting all forenoon—ever since the capture of the village. A third time he sent for me to tell me that Romeo had questioned the captive squaws and corroborated my discovery of the village below, and he then gave me orders to destroy all the captured property. I write this fully as I feel sure that the General did not know the direction Maj. Elliott had taken.

When we returned to the vicinity of the battlefield about a fortnight later, on our way to Fort Cobb, I was "officer of the herds" and could not get anyone to take my place, as all wanted to go over the battlefield. So the officer of the day, guards, and I had to remain in camp.

At sunset the whole command moved down the left valley of the Washita. The General had me ride with him so as to tell him when we should be able to sight the big village. As we neared the ridge beyond which the village could be seen—about five miles from the captured camp, as near as I could guess—it had become dark. We had seen no Indians on our way. The command now took the back trail and camped about midnight. The next day we marched until we came to our supply train. If the Indians followed us we did not see them.

I was placed in command of the captives that morning. On the third or fourth day I had a bit of a scare or worry. A squaw asked "to fall out." An old squaw had assumed the roll of speaking for the captives, and she assured me that the request was alright. As the squaw who made it did not want any one to remain with her I was a bit skeptical. Nearly an hour had passed, and I began to feel uneasy, but the old squaw laughed at my fears. Then, to my surprise and great relief, I saw the absent one coming in at a full gallop. She came up laughing, and on her back, slung in a blanket, was a papoose! Instead of losing a prisoner I had gained one.[17] The captives, who had sensed my worry, thought it a good joke. It seems to me that if the Indians had been following us they would have picked up my squaw.

Letter to Elizabeth B. Custer
December 15, 1918[18]

Cookstown, N.J.
Dec 15, 1918

My Dear Mrs. Custer:

I enclose [a] letter of Mr. W. M. Camp, Chicago, to whom I wrote after our conversation on 26th of Nov. Why didn't we think then, it was the eve of the anniversary of the *Washita*? Nor did it

---

[17]The woman with child was identified as Meotzi (Spring Grass), the daughter of Little Rock and Skunk Woman. Meotzi was a niece of Black Kettle.

Not mentioned by Godfrey is an incident of attempted child abandonment. Among the captives was an infant who was found on the battlefield near the body of its dead mother. This baby was handed over to the captive women for care. Yet it was noticed that the women used every opportunity to abandon this infant during the march, which was prevented only by the vigilance of the officers. Another case of cruelty was observed in the treatment of a two-year-old boy who was denied his share of rations and clothing by the other captives. The infant was fair-skinned with light hair and may have been born of a mixed-blood relationship. He was removed from the captives and eventually placed in the care of the Catholic sisters in Leavenworth. E. B. Custer 1966, 49; Burkey 1976, 73.

[18]This letter to Custer's widow is found on Reel 3, Elizabeth B. Custer Collection, Little Bighorn Battlefield National Monument, Crow Agency, Montana (microfilm).

dawn to the Gibsons and self when calling them. But on the 27th I wrote a note to Gibson.[19]

The next time we meet I want to talk about it a little for on reading "Life on the Plains" I find the General failed to give me credit for discovery of the large village down the creek. I gave him the first intimation and it was confirmed later by our captives.

The General recalled me several times during the day and again in the evening just before we marched down in that direction, to inquire as to the location, size and distance of the "Big Village."

The General gave me the task of destroying the village—with orders to destroy everything and not to allow any one to take anything. That accomplished, I was ordered to destroy the pony herd; that was more of a task and I had to call for assistance to kill the 800 or more ponies.

The next day after the battle I was given charge of the captives to guard them until after we arrived at Camp Supply.

I had a letter from Gen. J. M. Bell, Pasadena, Calif., the other day. He is 81, and in fairly good health. Mrs. Bell was in the hospital for operation for bladder troubles, but he expects her to be put in several weeks.[20] He, Gibson and myself are the only surviving officers of that expedition of '68 & 9—unless there are some of the 19th Kansas regt. living.[21]

It is hard to stop when I get to "Reminiscing."

Hoping this finds you well and wishing you a Merry Christmas and Happy New Year, in which Mrs. Godfrey joins,

Sincerely yours,

E. S. Godfrey

---

[19]The Gibsons were Capt. Francis M. Gibson; his wife, Katherine Garrett Gibson; and their daughter, Katherine Gibson Fougera. For information on Captain Gibson, see the introduction to chapter 9.

[20]Mrs. Emily Hones Bell had a successful operation and outlived her husband by twenty years. She died on June 1, 1940, at Hermosa Beach, California.

[21]Capt. Francis Marion Gibson died at age seventy-one on January 27, 1919, in New York City, a month after the letter was written. Gen. James Montgomery Bell died at age eighty-one on September 17 at Hermosa Beach, California. Gen. Edward Settle Godfrey himself died at age eighty-eight on April 1, 1932, in Cookstown, New Jersey. And Elizabeth Bacon Custer, widow of the Seventh Cavalry commander, died at age ninety-one on April 14, 1933, in New York City. Hammer 1995, 20, 79, 125, 129.

9

Francis M. Gibson, Seventh Cavalry

Francis Marion Gibson was a second lieutenant in A Company, which was assigned to Captain Thompson's squadron at the battle of the Washita. Born in Philadelphia on December 14, 1847, Gibson received a commission in the Seventh Cavalry in 1867 and served at Fort Leavenworth until 1868, when he joined the regiment for the winter campaign against the Cheyennes. He was promoted to first lieutenant in 1871 and participated in the Yellowstone expedition in 1873, the Black Hills expedition in 1874, the battle of the Little Bighorn in 1876, and the Nez Perce campaign of 1877. He was promoted to captain in 1880 and was granted a disability retirement in 1891. He died in New York City on January 17, 1919, and was buried in Arlington National Cemetery. The account that follows was written around 1907.

Extract of Narrative Account
ca. 1907[1]

The command had been halted and all officers were ordered forward to report to General Custer. He informed them briefly of

---

[1]This narrative is part of the Gibson-Fougera Collection, Little Bighorn Battlefield National Monument, Crow Agency, Montana. The manuscript appears to have been first printed in 1910, when it appeared in a regimental history, *Illustrated Review, Seventh Cavalry, USA*, published by Medley and Jensen, Denver, Colorado. Melbourne C. Chandler reprinted it in 1960 in his comprehensive work *Of Garry Owen in Glory: The History of the Seventh United States Cavalry Regiment*, published by Turnpike Press of Annandale, Virginia. In 1978 the late John M. Carroll, a Custer scholar and a prolific publisher of Custer literature, included an expanded version of Gibson's account in a pamphlet entitled *Washita!*

In the evaluation of primary data, one is confronted with the task of separating eyewitness observations from hearsay impressions. This task is especially difficult in the

what he had seen and heard, and suggested that they should all proceed as noiselessly as possible to the crest with him and he would point out the location of the village and the features of the country surrounding it. This was done and the general plan of attack was explained. The design was to surround the village as completely as it was possible for eight hundred men to do so, and at daylight at a given signal to make a simultaneous attack from all sides. There were still several hours before daylight and ample time for the attacking columns to get in position. The disposition was made as follows:

Major Elliott commanded the battalion composed of G, H and M Troops, which was to move well around to the left, to a position as near the rear of the village as possible. The officers with this column besides Major Elliott were Brevet Colonel Albert Barnitz, Brevet Colonel F. W. Benteen and Lieutenant Owen Hale, Troop Commanders, and Lieutenants T. J. March and H. W. Smith.

Colonel William Thompson commanded B and F Troops, which were to march to a corresponding position to the right, to connect if possible and cooperate with Elliott's battalion, but the distance necessary to be covered made it impracticable to get within communicating distance, and furthermore it could not have been accomplished without disclosing the presence of Thompson's command to the Indians. The officers of this command were Brevet Lieutenant-Colonel William Thompson and Captain Geo. W. Yates, Troop Commanders, and Lieutenants D. W. Wallingford and F. M. Gibson.

E and I Troops were commanded by Colonel Meyers [sic], and were posted down in the woods along the valley, about three-quarters of a mile to the right of the center. With this command were Brevet Lieutenant-Colonel Edward Meyers and Brevet

---

case of Washita due to the publication of Custer's *My Life on the Plains.* Published shortly after the events took place, the general's narrative was read by many battle participants and has influenced nearly every subsequent eyewitness account. One of the best examples is a Washita memoir attributed to Lt. Edward G. Mathey. Housed in the Brigham Young University Library, this manuscript is actually a verbatim extract of Custer's narrative. Since Gibson's account also suffers from lack of originality, I have extracted only those passages that reflect his personal observations or provide details not found in other chapters in this volume.

Captain Charles Brewster, Troop Commanders, and Lieutenant J. M. Johnson, but the latter before the close of the engagement was ordered to succeed Colonel Meyers in the command of E Troop, he having been incapacitated by snow-blindness.

The center column consisted of the Osage scouts, Brevet Lieutenant-Colonel W. W. Cook[e], with his detachment of sharpshooters, and Troops A, C, D and K, commanded respectively by Captain Louis McLane Hamilton, Brevet Captain M. Berry, Brevet Lieutenant-Colonel T. B. Weir, and Brevet Colonel R. M. West; the Lieutenants were Brevet Lieutenant-Colonel T. W. Custer, S. M. Robbins, E. S. Godfrey, and Edward Law. Brevet Captain A. E. Smith, who was Acting Regimental Commissary, also went into action with this portion of the command. General Custer accompanied by Lieutenant M. Moylan, the Regimental Adjutant, personally conducted this column into the fight. The medical officers present were Assistant Surgeon Henry Lippincott, U.S. Army, and Acting Assistant Surgeon William H. Rennick, and both had their hands full soon after the first shot was fired, and rendered efficient and valuable services. The different columns reached their respective positions in due season, and there silently awaited the coming of the morn. The weary vigil of that night left an impression that can never be effaced by the lapse of time. Daylight never seemed so long coming, and the cold never so penetrating. It was an infraction of orders to talk or move about, so there was nothing left to do but remain perfectly quiet and immovable, thus maintaining a death-like silence, while spending the night in moody meditation, broken occasionally by spasmodic shivers and involuntary shakes. At break of day, the band, which was with the main column, was to strike up "Garry Owen," the signal for each command to charge into the village. At last the first faint signs of dawn appeared while the morning star still shone in majestic splendor like a beacon light, as if to warn the silent village with its sleeping "braves" of approaching danger.

And now we listened intently for the signal notes of "Garry Owen," our charging call, and the death march as well of many a comrade and friend. At last the inspiring strains of this rollicking tune broke forth, filling the early morning air with joyous music. The profound silence that had reigned through the night was suddenly changed to a pandemonium of tumult and excitement; the wild notes of "Garry Owen," which had resounded from hill to hill were answered by wilder shouts of exultation from the charging columns. On rushed these charging cavalcades from all directions, a mass of Uncle Sam's cavalrymen thirsting for glory, and feeling the flush of coming victory at every bound, and in their impetuous eagerness, spurring their steeds to still greater effort, and giving voice to their long pent up emotions. There was no hope of escape for the surrounded savages. Their pony herd had been effectually cut off, and their slumbering village entered from all sides before they had time to realize the extent of their peril; but they fought with courage and desperation.

After charging into the village and taking possession of it, the battle began. The troops were quickly dismounted, the horses sent to a safer place of shelter, and a desperate hand to hand battle ensued. The command had practically changed places with the Indians. Now it was our camp, and they were the surrounding party, but victory was surely ours, while death and destruction were inevitably the lot of the savages. They sought cover behind every available tree, along the steep river banks, indeed behind anything that would afford the slightest protection, and as we were at very close quarters, and had exchanged places with them, the soldiers were in constant danger from hostile bullets fired from all directions. Every man was kept as busy as a bee, and every one knew that he was fighting for his life. The repeated caution to the new men not to waste their ammunition had no effect at all in the excitement of such a hazardous conflict, and had it not been for the timely arrival of Brevet Major J. M. Bell, the Regimental Quartermaster, who gallantly fought his way to the battlefield about an hour after the fight began, with a fresh supply, the Troops might have been required to husband their ammunition greatly to their disadvantage. The rattle of the constant fusillade, and the din of its answering chorus, as it echoed through hill and dale, and across the open plain, seemed to infuse new ardor and enthusiasm into the already fired souls of the zealous cavalrymen, and as the desperate fight progressed, its fury increased, and wilder and wilder grew the intense excitement, while louder and louder sounded the crack of our bullets as they sped on in their unerring flight, like a shower of hail into the very midst of our enemy. The desperation displayed by both sides in this bloody conflict beggars description, and the marked bravery of both friend and foe was beyond the need of praise.

. . . .

The death of Captain Hamilton was particularly sad, for aside from the fact that he was a thorough soldier and exceedingly popular, he should not have been a participant in the battle of the Washita, and was there only through courtesy, as I shall explain. When it was decided to abandon the wagon train, it became necessary to detail an officer to remain with it, and General Custer well knew there was not an officer of the Regiment who would be left behind if he could avoid it, so realizing the futility of calling for a volunteer for this duty, he very naturally decided that the officer of the day and his guard, with an additional detail, should remain with the wagons. When the Adjutant, Lieutenant Moylan, communicated this order to Captain Hamilton, who happened to be the officer of the day, it simply crushed him. He was in command of the squadron composed of A and D Troops, and the thought of [their] going into action without him was a blow to his soldierly pride and sensitiveness that almost stunned him, so he hastened to General Custer, and made such a strong and manly appeal to be permitted to lead his squadron, that the General acquiesced, provided he could find some other officer willing to take his place. As these were the best terms he could make, he hurried off to Lieutenant Mathey, who he remembered was suffering from snow-blindness, and pled and reasoned with him until Mathey very unwillingly, and entirely out of consideration and respect for Hamilton, consented to relieve him as officer of the day, and take charge of the wagon train. Thus Hamilton through the courtesy and kindness of a brother officer, rode to his death. Both Elliott and Hamilton were able and gallant officers, devoted to their profession and zealous and thorough in discharging every duty devolving upon them. Colonel Barnitz, who it was supposed had received a fatal shot, despatched two warriors before he fell, and bravely killed the "buck" who so seriously wounded him. He was later retired from active service in consequence of the disabling effects of that wound.

. . . .

The opportune arrival of the Regimental Quartermaster, Brevet
Major J. M. Bell, with an ambulance, two or three wagons, and a
supply of ammunition, is worthy, I think, of further mention. He
was not expected to come to the battlefield, but he boldly pushed
on to it, thinking that an additional supply of ammunition, which
he had thoughtfully collected, might be useful, and he reckoned
wisely, and luckily for himself and us, he reached us in the "nick of
time" for had he delayed a few moments longer, he would have
been effectively cut off by the hordes of Indians who took possession of the surrounding hills, and doubtless he and his little escort
would have met the same fate of Elliott and his party; as it was, he
had to fight his way through the timber skirting the Washita
River, and had a number of mules killed before he reached us.[2]

---

[2]For Lieutenant Bell's account, see chapter 11.

10

Charles Brewster,
Seventh Cavalry

Born in New York in 1836, Charles Brewster entered the Civil War in 1862 as a Union volunteer. In July 1863 he accepted a commission as first lieutenant with the Thirteenth New York Cavalry and the following year served on Custer's staff during Sheridan's Shenandoah campaign. Captured by Mosby's Rangers in September 1864, Brewster managed to escape, later serving in New Orleans, where he was honorably mustered out in July 1865, earning brevets to captain and major of volunteers for gallant and meritorious service during the war.

A year later Brewster received a regular-army commission as a second lieutenant in the Seventh Cavalry. He was promoted to first lieutenant in February 1867 and brevetted captain, U.S. Army, for his Civil War service. But his conduct as an officer during the next few years inspired little confidence. Col. Samuel D. Sturgis, his regimental commander during this time, informed a review board that Brewster brought "neither energy or industry into play in the execution of his duties and besides all this is unreliable and untrustworthy, never hesitating to tell a lie when it suits his purposes." Rather than facing a military board, Brewster requested a discharge, which was granted in November 1870.

Afterward Brewster made several attempts to secure reinstatement but failed each time. He died at Milford, Nebraska, on July 20, 1904. During the battle of the Washita, Brewster commanded I Company and was assigned to Captain Myers's squadron. The account that follows was published in the National Tribune, *May 18, 1899.*

Extract of Narrative Account
May 18, 1899

The 7th Cavalry, in light marching order, was . . . started southward in quest of Indians [on November 23]. A fall of snow one
night and a warm sun the following day aided the alert scouts in
the trailing of a number of mounted hostiles returning to their
tribes and families in their intended winter home on the Washita
River. These scouts which accompanied the command belonged
to the Osage and Delaware tribes[1] and were partly civilized, yet
with enough native instinct to enjoy the warpath and scalp-lifting
privilege, abundant food, and authority to seize all hostiles' property. At night their tents were separated a little from the main
camp, and the monotonous sound of beating the tom-tom was
heard at all hours.

The day on which the hostiles' trail was struck [November 26]
was made about noon. An officer with a detachment was designated to remain with the wagons, and we soon moved on, leaving,
by orders, all sabers and all dogs behind.[2] The trail in the snow was
about twenty-four hours old and easy to follow.

A rapid march was kept up until about 5:30 P.M., when we
halted in the timbered valley of the Washita to take coffee and
food and to feed the horses. Here Colonel Custer announced that
the troop which should report first as ready to move would be
accorded the right of the line—the head of the column. This was
an incentive for all to be expeditious during the halt for refresh-
ments, and it was not very long before Colonel Custer showed
surprise, while eating with his brother Thomas and Adjutant
Cooke,[3] when the officer commanding Troop I reported it ready
to move. Soon the march was resumed.

---

[1]Only Osage scouts were present at the Washita.

[2]Brewster's statement regarding the absence of sabers is supported by Benteen
(n.d.[b]). Yet Custer's memoirs make clear that the officers did carry sabers in the
engagement, which is corroborated by Godfrey, Ben Clark, and Indian survivors. G. A.
Custer 1874, 320; Clark 1899; Cometsevah 1999. See also "Extract of Narrative Account"
in chapter 8 and chapter 40.

[3]Lt. William W. Cooke served as regimental adjutant from December 8, 1866, until
February 21, 1867, when Lt. Myles Moylan was appointed to the position.

A little before dark silence was enjoined, and there was no talking above a whisper. Seen from an elevation as night approached, what a weird, serpentine specter was this body, outlined upon the white snow. As it wound around the tortuous valley, it had the semblance of a huge reptile, stealthily creeping to destroy its victim or foe. The silence was oppressive. Even the horses, by their rapid gait, showed that they, too, nervously partook of the quiet excitement and were imbued with the portent of some anticipated event. It was an experience long to be remembered. The colder atmosphere of the evening made the snow firmer. The moon was not quite visible, as the sky was overcast with fleecy clouds.

About 11:00 P.M. the column's gait was slackened and moved very slowly, and finally halted with its head at the base of a hill. The adjutant rode down the line and gave the order silently to the troop commanders to dismount, and for all officers to walk forward quietly to the crest of the hill and join Colonel Custer, whom we found lying upon the crust-covered snow near the ridge.

The Indian scouts—always a few miles in advance—had kept Colonel Custer advised of every sign of proximity to the hostiles' camp, and we had already passed two smoldering fires made by Indian boys while herding ponies during the previous day.

After we assembled where Colonel Custer lay prostrate, peering over the top of the hill with a field or marine glass, he called our attention to an occasional faint tinkling sound like that of a bell upon some animals, also to the sound of a barking dog. It was finally discovered that we were close to the upper end of the camp of Black Kettle's band. The other bands were successively camped down along the valley and stream in the woods, although we could see then but little more than the general contour of the valley. It is remembered that while waiting here, Lt. Edward Law, while conversing upon the possibilities of the next few hours, reached out his hand to the writer and said, "Well, let us shake hands, and it will be good bye if we don't meet again." This was declined as being too much preparation for an undesired end.

Colonel Custer indicated to us his plan of attack, which was by squadron from the other side of the camp. Crouching there upon the snow, in the dim light, with that group of fellow officers, this thought came to me: "How many of us will be together tomorrow evening? Probably some of us will be no more. Is it the last time we are all to meet?" Finally, evidences of approaching day became visible, and each squadron moved slowly and quietly to its appointed place of attack.

At last, with the earliest light of morning, there resounded, echoed, and reechoed over the valley the bugle call of the "Charge," and we braced ourselves in the saddles for the conflict. We were now to avenge the slaughter of the poor, helpless settlers of the Republican, Solomon, and Saline Rivers and the scattered laborers on railroad construction far to the north.

Soon the muffled sound of Cavalry horses' feet was heard, and it increased to a subdued roar, then instantly came the rapid discharge of arms. Fleeing from their lodges, tepees, and fighting as they fled from successive covers of knoll, bush, brush, ravine, and riverbank were the retreating Indians, pursued and failing. Amid the din was heard the mounted regimental band playing Colonel Custer's favorite battle tune, "Garry Owen."

The Indian boys and squaws fought as fiercely as did the bucks. They promptly killed all white prisoners. During the battle, one squaw was seen to kill a young white child by ripping open its abdomen. Another white infant was found mangled beside its dead captive mother with bullet holes in her head. It was a pathetic sight, which told of revengeful squaws.[4]

With the first rush of the charge, Chief Black Kettle sprang out from his lodge and shouted loudly to his people, reproaching them for disregarding his warnings in the past, that the whites were now upon them and that he was glad—then he fell with a bullet through his heart. He was not a bad Indian, but he could not control his warriors. Down through the valley for many miles the camps extended, consisting of a number of tribes and bands, and as they heard and learned of the progressing battle, they hastily mounted ponies and hurried toward the fray, continuously keeping along the hilltops, where they swarmed until the fight was

---

[4]No white captives were killed in Black Kettle's village. The first female victim referred to by Brewster was a Cheyenne mother who killed her full-blood infant out of despair. The second female victim was Clara H. Blinn. She and her infant son were found dead in an Arapaho village eight miles below the battlefield two weeks after the attack.

over. But many had no pony to mount, because of Custer's precaution to have them surrounded and herded by soldiers. They remained there to witness the destruction of hundreds of ponies, horses, mules, tepees, buffalo robes, dried meat, and a large amount of general plunder.

. . . .

The number of officers killed was two, and three were wounded. Twenty-one enlisted men were killed, and eleven wounded. That night the moon shone down upon the bodies of many who had not yet been found upon the battlefield.

Capt. Louis Hamilton, a grandson of Alexander Hamilton, was killed in the first charge. He was the officer detailed to remain with the wagons and supplies when the Indian trail was first struck, but his brave, restless spirit drooped at the thought of remaining away from an open engagement of his regiment, and he persuaded Lieutenant Mathey to serve as his substitute, which he did with the consent of Colonel Custer. Before the close of the War of the Rebellion, the sentiment became prevalent in the Union army that an officer did his duty sufficiently who served when and where ordered, instead of volunteering, whereby many lost their lives. But for this brave act, Captain Hamilton would perhaps be living today.

Lieutenants Custer and March were slightly wounded. Major Elliott and the sergeant major, with nineteen men who had become separated and cut off from the majority during the fight, were surrounded and killed by the Indians after a most desperate fight, their plight not being discovered by others of the command. Captain Barnitz was shot through the body and his death was expected, but he lived. A silk handkerchief was drawn through his body where the bullet made an opening or orifice.

11

James M. Bell,
Seventh Cavalry

James Montgomery Bell was a first lieutenant and served as the Seventh Cavalry's quartermaster at the time of the battle of the Washita. Born on October 1, 1837, in Williamsburg, Pennsylvania, Bell graduated with a master's degree from Wittenberg College (Ohio) in 1862. He immediately enlisted as a private in the Eighty-Sixth Ohio Infantry and was promoted to lieutenant the same year. Appointed captain in a Pennsylvania cavalry unit in 1863, Bell was engaged in sixteen operations before being wounded at Coggins Point, Virginia. He was mustered out in 1865 and earned brevets up to major for his gallantry in battle.

After the Civil War, Bell received appointment as a second lieutenant in the Seventh Cavalry in 1866. He was promoted to first lieutenant in 1867 and participated in the Washita engagement, where he supplied the regiment with much-needed ammunition transported from the rear through enemy lines. He was part of the Yellowstone expedition in 1873 but was on a leave of absence during the Sioux campaign of 1876, after which he was appointed captain due to the many officer deaths. He participated in the Nez Perce campaign in 1877 and was brevetted lieutenant colonel for gallant service.

Promoted to major of the First Cavalry in 1896, Bell fought in the Cuban campaign in 1898 and served in the Philippines in 1899 as a brigadier general of volunteers. He was appointed lieutenant colonel of the Eighth Cavalry in 1900 and retired in 1901 after his promotion to brigadier general in the regular army. Bell died on September 17, 1919, at Hermosa Beach, California, and was buried in San Francisco National Cemetery.

Bell served with the Seventh Cavalry for thirty years and was considered a well-educated and competent officer. The following items con-

sist of an interview by Walter Camp (ca. 1910); Camp's letter to Bell, dated May 12, 1911; and Bell's reply, dated July 28.

Interview by Walter M. Camp
ca. 1910[1]

The next summer after the [Medicine Lodge] council (several wagon loads [containing]) a large number of arms and ammunition were issued to the Indians. Two weeks after this we were fighting them on the Sully Expedition. The agent through whom these were issued was Col. Wyncoop [*sic*].[2]

On [the] Sully campaign in summer of 1868 there were six troops [of] 7th Cavalry: A, D, F, G, H, and I under Hamilton, Weir, Yates, Barnitz, Benteen and Keogh.[3] [The horse] Comanche had been bought just before this and was a troop horse, but Keogh rode him on the expedition and Comanche was wounded in it.[4] The regiment started out from Ft. Dodge and crossed the Cimarron and made camp.

On [the next] morning when [we] broke camp two men of F Company remained behind, going into [the] brush to answer a call of nature, and Capt. Hamilton, who was rear guard, passed without seeing them. After the rear guard had gone on some distance, Bell's

[1]Walter Camp's interview of Bell is found in Folder 1, Box 2, Camp Manuscripts, Indiana University Library, Bloomington; it is reproduced here by special permission. The text has been paragraphed.

[2]The Cheyennes signed the Medicine Lodge Treaty on October 28, 1867. The issue of arms took place at Fort Larned on August 9, 1868. The following day a large war party of two hundred Cheyennes attacked peaceful settlements along the Saline River and killed fifteen whites in the Solomon Valley on August 12.

[3]The Sully expedition consisted of nine companies of the Seventh Cavalry under Maj. Joel Elliott. This strike force was augmented by F Company, Third Infantry under Capt. John H. Page, with a howitzer and a supply train of thirty wagons. The column was guided by Ben Clark, chief of scouts, and left Fort Dodge on September 7, 1868, a force of nearly six hundred men. The troops returned ten days later. Albert Barnitz to his wife, Sept. 16, 1868, in Utley 1977, 188.

[4]Described as a clay-bank gelding, the horse Comanche became famous as Capt. Myles Keogh's mount and was considered the sole survivor of the battle of the Little Bighorn, having received seven gunshot wounds; Keogh was killed. Although the captain rode Comanche that day, he did not own the horse. Contrary to popular belief, Comanche was government property, a troop horse assigned to Pvt. John McGinnis, who was convalescing at Fort Lincoln when the regiment left on the Sioux campaign. Hardorff 1990, 30.

attention (he was QM) was attracted to some pistol shots, and looking back, saw that the Indians had slipped up and cut off the two men, who had mounted and just started to overtake the command. Their horses were badly frightened and were being driven off by the Indians.

Hamilton's men at once gave pursuit, and one of the men, when he saw he could not control his horse, threw himself out of the saddle. He was badly wounded, but finally recovered. The other man, a German, stuck to his horse and was run off and captured by the Indians, who burned him to death that night, their fire being visible from the cavalry camp.[5] Sully, learning of the trouble, came back and put Capt. Hamilton under arrest for permitting any men to be behind the rear guard. Lieut. Bell kept out of sight among his wagons until Sully's wrath had died down.

The night after [the] man [was] captured the Indians attacked the camp. This was anticipated and [the] wagons [had been] circled by Bell and horses [kept] within, and the men were ordered to sleep under wagons. About an hour before daylight [the] Indians charged right down to [the] camp, expecting to stampede the horses, but they received a hot fire and turned back. [The] Indians [were] well-armed, but still used bow and arrow a good deal.

[The] next morning after [the] attack [we] moved down Beaver Creek and came to [the] junction of Beaver and Wolf, following [the] trail of [the] three tribes. They had been across Wolf Creek and into [the] Sand Hills, and when he [Sully] got across, [the] Indians took advantage and attacked him with heavy force, so much so that Sully deemed it unwise to pursue [the] Indians any further and he turned back and camped that night at [the] junction [of] Wolf and Beaver, where Camp Supply [was] afterward located. One man of Yates' troop was killed and buried there that

---

5This incident occurred on September 11 and involved Pvts. Louis Curran and John A. Kennedy, who were assigned to Capt. George Yates, F Company, as cook and orderly. Curran was carried off by the Indians, but Kennedy was recovered by the rear guard and survived a bullet wound through the left lung. The Indians drove off three horses belonging to F Company and the private horse of Captain Yates. September Return, in U.S. Army 1868; Barnitz journal, in Utley 1977, 186 (which identifies the unfortunate man as James Curran).

night.[6] Next morning Sully took up [the] march northward. Sully's campaign having turned out a failure, Gen. Sheridan telegraphed [the] War Department that he must have Custer back.

On [the] Washita expedition, the first night out from Camp Supply [we] camped on Wolf Creek, and the next night on Hackberry Creek, and [the] third night on [the] Canadian near Antelope Hills. The march had been directly south. On the Canadian the ice was about three inches thick, and while breaking the ice a courier came in from Maj. Elliott, who was out scouting, saying that Elliott had struck a large, fresh Indian trail in the snow not far off.

Here Custer ordered Bell to corral his wagons and pick out some of his best mules to haul two wagons and four ambulances and follow as fast as he could. The officer in command of [the] rear guard (Capt. Hamilton) was ordered to remain with the wagons with forty men to guard it.[7] Capt. Hamilton went to Custer and requested to go along, saying he did not like to remain back when a fight was in prospect. Custer said that in as much as all the officers wanted to go he would not order any of them to remain behind, but if Hamilton could get any one of them to take his place he might do so; otherwise the duty of remaining to guard the wagons would have to fall on the officer in command of the rear guard. Hamilton persuaded Lieut. Mathey to remain and in this way happened to go with the regiment.

Bell, behind with four ambulances and two wagons with three days [of] rations, and [the] best horses,[8] kept right up with the column all night, and when [they] discovered [the] village Custer sent word back to halt [the] wagons and ambulances to prevent Indians [from] discovering [them]. [He] said [the] attack would be made at daylight and as soon as [Bell] heard firing to come on with [the] wagons. Benteen was Officer-of-the-Day and rear

---

[6]Pvt. Cyrus W. McCorbet, F Company, was killed in the Sand Hills on September 13, 1868. Not mentioned by Bell is the death of Pvt. Charles Kruger, I Company, who was accidentally shot by his own picket at daybreak on September 15. He was buried the next evening at Bluff Creek, Kansas. September Returns, U.S. Army 1868; Shirk 1959, 75.

[7]The escort consisted of eighty men, "with inferior horses," detailed from the different companies. G. A. Custer 1966, 303–304.

[8]The term "best horses" refers to the extra horses of the officers, which were led by orderlies assigned to the train.

guard, and Custer ordered him to join him on the hill at the front. Bell and [the] wagons were about a mile back from where Custer waited to attack the village.

When Benteen went forward Bell [was] left without any guard except deserters and four or five sick men. Bell was very uneasy about this and was tempted to anticipate the fight a little and moved up about half a mile. [He] found a very bad crossing of the Washita and had to get out pioneer tools and stopped there some time. Finally [he] got up to where [the] overcoats had been left in piles [and] thought they would be needed.[9] While packing these coats into [the] wagons, two columns of warriors came up on both flanks from [the] lower villages, to attack Custer. They started to corral Bell and [the] wagons, and Bell ordered drivers to put lash to the mules and ran down the hill toward Custer and just escaped by [the] skin of his teeth only.[10] [He] did not get all of the overcoats—only about half of them.

As Bell drove in he met forty or fifty squaws and children making away through [the] brush. Bell took his pistol and drove them back. In one of the ambulances with Bell rode Courtenay (with a camp stove), an Irish woman who had long been Custer's cook.[11] Bell asked her to make coffee, and while doing this the Indians around kept up firing. Suddenly a mule was shot down [on the] right side of her and she looked up toward the Indians and said, "Ye dirty devils ye," and kept right on making coffee.

---

[9]These piles contained the overcoats and haversacks of the center column. The property was left in the care of one private detailed from each of the five units in Custer's command. The five men were brought in safely with Bell's train. See "Interview by Walter M. Camp" in chapter 8.

[10]Although not mentioned by Bell, several of his mules were killed by Indian fire. This information comes from Charles F. Bates, Godfrey's son-in-law, who adds that during the headlong dash down the hill, some of the tar-soaked wooden hubs of Bell's wagons burst into flames due to the friction against the crusted snow. Bates 1936, 13.

In 1918 Rep. James V. McClintic of Oklahoma introduced a resolution in Congress to grant Bell the Medal of Honor for his valorous services at the Washita. This bill was pending at the time of Bell's death, but nothing came of it (Thoburn and Wright 1929, 428). A tributary of the Washita was named Quartermaster Creek in 1868 in Bell's honor.

[11]Mrs. Courtenay, a laundress, was married to a Sergeant Courtenay of F Company. She had led an extremely rough life as a camp woman and was known to Custer as the "awfulest" scold and most "quarelsomest" woman he had ever met. John Ryan, in *Newton Circuit*, May 21, 1909; E. B. Custer 1966, 12–13.

Bell was ordered to burn all plunder in the village. [The] Indians were now fighting all around [them] and [were] making it hot when Bell advised Custer to destroy the Indian herd, and Custer said [he] could not spare [any] ammunition, and Bell then told Custer [that] he had exceeded his orders of the morning before to him [to bring] only three days [of] rations and had brought along 20,000 rounds of ammunition. Custer then said [he was] very glad to hear that, and Troop F took herd up into [the] canyon and fired volley after volley until all [of the ponies were] shot down.[12] Then [the] Indians all left and Custer started down [the] Indian trail just at dusk. [He] followed it until darkness concealed [them] and Custer [then] countermarched and went right back on his trail until 11 PM, being fearful that the Indians would get at his transportation. When [we] got back to [the] Canadian, [we] found [that the] train [was] all right and no Indians had appeared.

Before leaving [the battlefield], Maj. Elliott was missed, but careful inquiry developed no knowledge of him, [and] so, the situation being pressing, the command went off without investigating, a thing for which Custer was sharply criticized in many quarters afterward.

Correspondence with Walter M. Camp[13]
1911

7740 Union Ave., Chicago, Ill.
May 12, 1911.

Gen. J. M. Bell,
1071 Ocean Ave.
New London, Conn.

Dear Sir:

I have received your letter of 11th inst. and also the photographs which you have so kindly sent, for both of which I thank you very much. I will take good care of the photographs and return them to

---

[12]Companies K and F and the sharpshooters destroyed the pony herd.

[13]These letters are housed in the Camp Collection, Brigham Young University Library, Provo, Utah; they are reproduced by special permission.

you by registered mail in about a week or ten days. I am much pleased with the notes you have given me of the campaign with Gen. Sully, in 1868, and of other engagements with the Indians.

Answering your question as to how soon I expect to complete the history, I will say that it will probably be more than a year yet. I still have a number of things to investigate, and this historical work, being one of leisure with me, does not move along as fast as though I was giving all my time to it.[14] Such time as I can get, however, I am giving to it, and I am getting splendid cooperation from the surviving officers. In regard to photographs, I now have one of every officer who took part in the battle of the Little Bighorn, and one of each company commander at the battle of the Washita except West, Myers and Brewster.

Since seeing you I have visited the site of the battlefield of the Washita, in company with Ben Clark.[15] The same trees are there in the bend of the stream, but the whole country is now settled up with farmers. Mr. Clark was able to point out to me the various landmarks connected with the battle, and in this connection I wish to enquire of you about a single matter.

You told me about getting out the pioneer tools during the night to get your wagons over a bad crossing of the Washita. I understood that this work was going on while Gen. Custer and his men lay waiting to attack the village. If I am correct about this, I will be glad to learn whether this crossing of the Washita *was on Custer's trail,* and about how far in the rear of the pile of overcoats that you told me about. Clark showed me where the pile of overcoats lay, but he did not tell me about any crossing of the Washita in the march up to that point. I am making a carefully prepared map of the country there, and I would like to know how many times Custer's trail crossed the Washita before coming to the point where the overcoats were left. Any information about this will be much appreciated. Not far in the rear of the point referred to where the overcoats lay there is a tributary of the Washita that the trail crossed.

Yours truly,

[Walter M. Camp]

---

[14]Camp died unexpectedly in 1925 before he could finish his research.

[15]Camp visited the Washita battlefield on October 22, 1910. See "Interview and Notes by Walter M. Camp" in chapter 18.

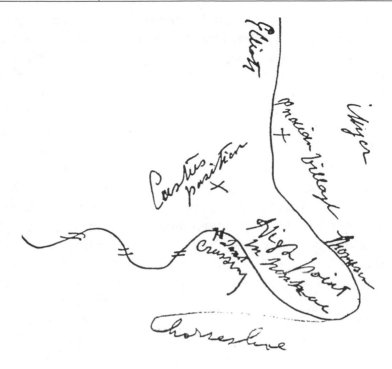

Route of the Ambulance Train, drawn by James M. Bell. This drawing was appended to his letter of July 28, 1911, addressed to W. M. Camp. The sketch shows the route of the ambulance train and identifies the squadron positions of Custer, Elliott, Myer, and Thompson. The numerous crossings of the Washita and its tributaries are indicated with hatch marks: "=". After a delay at the "last crossing," the train ascended a steep hill in the horseshoe bend and arrived at Custer's deserted bivouac. Indians attacked the train just beyond this location while it was loading up the overcoats and haversacks that the men of Custer's column had left behind. Reproduced courtesy of Brigham Young University Library.

July 28, [19]11

Mr. W. M. Camp

Dear Sir:

I should have replied to your letter of May 12th containing questions about the Washita fight much sooner, but some way overlooked it. As I stated to you when here, Genl. Custer sent word to me as soon as the camp of the Indians had been discovered, not to move any nearer the camp with the transportation for fear of giving the alarm to the Indians. The night was cold and the creaking of the wagons and ambulances could be heard for some distance. I was then about one mile in rear of the cavalry. I was informed that the attack would be made at daybreak and was expected to move forward as soon as I heard the firing, As I stated to you, I slowly moved up just as the first harbinger of day was visited in the east, and perhaps ten minutes or fifteen before the fight opened, and had reached the crossing spoken of just as the firing began. Having moved forward about a half mile, I examined the crossing, but found it not practicable for wagons, so hurriedly collected all the available men with tools and in ten minutes we were crossing and following the trail up a steep grade to where the overcoats were found and where Custer also made squadrons of his troops that morning. From the place where the coats were piled we could see the fight in progress in the village. The crossing was at the foot of the steep trail leading up to the top of the high sheer that ran out into the horseshoe of the stream, which made a sharp bend. The bed of the stream may have and very possibly has changed in over forty years, but my impression at the time was that it was the main stream, but it might have been in between the big bend of the stream, but its character was like the main stream. There was but little water in the stream at any point. The stream was very tortuous and the Indian trail, which we followed all the way, cut straight across the stream and we must have crossed it 20 times during the night, and at many places had to dig as at the last crossing. Should there be any other points on which you would like any information, write.

Bell

12

Anonymous Correspondent, *New York Daily Tribune*

This report appeared in the New York Daily Tribune, *December 29, 1868. Headlined "Gen. Custar's [sic] Battle," it was filed by "an occasional correspondent" of the* Tribune *and addressed from Indian Territory on November 29, 1868. There exists no doubt that the anonymous correspondent was an eyewitness, probably an officer, and may well have been Custer himself, who that same day sent a dispatch from Wolf Creek to Sheridan at Camp Supply. The* Tribune *piece may have been forwarded at the same time.*

Newspaper Dispatch
November 29, 1868

It was what the Boys in Blue call a nice little fight. We had surprised Black Kettle's band in their village. We had marched for days through sage-weeds, woods, morass, and sand, tediously, perseveringly. We had faced the pending storm of snow, wading wearily through its compressing depth, from its first fall; and had taken brief snatches of sleep upon its soft cold bed at night. We had finally abandoned our train and supplies, and had marched all day on the enemy's trail; and, turning our backs upon the setting sun at night, steadily and vigorously pushed on; at times nearly falling from our saddle with sudden sleep. It was after midnight, when two Osage Indian scouts in the advance, announced that they smelt the smoke of a wood fire, a fire which we came upon after going about a mile further. Around it were traces of Indian boys who had been herding ponies. On we pushed again, the crisp frozen snow rustling under the horses, feet, and our long, dark column winding through the valley like a huge black monster. Not a voice could be heard. Ten miles more were passed, and the scouts, who were ascending elevated ground, suddenly wheeled their horses and quickly moved to the rear, reporting that ponies were grazing nearly a mile ahead of us, and that a village was doubtless in the woods beyond, which skirts the stream in the valley. Strict silence was observed, but no white man who looked, could, by the utmost straining of the eyes, see a living object where the telescopic vision of the Osage Indian scouts had discovered so much. Soon a night-glass verified the presence of the animals. The officers were assembled by Gen. Custar, and all cautiously crept up to the little crest of the hill overlooking the valley below, and the surroundings were carefully noted. It was a moment of exultation, and the General's enthusiastic instructions were quietly and eagerly given and received. The hour was now about 2 o'clock A.M. Quickly the squadrons marched around to their respective positions, and there rested for the signal of the first gray tints of morning. It came at last; and, as the band struck up "Garry Owen," the platoons swept down with a yell from every side upon the doomed village. The savages sprang into ditches and holes, and behind trees and bushes, and opened a raking fire from every direction with bullets and arrows. Some fled with the terror-stricken squaws and papooses, fighting as they ran. They strove hard to reach the ponies to mount; but very few succeeded in doing so. Sharp and loud rang the rattling carbines, echoed back by the hills and bluffs on every side. Swift and sure rode the troopers, whose lines soon extended across the valley, furiously tearing after the fleeing enemy—many of whom bit the snow—miles beyond their village, where their bodies were not afterward seen nor counted. Two platoons were dismounted to fight to better advantage among the bushes. Gradually all the Indians were hunted from their cover like wild animals whose escape is cut off, and the fire slackened. One hundred and three bodies were found around the village proper, but many wounded escaped. A few of the squaws took part in the fight, using pistols. Others were spared, except those who had been seen to murder white captive children in their hands. These instantly met the fate of their warrior braves. The ground was strewn with blankets, robes, and clothing, etc., by the fugitives. Nearly 1,000 animals (horses, ponies, and mules) were surrounded and driven in by detachments when the fight opened. A great many rifles, pistols, saddles, lariats, bridles, robes, etc., were taken; also, large quantities of ammunition, dried meat, and other food, all of which we destroyed, together with the 51 lodges. When the squaws and children were overtaken, collected together, and turned back in their flight, they defiantly and resignedly chanted their war or death songs. Even the youngest did this, expecting to be put to death. Capt. Louis Hamilton, Major J. H. Elliott, and Brevet Lieut. Col. A. Barnitz fell in the fight. Black Kettle had for some time been disposed to keep peace with the whites, but had been overruled by his tribe. At the first sound of horses' feet, when the cavalry approached, he sprang outside his lodge, and sounded the war-whoop, then shouted that the whites were coming to kill them all, and that he was glad of it. Thus he fell, and died, with his faithless braves, though "seeking for the right." The village had no sooner been taken than swarms of mounted Arrapahoe warriors approached at full speed from their village a few miles below, drawn hence by the sound of firearms. They began circling around the village, after their custom—now dashing up and firing, now retreating in crooked circling courses behind hills and knolls. They cut off a few of our bravest, but more imprudent men. Yet, we well know that many a pony-saddle was emptied ere those few [with Elliott] fell. The battle is over, and the field covered with dead animals and savages, muddy and smeared, and lying upon each other in holes and ditches. The field resembled a vast slaughter pen. We have 53 prisoners.

13

Frederick W. Benteen, Seventh Cavalry

Frederick William Benteen was the captain of H Company and led a squadron of Major Elliott's command during the battle of the Washita. Born on August 24, 1834, in Petersburg, Virginia, Benteen entered military service in 1861 as a first lieutenant in the Missouri Volunteer Cavalry. He was appointed to captain the same year, to major of the Tenth Missouri Cavalry in 1862, and to lieutenant colonel in 1864, commanding the Fourth Brigade of Pleasanton's Cavalry Division in the engagements at the Big Blue and the Little Osage Crossing in Missouri. Benteen was mustered out in 1865, having been engaged in twenty-one actions, skirmishes, battles, and sieges. Thereafter he was appointed colonel of the 138th U.S. Colored Volunteer Infantry in July 1865 and the next year recommended for a brevet of brigadier general of the Missouri Militia, being mustered out of volunteer service soon after.

Benteen was appointed captain of the Seventh Cavalry in 1866. He earned brevets to major and lieutenant colonel in the regular army in 1867 for meritorious services in the battle of the Osage and the raid on Columbus. The following year he was awarded a brevet to colonel for gallant service against hostile Indians at the Saline River in August 1868. He participated in the battle of the Washita in 1868, the Black Hills expedition of 1874, the Sioux campaign of 1876, and the Nez Perce campaign of 1877. He was hailed the hero of the Little Bighorn by many survivors and in 1890 was awarded a brevet to brigadier general for gallant service in the campaigns of 1876 and 1877. He was appointed major of the Ninth Cavalry in 1882 and was granted a disability retirement in 1888. Benteen died on June 22, 1898, in Atlanta and was buried in Arlington National Cemetery.

Serving with the Seventh Cavalry for almost twenty years, Benteen was considered by many the ideal company commander. Gen. Hugh L. Scott spoke highly of him, remembering the officer as the idol of the Seventh Cavalry in 1877. Throughout his life, Benteen held an intense dislike for Custer. A comparison of personalities reveals that whereas Benteen was deliberate in his actions and reserved, Custer was impulsive and inclined to show off; Benteen at times indulged in liquor, while Custer was temperate. But both men were very brave and conceited.

The antagonism between the two came to a head with the publication of a letter written by Benteen to his friend William J. DeGresse of St. Louis that criticized Custer's actions at the Washita. Without authorization, DeGresse submitted the letter to the editor of the St. Louis Democrat *for publication, which the* New York Times *picked up on February 14, 1869. Custer was furious. He immediately assembled his officers and threatened to horsewhip the anonymous writer. When Benteen stepped forward and stated, "I am the man you are after, and I am ready for the whipping promised," Custer stammered, "Col. Benteen, I'll see you again, Sir!" and never brought up the matter again. A transcript of the contentious document follows.*

Letter to William J. DeGresse
December 22, 1868

Fort Cobb, I.T., Dec. 22, 1868.

My Dear Friend:[1] I wrote to you from Camp Supply, which place was left on the 7th, arriving at this post on the evening of the 18th. On the 11th we camped within a few miles of our "battle of the Washita," and Gens. Sheridan and Custer, with a detail of one hundred men, mounted, as escort, went out with the view of searching for the bodies of our nineteen missing comrades, including Maj. Elliott.[2]

---

[1]William J. DeGresse had been a captain in the Tenth Missouri Cavalry and had served in Benteen's regiment during the Civil War. Carroll 1974, 266.

[2]Only eighteen men were missing, including Elliott. See Appendix F.

The bodies were found in a small circle, stripped as naked as when born, and frozen stiff. Their heads had been battered in, and some of them had been entirely been chopped off; some of them had the Adam's apple cut out of their throats; some had their hands and feet cut off, and nearly all had been horribly mangled in a way delicacy forbids me to mention. They lay scarcely two miles from the scene of the fight, and all we know of the manner they were killed we have learned from Indian sources. It seems that Maj. Elliott's party was pursuing a well-mounted party of Cheyennes in the direction of the Grand Village, where nearly all the tribes were encamped, and were surrounded by the reinforcements coming to the rescue of the pursued, before the Major was aware of their position. They were then out of sight and hearing of the Seventh Cavalry, which had remained at and around the captured village, about two miles away. As soon as Maj. Elliott found that he was surrounded he caused his men to dismount, and did some execution among the Indians, which added to the mortification they must have felt at the loss of the village and herds of their friends and allies, and enraged them so that they determined upon the destruction of the entire little band.

Who can describe the feeling of that brave band, as with anxious beating hearts, they strained their yearning eyes in the direction whence help should come? What must have been the despair that, when all hopes of succor died out, nerved their stout arms to do and die? Round and round rush the red fiends, smaller and smaller shrinks the circle, but the aim of that devoted, gallant knot of heroes is steadier than ever, and the death howl of the murderous redskin is more frequent. But on they come in masses grim, with glittering lance and one long, loud, exulting whoop, as if the gates of hell had opened and loosed the whole infernal host. A well-directed volley from their trusty carbines makes some of the miscreants reel and fall, but their death-rattles are drowned in the greater din. Soon every voice in that little band is still as death; but the hellish work of the savages is scarce begun, and their ingenuities are taxed to invent barbarities to practice on the bodies of the fallen brave, the relation of which is scarcely necessary to the completion of this tale.

And now, to learn why the anxiously-looked-for succor did not come, let us view the scene in the captured village, scarce two miles away. Light skirmishing is going on all around. Savages on flying steeds, with shields and feathers gay, are circling every-where, riding like devils incarnate. The troops are on all sides of the village, looking on and seizing every opportunity of picking off some of those daring riders with their carbines. But does no one think of the welfare of Maj. Elliott and party? It seems not. But yes! a squadron of cavalry is in motion. They trot; they gallop. Now they charge! The cowardly redskins flee the coming shock and scatter here and there among the hills [and] scurry away. But it is the true line—will the cavalry keep it? No! no! They turn! Ah, 'tis only to intercept the wily foe. See! a gray troop[3] goes on in the direction again. One more short mile and they will be saved. Oh, for a mother's prayers! Will not some good angel prompt them? They charge the mound—a few scattering shots, and the murder-ous pirates of the Plains go unhurt away. There is no hope for that brave little band, the death doom is theirs, for the cavalry halt and rest their painting steeds.

And now return with me to the village. Officers and soldiers are watching, resting, eating and sleeping. In an hour or so they will be refreshed, and then scour the hills and plains for their missing comrades. The commander occupies himself in taking an inven-tory of the captured property which he had promised the officers shall be distributed among the enlisted men of the command if they falter or halt not in the charge.

---

[3]The "gray troop" was E Company, commanded by Capt. Edward Myers. While at Camp Sandy Forsyth in Kansas in November 1868, Custer "colored" the horses of the Seventh Cavalry by assigning similarly colored horses to each company. As a result of this process, bays were assigned to B, F, H, and L Companies; sorrels to C, I, and K Companies; chestnuts to G Company; browns to A Company; blacks to D Company; grays to E Company; and mixed colors to M Company. This decision coming two weeks prior to the winter campaign caused a lot of dissatisfaction among the officers and enlisted men. According to Benteen, "this act at the beginning of a severe cam-paign was not only ridiculous, but [was also] criminal, unjust and arbitrary in the extreme." Captain Barnitz held a similar view and stated that the order was "*foolish, unwarranted,* [and] *unjustifiable* [emphasis in original]." E. B. Custer 1966, 14; Benteen n.d.(b), 187, 192; Utley 1977, 204–205.

The day is drawing to a close and but little has been done save the work of the first hour. A great deal remains to be done. That which cannot be taken away must be destroyed. Eight hundred ponies are to be put to death. Our Chief exhibits his close sharp-shooting and terrifies the crowd of frightened, captured squaws and papooses by dropping the straggling ponies in death near them. Ah! he is a clever marksman. Not even do the poor dogs of the Indians escape his eye and aim as they drop dead or limp howling away. But are not those our men on guard on the other side of the creek? Will he not hit them? "My troop is on guard, General, just over there," says an officer. "Well, bullets will not go through or around hills, and you see there is a hill between us," was the reply, and the exhibition goes on. No one will come that way intentionally—certainly not. Now commences the slaughter of the ponies. Volley on volley is poured into them by too hasty men, and they, limping, get away only to meet death from a surer hand. The work progresses! The plunder having been culled over, is hastily piled; the wigwams are pulled down and thrown on it, and soon the whole is one blazing mass. Occasionally a startling report is heard and a steam-like volume of smoke ascends as the fire reaches a powder bag, and thus the glorious deeds of valor done in the morning are celebrated by the flaming bonfire of the afternoon. The last pony is killed. The huge fire dies out; our wounded and dead comrades—heroes of a bloody day—are care-fully laid on ready ambulances, and as the brave band of the Sev-enth Cavalry strikes up the air, "Ain't I glad to get out of the Wilderness," we slowly pick our way across the creek over which we charged so gallantly in the early morn. Take care! do not tram-ple on the dead bodies of that woman and child laying there! In a short time we shall be far from the scene of our daring dash, and night will have thrown her dark mantle over the scene. But surely some search will be made for our missing comrades. No, they are forgotten. Over them and the poor ponies the wolves will hold high carnival, and their howlings will be their only requiem. Slowly trudging, we return to our train, some twenty miles away, and with bold, exulting hearts, learn from one another how many dead Indians have been seen.

Two weeks elapse—a larger force returns that way. A search is made and the bodies are found strewn around that little circle, frozen stiff and hard. Who shall write their eulogy?

This, my dear friend, is the story of the "battle of the Washita," poorly told.[4]

---

[4]Questions raised about Custer's culpability in the alleged abandonment of a portion of his command caused a lasting rift within the regiment. Benteen neither forgot what happened nor forgave Custer for the rest of his life. After identifying the colonel's corpse at the Little Bighorn eight years later, Benteen remarked, "There he is, God damn him," and confided to a fellow officer, "What a big winner the U.S. Govt. would have been if only Custer and his gang could have been taken" (Graham 1953, 311; Carroll 1974, 271).

14

Winfield Scott Harvey, Seventh Cavalry

Winfield S. Harvey served as blacksmith in K Company and saw action with Captain West's squadron at the Washita. Born in Fayette County, Pennsylvania, on October 10, 1848, Harvey enlisted in his father's regiment, the Fourteenth Pennsylvania Cavalry, in August 1864 and was honorably discharged in 1865. He enlisted as a private in the Seventh Cavalry in September 1866, participating in the Sully expedition (September 1868), the battle of the Washita, and the Sweetwater campaign (March 1869). Harvey was discharged as a sergeant upon the completion of his enlistment term in 1871. After his discharge he settled in Belle Vernon, Pennsylvania, where he was known as a patriotic citizen and a successful businessman. Winfield S. Harvey died on March 5, 1931, and was buried in the Belle Vernon Cemetery.

Sergeant Harvey's diary covers his entire time in the regular army. Considering the rampant illiteracy among enlisted men, this diary is a rare and important document reflecting the daily impressions of a common soldier. The entries transcribed below focus on Custer's winter campaign and cover the period from November 21 through December 3, 1868. They are extracted from George H. Shirk's article "Campaigning with Sheridan: A Farrier's Diary," published in The Chronicles of Oklahoma *in 1959, and are reprinted by special permission from* The Chronicles of Oklahoma, *published by the Oklahoma Historical Society, Oklahoma City (copyright 1959).*

Diary Extract
November 21—December 3, 1868

Camp Supply, Ind. Ter. Nov. 21, 1868. Shoeing horses. The morning is cold; I think there will be snow soon. It is so cold and the wind blows so strong. We will march tomorrow if nothing is wrong. No mail has reached us since we left the Arkansas River;[1] we look for some today. I do not know whether it will reach us or not, it is so irregular. There is no way to reach us only by Pony Express, and it is some three hundred miles.

Camp Supply, Ind. Ter. Nov. 22, 1868. The morning is cold; it snowed all night and it is still snowing. Cleared up at noon and got warm. Still it snows. We took our horses out to graze at noon to let them pick all they can this Sunday. We did not move today. We will tomorrow.

[Marched] 25 miles.[2] North of Canadian River, I.T. Nov. 23, 1868. Reveille at three o'clock. We started on our scout. It snowed all day and very fast. Part of the time we could not find our road and at night we had to lay in snow eighteen inches deep with our clothes all wet and freezing, although we have plenty of wood and good fires to keep us warm. No news of Indians. All gone south. I am well.

[Marched] 18 miles. On Buffalo Creek,[3] Ind. Ter. Nov. 24, 1868. Broke camp at six o'clock; and the morning is very pleasant and warm, melting snow very fast. It melted it very near all off today. Saw some buffalo today and killed some of them. Killed some rabbits. Saw some deer, and had a fine chase after them but could not catch them.

[Marched] 22 miles. On the Main Canadian River, I. T. Nov. 25, 1868. The morning is very warm and we crossed over this morning at daybreak. We had a very hard march today and a lot of horses gave out today and mules also. Major Elliott and two squadrons started out on a scout up the river. They struck an Indian trail numbering two hundred warriors. We will have them.

[Marched] 30 miles. On the Night March, Ind. Ter. Nov. 26, 1868. Left our wagon train in the rear and started out in full speed. I think we will soon catch them. We marched all night, only two hours for supper, on the trail.

---

[1]The command moved south across the Arkansas on the morning of November 12. G. A. Custer 1966, 273–74.

[2]Lieutenant Godfrey of Harvey's K Company stated that camp was made after marching about fifteen miles. See "Extract of Narrative Account," in chapter 8. For an examination of Custer's route and daily marches, see Rea 1998, 244–61.

[3]Buffalo Creek is Wolf Creek.

[Marched] 10 miles. On the Washita River, Ind. Ter. Nov. 27, 1868. The morning is very cold. We found them at last. We charged at daybreak. Captured the entire Indian village, numbering fifty-two lodges, and killed 103 of their warriors, including their principal chief, Black Kettle. Captured 57 or 75 of their women and children, who are in our possession, prisoners of war.[4] Our loss is 23 killed and 11 wounded, including Major Elliott and Captain Hamilton, of Troop A, also our Sergeant Major.[5] Our officers wounded are Brevet Colonel Barnitz, of Troop G, Lieutenant March, and Lieutenant Custer, a brother of General Custer.[6] We captured eight hundred ponies and mules, afterwards killing them all and leaving them behind. We afterwards retreated back ten miles, where we laid overnight. No rations tonight. The Indians captured them all from us by us leaving it while charging. We will reach our old train tomorrow by noon, then we have plenty. I am very well so far. Plenty of snow.

[Marched] 10 miles.[7] On Dry Creek, Ind. Ter. Nov. 28, 1868. Reveille at six o'clock and we started without any breakfast. Met our supply train at noon. The Indians have not bothered us much. They ran into our pickets last evening, none hurt. Plenty to eat and drink now. There is plenty of wood.

[Marched] 24 miles. Camp on Skunk Creek, Ind. Ter. Nov. 29, 1868. Reveille at five o'clock. Packed up and started on back for Camp Supply. It is very pleasant to what it has been since we left on our scout. The snow has nearly all gone off. We have gone over some pretty country, and some nice streams. The Big Canadian River is from a mile to three-quarters wide.

[Marched] 30 miles.[8] On the Big Canadian River, Ind. Ter. Nov. 30, 1868. Reveille at five o'clock and we started on for a day's

[4]Custer's official report states fifty-one lodges and fifty-three captives.

[5]The casualties sustained by Elliott's detachment consisted of one officer and seventeen enlisted men killed; the casualties sustained at the village site consisted of one officer and two enlisted men killed and fourteen wounded. See "Official Report" in chapter 6 and Appendix F. One may wonder how everyone knew on November 27 that Elliott and his men had been killed instead of simply being missing. See Shirk 1959, 85.

[6]Capt. Albert Barnitz suffered a severe bullet wound in the stomach, Lt. Thomas J. March received a slight arrow wound in the right hand, and Lt. Thomas W. Custer sustained a gunshot wound in the right hand.

[7]The distance marched on November 28 was twenty miles. Rea 1998, 258.

[8]The distance marched on November 30 was ten miles. Ibid.

march. We marched over some hard looking country and made a big march. Arrived in camp about eight o'clock today. It is pleasant and warm.

Near Camp Supply, Ind. Ter. Dec. 1, 1868. The morning is very nice and pleasant. We had some fun today with seeing the Osage Indians having a war frolic on horseback. They would sing and fire their pieces off in the air so as to make it look nice. General Sheridan is here and is pleased at the victory we have won in his department. He gives us his thanks.

Near Camp Supply, Ind. Ter. Dec. 2, 1868. The day is cloudy but warm. I think it will rain before many days. There is no news yet of what we will do in order to go to our quarters. I think we are good for another march. I am satisfied to go if we can find any more Indians' camps. It is very hard out here.

Near Camp Supply, Ind. Ter. Dec. 3, 1868. The morning is cool and very pleasant. We are going to bury our dead today—Captain Hamilton, two soldiers of B Troop and one of H Troop.[9] They were buried in honors of war at three o'clock this afternoon. We are going back in a few days after the Indians. No more news.

---

[9]Pvt. Charles Cuddy and Pvt. Augustus DeLaney, both of B Company, died at the village site on November 27; Pvt. Benjamin McCasey, H Company, died at Camp Supply on December 1 from the trauma of a severe arrow wound in the chest. See Appendix F.

15

Dennis Lynch, Seventh Cavalry

Dennis Lynch was a private in F Company, commanded by Capt. George W. Yates. Born on February 22, 1848, in Cumberland, Maryland, Lynch enlisted under the alias "Bums" in the Eighth Illinois Cavalry in April 1864 and participated in the battles of Cedar Creek, Winchester, Shepardstown, and Yellow Tavern.

After the war he enlisted in the newly formed Seventh Cavalry on August 3, 1866. He participated in the Washita battle of 1868, the Yellowstone expedition in 1873, the Black Hills expedition in 1874, the Sioux campaign of 1876, the Nez Perce campaign in 1877, and the Milk River campaign in 1881. He was discharged as a private in September 1881 upon the expiration of his third tour of duty with the Seventh Cavalry.

After leaving the military, Lynch found employment as a civilian night watchman at the Depot Quartermaster Stable in Washington, D.C. He was admitted to the U.S. Soldiers' Home in 1914 and died on October 13, 1933, at Barnes Hospital, Washington, D.C.

Despite the errors of memory, the following interview is important because it describes the battle from the viewpoint of an enlisted man. The Interview is contained in MSS 57, Box 2, Walter Camp Interview Notes, Special Collections and Manuscripts, Brigham Young University Library, Provo, Utah; it is reproduced by special permission.

Interview by Walter M. Camp
February 8, 1909

In [the] Washita fight he was among 42 especially selected sharpshooters who went in advance guard with Custer.[1] Indians

---

[1]This *corps d'elite* of sharpshooters was commanded by Lt. William W. Cooke. In a

call Washita Creek the Sweetwater.[2] Among scouts were California Joe, a half-breed Mexican and Indian named Romeo, Stilwell,[3] Jim Curry,[4] of Hays City, Kans., and Jack Corbin.

---

letter written in November 1868, Custer mentions that this unit consisted of fifty sharpshooters. Yet in his memoirs the colonel states repeatedly that it consisted of forty marksmen, which agrees with Lynch's number. The regimental return for November 1868 identifies the names of only twenty-eight men who were on daily duty with the "Detachment of Sharpshooters." Ten additional marksmen served as Custer's bodyguard and are listed among those of fifteen men assigned to the headquarters staff. Lynch's name is absent (nor does it appear on the roster of sharpshooters reproduced as Appendix C). G. A. Custer 1874, 140–41, 159, 162; Benteen n.d.(b), 190–91.

[2]The Cheyennes called the Washita River "Hooxeeohe" (Lodge Pole Creek). It was named after an event during the pre-reservation era when the Cheyennes had found a hurriedly deserted camp in which the lodge poles had been left standing. Hart 1999, 60; J. H. Moore 1987, 247.

[3]Simpson E. "Jack" Stilwell was assigned to Crawford's Nineteenth Kansas Cavalry and did not arrive at Camp Supply until November 28. Born in 1849 along the Missouri River near present-day Kansas City, contemporaries described Stilwell as a sandy-haired youth who spoke Spanish and could handle a gun like a frontiersman. In 1868 he was hired as a scout at Fort Harker and fought under Forsyth at Beecher Island; on the second night of the siege, he slipped through the Indian lines to bring back a relief force from Fort Wallace. Later he scouted with William F. Cody on the plains and eventually was hired as chief of scouts at Fort Sill. Stilwell remained in government service until the close of the plains wars, after which he accepted employment on a ranch in Texas. Upon the opening of Oklahoma Territory in 1889, Stilwell became the first police judge in present El Reno, where he studied law and was appointed to the bar a few years later. In 1894, after serving two terms, he accepted appointment as U.S. commissioner at Anadarko. Being deficient in Kiowa, he became known as "Comanche Jack" for declaring Comanche the official court language for both tribes. Stilwell resigned his post in 1898 as a result of failing health and moved to Cody, Wyoming, where he died on February 17, 1903. General Sheridan characterized him as the bravest and most daring young man he ever knew. Stilwell's brother, Frank, was a deputy sheriff in Cochise County, Arizona; after being implicated in the murder of Morgan Earp, he was found shot to death in the railroad yards near Tucson on March 20, 1882, presumably killed by Wyatt Earp. Sneed 1936, 147–48; Peery 1935, 31; Roenigk 1933, 133; Conover 1927, 105–106; H. L. Scott 1928, 179; *Cheyenne Transporter,* Mar. 25, 1882; *Cheyenne Transporter* 1884; Criqui 1986, 219.

[4]Jim Curry was not present at the battle of the Washita but did fight under Forsyth at Beecher Island in September 1868. The report filed by Major Inman reveals that Curry was hired on August 28, 1868, and released on December 31. His activities afterward became legendary and gained him a reputation as a cold-blooded murderer. During a fracas between some black soldiers of the Tenth Cavalry and the citizens of Hays, Kansas, in 1869, several soldiers were wounded and left behind; Curry "blew the brains out of all who could not get away." Among the various occupations he held was that of railroad engineer. For a while he ran a construction train between Hays City and Ellsworth. One of his degenerate delights was to shoot at people from the cab of his engine, reportedly killing three men and wounding several others. Curry was also accused of killing a woman during a drunken brawl in a whorehouse at Ellsworth in 1870. Realizing the consequences of his actions, he fled to Texas before a vigilante committee could find him. While in Marshall, Texas, in 1879, he shot and killed an unarmed vaudeville actor named Ben Porter just for cracking a joke about him; Curry was acquitted on grounds of insanity

Corralled train near Antelope Hills on Canadian River between 8 and 9 P.M. Loosened girths and made coffee, and [Capt.] Yates reporting to him [the Adjutant] first, [his troop] took the advance. Marched all night to 3 A.M. Made a halt and heard cowbells on Indian ponies, and dogs barking in the camp.

First order Custer gave was for the 50 or 60 Kaw and Delaware Indians to crawl down between the village and herd and work the herd away from the village, which they did.[5]

Custer had a valuable greyhound that was barking when he heard Indian dogs bark. [The] General and Tom Custer choked him to death with a lariat.[6] Next [he] ordered sharpshooters to take off their overcoats, and some began to curse and grumble, the weather being very cold, and Custer said: "Stop that noise. It will be hot enough for you inside of an hour." We formed a skirmish line ahead of the eastern squadron. Had all twelve troops of 7th Cavalry there and none from [any] other regiment.[7]

When command [was] given to charge, Custer fired a sky-rocket[8] in [the] air and then the band struck up "Garry Owen." This [occurred] about half past 3 [A.M.]. Then [we] charged on village in four battalions from different directions. Village was on both sides of creek in series of groups of tepees in bends of creek. Maj. Elliott with 18 men had horses and followed Indians that ran out of village. They were killed about four miles from village by Kiowas and Arapahoes that came up.

---

caused by drunkenness. Eventually drifting to New Mexico, in 1888 he killed his partner during a gold-seeking venture. This time he was convicted and received a sentence of six years in the penitentiary. Curry died on September 11, 1899, in Spokane, Washington. Roenigk 1933, 204–205; Lockard 1927, 300–301; Criqui 1986, 76–77, 84.

[5]Only Osage scouts were present at the Washita. On November 6, 1868, ten Kaw Indians enlisted at Fort Hays and were assigned to Custer's second expedition into Indian Territory, which left on December 7. No Delaware Indians were used during the winter campaign.

[6]But Pvt. William C. Stair stated that Custer merely tied the dog's head up in an apron, which he probably got from Mrs. Courtenay, his cook. Stair added that he did not see the dog strangled, though it might have been done afterward. William C. Stair Interview, Box 3, Walter Mason Camp Collection, Brigham Young University Library, Provo, Utah.

[7]Only eleven companies of the Seventh Cavalry fought at the Washita: L Company was on detached service at Fort Lyon, Colorado.

[8]No skyrockets were fired at the Washita. A rising morning star on the eastern horizon was mistaken for a signal rocket. See G. A. Custer 1874, 162.

In the charge [we] did not see Indians until [we] got within 50 yards of village. Then Indians came running out with their guns and made for the bends in the creek. All [of us] charged mounted except sharpshooters. Mounted men charged through tepees and dismounted. Sharpshooters were charging in skirmish line and by bugle call. "Skirmishers to Left" was sounded and [we] made way for [the] black-horse squadron. (Troops "A," and "D")[9]

All mounted men dismounted after charging through camp and formed line round village and shot everything [they] could see. Killed some squaws in creek. One Mexican yelled that he would surrender, but in the confusion he was killed.[10] Firing around the village lasted fully two hours.

[Custer] next ordered all scouts under California Joe to round up all the herds, and sharpshooters ordered to form skirmish line around them and corralled them against foot of a bluff and shoot them down. Shot down 888 ponies. Did not stop to kill all of them, as Kiowas and Arapahoes came up and made it so hot [we] had to cease firing on ponies. [We] returned to this battlefield about six weeks later and saw where some of these ponies too badly wounded to get up had eaten all grass within reach of them and then died. Truly, Gen. Sherman was right in his definition of war [that it was "all hell"]. Band struck up "Getting out of [the] Wilderness" and [we] charged on Indians on ridges, and followed them up until dark and then returned to train in hurry, fearing that Indians would get it.

Picked up 106 dead warriors. Killed some squaws. Captured 65 squaws and great many children. These Indians had been killing stage drivers and settlers all summer.

He [Lynch] verifies the story of [the] Indian boy firing at Benteen, and Benteen killing him. Says one of the last Indians to be hunted out was a squaw who had a white boy, and when she saw that she was taken, she quickly drew a knife and disemboweled the

---

[9]Only Weir's D Company rode black horses; Hamilton's A Company was mounted on brown horses.

[10]This was a Mexican trader named Pilan, who was murdered by Myers's men. See "The *New York Sun* Interview" in chapter 18.

boy, whereupon California Joe took aim and shot her through the head, killing her instantly.[11]

(My own comment [by Walter M. Camp]): Although many settlers of the West did and do yet consider this a massacre of Indians, it reflects no discredit upon Custer. He was but obeying his orders as a commander of troops. The authorities who declared war upon the Indians necessarily took the responsibility for the results of the war.

---

[11]This was not a white boy but a Cheyenne baby killed by its mother out of despair. See chapter 18.

16

John Ryan,
Seventh Cavalry

John Ryan was a sergeant in M Company of Captain Benteen's squadron, which was commanded by Major Elliott at the Washita. Ryan was born on August 25, 1845, in West Newton, Massachusetts, where he enlisted in the Twenty-Eighth Massachusetts Infantry at age sixteen and served from 1861 through 1864. He then enlisted in the Sixty-First Massachusetts Infantry in January 1865 and was mustered out the same year, having been wounded three times during the war.

Joining the Seventh Cavalry in 1866, Ryan became a corporal of M Company. He participated in the fighting at the Washita and received a field promotion to sergeant. He was present with the Yellowstone expedition of 1873 and was promoted to first sergeant the same year. He participated in the Black Hills expedition in 1874 and the Little Bighorn in 1876. He was discharged in December 1876 upon expiration of service, noted as a "brave, capable, and trustworthy" first sergeant after serving with the Seventh Cavalry for ten years.

Following his discharge, Ryan returned to West Newton, where he received appointment as a patrolman in 1878. Promoted to police sergeant in 1891, he eventually retired with the rank of captain in 1913. John Ryan died in West Newton on October 14, 1926, and is buried in Calvary Cemetery, Waltham, Massachusetts.

In 1908 Ryan submitted a narrative of his army experiences to the Allen Megaphone, *a West Newton newspaper, which only published the first installment. Parts of the remainder of the narrative were serialized in the* West Newton Weekly, *the* Newton Town Crier, *and the* Newton Circuit. *The extract that follows deals with the battle of the Washita and appeared in the* Circuit *on April 2 and 9, 1909, under the heading "Ten Years with General Custer among the American Indians."*

Extract of Newspaper Account
1909[1]

When we advanced to the highest ground in the vicinity of the Indian camp [on the Washita] there were some dogs with some of the companies, and General Custer had his hounds with him. When the camp was discovered, Custer thought the dogs might alarm the Indians' dogs and arouse the camp, and I understood that Custer had to kill two of his hounds.[2] One dog in my company, of whom the men were very fond, was a little black dog called Bob, and as harmless as a kitten. We had to part with him, and one of our men drove a picket pin into Bob's head and he was left for dead. After that engagement was over and several days had elapsed, that dog joined us, and the men cured him and brought him to Kansas. . . .

When we discovered the Indian camp, General Custer assembled the officers, drew up his plans, and told them what he expected of them. This camp was situated in the valley of the Washita Creek, a small stream with considerable timber, some of it quite heavy on both sides. Custer's plan was to surround the camp, and he divided his regiment into four battalions. The division to which my company was assigned was commanded by Major Joel H. Elliott, and my company, Company M, was commanded by Lieutenant Owen Hale, Company G was commanded

---

[1]John Ryan was a "Custer man": he corresponded with Elizabeth Custer and was familiar with the general's memoirs, which may have influenced the contents of his own account. Regardless, I have extracted the entire narrative of the battle, adding some punctuation.

[2]Custer was an avid sportsman and had a close bond with his hunting dogs. Five of them, three staghounds and two greyhounds, where with him at the start of the Washita campaign. Perhaps the two dogs mentioned by Ryan as having been killed were the two greyhounds, Rover and Fanny. Josephus Bingaman, a private with the Nineteenth Kansas Cavalry, claimed from personal observation that Custer's greyhounds had been shot and that their cadavers had been thrown on a pile of haversacks. But this statement may be a combination of facts surrounding two different incidents, including the death of Blucher, Custer's favorite staghound, who was killed on the morning of November 27 when he dashed across the river and charged the Indians at the site where the overcoats had been left behind. The dog was killed at this location by an arrow shot through his body and was identified by Custer on his return from the Sweetwater in March 1869. E. B. Custer 1966, 12, 14; Schwarck 1992, 15; Bingaman n.d.; G. A. Custer 1874, 173–74.

by Captain Barnitz, Company H by Captain F. W. Benteen, and another detachment, consisting of 40 sharpshooters, was under Lieutenant Cook[e].[3]

In surrounding the Indians, some of the companies were obliged to travel several miles to get into their positions. In leaving the place where the divisions were formed, we received orders that no matches were to be lighted, not even to light our pipes. We also put our tin cups into the haversacks, so as to make no noise, and were ordered not to speak above a whisper. The battalions proceeded to their respective positions; mine made a detour through the valley in order to take its position. There was about 15 inches of snow on the ground; during the day it melted and at night froze hard again, forming quite a crust, and the companies made quite a noise with the horses breaking through. In about an hour we reached our position without alarming the Indian camp, and were obliged to sit in our saddles, as we were under orders not to dismount.[4] We were pretty cold, especially our feet, and we tried two ways of keeping them warm; first, to take the feet from the stirrups and let them hang down, thus allowing the blood to circulate; then to kick the feet against the stirrups and keep the blood stirring. The officers dismounted and with the capes of their overcoats drawn over their heads, sat in the snow. We could occasionally hear the Indian dogs barking, and the outcry of some infant, although we could not see the camp.

As soon as it became daylight enough to see, our band was to strike up Custer's favorite tune "Garry Owen." The command, "Attention" was given and we advanced at a walk, then a trot, then on a gallop, and charged when the command was given.

In entering the camp the troops were obliged to cross the Washita Creek, and as there was a very steep embankment on both sides, our speed was checked considerably. Finally we all

---

[3]Lieutenant Cooke's sharpshooters were assigned to the center column, personally commanded by Custer.

[4]On November 26 Captain Benteen was officer of the day and had charge of the rear guard, consisting of H and M Companies. Around midnight this squadron was ordered to the front to join Elliott's column but got lost in the hills in the darkness and only arrived just before dawn. It is unfortunate that Ryan did not provide more details about his escort duty with Bell's wagons and Benteen's difficult ride that night.

managed to get across and charged into the Indian camp, taking it completely by surprise.[5] The sleeping Indians sprang to [their feet and grabbed] their guns; some jumped behind trees, others remained in their lodges, and the rest threw themselves into low depressions in the ground and welcomed us with a murderous fire. In an attack on an Indian camp the squaws would use rifles or bow and arrows, and the boys from 12 to 15 years of age would engage in the fight.

We fought these Indians until most of them were killed or severely wounded, and then the squaws tried to drive off the ponies. California Joe caught a squaw in the act of driving away about 200 ponies, and he finally persuaded her to help drive them back.[6]

During our engagement a number of the Indians broke through the lines where they did not connect and started down stream. Quite a number of the squaws remained in the lodges and General Custer sent California Joe and Romeo to inform them they would not be molested.[7] In our first charge Captain Hamilton, commanding Company A, was shot by a rifle ball and instantly killed, and Captain Barnitz was also shot through the body. Two lieutenants, T. W. Custer and T. Z. Marsh [sic], were wounded.

As soon as the Indians were overcome, men were sent out to collect all the ponies they could find, and I, with five or six men of my company, was among that number. Presently, Major Elliott rode by with 18 men, trying to overtake those Indians who had broken through the lines. He sung out to me as he passed by, "Sergeant, take those Indians prisoners," referring to some squaws we were following. We did take some of them. We also captured the ponies

---

[5]Benteen later recalled that "My Fort Harker squadron [of H and M Companies] broke up the village before a trooper of any of the other companies of [the] 7th got in." Carroll 1974, 252; Benteen n.d.(b), 212.

[6]According to Benteen, "1st Sergt. Duane of M Troop, 2 privates, 'California Joe' and myself surrounded and drove in the ponies that were killed on that field by Custer—some 800. Custer, in his 'Life on the Plains' gives Calif. Joe the credit; but surely as there's sun, I conceived, and we carried it out, and Custer knew it. I turned the herd over to Col. West, who had his squadron intact, and was en route to find something" (Carroll 1974, 252). Benteen commented further that California Joe had been assigned to his squadron and that no Indian women assisted with the herd's capture (Benteen n.d.(b), 220, 222).

[7]Benteen later wrote that his squadron "protected the fifty-five squaws and children we captured" (Benteen n.d.(b), 252).

they were driving, and it proved to be very fortunate for me and my squad that we did not go with Elliott. Elliott followed the Indians who had broken through our lines, covering about a mile, and among his detail were Sergeant Major Kennedy, Sergeant Vanoski [*sic*], Corporal Thomas Fitzpatrick and five privates from my company. This was the last we saw of Major Elliott and his 18 men until two weeks afterwards [when] we found their dead bodies.

Upon bringing in our prisoners and the ponies I started with some other men to capture some more ponies, and was riding around the foot of a bluff when suddenly I came upon an Indian warrior who was about to shoot the second time at one of our men, who was dismounted, his horse having been shot. I was so close to the Indian that it was impossible for me to check my horse, so it flashed through my mind that the best thing to do was to ride over him. As I did so I fired, and dropped him with the first shot, and rode some distance before I could turn my horse. I returned and put two more shots into the wounded Indian, just as another person with a woolen blanket wound around him came in the same direction as I had taken. I mistook him for an Indian and was about to fire on him when I discovered he was Private Eagan of my company, who was born and brought up in East Milton, Massachusetts. I wanted very much to scalp that Indian, but being such a distance from the rest of the company I was a little shy about getting off my horse, as he was a spirited animal and might leave me in a bad place. I asked Eagan if he would hold my horse, and I dismounted, turned the Indian over on his face, put my left foot on his neck and raised his scalp. I held it up to Eagan, saying, "John, here is the first scalp for M Troop." I secured the rifle, which was a heavy muzzle-loading buffalo gun made at Lancaster, Pennsylvania, and of the style issued to the Indians for hunting purposes. I also took a 44-caliber Remington revolver and a sheath knife, but did not bother with trinkets, which he had. I believe some of these articles are in my collection at my home at the present time.

Hanging the scalp at the saber hook of my waist belt, I started to find our command, and on the way noticed that the skirt of my overcoat was covered with blood. So I threw the scalp away, and upon arriving at camp reported my experience to the company commander, Lieutenant Owen Hale. He asked me what I did with the scalp and I told him. He smiled and said that I should have kept it, as it was considered an honor on that occasion. . . .

When leaving camp I put this rifle in one of our wagons and thus was able to keep it with me. Soon after this engagement a detail from each of the companies began destroying the Indian lodges. The lodge poles were pulled down and the hides dropped onto the ground, and as there were fires in most of them they were burned up. In almost every one that was destroyed there was an explosion on account of the powder, which the Indians had secreted in them for use with their weapons.

Before going into the engagement at Washita Creek, two companies threw their overcoats and haversacks into a pile, to avoid being encumbered while fighting, some Indians rode around and captured the entire lot. During the remainder of the campaign these two companies were without overcoats, and they had to wrap blankets around them, as being a great many miles from any fort or settlement, new overcoats could not be obtained.[8] The ponies that were captured during the engagement were all driven into one herd and guarded by our men. Not long after General Custer saw about a mile and a half away some Indians assembling on the bluffs. Turning his field glass on to them he found they were warriors in full regalia, evidently waiting for their chiefs to lead them forward. Custer, through his interpreters, learned from some of the squaws that there was another large camp, some five miles below us, which extended for fully three miles and contained from 4000 to 5000 Indians. These were the parties that he had just discovered, and on their way to attack us they had probably met Major Elliott and his 18 men, and killed them.

Without much delay the Indians made their appearance, and Custer was ready for them with his available men dismounted and in position, with the horses on the further side on the lower ground, where they were well protected. The men, advancing to the top of the high ground, laid down; they had to wait but a few

---

[8]Actually four companies—A, C, D, and K—and the corps of sharpshooters suffered this misfortune. One can only imagine how these men must have cursed Custer when told of the loss of their coats and rations and learned that none of the other companies had been required to dress down.

minutes when several hundred of the Indians advanced and attempted to cut right through our lines. We opened fire on them with our Spencer carbines and mowed them down by the wholesale, while Custer ordered one of our captains with a detachment of two companies to attack the Indians. This captain did not fulfill the orders given him, and finally Captain F. W. Benteen, with a detachment of two companies, divided into four platoons, made a charge. That was the prettiest sight I have ever witnessed, and while they were charging the Indians we held our fire. The Indians were driven in great confusion, and I never saw troops in an engagement act in such splendid manner or keep their line under such a fire as these men did. Presently, the recall was sounded and they returned with a loss of but a few men.[9] A detachment of Indians moved around the other side of the camp in the direction opposite to where we were and commenced to fire upon us. General Custer took the squaw prisoners and placed them on the side of the camp, which was being fired upon. They sat up an awful yell whenever the bullets came close to them, and it caused the Indians to cease firing from that direction. While firing at the mounted Indians, there was one who made himself more conspicuous than the others, riding backward and forward in the opening between two bluffs, waving a black flag; waiting our chance, we dropped him and his pony the next time he put in his appearance. We found out he was Black Kettle, chief of the camp we were attacking, and it was claimed that Captain Benteen was the one who shot him. During the previous engagement Black Kettle had made his escape, and joining the Indians in this lower camp had joined in the attack on our lines.[10]

---

[9]This was Myers's squadron of E and I Companies. Since Myers was afflicted by snow blindness, Benteen was temporarily assigned to lead this force. The balance of the regiment looked on while the squadron executed its offensive maneuvers. Jim Bruton of Shamrock, Texas, found a number of Spencer and Henry cases, bullets, and metal arrowheads on two ridges in the north half of Section 7, east of the battlefield. These artifacts may well denote the action of this squadron. Benteen n.d.(b), 153, 225; Jim Bruton to author, Feb. 8, 2003; Bruton 1968–69; 2003–2004.

[10]Black Kettle was killed in the village early in the fight. His remains were found near the ford where Custer crossed to attack. Benteen shot and killed Blue Horse, Black Kettle's nephew. See chapters 29 and 32.

During this engagement a squaw was trying to make her escape with a white child, and when they were overtaken by some troopers, and she saw that the child was about to be rescued, she seized a butcher knife, and plunging it into the child's body, killed it instantly. No sooner had she committed this crime than the whole side of her head was blown off by our men.[11]

There was [a] trooper in my company named John Murphy, a tent-mate of mine, as we had both enlisted when the company was organized. During this encounter he was in pursuit of an Indian when suddenly the warrior let fly an arrow at him. Murphy threw himself to one side in the saddle, attempting to escape the arrow, but it struck him in the right side, penetrating several inches. Had he been sitting erect when he received it, the wound probably would have been fatal, but his leaning to one side caused the arrow to run up. It was withdrawn so quickly that his life was saved, as an arrow shot into the body must be withdrawn immediately or the head will remain. I attended Murphy during his hospital treatment, until we came in from the campaign. He survived and served his enlistment in the company. . . .

When we were ready to destroy the camp, General Custer selected some of the goods, such as saddles, bridles and other equipment belonging to the Indians. The balance was destroyed, as the enlisted men were not allowed to take anything from the camp; it would encumber our horses, and we expected to be engaged any moment with several hundred Indians. In the camp we found numerous coffee mills, frying pans, camp kettles, short handled hatchets, long handled axes, bags of flour, some marked "Department of the Interior," which showed that they were some of the party which made the treaty less than a year before at Medicine Lodge Creek, and had received those presents and supplies from the government. There was also found some scalps, a few of which had been taken from white men and women. Some of the Indians had their leggings decorated with scalps, which showed that they were the parties guilty of making raids during that season.

---

[11]According to Pvt. Dennis Lynch, California Joe killed this woman. Yet Ben Clark states that the shooter was a soldier, which is corroborated by an independent source who identified the man as T. P. Lyon. Spotts 1988, 169.

The men of Company M killed in this attack were Sergeant Irving Vanosky, Corporal Thomas Fitzpatrick, Privates Carl Sharpe, Meyers, Mier, Limeback and Stobias.[12]

When these Indians saw they could not break through our lines they went over to the other side of the creek and dismounted. While they remained there we were not further molested by them, and we were able to give our attention to the herd of ponies, which numbered about 900. In the herd were some government horses and mules, which probably had been run off from some fort. Then the wagon train that had been left in the rear put in its appearance and joined us. It has always been a mystery to me why the Indians did not attack this train before it reached us, as it would have been an easy matter for many of them to capture it. It must be that they did not see it in time. In the herd just mentioned there were some pretty good mules, and these were put in our wagons, replacing those which were played out. Each commissioned officer was allowed two ponies out of the herd, which their attendants picked out. Enough more were taken to mount the prisoners we had with us, numbering about 65. If we had known at the time that Major Elliott and his 18 men were killed, there probably would not have been one of those prisoners brought in, but we did not know of the slaughter for some two weeks afterwards. After picking what stock we needed, four or five companies surrounded the herd and shot all the animals [remaining]. It was hard, but there was nothing else to do under the circumstances. By leaving the ponies there the other Indians would have secured them, so Custer thought the best thing to do was to kill them.

After destroying everything in the camp—hundreds of robes, blankets, saddles, arms and entire Indian equipment—we moved out, carrying along our dead and wounded. General Custer kept a few articles, which were brought along in the wagons, and in leaving he had the wagons formed into columns of two, with troops in the front, on both sides and in the rear. This was the formation in which we moved in the direction of the bluffs on which the Indians were dismounted. They had again mounted their horses and

---

[12]For the correct names, see Appendix F.

moved down stream, and they did not try to molest us or interrupt our march after that.

After we had abandoned their camp, some of the Indians came in behind us to see the ruins. General Custer found out the number of Indians in the camp below and headed in that direction and we traveled until after dark, only to find on reaching the camp that it was deserted.[13] While the Indians had been fighting us at the upper camp, the squaws had pulled down the lodges and made their escape from this one. We immediately started on the return march for Camp Supply, and about two o'clock in the morning went into camp. We built large fires without fear of concealing our movements from the Indians, as we knew the course ahead was clear. The men made themselves as comfortable as possible around the fires, for they were pretty well fatigued from the exposure and hard marching, especially the companies that had lost overcoats, haversacks and canteens.

---

[13] According to Edward Godfrey, the regiment turned back on the trail before reaching the downstream villages.

17

J. C. Pickens, Seventh Cavalry

Born in 1846, J. C. Pickens was one of 137 recruits who enlisted in the Seventh Cavalry on November 10, 1868. Assigned to M Company, he saw action with Benteen's squadron at the Washita. After his discharge Pickens worked in a variety of civilian jobs and served as a police officer in Topeka, Kansas, during the 1890s, The following letter extract deals with the Washita fight and is found on Reel 3, Elizabeth B. Custer Collection, Little Bighorn Battlefield National Monument, Crow Agency, Montana (microfilm).

Extract of Letter to Elizabeth B. Custer
January 29, 1921

Mrs. G. A. Custer
Bronx,
     N.Y.

Honored Madam:

As one of General Custer's troopers, I make bold to address you. I first saw the 7th U.S. Cavalry at Ft. Dodge as a recruit, just as it was on the eve of the beginning of the Washita Campaign. I had seen service (2 years) in the volunteers, but had never seen any of the officers or men of the 7th Cav.

I found that Major Owen Hale was my troop commander. I soon learned to know the faces of many officers, Col. Cook[e], Keogh, Robbins, Myers, Benteen, and many others, names now forgotten. And, of course, General Custer and his brother, Col. "Tom."

Major Elliott I had not learned to designate before he fell at the Washita, though I was one of his detachment that struck the trail of the returning Indians and followed [it] in the snow south, on the day previous to our attack on Black Kettle's village. But I well remember the voice of the officer who, going around through our temporary camp, was giving this order, "Men, don't pitch your tents but be prepared to march after you have had supper." The men near me told us, "That is Major Elliott." My "bunky," Myers, was one of the men who fell with Elliott the next day.[1]

When after that night's march we were halted on the high plain and the General made the assignments for the attack, M Troop was ordered to dismount, and I being No. 4, it fell to my lot to hold horses.[2] So I did not have part in the attack, but we could distinctly hear the firing and, I think, the yelling. We were able to tell when the firing was mostly over that the fighting was done.

We men then began to clamor for a move to the scene. Our corporal in charge made a feeble objection at first, but on second thought yielded and we moved down into the valley. When we came in view of the yet distant tepees, they looked white, and I, in surprise, remarked, "Why, they have tents." It was the first wigwams I had ever seen.

I do not know if we were the only troop that was dismounted during the onslaught, but I have often recalled my impressions as to the very narrow escape we horse-holders had on that morning, for by the time we were in camp the Indians were swarming on the bluffs around us, and if we hadn't become restless our corporal

---

[1]M Company had two casualties named Myers: Pvt. John Myers and Pvt. Carson D. J. Myers. See Appendix F.

[2]This statement is not borne out by the facts. M Company did not leave any horse holders on the ridge where Custer divided his command. According to Sgt. John Ryan, M was mounted when it marched to Elliott's position east of the village. This is corroborated by Barnitz, who stated that Benteen's squadron "deployed into line at a gallop" at the signal of attack. The only men left behind on the high ridge west of the battlefield was a detail of five soldiers assigned to load the overcoats and haversacks in Bell's wagons upon arrival. These men were detailed from Custer's column, and none were from M Company. See "Extract of Narrative Account" in chapter 7 (Barnitz), and "Interview by Walter M. Camp" in chapter 8 (Godfrey), and chapter 16 (Ryan).

might have [kept] us there just a little too long, and M Troop would have lost its horses, etc.[3]

Our corporal was automatically promoted that day by the death of a Sergt. with Elliott.[4] I have a joke on that corporal. A few years ago he wrote an article in the National Tribune, saying that he was promoted for saving his Captain's life during the Washita battle. Major Hale was dead then, I think. I will not mention his name because he made a good record as a sergeant and also in civil life later. Many old soldiers are a little prone to forget just what deeds they performed at historic periods.

. . . .

Very Respectfully,
J. C. Pickens.

[3]In view of the facts stated in note 2 (above), it is difficult to make any sense out of this statement. Perhaps Pickens's recollection of the events had suffered from the passing of more than fifty years. The only troopers who were dismounted at the start of the battle were the baggage guards, the sharpshooters, and the right flank of G Company.

[4]Sgt. Erwin Vanousky of M Company was killed with Elliott. Cpl. John Ryan was promoted to sergeant on the same day to fill the vacancy.

18

Ben Clark,
Seventh Cavalry

Benjamin H. Clark was chief of scouts for the Seventh Cavalry at the battle of the Washita. Clark was born on February 2, 1842, in St. Louis, Missouri. In the summer of 1857, he was hired as a mule driver for a wagon train bound for Fort Bridger. There, in December, he enlisted in a battalion of U.S. volunteers and marched with Albert Sidney Johnston's army to Salt Lake City to impose the authority of the U.S. government upon the Mormons. Clark was mustered out at Camp Floyd in August 1858 but remained with the expedition in Utah to serve as a courier between Fort Bridger and Camp Floyd until the spring of 1861.

In October 1861 Clark enlisted in the Sixth Kansas Volunteer Cavalry. He engaged primarily in frontier service along the borders of Missouri, Kansas, and Indian Territory before being mustered out in July 1865. After the war Clark was employed by Indian traders until the summer of 1868, when he entered into scouting duty with the army. Clark served as chief of scouts for the Sully expedition and the Custer expedition in 1868 before assignment to General Sheridan's staff. After the winter campaign in 1869, he transferred to Camp Supply, Indian Territory, where he was the post guide and interpreter for the Cheyennes, often accompanying delegations of chiefs to Washington, D.C. His selection of a more direct wagon road from Camp Supply to Fort Dodge shortened the old "Custer Trail" by some twenty miles.

In 1871 Clark married a Cheyenne woman named Toch-E-Me-Ah. Born in 1853, she was well liked by the area whites, who knew her as "Emily." In January 1873 she was hit by a stray bullet fired during a brawl between drunken Indians at Camp Supply. Permanently disabled from the effects of the wound, Emily died on October 5, 1875, and was buried by Clark in the post cemetery. Their daughter, Jennie, born in 1872, died at Lawrence, Kansas, in 1893.

In 1874 Clark was chief of scouts for General Miles during the Red River War. At the urgent request of General Sheridan, he served briefly on General Crook's staff during the Sioux campaign of 1876. He then transferred to Fort Reno, Indian Territory, and in 1878, under orders from the War Department, accompanied a party of Nez Perce to the northwest provinces of Canada to induce the surrender and return of a refugee band. Later that year Clark served in the Dull Knife campaign and was in charge of the transfer of Little Chief's Cheyennes from Fort Lincoln, Dakota Territory, to Fort Reno, Indian Territory.

After the death of his first wife, Clark married a Cheyenne woman named Red Fern. This union resulted in the birth of another daughter, Emily, in 1878. Red Fern died at Darlington in 1880, and that same year Clark married Moka (also known as Bull Horn or Little Woman), a full-blood Cheyenne born in 1862. The couple had twelve children, of whom five had died by the turn of the century. In 1905 Clark guided a detachment of U.S. troops on a fatiguing practice march by way of the old trails from Fort Riley, Kansas, to Fort Houston, Texas. Despite his sixty-three years, Clark rode a distance of about eight hundred miles, spent each day in the saddle, cooked his own meals, forded every river on horseback, and slept in the open air each night. Upon the abandonment of Fort Reno in 1907, the War Department assigned him as caretaker of the military reservation. On May 6, 1913, Moka died and was buried at the Fort Reno Military Cemetery. Despondent over the loss of his wife and suffering from paralysis, Benjamin H. Clark ended his life on July 24, 1914, by a gunshot to the temple. He was laid to rest near Moka.

Ben Clark was fluent in Cheyenne and Arapaho. Known to the Indians as "Red Neck," from the hue of his burned skin, he was well trusted by them and often served as their intermediary. Contemporary records reveal that Clark had a fair complexion, with blue eyes and brown hair, and a slender build of medium height. He was the author of a 468-page manuscript, "Ethnography and Philology of the Cheyenne," prepared at the request of Sheridan. This scholarly work was completed in 1887 and was to be published under the auspices of the War Department. Unfortunately, the project was halted after the general's death in 1888.

Sheridan referred to Clark as "the most reliable and accomplished man of his class on the plains." Gen. William E. Strong met Clark in 1878 and described him as "a gentleman, and something of a scholar; gentle in manners, modest and truthful; a superb horseman, a good shot, and his knowledge of the plains, and of the Indians, surpasses that of any other man in his class living." These sentiments were also expressed by Gen. Nelson A. Miles, Gen. Hugh L. Scott, Col. E. P. Pendleton, and Col. Walter C. Short, all of whom had been acquainted with Clark during his service of nearly sixty years.

The items that follow consist of the following documents: Clark's interview with the New York Sun, *published on May 14, 1899, under the heading "Custer's Washita Fight"; his interview by Frederick S. Barde of the* Kansas City Star, *published on December 4, 1904, under the heading "Custer's Oklahoma Fight"; Clark's revision of the* Star *interview, dated October 22, 1910; his Washita interview by Walter M. Camp, dated October 22, 1910; and his letter to Frederick S. Barde, dated May 1, 1903, regarding the remains of Clara Blinn and her infant child.*

New York Sun Interview
May 14, 1899[1]

In September, 1868, the Seventh Cavalry, composed of between 800 and 900 men,[2] was in camp on Kiowa Creek, where it empties

---

[1]This interview was conducted by an unknown journalist at Fort Reno, where Clark was employed as corral master and interpreter. The dispatch was forwarded from Guthrie on May 10 and appeared in the columns of the *New York Sun* on May 14, 1899.

[2]Although Custer also speaks of a cavalry force of between 800 and 900 men, it appears that the strike force that attacked the village was much less than that. According to the regimental return for November 1868, the total of commissioned officers and enlisted men present after the battle was 837 troops. To determine the prebattle strength, we need to increase this total by 21 for the casualties who had died by November 30. The adjusted total of 858 needs to be reduced by 49 men from L Company, which was on detached service at Fort Lyon, Colorado. The subsequent total of 809 troops then needs to be reduced further by 17 men on duty with the Commissary and Quartermaster departments. If we adjust the new total of 792 with the 83 troops left behind with the wagon train, we arrive at a prebattle strength of approximately 700 men, which is the total reported by field correspondent DeB. Randolph Keim (1885, 102). The *New York Times* (Dec. 6, 1868) lists the regimental strength at 660, which is the troop total without Bell's ambulance train. For a further breakdown of the size of Custer's command at the Washita, see Appendix B.

into the Cimarron River, in Oklahoma. Sully, the commanding officer, was sick and Custer was in command. Custer had lately been under suspension, pending an investigation of charges that had been brought against him for shooting deserters, and was still smarting under the discipline.[3] He was impatient to proceed readily and harassed the men and his subordinates by his arbitrary conduct. He was a hard master, but his dash and cavalier bearing held the admiration of his troopers. The regiment began moving about November 1. It was announced the second night out that the march would begin the next morning at daybreak. The stars were still shining when Custer arose, swearing and charging around. His brother, Col. Tom Custer, had a particularly good appetite that morning and lingered at the table, to the disgust of Custer, who told him repeatedly to hurry and finish his breakfast. The Colonel still lingered, however, and brought on an explosion of wrath from Custer, who charged into the tent, kicked over the mess table and sent dishes and victuals flying in all directions. Three teamsters who failed to hear the bugle were several minutes late in getting their teams hitched and were made to walk all day in the snow. He worked his scouts hard and they would stay out as long as possible to keep from being run to death.[4]

The regiment arrived at the Washita River on the night of November 26. Early in the night, with my scouts, I struck a hostile trail leading southeast from the Panhandle. I had under me twelve Osage Indian scouts, bloodthirsty wrenches, who afterward disgraced the regiment. Two of these scouts discovered a campfire. Crawling cautiously toward it, they learned that the Indians had gone toward the river, having joined the war party. Several miles further down the river the tinkle of pony bells was faintly heard, and

---

[3]Custer was suspended from the army for one year without pay for leaving his command without authorization and for conduct prejudicial to good order and military discipline. The latter charge was supported by three specifications: excessive cruelty and illegal conduct in regards to deserters, abandonment of two soldiers attacked by Indians, and marching his troops excessively. The suspension was approved by the War Department on November 20, 1867, and was lifted on September 25, 1868, through General Sheridan's intervention.

[4]Although a man of ability, Custer's complicated personality rendered him difficult to command, or to be commanded. Shirk 1959, 70.

from the summit of a hill the ponies were seen in the valley below, their bodies standing out dark against the snow. Custer was in advance of the troops and came up to the scouts in a few minutes. He dismounted and the party lay down in the snow and peered over the ridge of the hill. It was a clear, frosty, starlit night, and the yelping of the dogs in the village could be plainly heard. The lodges were invisible, being hidden in dense timber in a low valley. The regiment was halted before it reached the hill. The troops were on the north side of the river. It was not known which side the village was on. The command was dismounted and each man told to hold his horse and make as little noise as possible. No cooking was allowed, and the hungry men made the best of it by chewing hardtack.

It was now about 1 o'clock in the morning. A council of officers and scouts was held. The group was startled by the remarkable brilliance of a star, which was at first sight mistaken for an Indian signal among the low-lying hills. Custer, who was impressed by such incidents, called it "the Star of the Washita," saying that it presaged victory for him.

I took with me several scouts, among them Joe and Jack Corwin [*sic*], and set out to learn the exact location of the village. We drew close enough to see the smoke curling from the tops of the lodges and found that the village was on the south side of the river. It was an admirable camping place, in a big bend of the river, on a level stretch of ground. Beyond the village and parallel to the swinging shore line of the river was an embankment, probably fifty feet high, with an almost perpendicular face. This embankment was the abrupt termination of an undulating prairie which stretched away still further to the south. The lowland close to the river continued for several miles down stream and merged gradually with the lessening height of the embankment into comparatively level ground. About a mile above the village was a trail which crossed the Washita.[5] On the north side of the river were

---

[5]Known to local residents as Custer's Crossing, this ford was located just below the present mouth of Plum Creek, near the northwest corner of the former John Wesner property, now the Washita Battlefield National Historic Site. Although the floodplain has been plowed, traces of a deeply cut pony trail are still visible on the river bench south of the crossing, as is an old roadbed with deep ruts just to the east and running parallel to the trail. Moore 1968; Briscoe and Watkins 1990, 23. See also chapters 28 and 32.

low spurs of hills, which increased in height northward until they reached much higher hills, to which they were almost at right angles. An Indian trail, followed by the war party, led down the river on the north side.

The officers removed their sabres for fear that the clanking would be heard by the dogs, and the village aroused. After learning from the scouts the topography of the camp, Custer mapped out his plan of attack. The regiment was divided into four detachments. Five troops were to remain with Custer and six were to take positions as follows: Major Elliott, with Troops I, H, and M,[6] and Col. Thompson, with Troops B and F, were sent by a circuitous route to positions parallel to each other and facing the village on the level ground below it on the east, to cut off flight in that direction. Col. Myers, with one troop, was to take up a position on the undulating terrain south of the village. Custer, in addition to his five companies, had the scouts and Col. W. W. Cook[e] with his forty sharpshooters. Shortly before the fight the sharpshooters were to advance on foot to a position on the north side of the river, opposite the village. Custer was to make the charge from above, fording the river at the trail crossing, and driving the Indians toward Elliott, Thompson, and Myers. As daylight approached a fog overspread the valley.

The village belonged to the Cheyennes, under Black Kettle. Below them were the Arapahoes, of whom Little Raven was head chief and Left Hand and Powder Face active chiefs. There were about 500 men, women and children in the Cheyenne village. There were other Indian villages extending for twenty miles down the Washita, composed of Kiowas, Comanches, Mescalero Apaches and Wichitas. The attack was to be at gray dawn and the regimental band was to strike up the tune of "Garry Owen" as the signal for battle. Custer said that this air more nearly suggested the trampling and roar of a cavalry charge than any other he knew of. The band was stationed near the river crossing. The hour was so still that a man could almost hear his watch tick.

---

[6] I Company (in addition to E Company) was assigned to Myers; Elliott commanded G, H, and M Companies.

With a crash the music burst upon the ears of the expectant men, who answered with a yell. As the tumult of trampling horses and cheering troopers went thundering by, the musicians lost control of their own horses and were carried away into the fight, the hills echoing again and again to the strains of "Garry Owen." Custer, surrounded by his scouts, led the charge. The Indians were taken completely by surprise and rushed panic-stricken from their lodges, to be shot down almost before sleep had left their eyelids. Many scrambled down on the ice of the Washita and ran under cover of the wooded bank along the river toward the other villages. Numbers fell before the crossfire of Cook's sharpshooters. Most of them encountered the detachments under Elliott and Thompson, and it was here that the greatest slaughter took place. Squaws with their children climbed the steep embankment south of the village and gained the prairie, where Myers's command lay in wait for them. The Osage scouts, before they could be intercepted, shot down the women and mutilated their bodies, cutting off their arms, legs and breasts with knives. An Osage brought in Black Kettle's scalp and asserted that he had the glory of having killed him. The old warrior was killed near a troop commanded by Capt. Hamilton, who was also killed at the beginning of the fight, being shot from his horse. I was riding to the south when I came in view of fully half [of] Myers's men, chasing the panic-stricken women and children. I immediately reported it to Custer, asking whether he wanted them killed. "No," he replied. "Tell Myers to call off his men and take the runaways to a big lodge and put a guard over them."

I got together about sixty women and children. The hunting and slaughter of fugitives continued during the greater part of the morning. The Indians fought desperately, but were wholly at a disadvantage. I estimate the Cheyenne loss at seventy-five warriors and fully as many women and children killed.[7] The number of wounded was never known, but there are still Indians in western Oklahoma who bear scars received on that cold November day. The dusk of the morning gave cover for escape, or the blood-

---

[7]For a comparison of Indian casualties reported by the Cheyennes and by the military, see "Aggregate Totals" in Appendix G.

shed would have been greater. Custer, with whom I rode stirrup to stirrup, killed only one Indian, a warrior who was about to fire at him from only a few feet. Custer killed him with a pistol.

After returning to the village with the women and children, I heard heavy firing down the river in the direction of Cook's sharp-shooters. I rode rapidly in that direction and found a small party of warriors, with their women and children, at bay under the embank-ment. During a freshet the bank had been undermined, causing it to cave in. The mass of dirt made an excellent barricade, the Indi-ans getting between it and the bank. They were protected from above by the overhanging turf, which had not been carried down with the dirt. The Indians were firing at the sharpshooters on the other side of the river. The latter were unable to dislodge them, but poured a hail of bullets at them. The shots of the Indians gradually grew fewer until they ceased altogether. The warriors were dead. It was then that I saw a terrible example of a Cheyenne mother's despair. A squaw arose from behind the barricade, holding a baby at arm's length. In her other hand was a long knife. The sharp-shooters mistook the child for a white captive and yelled, "Kill that squaw. She's murdering a white child." Before a gun could be fired the mother, with one stroke of the knife, disemboweled the child, [and] drove the knife to the hilt in her own breast and was dead. A trooper poked his carbine over the embankment and shot her through the head, but it was a needless cruelty.

Many of the Indians were armed only with bows and arrows, having grabbed up the first weapons within reach when they began their flight. Most of their shields and lances were left in the lodges. I came upon a wrinkled, gray-haired old squaw who stood at bay like an enraged tigress. She had an old cavalry sabre raised defiantly for battle. She was with difficulty persuaded to lay down the sabre after having been assured that her life would be spared.[8] In a ravine which traversed the plateau south of the village, Myers's men discovered a man hiding with a baby. He was a Mex-ican who had been captured by the Cheyennes when a child. He could speak a little English. When I rode up the troopers were

---

[8]Alvin Moore, a former Oklahoma state senator, as a young boy found numerous relics on the battlefield, including an old sword. A. Moore 1968.

discussing the question of killing their captive. The Mexican suspected his fate and stood stoically awaiting the end. Finally one of the soldiers said to him, "Move off, down the ravine." The Mexican hesitated and then asked beseechingly, "You will take the baby, won't you?" The trooper took the child in his arms and the Mexican darted away. He had run scarcely thirty feet when he fell, pierced through the back with bullets.[9] The little one grew to womanhood and married a white man in southwestern Oklahoma, where she lived until her death a few years ago.

It was from this spot that Major Elliott started on the foray which resulted in the massacre of himself and those who followed him. Shortly after the shooting of the Mexican, Elliott, looking down the river through his fieldglass, saw a number of Indians, mostly boys, who were skulking in the timber and moving rapidly toward the hostile villages. Elliott was separated from his command and when he said, "There is a lot of escaping Indians; come on boys, let's take 'em in," the men who joined him did so of their own accord. The party rode away, but I did not follow. Men and horses soon disappeared in the timber.

The news of the battle had been carried down the river and the warriors could be seen gathering on the hills to the north of Black Kettle's village. I never saw a more magnificent lot of Indians. The hills appeared to be alive with them. They were gorgeous in war bonnets and paint. Some were armed with guns and some with bow and arrows and gaudy shields. Their bracelets and armlets glistened in the sunshine and their ponies were adorned for battle with vermillion and feathers. They captured the overcoats of the sharpshooters, which had been left in the rear when the soldiers advanced to the fight. This pleased the Indians hugely and they dared the soldiers to come and get them.

9The name of this Mexican was Pilan. He was married to a Cheyenne woman and known to the Indians as "White Bear." He probably was a trader for William Griffinstein, who operated a supply post in Sedgwick County, Kansas, and was the licensed post trader for Fort Cobb in 1868. According to James R. Mead (1986, 117–18), a fellow trader, Griffinstein routinely furnished Black Kettle's camp with ammunition and had delivered "250 lbs of powder and 500 lbs of lead on one trip" a short time before Custer's attack. Griffinstein was married to "Cheyenne Jenny," a Wutapiu woman whose family lived in Black Kettle's camp. See also "Interview and Notes by Walter M. Camp" in this chapter.

The bugles sounded for the scattered troops to assemble. Nearly 1,000 ponies and mules had been captured. Custer decided to strike the hostiles a severe blow by destroying their ponies. The best animals in the herd, about 200, were divided among the officers and men, Custer taking four fine mules. The remaining 800 were bunched against the steep bank south of the village and two troops were detailed to kill them. One troop stood above the herd and the other in the valley below.[10] It took nearly two hours to kill all the ponies. The hostiles who were gathered on the hills witnessed their destruction and with shrill cries derided the soldiers as cowards and dared them to fight.

The ammunition was running low and Custer, surprised at the constantly increasing number of hostiles, was not anxious to risk a night attack. It had already become necessary to send Major Berry with a heavy line of pickets to drive the Indians further back into the hills and hold them at bay, as the Indians had a number of long-range rifles and were dropping bullets into the camp. The main wagon train was miles away in the Antelope Hills, with a rough, snow-covered country intervening. Major Bell, Quartermaster of the regiment, who had been stationed in the rear, came up before noon with several thousand rounds of ammunition. There was not enough, however, for prolonged fighting. It was therefore decided to burn the village, which consisted of about seventy-five lodges.[11] Some of them were very large, being from twenty to twenty-two buffalo hides in size. The average size was from ten to twelve hides. There was an abundance of cooked buffalo meat and bread, which had been prepared evidently for war parties. Large quantities of powder, lead, and percussion caps were found. I noticed four white and three Indian scalps. Many buffalo

---

[10]Numerous Spencer casings have been found on the ridges north and east of the present National Park Service overlook. This combat debris could have resulted from any of the following military actions: random firing at the village, shooting at refugees fleeing east, directed fire at Indian warriors coming from the east and southeast, or shots at the pony herd held in the valley below, to the north. Lees 1999, 35; Lees et al. 2001, 175–76.

[11]Like his estimate of the Indian casualties, Clark's total of the lodges in the village is too high. The official count by Lt. Algernon E. Smith, acting commissary, was fifty-one: forty-seven Cheyenne, two Sioux, and two Arapaho lodges.

robes and much clothing had been left behind. The village burned fiercely and made an intense heat, the Indians dancing and howling with rage at the sight.

The danger of being cut off from supplies in the Antelope Hills was growing hourly more serious. A lookout was kept for the return of Major Elliott and his men. It was feared that they had been killed. As the hours of the afternoon wore away Custer abandoned his original plan of following the Indians and prepared to retreat under cover of night. The troops started at sundown, crossing the Washita where they had gone thundering over at daybreak. For several miles down the north side of the river was level bottom land. Strategy was employed to deceive the hostiles. The regiment was drawn up in close marching order. Three hundred yards ahead of the advance guard of one troop were the scouts. A quarter of a mile in the rear of the advance guard was another troop, close behind which were the captives on ponies. Then came the main body of troops, the wagon train and the rear guard. It was apparently a general movement to attack the villages. The hostiles deserted the hills and rode as rapidly as possible toward the villages, firing at long range. Troop flankers were thrown out near the river to guard against surprise and to look for Elliott. After marching slowly for six or seven miles an order was given to countermarch and to move briskly. The rear guard now grew very restless, expecting a general assault by the Indians, but the latter failed to suspect the ruse. Camp Supply was reached without trouble from the Indians.

Gen. Sheridan had reached Camp Supply the day after the regiment had left,[12] and was there when it returned, as was the Nineteenth Kansas. Another expedition was now formed and Gen. Sheridan assumed command. The troops were in motion in about a week, headed south, to deliver a crushing blow to the hostiles and to succor Elliott and his men if they were alive. Soon Elliott and his men were found dead. On the south side of the Washita, about three miles below the ruins of the Cheyenne village, a searching party was startled at the sight of a pile of naked bodies.

---

[12]Sheridan arrived at Camp Supply on the afternoon of November 21, two days before Custer commenced the winter campaign. Utley 1977, 208–209.

They were as white as the snow around them and stiff in the rigor of death. Strange as it may seem, they had not been molested by the wolves and other wild animals so numerous in that region. Every body except Elliott's had been mutilated. Skulls were crushed in with war clubs, ears and noses and legs had been cut off, scalps torn away and the bodies pierced with bullets and arrows. Elliott had been greatly admired by the Indians for his bravery long before the fight. They remembered this when he was dead and treated him as a valorous foe by severing his right hand at the wrist and his left foot at the ankle, leaving each attached by a tendon. The body bore no other marks save the death wounds.[13] It was evident that the bodies had been brought to this place and a war dance held around them.

The charge was made against Custer in after years that he gave the order which led Elliott to his death and then abandoned him to his fate. This accusation was false. Custer knew nothing of Elliott's going. Half an hour after Elliott and his men rode away Custer came up and asked me what had become of Elliott. The enmity between Custer and Col. Benteen, which afterward grew very bitter, showed itself a day or two after the fight. Benteen, anxious to weaken Custer's prestige, came to me after it was believed that Elliott and his men were lost and asked me if I would be willing to make the statement that Custer knowingly let Elliott go to his doom without trying to save him. I refused to have anything to do with the matter.

After the bodies of Elliott and his men had been found the troopers were commanded to deploy in all directions in order not to miss any of the dead. A short distance up the river the naked body of a white woman was found and near by was the body of her baby. Both had been stabbed with knives. This woman and her child had been captured during a Cheyenne raid in Colorado near where

---

[13]Elliott's body revealed the following wounds and mutilations: two bullet holes in the head and one in the left cheek; the right hand was cut off and the left foot was almost severed; the throat was cut; the right groin and the calves of both legs contained deep gashes; the little finger of the left hand was cut off to remove his ring; and the penis was cut off and stuck in the victim's mouth, though the medical report is silent on this latter point. G. A. Custer 1868c; Thomas B. Murphy to Joseph G. Masters, Oct. 15, 1928, Letter Collection, Western History Department, Denver Public Library.

Sand Creek empties into the Arkansas River. In the uproar of battle they had been killed by squaws to prevent their being rescued.[14]

The story of the death of Elliott and his men was not learned until after the Indians came in from the warpath. The hostiles who killed him were led by Left Hand, now the head chief of the Arapahoes and the most eloquent Indian orator in Oklahoma. He lives at this time on the North Canadian River, about four miles from the little town of Geary. Elliott had captured about a dozen Indian boys and left them in [the] charge of a detail of his men. As he advanced he came in sight of about forty advancing warriors. He thought he was much nearer the main body of troops than he really was and felt himself comparatively safe. He fell back to where the captives were, massed his men and began firing. The advancing Indians knew that they were followed by hundreds of warriors who were coming through the timber along Sergeant Major Creek. They were joined at intervals by reinforcements and came steadily ahead to where the troopers had dismounted. The Indians, charging like a whirlwind, rode down the troopers as if they had been blades of grass. Not a man escaped. The Indians said that only one warrior was killed,[15] and that if Elliott had been less daring and retreated he would have escaped, as the Indians were afraid to follow him.

Custer, in his story of the Washita fight, gives the killed and wounded as follows: Major Elliott, Capt. Hamilton and nineteen enlisted men killed; Col. Albert Barnitz, Col. T. W. Custer, Lieut. B. Marsh and eleven enlisted men wounded. I know positively, however, that thirty-two lives were lost in the Elliott disaster, but all of them may not have been enlisted men.[16]

---

[14]Clark's comments regarding the white woman and her baby are incorrect. The reference, of course, is to Clara Blinn and her infant son. Their remains were found in Yellow Bear's Arapaho camp, which stood some five miles downstream from Black Kettle's village. The Arapahos and not the Cheyennes captured these two victims. (Clark corrects himself in "Letter to Frederick S. Barde" later in this chapter).

[15]The name of this Arapaho casualty was Tobacco, or Smokey. Being the owner of a flat war club, it was expected that he would perform a great feat during the Elliott fight. Living up to this expectation, Tobacco spearheaded the assault on Elliott and was shot in the breast while riding over the troopers. A second Arapaho, Lone Coyote, was mortally wounded and died some time later. Grinnell 1956, 304–305; Nye 1969, 68.

[16]No evidence has come to light to support this statement. It is possible that the

The expedition under Sheridan and Custer never came within striking distance of the hostiles, who finally surrendered after seeing that flight was hopeless.

***

Kansas City Star Interview
December 4, 1904

Thirty-six years ago last Sunday General Custer and his Seventh Cavalry troopers fought the battle of the Washita, destroyed Black Kettle's band of Cheyennes and suppressed one of the most powerful Indian uprisings that ever menaced the Western frontier. The entire tribes of the Southern Cheyennes and Arapahoes were preparing for war, and it seemed more than probable that they would take with them the Kiowas, Comanches and Mescalero Apaches. The campaign was historic in Indian warfare.

Ben Clark, now post interpreter at Fort Reno, was Custer's chief of scouts in the fight. Clark accompanied a correspondent of The Star to the battleground several weeks ago, and went over it in detail to point out accurately the different points of interest. The battleground is about two miles northwest of the town of Cheyenne, and is located on a farm belonging to G. F. Turner,[17] a merchant at Cheyenne. Clark has not seen the battleground in many years, but greatly to his surprise it showed little change. Much of the heavy timber along the Washita had been cut, but enough remained to make the loss scarcely noticeable.

Where Black Kettle's village stood is now a meadow. The land has never been plowed, as the Washita rises and overflows it every spring. The Washita flows from the west against an almost perpendicular bank, which marks the break of the high prairie on the south as it descends suddenly to the level floor of the river valley. Then the river turns northwest for about a thousand yards and

---

journalist misunderstood or may have forgotten the exact meaning of some of Clark's answers by the time he wrote his report, which was the case with the *Kansas City Star* interview.

   [17]The G. Frank Turner farm stood a short distance south of Major Elliott's death site, just north of the town of Cheyenne (NW1/4, Sec8, T13N, R24W). But the village and the battlefield are located about two miles west of Cheyenne (N1/2, Sec12, T13N, R24W). See map on p. 232.

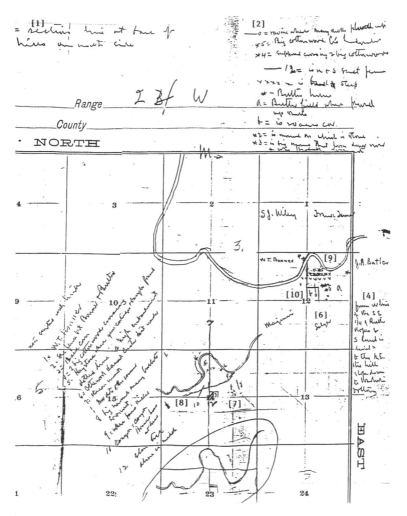

Historical Locations on the Washita Battlefield, drawn by Fred S. Barde. Although the Barde map is not dated, we know that Barde visited the battlefield with Ben Clark in November 1904. However, some of the information then obtained by Barde contradicts the text recorded on the map, suggesting the possibility that the map did not originate in 1904. A clue about the date of origin may be found in the reference to J. A. Butler, who is listed on the map as one of the landowners. As Butler sold his property to W. T. Bonner in July 1900, we may assume that Barde drew his map prior to that date, perhaps as early as May 1899, after the publication of the *New York Sun*'s Washita article. The map reproduced here, which is only a section of the original, contains two similar pencil drawings of the battlefield, each with its own legend. Because the text is difficult to read, a transcript has been provided, which includes the entire text listed on the original map. The Barde map is a long-neglected, valuable document that describes the battlefield, its landmarks, and the locations of artifacts before white settlements and the forces of nature permanently altered the evidence. Reproduced courtesy of the Oklahoma Historical Society.

216

1. Section line at base of lines on north line
   Range 24 W

2. —— o   = ravine where many shells plowed up
       x5   = Big cottonwood Cr's headquarters
       x4   = supposed crossing 2 big cottonwoods
   —— 12   = is N and S sect fence
     xxxx   = is broad and steep
        *   = Butler house
        a   = Butler field where plowed up shells
        b   = 20 acres corn
       x2   = is mound on which is stone
       x3   = is big mound that looks down river and was probable lookout

3. S[amuel] J. Wiley, Frank Turner, W[illiam] T. Bonner, J[onathan] A. Butler, [Fleming] McGinnis, [John M.] Salyer

4. from W line of the SE ¼ of Butler [the land] slopes E. S land is level; to the NE the hills slope down to the Washita bottom

5. river skirted with timber
     1 = W. T. Bonner
     2 – sec fence bet Bonner and Butler
     3 = 18 acres corn
     4 = 2 big cottonwood crossing
     5 = Haystack where gun cartridges and bangles found dotted line is high
       embankment
     6 = cottonwood claimed Custer tend under two dots other mound
     7 = stone on mound
     8 = big mound may bullets
       Lookout
     9 = where ponies killed
     10   canyon = canyon Bonner's house at head
     12   elm tree alone in middle

6. Salyer ploughed up bullets in field
   thousand bullets in field house
   5 = elm tree and haystack — [illegible word]

7. monument erected east of 18 acre field
   bet 1/4 and 1/2 mile west is old muddy crossing which Myers crossed
   Custer's headquarters was here

8. next to rim of hill Washita has flushed in and filled up

9. NW 40 of Butler
   x = hill [and] stone on it

10. stone was near SW corner of field[;] lots of shells in field

turns again to the wall-like embankment of the prairie. Surrounded on two sides by this gooseneck bend of the river and
flanked on the south by the higher ground, is a track of land of
about twenty-five acres, the old camp ground.[18]

Less than two miles northwest of the village on a farm owned
by a man named Kirtley,[19] Clark stood on the backbone of one of
these ridges, and pointing still further northwest, said:

"There is where the troops came down from the divide, and in
that cotton field is where the men dismounted when the scouts
and Osage trailers reported in looking over the crest on which we
stand they had heard dogs barking and seen a herd of ponies in the
valley beyond us. Custer and his officers lay on this very spot and
spied out the village and the lay of the land. The stiff short grass
and the unusual hardness of the ground were noticed at that time.
The weather was bitter cold and snow lay upon the ground.

"Custer quickly formed his plan of battle. Captain Myers was
sent to the right, and told to occupy the high ground south of the
village, to cut off retreat. He moved cautiously, forded the river close
to where a little stream empties in from the south,[20] and passed up
this little tributary several hundred yards to the higher land. Hamilton and Barnitz went with their detachments to the heavy timber
down the river northeast of the village.[21] Cooke's sharpshooters
took a stand on the north side of the Washita. In that cotton field
about half a mile north and west of the village, Custer formed his
five troops in line of battle. Close by was his regimental band, which
was to signal the attack by playing 'Garry Owen.'

"The night was changing to the first gray of dawn when Custer
gave the word and the silence was broken by the crash of music.
The horses sprang forward on a run, the troopers shouting in

---

[18]From the description given by the reporter, it appears that the village stood in the
loop shown in the northwest quarter of Section 12. The historical channel has shifted
over time so that the left leg of the loop is now a short distance east from its 1868 bed.
Briscoe and Watkins 1990, 23.

[19]The James A. Kirkley farm stood about a mile northwest of the battlefield (SE1/4,
Sec2, T13N, R24W).

[20]This could have been Plum Creek, though it seems more like that the tributary
mentioned entered the Washita a little farther to the west.

[21]Hamilton's squadron was assigned to the main column commanded by Custer.

anticipation of battle. The musicians had little time for music. Their horses became uncontrollable in the rush and rumble of the charge and a number of the musicians were drawn into the very teeth of the fight. Custer was riding a black stallion and cleared the trail crossing of the Washita at a single jump. I had a good horse and made the jump with him.

"The story of the surprise and slaughter of the Indians has been told too often in detail to be repeated. Custer fired at one Indian as he ran through the village and his horse knocked down another. He rode straight to a little knoll that overlooks the village on the south, and from that point issued many of his orders. On this knoll stands the brown sandstone marker which Captain Scott of Fort Sill erected several years ago.[22]

"As the Indians fled from the village they tried to pass down the river to the big camps, which stretched for miles below, and ran into the troops under Hamilton and Barnitz, and there the fight was heaviest. Hamilton, a grandson of Alexander Hamilton, was shot squarely between the eyes and killed.[23] Barnitz was shot through the lungs and so badly injured that he never fully recovered and had to retire from the service.[24]

"In making its sharp bend around the village, the Washita had cut into its north bank till heavy portions of the bank fell away and

---

[22]There is a small elevation on the bench land some 250 yards southeast of Custer's Crossing, just north of Highway 47A. This little knoll rises some fifteen feet above the valley floor and commands a view of the loop described in note 18 above. Yet a National Park Service survey conducted in 1997 failed to locate any artifacts at this location. Moreover, Clark's statements locate Custer's Knoll (Headquarters Hill) nearly a mile father to the east, which is validated by the firing refuse found at this site. Lees et al. 2001, 175. See also "Interview and Field Notes by Walter M .Camp" later in this chapter. For information on the marker and Captain Scott, see chapter 27.

[23]Hamilton died instantly from a gunshot wound near the heart. The medical report reveals that the ball entered the ribcage five inches below the left nipple and exited near the inferior angle of the right shoulder blade. Hamilton's face was extremely lacerated from striking the frozen ground after he fell from his horse. These bloody cuts may have given rise to the speculation that the captain was shot "squarely between the eyes." Hamilton's shell jacket, cap, belt, boots and some mementos were donated by his brother to the Oklahoma Historical Society in 1908. The shell jacket shows a hole in the back, with a rust-colored stain below it on the inside. It is believed that Hamilton had his jacket buttoned only at the top for greater maneuverability in the saddle. Keim 1868, Dec. 24; Reed 2000, 238.

[24]Barnitz retired from the army on December 15, 1870, and died on July 18, 1912, from a growth around his old Washita wound. Utley 1977, 247.

made a natural breastwork in the river below. About twenty men, women and children took refuge in this place and hid from sight during the heaviest fighting. When a lull came they were discovered. They refused to surrender and all were killed. I saw a Cheyenne woman, the last survivor, kill her child with a butcher knife, and then bury the blade in her own breast. The Cheyenne babies are almost as fair as white children. Several of the soldiers thought she had murdered a white child, and one of them poked his carbine over the embankment and sent a bullet into her brain. In relating this incident in his history of the battle, Custer made the mistake of saying that this woman killed a captive white child.

"While standing on the knoll to which Custer had ridden, I saw a large number of women and children near two buttes on the prairie south of the village, pursued by Myers's men, who were killing them without mercy. I asked Custer if it was his wish that they should be killed, and he ordered me to stop the slaughter, which I did, placing the captives in a big tepee under guard.

"Major Elliott was standing on a larger mound further east,[25] and later in the day, looking down the river with a field glass, he discovered a number of Indian men and boys skulking in the timber, about a mile north of the present town of Cheyenne. He called for men to go with him, and disappeared, never to return. Warriors were coming up the Washita to engage the troops. Sergeant Major Creek and the Washita run parallel for nearly a quarter of a mile before they join, and the two streams are almost within a stone's throw of each other. A big band of these Indians went from the Washita to the Sergeant Major and were in the timber when they saw Elliott and his men advancing across the meadowland. The Indians charged from the timber in overwhelming numbers, killed every man in the detachment and afterward mutilated them at a war dance. In later years I was told by Indians that Left Hand, an old Arapahoe chief, now living on the Canadian near Geary, was in command of this hostile band.

---

[25]According to Alvin Moore, the location pointed out by Ben Clark as where Elliott stood was on "the easternmost red hill on the John Wesner farm, formerly the Butler place [NE1/4, Sec12]." This elevation is on a spur of the present National Park Service overlook. (See map on p. 232.) Moore was a young boy when he accompanied Clark to the battlefield, which probably took place in 1904. Moore 1968.

"The very flower of the hostile tribes of the Southwest massed themselves on the buttes north of the battleground in the afternoon. There were 1,200 or 1,500 mounted warriors, armed with guns, lances and bow and arrows.[26] They wore a profusion of metal wristlets and armlets, which glistened in the sunlight. They taunted the soldiers and dared them to fight, but seldom approached within range. When the herd of nearly 1,000 ponies was driven against the hillside south of the village and shot to death by two troops of cavalry to put the Indians afoot, the warriors on the hills yelled with rage.

"In a forced march that night, Custer met his wagon train coming from the Antelope Hills to join him, and the danger of a greatly diminished supply of ammunition was overcome. He had not expected to find the Indians in such numbers, and returned to Camp Supply to outfit for a heavier campaign. He returned to the pursuit a week later, accompanied by General Sheridan. The hostiles were subdued and brought back to their reservations."

Revision of *Star* Interview
October 22, 1910[27]

This abstract of [the] article of the *Kansas City Star* was verified by Ben Clark on Oct. 22, 1910. The parts worked out are incorrect. The matter left standing is correct. Some of it (page 7 [of the *Star*]) has been revised in my own language—W.M.C.

Kansas City Star, December 4, 1904. According to Clark the troops came in from the northwest. Capt. Meyers' was sent to the right and told to occupy [the] high ground south of the village. He forded the river close to where a little stream empties in from the south and passed up this little tributary several hundred yards to the higher land. He took part in charging [the] village. Hamilton

---

[26]For an excellent discussion of the strength and temper of the Indians, see Milo Milton Quaife's editorial comments in G. A. Custer 1966, 353–55. Clark's total corroborates Quaife's conclusions.

[27]This revision of the 1904 *Kansas City Star* article resulted from Ben Clark's interview with Walter Camp at the Washita battlefield in 1910. The abstract is in Box 3 (Battle of the Washita), Camp Manuscripts, Indiana University Library, Bloomington; it is reproduced by special permission.

and Barnitz went to the heavy timber down the river, northeast of the village. Cooke's sharp shooters took a stand on the north side of the Washita. About half a mile north and west of the village Custer formed his four companies in line of battle.

Custer, as he entered the village, fired on one Indian, and his horse (a black stallion) knocked down another. He rode straight to a little knoll that overlooked the village on the south side, and from that point issued many of his orders. On this knoll stands the brown sandstone marker which Capt. Scott of Fort Sill erected several years ago.

As [the] Indians ran from [the] village they tried to make their way down the river to the other Indian camps and ran into the troops of Hamilton and Barnitz, and there the fight was the heaviest. Capt. Hamilton, a grandson of Alexander Hamilton, was shot squarely between the eyes and killed. Barnitz was shot through the lungs.

During the heaviest fighting about twenty men, women and children took refuge behind the bank of the river in the bend. When a lull came they were discovered. They refused to surrender and all were killed. I saw a Cheyenne squaw, the last survivor, kill her child with a butcher knife and then stab herself. Several of the soldiers thought she had murdered a white child (some Cheyenne babies being almost as fair as white children) and one of the soldiers poked his carbine over the bank and shot her through the head. "In relating this incident in his history of the battle Custer made the mistake of saying that this woman killed a captive white child."

"While standing on the knoll to which Custer had ridden I saw a large number of women and children on [the] high ground southeast of two buttes[28] pursued by Meyers' men who were firing into them. I called this movement to Custer's attention and asked him if it was his wish that these people should be killed, and he

---

[28]The revised language enables us to identify these two buttes, which stand directly south of the former John Wesner residence some six hundred yards southwest of the National Park Service overlook. The fleeing noncombatants ascended a wooded drainage swell near the buttes and then turned east on the high ground near present Highway 47. See also chapter 29.

said (apparently with some reluctance): 'No. Ride out there and give the officer commanding my compliments and ask him to stop it.[29] Take them [the captives] to the village and put them in a big tepee and station a guard over them,' which I did, and the women seemed well pleased that I said so.[30] When I rode out, one of these women had been shot in the jaw and was standing on defense with a saber."

"Major Joel Elliott was standing on a larger mound further east, and later in the day, looking down the river with a field glass, he discovered a number of Indian men and boys flitting through the timber about a mile north of the present town of Cheyenne. He called for men to go with him and disappeared, never to return. Warriors were coming up the Washita to engage the troops. Sergeant Major Creek and the Washita run parallel for nearly 1/4 mile before they join, and the two streams are almost within a stone's throw of each other. A big band of these Indians went from the Washita to Sergeant Major and were in the timber when they saw Elliott and his men advancing across the meadow land. The Indians charged from the timber in overwhelming numbers, killed every men in the detachment and afterward mutilated them at a war dance. In after years I was told that Left Hand, an old Arapaho Chief, now living on the Canadian near Geary (still lives there), was in command of this hostile band."

In the afternoon 1200 or 1500 warriors massed themselves on the battlefield, armed with guns, bows and arrows, and lances. When the herd of Indian ponies was driven against the hillside south of the village and shot to death by two troops of cavalry the warriors on the hills yelled with rage. "Some of the warriors slipped around within shooting distance and Berry went out and drove them off."[31]

---

[29] If this statement is true, then the killing of the women and children was not entirely accidental, as suggested by Custer in his official report.

[30] The guard consisted of A Company, Captain Hamilton's unit, which upon the captain's death was commanded by Lt. Thomas W. Custer, who himself was wounded in the hand. The captives were initially guarded by Benteen's squadron. Custer 1869c; Benteen n.d.(b), 212.

[31] The reference is to Lt. Matthew Berry, who commanded C Company.

"In a forced march that night Custer met his own wagon train coming from Antelope Hills to join him, and the danger of a greatly diminished supply of ammunition was overcome. He had not expected to find the Indians in such numbers and returned to Camp Supply to outfit for a heavier campaign. He returned to the pursuit ten days later accompanied by Gen. Sheridan."

In the above much is put in quotation marks and a good deal of the rest is taken down nearly in the words in which it appeared in the newspaper.

Interview and Field Notes by Walter M. Camp
October 22, 1910[32]

[We] were following the trail of a war party of at least 100 warriors and perhaps 200 horses down the Washita and all of a sudden smelled smoke and began to investigate. Found by marks in [the] snow that a village had been at the place and moved the previous day. When the Indians moved they left a rotten log burning. This was at a point [about] six miles above Black Kettle's [village].

We followed the trail and came in from [the] northwest, about past where the barn of A.C. Smith now stands.[33] As we made the rise about a mile N.W. of [the] village, [we] came upon the Indian pony herd and heard a bell tinkle, one of the horses having a bell on its neck. Soon the dogs in the village began to bark and we then knew we were near it. The command fell back on the trail over the rise of ground to a flat place where Custer's part of it remained between 1 A.M. and daylight. Mr. Bonner thinks this flat place [is] on Frank Turner's place.[34] (This should be verified.)

---

[32]Clark's interview with Walter M. Camp and the appended field notes are contained in Box 2 (Ben Clark), Box 3 (Battle of the Washita), Camp Manuscripts, Indiana University Library, Bloomington; they are reproduced by special permission.

[33]The Andrew C. Smith barn stood in the horseshoe bend of the Washita, about one and a half miles northwest of the battlefield (NW1/4, Sec2, T13N, R24W).

[34]The Frank Turner homestead stood on the north side of the Washita, across from the battlefield (SE1/4, Sec1). The William T. Bonner homestead stood south of the Washita (NW1/4, Sec12). In 1945 John Wesner purchased the Bonner property and the adjacent John A. Butler homestead (NE1/4, Sec12). These properties were sold to the U.S. government in 1997 by Wesner's daughter-in-law, Betty Wesner, and her son Brian.

When the command fell back Custer called a council, and in [the] course of it Thompson said, "General, suppose we find more Indians there than we can handle,["] etc. Custer said gruffly "Huh, all I am afraid of we won't find half enough. There are not Indians enough in the country to whip the 7th Cavalry."

The village which had pulled up the day before and moved, had gone down the north side of the Washita and on past Black Kettle's village without crossing the stream,[35] but the trail of warriors we had been following split from it near Black Kettle's village and entered the village. When we charged on the village Custer's battalion followed this trail right into the village.

I rode right beside Custer, just ahead of the command. He would allow no one to get ahead of him. His horse cleared the stream at one jump, and up the bank we went and into the village. When Custer started to charge from a point 1/2 mile or more back he had the band start playing Garry Owen, but they did not play much and drew their pistols and followed right along.[36] This music had aroused the camp and as we entered the village the Indians were up and running to get away, although a few stood their ground and fired at us.

It was hardly yet daylight when we charged into the camp. California Joe and some of the white scouts got the herd as Custer charged into the village. As Custer charged straight into the village the Indians ran downriver and Custer rode immediately out to Headquarters Hill. I rode right at [the] side of Custer all [the] time.

Meyers' men took no part in charging on the village, but followed [the] women and children who had run first westward and then southward up the tributary [of] Broken Leg Creek, coming

---

[35]The pony trail on the north side of the river followed an old river road that curved around the big bend of the Washita and led to many of the traditional Indian campsites scattered along the river. Custer's Bend, a pioneer settlement ten miles below the battlefield, was established on one of these campsites and later became known as Strong City.

[36]The Seventh Cavalry was equipped with the .50-caliber Model 1865 Spencer carbine and the .44-caliber Model 1861 Remington pistol. Yet the ordnance statements reveal that few troopers actually carried a pistol. The musicians did have sidearms, as did Hamilton's squadron, A and D Companies, which, however, carried .44-caliber Model 1861 Colt Army revolvers. See Lees et al. 2001, 172; Editor, "In Memoriam," *Chronicles of Oklahoma* 66, no. 4 (1988): 381.

in 1/2 mile to the west.[37] When they started east over [the] high ground to [the] south and east of the two buttes, Meyers' men began firing into them, and at Ben Clark's suggestion Custer had it stopped.

After this they found a Mexican named Pilan with his little girl, making their way along a ravine on the south side of the Washita. The Mexican said in broken English, "Don't kill me. Me Mexican." He was not armed. The soldiers took the little girl and they told the Mexican to go, and as he got a little way off they shot him in the back, killing him in cold blood. Ben Clark says he saw this done. This little girl was by a Cheyenne mother. She grew up and was married and Clark thought she might be living in 1910.

Major Elliott left the hill where Ben Clark was standing and started down [the] river between 9 and 10 A.M. [He] never came back. The Sergeant Major also had been standing there with Clark. A prominent Indian against Maj. Elliott—the one who took the leading part—was Left Hand, an Arapaho. [The] Indians say [that] when they met Elliott, he had about a dozen Indian boys whom he had captured.

As the warriors came up from the camps below they met and killed Maj. Elliott and his men, and then came on us and swarmed on [the] hills north of the village so as to hold us in check and give [the] villages below [a] chance for [the] squaws to get the tepees away. They got up on Barnitz Sugar Loaf [Hill] in large numbers and did some firing at long range, and a party worked around [to the] west and were beginning to make it warm for us when Custer ordered Berry to charge out with one troop and run them off. This Berry did very nicely. This was about 1 P.M.

No squaws were killed by soldiers in cold blood. Some were killed unavoidably. The Osage Indians killed all they could purposely until [they were] stopped. [We] did not begin to destroy [the] village until [the] afternoon. Custer left the valley (on west side of river opposite [the] village) about 9 P.M. This was after [we] came back from downriver.

---

[37]Plum Creek entered the Washita about a half-mile west of the Indian village, which according to Clark, was located in the northeast quadrant of the present battlefield site. See map on p. 232.

Broken Leg comes into the Washita from [the] south. It is west of Bonner's house, [about] half a mile.[38] Mrs. Blinn [was] captured near Sand Creek in Colorado about September. On second expedition Mr. Blinn came with us to look for her.[39] Her body and that of her baby were found the same day that Elliott was found. It was in [an] Arapaho village five miles below Black Kettle's.

Ben Clark says that after the battle of the Washita Benteen was quietly making pointed inquiries of him (Clark) to see what blame he could place against Custer for going off and leaving Maj. Elliott. In Custer's charge down the stream below Black Kettle's village nothing had been seen of Elliott, although the command had passed not far from him, but on [the] north side of the river.

Some of [the] Washita scouts:

Ben Clark, Chief

Jack Corbin. Killed near Wichita in early 70s by a vigilance
    committee who hung him.

California Joe. [Actual name was] Joe Milner. Not much of a scout,
    but Custer took a notion to him, and his peculiar personality
    gave Custer something to write about.

Raphael Romero. [Nickname was] Romeo. [A] Mexican [who]
    lived with Arapahoes two years after Civil War. Had been in
    Civil War in a Colorado regiment. Romero was a fairly efficient
    scout.

[We also] had a half breed Arapaho named John Poisel [*sic*] and his nephew [who was] 1/4 Arapaho and 3/4 white [named] Jack Fitzpatrick.[40] [Also] a youngster named Smalsle who afterward worked as a scout for Miles in 1874.[41] [There were] twelve Osages

---

[38]Broken Leg Creek empties into the Washita about one and a half miles west of the former Bonner house (SE corner, NW1/4, Sec12). Camp is probably referring to Plum Creek.

[39]Richard F. Blinn never saw his wife again after her capture at Sand Creek in October 1868. Clark is probably referring to Daniel A. Brewster, the brother of Anna Belle Morgan, who was captured by Cheyennes in the Solomon Valley in August 1868. Brewster accompanied Custer's troops to the Sweetwater, where Anna Belle was released into his custody. Spotts 1988, 207–10.

[40]For information on John Poisal and Jack Fitzpatrick, see chapter 24.

[41]Of German descent, William Schmalsle was perhaps best known for his ride to Camp Supply with a relief message from Capt. Wyllys Lyman's wagon train, which was besieged by Indians near the Washita River in September 1874.

in [the] fight and a half breed Osage named Chateau [*sic*] who
was interpreter for [the] Osage.[42] One of the Osage claimed the
honor of having killed Black Kettle.

Field Notes

Ben Clark. Did the [Indian] trail keep on the same (north) side
of the Washita all along? How about Bell getting out pioneer tools
to get wagons across what he says was the Washita? Where was
this, or was it a tributary of the Washita? He says he must have
crossed it twenty times during the night. Use the map. Clark says
[Bell] did not cross the main stream at all, but [only] tributaries.

Ben Clark. The first camp below Black Kettle's was down the
river five miles. It was an Arapaho camp. Kiowas and others were
camped along the river at intervals for fifteen miles downstream.
Among these other villages were more Cheyennes.

Inq[uiry] Washita. Maj. Elliott's battalion [consisted of] G, H,
and M, which was to move around to [the] left of [the] village and
get in rear of it. Capt. Thompson had B and F Troops which were
to get in rear of [the] village by a detour to [the] right and [were]
to connect and cooperate with Elliott, but they did not connect.
Meyers commanded E and I Troops and were posted down in
[the] woods along [the] valley about 3/4 mile to right of center.
Custer's column consisted of Osage scouts, under Cook[e] with
sharpshooters, and Troops A, C, D and K. Custer commanded
this column personally.

---

[42]Born in 1822, Gessau Chouteau was the mixed-blood son of Auguste L. Chouteau,
whose family founded St. Louis and built a trading empire in the Indian country. After
the outbreak of the Civil War, Gessau enlisted in the Confederate army and served in
Company D of Stand Watie's Second Cherokee Mounted Rifles. After surrendering to
Union cavalry stationed at Osage Mission, Kansas and taking the oath of allegiance in
the spring of 1865, he settled on a section of land southwest of the mission. In 1868 Gessau's relative Louis P. Chouteau became U.S. interpreter for the Osage Indians. At
General Sheridan's request, Louis Chouteau supplied the Osage scouts for Custer's regiment and assigned Gessau as their interpreter. Captain Benteen knew the interpreter
as "Yasso," while other contemporaries recorded his name as "Gesso." Westbrook 1933,
942–66; Sanders 1928, 196; Graves 1986, 253.

Before the herd was shot down Custer picked out some mules, the Osages were given what horses they wished to pick, and some others [also] selected horses for themselves.

Washita Battle. Custer gave about 50 horses to officers and picked out four fine mules for himself; and other officers [also] had captured horses.

Inq[uiry] Ben Clark. Red Moon personally was in Black Kettle's camp when Custer charged it. Who was Red Moon?[43] Cheyenne. About Jim Bridger, was he at Camp Supply at all? Don't know. Did not hear anything about him says Ben Clark. About wounded and dead Indians. What was done with wounded Indians? None taken away. All [were] killed.

Wounded Indians [at] Washita. Only one male Indian wounded and later [taken] captive, and this [was] a boy about twelve years old.[44] This was the oldest male captured. Pilan (Mex-

---

[43]Red Moon was a Southern Cheyenne married to a Sioux woman from Black Kettle's Wutapiu band. His family was camped in the village on the day of Custer's attack. Born about 1835, he was the son of Yellow Wolf, a council chief of the Hair Rope band who was murdered with his brother Big Man at Sand Creek in 1864. Red Moon, actually Red Sun, was named after a younger brother of his father. After the attack at the Washita, Red Moon led eighteen families to Camp Wichita, where they surrendered in March 1869. Known as Red Moon's band, his followers were conservative people who adhered to the traditional Cheyenne way of life, termed "non-progressive" by whites. Although Red Moon fought against buffalo hunters at Adobe Walls in 1874, he refrained from any further hostilities with whites and brought his band of one hundred people to Darlington Agency in April 1875. His successful negotiations with the remaining hostile Cheyennes led to their return to the reservation and ended the Red River War of 1874–75. By the late 1880s his band had camped along the Fort Elliott Trail, where they collected "tax" from the cattle outfits moving through the reservation. Now labeled hostile to whites, Red Moon steadfastly refused to negotiate the sale of reservation land and eventually moved his band farther away from Darlington. They settled near the present town of Hammon, not far from the Washita battlefield, where they reluctantly accepted three separate blocks of allotments. There, on the south bank of the Washita, the Red Moon School was opened in 1896, followed by the construction of a Mennonite mission in 1899. Red Moon and his Sioux wife had one son, Black Coyote, and four daughters, Sitting With, Path, Fish, and Little Sioux Woman, though some of the latter may have been adopted. His daughter Sitting With later married the Cheyenne White Shield, who eventually succeeded Red Moon as the leader of the Wutapiu. Red Moon died near Hammon on July 1, 1901. See Hyde 1968, 43, 294; Grinnell 1972, 1:234; J. H. Moore 1987, 225, 241–42, 273.

[44]Among the Washita captives was a twelve-year-old Arapaho boy named Isidore

ican) had a baby in his arms and said: "Don't kill me; me Mexican." The soldiers took the child away from him and motioned him to go on and then, when he was a little way off, shot and killed him. Pilan was totally unarmed. When Clark called his (Custer's) attention to [the] killing [of] squaws, Custer seemed to consider it as a little officiousness. I said. "General, do you want the women and children killed?" Custer hesitated and then said impulsively: "No, why?" Clark then called his attention to a company of soldiers firing on squaws who were trying to get away.

Wounded Indians at the Washita. As wounded Indians were supposed to or known to fight as long as they could, all of the wounded Indians in the fight were promptly shot to death by the soldiers without discrimination as to appearance of danger, just exactly as Indians would have treated wounded soldiers.

Inq[uiry] Ben Clark. About the squaw who killed a child, thought to be a white child, and then a soldier shot her. Yes. In [the] Kansas City Star, December 4, 1904, Clark is quoted as saying that she killed her own child. Clark says this was so. Says he had called upon these Indians to surrender, but they would not do it. First village below Black Kettle's was [an] Arapaho village, five miles down [the] Washita, on the south side.

Washita. Regarding the squaw who killed a child. One of the squaws, thus closely surrounded, pulled out a knife and ripped open the bowels of a child. A soldier, seeing this, drew his gun over the bank and shot her dead because presumably the child was a captive white one, but he made a mistake. He killed a mother, who, in despair, had killed her own child rather than see it fall into the hands of the victorious soldiers. Ben Clark, chief of scouts, has vouched for the fact that the child was an Indian.

Washita. Ben Clark says (but not to be quoted) that many of the squaws captured at the Washita were used by the officers. Says

---

Bittle, who was blind in one eye. Nicknamed Little Bittle, this boy left Fort Hays with an escort on June 4, 1868, and was released into the custody of the Arapaho chief Little Raven at Camp Supply a week later. Burkey 1976, 68, 71.

[that] Romero was put in charge of them, and on the march Romero would send squaws around to the officers' tents every night. Says Custer picked out a fine looking one and had her in his tent every night with old Mrs. —— for a guise.[45]

Benteen and Custer. Benteen wanted to find out if Elliott went off by Custer's order, or, if Custer knew he had gone at the time. About two hours after Elliott went off, Custer asked Clark if he knew where Elliott had gone and Clark told him Elliott had gone east.[46]

Ben Clark says Maj. Elliott at Washita was not scalped, but one foot and one hand [were] nearly cut off.

[Ben Clark] says that Lieut. J. M. Bell made him trade horses on one of the expeditions in 1868, Clark's horse being better and

---

[45]Clark here is referring to Mrs. Courtenay, who was Custer's cook. Sgt. John Ryan recalled that a Washita captive assisted Courtenay with her daily duties. He added that she learned to speak English fairly well and became quite a favorite with the regiment. There is no doubt that Custer was sexually involved with her. Captain Benteen recalled that Custer invited the other officers "to avail themselves of the services of a captured squaw" and that "Custer took first choice." In the margin of his copy of *My Life on the Plains,* he wrote that "Custer lived with her during the winter of '68–'69 at [Camp Wichita on] Medicine Bluff Creek, I.T." Benteen later elaborated that Dr. Rennick had caught the colonel in a compromising position with this woman and that "Custer slept with her all the time, although she was pregnant and gave birth to a male child" (n.d.[b]) on January 12, 1869, and was jokingly called "Tom" after Tom Custer, with whom she also had been sexually involved. Colonel Custer retained her services as "interpreter" from December 7, 1868, until April 17, 1869, when she was transferred to the prisoner stockade at Fort Hayes shortly before the arrival of his wife. The identity of this captive mistress was revealed by Elizabeth Custer, who called her Monahsetah (actually Meotzi, or "Spring Grass"), the daughter of Chief Little Rock, though she was known among the officers as "Sallie Ann," a name given to her by Tom Custer.

An old army expression said that "Indian women rape easy." In the case of the Washita captives, there is no doubt that the women were sexually abused and that this was common knowledge among the officers. The fact that this was not exposed at the time probably reflects a "gentleman's agreement" to keep quiet about a dark secret of the frontier army. *Newton (Mass.) Circuit,* May 21, 1909; Carroll 1974, 258, 271; Mills 1985, 177; E. B. Custer 1966, 49, 90, 97; Watson and Russell 1948b, 60; Hutton 1985, 389.

[46]Before going east in pursuit of the fleeing refugees, Elliott went back to his command at the village site to gather volunteers. This conclusion is based on Keim's statement that Sheridan's party left the village and "moved down the south bank of the Washita, over the route taken by Major Elliott and the missing men." See "Extract of Dispatch, December 11," in chapter 19.

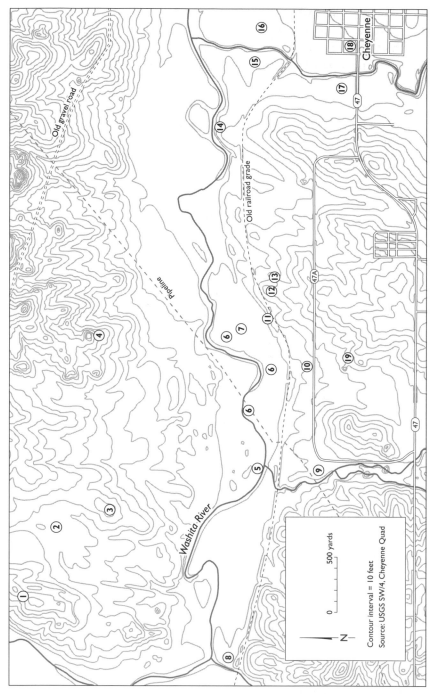

Washita Battlefield Landmarks, identified by Ben Clark.

Washita River

Old gravel road

Pipeline

Old railroad grade

Cheyenne

47

47A

47

N

500 yards

0

Contour interval = 10 feet

Source: USGS SW/4, Cheyenne Quad

1. Site of the Andrew C. Smith barn in 1910 (50 W of N), where soldiers crested the ridge.
2. Baggage site, where Jim Bruton of Shamrock, Texas, found buttons, impacted Spencer rounds, and other bullets.
3. Site of the James E. Kirkley farm in 1904, from where Osage scouts discovered the village.
4. Barnitz Hill (15 W of N), ascended by Barnitz and Elliott during night march.
5. Pony crossing, later known as Custer's Crossing.
6. Location of tepee clusters according to Magpie.
7. Village location (54 W of N) according to Ben Clark.
8. Streambed of Broken Leg Creek.
9. Streambed of Plum Creek.
10. Site of the William T. Bonner house in 1910.
11. Pony Kill Site (105 W of N).
12. Headquarters Hill.
13. Elliott Hill (69 E of S).
14. Probable location where Little Rock was killed.
15. Kill Site of lone soldier detached from Elliott's Last Stand. Camp's notes identify a different location about a mile further northeast.
16. Location most often identified as Elliott's Last Stand. Camp's notes identify a different location about a mile further northeast.
17. Present-day streambed of Sergeant Major Creek.
18. West side of City of Cheyenne.
19. The Twin Knolls, where Myers' men fired into women and children.

less used up. He submitted to Bell's order to give up the horse and take Bell's, but told Bell that if he (Bell) were not an officer, he would not obey. He told Bell [that] he considered he [Bell] was taking undue advantage of him. He and Bell did not like each other after that.

Custer [was] called Red Nose by Southern Cheyennes. Myase, or conveniently, Myes. They happened one time to see him when he had his nose sunburned. Sheridan was called Three Stars, Hotahci o Niis (pronounced Nice), [or,] Hotahcio Nys. Cheyenne has no sound of r and f.

Landmarks of the Washita Battlefield
(as Identified by Ben Clark)[47]

Village was in NE 1/4 Sec. 12, Twp. 13 N, Range 24 W. Bluff where [Custer] shot ponies [is] right near NE [corner] of Mr. W. T. Bonner's house. It rises at south edge of that piece of land on which village stood. Bearings [taken] from Headquarters Hill where monument is [in 1910], to hill from which Maj. Elliott started to pursue Indians is 69 degrees E of South. To Barnitz Sugar Loaf Hill on N side of river [is] 15 degrees W of North. To barn near which Custer halted command when [they] first were aware of the village is 50 degrees W of N. The command was halted on flat ground right north of this barn. This barn is on [the] place of A. C. Smith ([in] 1910). Flat where [command] halted between 1 A.M. and daylight [was] on Frank Turner's place. It is on flat ground lower than the barn, and north of barn. To bluffs where ponies [were] shot [is] 105 degrees W of N, or 74 W of S. To center of village is 54 [degrees] W of N. Distance from Bonner's gate to section corner in Cheyenne [is] 1 1/2 miles along half section line (exact distance). This road [is] east and west right through middle of section 12.

---

[47]Walter M. Camp's field notes are housed in Box 3 (Battle of the Washita), Camp Manuscripts, Indiana University Library, Bloomington; they are reproduced by special permission.

The river bends sharply to the north, and from the bluffs where the horses were shot, out to the bend, the area is about 30 acres. The village was in the northwest corner of the bend and consisted of about sixty lodges. Sheridan's account says 51 lodges.

L. M. Sheppard & Co., El Reno, Oklahoma. Blue print map, Roger Mills Co[unty], Oklahoma. Elliott [was] killed in SE 1/4 Sec. 5, Town[ship] 13 N, R[ange] 23 W.[48] It is 2 1/2 miles straight east of Black Kettle's village.

Letter to Frederick S. Barde
May 1, 1903[49]

Fort Reno, O.T. May 1, '03

Mr. Barde,

Dear Sir: I hav'nt seen the story you mention, though if you have the paper I would like to look at it.

We found Mrs. Blinn's and her child's body where an Arapaho village had been camped at the time of the attack on Black Kettle's camp. The Arapaho village stood on the east side of the river, 4 or 5 miles below the Black Kettle village. It was afterwards said that in the excitement of the Indians hurrying to get their families out of danger, one of the Indian women killed her.[50]

---

[48]Today Sergeant Major Creek enters the Washita in the southwest corner of Section 5. In 1910, however, it curved east just before reaching the Washita and ran parallel with the river for a mile. The streams then joined in the southeast corner of Section 5. This parallel flow probably existed in 1868 and continued until 1934, when the Hammon flood changed the course of Sergeant Major Creek and formed the present channel. The discovery of artifacts suggests that the Elliott death site was farther upstream (south), in the northwest corner of Section 8. Ammunition, gun parts, uniform fragments, metal arrowheads, and military equipage are said to have been recovered in the early days along the east side of Sergeant Major Creek in an area about a quarter-mile long. But more-recent surveys by Jim Bruton in the 1970s and the National Park Service in 1997 have failed to locate the Elliott site. Channel cutting and the filling in of Sergeant Major Creek by landowners, the leveling of adjacent land, and the destructive forces of nature may well have destroyed the historic site. Briscoe and Watkins 1990, 4; Bruton to the author, Jan. 17, Jan. 29, 2004; Lees et al. 2001, 175.

[49]This letter is from the Frederick S. Barde Collection, Oklahoma Historical Society, Oklahoma City; it is reproduced by special permission.

[50]Clara Blinn and her son, Willie, were killed in Yellow Bear's Arapaho camp on the morning of Custer's attack. During the rush to take down Yellow Bear's lodge, the little

When we came on the second Expedition from Camp Supply (which was commanded by Sheridan in person) we struck the Washita where it bends the farthest north, some six miles or so below the Black Kettle camp.

In the search being made for the Elliott party, Mrs. Blinn's body was found. She had been captured by an Arapaho war party. I was out scouting the day she was buried, but I understood she was buried where the soldiers of the Elliott party were; that is, just above or west of our camp.[51]

I have never heard whether Mr. Blinn had her body removed afterwards or not.

As the Expedition went into camp in the latter part of Dec. 1868 on Medicine Bluff Creek and as Gen. Sheridan soon after determined on establishing a post there, and did so, (Fort Sill), I think the soldiers' bodies were taken to Sill and possibly Mrs. Blinn. As I have never been stationed at Sill, being assigned to Camp Supply in April 1869, and I never thought of inquiring or looking in the cemetery at Sill, I can't say for sure where the bodies were finally taken.[52]

Truly yours,
[Signed:] Ben Clark

----

boy was in the way of the women and was killed along with his mother, who refused to leave her son's remains behind. Undated *Star* clipping, Blinn Collection.

[51]The remains of the Blinn victims were taken to Fort Arbuckle and buried in the post cemetery on December 25, 1868. The following January Clara's grief-stricken husband, Richard, visited the graves and built a sturdy fence around them. Richard Blinn died on September 18, 1873, from tuberculosis (and perhaps a broken heart). Justus 2000, 19; Ross 1988, 47.

[52]After the abandonment of Fort Arbuckle in 1870, the remains of Clara Blinn and her son were exhumed and transferred to the Fort Gibson National Cemetery, established in 1868 on land donated by the Cherokee Nation. The Blinn graves are identified as No. 2216, "Unknown Woman," and No. 2211, "Unknown." In a strange twist of fate, their burial sites are located not far from marker No. 2233, which identifies Maj. Joel H. Elliott's grave. The remains of Elliott's men were never exhumed. While camped near the mass grave on March 11, 1869, Pvt. Winfield S. Harvey wrote in his diary, "The bones of our dead lay all over the ground; the wolves dug them up and ate off all of the flesh of them." Harvey's company was then camped at Inman's supply depot, which was established about five miles downstream from the Washita battlefield. Justus 2000, 18; Interment Register, Fort Gibson National Cemetery, Okla.; Shirk 1959, 102; Runyan 1940, 72.

19

DeB. Randolph Keim,
New York Herald

DeBenneville Randolph Keim was a correspondent for the New York
Herald *and accompanied Sheridan's staff during the winter campaign
of 1868. He recorded his impressions in numerous dispatches and a book,*
Sheridan's Troopers on the Border, *which was published in 1870.
Born in 1841 in Reading, Pennsylvania, Keim was an ambitious
reporter who spent three years covering the Civil War for the* Herald.
*He had been at Vicksburg with Grant, had marched with Sherman
during the Atlanta campaign, and had been at Richmond in 1865 to
report on the closing days of the war. He was confident, self-assured,
and opinionated and was considered a veteran reporter, having filed
dispatches from twenty-six battlefields.*

*After his Indian wars assignment, Keim became a Washington
correspondent for the* Herald *and other papers. His position was solid-
ified by a confidential relationship with President Grant, which was
established at Vicksburg during the war. He was said to have been the
only reporter who had access to the White House during the Grant
administration.*

*The excerpted dispatches that follow describe Custer's fight and
Keim's visit to the battleground. They were published in the* New York
Herald *on December 24 and 26, 1868, and January 4, 1869.*

Extract of Dispatch, December 1
Published December 24, 1868

Yesterday a courier from General Custer announced that his
column would encamp that night within ten miles of this point
[Camp Supply], and would be in this morning. Every one was

more than anxious to see the victors of the Washita, and it was with considerable impatience the appearance of his column was looked for. The day was a bright one, and the temperature, materially affected by the moderating influence of the sun, gave additional interest to the anticipated display. Shortly after the sun had passed its meridian a cluster of dark and almost indefinable objects appearing upon the crest of a hill about a mile distant, simultaneously accompanied with shouts and the firing of musketry, announced the approach of the column. The mules and horses grazing in the valleys nearby hearing these unusual sounds stampeded from all directions towards camp, as if by instinct, interpreting these demonstrations of triumph for the defiant shouts of hostility. On the summit of the hill the head of the column halted a few moments. Meanwhile General Sheridan, accompanied by Brevet Brigadier General J. W. Forsyth,[1] Brevet Lieutenant Colonel A. J. McGonnigle[2] and Dr. Morris J. Asch, Surgeon, all of the staff, and a number of officers of the garrison here, took position in the valley to await the column, which the commanding general was to witness in passing review. At the same time Brevet Lieutenant Colonels J. Schuyler Crosby and T. W. C. Moore,[3] of the staff, were to conduct the column by proper line of march. All

---

[1]James William Forsyth was an aide to General Sheridan and brother of George A. "Sandy" Forsyth of Beecher Island fame. Born in Ohio in 1834, he graduated from West Point in 1856 and was assigned to frontier posts in Washington Territory until 1861. He returned east to serve in the Civil War and was mustered out of volunteer service in 1866 as a brevet brigadier general of volunteers. Afterward he became major of the Tenth Cavalry but was reassigned to Sheridan's staff in 1868 at the rank of lieutenant colonel. Serving as a military secretary through 1878, Forsyth was assigned to the First Cavalry until 1886, when he was promoted to colonel of the Seventh Cavalry. In 1890 he commanded the Seventh in the last conflict with the Sioux, seeing action at Wounded Knee and White Clay Creek, South Dakota. Forsyth died in 1906.

[2]Andrew Jackson McGonnigle served during the Civil War as a captain in the Quartermaster Department. In March 1867 he received promotions up to the rank of lieutenant colonel for gallantry at Fisher's Hill, Cedar Creek, Five Forks, Sailor's Creek, and Appomattox. Assigned to Sheridan's staff in 1868, he was promoted to colonel in February 1869 for meritorious services against the Indians during the winter campaign. McGonnigle retired in March 1893 and died on January 25, 1901.

[3]Thomas William Channing Moore entered the Civil War as a private in the Twenty-First Wisconsin Infantry but was honorably mustered out in August 1866 with brevets up to lieutenant colonel for gallant and meritorious services at Todd's Tavern and Cedar Creek. Upon the reorganization of the regular army, he was appointed a sec-

the officers and soldiers not on duty assembled in the vicinity of the fort to witness the warlike pageant. The column now resumed its march, and as it descended the hill the flashing of sabres and carbines and the shouts of the men were in wild counterpart of the dreary surroundings of their departure from this point about a week since. The column was now within a short distance of the commanding general; the Indians shouted, the band reiterated the stirring tones of "Garryowen" and the troopers cheered. In response rounds of huzzas from the troops of the fort shouted welcome and congratulations. In the advance were the Osage Indian trailers. Before leaving camp this morning they had arrayed and decorated themselves in a manner becoming the importance of the occasion. Their faces were painted in the most fantastic and hideous designs. About their persons were dangling the trophies which they had captured in battle. Spears, upon which were fastened the scalps of their Indian foe, were slung upon their shoulders; from their own plaited scalp locks were suspended long trails of silver ornaments and feathers; over their shoulders hung shields and bows and quivers full of arrows, while in one hand they held their trusty rifle and with the other grasped the reins. Even the animals which the Osages bestrode were decorated with scalps and strips of red and blue blankets. At the head of the little band rode Little Beaver, the chief, with a countenance as fixed as stone. Yet, in his bearing showing indications of an inward self-glorification, which was apparently kept stirring and swelling higher and higher by gesticulations and wild notes of the war songs shouted by his warriors, intermingled with whoops and the discharge of rifles. In a moment of enthusiasm the chief shouted, "They call us Americans; we are Osages," to which sentiment went up a responsive yell of approval. Conspicuous in this party was the young Osage warrior Koom-la-Manche (Trotter). It was he, under the impulse of the highest ambition of Indian valor, that singled out the great chief Black Kettle, the terror of all the Osages, as his victim. After a severe conflict he reached the crowning point of his efforts, and

---

ond lieutenant in the Eleventh Infantry but was transferred shortly thereafter to the Fortieth Infantry with the rank of captain before assignment to Sheridan's staff in 1868. Moore was honorably discharged in August 1870 and died on November 6, 1881.

bore away the ghastly scalp of the terrible chief as the trophy attaching [attesting?] to his success.[4] With a mark of special attention this scalp was carefully and fantastically decorated and hung prominently among the most sacred possessions of the young warrior.

Following the Indians were the scouts, led by California Joe, a veteran pioneer of over forty years. Joe is a hirsute-looking specimen of humanity, exhibiting an altitude of six feet, a mat of red whiskers hiding two-thirds of his face, and a long, knotty head of hair, well powdered in a series of coats of dust, intermixed with stray blades of grass, leaves and sticks as the vestiges of his previous night's slumber upon the bosom of Mother Earth. Joe was a suitable figurehead for his motley band of curiously clad, brave, adventurous and rugged men. Next came General Custer, riding alone, mounted on a magnificent black stallion, and dressed in a short, blue sack coat trimmed with the color of his arm of service, with fur collar and cuffs; on his head was an otter cap. When General Custer came within fifty yards of the commanding general he left his position in the column and dashed up to his chief, when a warm and hearty exchange of salutation was made between the commander and his distinguished and successful lieutenant. General Custer was followed in the column by the members of his staff, arranged in platoon: First Lieutenant M. Moylan, Assistant Adjutant-General; First Lieutenant S. M. Robbins; Brevet Major J. M. Bell; Brevet Captain A. E. Smith, after whom came the mounted band.

Next followed the living evidences of the victory—over fifty squaws and their children, surrounded by a suitable guard to prevent their escape. These were mounted on their own ponies, seating themselves astride the animals, their persons wrapped in skins and blankets, even their heads and faces being covered, leaving nothing visible but their eyes. The mothers had their offspring mounted behind them, the papoose being visible only by its diminutive head, peering up over the back of the head of its mother. As many as three

---

[4]Yet Charles Brill (1938, 25) claims that Black Kettle was not scalped, naming Chief Magpie as his source of information.

were mounted on some of the ponies. Without a sight, without a glance to the right or left, these remnants of the band of the once powerful Black Kettle followed with all the submission of captives. Following them came the keen-sighted sharpshooters, commanded by Brevet Lieutenant Colonel W. W. Cook[e], and following them the bravest men of the different companies of the regiment, in column by platoons, under their proper officers.

On a separate line of march from the summit came the wagon train pouring over the hill. In the lead were the ambulances conveying the dead and wounded. The train was formed in a double column, and in the centre were the led ponies.

The regiment moved up the Beaver about half a mile from the fort and there went into camp. The scene during the remainder of the day was that of a joyous holiday. Officers and men recounted the perils and hardships of the march and the battle and exhibited the trophies which had been saved from the burning village. General Custer's Sibley raised its cone-like outlines in the centre; on the left, a hundred yards off, were the prisoners, the Osages and the scouts; in front, the long lines of picketed horses and the wall and shelter tents of officers and men.

Returning now to the operations of the advancing column [on November 26, 1868], having crossed the Canadian River General Custer sent a detachment under Major Joel H. Elliott up the river to reconnoitre for trail and with orders, should any such exhibitions of the presence of Indians be discovered, that a courier should be sent back with the announcement of the gratifying intelligence. Meanwhile, General Custer, with the main column, would proceed down the stream and encamp at a distance of five or six miles. Hardly had General Custer reached his camp for the day than couriers came dashing in, informing him that a trail hardly twenty-four hours old had been found in the snow and leading southward. Everything was now excitement, and officers and men were anxious and ready to abandon the few comforts they had with them to set out in pursuit. While Major Elliott kept the trail at a trot, General Custer, leaving the train and all tents in charge of Lieutenant E. G. Mathey, with a guard of eighty men, and taking but a few wagons containing three days' rations, started cross country. Fortunately the General struck Major Elliott's column. The entire command now hastened forward at the utmost speed the animals could endure. When the report of the Osage trailers of the discovery of the village reached General Custer's ears the General, with several officers, crept up stealthily to the crest of a hill overlooking the village. At first he doubted the authenticity of the Osages' report. The light of the moon was not sufficiently bright to enable him to define the dark objects which he saw in the valley. At first he remarked they were buffaloes, as it was an extraordinary occurrence to get so close to a village without an alarm being given. In his opinion that the objects they saw were buffaloes the General had also the like opinions of the officers with him. All were as silent as if the presence of a hostile force were not there to break the wild solitude of the scene. Suddenly the distant tingling of a bell broke upon the alert ears of the party. This slight and welcome sound solved the mystery. The Osage chief repeated his words, "Heap ponies." The General, turning to those with them, said in a whisper, "I am satisfied they are ponies, the herd of the village. Buffaloes are not in the habit of wearing such ornaments as bells in this country." The party now returned and fearing that the untimely neigh of a horse or some unusual sound might signal their presence to the sleeping savages the column was withdrawn for a distance. The men were ordered to stand by their horses and [were] not allowed to build fires or even to stamp their feet for fear of defeating the success of the attack. A small detachment of dismounted men were left to watch the village, with instructions to attack immediately should the savages show any sign of suspicion by issuing from their lodges.

General Custer now took his principal officers with him to a point giving an idea of the village. He then explained to each officer what he proposed as a plan of attack. The village lay upon the south bank of the Washita. The Cheyenne lodges were in the centre, the Arapahoes above and the Sioux below, all ranging along the banks of the stream. The nature of the ground, as it could be indistinctly traced by moonlight, seemed to indicate that the village was accessible from all points. The General and his officers now retired to a ravine near the column and determined upon the following plan of attack. Four columns, composed as follows, were to attack the village from different directions:—

Right column—Companies B and F, Brevet Colonel William Thompson commanding; Captain G. W. Yates, Lieutenants D. M. Wallingfort and F. M. Gibson on duty with column.

Right centre column—[Companies E and I,] Brevet Lieutenant Colonel Edward Myers commanding; Brevet [Captain] Charles Brewster and First Lieutenant J. M. Johnson on duty with column.

Centre column—Companies A, D, C and K, Brevet Major General George A. Custer commanding in person; First Lieutenants M. M. Moylan [and] G. M. Robbins, Brevet Major J. M. Bell, Brevet Captain R. M. West, Captain L. M. Hamilton, Brevet Lieutenant Colonel T. B. Weir, Brevet Lieutenant Colonel T. W. Custer, Brevet Captain M. Berry and Lieutenants E. S. Godfrey and Ed. Law on duty with column. A detachment of sharpshooters, under Brevet Lieutenant Colonel W. W. Cook[e], with centre column.

Left column—Companies G, H and M, Major Joel H. Elliott commanding; Brevet Lieutenant Colonel F. W. Benteen, Lieutenants Owen Hale and H. W. Smith on duty with column.[5]

The signal was to be the firing of a shot, or the gray of dawn if beyond hearing. The columns took position, and at the preconcerted time every command began its appointed offensive. As the cavalry came dashing towards the village Black Kettle broke from his bed of robes and in an instant appeared without [outside?] his lodge. He had heard the trampling of horses on the snow. He looked around him and, witnessing the approaching columns, fired his rifle and gave one wild whoop. Each warrior, springing up as if by magic, seized his rifle and responded to the yell of despair which broke from the lips of the chief. Some of the warriors fled to the river and began fighting at the same time, standing waist deep in the water; others took to a ravine nearby. The squaws fled towards the high hills south of the village. It was as the centre column was charging down the precipitous bluffs to cross the river and take the village that Captain Hamilton was killed. When struck he gave one convulsive start, stiffened in his stirrups and

---

[5]The dispatch fails to list Bvt. Lt. Col. Albert Barnitz and 2nd Lt. Thomas J. March.

was thus carried a corpse for a distance of several yards, when he fell from his horse, striking upon his face, which was from this cause terribly lacerated and disfigured. Colonel Barnitz fell, seriously wounded, while charging with Elliott's column up the river. As the fight became general each man picked his antagonist and started for him. It was after this mode of fighting had commenced that Major Elliott, with the Sergeant Major of the regiment and a handful of men, started down the river after a small band of Indians. During the excitement of the fight the Major was not missed. At one time heavy firing was heard at a distance, which was supposed to be signals to the village below. When the conflict lulled the question was carried along the line, "Where is Elliott? Where is Elliott?" The only reply was that he was last seen charging some fugitives fleeing down the river. There is now no doubt that he and his party struck the approaching Kiowas and Arapahoes coming to the rescue of the Cheyennes and were cut off by them. There is no question that each man of this ill-fated band sold his life as dearly as possible and died at his post. For these unfortunate men there was no possibility of escape. Their alternative was death by some friendly bullet or death by the horrible torture which the hellish ingenuity of the savage alone can invent.

Before the fight the Osage Indians seemed to have some misgivings as to their own part in the affair. It is known they hesitated, and for some cause or other they took it into their heads that our troops would there dictate a peace, and that ten Osage warriors, to be given to the Cheyennes, were to be the price of so dishonorable transaction. The Osages, not to be caught, determined to fight on horseback. The chief, Little Beaver, took position behind the color-bearer of the regiment and followed him. After the fight was over and the victory complete the Osages were probably the proudest of savages. They saw they had mistaken the sincerity of the whites in securing and using their services according to the stipulations. After the fight had commenced a party of Osages discovered the squaws trying to escape. They immediately started in pursuit, and, seizing switches gave the fugitives a severe whipping, telling them if they tried to escape again they would give them another beating. After this exercise of authority the squaws became exceedingly submissive and made no further efforts to get away, and have since manifested the greatest terror of the Osages.

While the fight was the thickest a diminutive person closely wrapped in a blanket took refuge among the squaws. At that time Lieutenant H. W. Smith was charging by, followed by a bugler. He ordered the bugler not to fire upon the woman. Hardly had the words fallen from his lips than an arrow was seen to take its flight from beneath the blanket of the diminutive figure, taking effect on the right temple of the bugler and ranging around, the blade tearing the scalp half the circumference of the head. The wound had the appearance of producing a contusion of the skull, but upon examination it was discovered to be merely a laceration of the scalp.[6] In retaliation as he rode by, the wound not having dismounted him, the bugler despatched the individual who had wounded him. The diminutive figure was found to be that of an old man and from under his blanket was taken a bow and quiver full of arrows. A number of squaws also participated in the fight, and were seen firing with all the energy and precision of warriors. The encounter between Colonel Benteen and the son of Black Kettle was at close quarters and quite hot for some time. Colonel Benteen made an effort to capture the young warrior, who responded to these overtures of humanity by refusing to surrender, and fired several times at the Colonel when but a few yards distant. His escape was miraculous, one ball taking effect upon the Colonel's horse, killing him. The young warrior made a rush at the prostrate officer, but was arrested in his murderous design by being despatched with a pistol.

It would be impossible to enumerate the hairbreadth escapes and hand to hand encounters which were had with the Cheyenne

---

[6]H. Walworth Smith was a second lieutenant in M Company. Although the identity of the injured bugler is not given, it has been presumed that he was assigned to the same unit. Lippincott's medical report does indeed list a bugler from M Company, John Murphy, who sustained a severe arrow wound, but the injury is listed as a chest wound, which is confirmed by Sgt. John Ryan, who attended to Murphy during his convalescence (1909, Apr. 9). Custer also mentions the head trauma described by Keim, so there can be no doubt as to the location of the injury. The only casualty listed with an arrow wound in the head (right temple) was Pvt. Daniel Morrison of G Company and was probably the trooper referred to by Keim and Custer. See "Extract from *My Life on the Plains*" in chapter 6.

warriors. The appearance of the Kiowa and Arapahoe warriors from the villages below was an unexpected attempt at rescue. The fighting for several ensuing hours was even increased in desperation. Brevet Lieutenant Colonel Weir was detached with his squadron to encounter the fresh warriors who had now come upon the field. The Kiowas and Arapahoes fought with unusual courage, maintaining, however, the customary mode of Indian fighting, circling around and making dashes upon vulnerable points. When the savage allies of the Cheyennes saw that their effort could be of no avail they took to flight, seeking their own safety.

On the morning of the discovery of the first signs of Indians the Osage chief, through the medium of some superstition, remarked to General Custer that Indians would be seen that day. To the credit of this mysterious prompter the Osage was right. During the pursuit the same day at sunset the Osage chief again said to the General, through the interpreter, that the signs were favorable, that the sun had gone down covered in a slight haze, which was an omen always when the Osages went to battle that they would be successful, or, in his own words, "It was good medicine." Prior to the fight one of the Osages was in mourning for the murder of his squaw some months before by a party of Cheyennes. Every night and morning he kept up his wail of grief. When the fight began, while all his companions were covered with war paint and presented more the appearance of so many devils rather than human beings, the mourning warrior sat down mumbling over his mournful strains. He was not painted. As soon as the conflict began in earnest an Osage warrior, having shot a Cheyenne, rushed upon his fallen foe and in an instant with his knife severed the head from the body. With a wild whoop he took the ghastly object to the mourning warrior and threw it down before him. The warrior seized the trunkless head and in an instant had the scalp. His bowl of blood was full. As if by magic the face of the sorrowing warrior was bedaubed with war paint. Starting to his feet he gave one yell, and, waving the proprietary scalp in mid air, he cast his woes aside and disappeared in the thickest of the fray. A few moments after, the same warrior was seen standing over the lifeless form of a Cheyenne warrior. He had discovered the murderer of his squaw. Stooping, knife in hand, he was about to take the scalp, when he discovered it had already been taken. Such an expression of fiendish disappointment was probably never exceeded. Raising himself full length, with spasmodic and fearful emphasis he articulated, "Ugh, ugh." Frantically again gesticulating he fell upon the body with the ferocity of a beast of prey and severed the throat from ear to ear. Again he stood erect, his whole frame quivering with rage. Once more he fell upon the lifeless body and, this time completely severing the head from the trunk, now took his knife between his teeth, then clutched the gory head in both hands and raising it high above him dashed it upon the ground at his feet with an imprecation and a convulsion of his entire frame.

During the fight, after the squaws and children had been beaten back by the Osages, they were placed for safe keeping in a lodge. As the number was considered too great for one lodge General Custer directed that they should be divided, part to be put in another lodge. When told that they were to be separated those designated started out. The remainder became panic-stricken and like so many sheep crowded to the exit and rushed out until the lodge was quite empty. When they got out into the open air and could see their warriors fighting all around them they set up a mournful wail, which was answered by the warriors from the hills. Hitherto the warriors shouted defiance. When they found their families were in possession of the troops their shouts were changed to mourning and they seemed to realize that the star of Black Kettle's band of Cheyennes had set.

The very ponies of the village seemed to feel an instinctive hostility towards the white man. Repeated efforts were made to take them, but they eluded capture, and when taken struggled violently to be released. As time was now precious a few squaws were sent out to bring in what they could catch. The ponies now recovered from their frantic efforts to escape. The squaws walked up to them, the animals quietly submitting to be bridled and saddled, but displaying a disposition to fight whenever a white man came near. About 200 ponies were thus taken and brought in, while over 700 were shot to prevent their being retaken by other Indian bands. Next to the loss of a warrior or a squaw the savage laments the loss of a pony.

The troops had won a great victory. The General commanding the expedition found, after a brief pursuit, that to overtake the Kiowas and Arapahoes would involve a long pursuit. His train was some miles in the rear and, being guarded by a mere handful of men, he feared an attack by the Indians getting in the rear, and as it was a question whether so few men could prevent at least the destruction of a portion of the train, he therefore returned, and found to his satisfaction that though the wagons had made but little progress the train was intact.

On the return trip no Indians were seen. They were evidently in great alarm at the just and terrible punishment meted to the Cheyennes. It was anticipated that at least a small party would follow, in order to watch the movements of the column; but such was not the case. Night and morning the prisoners set up their mourning songs, but received no response from warriors lurking about the camp. While thus giving vent to their grief the sister and niece of Black Kettle,[7] who were also taken, passed among the sorrowing party, placing their hands upon the head of each, simultaneously repeating a few sounds. At the first camp on the return, according to custom, the Osages hung their scalps outside their tents and fired several volleys over them. They have a superstition that such demonstrations of hostility drive away the spirits of those from whom the scalps were taken, and that in the event of the neglect of so important a precaution these spirits would come and rob them of their hard-earned and ghastly evidences of their prowess. Another rather singular superstition was witnessed before the column arrived. Before the fall of the snow the Osages were sitting in their usual sullen manner around their campfire. One of them suddenly espied a few yards off a whirlwind stirring up sand and sticks. The Osage jumped up and was followed by half a dozen of the warriors. The warriors kicked forcibly at the whirlwind until it disappeared. Upon inquiry the warriors said the whirlwind was the spirit of an Arapahoe warrior who had been killed on the Solomon, and was then on its way south to alarm the

---

[7]The name of this sister was Mahwissa (Red Hair), who actually may have been a sister-in-law or cousin to Black Kettle. His niece was Meotzi (Spring Grass), daughter of Little Rock. Dyer 1896, 96.

tribe of the approach of danger, but they had now driven the spirit away. The Osages having been promised all the Indian ponies they could capture, the niece and sister of Black Kettle were told [of] the fact. They replied with an air of contempt, "Let them have them; the Osages are poor."

Extract of Dispatch, December 4
Published December 26, 1868

Captain Louis M. Hamilton, killed in the battle of the Washita, was buried this afternoon with military honors. The entire regular troops at present have turned out here. The body of the deceased captain was carried in an ambulance as a hearse and covered with a large American flag. The ambulance was preceded by Captain Hamilton's squadron, commanded by Brevet Lieutenant Colonel Weir, as escort, and was followed by his horse, covered by a mourning sheet. Major General Sheridan, Brevet Major General Custer, Brevet Lieutenant Colonels Crosby, Cooke[e] and T. W. Custer; Brevet Major Beebe and Lieutenant Hale acted as pall-bearers.

A meeting of the officers of the Seventh United States Cavalry was held in the camp of the regiment, on the north fork of the Canadian River, Indian Territory, the 3rd day of December, 1868, to take into consideration the untimely death of Major Joel H. Elliott, of the regiment, who was killed in the battle of the Washita, November 27, 1868, and to testify by resolution the respect and estimation in which the deceased was held by his comrades in arms. Brevet Major General George A. Custer was chosen to preside over the meeting, and a committee was appointed to draft resolutions. The following were reported by the committee:—

Resolved, That the officers and soldiers of the Seventh United States Cavalry unite in their expression of sincere and profound sorrow for the death of Major Joel H. Elliott, who was killed in the battle of the Washita, November 27, 1868. That his earnest devotion to duty and to the best interest of the service, renders his death a loss to the profession and to the regiment which he had labored so zealously to improve.

Resolved, That in all the vicissitudes of his eventful life, from the ranks where he first served as a soldier during the late war to the position he had attained when he died, our lamented Major performed all the duties and obligations of his station with rare fidelity and truthfulness; that his correct example is worthy of imitation by every one who aims at distinction in the profession of arms.

Resolved, That the gallant bearing of Major Elliott in the battle which brought him suddenly to the end of his earthly career is deserving of the highest praise; that he fell in the attitude of defiant daring, heroically rallying his men, and by example inciting them to deeds of valor worthy of the greatest encomiums that can be bestowed.

Resolved, That to the bereaved mother and relatives of the deceased the officers of this regiment especially tender their heartfelt sympathies.

Resolved, That the secretary of this meeting be directed to send a copy of these proceedings to the family of the deceased.

The report of the committee was adopted and the meeting adjourned *sine die.*

A meeting of the officers of the Seventh United States Calvary was held in the camp of the regiment, on the north fork of the Canadian River, Indian Territory, on the 4th day of December, 1868, to take into consideration the untimely death of Captain Louis M. Hamilton, of that regiment, who was killed in the battle of the Washita, November 27, 1868, and to testify by resolution the respect and estimation in which the deceased was held by his comrades in arms. Brevet Major General Custer was chosen to preside over the meeting, and a committee was appointed to draft resolutions. The following was reported by the committee:—

Resolved, That the death in battle of our late comrade, Captain Louis Hamilton, has bereft us of a dear and valued friend, whom while living we cherished as a rare and gifted gentleman of unsullied honor and spotless fame; that we miss the genial face, the sparking wit, the well tried, warm and trusty heart of him whose loss we mourn more deeply than words can tell.

Resolved, That by the death of the heroic Hamilton the army has lost one of the brightest soldiers; that he was a thorough, gallant soldier, with heart and hand in his work, whose highest aim was to be perfect, "without fear and without reproach," in all things pertaining to his profession; that among the brilliant soldiers who were selected after the closest scrutiny from the armies of the East and West for the new army which was organized at the close of the late war, our Lieutenant Hamilton stood in the foremost rank; that the genius of his mind and the qualities of his heart stamped him as one of the purest and brightest soldiers of his years and time; that his blameless life and glorious death entitle him to a place among the departed heroes of his race.

Resolved, That the patriotic ardor and devotion to country and duty which rendered the grandsire, Alexander Hamilton, illustrious, were truthfully perpetuated in his grandson, the best efforts of whose life were directed toward the reestablishment of the government which his progenitor had aided to build, whose life blood was shed in visiting just retribution upon those who had savagely outraged every principle of humanity and who persistently refused to recognize the authority of that government which he had learned from infancy to venerate and for the supremacy of which he had fought on many famous fields.

Resolved, That the officers and soldiers of the Seventh Cavalry do hereby express their heartfelt sympathy with all who mourn the loss of the deceased. Especially do they tender the same to his relatives and family friends.

Resolved, That the secretary of this meeting be directed to transmit a copy of these proceedings to the relatives of the deceased.

The report of the committee was approved and the meeting adjourned *sine die*.

During the first few days of the captivity of the squaws of Black Kettle's band of Cheyennes there was considerable anxiety felt by them. They all expected they were to be killed in retaliation of the atrocities committed by their band. At first the wounded ones refused to go to the hospital, fearing they were the first singled out for vengeance. The soldiers talking to each other not in tones the most gentle and euphonious and in a language they could not understand, they construed it into a controversy as to when and how they were to be disposed of. In constant dread of what disposition was to be made of them several of the squaws visited General

Sheridan's interpreter, Mr. Curtis,[8] and asked him whether they
were all to be killed. When assured that the white man did not kill
women and children for what the warriors did they felt materially
relieved. Since then the wounded squaws have appeared more
lively and exhibit an unusual feeling of gratitude for the kind treatment they have been receiving. This feeling they manifested by
shaking hands with the surgeon whenever he visits them. The most
remarkable instances of fortitude are exhibited in the cases of the
wounded Indian children. The desperation of the fighting at the
battle of the Washita on the part of the savages may be judged from
the fact that no male prisoners were taken over eight years old, the
rest taking up arms and joining in the fight. There are now in the
hospital several very young boys and girls badly wounded, but from
not a single one of them has come the slightest audible indication
of their suffering; yet the expression of their faces, the wild glances
of their eyes, betray that they do suffer. During such painful operations as probing and cleaning out their wounds, placing the thumb
on one temple and stretching the hand across the forehead, fixing
the second finger on the temple opposite, they close their eyes and
patiently submit to such operations as the teachings of surgery
require. One little girl about six years of age has a bullet hole
through her body, on the left side, and yet she sits up and makes no
complaints. All the wounded squaws and children rode in on their
ponies, refusing to have anything to do with ambulances. Another
singular feature in the wounded is the peculiarly offensive odor of
the sloughing wounds. The well squaws are still encamped with the
cavalry and seem to be contended with their lot. The male children
amuse themselves throwing reeds as if they were spears at different

---

[8]A native of Onaudague County, New York, Dick Curtis was employed by both the
Indian Bureau and the U.S. Army. In the fall of 1865, he served as chief of scouts for
General Sherman and the Indian commissioners during the treaty negotiations with
the Kiowas and Comanches at Council Springs, Kansas. In 1867 he served at Fort
Larned as an interpreter for Col. Edward Wynkoop and accompanied the Hancock
expedition as an employee of the Indian Bureau. After Wynkoop's resignation, Curtis
was hired by the military and assigned to Camp Supply as post interpreter. Married to
a Sioux woman, he was described by a contemporary as "a shrewd, plain man, up to all
the tricks of the Indians, and thoroughly conversant with their dialect." Curtis died
about 1872. Davis 1867.

objects, thus displaying the cultivation of their expanding merit as future warriors.

Among the trophies brought in was a handsome lodge, which belongs to General Custer. Today this was unloaded from the wagon, and having sent for several squaws the General had the lodge put up in true Indian style. This is part of the duties of the squaws, and in a very few minutes they displayed their proficiency to an extent which surprised every one. The lodge is of skins and perfectly white. It is not at all surprising that the loss of their lodges is looked upon by the squaws as so great a calamity. The number of skins, the proper tanning of them, fitting and stitching them together constitute evidently a labor and expense of considerable magnitude. In setting up a lodge the squaws get around with the lodge poles in their hands; these they lock at the proper extremities and set them in position forming the skeleton of the lodge. The lodge skin, one end attached to a pole, is laid in an upright position against the lodge poles already up; the skin is then unrolled and wrapped around the outside of the lodge poles. The ends are then fastened with thongs, leaving an aperture about three feet high for an entrance and at the top for the egress of smoke.

The captives, sick and well, have not lost appetite or flesh since in our hands. Their capacities for stowing away food are truly amazing. Hardtack to them is a great luxury, and old and young, sick and well, devour it with all the relish of the choicest and richest cake.

Extract of Dispatch, December 6
Published December 26, 1868

Brevet Major Henry Inman, who left here with a train of two hundred and fifty wagons, returned yesterday from Fort Dodge, after a trip of two hundred and ten miles in twelve days. Arriving at Mulberry Creek the Major found a piece of pantaloons covered with blood, a coat filled with bullet holes and other signs of a fight. Reaching a ravine nearby a pack of thirty wolves started up. A number of letters were now found strewn around, one of which was a despatch from your correspondent, dated at Bluff Creek, November 18, 1868. The despatch was returned to your correspondent by

Major Inman, and was considerably torn, evidently by the wolves. On the morning of November 18, before leaving Bluff Creek, General Sheridan sent two couriers to Fort Dodge with despatches. It would appear that these couriers fell into an ambuscade while crossing Mulberry Creek, which vicinity is much broken by ravines covered with underbrush. On his return Major Inman, after diligent search, found fragments of the bodies. One skull was broken as if struck by a tomahawk. The fight was evidently a desperate one. The route of the couriers could be traced for a mile by the empty cartridge shells. A tree was discovered with the head of a spear sticking in it and full of bullet holes. It is probable the couriers took position here after they had lost their horses. The remains of the men, such as could be found, were gathered together and buried. The names of the two men were Davis and Marshall.[9] On the return trip a small party of Indians were seen and pursued by Major Inman and Lieutenant Borden,[10] Fifth United States Infantry, with a detachment of Kansas cavalry.

The following document was taken from the body of one of the warriors slain at the battle of the Washita. It emanates from a peace commissioner and is a fit commentary upon their labors:—

United States of America,
Department of Interior,
Office of Superintendent of Indian Affairs,
Northern Superintendency,
Fort Laramie, June 28, 1868.

---

[9]Nate Marshall and Bill Davis carried dispatches from General Sheridan when they were killed by a Cheyenne and Arapaho war party along Mulberry Creek south of Fort Dodge on November 18, 1868. Both were experienced frontiersmen who had been hired as government scouts. Marshall had a great admiration for the Indian way of life. Having lived with the Cheyennes, he considered himself integrated with them, though he had been warned several times by Edmund Guerrier of the danger of this association. Not far from the scene of the fight, Inman found the remains of several dead Indians hidden in the brush. A funeral lodge in a nearby ravine contained a dead warrior with all his paraphernalia and a woman slumped by his side, frozen to death. R. M. Wright 1913, 103–105; Inman 1898a, 239–40.

[10]George Pennington Borden served as a private in the 121st New York Infantry from July 1862 until October 1863, when he was admitted as a cadet to West Point (though discharged from the academy in January 1864). In October 1866 Borden obtained a commission as a second lieutenant in the Fifth Infantry and eventually obtained the rank of lieutenant colonel by November 1902.

This is to certify that Black War Bonnet[11] is a recognized chief of the band of Ogalallah Sioux. He is under treaty stipulations with the United States government, and has promised his Great Father to be always friendly towards white men, and any white man to whom he may show this paper is requested by the government to treat him in a friendly manner, and to be careful to give him no cause to break his promise.

(seal.)   R. W. McLaren,
President *pro tem,* Peace Commission.

Extract of Dispatch, December 11
Published January 4, 1869

Camp Washita River, I. T., Dec. 11, 1868. Having reached this point in the chosen valley of the hostile Indians the Commanding General determined to spend the entire day in camp, in order to give the animals rest and an opportunity to avail themselves of the luxuriant pasturage in this vicinity. We were now, it was known, but eight miles from the scene of General Custer's decisive victory over the Cheyenne band of Black Kettle but two weeks ago. General Custer, still feeling considerable anxiety to know the fate of Major Elliott and the missing men of the Seventh Cavalry, who disappeared in the battle of the Washita, and hopeful of at least finding traces whereby some certainty might be arrived at relative to their death or captivity, he determined to organize a small expedition to the battlefield.

At eight o'clock this morning the horses of the party were saddled and mounted and the bugle had sounded the escorting squadron to horse and forward. The party consisted of Major General P. H. Sheridan, commanding the department; Brevet Major General George A. Custer, commanding the expedition; Brevet Brigadier General J. W. Forsyth, Brevet Lieutenant Colonels J. Schuyler Crosby, A. J. McGonnigle and W. W. Cook[e]; Dr. Morris J. Asch, Brevet Captain Charles Brewster;

---

[11]Black War Bonnet may also have been known as Tall Hat (Tall War Bonnet), a Sioux casualty identified by the captive women. This Oglala Lakota may have been a visitor to the Moisiyu (Sioux) lodges in Black Kettle's village.

Lieutenants Owen Hale, M. Moylan and Samuel Robbins, and your correspondent. The escorting squadron consisted of detachments from each of the companies of the Seventh Cavalry, commanded by Brevet Lieutenant Colonel T. W. Custer, Captain G. W. Yates and Lieutenant J. F. Weston. Several of the Osage and Kaw Indian trailers were sent in advance as scouts. The morning was clear but cold. The hard frozen ground and the biting air made both men and animals move quickly.[12] A ride of an hour and a half brought the party in the immediate approach to the battlefield. At a distance, looking down from the divide which the column was crossing, the scene was one of the most intense solitude. The sunlight, glistening upon the hoarfrost settled upon the grass and trees, lent a tranquil charm to the landscape; the leafless and inert vegetation and painful silence was the picture of desolation. We had now followed for several miles the trail of General Custer's pursuing column,[13] after the battle, endeavoring to overtake the fugitive Kiowas and Arapahoes and treat them to a dose of martial solution of Indian hostilities. At length our column crossed the line of formation taken by the left centre column under the unfortunate Elliott. The horses' tracks were quite visible. It was here, with their comrades of the other columns, that Elliott and his men stood for several hours awaiting the first finger of dawn upon the eastern horizon to launch forth at the charge converging upon the fated village.[14] Crossing this line the party now trod the ground rendered historical by a decisive and demolishing blow at the heart of Indian hostility. As the party entered within the area of the fight the alarm of the approach was the signal for the flight of numerous beasts and birds of prey. Thousands of ravens and crows, disturbed in their carrion feast, rose in one

---

[12]"Our line of march was along the north side of the steam. A heavy growth of timber and underbrush skirted the bank" (Keim 1885, 142).

[13]Keim's observation about Custer's trail confirms Edward Godfrey's statement that the regiment retreated before it reached the next village downstream.

[14]"The foot prints of the charging squadrons could be followed in one extended front through the tangled brush" (Keim 1885, 143). These were the footprints of Barnitz's men, who deployed dismounted on the south side of the Washita. Benteen's squadron remained on the north bank and advanced upstream *mounted*. Keim's observation implies that Sheridan had crossed to the south bank of the river, following Barnitz's trail. See "Extract of Narrative Account" in chapter 7.

dense, black mass, filling the surrounding air with their mournful notes, and, soaring over the field, seemed to shower down imprecations in return for their molestation. The sly, cowardly wolf started from his abundant repast, at intervals casting a savage look behind, retired to the summit of the surrounding hammocks and ridges out of range of danger, and here, seating himself upon his haunches, boldly watched the results of the intrusion.

A few yards in advance of the first position taken in the opening of the battle by Major Elliott an object having the appearance of a bundle of blankets was discovered in the bushes.[15] Upon opening the blankets an Indian warrior was found, scalped. At intervals these evidences of the just retribution given the savage Cheyenne in the battle of the Washita were seen. About thirty bodies of warriors were counted, also several squaws accidentally shot in the melee.[16]

Entering the space occupied by the Indian lodges, on all sides lay the ruins of the village of Black Kettle's band. The conflagration started by the troops was so complete that scarcely anything of a combustible character escaped, and today the debris of the village consisted in broken and burned lodge poles, small pieces of untanned and tanned hides. From the immediate site of the village the party rode to the top of a hill, about a hundred yards distant, from which point General Custer repeated to General Sheridan the details of the battle and the positions taken by the different columns.[17] The former site of the lodges could be distinctly seen by the pins ranging in a circle and the fireplace in the centre. On the right of the village, at a distance of 150 yards, lay the

[15]"A large quantity of underbrush had been gathered and deposited around [the sepulchers] to prevent disturbance or molestation" (Keim 1885, 143).

[16]"Many of the warriors left on the field were carefully tied up in two or three thicknesses of blankets. Some were laid in the branches of trees, out of reach of the hungry wolf, while others were deposited under the protections made of brushes" (ibid., 143).

[17]This hill was probably the same elevation from which Custer and Ben Clark watched the battle. Identified now as Headquarters Hill, this observation post was on the south side of the village, on a spur containing the present National Park Service overlook. Yet Sheridan (1888, 2:328) states that the escort crossed to the south bank after Custer briefed him about the battle. But the sequence of Keim's observations regarding the foot prints on the south bank, his detailed description of the village debris, the distance from the village site to the hill where Custer briefed Sheridan, and the distance from the said hill to the pony kill site indicates that the command had already crossed to the south bank when these observations took place.

carcasses of the ponies of the Cheyennes. These covered about four acres, and numbered not less than 700.[18] After the battle was perfectly understood and the ground well surveyed Generals Sheridan and Custer, accompanied by Lieutenant Hale, your correspondent and a small detachment of troops, moved down the south bank of the Washita, over the route taken by Major Elliott and the missing men, in hopes of recovering the bodies. The remainder of the party spent some time longer in the village and moved down the bed of the valley of the river.

The General's party, moving down the south bank, ascended a high divide, from which an extensive view could be had of the surrounding country. Descending on the other side the party had proceeded but a hundred yards when the body of a white man was found, perfectly naked and covered with arrow and bullet holes. The head presented the appearance of having been beaten with a war club. The top of the skull was broken into a number of pieces and the brain was lying partly in the skull and partly on the ground. At first it was supposed that the body was that of Elliott, but upon minute examination this was found not to be the case.[19]

---

[18]This field of carnage "covered a full quarter of a mile in length." The bones were scattered all along the base of the terrace wall south of the village, commencing near the center of Section 12 and extending east to Headquarters Hill. After the opening of the Cheyenne-Arapaho Reservation in 1892, the bleaching bones were loaded by freighters into huge wagons and hauled to Texas for fertilizer. But plenty of skeletal remains were left behind, for a visitor observed in 1933 that horse bones of every description still lay in the underbrush for a distance of several hundred yards. Today none remain. Soil samples taken for radiocarbon dating suggest that extensive flooding of the river may have washed away the historic soil from the valley floor, including the debris of the village, the combat artifacts, and any bone remains at the pony kill site. But recent soil tests taken along the terrace wall have revealed the presence of calcium deposits near several culverts placed under the railroad tracks in 1928. Van Zandt 1984, 61, 65; Lees et al. 2001, 174; Betty Wesner to author, Nov. 18, 2002. See also the map on p. 232, which clearly establishes the location of the pony kill site. The discovery of an antique crowbar, old barbwire, and other items found *four feet* below the surface of the floodplain renews the hope that some part of the historic ground may still remain. These items were recovered by Jim Bruton in the northeast corner of the battlefield in the early 1970s and perhaps date back to 1892, when the first pioneers settled the land (Bruton to author, Feb. 3, 2004).

[19]The identity of the "Lone Soldier" has been the subject of speculation. George Bent knew many of the Washita survivors, including White Buffalo Woman, the sister of Little Rock, who was a witness to the Lone Soldier's death. But she never identified the victim by name, nor did Bent in his correspondence on the subject. Neither did George Grinnell, who also interviewed White Buffalo Woman and received additional

Marking the spot where the body was found, the party continued moving down stream. Crossing with some difficulty a small ravine, about the centre of an expansive swell, at a distance of two hundred yards further on objects were seen lying in the grass and supposed to be bodies. Their attention attracted in this direction, the party moved off for the spot at a gallop. A few minutes after a scene was witnessed sufficient to call forth the rebuke of every benevolent and enlightened mind against the darkened intellects of the so-called philanthropists. Within an area of not more than fifteen yards lay sixteen human bodies, all that remained of Elliott and his party. The winter air swept across the plain and with its cold blasts had added to the ghastliness of death the additional spectacle of sixteen naked corpses frozen as solidly as stone. The party here dismounted and an examination of the bodies was made. There was not a single one that did not exhibit evidences of fearful mutilation. The bodies were all lying with their faces down and in close proximity to each other.

---

information about Elliott's fight through the research of George Hyde. The latter's friendship with Bent resulted in an exchange of letters that eventually became the basis of the *Life of George Bent*. Published in 1957, this volume mentions the death of the Lone Soldier who is identified by the editor, Savoie Lottinville, as Walter Kennedy. Although Lottinville does not disclose his source, it is possible that he obtained his information from Charles Brill's 1935 article, "The Battle of the Washita," or more likely from his *Conquest of the Southern Plains*, a more-extensive treatment of the same subject, published in 1938.

Charles Brill based his work on his 1930 interview with two Cheyennes, Magpie and Little Beaver. In the interview (reproduced in chapter 29), neither informant mentions either Walter Kennedy or Elliott's desperate struggle, though it is possible that the subject was bridged at a later date. Yet since both informants were only boys at the time of the battle, it seems very unlikely that they could have identified any enlisted soldier, especially by name. Despite Brill's statement that Elliott's soldiers captured Little Beaver, the latter never mentions this during another interview in 1933. Asked how he had survived the soldier guns, Little Beaver shows on a crude map his escape route across the floodplain south of village and to the hills beyond. It appears, therefore, that his identification of Walter Kennedy never took place. It may also be possible that Brill misunderstood his informants, which would have contributed to his erroneous conclusions. Using contrived dialogue and pretending to know the thoughts and behavior of Kennedy, Brill reconstructs a series of convincing incidents that led to the sergeant major's death. Kennedy's rank association with Sergeant Major Creek furthered the belief that he was slain near this location.

Since neither Bent, Grinnell, Hyde, nor any of the Indian informants identified the Lone Soldier by name, who then was this casualty? Keim's description of the head trauma excludes Kennedy as the victim because his skull was not broken. The most likely candidate is Pvt. John Myers of M Company, whose cranial vault was "extensively fractured." Grinnell 1956, 303; Hyde 1968, 319–20; Brill 1930; 1935a; and 1938, 164–67; Van Zandt 1984, 69. See also "Letter to Robert Beck" in chapter 42.

Bullet and arrow wounds covered the backs of each, the throats of a number were cut and several were beheaded. The body of one of the horses which the men had ridden out was seen lying at a distance of fifty yards from the pile of bodies. Owing to the mutilation of the bodies, and no one present having been sufficiently acquainted with Major Elliott while living, his body was not at the time recognized. Judging from the position of the bodies and the nature of the ground surrounding, it is probable that Major Elliott (by some it is thought his horse ran away with him) set out in the direction of a party of fugitive Indians.[20] Some of the men seeing the Major start followed and joined him. It is very probable the party pursued several miles when they struck the Arapahoes coming up to the support of the Cheyennes.[21] The party being vigorously pressed commenced retiring, and descending the second divide on the return found themselves cut off by a party of warriors who had moved up under cover of the timber on the banks of the Washita and took position in the ravine, which cut them off entirely from the rest of the command.[22] Not being missed in the command until too late, the little band was compelled to defend itself against the whole force of the Arapahoes and doubtless a number of Kiowa warriors. The party abandoned their horses and probably attempted to force their way down to the river and take protection behind the trees where they could fight to greater advantage. It is likely when all hope of rescue and escape was given up they determined to sacrifice their lives as dearly as possible. The grass where they lay was trodden down and a number of cartridge shells testify to the valor of their defense, until some friendly, fatal bullet gave them the only

[20]"Three warriors, the only fugitives, had left, on the first alarm, to arouse the bands below. Elliott, seeing them break through the lines, started in pursuit. According to the Indian account, which I subsequently obtained, two of the three were killed, but the third gained the nearest village with tidings of the attack on Black Kettle's people" (Keim 1885, 145). These warriors were identified as Little Rock and Packer, both Cheyennes, and Trails the Enemy, a Kiowa. Only Little Rock was killed. Grinnell 1956, 303; Hyde 1968, 319. See also chapter 40.

[21]"An Arapaho warrior, braver than the rest, in hopes of inspiring his people with courage, led off at a gallop, with the intention of riding down the party. As he came near, followed by one other warrior, a volley from the troops finished both" (Keim 1885, 146).

[22]George Bent corroborated Keim's description of the Elliott fight. See "Letter to Robert Beck" in chapter 42.

alternative of escape from the terrible torture to which they would unquestionably have been subjected if taken alive. It is not likely that the entire party was killed before taken, but whether any and who were taken alive and the trying and terrible moments which followed will always remain a mystery, All the missing bodies were now found. Not one had been left to narrate the terrible story. The last offices of humanity—a proper burial—was all that remained.

Generals Sheridan and Custer now considered that all had been accomplished and set out on [their] return. Moving towards the creek the party followed down the banks of the stream. The bodies of several dead warriors were found, probably killed by Elliott and his men.[23] After a short ride of several miles the remains of the villages of the Arapahoes and Kiowas, who came to the support of the Cheyennes, were found. It was evident that both these nations cleared out with their families as hastily as their means of locomotion would allow. Camp kettles, coffee pots, cups, Peace Commission and Interior Department powder kegs (empty), several philanthropic rifles, hundreds of untanned robes, hundreds of lodge poles and a variety of other things was left behind. Orders were given to destroy everything found. It was not long before a stream of consuming smoke and fire could be described following the line of the Washita for a distance of six or seven miles all the way to our present camp. Not less than 1,000 lodges occupied the stretch of country at the time of the fight. It was quite evident after the troops had left the scene of the battle that a party of warriors had returned to contemplate the lesson prepared for them. It was noticeable that all the bodies left were those which had been scalped. As the Indians consider a warrior losing his scalp as debarred from the privilege of entering the happy hunting grounds, these bodies were left, the Indians merely wrapping them in a blanket and laying them at the foot of a tree. The others were removed and probably taken to a distance and there buried according to the rites of their nation.[24]

---

[23]Two Arapahos, Lone Coyote and Tobacco, were mortally wounded in the Elliott fight and may have been buried near the battlefield. Grinnell 1956, 304–305.

[24]This statement is pure speculation and is not supported by facts. The Osages scalped every victim found on the battlefield, regardless of age and sex. Some of the officers and enlisted men also took scalps. Among the trophies taken by Lt. Thomas Custer was a scalp lock removed from Little Rock's head, donated afterward by General Custer

Upon reaching camp this afternoon General Custer sent out two wagons, with an escort, commanded by Lieutenant Owen Hale, to bring in all the bodies. It was determined that the men should be buried on a beautiful knoll near this point. The remains of Major Elliott will be taken to Fort Cobb for interment. The wagons returned with all the bodies shortly after dark this evening, which were conveyed to the grave prepared for them.[25] Previous to burial Dr. Henry Lippincott, Assistant Surgeon, United States Army, made a minute examination of all the bodies and the extent of their mutilations.

. . . .

During the journey to the battlefield this morning a detachment moving along the river found, near the recent camp of the Kiowas, the body of a white woman and child.[26] The body was brought into camp and examined. Two bullet holes penetrating the brain were found; also the back of the skull was fearfully crushed as if by a hatchet. The body of the child presented the appearance of star-

---

to the Audubon Club in Detroit. Keim apparently tried to offer an explanation for the large difference between the actual Indian dead count and the absurd number claimed by Custer. Kiowa war parties passing by the battlefield in the fall of 1869 reported that the Cheyenne skeletons still lay where they had fallen the previous year. Some bodies were indeed removed. One such case took place in March 1869. While waiting for Custer's return from the Sweetwater, soldiers from Inman's supply train visited the battlefield and returned with the desecrated remains of a sepulchered Cheyenne, brought along for a prank. Nye 1962, 155–56; Inman 1898a, 282.

[25]"By three o'clock in the afternoon we reached camp. Immediately several wagons were detailed, under Lieutenant Hale, with an escort, to bring the rest of the corpses. It was nine o'clock at night before the wagons returned with the load of stark and ghastly dead. During the afternoon a trench had been dug on the crest of a beautiful knoll, overlooking the valley of the Washita. Large fires were built at night to enable the burial party to perform their sad work. Each body was examined, and several men from each of the companies, to which the deceased soldiers belonged, were present to identify the remains. Each corpse was now wrapped in a blanket and laid in the trench. At the hour of midnight, the solemn duty was consummated" (Keim 1885, 150–51).

[26]This was a detachment from the Nineteenth Kansas Cavalry. The remains of Clara Blinn and her son were discovered at an abandoned Arapaho camp two miles upstream from Sheridan's bivouac, six miles below Custer's battlefield (H. L. Moore 1900, 41; Sheridan 1868b). But see the statement by Capt. George B. Jenness that the Blinn bodies were found near Black Kettle's death site, close to the remains of five or six squaws. This is contradicted by Jenness's orderly, Pvt. Joseph Phelps Rodgers, who recalled that the Blinns were found a "short distance" downstream from the Elliott death site. Rodgers remembered seeing "a woman with her skull crushed in, laying on a cottonwood log and her little boy lying on top of her." Jenness 1869; Rodgers n.d.

vation, being reduced to a perfect skeleton. There were no marks on the body except a bruise on the cheek, which leads to the conclusion that the child was seized by the feet and dashed against a tree. When brought in the body of the woman was recognized as Mrs. Blynn [*sic*]. The woman was captured by Satanta, chief of the Kiowas, near Fort Lyon, while on her way to her home in the East. At the time of her capture she was in a wagon in the centre of a civilian train. The men with the train, it appears, fled like a pack of cowards and left Mrs. Blynn and her child to fall into savage hands. Satanta kept her as his squaw until the time of the flight of the Kiowas, when she was ruthlessly murdered. The body was dressed in the ordinary dress of a white woman; on the feet were a pair of leather gaiters, comparatively new. Upon the breast was found a piece of corn cake, and the position of the hands indicated that the woman was eating when she unexpectedly received a fatal blow. The body presented the appearance of a woman of more than ordinary beauty, small in figure and not more than twenty-two years of age. The body will be taken to Fort Cobb and there buried.

20

Milton Stewart, Nineteenth Kansas Cavalry

Milton Stewart enlisted in the Nineteenth Kansas Volunteer Cavalry on October 29, 1868, at Topeka and was commissioned a captain in Company K. He was promoted to major on March 8, 1869, and was mustered out of service with his regiment on April 17. During the expedition, Stewart served as an occasional correspondent for the Junction City (Kans.) Weekly Union. *In a letter mailed from Fort Cobb on December 20, 1868, Stewart describes his visit to the Washita battlefield and the discovery of the remains of Clara Blinn and her infant son. An extract of the correspondence published on February 6, 1869, follows.*

Letter Extract
December 20, 1868

Our [march from Camp Supply] . . . commenced on the 7th inst. and terminated day before yesterday. On the line of march the 7th Cavalry occupied the right, the 19th [Kansas] the left, with a train of about 200 wagons intermediate, the whole under supervision of General Sheridan who accompanied us to this place.

The weather at first proved squally, but lately has been as mild and pleasant as a May day. Our route ran southeast across the South or Main Canadian to the Washita River, whose meandering course we followed to this post [Fort Cobb], a distance of about 150 miles. The only incidents of the march worthy of note are two in number.

On the fifth day out, five miles from where General Custer had his fight with the Indians a week previous, General Sheridan wishing to view the battlefield and also to institute a search for the missing body of Major Elliott, halted the command for one day, and selecting a small party—myself included—rode over to the field where Custer won another laurel, and Black Kettle gained admittance to the "happy hunting grounds" of his race. For some distance off the exact spot could be discerned from the large number of ravens hovering over it. On our approach the yelping of numerous dogs could be heard who, still faithful to their masters, kept watch over their stiffened remains. Commencing our search, we first observed underneath a clump of bushes the inanimate form of a brave, his bald [head] shining pale, giving evidence that he and his topknot had parted company not long since. Soon we found a defunct squaw, calmly reposing on the lap of mother earth, and not long after another, and then more of the fallen bucks. Next we beheld the charred debris of 51 lodges, and a stone's throw beyond about two acres thickly strewn with the bodies of slaughtered ponies, which cruel, *cruel* Custer had made short work of.

Soon a much sadder and more revolting sight than dead Indians or slaughtered ponies met our vision. It was the naked, mutilated bodies of Major Elliott and seventeen of his men, in one small spot of ground, where they had yielded up their lives, standing back to back, with face to the foe. Their bodies were literally hacked to pieces. Here a head was severed or a throat cut, there an arm or a leg, and huge gashes in the back and abdomen. The fiends had done their work well, and "none were left to tell the tale." Turning from this sickening sight with a shudder, my companion and I proceeded homeward, pursuing a different trail from the one outward bound, and continuing our course to the banks of a narrow, wooded stream.

We were surprised to find before we had proceeded far, evidence of a large Indian camp which had been hastily deserted, as their lodge poles were left standing and camp equipage of every variety in use among them lay strewn about in the wildest confusion. For a distance of four miles our eyes were regaled with such a scene when Linden saw another sight, a sad incident to relate. The frail, delicate form of a white woman, apparently not more than twenty years of age, lying face downward, her skull smashed in, and every particle of hair removed, lay before us. Close by was her little boy baby, scarce two years old, his white, curly hair dabbed with blood, the brains oozing there from, and on the same spot also lay a dead squaw, partially concealed in a robe.[1] No marks of violence were on her person save a slight contusion on the back of the head, evidently the effect of some weapon. The [white] woman was clad in a dark calico dress, balmoral skirt and boots, and white cotton stockings. In the pocket of her dress we found a crust of bread, but no signs by which the slightest knowledge of her identity could be gained. To account for the dead squaw, we concluded that the Indians, fearing a rescue, had dispatched this poor woman and child—their prisoners—and that the squaw, a little more humane than the rest, had interfered to save them, and received her death blow from some enraged buck. We reported the facts to General Sheridan who had the first two bodies removed and with Maj. Elliott brought to this place [Fort Cobb] for interment. They are now supposed to be the bodies of Mrs. Blinn and child, who were captured some two months since near Fort Lyon.

. . . .

Yours,
M. S.

---

[1] This sepulchered Indian woman is also mentioned by U.S. Indian Agent Albert G. Boone in his condolence letter to Mrs. Harrington, dated January 2, 1869 (Blinn various).

21

Henry E. Alvord,
Tenth Cavalry

Henry Elijah Alvord was a captain in the Tenth Cavalry on special assignment at Fort Cobb in 1868. Born in Greenfield, Massachusetts, in 1844, Alvord was educated at Norwich University and entered the Civil War in 1862 as a sergeant in the Rhode Island Volunteer Cavalry. In November 1862 he enlisted as a second lieutenant in the Second Massachusetts Cavalry, promoted to first lieutenant in January 1864 and to captain the following December. He was honorably discharged in August 1865. In July 1866 Alvord received a commission as a first lieutenant in the Tenth Cavalry, becoming a captain in July 1867.

That same summer Alvord was transferred to Indian Territory to serve chiefly on the staffs of Generals Hancock and Sheridan. His principal duty was to collect information on the Indians, and for that purpose he organized an intelligence force of white scouts and friendly Indians that enabled him to keep his superiors informed through semiweekly reports about the movements of hostile Indians in 1868. He also assisted Gen. William B. Hazen with his duties as special agent to the Indians south of the Arkansas River.

In 1869 Alvord was assigned to the Massachusetts Agricultural College, where he served as a military instructor. He was transferred to the Ninth Cavalry in January 1871 but resigned his commission on December 9. Afterward he became active in the field of agriculture, serving on the faculties of several universities. Alvord died in 1904 at Spring Hill, Virginia, having devoted his last ten years to the U.S. Department of Agriculture.

The Alvord documents that follow consist of two items. The first is an extract of a semiweekly intelligence report dated December 7, 1868, regarding the Washita casualties sustained by the Indians and the military. This item is contained in U.S. Senate, Indian Battle on the

Washita River, *40th Congress, 3rd session, Senate Executive Document 18. The second is an extract of Alvord's letter to General Hazen dated April 4, 1874, regarding the Kiowa presence at the Washita battle. This letter was printed in Hazen's 1874 pamphlet,* Some Corrections of "Life on the Plains."

Extract of Report
December 7, 1868

SUMMARY OF INFORMATION REGARDING
HOSTILE INDIANS
Semi-Weekly Report No. 5

> Camp at Old Fort Cobb, Indian Territory,
> December 7, 1868.

. . . .

The latest accounts of the fight by eyewitnesses and persons who have been over the field since, confirm reports heretofore rendered. The camp surprised was that of Black Kettle, Cheyenne chief, rather isolated and of about 30 lodges. The bodies of 29 soldiers (including three officers) and one Osage Indian were found dead upon the field. The Indians lost five chiefs and distinguished braves, Black Kettle among them, and about 75 of their ordinary fighting men were killed. Thirty-seven Cheyennes, boys, women, and girls are missing, supposed to have been taken prisoners.[1]

The last heard of the troops, they had crossed to the north side of the Canadian, followed only by two well-known braves of the Cheyennes whose relations were among the missing, and who announced their determination of rescuing their people or dying in the attempt.

. . . .

> Henry E. Alvord,
> Captain 10th Cavalry,
> A.A.I.G. Dist. Ind. Ter.

---

[1]The accuracy of Alvord's intelligence reports leaves much to be desired. Fifty-one lodges were destroyed and fifty-three women and children were taken captive. The military casualties abandoned on the field amounted to one officer, Major Elliott, and seventeen enlisted men. None of the Osage Indian scouts were killed. But see also Ben Clark's assertive statement to the *New York Sun* that thirty-two lives were lost in the

Letter Extract
April 4, 1874

Easthampton, Mass., April 4, 1874.
Col. W. B. Hazen, 6th Regt, Inf.,
Bvt. Major Gen. U.S. Army.

General:

. . . .

Some of the earliest and most disinterested accounts of that [Washita] affair, and in my opinion, the most accurate, came from friendly Indians, and were subsequently fully corroborated as to the participants on the Indian side. These united in the statement that but one Kiowa was killed in action[2]—he was a casual visitor at the camp of Black Kettle, a returning hunter or runner, who merely happened to pass that way with the Cheyennes. And no reliable report ever reached us of there being any number of Kiowas engaged in the fight. We know that the Kiowa chiefs and the greater portion of their people received their rations in person from us at Fort Cobb only the day before, and on the night of Nov. 26th the camp of the entire tribe was much nearer ours than to that of the Cheyennes. It was a ride of some hours, from the Kiowa camp to the scene of the battle, and using every moment from the first alarm, but few, if any, could have reached the place during the progress of the conflict. My best information was to the effect that a few Kiowas witnessed the closing scene, but that none reached the ground in time to take part in the action.[3]

. . . .

Very Respectfully,
Your obedient servant,
Henry E. Alvord.

Elliott disaster ("*New York Sun* Interview" in chapter 18). Clark may have gained this erroneous information from Alvord's report.

[2]Known as High Bank, or Bad Bank, this Kiowa was also identified as a Sioux. See chapter 32.

[3]Throughout their history, the Wutapius maintained a close relationship with the Kiowas. Many of the Washita survivors preferred to join their Kiowa relatives at Fort Cobb rather than unite with the Dog Soldiers at the Sweetwater. This intertribal relationship continued during the early reservation years, when the remnant of the old Wutapiu band remained aloof from other Cheyennes. See J. H. Moore 1987, 224–25.

22

Thomas Murphy, Bureau of Indian Affairs

Thomas Murphy was the superintendent of Indian affairs for the Central Superintendency and made his home at Atchison, Kansas. He had been a member of the peace commission at the Little Arkansas in 1865. His cousin was John Murphy, who entered the Indian service in 1869 and served at the Cheyenne and Arapaho Agency until 1886.

On December 4, 1868, Thomas Murphy filed a report with Commissioner Nathaniel G. Taylor in which he was critical of the army's attack on Black Kettle's village. Although Murphy had condemned the Cheyennes for their raids on the Saline and Salomon settlements, his report to Taylor praises the virtues of the slain chief and recites his services to the whites. The document is contained in U.S. House, Difficulties with Indian Tribes, *41st Congress, 2nd session, House Executive Document 240.*

**Report
December 4, 1868**

Fort Cobb Indian Territory,
December 4, 1868.

Hon. N. G. Taylor
Commissioner,
Washington, D.C.

Sir: I have the honor to report that on my return yesterday from Paola, whither I had been to pay the fall annuities to Indians of the Osage River agency, I found in the public journals General Sheridan's report of what he calls "the opening of the campaign against the hostiles Indians," the perusal of which made me sick at heart. Had these Indians been hostile, or had they been the warriors who committed the outrages upon the white settlers on the Solomon and Saline Rivers, in August last, or those who subsequently fought Colonel Forsyth and his fifty scouts,[1] no one would rejoice over this victory more than myself. But who were the parties thus attacked and slaughtered by General Custer and his command? It was Black Kettle's band of Cheyennes. Black Kettle, one of the truest friends the whites have ever had among the Indians of the plains; he who, in 1864, purchased with his own ponies the white women and children captured on the Blue and Platte Rivers[2] by the Dog Soldiers of the Cheyennes and by the Sioux, and freely delivered them up at Denver City to Colonel Chivington, who was at the time the military commandant at that place. After this he was induced, under promises of protection for his people, to bring them into the vicinity of Fort Lyon, where they were soon afterward pounced upon by the military, led by Chivington, and cruelly and indiscriminately murdered. Black Kettle escaped, but his people, in consequence of the step he had taken to induce them to come to the vicinity of the fort, refused to recognize him as their chief, and he thus remained in disfavor with them up to the time of the treaty of 1865, at which time, after explanations on the part of the commissioners, he was reinstated.

In 1867, when General Hancock burned the villages of peaceful Cheyennes and Sioux, Black Kettle used all his influence to prevent

---

[1]George Alexander "Sandy" Forsyth is chiefly remembered for his valorous defense of Beecher Island in eastern Colorado against a large force of Cheyenne, Sioux, and Arapaho warriors in September 1868. Born in 1837, Forsyth entered the Civil War as a private in the Chicago Dragoons in 1861 and was honorably mustered out in 1866 with the regular rank of major and a brevet of brigadier general of volunteers. In July 1866 he received a commission as major of the Ninth Cavalry and was assigned by Sheridan to lead a company of fifty frontiersmen selected for Indian service. In the subsequent engagement at Beecher Island, Forsyth was seriously wounded three times, his gallant conduct earning him a brevet to brigadier general in the regular army. After his convalescence, he served on Sheridan's staff as lieutenant colonel from 1869 to 1881, when he was assigned to the Fourth Cavalry. Forsyth retired in March 1890. He was the author of two books about army life and died in Massachusetts on September 12, 1915. His brother, James William Forsyth, also served on Sheridan's staff.

[2]During August 1864, at least fifty people lost their lives along the Platte River, while at the same time a number of women and children were carried off into captivity. Four of these young children—Laura Roper, Isabella Eubanks, Ambrose Usher, and Daniel Marble—were released on September 17, 1864, through the intervention of Black Kettle. Berthrong 1963, 208.

the Cheyennes from going to war to avenge the wrong, and so persistent were his efforts in this behalf, that his life was threatened and he had to steal away from them in the night with his family and friends and flee for safety to the lodges of the Arapahoes.

In August, 1867, when I was sent out by the Indian peace commission with instructions to assemble in the vicinity of Fort Larned all the friendly Indians belonging to the Kiowas, Comanches, Apaches, Cheyennes, and Arapahoes, with a view of using them to get into communication with the hostile Indians, Black Kettle was among the first to meet me at Fort Larned, cheerfully proffered me his assistance and protection, and from that day until the conclusion of the treaty of Medicine Lodge Creek no man worked more assiduously than did he to bring to a successful termination the business then in hand, and no man, red or white, felt more happy than did he when his people had finally signed the treaty by which they once more placed themselves upon friendly relations with the government. And when he ascertained that some of the young men of his tribe had committed the atrocities upon the Solomon and Saline in August last, I have been credibly informed that so great was his grief he tore his hair and his clothes, and naturally supposing that the whites would wreak their vengeance upon all Indians that might chance to fall in their way, and remembering the treachery that had once wellnigh cost him his life, (I refer to the massacre at Sand Creek,) he went south to avoid the impeding troubles.

The same report says the family of Little Raven, of the Arapahoes, are among the prisoners, and that he too was engaged in the fight. When I recollect that he was one of those who met me at Fort Larned in September, 1867, furnished me with a guard of his young men from that post to Medicine Lodge Creek, protected myself and the few white men with me while there, vigilantly watching over us both day and night, continually sending out his warriors as messengers to the hostile Indians for the purpose of inducing them to abandon the war path and to come in and meet the commissioners, and firmly believing that Little Raven has not been engaged in the recent depredations, nor would have permitted any of his warriors to go upon the war path could he have prevented it, I cannot but feel that the innocent parties have been made to suffer the crimes of others.

It is likewise said in the report that Sartau-ta [Satanta] came to the assistance of Black Kettle. I regret that he has been drawn into these difficulties. He is one of the most powerful chiefs among the Kiowas, and his influence for the last three years has been exerted in favor of peace. Had it not been for him in August last, a desperate fight might have taken place at Fort Zarah, between the Kiowas and the soldiers of that post. . . .

Knowing these chiefs as I do, I feel satisfied that when all the facts pertaining to the late attack shall become known, it will be found that they and the few lodges with them composed that portion of their tribes who desired to remain at peace, and who were endeavoring to make their way to Fort Cobb for the purpose of placing themselves under the care of their agents on their new reservations.

Judging from the map of the Indian country, this fight took place within some sixty or seventy miles of the latter post,[3] and being so near, it confirms the fears I entertained as expressed in my letter to you of the 15th ultimo, and will have the effect, I apprehend, of frightening away all those Indians who were expected to congregate in the vicinity of Fort Cobb, and of starting upon the war path many Indians who have been friendly disposed toward the government, thus costing the nation many valuable lives and millions of treasure.

Had Congress, at its last session, appropriated sufficient funds to continue the feeding of these Indians last June, I believe we could have kept them at peace, and that by this time they would have been quietly located on their new reservations, where we could control and manage them and gradually wean them from their wild and wandering life, and in doing which it would not have cost the government as much per year as it is now costing per month to fight them, and this course would have been far more humane and becoming [to] a magnanimous and Christian nation.

Very respectfully, your obedient servant,

Thos. Murphy,
Superintendent Indian Affairs.

---

[3]The Washita battle took place 119 miles west of Fort Cobb. "Record of Troop G, Distances Marched, December 1868," in Chandler 1960, 28.

23

Philip H. Sheridan,
Department of the Missouri

Gen. Philip Henry Sheridan was the commander of the Department of the Missouri, responsible for the winter campaign of 1868. Born in Albany, New York, on March 6, 1831, he graduated from West Point in 1853 and was assigned to the First Infantry in Texas. The following year he was transferred to the Fourth Infantry in California and distinguished himself during the Yakima Indian War in 1856. At the close of hostilities, he was assigned to the Grande Ronde Indian Reservation in Oregon.

At the outbreak of the Civil War, Sheridan was promoted to captain and transferred to the Thirteenth Infantry. After serving on the staff of Gen. Samuel R. Curtis's Army of the Southwest, he gained an appointment as colonel of the Second Michigan Cavalry in 1862. This was followed by swift promotions to brigadier general of volunteers and major general of volunteers in recognition of his courage at Perryville, Kentucky, and Stones River, Tennessee. In 1864 Sheridan commanded the Army of the Potomac's cavalry and operated in the Shenandoah Valley. His defeat of Gen. Jubal Early's Confederates earned him the rank of brigadier general in the regular army in September 1864, which was followed by appointment as major general in November by President Lincoln in grateful recognition of Sheridan's services. By resolution in 1865, Congress extended to him its thanks for his gallantry, military skill, and courage displayed for his Shenandoah Valley campaign, especially at Cedar Run, where he averted a great disaster and turned it into a Union victory.

After a short service in Texas after the war, Sheridan was reassigned in 1867 to assume command of the Department of the Missouri. After the devastating Indian raid on the Saline and Solomon settlements in

Kansas in 1868, the general declared war on the Cheyennes, culminating in the battle of the Washita and the surrender of the Cheyennes the following year. Although some easterners sharply criticized Sheridan for the slaying of innocent Cheyenne women and children, President Grant promoted him to lieutenant general and command of the Division of the Missouri in March 1869. Sheridan's subjugation of the Plains Indians was completed with the Red River War of 1874 and the Sioux War of 1876.

In November 1883 Sheridan became commander in chief of the army. But his health had been declining for years, and he had barely finished writing his memoirs when he collapsed in May 1888 from a severe heart attack. Phil Sheridan died on August 5, 1888. Intemperate and coarse in language, "Little Phil" had earned the adulation of his soldiers, the civilian population, and the government for his Civil War achievements and his later accomplishments on the western frontier.

Three of his official reports, dated December 3 and December 19, 1868, and January 1, 1869, follow. The 1868 reports are from U.S. Senate, Indian Battle on the Washita River *(40th Congress, 3rd session, Senate Executive Document 18, part 1), and describe Sheridan's interview with the captured Cheyenne women and his march to the Washita battlefield and Fort Cobb. The 1869 report is from U.S. Senate,* Indian Battle on the Washita River *(40th Congress, 3rd session, Senate Executive Document 18, part 2), in which he gives his justification for the decimation of Black Kettle's people.*

Official Report
December 3, 1868

Headquarters Department of the Missouri,
    In the field, (depot on the North Canadian, at the
    junction of Beaver Creek,) December 3, 1868.

Brevet Major General W. A. Nichols,
Ass't Adj. Gen.,
Military Division of the Missouri,
St. Louis, Mo.

General: I had an interview today, through the interpreter, Mr. Curtis, with the sister of Black Kettle, from whom I learn as follows, and which seems to be, after close questioning, a correct statement of the Indians who were located in the vicinity of where Custer had his fight on the 27th ultimo, on the Washita River, about 75 or 80 miles northwest of Fort Cobb, and immediately south of Antelope Hills. The Indians there were encamped on the Washita as follows: First, Black Kettle and other chiefs of the Cheyennes, and a small party of Sioux, in all numbering 51 lodges. Eight miles down the stream were all the Arapahoes and 70 additional lodges of Cheyennes; also the Kiowas, then the Apaches and Comanches.[1] While thus encamped three war parties were sent out north. One, composed of Cheyennes, Kiowas and Arapahoes, went north in the direction of Larned, and the trail of which we crossed in coming down; it was still out. Another party, composed of Cheyennes and Arapahoes, which party returned, and the trail of which led General Custer into Black Kettle's village. This party brought back three scalps, one of which was the expressman killed and horribly mutilated just before I had left Fort Dodge; the mail on his person was found in Black Kettle's camp. The other party was a mixed party and went out on foot in the direction of Lyon, and is still out.

About the time the first of these parties left, Black Kettle and a representation of one sub-chief from each of the bands visited Fort Cobb, and all brought back provisions from General Hazen or some one else there,[2] and while they were gone, or about the time of their return, the last war party was sent out, which is the

---

[1]Within a distance of six miles below Black Kettle's village, and extending for six more miles downstream, the following camps were strung along the Washita: the Arapahos with 180 lodges under Little Raven, Big Mouth, Yellow Bear, and Spotted Wolf; a Cheyenne camp of 70 lodges under Little Robe; another Cheyenne camp of 60 lodges under Whirlwind; a small Kiowa camp of 30 lodges under Big Bow and Little Mountain; the main Cheyenne camp of Dog Soldiers, containing 200 lodges under Medicine Arrows; and a camp of 50 lodges of Quahada Comanches. Alvord 1868; McCusker to Hazen, July 19, 1874, in Hazen 1925. See also chapter 38.

[2]The supplies consisted of coffee, sugar, flour, and crackers, which were issued by post trader William Griffinstein upon General Hazen's authorization. In February 1869 Griffinstein reminded the commissioner of Indian affairs that this account had not been settled yet. See Indian Trader Information in Blinn various.

one first alluded to as going in the direction of Fort Larned, and whose trail we crossed.

The women are of the opinion that they will sue for peace at Cobb, since the blow received by them on the 27th. They would have come here had the opening there not been held out to them.

I will start for Fort Cobb as soon as the trains from Dodge arrive. If it had not been for the misfortune to the Kansas regiment of getting lost from the trail while enroute from the Little Arkansas to this place, and the heavy snow storm which reduced and jaded their horses so as to render them on arrival unfit for duty, we would have closed up this job before this time. As it is, I think the fight is pretty well knocked out of the Cheyennes. Thirteen Cheyennes, two Sioux, and one Arapaho chief were killed, making 16 in all.[3]

The government makes a great mistake in giving these Indians any considerable amount of food under the supposition of necessity. The whole country is literally covered with game. There are more buffalo than will last the Indians for 20 years; the turkeys are so numerous that flocks as large as from 1,000 to 2,000 have been seen; and the country is full of grouse, quails, and rabbits; herds of antelope and deer are seen everywhere, and even ran through the wagon trains of General Custer on his march.

The buffalo here are a separate band from those ranging during the fall north of the Union Pacific railroad, where I have seen myself not less than 200,000 in one day.

The reservation laid off for the Arapahoes and Cheyennes, by the treaty of 1867, is full of game and the most luxuriant natural grasses, as reported by Colonel Crawford of the 19th Kansas, who just passed through this reservation in coming here. Others familiar with the reservation report the same.

Black Kettle's sister reports three white women in the lodges below Black Kettle's camp.[4]

Very respectfully, yours,

P. H. Sheridan,
Major General United States Army.

---

[3]For the names of these casualties, see "The Keim Listing: Extract of Newspaper Dispatch, December 1, 1868," in Appendix G.

[4]These were Clara Isabel Blinn, Anna Belle Morgan, and Sarah Catherine White.

Official Report
December 19, 1868

Headquarters Department of the Missouri,
In the Field, Fort Cobb, Indian Territory, December 19, 1868.

Brevet Major General W. A. Nichols,
Assistant Adjutant General,
St. Louis, Missouri.

General: I have the honor to report, for the information of the Lieutenant General [William T. Sherman], my arrival at this place yesterday evening, with the 7th Cavalry, and 10 companies of the 19th
Kansas, the Osage and Kaw scouts, numbering about 1,500.

We crossed the North Canadian from Camp Supply, proceeding in a southerly direction across the main Canadian, striking the
Washita about eight miles south of Custer's battleground, and
distant from Fort Cobb 113 miles.

Here we rested one day and searched for the body of Major
Elliott, which we found, and 16 soldiers killed in the battle. They
followed in pursuit of some fleeing Indians, and warriors coming up
from the river below surrounded them in large numbers, and killed
them, and mutilated them in the most horrible manner.[5] We also
found the body of Mrs. Blinn and her child in one of the camps
about six miles down the river; Mrs. Blinn shot through the forehead, and the child with its head crushed by a blow against a tree.[6]

---

[5]"[We] pushed across the river where Elliott had crossed. Moving directly to the
south, we had not gone far before we struck his trail, and soon the whole story was
made plain by our finding, on an open level space about two miles from the destroyed
village, the dead and frozen bodies of the entire party. The poor fellows were all lying
within a circle not more than fifteen or twenty paces in diameter, and the little piles of
empty cartridge shells near each body showed plainly that every man had made a brave
fight" (Sheridan 1888, 2:328).

[6]Dr. Lippincott's medical examination revealed a bullet hole above the victim's left
eye, extensive fractures in the back of the skull, and that she was scalped. Keim, however, observed two bullet holes in Blinn's head, which may have been the entry and exit
wounds of the same projectile. The emaciated body of Clara's infant son showed bruises
to the head and face. The identity of the two victims was not known until the morning
of May 12, 1868, when the bodies were recognized by soldiers of the Nineteenth Kansas
Cavalry who filed past the remains laid out on a blanket. H. L. Moore 1900, 41–42.

All the Indians heretofore enumerated were encamped from a point about three miles below the battleground, for a distance of about six or eight miles. They abandoned their camps and fled in the greatest consternation, leaving their cooking utensils, mats, axes, lodge poles, and provisions. As much of this property as we could spare time to destroy was burned.

We then took up the trail of the Indians, and followed it down the Washita for a distance of 76 miles, and 36 miles from Fort Cobb, we came near the camp of the Kiowas, who were unconscious of our presence, but discovered it late in the evening, and hastened to Fort Cobb, and next morning presented a letter from General Hazen, declaring them friendly. I hesitated to attack them, but directed them to proceed with their families to Fort Cobb. This they assented to, and nearly all the warriors came over and accompanied the column, for the purpose of deceiving me while their families were being hurried towards the Washita mountains, but suspecting that they were attempting to deceive me, as they commenced slipping away one by one, I arrested the head chiefs, Lone Wolf and Satanta, and on my arrival at Fort Cobb, as I suspected, there was not a Kiowa; so I notified Lone Wolf and Satanta that I would hang them tomorrow if their families were not brought in today, and I will do so. They have been engaged in the war all the time, and have been playing fast and loose. There are over 50 lodges [of Kiowas] with the Cheyennes now. They have attempted to browbeat General Hazen since he came here, and went out and ordered the two companies from Arbuckle for protection to General Hazen to return. I will take some of the starch out of them before I get through with them.

The Cheyennes, Arapahoes, one band of Comanches, and the 50 lodges of the Kiowas, are at the western base of the Washita mountains.

The following is what I propose to do, and I have submitted it to General Hazen, who approves. I will punish the Kiowas, if they come in; if not I will hang Lone Wolf and Satanta. I will send out Black Kettle's sister tomorrow, ordering the Cheyennes and Arapahoes to come in and receive their punishment, which will be severe. She says they will come in, as they are now willing to beg for peace, and will have done so already since Custer's fight. If they do not come in I will employ the Caddoes, the Wachitas, and Asa-habet's band of Comanches against them, with my own forces, and will compel the other Comanches to go out against them, or will declare them hostile. They have all been working together as one man, encamping together, and holding intercourse and trading in captured stock, and they must assist in driving them out of the country, or compel their surrender. I will then leave a sufficient force with General Hazen to keep him from being browbeaten; he is helpless as he is.

The Comanches are now under my thumb, and the Kiowas will be, I hope; and I hope that the Cheyennes and Arapahoes may soon be in the same condition. In the trip down here the distance was 187 miles; snow was on the ground most of the way, and the cold on the high tablelands and the crossing [of] the rivers was intense. The country travelled over was terrible, the surface of the earth was defaced by canyons, hummocks, scooped-out basins, making constant labor f or the men. I lost some horses, but in this beautiful valley, with splendid grass, will soon have the command in good trim. The Indians for the first time begin to realize that winter will not compel us to make a truce with them. I am a little sorry that I did not hit the Kiowas, but I did not like to disregard General Hazen's letter, and perhaps we can do as well by other modes. Only two men are sick in the 7th Cavalry, and six in the 19th Kansas. The whole command is in shelter-tents, as we could not spare transportation for others, but the men now prefer the "shelter," even at this season of the year. Everybody is feeling well and enthusiastic.

I am, general, very respectfully, your obedient servant,

P. H. Sheridan,
Major General United States Army.

Official Report
January 1, 1869

In the Field, Fort Cobb, Indian Territory,
January 1, 1869.

Brevet Major General W. A. Nichols,
Assistant Adjutant General,
Military Division of the Missouri.

General: I have the honor to forward the following for the information of the Lieutenant General [William T. Sherman].

. . . .

Yesterday we received a few papers, the first for one month, and I see it alleged by Indian agents that Black Kettle's band was on the reservation at the time when attacked. This is a falsehood. The reservation extends but thirty miles up the Washita from Fort Cobb. The battle took place 120 miles up the river from Fort Cobb. It is also alleged the band was friendly. No one could make such an assertion who had any regard for truth. The young men of this band commenced the war; I can give their names. Some of Black Kettle's young men were out depredating at Dodge when the village was wiped out. Mules taken from trains, matter carried by our murdered couriers, photographs stolen from the scenes of outrages on the Solomon and Saline, were found in the captured camp, and, in addition, I have their own illustrated history, found in their captured camp, showing the different fights or murders in which this tribe was engaged; the trains attacked; the hay parties attacked about Fort Wallace; the women, citizens, and soldiers killed. It is at the service of any one desiring information on the subject. It should be known, also, that I invited Black Kettle and his family to come in through the Arapaho chief Little Raven, in my interview with that chief at Fort Dodge in September last. They did not come.

Yours, respectfully,

P. H. Sheridan
Major General United States Army

24

James S. Morrison,
Agency Employee

James Stuart Morrison (whose real name may have been Jesse Stuart Morrison) was an agency employee of the Interior Department in 1868. Better known as "Jimmy," he had been a clerk and Arapaho interpreter for Indian Agent Edward Wynkoop at Fort Larned until the latter's resignation that November. Morrison was married to Emma, daughter of the Arapaho chief Big Mouth. Like her father, Emma had made quite a name for herself. She wore "American clothes" that she made on a sewing machine and was considered a good housekeeper, a devoted mother, and an excellent cook. Emma Morrison passed away from tuberculosis near Camp Supply in 1872. Although Gen. Nelson A. Miles arranged for a Christian funeral, her grieving kinsmen gashed their arms and legs and shot their favorite ponies at her gravesite after the service.

In 1875 Morrison and his three children, Jennie, Nellie, and Ned, settled on a cattle ranch along the North Fork of the Canadian River at Darlington Agency. In February 1882 tragedy struck the family again when Jennie, the youngest daughter, perished in a fire at the Mennonite mission school near Darlington. Despite his personal hardships, J. S. Morrison became known as a successful rancher and later a prominent citizen of El Reno, Oklahoma.

The letter extract that follows was written on December 14, 1868, upon the arrival of the Cheyenne captives at Fort Dodge. Addressed to Colonel Wynkoop, it repudiates the exaggerated claims made by Custer about the Indian casualties. The letter is reproduced in U.S. House, Difficulties with Indian Tribes. *41st Congress, 2nd session, House Executive Document 240.*

Letter Extract
December 14, 1868

Colonel Edward W. Wynkoop,
U.S. Indian Agent.

Fort Dodge, Kansas, December 14, 1868.

Dear Colonel:

John Smith, John Poysell,[1] and Jack Fitzpatrick[2] have got in today. John S. was not in the [Washita] fight, but John P. and Jack were. They all agree in stating that the official reports of the fight were very much exaggerated; that there were not over twenty bucks killed; the rest, about forty, were women and children. The prisoners have got in today; they consist of fifty-three women and children. One boy is an Arapaho; the rest are all Cheyennes. Mrs. Crocker is among them; she is badly wounded; she says her child is killed.[3] The women say that Black Kettle was killed. The prisoners will be taken to Fort Riley. It is probable that I will be sent in charge of them. Generals Sheridan and Custar [sic] have started

---

[1]Born in 1850, John Poisal Jr. was the son of a French Canadian trader and Snake Woman, sister of the Arapaho chief Left Hand. His father was employed by the Bent firm and died in a cabin at Cherry Creek in Denver in 1861. Afterward Snake Woman and her five children—Margaret (b. 1834), Mary (b. 1838), Robert (b. 1838), Mathilda (b. 1845), and John Jr.—returned to her brother's Arapaho band at Sand Creek. She and her children miraculously escaped the carnage unleashed by Chivington's troops in 1864. In reparation for the Sand Creek Massacre, each of the Poisal children was granted 640 acres under the Treaty of the Little Arkansas of 1865. John Jr. and his brother later settled on a cattle ranch in the unassigned lands just east of Darlington Agency, where Robert was murdered in 1883. Lecompte 1968, 355; *Cheyenne Transporter*, Aug. 1, 1883.

[2]Andrew Jackson "Jack" Fitzpatrick was the son of Indian Agent Thomas Fitzpatrick and Margaret Poisal, the mixed-blood daughter of John Poisal Sr. Born on October 8, 1850, Jack was described as an educated, handsome man with long black hair and was a noted marksman. His father died in Washington on February 7, 1854, a few months before the birth of Jack's sister, Virginia Thomasine. Under the Treaty of the Little Arkansas, the mix-blood children of Thomas Fitzpatrick were each granted 640 acres of land. Jack Fitzpatrick died in a train accident in California in 1883. His sister died in El Reno in 1929. E. B. Custer 1967, 25; Hafen 1931, 318, 320.

[3]Mrs. Crocker was a full-blood Cheyenne named Ne-sou-hoe. She was the wife of a Lieutenant Crocker, who served with the Second Colorado Volunteers. Ne-sou-hoe and her young daughter, Jennie Lund Crocker, were visiting relatives in Black Kettle's Washita village when Custer attacked. Jennie was killed during the fighting. Charles J. Kappler, *Indian Treaties, 1778–1883* (New York: Interland, 1972), 889.

on a new expedition. The officers say that he is going direct to Fort Cobb, swearing vengeance on Indians and Indian agents indiscriminately. When John's wife heard of the fight she tried to kill herself, first with a knife and then with strychnine,[4] but Dr. Forwood saved her from the effects of it.[5] John starts for Larned tonight.

. . . .

Very respectfully,

James S. Morrison

---

[4]This was Na-to-mah, the Cheyenne wife of John Simpson Smith. Her father, Chief Yellow Wolf, and her son, Jack Smith, were murdered at Sand Creek in 1864. Na-to-mah's brother Red Moon and his family were present in Black Kettle's village when it was destroyed by Custer in 1868. She did not know that her brother had survived. Hoig 1974, 48–49; Hyde 1968, 156.

[5]William Henry Forwood entered the Civil War in August 1861 as an assistant surgeon and earned brevets to captain and major by March 1865 for faithful and meritorious services. He was stationed at Fort Wallace in 1866 and served at several other posts in Kansas. Commissioned as surgeon with the rank of major in June 1876, he would later gain appointment as assistant surgeon general, with the rank of colonel, in May 1897. Forwood retired in September 1902 after becoming surgeon general, with the rank of brigadier general.

25

Benjamin H. Grierson, Tenth Cavalry

Benjamin Henry Grierson served as colonel of the Tenth Cavalry from 1866 to 1890 and was responsible for the establishment of Camp Wichita in March 1869, renamed Fort Sill shortly thereafter. Born in Pittsburgh, Pennsylvania, in 1826, Grierson entered the Civil War as a captain on the staff of Gen. Benjamin H. Prentiss. He was commissioned as major of the Sixth Illinois Cavalry in 1861, promoted to colonel in 1862, and appointed brigadier general in 1863 to command the First Cavalry Brigade. He took part in the Vicksburg campaign and became widely known for his spectacular raids through Mississippi in 1863 and 1864, receiving high praise from General Grant and President Lincoln.

In recognition of his Mississippi services, Grierson was awarded a brevet of major general of volunteers in 1865, and after the war he served as colonel of the Tenth Cavalry. he was promoted to brigadier general in 1890 and retired that same year. He died at his summer cottage in Omena, Michigan, in 1911 and was buried in Jacksonville, Illinois. Grierson was known as a talented musician and was instrumental in the organization of the Tenth's regimental band. Labeled an eccentric cavalryman, he was an advocate of the Quaker peace policy, which called for fairness and justice in dealing with the tribes.

The letter extract that follows was written by Grierson to his father-in-law, John Kirk, on April 6, 1869, and comments on Custer's exaggerated count of Indian casualties at the Washita. The original letter is in the Grierson Papers, Edward E. Ayer Collection, Newberry Library, Chicago, Illinois; this portion is reproduced by special permission of the Newberry Library.

Letter Excerpt
April 6, 1869

Camp Wichita
Wichita Mts., I.T.
Apl. 6th, 1869.

Father Kirk[1]
  My Dear Sir

. . . .

I arrived here on the 4th of March. Established the Hdqtrs. of the District, and a permanent Camp designated as per heading of this sheet, and in addition to my other duties assumed in compliance with instructions, the command of the garrison at this point. *Like yet very unlike Grant,* I, too, was duly *inaugurated.*

Gen. Sheridan left me plenty of work to do. A new Post is to be built upon the very ground selected by me last summer. It is the finest location for a Military Post in the United States—is situated about the center of the Kioway, Comanche and Apache reserve. I am having a military reservation surveyed of about eighteen square miles, maps made showing the lay of the land, direction of streams, location of timber, stone and other building material, elevation of the plateau as site for the Post, plans of buildings, etc. I have a saw mill already up, and in working order, about 200 fine saw logs cut, and will soon have at least temporary quarters erected for the troops. Immediately south of the military reservation is, or will be located the Indian Agency, buildings, workshops, etc. There are now about 3000 Indians, Kioways, Comanches, Apaches and Arrapahoes [*sic*] in this vicinity. The latter will soon be moved north to their Reservation south of the Arkansas River. About 3000 more Indians who properly belong to this reservation, are still out near the Llano Estacado or Staked Plains, determined perhaps to fight it out on that line if it should take all summer.

You must not believe all you have heard or read in the papers about this Indian war. Instead of a grand success, it has been like

---

[1]"Father Kirk" was John Kirk, the father of Alice Kirk, Grierson's wife. For Grierson's biography, see Leckie and Leckie 1984.

most other Indian wars—a grand "fizzle"—and has cost the Government over $200,000 for every Indian killed. More soldiers have been killed than Indians, leaving out the women and children of the latter. Custer's fight was a big thing on paper. The 102 warriors he reported killed, has dwindled down, according to Indian count, to just *eighteen*,[2] and he reported more material captured and destroyed than all the hostile Indians had put together. Sheridan has however made the most out of it and reported the *war over*, just in time for it to have effect at Washington and was *elevated* thereby to the position of Lieut. General. So far as any credit, gain, or glory is concerned, I am merely left here to hold the empty bag, out of which he sloped with all that could be turned to any account, but it will all be the same in a hundred years, hence "*it makes no difficulty with me.*"

. . . .

Regards to all,
Yours Truly
B. H. Grierson

---

[2]Grierson's low casualty count is corroborated by independent information obtained by Commissioner Vincent Colyer from surrendering Cheyenne leaders three days later. See chapter 43.

26

William B. Hazen,
Southern Indian Military District

William Babcock Hazen was an army officer on special assignment as military Indian agent of the Southern Indian Military District in August 1868. Stationed at Fort Cobb, he was to supervise all issues and disbursements to the Indians and was to segregate the peaceful bands from those declared hostile. But Sheridan's winter campaign and the meddling of Indian Bureau agents complicated his task. He concluded his services as a special agent in June 1869 and briefly served as a member of the Southern Superintendency, leaving the Indian service entirely in 1870.

Born in West Hartford, Vermont, on September 27, 1830, Hazen graduated from West Point in 1855 and served briefly as a brevet second lieutenant in the Fourth Infantry before being assigned to the Eighth Infantry. He was brevetted first lieutenant for gallant conduct while severely wounded in the left hand and the right side of his chest during an engagement with Comanches in Texas in 1859. Promoted to captain in 1861, with the outbreak of the Civil War he was commissioned colonel of the Forty-First Ohio Infantry, followed by promotions to brigadier general of volunteers in 1862 and major general of volunteers in 1864. He was cited for gallant and meritorious services at Chattanooga in 1863 as well as during the capture of Atlanta and Fort McAllister, Georgia, in 1864. Hazen's services were further recognized with a brevet to major general (regular army) in 1865 for gallant and meritorious conduct in the field during the war.

Honorably mustered out of the volunteer service, Hazen was assigned as colonel of the Thirty-Eighth Infantry in 1866. He was transferred to the Sixth Infantry in 1869 and was promoted to brigadier general as chief signal officer in 1880. He died on January 16, 1887, and was buried in

Arlington National Cemetery. Hazen was a complex character, described by some as a courageous crusader and by others as a chronic troublemaker. He held an intense dislike for both Sheridan and Custer as a result of false imputations and "mischievous errors" propagated by them immediately after the Washita battle.

The extract that follows is from a letter addressed to James A. Garfield, chairman of the House Military Affairs Committee, which also appeared in the New York Times *on February 21, 1869. In it Hazen refutes newspaper charges that he had misled Black Kettle into a false sense of security.*

Letter Excerpt
January 18, 1869

Fort Cobb, I. T., Jan. 18, 1869.

My Dear Garfield:

. . . .

I see a great deal [in the papers] about the killing of Black Kettle; that he was on his way to his reservation, where he had been invited by the Government. These are all fabrications. Seven days before he was killed, he came to my camp, having previously been called down from the camp where he was afterward attacked, by a trader who had just lost his Cheyenne wife, to claim her estate.[1] Being down for that purpose, and by the advice of the trader, he came to sue for peace for all the Cheyennes. He made a fair and I have no doubt a truthful talk. He said he deplored the war and wanted peace. That many of his people were then on the warpath above the Arkansas, and that his band had been at war all summer.[2] He wished the war

---

[1]Post trader William Griffinstein had married two women from Black Kettle's band. His first wife (deceased) was known as "Cheyenne Jennie," the daughter of a noted Wutapiu chief. She was a woman of great ability and had considerable influence with all the Indian leaders, engaging in the commercial Indian trade on her husband's behalf. Being an invalid, Jennie rode in an ambulance when she was unable to sit up. She was best known among whites for her humanitarian efforts that led to the release of captive white children on a number of occasions. Jennie Griffinstein died about October 10, 1868. Blinn various; Mead 1986, 129.

[2]This is a deliberate distortion of Black Kettle's speech. The chief stated that while

confined to Kansas, but we had brought it below the Arkansas, and he wanted it stopped.

I told him that I did not control the war, and could not make peace if I would. Also, that the two previous summers his people had made war so long as the season permitted; then made peace, only to commence war again when the spring came; that now he must make peace with the people he was fighting, and that there must be some assurance that they would not fight again in the spring.

He said he thought it hard he could not make peace when he wanted to, but understood perfectly why I could not make peace with him. I told him of the troops then approaching the Washita, liable to attack him at any time. I again asked him whom he represented, hoping to give him personally, with his families, the protection of the Government, but he replied that he spoke for all the Cheyennes,[3] nearly all of whom were then at war, and with whom I could not and ought not to deal, as they were not only deserving punishment, but were actually in the face of an army I did not and could not control.

Black Kettle returned to his camp with as full a knowledge of his own *status*, and that of our forces, as I had myself, and two days after was attacked and killed. He was neither on his reservation nor going toward it, nor had he been invited to do so since the breaking out of hostilities, but, on the contrary, was distinctly told (which fact he equally well knew,) that all of his people, with himself, were considered at war, and would be treated accordingly.

> Very respectfully, your obedient servant,
> [Signed,] W. B. Hazen
> Brevet Major General.

------

he exerted himself to keep the "young men quiet, but some will not listen" and had joined in the fighting, he and his band of 180 lodges wanted peace. Hazen's letter to General Sherman of December 31, 1868, reveals additional distortions of Black Kettle's words.

[3]Black Kettle did not say that he spoke for all the Cheyennes; he said, "I speak only for my own people; I cannot speak nor control the Cheyennes north of the Arkansas." His "own people" consisted of Black Kettle's band (fifty lodges), Little Robe's band (seventy lodges), and Whirlwind's band (sixty lodges).

27

Hugh L. Scott,
Seventh Cavalry

Hugh Lennox Scott was born in Danville, Kentucky, on September 22, 1853. After graduating from West Point in 1876, he was assigned as a second lieutenant to the Ninth Cavalry but immediately applied for a transfer to the Seventh Cavalry to fill one of the many vacancies created by the destruction of Custer's battalion at the Little Bighorn. Scott participated in the Nez Perce campaign in 1877 and was promoted to first lieutenant the following year. He was commissioned a captain in 1895 and during the Spanish-American War achieved the ranks of major of volunteers in 1898 and lieutenant colonel of volunteers in 1899. He was honorably discharged from the volunteer service in 1901.

Scott became major of the Third Cavalry in 1903 and was shortly thereafter transferred to the Fourteenth Cavalry. He served as adjutant general of Cuba from 1898 to 1903, when he became commander of troops in and military governor of the Philippines. Scott was superintendent of West Point from 1906 to 1910 and served as major general, chief of staff, from 1914 to 1917 before seeing action in France during World War I. He retired in 1919 and died in Washington, D.C., on April 30, 1934.

In 1888 Scott was transferred to Fort Sill to monitor disturbances among the Indians of the southern plains. In 1892 he enlisted Company L, Seventh Cavalry, composed of Kiowa, Comanche, and Apache Indian scouts, which remained active until 1897, when the company was mustered out of service. Scott was an expert in Indian sign language and had gained the trust and respect of the Fort Sill Indians.

The following papers consist of two items: the first is a letter written by Scott to Walter M. Camp on December 4, 1910, regarding the presence of a commemorative marker on the Washita battlefield; the second consists of several field notes by Camp containing Scott's comments about the Washita battle.

Letter to Walter M. Camp
December 4, 1910[1]

Decr 4th 1910

My dear Mr. Camp:

. . . I was very glad to see that you had a good visit to the Washita with Ben Clark. As you say he is a fine old fellow for whom I have a sincere affection and admit he [is] the last of his kind. I was especially glad to know that the 7th Cavalry stone is still there [on the Washita battlefield]—the boomers that go into a new country have little reverence for such things and we had to hunt that country for three days in order to find a stone suitable for that purpose.[2] I don't suppose that "Smokes road"

---

[1]The original letter is housed in Folder 15, Box 1, Walter Camp Collection, Brigham Young University Library, Provo, Utah; it is reproduced by special permission.

[2]In 1890 Lt. Hugh L. Scott placed a sandstone monument on the Washita battlefield to commemorate the action of his regiment and to mark the historic site for future generations. The memorial consisted of a large flat stone, inscribed with the words "7th Cav. Nov 27, 1868," that stood on top of a four-foot cairn of rocks. Sgt. Thomas Clancy of the Seventh Cavalry, a stonemason, chiseled the letters on the monument and placed his initials, "TC," on the back. The monument was erected on the floodplain at the battlefield site, but the exact location is now unknown. Alvin Moore, a local resident, claimed that it originally stood on the site where Elliott's soldiers were buried. But since the burial site is eight miles below the battlefield proper, it contradicts Scott's statement that the monument was erected at the "site of Custer's battle." In the succeeding years the cairn of stones was leveled several times by the force of rushing floodwaters as well as by grazing cattle that roamed the area after the opening of Cheyenne and Arapaho lands in 1892. The last person to rebuild the cairn was Capt. Allyn K. Capron of the Seventh Cavalry. Capron intended to raise funds for a permanent monument commemorating the soldiers who fell in the fight, but this project never materialized due to his death in Cuba in 1898.

Sometime after the turn of the century, probably in 1901, the Scott monument was "moved to a high nearby point to make way for the plow." This "nearby point" was an elevation near the present National Park Service overlook. Named Custer Knoll, or Headquarters Hill, this new location was identified in 1904 by Ben Clark, Custer's chief of scouts, who pointed out the landmark to Fred S. Barde, a correspondent for the *Kansas City Star*. In 1910 Clark revisited the monument, this time in company of Walter M. Camp, a railroad engineer and scholar of the Indian wars. Camp noted that souvenir hunters had knocked off chunks from the stone slab, which had been reduced in

[?]3 is still marked or that the new settlers have spared Black Kettle's tree.4 There used to be a newspaper published at Minco on the Rock Island, the "Minco Minstrel." I sent photographs of that monument and a short story asking them to publish it and request the newcomers to cherish the monument and trees.

When we made the monument, we piled a great many pony skulls of those killed by Custer from the captured Indian pony herd against the monument and there were still many left altho some one from the southwest had hauled away a great many to sell. I wish those old Indian days were back again. . . .

---

size to half a bushel; he was able to lift it off the ground and place it on top of a little heap of rocks, where it would appear to better advantage. Writing to Scott in 1918, Camp informed him that "the stone is still in existence, though it had been moved from the location where you left it." But the vandalism and erosion of the monument continued. By 1928 the damage had become so severe that it alarmed the current landowner, James H. Williams, who notified the authorities and requested the immediate removal of the crumbling stone to ensure its preservation. Accordingly, Sheriff Jim Lester transferred the artifact to the Roger Mills County Courthouse in Cheyenne.

In 1930 the remains of an unknown Indian were interred at the battlefield during a military ceremony conducted by the American Legion in the presence of a crowd of more than five thousand people, resulting in renewed public interest in the Washita battle. As a result the monument was taken from its obscure place in the courthouse and loaned to John C. Casady, founder and editor of the *Cheyenne Star* and an avid student of the battle. Casady, whose collection of artifacts included several skeletons, exhibited the stone with other battlefield relics in a window of the Star building on Main Street in Cheyenne. A local resident recalled that the transfer took place in 1934, which is probably the correct date, for in 1935 a tourist reported seeing the stone on display in the storefront along with the alleged skull of Black Kettle. Casady maintained custodianship over the monument until 1959, when it was transferred to the newly built Black Kettle Museum in Cheyenne. Eventually, the artifact will be returned to the Washita battlefield to be displayed in a glass case in the new National Park Service visitor center planned for the near future. H. L. Scott 1928, 153; Scott to Joseph B. Thoburn, Mar. 26, 1918, Thoburn Collection; *New York Sun,* May 10, 1899; *Daily Oklahoman,* July 27, 1930; *Kansas City Star,* Dec. 4, 1904; Camp 1910; Camp to Scott, Apr. 3, 1918, Camp Collection, Little Bighorn Battlefield National Monument Library, Crow Agency, Mont.; *Cheyenne Star* 1930b; Young 1929; A. Moore 1968; Betty Wesner to Bruce Liddic, e-mail, Dec. 3, 2001, Feb. 4, 2002, copies in author's files. See also chapter 30.

3This appears to be a reference to Smoke (or Smokey), an Arapaho who was known to the Cheyenne as "Tobacco." This man had made a daring charge on Elliott's soldiers and was shot to death right among them. In commemoration of Smoke's valorous deed, his tribesmen later marked the path of his charge by two cottonwood poles placed upright in the ground. H. L. Scott 1931.

4Black Kettle's lodge stood under a giant cottonwood, which was scorched when his lodge was set on fire during the destruction of the village. But Scott states elsewhere that the cottonwood was blazed by Cheyennes shortly after the fight. H. L. Scott 1928, 153.

Very sincerely yours,
H. L. Scott
War Dept., Washington, D.C.

Interview Notes by Walter M. Camp
Undated[5]

Scott says he was told by some of the warriors who killed Major Elliott and [his] men that Elliott and [his] men could easily have escaped during some little time before [they] were completely surrounded. The Indians at first came up straggling along as they got their mounts and for some time were not strong enough to attack [the] soldiers. They expected the soldiers to leave, but they did not and held their ground until overwhelmed.

Col. H. L. Scott, who had an intimate acquaintance with some of the old warriors who were in the Washita fight and in the Kiowa and other camps further down the river, says that all these Indians, as well as Black Kettle's, were poorly armed. Elliott went southeast from Black Kettle's village.

Scott says Custer had the right ideas of Indian fighting. Indians could not be maneuvered by "threatening their flank" as in civilized warfare—they had to be grabbed, as at [the] Washita and as [Gen. Nelson A.] Miles afterward did.

---

[5]These notes are found in Unclassified Miscellaneous Envelope 8, Camp Manuscripts, Indiana University Library, Bloomington; they are reproduced by special permission.

28

Homer Heap of Birds, Cheyenne

Homer Heap of Birds was born about 1860 and was the son of Chief Heap of Birds, a signatory of the Medicine Lodge Treaty of 1867. The elder Heap of Birds was arrested at Darlington Agency in April 1875 for depredations committed against whites and died in October 1877 at the age of fifty-one while imprisoned at Fort Marion, Florida. The chief's two sons, Homer and Alfrich, served with the Indian Scouts at Fort Reno from 1883 until 1895, when the company was disbanded.

The comments that follow are from a feature article written by Alvin Rucker and published in the Daily Oklahoman, *July 27, 1930.*

Comments Recorded by Alvin Rucker
With Excerpts from His Commentary
February 15, 1930

Standing Bull,[1] accompanied by his aged father, Chief Heap of Birds, and by Chief Little Hand and by Walter Bear Bow, a youthful Cheyenne, recently visited the five-mile long campsite which includes the Washita battlefield and Black Kettle's camp-site. Chief Heap of Birds, as a boy, was in camp when Custer made his attack sixty-one years ago. Chief Heap of Birds is about 70 years old. Chief Little Hand, about 75 years old, was in Kansas at the time of Custer's attack. His present wife, about 78 years old,

---

[1]Clyde Standing Bull was born in 1896 and was the son of Homer Heap of Birds and Little Woman. A veteran of World War I, he was gassed by the Germans while in the frontline trenches and was severely wounded by shrapnel. Clyde Standing Bull was also known as Many Magpies. Rucker 1930.

was in the camp when the daybreak attack was made on the sleeping village.

Chief Heap of Birds experienced no difficulty in piloting the visiting party to the east end of the five-mile long campsite where the Cheyennes, Arapahos, Kiowas, Comanches and Apaches camped sixty-one years ago, and [the party then drove] from the east end to near the west end where most of the fighting occurred. En route he explained through his son, Standing Bull, the location of the various tribes on the campsite. The east end of the campsite is about three miles north and east of the town of Cheyenne. [Between] . . . the west end, where Black Kettle's village [stood] at the extreme western end of the area, and the western end of the main camp there was an intervening, unoccupied area of about one mile. It was in that unoccupied area that all the fighting occurred after Custer charged at daylight upon Black Kettle's detached village. It is in that space of one mile that old cartridge shells, rifles, arrow heads and other relics of the battle have been found, and are still being found.[2]

Here is the order in which the various camps were pitched, as Chief Heap of Birds explained while standing on the battlefield: "Black Kettle's village was over there to the west; then came the unoccupied area; then the Arapahoe camp; then the main body of Cheyenne camp; then Kiowa camp; then the Comanches and Apaches."

. . . .

While Chief Heap of Birds stood in the area where so many relics of the battle have been plowed up during the past thirty-eight years, he asked to be driven to the mouth of a creek, which he said should be nearby. The car lumbered over the furrows of a rye field to an old creek bed west of the battleground, and came to a stop without much effort. Chief Heap of Birds shook his head, indicating that the creek was not the one he had in mind. The car

---

[2]Alvin Moore was a young boy in 1899 when his family rented the Butler farm in the northeast corner of the battlefield. He recalled that "there still existed much evidence of the carnage, consisting of the bones of Indian ponies, bones of human beings, spent bullets galore, and some unused ammunition. After a rain I would go to the battlefield and gather a tomato can full of bullets to use as fish line sinkers." Moore added that he also had found a sword, a peace pipe, an old rifle, and a canteen. A. Moore 1968.

was again set in motion westward and was driven through a gate into a north and south highway.[3] "There is where Black Kettle's village stood," he said in Cheyenne, and pointed to a creek traversing part of the farm on the west side of the road. By his direction the car was driven south a short distance, the ground at that point being higher and from which a better view of the surrounding area could be obtained.

"Black Kettle's village was all along here," he said, supplementing his statement with a generous sweep of the hand. He asked that the car be stopped so that he might get out and look around. All got out of the car, and while Heap of Birds was pointing out the route of an old army trail between Fort Elliott, a short distance beyond the Oklahoma-Texas boundary line, and old Fort Reno, more than 100 miles northeast, Walter Bear Bow, the youthful Cheyenne, pointed to a sector of sandstone exposed by a road scraper which had recently passed. It was fast in virgin soil, and about four inches beneath the surface. With some effort he wrenched it from the earth.

It was a Cheyenne pounding rock, a familiar domestic utensil to the older Cheyennes. The rock was used in pounding meat, berries, corn and other foods, the foods being placed on the rock and pounded with a similar rock. It was circular in shape and weighed about three pounds. The pounding rock had lain here sixty-one years, two months and nineteen days, in the position where it was abandoned when Black Kettle's people fled from the village at the time of Custer's charge. Windblown sand had covered it to a depth of about four inches. It was in soil that has never been plowed and has never been part of the beaten highway. It was exposed when the driver of the road scraper edged the machine off the beaten road to turn his machine around. He did not lift the blade clear of the shoulder of earth, and the blade had cut a swath from the shoulder, leaving the rock exposed but not damaging it.

. . . .

---

[3]This county road is no longer used. It ran north along the west side of the James H. Williams property, now the Washita Battlefield National Historic Site. After crossing the dry bed of the 1868 Washita channel, the road continued north to the bridge across the new channel of the river, dug by Williams in 1929. Ibid. See also maps on pp. 298 and 313.

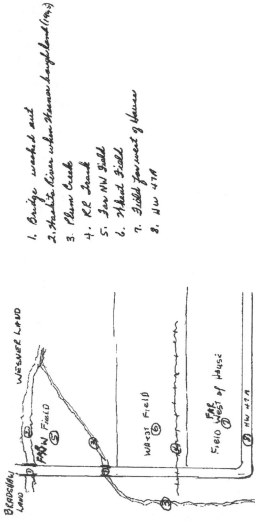

1. Bridge washed out
2. Washita river when Wesner bought land (1945)
3. Plum Creek
4. RR Track
5. Far NW Field
6. Wheat Field
7. Field far west of House
8. HW 47A

Dale told me that Plum Creek was on the Wesner land when John purchased the Battlesite. Dale had a little trouble explaining this so he made a drawing to show me. I did add the Field that is far west of our house.

—Betty Wesner, 2002

Washita Course in Northwest Corner of Battlefield, drawn by Dale Wesner.

In 1926 James H. Williams purchased the north half of Section 12, which contained the site of the Washita battlefield. He and his family lived in the old Bonner homestead on the property until 1928 when Williams began construction on a new two-story home. The Williams house was built northwest of Bonner's place and overlooked the valley and the curving tracks of the Panhandle Short Line. In 1929 Williams decided to reroute the Washita north of its original channel to gain easier access to his cultivated land. The new channel commenced just west of his property where the Washita entered his neighbor's land. From there the channel extended east along the north edge of Williams' property and rejoined the Washita after half-a-mile. As a result of Williams' reroute, Plum Creek no longer emptied in the Washita on his neighbor's property, but instead drained in the man-made channel in the northwest corner of Williams' land.

In the same year, 1929, Roger Mills County began construction of a county road along the west side of Williams' property. This road commenced at Highway 47 and ran north across the dry bed of the historic Washita channel. After crossing Plum Creek, the dirt road continued toward the Williams Channel where a wooden bridge allowed access to the north bank. Elderly Cheyennes who visited the battlefield in 1930 were confused by the new course of the Washita and remarked that the "white man change everything." Williams had been forewarned by his Cheyenne friend Sam Standing Water that the river could not be conquered and that sooner or later it would leave its new channel. Despite this warning, the Williams Channel survived the devastation of the flood of 1934 that took the lives of seventeen people in the Hammon area. The flood destroyed the Washita River Bridge over the Williams Channel, which was used by farmers north of the river to haul their loads of wheat across, and which was then the only way to town.

In 1945 James H. Williams sold his property to John Wesner. At this date the Washita continued to flow through the Williams Channel. However, in 1951 the Washita returned to its historic 1868 channel after heavy flooding in the Cheyenne area. Despite this setback, Wesner was determined to push the river back into the Williams Channel. The excavation work was completed in 1953. The restored Williams Channel was protected by wide berms of excavated dirt. Unfortunately, the improvements were no match for the unpredictable forces of nature. A devastating flood in 1954 destroyed the Williams Channel and caused the Washita to flow through its historic channel once again. This flood also destroyed John Wesner's new well, irrigation pipes, and fences. After this financial loss, neither he, nor his son Dale, made any further attempts to change the course of the Washita.

Today the outline of a berm and the rotted timbers of a bridge abutment near the northwest corner of the battlefield provide mute evidence of the Williams Channel and man's struggle to control the river. The bridge remnants stand 1056 feet north of the present Washita streambed. From here the river curves northeast towards the old Williams Channel and then loops south. Black Kettle's camp stood within this loop, about 600 feet south of the Williams Channel.

In the town of Cheyenne, about two miles east of the Black Kettle campsite, John C. Casady, editor of the Cheyenne Star, has a battered copper kettle which was picked up on the Arapaho campsite about twenty years ago by John Plunkett. The manufacturer's imprint shows that the kettle was patented February 13, 1866. Casady has several old revolvers, one of which is still loaded, and a rusted rifle picked up in the Cheyenne area.

In the courthouse at Cheyenne there is a large sandstone rock on which is etched an inscription indicating that Custer attacked the Cheyennes November 21 [sic]. The rock originally stood on the battlefield. After whites settled in the area the stone was moved to a high nearby point to make way for the plow. Souvenir hunters chipped away at the rock so much that J. M. Lester, then sheriff of Roger Mills County, moved the rock to the corridor of the courthouse for safekeeping.

. . . .

Due to the necessity of fleeing from the field when threatened by several thousand warriors who appeared during the day from the lower camps, Custer's men were forced to abandon overcoats and much other baggage which they had stacked preparatory to making the charge, the coats and baggage failing into the hands of the Indians. In sharp contrast to prevailing prohibition conditions, nearly all of the overcoats contained bottles partly filled with whiskey, according to tribal history related by Chief Heap of Birds.[4]

It is the Indians' understanding that whiskey was issued as part of the regular rations to frontier soldiers of those days, and as a blizzard was raging throughout the time of Custer's march upon Black Kettle's camp, and fire of any kind [being] prohibited, inward heat was doubtless needed. Custer killed 103 men, women and children during the charge upon Black Kettle's camp. The Cheyennes today take a charitable view of the killing of the women and the children and attribute it to the influence of liquor rather than inhumanity, or reckless indifference to the accidents of battle.

---

[4]The Sioux and Cheyenne made similar observations about the presence of whiskey at the Little Bighorn in 1876. They were convinced that the alcohol made the soldiers "crazy." See Richard G. Hardorff, comp. and ed., *Lakota Recollections of the Custer Fight: New Sources of Indian-Military History* (Spokane: A. H. Clark, 1991), 86–87.

29

Magpie,
Cheyenne

Born about 1852, Magpie was the son of Big Man and Magpie Woman of Stone Calf's band. After the Sand Creek Massacre in 1864, Magpie and his family joined relatives in the Wutapiu band and were present in the Washita village when Custer attacked in 1868. After the battle his family joined Medicine Arrow's band and surrendered at Fort Cobb in 1869. Fearing a renewal of hostilities, his family left the reservation in the 1870s and traveled north to join the Northern Cheyennes in the Powder River country of Montana. In June 1876 Magpie participated in the battle of the Rosebud, during which he was wounded twice by General Crook's soldiers. A week later he was present at the defeat of Custer at the Little Bighorn.

Magpie returned to the reservation in 1878. He enlisted as an Indian scout at Cantonment in 1879 and served through 1885, when the scouts were discharged. Magpie married Walking Woman, the daughter of Afraid of Beavers, who was a close friend of Magpie's father. In later years Magpie was elected to the Cheyenne Chiefs' Council and converted to Christianity to become the first adult Indian in the Cheyenne church at Cantonment. Chief Magpie died about 1936.

The account that follows was recorded by Charles Brill during an interview with Magpie at the Washita battlefield in September 1930. Brill submitted the interview with his commentary to the Daily Oklahoman, *which included it as a feature article in the Sunday issue of November 23, 1930.*

Narrative Account Recorded by Charles Brill[1]
With Excerpts from His Commentary
September 19, 1930

When the Oklahoma State Park Association listed this battle-field, some two years ago, as a possible state monument or state park, it appealed to Frank Rush,[2] one of the founders of the association, to assist it in locating these survivors. Frank Rush, who for more than half a century had been in sympathetic contact with these plains tribes, began inquiring among his Indian acquaintances for those whose testimony could be relied upon. Several times he followed clues only to find they led to imposters. Then, during the last all-Indian fair at Craterville Park, he learned through John Otterby,[3] former Indian scout and an educated

---

[1]Charles J. Brill was the secretary of the Oklahoma State Park Association and the coeditor of the outdoor magazine *Southwest Wilds and Waters.* This interview formed the basis for his book *Conquest of the Southern Plains,* which was published in 1938 and reprinted recently by the University of Oklahoma Press. Brill died on August 20, 1956, at the age of sixty-seven.

[2]Born in Kentucky in 1865, Frank Rush came to Oklahoma Territory from Kansas and worked the range as a cowboy and a ranch foreman, later becoming owner of a cattle ranch. In 1907 he accepted an appointment with the ranger force at the Wichita National Forest and Game Preserve, retiring after fifteen years' service. In 1923 he purchased Craterville Park near Lawton, Oklahoma, which he developed as a summer resort. As part of the attractions, Rush sponsored an all-Indian agricultural fair that included the customary Indian parade, traditional Indian dances, an arrow-shooting contest, horse races, and agricultural and livestock exhibits. In 1931 the all-Indian fair was expanded, with the financial backing from the state, and renamed the Oklahoma State Indian Fair. Widely known as "the Indian's Best Friend," Frank Rush died at his ranch at Craterville Park on April 7, 1933. See Muriel H. Wright, "The American Indian Exposition in Oklahoma," *Chronicles of Oklahoma* 24, no. 2 (Summer 1946): 160–61.

[3]Born in Colorado about 1858, John Otterby Jr. was the son of a French mixed-blood and a Southern Cheyenne woman named Picking Bones. His father was born in 1837 and served as an army scout at Fort Laramie, while his grandfather, Charles Autobees, had been employed as a trapper for William Bent and was known as Hoarse Voice among the Cheyennes. (The Autobees name was a phonetic derivative of Ortivi, which was variously spelled as Ortibi, Otterbees, and Otterby.) After the establishment of Darlington Agency in 1874, John Jr. was enrolled at the agency school, where he was listed as a full blood. In 1885 he enlisted in Lt. Homer H. Wheeler's Indian Scout Company at Fort Reno and by 1889 had been promoted to the rank of sergeant. Otterby was a member of the Cheyenne-Arapaho Tribal Council when he died about 1939. He was survived by his wife, Wolf Belly Woman, daughter of Chief Whirlwind (for her account, see chapter 38). Brill 1938, 26; George Bent to George Hyde, Oct. 20, 1902, Grinnell Collection, Southwest Museum Library, Los Angeles; Lecompte 1957, 163–79; Berthrong 1976, 196; Wheeler 1923, 280, 285.

member of the Cheyenne tribe, there would be at the Cheyenne campfire at El Reno in September, a veteran Cheyenne chief who had been wounded in the battle of the Washita. Through Otterby, as interpreter, an interview was arranged. . . . That is how Chief Magpie, Little Beaver,[4] another survivor, interpreter Otterby, Frank Rush and the writer came to make the pilgrimage one week later, which resulted in marking the exact location of Black Kettle's camp, in the creation of this narrative and in the determination of the citizens of Cheyenne to formally commemorate the sixty-second anniversary of the so-called battle.

. . . .

The big bend of the Washita in which Black Kettle's village stood lies two miles west of the city of Cheyenne. Topping the rise, which brings it into view from the highway, we brought our cars to a stop [so] that the Indians might get their bearings. It was their first visit to the spot since the day of the massacre. For several minutes there was silence. "White man change everything," Chief Magpie finally remarked through the interpreter. "Everything except hills. He can't change them. . . ." Chief Magpie was right. [The] white man had changed everything in the region of the Washita battlefield, except the hills. He has cut the timber, which had fringed the banks of the Washita along the big bend where Black Kettle's camp had stood. Not content with this, he has changed the course of the Washita to straighten it so that it flows several hundred yards north of the original channel. In some places the faintest trace of the old channel remains; but the Black Kettle bend still is distinctly marked by the precipitous sides of the old stream.[5]

No sooner had these things been explained to Chief Magpie after reaching the bend, than, taking his bearing from the prominent buttes on the ridge to the south, a creek to the west, and tracings of the old channel, he began searching in the weeds which

---

[4]Born about 1856, Little Beaver was the son of Wolf Looking Back and Red Dress Woman. Although Little Beaver and his father escaped from the village, his mother was captured and later forced to endure the sexual abuse of Custer's officers; she died near Watonga about 1925. Little Beaver married Turtle Woman (b. 1858) and settled on an allotment near Geary with their son, Young Little Beaver. Brill 1938, 22; Van Zandt 1984, 67.

[5]Traces of some of the old river channels are still visible today.

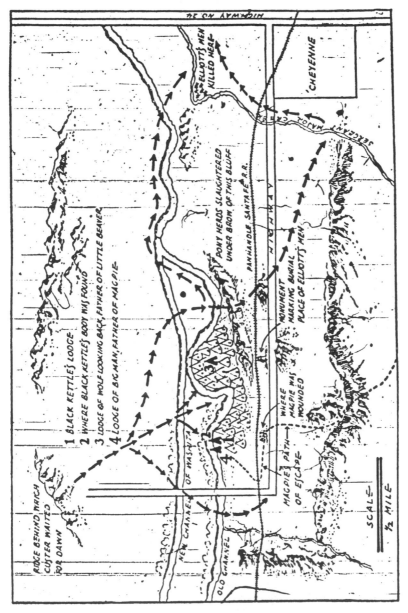

Location of Black Kettle's Village, drawn by Frank Rush. This map of the Washita battlefield is based on information he received from two elderly Cheyennes in 1930. Contrary to the annotation, the bodies of Elliott's soldiers were buried in a mass grave near present Strong City. Courtesy of *The Cheyenne Star*.

grow along the old bank for some familiar landmark. Asked for the object of his search he replied: "An immense tree stood near Black Kettle's lodge." Immediately Frank Turner,[6] who had joined the party and who had staked out a claim just north of the battle-field when that county was opened to white settlement in 1892, came to the rescue. "I helped cut that tree down. Part of the old stump is still there," he said.[7] And he led the chief to the spot. For some time the old chief was lost in meditation.

· · · ·

Now for Chief Magpie's story: "My heart is sad. I never had expected to return to the spot where so many of my people were killed and where the soldiers wantonly slaughtered our ponies; now that I am here, I feel I should tell what I knew to be the truth about the Black Kettle fight so the people will know the Indians were not the blame. They were not bad. They were not on the warpath. They had come here to be out of the white man's way, so they would not have to fight the white soldiers, but Custer's soldiers hunted them out and tried to kill or to make slaves of them.

---

[6]Born in Texas, Hannibal Frank Turner and his half-brother William E. Turner participated in the Cheyenne-Arapaho Land Run of 1892, settling on the south half of Section 1 north of the battlefield. William Turner died at his homestead in the 1920s. Frank Turner moved back to Texas in 1932. After a short stay, his family moved to Cold-water, Arizona, while Frank went on to Nevada to find employment in the construction of Hoover Dam. Frank Turner died in Texas in 1938 at the age of seventy-three. Wesner to Liddic, e-mail, Mar. 20, 2002, copy in author's files.

[7]This tree stood on land owned by James H. Williams, who had purchased the north half of Section 12 in 1926. Being present during Magpie's visit in 1930, Williams learned that Black Kettle's lodge stood on the south bank of the river, only a few feet from a tall cottonwood that leaned to the north, while five yards downstream another tree stood on the north bank, leaning south. Although Williams and his neighbor cut down these trees in 1928, the remaining stumps were still visible in 1930, confirming to Magpie that this location had once been the site of Black Kettle's camp. Unfortunately, the site was not marked in 1930, and the exact location is now no longer known. Based on information provided by Chief Heap of Birds in July 1930 and by Chief Magpie the following September, however, it is believed that Black Kettle's lodge stood a few hundred yards east of the pony ford. This crossing on the Washita is near the west section line of Williams's property. In 1929 a bridge was built a short distance north of the old ford. When the Hammon flood of 1934 destroyed this bridge, a road crew discovered an Indian skeleton near the abutment on the north bank. Van Zandt 1984, 62–63; *Cheyenne Star*, Apr. 10, 1952; see also chapter 28. Some of the larger trees that were cut down were hauled to a sawmill on the west side of Cheyenne. When the trunks were ripped into planks, the teeth of the large saw wheel sustained damage from the bullets imbedded in the wood. These slugs were collected in a bucket, said to have been half full at one time. Gary Scott to author, Feb. 16, 2004.

"Black Kettle's village stood on the south side of the big bend in the creek. There were sand hills and scattered timber north of the stream. There was a fringe of larger trees along the creek, which gave partial shelter from the cold north winds. There was snow on the ground, but in the village the snow had been beaten down by many feet. Our pony herds grazed in the valley and up on the sides of the hills to the south when snow did not hide the grass. Some horses, however, were kept always in the village for emergencies or to be ridden after the herds. That night some of them were across the creek in the sand hills.

"My father's lodge was the farthest west in the entire village. Next to it was that of Black Kettle. My father's name was Big Man. I think Black Kettle's people and my people were related. My mother told me I was a sort of nephew to Black Kettle. (Probably a second cousin.) My name was Magpie. Black Kettle's daughter was Magpie Woman, so we must have been some relation. There were about fifty or sixty lodges in the village. (Custer reports fifty-one.) That at the farthest end of the village was close to the monument.[8]

"The day before Custer came, Black Kettle and some of the other chiefs (Wolf Looking Back, father of Little Beaver, was one of these) had returned to the village from a visit to the soldier camp down the Washita. (Fort Cobb.) While there they had been informed by the chief officer (General Hazen, a classmate of Custer's at West Point) that the soldiers were coming after the Indians from the north. Black Kettle protested that all the Indians on the Washita were at peace with the whites and begged the chief officer to tell the soldiers who were coming that this was so. The chief officer shook his head sadly and replied that while he knew this to be so, the man in charge of the soldiers from the north was of higher rank than he. (General Sheridan was at [Camp] Supply when the expedition started and General Hazen supposed that he

---

[8]There was no monument on the battlefield in 1930: Scott's Seventh Cavalry monument had been moved to Cheyenne in 1928, and the Platonic Club's commemorative Indian marker would not be erected until 1932. Yet the map published with Brill's article shows a marker on the bluffs, with the annotation "monument marking the burial place of Elliott's men." But this too contradicts the facts, for Elliott's men were buried in the big bend of the Washita, northwest of present Strong City. See Keim 1885, 150–51.

would head the expedition.) Therefore he merely could transmit Black Kettle's message and testify to the peaceful nature of the villages on the Washita, which were all within the district administered by General Hazen. He could not give orders to the new soldiers.[9]

"It was a troubled group which gathered in Black Kettle's lodge that night to partake of crackers, hardtack, and other supplies brought back from the soldier camp down the river and to discuss the disturbing information received here. My family was there, including myself. There was some talk of moving camp; and it might have been done except for the fact that it was winter with deep snow on the ground. We did not know that even then the soldiers were almost upon us. (This statement is rather significant in view of the fact that in Custer's memoirs he says that some of the chiefs and warriors had spent the night in carousal, celebrating the return of a victorious war party, hence were caught napping when he charged the village. Apparently it was the bad news from Fort Cobb, which kept the chiefs up late that night.)

"Early next morning when my father stepped outside his lodge, he heard dogs barking. An instant later a woman came running from the timber across the creek to tell Black Kettle that soldiers were riding down on the camp. Remembering the Sand Creek massacre and fearful this might be a repetition of that tragedy, Black Kettle quickly sent word for women and children to save themselves. Scarcely had he spoken when the soldiers poured a volley into the camp and came charging across the creek.

"I had just pulled on a few clothes and was buckling on one of my father's pistols when this volley struck camp. I rushed out just as Black Kettle and his wife mounted a pony and started to ride into the timber. With two companions I headed for the cover of

---

[9]After a disappointing conference with General Hazen at Fort Cobb on November 20, the Cheyenne delegation arrived back at their village on November 26, having traveled 240 miles in thirteen days on weakened ponies in severe weather. Black Kettle's journey to Fort Cobb may have been undertaken at the advice of William Griffinstein, who was married to a woman from Black Kettle's village. After his wife's death about October 10, 1868, Griffinstein sent a runner to her parents to inform them of their daughter's passing. At the same time he may have sent a message to Black Kettle to warn him about Sheridan's winter campaign and to urge him to see Hazen. Justus 2000, 13.

the creek about a quarter of a mile west.[10] We had traversed only half the distance when we ran into soldiers swooping down from that direction. We turned to the south, finally dropping into a slight depression in which was growing a small thicket of chinaberry bushes and tall grass. Creeping to the edge I pulled out my pistol ready for action. A shower of bullets told us that our hiding place had been discovered. One of these bullets struck me just below the left knee, on the outer side of the leg, passed through the calf and came out just above the ankle. (He exhibited the scars, showing where the bullet had entered and where it had come out.)

"In spite of my wound, I jumped up and joined my companions in our flight, closely pressed by soldiers. Just when I thought they would kill us, they spied a large group of women and children coming from the southeastern end of the village. So they quit chasing us and took after the larger bunch of fugitives.[11] We ran over the ridge to the south, passed those two buttes (pointing to twin knolls near the top of the hill), turned down the next valley and kept going east until we encountered reinforcements coming from the lower villages.[12] These bound up my leg and I went on out of the battle zone. From the top of a high ridge I watched the battle and saw the soldiers burn the village and slaughter our ponies. This made the Indians very angry and they would have attacked the soldiers had they not been afraid that such an attack would bring death to the women and the children the soldiers had captured and were holding in the village. Shortly after dark, the soldiers suddenly fell into line and with the women and children in the center

[10]Magpie, his father, and a man named Pushing Bear "headed for the cover of a creek some three hundred yards south and West [from Black Ketttle's lodge.]" (Brill 1938, 161). This was Plum Creek, which flows into the Washita near the northwest corner of the present battlefield site. Black Kettle's camp was a few hundred yards east of this ford.

[11]Ben Clark also mentions the plight of these fleeing women and children and describes their escape route. See "Revision of the *Star* Interview" in chapter 18.

[12]Although not mentioned in this article, Brill later reveals that Magpie shot a mounted soldier near the twin knolls, along the bluffs south of the village. This soldier, according to Brill, was Capt. Albert Barnitz, who sustained a pistol shot to the stomach fired at point-blank range by Magpie, who then captured the officer's horse and made his escape. Yet Brill's identification of the victim merits skepticism based on the following facts: Barnitz killed his adversary; the victim was armed with a Lancaster rifle; and Barnitz's horse was not captured. Brill 1938, 162, 304–305.

marched out in the direction from which they had come—to the northwest. Some of the Indians started to follow them but were called back for fear harm might come to the prisoners.

"After the soldiers had left I went with other Indians to the village to help bury the dead. We found Black Kettle's body at the edge of the stream within a few yards of his lodge. All of it was under water except his face. His body had two bullet holes in it. One bullet had entered from the front, through the abdomen. The other had struck him in the back just below the shoulders. This bullet had shattered his backbone. It is possible one of these same bullets may have killed his wife whose body was found a few steps up the bank. One of the two braids in which she wore her hair had been cut off.[13] We carried these bodies to a small Sand hill north of where they had been found. That was the last I saw of them, for I went back to the village to try to find the body of an aunt who had been reported killed. When I left the group around the bodies of Black Kettle and his wife, the men were discussing carrying them farther from the stream for burial. Whether this was done or whether they were buried on that little sand knoll I do not know.[14]

"Most of those who escaped were those who ran for the creek. Most of those who tried to take to the hills ran into the soldiers and were captured or killed. It was freezing cold and there was ice on the creek except where the water ran swift. Although many of the women and children were barefooted and only scantily dressed, they plunged into these icy waters and waded down them believing this temporary misery [was] better than the showers of bullets the soldiers were raining into the brush. They tell me a lot of women and children were killed under one bank when the soldiers came upon them.[15] They also tell me Custer said he killed

---

[13]Black Kettle's wife was a Ponca captive known as Medicine Woman Later, or Medicine Woman Hereafter. She was a Sand Creek survivor despite having suffered nine gunshot wounds during that attack. Her grandson described her as a very large woman, weighing more than two hundred pounds. Hyde 1968, 155, 316. See also chapter 31.

[14]For a discussion of Black Kettle's death and his burial location, see chapter 32.

[15]A portion of the north bank in this gooseneck bend of the river had caved in and had formed a large mount of dirt. The bodies of some twenty men, women, and children were found huddled behind this natural breastwork after the battle. See "*Kansas City Star* Interview" in chapter 18.

103 braves; but he did not. Only fifteen or twenty of our men were killed.[16] All the others killed were women and children. (Custer in his letter to his wife admits 'some' women and children inadvertently were killed and wounded.)

"I do not know either how many soldiers were killed. Not many, for there was little or no shooting at the soldiers in the village. The Indians did not fight back there. The soldiers started shooting into the village even before we could see them and kept shooting everywhere so flight was all the Indians were interested in at the time. About the only fighting by the Indians in the vicinity of the village was done by men trying to hold back the soldiers who were trying to kill our women and children running down the creek. They told me afterward that three Indians hidden behind a fallen tree killed several soldiers who were trying to get to the women and children in the creek, but I did not see this done. I think most of the soldiers killed were those who chased some Indians away down the Washita and ran into our reinforcements from the camps below. (Elliott's command.) These soldiers became separated from the others and all were killed, but they were not many. They were all killed in that ravine just this (west) side of Cheyenne."

Included in the prisoners carried away was the mother of Little Beaver. Another was the sister of Black Kettle. Black Kettle's son and daughter made their escape.[17] When the soldiers marched away with the prisoners, those left behind feared they never would be seen again, but all were returned to their tribes several months later.

. . . .

The loss which stirred the Indians more than all others was the wanton slaughter of their ponies. While hundreds of Indians looked on from the rugged ridges, which flank the north and south banks of the Washita valley at this point, the pony herds

---

[16]Although Magpie and Little Beaver stated the names of twelve Indian casualties, Brill only mentions seven by name: Black Kettle, Little Rock, a boy known as Crazy, two young men called Hawk and Blind Bear, a Sioux identified as Bad Bank, and an Arapaho named Tobacco, who Brill misidentifies as a Cheyenne. Brill 1938, 16, 155–56, 161, 163–64, 169–70.

[17]Black Kettle had four wives and fathered a total of seventeen children, according to White Buffalo Woman, sister of Little Rock. Two of these wives and several children were killed during the Washita attack. J. H. Moore 1987, 272. See also Appendix I.

were rounded up under the bluffs south of the village and these were shot down. Custer's report says it took three companies more than an hour and a half to complete this detail. Magpie pointed out the bluffs where this took place. His identification of the location was confirmed by Frank Turner, the pioneer settler who was with our party and also by Alvin Moore, an attorney of Cheyenne and member of the Oklahoma senate, whose father once owned the land upon which the battlefield stands. Frank Turner said long after he had staked his claim north of the battlefield he watched freighters load bones of these animals into huge wagons to be taken to Texas and sold for fertilizer.

Numerous incidents of more than passing interest were related by both Chief Magpie and Little Beaver during our stay on the battlefield. Included among the guests in Black Kettle's village on the occasion of Custer's attack was Black Beaver, a famous Kiowa. Being only a visitor, Black Beaver kept his horse with him and had it tied just outside his lodge. When awakened by Custer's opening volley he rushed out only to find someone had beaten him to his mount. He then fled afoot and made good his escape.

Another visitor was a Sioux named Bad Bank and his family, consisting of his wife and three daughters. These learned from those who had returned from Fort Cobb with Black Kettle the report that soldiers were coming out of the north. His wife urged that they move immediately to one of the larger camps, which stretched out from six to twelve miles farther down the Washita. Bad Bank said it was too late in the day to move then but that they would do so next day. Next day was too late. Bad Bank, his wife and one daughter were killed. The other two daughters got away.[18]

A unique character in camp was Pegleg, so called because he possessed only one leg. He had lost the other during a fight with an Arapahoe. Though many with two good legs were killed, Pegleg managed to make good his escape. It is possible it was he who appropriated Black Beaver's pony.

---

[18] Also known as High Bank, this Sioux man and his family camped with Black Kettle's relatives at the western end of the village. Bad Bank's wife and daughter were the only Sioux women killed. See chapter 32 and "The Grinnell Letter" in Appendix G.

30

Judson Cunningham, Roger Mills County Recorder

Judson Cunningham was a longtime resident of Cheyenne, Oklahoma, where he served as the court recorder for Roger Mills County. He held a lifelong interest in the battle of the Washita and had searched the area for artifacts on numerous occasions. Cunningham chaired a committee to raise funds for a commemorative monument to the "Unknown Indian," which became a reality in 1932 through the efforts of the Cheyenne Platonic Club.

The interview that follows was conducted by Joseph G. Masters in July 1935. Masters was a principal at Central High School in Omaha, Nebraska. An avid student of the history of the Santa Fe Trail, he made a side trip to Cheyenne in 1935 to view the Washita battlefield. The interview is housed in the Joseph G. Masters Papers, Kansas State Historical Society, Topeka; it is reproduced by special permission.

Interview by Joseph G. Masters
July 29 and 30, 1935

July 29, 1935

Battle of the Washita, July 29, 1935. Told to me by Judson Cunningham who got much of the tale from Chief Magpie as this Indian related it at the dedication of the monument to the Unknown Indian in 193-.[1]

---

[1]The dedication of the monument to the Unknown Indian took place in November 1932. The triangular granite marker was donated to the Platonic Club by Peller Brothers of Granite, Oklahoma, inscribed "Custers Battle, Nov. 27, 1868." It was erected at the grave of an unknown Indian who was buried in 1930 on the slope near the present National Park Service overlook. See Appendix H.

Magpie relates that Major Elliott and his men were following down Sergeant Major Creek and were after Indians. He moved on and on east until he had reached the red hills in the east which were about 1 1/2 miles from where the first attack was made. Then, Major Elliott saw Indians from the camps below coming through the hills from the east. Major Elliott saw they were too many for him and began to retreat toward the southwest, but unexpectedly met Indian warriors coming down Sgt. Major Creek. He seemed to veer to the north (he was still on the east side of Sgt. Major Creek, which he had to cross to get back to Custer). He was com-

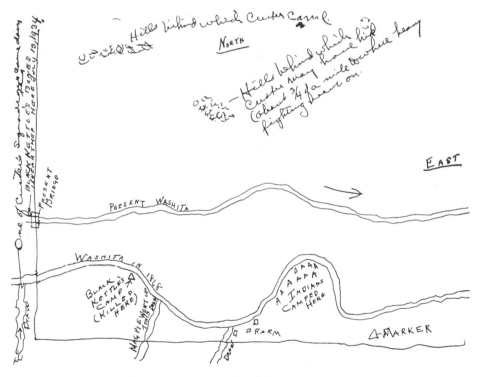

Washita Battlefield, drawn by Joseph G. Masters, 1935. Masters's map shows the dry channel of the historic Washita and the excavated replacement to the north by James Williams. The map gives the location where "Black Kettle's bones" were exhumed and the marker to the Unknown Indian, placed in 1932. Also shown are the old Bonner house near the "draw" and the new farmstead of the Williams family, located east of the Bonner house. Courtesy of the Kansas State Historical Society.

pletely surrounded when he and his men fought to the last ditch as has been described. He and his men fell about a mile east from where the main engagement began.

Black Kettle was far up the west end (possibly 200 yards upstream from the main body of Indians) and was running west when he ran onto soldiers, was killed, and fell into the water. His warriors, thinking to honor his memory, took him to a knoll of sand some 200 to 300 yards northwest where they buried him with many remembrances. Strangely enough the Washita River shifted its course a hundred or 200 yards north. A bridge was built across the new channel. Then, when the north approach washed away, the teamsters found all of his bones. They took the beads and trinkets, but many were allowed to go with the dirt. The skull and bones now (July 29, 1935) adorn a show window of a drugstore in Cheyenne, Oklahoma.[2]

From the high hills northwest where Custer came in, one can look over the field of battle very clearly ([took] 3 photos here). Distance may be calculated from data.

Black Kettle's body was taken some 200 or 300 yards northwest and buried on a sand knoll with many beads, trinkets, pipe stem, etc. His body strangely enough was buried where later a bridge over the new Washita was built and where the north approach was washed away in the summer of 1934. Graders were scooping out dirt on the west side of the north approach to the bridge and came to Black Kettle's bones. These are now in a show window of the Cheyenne store. (Owner John C. Cassidy.) (Got photos of the 7th Cavalry marker and skull of Black Kettle; photos against my car were taken in the sun.)[3]

------

[2]The skeleton was found by a road crew on July 13, 1934, during excavation work near the Washita River Bridge in the northwest corner of the battlefield. Two laborers named George Parker and Jeff Lacy carefully collected the bones and ornaments and brought them to the *Star* office in Cheyenne, where they were displayed as Black Kettle's remains. The "identification" was made by Black Kettle's grandson Stacy Riggs and by Charles J. Brill. But a forensic examination by Dr. Clyde Snow of the Oklahoma State Medical Office in 1968 revealed that the victim was a young Indian woman. *Cheyenne Star,* Apr. 10, 1952; Thetford 1969a.

[3]In addition to the 1890 commemorative monument and the "Black Kettle skeleton," the following battlefield artifacts were also exhibited in John Casady's office window: a .44-caliber Remington Model 1861 pistol, a rim-fire cartridge and bullet, a barrel

July 30, 1935

Major Elliott rode almost two miles east after Indians and [was] killing one once in a while. He rode down Sergeant Major Creek over to the red hills east of town where he saw Indians come through the hills and knew he must turn back to escape. He started to ride to [the] top of [a] hill about 200 yards east of [the] present town of Cheyenne for observation and to get his bearing to find his way back to camp. He then started almost northwest where he began to meet Indians. By the time he reached Sgt. Major Creek, Indians were coming down that [stream] in such numbers as to stop him, where Indians completely surrounded him and cut him and his men down. (See other accounts.) General Custer must undoubtedly have heard the firing that killed Maj. Elliott and must have been reasonably sure of his death before leaving the battlefield.

Battlefield General

It was a running battle. Indians escaped to the south. Tried to get out other ways and could not. Magpie escaped up a draw to [the] west and south and hid in tall grass. Later when soldiers came that way he jumped up and started to run, when the soldiers shot him in the leg, but [he] ran on and escaped. He saw Maj. Elliott and has given us this account of the escape. Indians were strung up and down [the] river over a quarter of a mile in Black Kettle's camp.

In [the] early days [the] Washita was not over 20 feet wide, with steep grassy banks and deep water, but easy to cross. There was heavy timber on both sides in 1868. [There] was heavy timber along Sgt. Major Creek. Elliott sought to hide in this as he went down (or east).

July 30. In going over [the] battle this afternoon it is clear that Maj. Elliott was killed a good 1½ miles east of where Custer made his big attack. He was killed on the banks of the Sergeant Major

---

from an Indian percussion rifle, a Minié ball fired from an Indian muzzleloading rifle, a mess kettle, a cavalry stirrup, and a bridle bit (Casady n.d.). Casady also became the custodian of four sets of Indian remains, three of which are believed to be those of Washita victims.

Creek (on east or south side). He had gotten to the red hills almost a mile east of the point where he was killed. When he saw Indians coming through the red hills he lit out to escape them but was confronted by many Indians [who] surrounded [him] on the east bank of Sgt. Major Creek, and could not escape. Probably he got at least ¾ of a mile east of where he was killed.

31

Stacy Riggs,
Cheyenne

Stacy Riggs was born about 1860 and was the son of Black Kettle's daughter. His father was killed by Ute Indians near Bent's stockade in March 1864 after an unsuccessful raid on their pony herds. (He was scalped and all of his fingers were cut off—exactly as had been revealed to him in a premonition.)

Riggs was known during adolescence as Red Bird and was given the name Lone Wolf by his father, just before the latter's death. He had a younger sister, who was born about 1862. After the Washita battle she was adopted by some of her father's relatives and raised among the Northern Cheyennes in Montana. Riggs, however, remained in Indian Territory and was brought up by aunts and uncles. About 1875 his relatives joined the Northern Cheyennes and were present in Dull Knife's village when it was destroyed by General Mackenzie's troops in November 1876.

After his return to Indian Territory, Riggs was enrolled at Carlisle Institute, where he adopted the Christian name Stacy Riggs from a missionary he greatly admired. Upon graduation he returned to the reservation and married Marry Ella Poisal, the granddaughter of French-Canadian trader John Poisal and his Arapaho wife, Snake Woman, the daughter of Chief Left Hand. Marry Ella was simply known as Arapaho Woman and was praised among the Cheyennes for her beautiful beadwork.

After a short enlistment as an Indian scout, Riggs was employed by the agency as an assistant farmer and interpreter. He embraced Christianity and was enrolled as a member of the Episcopal Church. He also operated a small general store at Whirlwind's village along the Canadian River near Fay, Oklahoma. In later years Riggs moved to

Washita County, where he lived on his allotment near Clinton with his grandchildren. It was said that he was a good-natured man who enjoyed reading and had mastered the use of a typewriter to prepare articles for the Cordell (Okla.) Beacon. *Stacy Riggs, Lone Wolf, died in Clinton, Oklahoma, in 1947.*

The statements that follow consist of two items: an account by Stacy Riggs's mother given to her son and retold to Thomas Benton Williams on November 18, 1936; and a letter written by Riggs in July 1934 regarding the death of his grandparents.

Account of Black Kettle's Daughter
As Told to and Related by Her Son, Stacy Riggs
November 18, 1936[1]

Me [Riggs's mother] and my three sisters, Pipe Woman, White Buffalo Woman[2] and Ma-wota, Red Feather [Woman], and one brother, Motovata, (Black Kettle, Jr.)[3] left our village for Whirlwind Camp where the river comes back to east of our village.[4] White Shield (Gentle Horse)[5] had had [a] vision and had seen

---

[1]This interview was conducted by Thomas Benton Williams, who included it in his provocative volume *The Soul of the Red Man.* Williams was an Indian-rights advocate, and his probing work, published in 1937, is a sensitive testimonial to the injustices done to the indigenous people.

[2]One genealogical source suggests that White Buffalo Woman was the mother of Stacy Riggs. But Riggs himself makes clear that this was not the case. Nonetheless, White Buffalo Woman, his aunt, may have raised Riggs because his granddaughter recalled that he became an orphan after Washita and that relatives adopted him. Thetford 1969a; Lone Bear 1999.

[3]This son, known as Young Black Kettle, was born about 1831 and died in 1902. Two of his children were still living in 1969: Jay, born in 1880, and Nettie, born in 1884. Their last name had been shortened to "Black" during their youth as a result of misguided government efforts to Anglicize Indian names. Thetford 1969a.

[4]The Whirlwind village stood on the east side of the big bend in the Washita, some ten miles downstream from Black Kettle's camp. The distance between the two camps was only five miles when going straight across the base of the bend. Whirlwind was a nephew of Black Kettle.

[5]Gentle Horse was born in the Black Hills about 1800. He was the second son born to Black Hawk Lying Down and Sparrow Hawk Woman, who were both Sutai. In 1883 Gentle Horse changed his name to White Shield to honor the memory of a deceased nephew. Gentle Horse died in 1896. Most of his life he lived with the shame of killing the abusive husband of his sister. See Grinnell n.d.; Powell 1981, 1:638; Hodge 1907, 2:975; Grinnell 1972, 1:356.

and foretold this danger. White Shield said he had seen a big wolf, with [a] wound on [the] right side of its head, mourning for its little ones who were all scattered and dead, by the mighty enemy, which we were unable to resist.[6] White Shield told his older brother Black Kettle, "Let's leave our village for [the] other camp," but Chief Black Kettle answered, "No, that wouldn't be right if I leave my village for safety. I am chief of this band and I [am] suppose to die first, before all of my people. Take our children to another camp for they are too young to scare."

We came to Whirlwind Camp nearly [at] midnight and was awake all night. I was thinking about our relatives we left behind. Whirlwind Camp was in hearing of the main camp at [the] Washita. I suddenly hear the firing at [the] main camp before daylight. I jump up from my bed and all my sisters were up at the same time and all went out to saddle our horses [to] go back to see the battle at home.

We went up Red Hill east of our village, looking [down] on our village, [which] was covered with [the] smoke of powder. Some of our young men arrived in time to save some women and children, who were hiding on the deep water in the creek below our village and white soldiers followed them and keep fire on them on their flight for safety.[7] Then we saw our young men charge fearlessly to the main battlefield at our village. They cut the detachment [of Elliott's soldiers] off from the main body of Custer's men as our young men keep arriving and charge the soldiers; but they were kept back by the heavy fire. Then, [an] Arapaho youth named Tobacco and [a] Cheyenne youth named Roman Nose Thunder[8] [charged], and then all [the] other warriors rush to [the] white soldiers, fighting by hand, and finish as we watched our village burn.

All our horses were killed south of our village, and soon the great smoke of the burning of our tepees and everything we had for our winter use was all we could see. We had a great herd of fine

---

[6]But see also "Extract of Letter to *Cheyenne Star*" following, which credits Black Kettle with the premonition.

[7]The flight of these women and children is described in detail in "Letter to Robert Peck" in chapter 42.

[8]For information on Roman Nose Thunder, see "Letter to Robert Peck" in chapter 42.

spotted horses. The white soldiers kill all of them except the few of the prettiest ones, which they take for themselves. We stay on [the] hill where we can see our village until toward evening. We watch the soldiers march up the river with the band play[ing]. After the soldiers left we took [their] overcoats which they had not used when they were making the charge, and can't use in fighting. And our boys help themselves to good warm overcoats, which they would not give back to Longhair because he destroyed our property. The snow was deep and it was covered with the blood of our people and our ponies.

My mother and aunts mourn and unbraided their long hair and cut it short. Their cousins and other relatives were all gone, either killed or taken prisoners to Camp Supply. Some of our brave young men follow the soldiers, who thought they had [a] chance to steal the prisoners in the night. But the guards watched them close[ly], and the Indians returned and inform us that the prisoners were not at Camp Supply. Then we move toward the south and our men chase buffalo to get hides for robes and shelter and meat for food. We suffered very much, but soon after we reached Texas it gets a little warmer and warmer, and we thought spring is approaching and we moved back north to our hunting grounds.

Extract of Letter to *Cheyenne Star*
July 1934[9]

I was three years old when my people were massacred by Gen. Custer and I am now an old man,[10] but I still remember where our tepee was located [at the Washita in 1868]. It was located near the

---

[9]This typed letter by Riggs was addressed to George Parker of Cheyenne. It appeared in the *Cheyenne Star* on July 26, 1934. Some grammatical changes have been made in the text, which has been divided into paragraphs.

[10]According to Riggs's account, he was born about 1865. But since Riggs was given the name Lone Wolf by his father, who was killed in 1864, he must have been born prior to his father's death. Riggs told Thomas Benton Williams that "he was a little boy of eight years when his grandpa smoked with . . . [Custer] at Captive River [in 1869]." This statement suggest that he was born about 1860, which is corroborated by his granddaughter, who added that he was about eighty-seven years old when he died in 1947. The "grandpa" was Stone Forehead, who was a cousin of Black Kettle. Lone Bear 1999; Grinnell 1972, 1:84; Williams 1937, 238.

river and [I] use to play with the other Indian children at the river. There was a large log in front of our tepee, which I use to ride on it. My people were busy cutting and drying buffalo meat for winter use, but the soldiers burned everything what we had. There were very few men [who] remained at home when General Custer attacked our village, so the women and children had no chance to be saved.

We had a blue pony tied in front of our tepee, which Uncle Bear Feathers was going to use when he went after horses early in the morning. But before everybody was up, our village was under fire and Uncle Bear Feathers tries to put grandmother, Mrs. Black Kettle, on the pony. But [the] pony was frightened and tries to start, but grandfather stood in front of [the] pony holding the pony so grandmother can get on with help of Uncle Bear Feathers. But grandfather fell and the pony was shot on the right hind leg, and then grandmother also fell. Grandmother was [a] very large woman [who] would weigh over two hundred [pounds]. Uncle Bear Feathers tries to drag her over a tree, but grandmother begs him to leave her.

He [Bear Feathers] leaves her to run down the river to save a large number of women and children from being shot down by the soldiers. Uncle Bear Feathers was carrying a baby boy in his arm and he uses his other arm in defending the women and children. Uncle Bear Feathers is known to be the swiftest runner in his day. I have this history and [it] will be published in the near future. I am [an] Indian, but I have been educated at Carlisle Indian School in Pennsylvania.

I had been visiting that old [Washita] battlefield and found many bones of our horses from 1885 through 1887 as United States Indian Scout at Fort Elliott, Texas, where Gen. Custer had smoked the pipe of peace with Priests Stone Forehead and Wooden Legs the next year after the massacre [of] my people. But [he] disobeyed the rules of the pipe. He took three old Indians, Curley Hair, Fat Bear and Island, as his prisoners, but the Indians never tried to fight him, for [the] Indians had to obey the code of their peace pipe.[11]

---

[11]For information on Stone Forehead and the Sweetwater captives, see "Letter to George Hyde" in chapter 42.

[Comments by the *Star* editor:] Stacy Riggs of Clinton, whose Indian name is Lone Wolf, grandson of Chief Black Kettle ..., is a Cheyenne Indian, educated at Carlisle University. He is nearly 70 years of age and is a correspondent for the *Clinton Daily News*. He was accompanied to this city by his son, Evert Riggs, part white, a printer of Enid, Oklahoma.

. . . According to his [Stacy Riggs] story, Black Kettle had a dream in which he saw a wolf with blood on its face, so he said, "Indians would die," and had sent his mother and him on east of the camp for safety, and that after the battle, some ten days, his mother and others came back to bury Black Kettle. The wolves had eaten part of the flesh, so he was buried in the ground, although it was custom to bury in trees.[12]

---

[12]According to a creditable Arapaho source, Black Kettle's remains were exhumed by his Arapaho daughter and buried on the North Canadian near Cantonment sometime after 1880. A. Heap of Birds 1999; Briscoe 1987, 3.

32

Moving Behind Woman, Cheyenne

Moving Behind Woman's recollections were recorded by Theodore A. Ediger in 1937. Ediger was a correspondent for the Associated Press and was then living in western Oklahoma. Well known among the Cheyennes, he had been given the name She Wolf after a brave man who fought at the Washita. The narrator was an elderly, blind Cheyenne named Moving Behind Woman, better known as Mrs. Black Hawk of Hammon, Oklahoma. Born about 1854, she had lived with the Wutapiu band of Chief Black Kettle and still vividly recalled the carnage of Custer's attack. Moving Behind Woman died shortly after the interview. Ediger was assisted by Mrs. Vinnie Hoffman, a formally educated Cheyenne who provided the translation for the interview. Hoffman was the granddaughter of Chief Heap of Birds, who died in prison at Fort Marion, Florida, in 1877.

The following is a reprint of "Some Reminiscences of the Battle of the Washita" by Theodore A. Ediger and Vinnie Hoffman, published in The Chronicles of Oklahoma *in 1955. It is reprinted by special permission from* The Chronicles of Oklahoma, *published by the Oklahoma Historical Society, Oklahoma City (copyright 1955).*

Narrative
1937

I have lived all these years, and before this no one ever has asked me to tell the story about how the soldiers approached the Black Kettle camp one morning at daybreak. You should have asked me long ago, before I went blind. Then I could have gone with you to that place and shown you where we camped and hid—if that place

323

is still the same. From what I hear, the place and the river are different now.

I was there, and know what happened to us that morning, about dawn. That was where Black Kettle was killed, as well as many other Cheyennes.

I was an orphan since I was a child, and my close relatives reared me. I was a young girl, and began to know a little about love at that time. I lived with my aunt, Corn Stalk, and her family. As I remember, my aunt and her husband, Roll Down, were well acquainted with Black Kettle and his family, and used to camp near him whenever they pitched camp.

Now, I will mention the names of some families who also camped near Black Kettle: Clown, Bear Tongue,[1] Scabby Man, Half Leg,[2] and some others I do not recall. These families all used to camp together. One Kiowa man named High Bank also camped there.[3] The rest of the Cheyennes camped east and west along the Washita River.

Bear Tongue and Statue[4] were the bravest men, and fought valiantly until they were shot and killed.

Black Kettle and some of the other Cheyennes had gone off somewhere during that time, and had just returned to the camp the day before the attack was made. With them they brought plenty of sugar, coffee, and other stuff.[5]

Someone in the camp said that a warning had been issued for us to move at once. They planned to have the camp move. But somehow they refused to move away at once. If they only could have listened and done what they were told to do! They did not feel sure

---

[1]Bear Tongue was the camp crier of Back Kettle's village. He was an older man who had fought conspicuously during the Pawnee Wars of the 1850s. Bear Tongue survived the Sand Creek Massacre but was slain at the Washita. Hyde 1968, 269.

[2]Also known as Peg Leg, this man had lost a limb during a battle with Arapahos. He was a Washita survivor. See chapter 29.

[3]High Bank was also identified as a Sioux; he was also known as Bad Bank. He, his wife, and one of his two daughters were killed during the attack. See chapter 29.

[4]Statue may also have been known as Standing Out or Sun Bear.

[5]The Cheyenne delegation returned on November 26 after a disappointing conference with General Hazen at Fort Cobb.

about the warning.[6] Not a soul knew about the secret plans that were being laid.

I felt rather strange late that evening.

Black Kettle's wife became very angry, and stood outside for a long time because they were unable to move that evening. She was disappointed. Sometimes your own feelings tell you things ahead; perhaps this was what the woman felt. She talked excitedly, and said, "I don't like this delay, we could have moved long ago. The Agent sent word for us to leave at once. It seems we are crazy and deaf, and cannot hear."

The next morning, just before daylight, someone must have suspected that the soldiers were near the camp, for many awoke earlier than usual.

We heard a woman saying in a low voice: "Wake up! Wake up! White men! White men are here! The soldiers are approaching our camp."

We became frightened, and did not know what to do. We arose at once. At that instant, the soldiers let out terrible yells, and there was a burst of gunfire from them.

My aunt called me, but as I started to go out, the girl with whom I had stayed all night grabbed me by the arm and pulled me back, saying, "Don't go out, stay inside; the white men might see you outside and shoot you." My aunt called me again, and told me to hurry up and come out. I became so frightened that I was trembling, but went outside.

I could see dark figures of persons running here and there in a mad rush. When a burst of gunfire was heard, my aunt would catch my hand, and say, "Hold my hand tightly, don't turn it loose whatever may happen. We will go somewhere and hide."

---

[6]The Cheyennes had ample warnings of the coming danger. General Hazen warned Black Kettle at Fort Cobb that troops were in the field to punish the Cheyennes. In addition, Black Kettle's younger brother, Gentle Horse, had a dream vision that the camp would be attacked. Moreover, a Kiowa war party reported a soldier trail near Antelope Hills and informed the Cheyennes of the danger. The Kiowa report was confirmed by a Cheyenne named Crow Neck, who had seen a line of moving figures coming from the Canadian River toward the Washita. In view of all these warnings and the lesson learned at Sand Creek, it seems incredible that Black Kettle did not move the village immediately. Powell 1981, 1:598; Grinnell 1956, 301–302. See also chapter 31.

The young men had guns, and they uttered the most terrifying war whoops when the fight began. Black Kettle and his wife were last seen when they rode off on a horse.

The brave man, Statue, on horseback, trotted his horse back and forth at the camp, talking in a loud voice to the chiefs. He said, "That is exactly how I always have felt toward you chiefs, that some day you would turn out to be cowards. Leaving the poor, helpless women and children behind, and letting them suffer!"

They say that some [Indians] got away before daylight, but no one saw who they were.[7] Many Indians were killed during the fight. The air was full of smoke from gunfire, and it was almost impossible to flee, because bullets were flying everywhere. However, somehow we ran and kept running to find a hiding place. As we ran, we could see the red fire of the shots. We got near a hill, and there we saw a steep path, where an old road used to be. There was red grass along the path, and although the ponies had eaten some of it, it was still high enough for us to hide.

In the grass we lay flat, our hearts beating fast; and we were afraid to move. It was now bright daylight. It frightened us to listen to the noise and cries of the wounded. When the noise seemed to quiet down, and we believed the battle was about to end, we raised our heads high enough to see what was going on. We saw a dark figure lying near a hill, and later we learned it was the body of a woman with child. The woman's body had been cut open by the soldiers.[8]

The wounded ponies passed near our hiding place, and would moan loudly, just like human beings. We looked again, and could see the soldiers forcing a group of Indian woman to accompany them, making some of the women get into wagons, and others on horses.

---

[7]Gentle Horse took some of Black Kettle's children and grandchildren to Whirlwind's village on the evening of November 26. There is also a report that a woman and her children fled the village after seeing soldiers moving on the hillside just before dawn. Nye 1969, 65. See also chapter 31.

[8]This atrocity could have been committed by the Osage scouts, who brutally mutilated their slain victims without regard to sex or age. But other survivors also spoke of atrocities committed by Custer's soldiers. Black Kettle's daughter, Walking Woman, saw a pregnant woman being chased by soldiers, who shot her near the river. "As she fell, one of them jumped off his horse and sliced her stomach and he held that unborn baby on his saber" (Cometsevah 1999, Aug. 20).

The Indian ponies that were left were driven toward the bottoms. Some horses would run back, and the soldiers would chase them, and head them the other way.

The soldiers would pass back and forth near the spot where I lay. As I turned sideways and looked, one soldier saw us, and rode toward where we lay. He stopped his horse, and stared at us. He did not say a word, and we wondered what would happen. But he left, and no one showed up after that. I suppose he pitied us, and left us alone.

Before leaving, the soldiers shot all the Indian ponies, which they had driven to the bottoms.

It was getting late in the day, and when all was quiet my aunt raised her head and looked around. "Look, we are safe!" she cried. "I can see someone walking up the hill. Let us get up now, and go there too."

Some more Indians were walking toward the first one on the hill. We got up, and ran to where the men were standing. Some more men and youths were coming from all directions. Some where on horseback.

"They (the soldiers) are right across the river, and are going slowly, let's shoot them," suggested someone. Others said not to shoot, for fear of hitting the Indian women who were being taken away by the soldiers. My aunt's husband happened to be there. Scabby and Afraid of Beaver[9] were there also, with two extra ponies, one of them my aunt's slow pony. While we stood there, some young men rode up, and one of them recognized me as his girlfriend. He got off, and as he shook hands with me, he asked, "Is this you, Moving Behind?"

I said "Yes." We both cried, and hugged and kissed each other. This young man, named Crane, was my sweetheart in the good old days when I was young. As I was about to leave, he said, "I will lend you my saddle, and you can return it sometime." He took his saddle off his horse, and brought it to me. I took it and used it.

---

[9]Afraid of Beavers was the brother of Medicine Woman Later, wife of Black Kettle. His daughter, Walking Woman, later married Magpie. *The (Washita Battlefield Historical Society) Washita Newsletter* 6, no. 3 (2000): 4.

We all got on our ponies, and rode down to the river to find the spot where Black Kettle and his wife were killed. There was a sharp curve in the river where an old road crossing used to be. Indian men used to go there to water their ponies.[10] Here we saw the bodies of Black Kettle and his wife, lying under the water. The horse they had ridden lay dead beside them. We observed that they had tried to escape across the river when they were shot.

Clown, Afraid of Beaver, and Roll Down got off their horses, and went down to get their bodies. They were too heavy to lift, so they had to drag them in the water, then bring them up. Clown got his red and blue blanket, and spread it on the ground beside a road a short distance from the river, and the bodies were laid on the blanket and covered with the same blanket. Clown got the saddle from the dead horse, and gave it to my aunt to use, saddling her pony with it.

It was getting late, and we had to go, so we left the bodies of Black Kettle and his wife. As we rode along westward, we would come across the bodies of men, women, and children, strewn about. We would stop and look at the bodies, and mention their names.[11]

We went farther west, up the Washita River, until we got to where Afraid of Beaver's father, named Crooked Wrist, was camping. There were some of my relatives there, and they told me to remain, that I was welcome at their tepee. I dismounted, and went in, and I lived with this family until I married.

A long time later, when the whites and Indians had quit fighting, George Bent asked us to go and shake hands with a soldier. We went, and he said that this was the soldier who saw us hiding, and pitied us and saved us. Of course, we shook hands with the tall soldier. I recall that he had a brown mustache and blue eyes.

---

[10]This pony crossing, later known as Custer's Crossing, was near the northwestern corner of the Washita battlefield.

[11]Some of the nude bodies of Cheyenne men and women were propped in sexually suggestive positions by Custer's soldiers. Several other corpses had been thrown on the huge bonfires during the burning of the village. One of the victims was a Cheyenne woman "with her lips burned off, stiff and cold, [who] was propped up against a tree, a horrible, grinning spectacle." Methvin n.d., 41; and 1899, 88.

33

John L. Sipes Jr., Cheyenne

John L. Sipes Jr. is a Cheyenne chief and a member of the Chiefs' Council of Forty-Four. He is also a tribal historian and is presently preparing a manuscript of Cheyenne oral histories. Sipes is a descendant of both peace chiefs and war leaders. One of his ancestors was Alights on a Cloud, a signatory to the 1851 Fort Laramie Treaty. Alights on a Cloud visited Washington the year of the accord and was killed in 1852 during the tribal wars with the Pawnees. His brother, Man on a Cloud, also became a council chief and visited Washington in 1880.

Another ancestor of Sipes was Medicine Water, son of Old Medicine Water and Yellow Haired Woman, who was the leader of the Bowstring Society. He is chiefly remembered by whites for his involvement in the killing of Oliver F. Short's surveyors crew, the destruction of the Patrick Hennessey wagon train, and the capture of the John German family, all in 1874. For these acts he was imprisoned at Fort Marion, Florida, for several years. Medicine Water was the great-great-grandfather of John L. Sipes Jr. and died in 1925.

The following account describes Custer's attack at the Washita and the subsequent death of Red Bird, great-granduncle of John L. Sipes Jr. The article originally appeared in the Watonga Republican *on June 18, 1997; it is reproduced with Sipes's permission.*

Account
June 18, 1997

Red Bird was born in 1850 in the Yellowstone River Country (Wyoming).[1] He had three brothers, Standing Bird, Bird Chief and Little Wolf, and three sisters, White Buffalo Woman, Little Woman and Double.

In the winter of 1868, while camped with his family on the Lodge Pole River (Washita River), Custer attacked their village. The troops were under orders to destroy a village and hang all the men and take all the women and children as prisoners. This was the second stealthy and unexpected attack by troops for Red Bird and his family since Sand Creek.

He was only 18 years old at this time. As he fought off the troops while his family escaped by crossing the icy waters of the Lodge Pole River, he fought bravely, standing in between the troops and his fleeing family. He was not married at this time.

Red Bird had a warhorse that stood beside him, never moving as he fought. This warhorse would not get exited if it heard loud noises such as gunfire or sounds of fighting for it was trained by Red Bird himself to be a warhorse.

Finally, Red Bird was overcome by the troops and killed. A family member took aim and shot Red Bird's warhorse that continued to stand by his fallen owner as he lay on the snow-covered ground. The horse fell beside Red Bird, as [it] was the custom of the Cheyenne warrior to be with his warhorse spirit in the journey along the Seana (Milky Way) to Maheo (God). This was also to insure that the troops didn't get this fine horse.[2]

A few days later, his sisters, Little Woman and White Buffalo Woman, moved his body to the southwest of the site. They put

---

[1]Red Bird was the son of Cut Arm, also known as Walks Different. Cometsevah 1999. Colleen Cometsevah was the great-granddaughter of Red Bird's sister, Little Woman, who was born in 1853.

[2]Red Bird received a fatal gunshot wound to the stomach while mounted, which caused his intestines to protrude from his abdomen. He died shortly thereafter in the presence of his grieving father, who shot his son's pony at the death site. Cometsevah 1999, which are based on a written account by Little Woman's son, Paul Mouse Road. George Bent was told that Red Bird was shot through the hand and in the breast.

him on a burial scaffold. They sang the proper death songs and warrior-going-home songs of the Cheyenne.

Two years later, Little Woman and White Buffalo Woman returned to Red Bird's burial scaffold. His remains had fallen to the ground. Little Woman gathered his remains and wrapped them in a specially prepared buffalo robe. She had the five (customary) food components and sang the proper songs again as she buried his remains somewhere in the deep canyons to the southwest of the site. Here he rests today with many of his extended kinship that died needlessly at the orders of the white soldiers.

Red Bird's sister-in-law, Tahnea or Measure Woman Standing Bird, was five years old at the time of Custer's attack. She was wounded by a soldier's bullet as she waded across the icy waters to escape. The wound was in the right hip. She walked with a slight limp the rest of her life (Measure Woman Standing Bird to Cleo Wilson and Everett Wilson as Oral Family Historians). Measure Woman was one year old at the Sand Creek Massacre in 1864.[3]

[During Custer's attack in 1868,] women, children, old people and even dogs in the camp were shot as if at a turkey shoot. Some people say this was a battle, but women and children don't fight battles.

---

[3]Measure Woman was the daughter of Big Shield Woman and Medicine Water, who had two wives. Measure Woman married Standing Bird, a brother of Red Bird. Born in 1864, Standing Bird and his brother Bird Chief served as members of Lieutenant Wheeler's Indian Scout Company at Fort Reno during the 1880s. C. S. Greene 1992, 52.

34

Mrs. B. K. Young Bird,
Cheyenne

Mrs. B. K. Young Bird was born in 1854 and was the daughter of Fly-ing Woman, a Southern Cheyenne. In 1937 Mrs. Young Bird related her story of the attack on Black Kettle's camp to her son-in-law, Joe Yellow Eyes, who wrote down her recollections for posterity. Mrs. Young Bird passed away on August 13, 1937, at Watonga, Oklahoma, shortly after this interview. The account that follows is housed in the Indian-Pio-neer History Collection, Archives Division, Oklahoma Historical Soci-ety, Oklahoma City; it is reproduced by special permission.

Narrative
June 22, 1937

We were camping very near the banks of the Washita, near the present site of Cheyenne, in Roger Mills County. Previous to this happening, there had been a Treaty of Peace signed by Chief Black Kettle. All of Black Kettle's band of Cheyennes felt very secure on account of that recent treaty of peace, but we were very much disappointed when Long Hair Custer made his surprise attack on us.

I was only fourteen years old and I remember well the happen-ings there. I was staying with my uncle. His name was Lays-on-top-of-a-Hill.[1] Very early that cold morning there was a little snow on the ground.

---

[1]Young Bird's parents were members of Whirlwind's band of the Hair Rope Peo-ple. This sub-band consisted of sixty lodges and camped separately in the big bend of the Washita, near present Strong City. Young Bird was visiting her relatives in Black Kettle's camp when the village was attacked.

There was no warning; up from our sleep we jump, we did not have time to gather our clothing; just as we got up from our sleep we ran for safety in the best way we knew. I heard very much firing all around us. I did not look to see whom it was that was doing all that firing but we all knew that Long Hair Custer was out hunting the Indians and we knew that he had found us.

We ran all our women folks and our girls and all of our children down to the banks of the Washita River for safety, but we found no safety. The soldiers were on both sides of the Washita River shooting a crossfire. There was no escape; we waded down the stream, all of us who were making an attempt to escape. Quite a few were shot down and some escaped I guess by a miracle. We could hear the women singing; they sang some war songs and some death songs, because all the men were now trying their best to defend us and themselves, and many were lying on the ground dead and very many were wounded; they were needing someone to come to take them to safety, where they might be given treatment to try to recover.

A lot of little children were still barefooted and lots of their feet were frozen. I experienced that myself, for up to the present time I'm having lots of trouble with my feet and also with my legs.

I cannot tell the horror that was experienced that awful cold morning when the soldiers started shooting and we jumped out of our sleep and ran for safety and very many of our people were shot down like rabbits. No mercy was shown to either the babies or children of any age and no mercy was shown to the women.

There was crying everywhere, all around us, and the shouting of war and death songs, and after the battle we looked from our place of safety and we saw smoke, very much of it, coming from where our camp had been. We learned soon that the soldiers had plundered and burned our whole camp and had taken our belongings and very many of the women and girls, and even smaller boys were driven away, taken prisoners to somewhere to be held there until our people were subjected by the government.

And from the main camp on down below the Washita River east came the Indians principally to rescue us, the survivors. I could see then my mother, Flying Woman, coming [showing?] both of very much sorrow and gladness and she seeing me, came running to embrace me, and I, too, was very much overjoyed, thanking the Great Spirit who watches over us in times of trouble.

After all was settled and the camp crier having made known that the soldiers were gone and far away, we all felt more at ease. Still orders were for each band of the Cheyennes to go off in hiding lest Custer might return.

My father and mother with us two children, a younger brother named Young Bear and myself, hurriedly broke camp with the main band which had decided to try to be on safe terms with the Government. This band of Cheyennes went east to Fort Cobb near Anadarko.

Later we were escorted by some troops to the Darlington Agency[2] where we were kept under strict military discipline, yet we felt safer under those conditions than we would have felt out hiding away from the military.

All of our chiefs had seen and learned that to live at peace with the Government was very much better, so our head chiefs very rapidly signed any agreements that the Government made with the chiefs in order that the Cheyennes could be safer.

As I think back to those times how terrible those days were it makes tears roll off my eyes to think of our loved ones as they were suddenly taken away from us, and the sad ordeal we went through with. Now it is all different; we live in peace and enjoy our living as never before.

I am now eighty-three years old and I am thankful to live to know that the coming generations of our Cheyennes will enjoy the benefits the white man's civilization is here to offer.

---

[2]In 1870 the Cheyenne-Arapaho Agency was relocated from Camp Supply to the North Fork of the Canadian River, just north of present El Reno. Named after the Quaker agent there, Brinton Darlington, the agency stood on the north bank of the river, where the military road from Fort Harker to Fort Sill crossed the stream. The complex consisted of a sawmill, several buildings, and two small schools, one for each of the two tribes. Much beloved by the Indians, Brinton Darlington passed away on May 1, 1872, at the age of sixty-eight. Berthrong 1963, 349.

35

Mrs. Lone Wolf, Cheyenne

The account that follows was given by Mrs. Lone Wolf to J. L. Puckett in 1905. Born about 1852, Mrs. Lone Wolf was a Southern Cheyenne who lived with her husband on an allotment near Hammon, Oklahoma. Although hesitant at first to relate her experiences, she relented after Puckett assured her through the interpreter that no harm would come to her. Puckett included the interview in his History of Oklahoma and Indian Territory and Homeseekekers' [sic] Guide, *published in 1906.*

Narrative
1905

I was about sixteen years old. We had camped at this place [on the Washita] but a few days. When we first went into camp there a white cloth about the size of a blanket had been taken and sewed on a long pole, and Black Kettle gave orders that if anyone saw the soldiers they must raise this pole. That night it was very cold, and my father staid on guard until after midnight. The moon shone all night long.

When my father lay down another Indian by the name of Double Wolf took his place. It was so cold that Double Wolf came in and lay down. Day had just begun to break when I heard somebody halloing. Double Wolf jumped up and ran outside. Instead of raising the white flag he fired his gun. My father jumped up. Just then several shots were fired. My father and Double Wolf fell dead. Then the shooting stopped for a moment.

We all ran out of our tepees and tried to run out through the narrow entrance. We saw white men in front of us motioning to us

335

to go back. Then the battle began. I don't know which side began shooting first. I fell on my face in the snow and could hear nothing but guns. At last the shooting stopped, and the next thing I knew a soldier punched me with his gun and motioned me to get up. There were several other women lying close to me. Men, women, and children lay dead everywhere. I saw many of the warriors lying dead with their guns in their hands.

The ponies, after being shot, broke away, and ran about, bleeding, until they dropped. In this way the snow on the whole bend of the river was made red with blood. This is the reason we call it the [battle of] the red moon.

We crossed the river on the ice, and the women and children were put on horseback. We started north towards Fort Supply. I saw Major Elliott and a number of other men start down the river. I knew Major Elliott, as I had seen him many times before. We camped on the South Canadian, had made a big fire, and were warming ourselves when a bunch of Tonkawa scouts came in and brought the news that Major Elliott and his entire party had been killed.[1]

We had a law among ourselves that if we had any prisoners, and any of our people should be killed by the prisoners' friends, we should kill that many prisoners. We thought, therefore, when we heard this news, that a part of our people would be killed in retaliation for the killing of Major Elliott and his men. So our warriors asked how many were to be killed, so that they might prepare to die. They sent me to General Custer to find out. I went to the interpreter and told him I wanted to see General Custer. I was taken close to him, and I asked him through the interpreter how many prisoners he was going to kill for Major Elliott. He covered his face with his hands and refused to speak for a minute. One of the soldiers started to drive me and the interpreter away, but Custer raised his head, saw that we were going away, and made the soldier bring us back to him.

---

[1]There were no Tonkawa Indian scouts with Custer's command during the two Washita expeditions. But ten Kaw scouts were enlisted at Fort Hays on November 6, 1868, and were assigned to the second Washita expedition, which left Camp Supply on December 7. Keim 1885, 86.

Then he said, "White people don't kill prisoners." He told me further that as long as we did not try to run away, and as long as we behaved ourselves, none of us would be hurt. So we built a big fire, and the smoke went straight up into the sky, so that the old Indians said that the great spirit was with us and would deliver us back into our tribe. Then we took meat and ate it, the first we had eaten since the night before, though it had been offered us before that day. From that time on we had plenty to eat and good warm blankets to wear, and I am sure if Double Wolf had done what Black Kettle told him to do, there would not have been a gun fired. Though many of my people deny it, I know that Double Wolf fired the first shot.

36

Red Bird Black,
Cheyenne

The statement that follows was recorded in the early 1930s by Paul I. Wellman at Concho, Oklahoma. Born about 1854, Red Bird Black was a Southern Cheyenne who married into the Hotametaneo (Dog Soldier) band. He later settled on an allotment along the North Canadian River near Fonda in Dewey County, where he engaged in crop farming. Wellman, who was a historian, included Red Bird Black's statement in his 1934 book, Death on the Prairie: The Thirty Years' Struggle for the Western Plains.

Statement
Undated

Red Bird Black, now living in Concho, Oklahoma, was a boy of fourteen when the [Washita] fight took place. He remembers vividly the terrific cold and how the Indians, rudely awakened, ran naked except for their breechclouts into the ice-covered stream. Some of them were cut by the razor edges of the broken ice until the water ran red with their blood.[1] Children were trampled under the hoofs of charging horses. A few brave Cheyenne men, behind the riverbank, fought and fought, until all were dead, in heroic self-sacrifice, so their families might get away.

---

[1]The psychological power of Custer's surprise dawn attack left deep emotional scars with the Cheyenne survivors, altering behavior patterns in some forever. This was the case with Spirit Woman, who was only a young girl when the brutal attack took place. She told her grandchildren that her feet were sliced open while running across the frozen snow and that she left a trail of bloody footsteps. From that day on she was afraid to go to bed without wearing her moccasins. She reminded her grandchildren how fortunate they were to be able to go to sleep without their moccasins because they no longer had to fear surprise attacks by soldiers. Bull Coming 1999.

37

George W. Yates,
Seventh Cavalry

Capt. George W. Yates commanded F Company, Seventh Cavalry and was assigned to Captain Thompson's squadron at the battle of the Washita. Born in Albany, New York, on February 26, 1843, Yates served in the Civil War as a private and was mustered out in 1866 as a captain in the Thirteenth Missouri Cavalry. His conspicuous gallantry at Beverly Ford, Fredericksburg, and Gettysburg earned him a brevet of lieutenant colonel of volunteers.

After the war Yates was appointed a second lieutenant in the Second Cavalry. In 1867 he was assigned to the Seventh Cavalry to fill a vacancy and was promoted to captain the same year. He participated in the Black Hills expedition of 1874 and the Sioux campaign of 1876. Captain Yates died at the Little Bighorn on June 25, 1876, along with Custer and the men of five Seventh Cavalry companies, all slain by Sioux and Cheyenne warriors. He is buried in the Fort Leavenworth National Cemetery.

The statement that follows was recorded by Elizabeth B. Custer, widow of General Custer, who included it in her 1890 book, Following the Guidon *(republished in 1966 by the University of Oklahoma Press).*

Statement
Undated

The attention of Captain Yates was attracted to the glittering of something bright in the underbrush. In a moment a shot from a pistol explained that the glistening object was the barrel of a pistol, and he was warned by his soldiers that it was a squaw who had

339

aimed for him, and was preparing to fire again. He then went round a short distance to investigate, and found a squaw standing in the stream, one leg broken, but holding her papoose closely to her. The look of malignant hate in her eyes was something a little worse than any venomous expression he had ever seen. She resisted most vigorously every attempt to capture her, though the agony of her shattered limb must have been extreme. When she found her pistol was likely to be taken, she threw it far from her in the stream, and fought fiercely again. At last they succeeded in getting her papoose, and she surrendered. She was carried forward to a tepee, where our surgeon took charge of her.

38

Wolf Belly Woman, Cheyenne

This testimony was recorded in 1939 by Theodore A. Ediger in Clinton, Oklahoma. Wolf Belly Woman was born about 1857 and was the daughter of Old Whirlwind, chief of the Hair Rope (Hevhaitaneo) band of Cheyennes. She later married an educated mixed-blood Cheyenne named John Otterby, who was a member of the Cheyenne-Arapaho Tribal Council. Wolf Belly Woman died in 1941. Ediger was an Associated Press correspondent in western Oklahoma, where he was well known among the Cheyennes.

The account that follows is a reprint from "Some Reminiscences of the Battle of the Washita" by Theodore A. Ediger and Vinnie Hoffman, published in The Chronicles of Oklahoma *in 1955. It is reprinted by special permission from* The Chronicles of Oklahoma, *published by the Oklahoma Historical Society, Oklahoma City (copyright 1955).*

Statement
1939

I was about ten or eleven years old during the Battle of the Washita. My father's camp was not far away from Black Kettle's, and I could hear the battle. But let me tell you how narrowly I escaped being in the battle. Black Kettle's camp was the farthest west on the Washita. Thus it was the one that was attacked. Next to it there was an Arapaho camp, then another Cheyenne camp, then my father's, then a Kiowa camp.[1]

---

[1]See also chapter 23, note 1.

The evening before the battle, I was visiting at Black Kettle's camp with Carrying Quiver, a woman who was a friend of my family. At Black Kettle's camp they wanted Carrying Quiver and me to stay overnight, but she said that she had to take me home. I am thankful that we did not remain.

39

Sarah C. Brooks, White Captive

Sarah Catherine (White) Brooks was a captive in a Cheyenne village located in the big bend of the Washita some distance downstream from Black Kettle's village. Born on December 10, 1850, in Elk Grove, Wisconsin, Sarah White was abducted from her father's homestead at White Creek, Cloud County, Kansas, during the Indian raids of August 1868. After enduring many hardships, she was released by the Cheyennes after a confrontation with Custer's troops on March 18, 1869, near Sweetwater Creek, Texas.

Upon her return from captivity, Sarah became a schoolteacher in Clyde, Kansas. She married a neighboring friend, H. C. Brooks, and raised a large family of seven children. After the death of her husband in 1926, she resided at her son's house near Concordia, Kansas, where she died on May 11, 1939.

The following statement was recorded by Joseph G. Masters at the Brooks farm near Concordia on July 27, 1935. Housed in the Joseph Gallio Masters Collection, Kansas State Historical Society, Topeka, it is reproduced by special permission.

Statement
July 27, 1935

Mrs. Brooks refused to let me have [her] photograph. Has been bothered too much by the reporters. She spoke highly of General Custer. Says she heard the firing of the rifles and revolvers in the battle of the Washita. She was down the river a short distance in the other camps. As soon as the battle started

343

the Indians spirited her away and took her farther down the river. It was so cold that her feet (the bottoms) were frostbitten she said.[1]

---

[1]For the capture and release of Sarah C. White, see Brooks 1933; and White 1969, 335–37, 340–42.

40

Trails the Enemy,
Kiowa

Trails the Enemy was a Kiowa Indian whose valorous conduct at the battle of the Washita saved the lives of a number of Cheyenne women and children by shielding them from Elliott's soldiers. His Kiowa name was Eonah-pah (Trails the Enemy), which was abbreviated to Yoo-nap on the agency rolls. Born about 1838, Trails the Enemy was married to Ah-toh-nah, the daughter of the Kiowa chief Satanta. He served as an agency policeman at Anadarko and later rode the range as a cowboy for the Chain Ranch for many years. Trails the Enemy died about 1925.

The following narrative was recorded by George Hunt, a prominent Kiowa leader. Known as Set-Maunte (Bear Paw), Hunt was born in the Wichita Mountains near Lawton in 1878. He grew up near Fort Sill, where he learned to speak English as a child while associating with the officers' children. Hunt was married to the daughter of Chief Satank, and after her death, he married Lillian Goombi, the daughter of a white captive. Educated at agency schools, Hunt became known as the leading Kiowa historian. He assisted a number of researchers with their fieldwork, among them Wilbur S. Nye, Alice Marriott, and James Mooney. Hunt was a deacon of the Kiowa Church of Rainy Mountain, Oklahoma, and died on April 16, 1942.

This account is housed in Folder 1, Box 38, William Carey Brown Collection, Norlin Library, University of Colorado at Boulder. The original manuscript is titled "Eone-Ah-Pah, the only Kiowa Indian Who Participated in the Battle of Washita, on November 27, 1869 [sic]"; it is printed here in edited form by special permission.

Narrative
Undated

The name of Eone-ah-pah means Trails the Enemy. Eone-ah-pah is well-known among the Kiowa tribe, and has a record of being a fast runner. Many times he would tell his story of his experience at the time that he took part in the battle of the Washita. He said that the Cheyenne were having a great dance in honor of the returning war parties and that it took nearly until midnight. Most of the Cheyennes were taking part in this dance, and were not thinking of any possibility of an attack by the soldiers, and were unprepared for the unexpected emergency of the villages.

Eone-ah-pah was returning from some of the other war parties, and was on his way to the Kiowa camps that were below the other tribes of villages, the Kiowa camp being several miles down on the same Washita River. When he came to the Cheyennes he decided to stay overnight near the Cheyenne village.[1] He also stayed up late, looking on at this dance, and after this dance was over he retired near the village. After he had hobbled his mule and his horse, he unsaddled his mule and turned them out for grazing, thinking of getting an early start on his journey to the Kiowa camp. Being so uncomfortable through the cold on the carpet of snow with heavy frost on top of the snow, it was hard enough without an attack by the powerful soldiers. He kept his quiver of bow and arrows next to his breast to keep it from the dampness of the snow.

Just before or about daybreak, with hardly any Indians awake, the galloping and roaring of the mounted cavalry and the shouts of the soldiers, the sounds of bugles and the firing of guns began, shooting into the village, onto the sleeping women and children. Like any of the other warriors, Eone-ah-pah jumped to his feet, and the only thing for him to do was to run for the safety of his life. He did not have any time to get his horse or his mule so that he might get away. His only hope for life was to run to the timber,

---

[1]While returning from a foray against the Utes, a Kiowa war party came across a broad trail of shod horses near Antelope Hills and immediately warned Black Kettle's village. Trails the Enemy fails to mention this. Nye 1969, 64. See also chapter 41.

and about this time a few shots were returned at the soldiers by the warriors of the camp.

He said he had left his blanket, but had on his moccasins, which were of help to him on the frozen snow. The soldiers were firing on several different parts of the village. The roaring of the guns and the wailing of the women and children caused great excitement. The warriors were busy in getting the women and children to places of safety in the timber; but this was so impossible for it was quite a distance to the river and it took a hard run to get to a place of safety for defense. As he was running toward the river, he saw about twenty Cheyenne women who were running with two or three warriors behind them,[2] doing their best to defend the women, and at this point he felt it his duty to help defend these women. At this time it came to mind that he had his bow and arrows in his quiver, and he turned his quiver around to his front side for quick use. In the meantime splashes of snow showed where the bullets were hitting the snow, making it splash.

Every now and then one would fall when they were hit by the shots. He saw one of the other warriors get shot and fall down.[3] One of the warriors called to him and handed him more arrows,[4] and at this time he told the women to scatter out so they would not be hit so easily, and he said that he began to defend them. Once in a while the soldiers would charge them as if they wanted to run them over to shoot these women; but it gave him the best advantage to shoot them. Once in a while a cavalryman charged on his horse, and he had a good shot at his horse, at the flank of the horse. He had his mind made up that it was important to shoot the soldiers' horses, then to shoot the soldiers. And so the first one dashing up toward him with his saber in his hand, acting as if he was going to make a fancy coup, was unable to use his saber because he jerked his horse with his spurs, and he, Eone-ah-pah, sent an arrow in the flank of the horse's belly, which made the horse pitch so hard that it threw the soldier off the horse.

---

[2] The two Cheyennes were identified as Little Rock and She Wolf, who was also known as Packer. Hyde 1968, 319.

[3] Little Rock received a gunshot wound to the forehead and died instantly near a horseshoe bend some distance below the village. Grinnell 1956, 303; Hyde 1968, 319.

[4] This was Little Rock's quiver. It contained only six arrows. Hyde 1968, 319.

After that he decided that it was best to shoot their horses, causing the horses to buck so hard that they threw the cavalry men off, which makes it easier to fight them. But there was no chance to get hold of a horse, for it made them buck hard and run fast so that hardly any one could catch them. About this time he had reached the timber, which provided safety for the women.[5] At about the same time help from reinforcements from the camps below were upon them and took them on to get their feet warm.

The record of this Kiowa is still being told by the warriors of the Cheyenne who saw this Kiowa and who has been of great service to the Cheyenne tribe. He was told by the Cheyenne that it is a custom of their tribe that if a man saves a woman or women during battles, he should have the right to marry one or all of them regardless of any of them being married. But he said that the custom of the Kiowa tribes is that if a man saves a woman or women during battles, she or they shall be his sister or sisters, and so, he said, he would have inherited about fifteen sisters. Otherwise, if he had accepted the custom of the Cheyennes, he would have inherited about fifteen wives.

Eone-ah-pah died about nine years ago. He was well known by many of the great cattlemen in the early days for he was a cowboy for the chain (o-o-o) ranch for fifteen years in the southwest part of the state of Oklahoma. He also served as an U.S. Indian Policeman at the Kiowa Agency at Anadarko, Oklahoma.[6]

---

[5]In addition to Trails the Enemy, a second Kiowa was present with the little group of people pursued by Major Elliott. Known as High Forehead or Shingled Hair, this young man was born in 1852 and was the great-grandson of Kiowa chief Mountain. High Forehead was arrested in 1875 for killing several white men and was imprisoned at Fort Marion, Florida. Upon his release in 1878, he enrolled at Carlisle Institute, graduating in 1880. After his return to the reservation, he was variously employed as a teacher and school recruiter, a timekeeper for Indian employees, a farmer and stock raiser, a carpenter, and a policeman. He was also an assistant to ethnologist James Mooney. High Forehead died in 1934 at his home in Anadarko. Petersen 1971, 161–62.

[6]For another account of Trails the Enemy, see Perez 1999. Martha Koomsa Perez is the great-granddaughter of Trails the Enemy. The oral history passed down to her differs in some details with the account obtained by George Hunt.

41

Philip McCusker,
Interpreter

Philip McCusker was an Interior Department employee who served as Kiowa-Comanche interpreter for Indian agent Jesse H. Leavenworth in 1868. Thought to have been of Scottish descent, his parents settled in New Jersey, from where McCusker ventured west in the 1850s. He enlisted in the Sixth Infantry and was a member of Maj. Earl Van Dorn's command that established Camp Radziminsky near the Wichita Mountains in 1859. That same year he assisted in the removal of the Penateka Comanches from Texas to their new reservation near Fort Cobb. Despite being from New Jersey, McCusker was a Southern sympathizer, and upon the expiration of his enlistment in late 1859, he reputedly joined the Caddo Frontier Battalion, commanded by Maj. George Washington, the renowned Caddo chief. In 1862 McCusker was at Fort Cobb and barely escaped with his life when Indians from the Kansas Agency massacred a band of Tonkawa Indians.

McCusker was married to a Comanche woman and had several young children when he accepted employment as interpreter for Agent Leavenworth. He was the principal Comanche interpreter at the Medicine Lodge talks in 1867. For some time thereafter, he seems to have been employed by the commissioner of Indian affairs as an informant on matters pertaining to the southern-plains frontier. McCusker may have had ambitions of becoming Leavenworth's replacement as Kiowa-Comanche agent, a hope that did not materialize upon the latter's resignation in May 1868. Occasionally, McCusker worked as a part-time trader for James R. Mead, who had a trading house at the big bend of the Arkansas River, and in 1871 accompanied a delegation of Indian chiefs to Washington, D.C. He was employed by the War Department during the Red River War in 1874 and was assigned as interpreter to the Tenth Cavalry, commanded by Col. John W. "Black Jack" Davidson.

After serving as an interpreter at both Fort Reno and Fort Sill, McCusker left the Indian service to raise stock. In 1883 he was arrested for the illegal sale of whiskey to reservation Indians. McCusker died near the Wichita Agency about Christmas 1885, when he froze to death after fording Deep Red Creek while carrying dispatches from Fort Sill to Camp Augur during a blizzard. His contemporaries described him as a very intelligent man who enjoyed his liquor. He was proficient in sign language and was fluent in Comanche, the court language of the Southwest. George Bent, who was well acquainted with him, commented that McCusker was a masterful Comanche linguist and spoke Kiowa and Kiowa-Apache as well.

On December 3, 1868, McCusker filed a report about the Washita battle based on information related by a friendly Kiowa chief. Despite a few errors, the Kiowa's statements proved accurate. The report that follows is from U.S. House, Difficulties with Indian Tribes, *41st Congress, 2nd Session, House Executive Document 240.*

Report
December 3, 1868

Fort Cobb, I.T., December 3, 1868.

Colonel Thomas Murphy,
Superintendent Indian Affairs,
Atchison, Kansas.

Sir: I have the honor to report the following statement of Black Eagle, chief of the Kiowas, concerning an action that recently occurred on the Washita River near the Antelope Hills, between a column of United States troops and the Cheyennes and Arapahoes and a small party of Kiowas and Comanche Indians.

On the night of the 25th November [*sic*] a party of Kiowa Indians, returning from an expedition against the Utes, saw, on nearing Antelope Hills, on the Canadian River, a trail going south towards the Washita. On their arrival at the Cheyenne camp they told the Cheyennes about the trail they had seen, but the Cheyennes only laughed at them. One of the Kiowas concluded to stay all night at the Cheyenne camp, and the rest of them went on their way towards their own camps, which were but a short distance off.

About daylight on the morning of the 26th of November [*sic*], Black Kettle's camp of Cheyennes, containing about thirty-five lodges, was attacked by the United States troops. The Indians all fled towards some other camps of the Cheyennes, closely pursued by the troops. After the Indians had run a short distance they separated in two parties, the braves and young women, who were fleet of foot, taking to the right, and the old and infirm taking to the left and running into some brush, where they were soon surrounded by the soldiers. The other party of Indians, who ran to the right, (and among them was one Kiowa,) were hotly pursued by a party of eighteen soldiers, who were all riding gray horses.[1] They overtook and killed some Indians, when they were met by a large party of Indians who had rallied from the other camps. Here a sharp action took place, both parties fighting desperately, when one Arapaho brave rushed in, and with his own hands struck down three soldiers, when he was shot through the head and instantly killed.[2] Here the soldiers all dismounted and tied their horses. About this time a Cheyenne brave rushed in and struck down two soldiers, when he was shot through the leg, breaking it, and knocking him off his horse.[3] The Indians then made a desperate charge and succeeded in killing the whole of the party of eighteen men. Then they rushed down to the rescue of the party that the troops had surrounded at first, but found that they were all killed or taken prisoners. By this time the soldiers had collected together a large number of the Cheyenne horses, which they shot. The Indians then attacked the troops, who dismounted and commenced to retreat slowly. The Indians also dismounted and took every advantage of cover, getting ahead of the troops and ambushing them whenever

---

[1]Gray horses were assigned to E Company. But the narrative at this point makes reference to Major Elliott's party of eighteen men, which included only three soldiers from E Company. The balance of Elliott's troopers rode bays (H. Company), sorrels (I Company), and a mixture of all other colors (M Company).

[2]This was probably Smoke, or Smokey, an Arapaho who was known as Tobacco among the Cheyennes. See Grinnell 1956, 304–305.

[3]This man was identified as Roman Nose Thunder.

possible. They continued fighting in this way until near night, the soldiers slowly retreating, until they met their wagon train, when the Indians retired.

The troops did not commence the retreat until the second day, both parties holding the battleground.

The Indians report having counted 28 soldiers killed, and acknowledge a loss of 11 Cheyennes (men) killed, including Black Kettle; the Arapahoes had three men killed; they also had a great many women and children killed in both tribes, as well as a great many taken prisoners.[4] One Comanche boy was badly wounded. The Kiowas report one Osage Indian killed, supposed to have been a guide for the troops.[5] Black Eagle says he does not vouch for the correctness of this report, but that the above statement is just as he has heard it.

The above statement is respectfully submitted for your information.

Philip McCusker,
U.S. Interpreter for Kiowas and Comanches.

---

[4]The military casualties consisted of eighteen men who were abandoned on the battlefield and four men who were buried at Camp Supply. The Arapaho casualties were Lone Coyote, Smoke, and Lame Man. For a composite list of Indian casualties, see "Composite List of Names" in Appendix G.

[5]All twelve Osage scouts and their interpreter survived the battle and were discharged at Fort Hays in March 1869.

42

George Bent,
Interpreter

George Bent was one of four children born from the marriage of William Bent and Owl Woman, daughter of Tail Woman and Gray Thunder, the Cheyenne Arrow Keeper. George was born on July 7, 1843, in a tepee near Bent's Fort on the Arkansas River. He attended public school in Westport (present Kansas City), Missouri, from 1853 to 1857, then enrolled at Christian Brothers College in St. Louis. He transferred to Webster College in 1858 and graduated three years later.

When nearly eighteen years old, George Bent enlisted with the cavalry of the pro–Confederate Missouri State Guard and fought at Wilson's Creek and Lexington in 1861. The next year he saw action at the battle of Pea Ridge in northwestern Arkansas and was present at the siege of Corinth, Mississippi. While near Memphis in August 1862, Bent was captured by Union forces and sent to military prison in St. Louis. He was paroled the same year through the intervention of family members.

Upon his return to Bent's Fort, George settled with his mother's people. She had died in 1847 of complications from the difficult birth of her daughter Julia. His maternal grandfather, Gray Thunder, had been killed in a battle with the Kiowas in 1838 and Bent's grandmother, Tail Woman, had died from cholera in 1849. In 1864 he and his half-brother Charles barely escaped death when Col. John M. Chivington massacred a village of peaceful Cheyennes and Arapahos at Sand Creek, Colorado. In the bloody war that followed, the Bent brothers rode with the Cheyenne Dog Soldiers and helped ravage the Platte Valley to avenge the massacre.

On August 17, 1865, Pawnee Indian scouts killed a small Cheyenne raiding party along the Powder River in present Montana. Among the slain was George's stepmother, Island Woman. She was the sister of Owl Woman, whose children she had raised. Two years later, in November 1867, Charles Bent attempted to avenge her death but was critically wounded by his Pawnee adversaries near Walnut Creek in Kansas. He died in a Cheyenne camp on November 20 and was sepulchered in the forks of a cottonwood tree north of present Fort Supply. Tragedy struck the Bent family again on May 19, 1869, when Gorge's father, William Bent, died of pneumonia.

In 1866 George Bent was hired as a Cheyenne interpreter by the Department of Indian Affairs. Although the War Department offered him twice the pay, he steadfastly refused to work for them on moral grounds. Instead, he remained with the Indian service for more than fifty years. In the spring of 1866, he married Magpie Woman, the niece of Black Kettle, chief of the Wutapiu band. The following year Bent assisted the peace commission at Medicine Lodge Creek, where his daughter Ada was born on October 19, the first of five children. He also worked for David Butterfield, a licensed trader who engaged in clandestine arms trafficking with the Indians. After the establishment of the Cheyenne-Arapaho Agency, Bent became an employee for the trading firm of Lee and Reynolds.

He took a second wife in 1869, a young Kiowa girl known simply as Kiowa Woman, whose parents had been killed during Custer's attack on Black Kettle's village. Kiowa Woman gave birth to a daughter named Julia in 1871. A son named George W. Bent Jr. was born in 1877. He was educated at Haskell Institute in Kansas and at Wabash Quaker College in Indiana. George Jr. settled in Salem, Oregon, where he worked for the Boy Scouts of America and was first chair in the cornet section of the Salem Symphony Orchestra. He never learned to speak Cheyenne or Kiowa and considered himself the "dark horse" of the family.

The Cheyenne-Arapaho Agency moved from Camp Supply to Darlington, near present El Reno, in May 1870. Bent was assigned to the new agency as interpreter for Brinton Darlington, newly chosen Indian agent for the Cheyennes. Darlington died in 1872, but Bent stayed on as interpreter. In 1878 Kiowa Woman left him. The following year he married Standing Out Woman, a Northern Cheyenne who arrived at Darlington Agency from Montana with Little Chief's band. In 1882 Bent importuned the Cheyennes with funds provided by cattlemen to lease grazing land. The Indians later accused him of having profited most from the lease agreement by col-lecting and keeping rental money.

By 1885 George Bent and his older brother, Robert, had cleared a farm near Darlington Agency and planted large fields of corn. George had built a model home, surrounded by a picket fence and containing five rooms, a bathroom with a tub, and equipped with the latest "heat-ing apparatus." He also kept a pet buffalo, a relic of the past that was visited frequently by the older Cheyennes and their children. Magpie Woman, Bent's first wife, died that same year.

In 1889 Bent was involved in a scheme to cede Cheyenne land for individual allotments. He worked as an interpreter for U.S. commis-sioners and was employed at the same time by attorneys whose fee was contingent upon the ratification of the land agreement. Bent, with oth-ers, devoted all of their energies to bribe the Indians to sign a treaty that robbed them of at least three-fourths of their property's value.

In the early 1890s he and Standing Out Woman left Darlington and moved to Seger Colony in present northeastern Washita County. He began to correspond with former soldiers, army officers, frontiersmen, and historians about the battles fought between the Indians and the whites. He also assisted ethnologists James Mooney and George B. Grinnell with their fieldwork among the Cheyennes.

While at Seger, Bent began to focus more on his Indian heritage and wrote a history of the Southern Cheyennes. It was serialized during 1905 and 1906 in The Frontier: A Magazine of the West *under the title "Forty Years with the Cheyennes." His friendship with George Hyde, editor of the article, resulted in an exchange of letters over the next thirteen years about Bent's Indian life. These became the founda-tion for Hyde's work* Life of George Bent, *which finally saw publica-tion in 1968. George Bent died from pneumonia on May 19, 1918. Penniless, he was buried in a small Indian cemetery at Seger.*

A contemporary once described George Bent as a fine specimen of physical manhood, well proportioned and weighing about 200 pounds. His complexion was of a swarthy hue peculiar to half-breeds, which gave him a striking appearance. He was blessed with a marvelous mem-ory and was a walking encyclopedia of Great Plains history. A member of the Crooked Lances, a military society of the Cheyennes, his Indian name was Hi-my-ike (Beaver), though he was also known by the nick-name "Tejanoi" (Texan) for his Confederate service. Throughout his life, George Bent lived in the middle of two conflicting cultures and constantly had to balance Indian with white. When accepted by one culture, the other rejected him, and often times he was misunderstood and mistrusted by both.

The letters reproduced in part below consist of the following: Bent to Robert M. Peck, written in December 1907, regarding Elliott's fight; Bent to George E. Hyde, written in September 1905, about Custer's confrontation at the Sweetwater; and Bent to Joseph B. Thoburn, December 27, 1911, and January 9, 1912, which contain information about Black Kettle.

Letter to Robert Peck
December 1906[1]

Robert M. Peck,
Whittier, California.

Your letter of December 7 received. First, I will tell you what Cheyennes say about [the] killing of Major Elliott and his men at the battle of Washita.

She Wolf, Cheyenne Indian, Little Rock, Cheyenne, and a Kiowa Indian[2] were running down [the] Washita River with squaws and children after Custer's attack on Black Kettle's village. She Wolf, who is living here now, tells me this.[3] He says they all came to a very deep hole of water, and high banks on each side of it, so they all had to get out of the creek bottom into [an] open place to get around this deep hole. Soon as they came up in open

---

[1]This letter reports the recollections of three Cheyennes who witnessed Elliott's last fight. Recognizing the historical value of its contents, Peck submitted a copy of the letter to the Kansas Historical Society, which included it in volume 10 of its *Collections*, published in 1908. An extract of this letter is reproduced here with the kind permission of the Kansas Historical Society. Peck served as a private in the First Cavalry from November 1856 through October 1861. For an account of his experiences, see Peck 1904. The contents of this letter are very similar to the details of Bent's letter to George Hyde, published in Hyde 1968, 319–21.

[2]The Kiowa was Trails the Enemy.

[3]She Wolf became known by his nickname "Packer" after he bestowed his formal name upon Theodore A. Ediger, who was an Associated Press correspondent. Ediger lived in western Oklahoma and was well liked by the Cheyennes. She Wolf married a woman from the Masikota (Grasshopper) band and lived in Colony. See Ediger 1940, 293.

view, Elliott and his men saw them, and charged towards them. Little Rock told the squaws and children to run back for the creek. These three men stayed behind the women and children to fight for them. Elliott and his men charged upon them, and commenced firing into them. Here Little Rock was killed.[4] The Kiowa Indian, now living, ran to Little Rock and picked up his arrows (this Kiowa had only two arrows left), he picked up six arrows of Little Rock.[5] Understand, these people were running from Black Kettle's camp or village. A Cheyenne woman called White Buffalo Woman,[6] now living with her sister, had been running so long [that] the girl gave out here. One soldier rode up to them and made [a] motion to them to walk back towards the camp.[7] The soldier got off his horse and walked behind them. Just

---

[4]About a half-mile below the eastern boundary of the Washita Battlefield National Historic Site is a small horseshoe bend that is about eight hundred feet wide at its base. During a flood many years ago, the river left its historic channel and forced a new streambed across the base of this bend. In 1868 the water in this horseshoe bend ran very swift, the bottom was very deep over its whole width, and this made it impossible for a person to walk in the water or hide under the steep banks. Little Rock was shot while crossing the tongue of land in this bend. See Grinnell 1956, 302; Briscoe 1987, 4.

[5]George Grinnell (1956, 303) states that Trails the Enemy took Little Rock's rifle and powder horn. But in his recollection of this incident, Trails the Enemy does not mention taking the muzzleloader, stating that "one of the warriors called out to him and handed him more arrows." See chapter 40. See also Hyde 1968, 319.

[6]At least four women in Black Kettle's village were named White Buffalo Woman, including the chief's own daughter. The White Buffalo Woman spoken of by Bent was born in 1852 and was the youngest sister of Little Rock. Named after one of her father's female relatives, her birth name, White Buffalo Girl, was changed to White Buffalo Woman upon puberty. At the Washita the soldiers captured her pregnant niece, Meotzi, as well as her eighty-year-old mother, who was unable to climb down the steep riverbank. White Buffalo Woman later married Big Red White Man, who was listed on the agency rolls by the Euro-American name "Mann." She gave birth to two children: a daughter named Crooked Nose (Miriam Mann), born in 1887, and a son, Spotted Horse (Fred Mann), born in 1890. White Buffalo Woman died in 1936. Her great-granddaughter, Dr. Henrietta Mann, was the first Cheyenne to receive a Ph.D. degree and is presently the director of Indian Studies at the University of Montana. Mann 1997, 12, 13, 15, 24; Berthrong 1989, 108.

[7]This party of captives consisted of White Buffalo Woman, her sister, and three children. Although it has been alleged that Little Beaver was one of these children, he himself states that he eluded the soldiers and escaped over the bluffs south of the village. Contrary to Bent, Grinnell states that the captives were guarded by a soldier whose horse had been killed earlier by Little Rock and, for that reason, was given the guard detail. Hyde 1968, 319–20; Brill 1938, 163; Van Zandt 1984, 69; Grinnell 1956, 303.

Attempts to locate the Washita interviews in the Grinnell notebooks and diaries have been unsuccessful since 1975, when Peter J. Powel searched in vain for the docu-

in front of them a lot of warriors, running from Black Kettle's village, rode up out of the creek timber. The soldier fired at the Indians as they were charging toward them. This soldier, White
Buffalo Woman says, shot at them warriors two times, and then
got [a] cartridge fast in his carbine, Bobtail Bear rode up to the
soldier and tomahawked him.[8]

Elliott and his men were still chasing She Wolf and the women
and children down [the] Washita River when these warriors cut
him off from Custer. Bobtail Bear and his warriors pushed Elliott
and his men right into a lot of warriors that were coming up from
the big village of Cheyennes and Arapahos. When Elliott saw he
was surrounded they turned their horses loose, [and] then himself
and his men got in among high grass and were all lying down when
the Indians rode around them. Touching the Sky[9] tells me he got
off his horse and crawled up towards them in [a] small ravine and
could see them lying down. When he motioned to Indians to bring
their guns he says several came running, stooping down. These
opened fire on Elliott and his men and must have hit several of
them, as it was very close. Those Indians on horses commenced to
close in on Elliott, and those in the ravine kept shooting at them
[Elliott's men]. In a little while Roman Nose Thunder, Cheyenne,

---

ments at the Braun Research Library. Mrs. Kim Walters, head of the Braun Library,
stated in 1999 that she vaguely remembers that Grinnell's informant was a woman. If
this is indeed the case, then the informant was probably White Buffalo Woman because
Grinnell's *Fighting Cheyennes* contains details of her capture that are not mentioned in
the Bent letters to Robert Peck or George Hyde. It is known that Grinnell visited the
Southern Cheyennes in 1901 and 1902 and that he returned to Oklahoma once more in
1908 and 1912. Unfortunately, his notebooks for these years fail to mention White Buffalo Woman or the battle of the Washita. Yet upon examination of the remaining notebooks, it was discovered that some pages were removed from Notebook 341, "Field notes,
1905." This notebook was compiled by John J. White Jr., who traveled to Oklahoma on
Grinnell's behalf to conduct fieldwork among the Southern Cheyennes. It is a remote
possibility that these missing pages may have contained the Washita interviews.

[8]But George Grinnell (1956, 303) states that this soldier was killed by Little Chief,
an Arapaho. For the names of Little Chief's companions, see Brill 1938, 166–67. For the
possible identity of this soldier, see chapter 19, note 19.

[9]Born about 1845, Touching the Sky was the youngest son of Alights on a Cloud,
who was a signatory to the Fort Laramie Treaty of 1851. Alights on a Cloud refused to
establish friendly relations with the Pawnees, hereditary enemies of the Cheyennes. He
and his brother, Ear Ring, were killed in the great battle with the Pawnees in 1852.
Touching the Sky became a council chief in the 1870s and was a member of the chiefs
delegation that visited Washington in 1880. Grinnell 1956, 74, 79.

now living, was first to ride over Elliott and his men.[10] Then the
Indians all made [a] charge on them. Elliott and his men did not
do much shooting for some reason, and Elliott and his men were
all killed inside of two hours. She Wolf and squaws then went to
where Elliott and his men were killed. They had stopped in the
creek soon as Elliott had left them, to rest up. The warriors after
killing Elliott and his men went on up to where Custer's command
was, and fought him again.

Ben Clarke [*sic*], now interpreter at Fort Reno, was with Custer
at the battle of Washita. He told me that Custer's officers told him
that Custer ordered Major Elliott to take some of his men and
drive those Indians out of the creek that were firing at his men.[11]
Over 200 Cheyennes and Arapahos are now living that were in
that fight with Elliott and his men. Only one Indian was killed in
this fight with Elliott; several were wounded. Black Kettle's village
was further up [the] Washita River. Other villages were down the
river. Indians in these villages heard the firing, so the men ran for

---

[10]At the Sun Dance near Cantonment in 1913, Roman Nose Thunder recounted his
valorous charge on Elliott's soldiers. He stated that at first the Indians could see nothing but gunpowder smoke at the spot where the soldiers were lying in the grass. He circled around the location a few times and was getting closer to the white smoke every
time. Soon Roman Nose Thunder was near enough to see some of the soldiers through
the smoke. "They were all shooting—not taking aim—just shooting. So then I charged
right in among them. When my horse came along the first soldier lying there I wanted
to strike him. I had a bow in my hand, and leaned down to strike him. He saw me coming, rolled over, and fired at me. His bullet hit my arm. But I did not flinch. I struck
him in the face, on his cheek. I counted the first *coup* in that fight." Fortunately, the
gunshot to his arm only caused a flesh wound. From a safe distance, Roman Nose
Thunder noticed that "everyone charged in and began to kill the soldiers and count *coup*
on them. Warriors of all the tribes charged in. People were running up from all sides to
see the end of the fight. But before they could get close, all the soldiers were dead. The
shooting was over. The fight did not last longer than it would take a man to smoke a
pipe four times." Vestal 1948, 159.

[11]A somewhat similar statement appears in Grinnell, *Fighting Cheyennes* (300),
which quotes Clark as saying, "When the first people appeared from the lower villages,
General Custer ordered Major Elliott to take a few men and disperse those Indians."
Yet in his 1899 *New York Sun* interview, Clark refutes the allegation that Custer had
given the order that led to Elliott's death, adding that "Custer knew nothing of Elliott's
going." Custer himself stated that he did not know why and when Elliott disappeared.
But Elliott stood only a short distance from Custer, and when the major left Headquarters Hill, he was accompanied by Sergeant Major Kennedy, a member of Custer's
staff. It has never been explained why Kennedy would have joined Elliott unless he was
directed to do so by Custer.

their herds of ponies and ran them into the villages. Meantime, Indians from Black Kettle's village began to come to [the] first village next to Black Kettle's village. Of course they told what took place. Most all women got on horses and carried the news to other villages. All the men, as fast as they got on their warhorses, rode for the battlefield. They met men and women and children of those that had got away. She Wolf and Little Rock's party were [the] last ones coming down the creek, and Elliott and his men lost their lives by following them too far down.

I knew Major Elliott and Captain Hamilton. Hamilton was also killed in Black Kettle's fight. I met both these officers in 1867, at the treaty in Medicine Lodge Creek. They were there with four companies to guard the annuity goods. Fourteen months afterwards they were both killed. I was camped [on the] south side of Medicine Lodge Creek at that time. They were on the north side. Both these officers and Doctor Ranick [*sic*], whom I went to school with in St. Louis, used to come over to my lodge every day and smoke with Black Kettle. I was then married to Black Kettle's stepdaughter.[12] She died some years ago. I suppose you saw my picture [with her] in the *Frontier Magazine.* She had [an] elk teeth dress on.

Ben Clarke told me that at the Black Kettle fight, a Mexican that used to live with my father,[13] came up with a little girl in his arms to give her to some one to save. A sergeant took the little girl, then told the Mexican to run, then shot him in the back as he ran. Ben Clarke says this was a cowardly act. He said he would have stopped this or else had a fuss over it, but did not see it done. He was told of it by teamsters or packers. Ben Clarke has an Indian wife and has a large family of half-breeds. I was talking to some old Indians today.

. . . .

Respectfully,
Geo. Bent.

---

[12]On other occasions Bent referred to Magpie Woman as Black Kettle's niece. In an attempt to clarify this matter, Bent's biographers write that "in fact she was his [Black Kettle's] niece and stepdaughter, because the Cheyennes made no distinction between daughters and nieces." Halaas and Masich 2004, 259.

[13]This man had worked for the Bent firm and was known as Pilan.

Letter to George Hyde
Sept. 1905[14]

Colony Okla
Sept 1905

Geo. E. Hyde
    Omaha Neb

Dear Sir

After [the] Washita fight, all the Cheyennes, Arapahoes, Kiowas, Apaches and Comanches moved south towards Red River on [the] Texas [border] line. Most of them were camped [on the] North Fork of Red River. Women and children prisoners that Custer captured on Washita were taken to Fort Hayes. One of these, [an] old squaw named Red Hair, was taken to Ft. Sill and was sent from there to the Indian camps to notify them to come to Ft. Sill and make peace. After she had started with some friendly Indians for the camps, Custer started also for the camps, as he had learned just where [the] Cheyennes were camped, instead [of] waiting for the chiefs to come in to Ft. Sill.

He rode into [the] Cheyenne village after [the] woman, Red Hair, notified the Cheyennes. Custer met Sand Hill,[15] Cheyenne,

---

[14]This letter is housed in the George Bent Letters, Stephen H. Hart Library, Colorado Historical Society, Denver; it is reproduced in part by special permission.

[15]Born about 1825, Sand Hill was a council chief of the Hill band, also known as the Aorta (Haviksnipahis) band. He survived the massacre of Sand Creek in 1864 and the next year captured a young white girl named Mary Fletcher at the North Platte. Fletcher was treated very kindly by Sand Hill and his Sioux wife and was later released into the custody of Indian Agent Edward W. Wynkoop. Sand Hill remained on friendly terms with the whites despite his brother's involvement in the Cheyenne raids on the Kansas settlements in August 1868. In the spring of 1875, he and his followers left Indian Territory for Montana. While camped along Sappa Creek in Kansas on April 23, his band was jumped by a detachment of the Sixth Cavalry, resulting in the death of twenty-seven Cheyennes, including eight women and children. Severely wounded, Sand Hill, with his wife and son, was able to reach the Northern Cheyennes in the Powder River region of Montana. After staying with the Northerners for a year, the family returned to Indian Territory and surrendered to the military on July 10, 1876. Some of the more irreconcilable elements of the Hill band remained in Montana with Sand Hill's son Yellow Horse and participated in Custer's annihilation at the Little Bighorn in June 1876. Sand Hill died near Cantonment shortly after his surrender. His son Robert Sand Hill assisted Missionary Rodolpho Petter at Cantonment with the translation of the Gospel of Luke into Cheyenne during the 1890s. Hyde 1968, 121, 159, 251; Berthrong 1963, 404–405; Petter [1936], 38.

who was hunting, and rode with him to the Medicine Arrow
Lodge. Sand Hill told Custer to dismount and go into the lodge.
The Owner of Arrows filled his pipe and when Custer came in
and sat down, this owner, called by white men Medicine
Arrows,[16] held in his hand the pipe and told Custer to smoke
while he held the pipe. He said in Cheyenne to Custer, ["]If you
are acting treachery towards us, some time you and your whole
command will be killed.["] After Custer got through smoking,
Medicine Arrow took [the] pipe stick used for cleaning the pipe.
After he loosened the ashes he poured this on Custer's toes to give
him (Custer) bad luck.[17] Custer was by himself [and] had no
interpreter, so he did not know what Medicine Arrow was saying
when he was talking while smoking. They made room for him to
sit right under the Medicine Arrows. These were hanging on [a]
fork of stick made [for the] purpose to hang them on.

---

[16]Medicine Arrow, whose actual name was Rock (or Stone) Forehead, was born
about 1795 and was a cousin of Black Kettle. After his appointment as Keeper of the
Sacred Arrows in 1850, whites referred to him as Medicine Arrows; he was also known
to Cheyennes by the nickname "Walks with His Toes Turned Out.." Nearly all of his
children were involved in violent confrontations with whites. His youngest son, Fox
Tail, was wanted for the killing of a Mexican herder during a drunken brawl near Fort
Zarah in 1866. His oldest son, Tall Wolf, was one of the principal men implicated in the
violent raids on the Saline and Solomon settlements in 1868. Rock Forehead's daughter was married to a Dog Soldier of Tall Bull's band and was present during the band's
destruction on July 11, 1869, by the Fifth Cavalry; she and her four children were taken
prisoner but were later released. In 1874 Rock Forehead was caught up in the turbulence
of the Red River War. Fearing reprisals by military personnel who might seize the
Sacred Arrows, he fled his agency in January 1875 and joined his northern kinsmen in
Montana. That April his son Black Hairy Dog and the latter's wife and stepson, White
Bear, attempted to join him with a small group from Sand Hill's band. During the surprise attack at Sappa Creek, White Bear was killed. Black Hairy Dog and his wife
escaped to Powder River and joined Rock Forehead, who died peacefully in 1876. The
Cheyennes regarded him as a man of wisdom and peace, whose advice was respected in
tribal affairs. Black Hairy Dog, born in 1823, became the new Keeper of the Sacred
Arrows. Upon his death in 1883, Black Hairy Dog was succeeded by Little Man, a
cousin. See Grinnell n.d.; Berthrong 1963, 349, 391; Hyde 1968, 368.

[17]This pipe passed through three generations of Rock Forehead's descendants
before it came into the possession of Mike Balenti, a former soldier stationed at Fort
Reno. Balenti had married Cheyenne Belle, the daughter of Charlie Rath, founder of
Dodge City, and his full-blood Cheyenne wife, Road Maker. Balenti sold the pipe to a
Mr. Barnhill in 1933. Claude E. Hensley, a prominent newspaper editor in Oklahoma
City, eventually acquired it from Barnhill's widow and loaned the artifact to the Fort
Sill Museum in 1957 for permanent exhibition. "Notes and Documents," *Chronicles of
Oklahoma* 36, no. 1 (1958): 89–92.

Custer went back to his command which was coming towards the camp. Custer told them that he was going to camp below them and he wanted all the chiefs to come to his camp, so all the Indians (men) went to his camp to talk to him about the prisoners he had at Fort Hayes. Cheyennes thought it was [a] good time to get women and children back from him. Custer's plan, I understood afterwards, was to take as many men prisoners as he could get hold of, [and] then have the whole village surrender to him. But instead [of] getting [a] lot of the men, he got only two old men and one middle-aged man. Two of these men got killed at Ft. Hays afterwards by [the] guard. Slim Face was 80 years old and Curly Hair [was] 50 years old. These men were killed. Little Bear, the other man, got wounded.[18] Of course, these men had no

[18]Scholars continue to speculate about the correct identification of these three captives. The names of all three appear as signatories on the Medicine Lodge Treaty documents. Two of these men, Curly Hair (born ca. 1819) and Lean Face (born ca. 1789), were killed by guards during a struggle in the prison stockade at Fort Hayes on May 9, 1869. The third man, Fat Bear (or Little Bear), died a violent death at Sappa Creek on April 23, 1875. All three appear in a photograph taken by William S. Soule either at Camp Supply on March 29 or at Fort Dodge on April 2, 1869. During the previous December, Soule had arrived at Fort Cobb with Colonel Inman's wagon train and on the twenty-eighth photographed General Grierson at the future site of Fort Sill. At this same location, then called Camp Wichita, he also photographed a bearded Custer wearing a fur cap, probably on February 9, 1869. Possibly at the same time Soule photographed Meotzi with her newborn child. Burkey 1976, 68, 70; Nye 1969, 138 (Soule's image of Fort Sill site, Dec. 28, 1868); McChristian 2000, 4; E. B. Custer 1966, 96.

Bent's identification of the three captives—Curly Hair, Little Bear, and Slim Face—is supported by Ben Clark, who lists Little Bear's name as Fat Bear, which conveys the same meaning; Clark obtained his information from his Cheyenne wife. Raphael Romero, Custer's interpreter, refers to Slim Face as Dull Knife and identifies Curley Hair as Big Head, though Clark comments that it was Fat Bear who was sometimes called Big Head. Clark states further that Romero's translations are suspect because the latter spoke very little Cheyenne and conversed with them primarily in sign language. To complicate matters more, Cheyennes told Grierson in April 1869 that Custer had captured Big Head's half brother. But the person identified by Romero as Big Head wore a large treaty medal, which suggests that he was indeed Big Head (or Curly Hair), the Dog Soldier headman whose name is listed on the Medicine Lodge Treaty. Some of the confusion may be attributed to the interpreters' inability to grasp the finer nuances of the Cheyenne language. This is particularly the case with the translations rendered by Romero. His lack of proficiency is clearly exposed by garbled Cheyenne words that modern Cheyenne speakers are unable to translate. Unfortunately, his mistranslations appear in Custer's reports and letters as well as his wife's publication, and they have been quoted frequently. In later years two Cheyennes provided additional information on the figures in the Soule photograph. One of these informants was Yellow Hair Woman, born in 1832, who was the daughter of Old Stands in Timber. She told Grinnell in 1912 that the man identified by others as Lean Face was her uncle,

weapons, only knives, when killed by a guard. A woman was also killed with these men. Soldiers do lot of things that people do not know about in [the] States. [In] those days only officers and their men knew these things.[19]

In the spring Kiowas and Comanches went to Fort Sill and made peace. Cheyennes and Arapahoes went to Fort Supply and made peace. The women and children that were taken prisoners on [the] Washita were turned over to [the] Cheyennes there.

. . . .

. . . [Elliott's stand was in tall][20] grass the Indians say, as lots of them were in this fight that are living here in Colony. They could only see smoke from their guns when they shot. Soldiers were lying down in high grass. Indians got all around them and very close. The Indians soon found out that Elliott's men were firing wild so they closed in on them. Before the soldiers could get up from lying down, they had them all killed. The Indians say to this day [that] they do not know who counted "coos" on Maj. Elliott and Lieut. Hamilton, as they all jumped on them [at the] same time. Roman Nose Thunder, now living, first counted "coo" on a soldier private. He was [the] very first [one] to run in on them. Then the big crowd jumped on them. I know the whites never got it straight how Elliott and his men were killed. I have heard Indians talk about this lots of time.

. . . .

Respectfully
[Signed:] Geo. Bent

---

whose name was actually Island, which was probably his formal name. A relative of Yellow Hair Woman, John Stands in Timber, made the same identification in 1960. Yet their identification of the other two captives is so different from the other informants that it defies reconciliation at this late date. In retrospect, Bent's identification appears to be the most reliable since he met the Washita captives at Camp Supply on June 21, 1869, and learned firsthand about their suffering. Clark 1910c; Burkey 1976, 69n61; P. Harrison 1998, 24n43; Grinnell 1956, 308n3; Bent 1869.

[19]Ever since the massacre at Sand Creek in 1864, Bent held an intense dislike for the military. When in 1869 he was offered the position of chief of scouts at Fort Lyon at ten dollars a day, he declined, preferring to work as interpreter for the Indian Bureau at five dollars daily, stating, "I did not want to go against my own people." Enlisted soldiers were then paid about ten dollars per month. Bent 1905.

[20]The sudden transition in the middle of a sentence at the end of the fifth page suggests that a page of the letter is missing. See also Hyde 1968, 318–20.

Letters to Joseph B. Thoburn
December 27, 1911[21]

Joseph B. Thoburn

Colony Oklahoma
Dec 27th, 1911

Dear Sir

Jack Fitzpatrick was son of Col. T. J. Fitzpatrick who had a big council with some tribes of Indians at [the] mouth of Horse Creek in Wyo. in 1850. He had two children, [one of whom is] Jennie, now living in El Reno.[22] Col. A. G. Boone was my guardian in 1853 when I went to school at Westport, Mo.[23] I was Maj. E. W. Wynkoop's interpreter in 1867, while he was an agent for the Cheyennes and Arapahos. Col. J. H. Leavenworth was [the] agent for Kiowas, Comanches and Apaches.[24] Knew him

---

[21]These two Bent letters in their entirety are housed in the Joseph B. Thoburn Collection, Oklahoma Historical Society, Oklahoma City; they are reproduced by special permission.

[22]For information on the Thomas J. Fitzpatrick family, see chapter 24, note 2. The negotiations took place in 1851 and resulted in the Fort Laramie Treaty.

[23]Albert G. Boone was born in Kentucky in 1806, the grandson of Daniel Boone. During his early life, he worked as a trapper and a trader, later serving the U.S. government as an Indian agent and as commissioner. In the 1830s Boone opened a trade firm at Westport, Missouri, where he outfitted westbound travelers and loaded his trains for the Indian commerce. At the request of his friend William Bent, Boone acted as guardian for George Bent from 1853 to 1857 while the boy attended school in Westport. In 1860 Boone relocated his mercantile operations up the Arkansas River to near Bent's Fort and founded the town of Boonville, Colorado. That same year he was appointed Indian agent for the Cheyennes and Arapahos at the Upper Arkansas Agency. His skill in dealing with Indians was instrumental in the successful treaty negotiations with several tribes. Boone died at La Veta, Colorado, on July 14, 1884. Hyde 1968, 94; Thrapp 1988, 1:137.

[24]Jesse H. Leavenworth was born in 1807, the son of Gen. Henry Leavenworth, for whom Fort Leavenworth was named. Jesse graduated from West Point in 1830 and appointed as a second lieutenant but resigned his commission in 1836 to pursue a career as a civil engineer in Chicago. In 1862 he was appointed colonel of the Second Colorado Volunteers. The following year he was assigned to Fort Larned, Kansas, and placed in command of all troops operating on the Santa Fe Trail. Leavenworth was dishonorably discharged in 1863 for enlisting a unit without proper authorization. After a hearing with the judge advocate general in Washington, he was exonerated in 1864 by order of President Lincoln. From then until 1868, Leavenworth served as an Indian agent to the Kiowas, Comanches, and Plains Apaches. His critics accused him of numerous irregularities during his administration, but none of these charges turned out to be true. After his resignation Leavenworth returned to his family in Milwaukee, where he died on March 12, 1885. Unrau 1964, 301.

well also. I knew all these people that I speak of. I was married to Black Kettle's niece. He was past 60 years when he was killed. He was born near Black Hills. I was living in Colorado at the time he was killed on [the] Washita. Last time I was with him was near Fort Dodge, Kansas, in 1868. Col. E. W. Wynkoop told him [that] if he would move to Fort Larned he would take care of him, but [he] moved south of [the] Arkansas River with [the] Cheyennes. . . .

Yours Respectfully
George Bent

Letter
January 9, 1912

J. B. Thoburn

Colony Oklahoma
Jan 9th 1912

Dear Sir

I received your letter and book some days ago and I am very much obliged to you for the book. The reason I did not answer your letter [was that] I was waiting for the woman that was [a] relative of Black Kettle and was with him when he was killed. I thought [that] maybe she would know about his Washington medal. I have an idea that some one got it. She says she does not know anything about it.[25] Black Kettle was not in the Solomon Valley Raid. I know this to be the fact.

Yours respectfully
George Bent

---

[25]Black Kettle never went to Washington. The medal spoken of by Bent probably was an Indian Peace Medal bearing the image of Pres. Andrew Johnson. This may have been issued to Black Kettle during the Little Arkansas Treaty talks in 1865 or, more likely, at the Medicine Lodge talks in 1867. Many years later it was alleged that Trooper Joseph Bell of I Company had taken a medal from Black Kettle's body (Charles M. Harvey to William J. Ghent, June 21, 1935, Box 31, Ghent Papers, Library of Congress).

43

Vincent Colyer,
Special Indian Commissioner

In 1869 Vincent Colyer, U.S. special Indian commissioner, visited the West to obtain by personal observation and inspection the condition of the Indian tribes in several western territories. As a member of the Indian commission, he served without salary, while his escort and transportation were provided for by special order of President Grant. Colyer departed on his journey from Fort Leavenworth in the middle of February and arrived at the Wichita Agency, Indian Territory, on March 29, 1869.

On April 9 Colyer held an interview with Little Raven, chief of the Arapahos. This was followed by an interview with the headmen of the Cheyennes, who gave their version of the confrontation with Custer at the Sweetwater in March 1869. Of particular interest is their statement about the Washita casualties, which refutes the inflated number reported by Custer.

Colyer's full report is included in the Annual Report of the Secretary of Interior for 1869, *41st Congress, 2nd session. The extract for April 9, 1869, follows.*

Extract of Report
April 9, 1869

April 9, 1869, I had an interview with Oh-has-tee or Little Raven, chief of the Arapahos, in the tent of Major General Grierson, and received a distinct statement from him as to the entire ignorance of himself and his people, and also of the Cheyennes, about the precise location of the reservation set off for them by United States peace commissioners, in 1867. It was because the Cheyennes, under Black Kettle, and the Arapahos, under Little

Raven, were not on the reservation, that they, with their tribes, were held guilty, and this was one of the reasons why they were attacked by General Custer at the battle of the Washita, last fall. You may remember that Colonel Wynkoop stated that he thought they were on their reservation at the time they were attacked. By the following statement, you will see now how easily these people are made to sign treaties of the character of which they are not familiar, and are afterwards so severely dealt with for not understanding:

Little Raven, chief of the Arapahos, being questioned as to his knowledge of the location of the reservation allotted to his people and the Cheyennes, by the Medicine Lodge treaty, in 1867, declared in our presence that at the time he signed the treaty he fully supposed that the land upon the Upper Arkansas, between Bent's Fort and the Rocky Mountains, was the reservation, being the same as previously set apart to them in the treaty of 1865; and he believes the Cheyennes were also of that opinion. Nor had he any doubt about [this] until he met General Sheridan at Medicine Bluff headquarters, 15th February 1869, and until today he did not know precisely where the new reservation was located.

Little Raven says he supposes that his misunderstanding arose from the hasty way in which the treaty was made and read to them and by mistaken interpretation.

his

Little X Raven,

mark.

Chief of the Arapahos.

B. H. Grierson,

Colonel and Brevet Major General United States Army.

H. P. Jones,

United States Interpreter.

Henry E. Alvord,

Captain Tenth United States Cavalry.

After the above interview with Little Raven, a party of twenty-six Southern Cheyennes with their head chiefs, Little Robe, Minnimic, and others, came up and had a talk. They are a fine-looking body of men, and when on horseback beat anything in the way of Cavalry I have ever seen.

This is their version of General Custer's meeting with them [in March 1869], on his way home to Camp Supply, after his raid last spring:

At an interview with Little Robe,[1] Minnimic or Bald Eagle,[2] Red Moon, Gray Eyes, and other chiefs of the Cheyennes, held in

---

[1]Born about 1828, Little Robe was the headman of the Dog Soldier band. He was married to several wives, one of whom was the daughter of a Kiowa chief. In 1864 several members of his family were killed at Sand Creek. Little Robe escaped the decimation as did his two sons, White Bird and Sitting Medicine (also known as Young Little Robe). The elder Little Robe was a signatory of both the Little Arkansas Treaty of 1865 and the Medicine Lodge Treaty of 1867. At the Washita in 1868, his band of seventy lodges escaped the fate that befell Black Kettle's band because they camped separately. Little Robe surrendered to General Sheridan at Fort Cobb on December 31, 1868, and from then on exerted his influence among the Cheyennes in favor of peace. He visited the East in 1871 with a Cheyenne delegation and toured Washington, where he was granted an interview with President Grant. The headman returned to Washington two years later to sign documents that redefined the reservation area as established by the Medicine Lodge Treaty. In 1874 Little Robe's son Sitting Medicine sought redress for ponies stolen from his father's band by a gang of white horse thieves from Kansas. He and two companions captured a number of horses, mules, and cattle near Sun City, Kansas. During their return to the reservation, Sitting Medicine was severely wounded in a skirmish with troopers of the Sixth Cavalry. Despite this and other confrontations with whites, Little Robe continued to counsel peace and remained at Darlington Agency during the Red River War. By 1877 his band of 179 lodges had settled at the North Canadian near Cantonment, now known as Canton. He was joined by the bands of Stone Calf and White Shield, and together they opposed the grass-lease program of Agent John D. Miles in order to keep the herds of white cattlemen off the reservation. Distrustful of white reform, Little Robe did not allow children of his band to attend white schools and also refused to join a program whereby the Cheyennes freighted their own goods from Kansas. In 1882 his daughter Issenon passed away, followed in 1885 by the killing of Sitting Medicine, who had been an U.S. Indian scout at Cantonment since 1879. Burdened by grief, Little Robe died in 1886. Hyde 1968, 256, 355; Grinnell 1956, 305–306, 321; Berthrong 1963, 382–83; Mooney 1907a, 1:400; Schukies 1993, 244.

[2]Known also as Eagle Head, Minimic was born about 1825 and was a headman of the Bow String Society. His wife and two daughters were killed at Sand Creek in 1864. A signatory of the Little Arkansas Treaty of 1865, he refused to sign the Medicine Lodge Treaty of 1867. After Sheridan's winter campaign, Minimic surrendered his band on December 31, 1868. He was elected to council chief in 1873 but engaged in hostilities the following year and fought white buffalo hunters at Adobe Walls. He and his son Howling Wolf (born ca. 1850) surrendered at Darlington on March 6, 1875, and were arrested a month later as ringleaders. Both were imprisoned at Fort Marion, Florida. Minimic was the principal Cheyenne among the prisoners and acted as peacemaker and mediator, exerting his influence for good relations whenever disputes arose. He converted to Christianity, and after his return to Darlington in 1878, he secured contracts with agency headquarters and Fort Reno to provide the whites with wood. Minimic performed this job until his death on May 6, 1881. His son Howling Wolf is perhaps best known for his colored sketches of Cheyenne life drawn while imprisoned with is father. Howling Wolf was elected to council chief of the Dog Soldiers in 1884 and died in July 1927 after a car accident near Waurika, Oklahoma. Rath 1961, 27; Hoig 1961, 161; Petersen 1968, 21–30; *Cheyenne Transporter*, May 25, 1881.

the headquarters tent of Major General Grierson, they gave the following account of their interview with General Custer on the 8th or 9th of March, 1869:[3]

They (the Indians) were on their way to Camp Supply, and this interview with General Custer turned them back and delayed their progress there.

The first notice they, the Cheyennes, had of the approach of Major General Custer and his regiment was from a Cheyenne woman who had been captured by General Custer in the fight against Black Kettle, on the Washita. She had been turned loose, or ran away, from General Custer some days before. The chief went out to see and met General Custer coming in with two men, no other soldiers at that time being in sight. He went on to Medicine Arrow's tent and shook hands. Soon afterwards a young man came in and told them that there were a great many troops coming on the warpath, which frightened the women, and they immediately began to saddle up their ponies; but the chief went out and quieted them down. General Custer then left them, and thirty of the chiefs and warriors went over to visit General Custer and his camp. He surrounded them with his soldiers, and told them he was going to keep them. They immediately drew their revolvers and said that if they were to die, they would die in trying to escape; and they made a rush and all but three broke through the guard. They were desperate and determined and brave about it, so they were allowed to go unguarded. General Custer told the chiefs to go and bring in two white women who were in the camp, or he would hang the three young men. They brought him the two white women, and then expected that he would release the three young men; but he would not do so. Some times he would talk good and sometimes bad to them; they could not understand him. He staid near them only a little while, and started for Camp Supply. He told them he wanted them to follow him on to Camp Supply; but he talked so strangely to them they would not trust him. This over, seventy lodges started for this post, (Camp Wichita.) They left the others, about one hundred and twenty lodges, on the headwaters of the Washita; but the interview with Custer was on

<hr />

[3]Little Robe's interview with Custer took place on March 16. Spotts 1988, 151–53.

the North Fork, or small branch of the Red River. They say there were only thirteen men, sixteen women, and nine children killed at the Washita fight. (General Custer reported one hundred and —— [three] killed.)

. . . .

Henry Bradley, *Interpreter.*

Appendix A

Military Records of the Seventh Cavalry Officers Present at the Washita

Barnitz, Albert. See the introduction to chapter 7.

Bell, James Montgomery. See the introduction to chapter 11.

Benteen, Frederick William. See the introduction to chapter 13.

Berry, Matthew. A native of Ireland, Berry served as a private in the Second Cavalry from 1857 to 1861. At the outbreak of the Civil War, he enlisted in the Fifth Pennsylvania Cavalry with the rank of second lieutenant and was promoted to first lieutenant in December 1863. After his honorable discharge in February 1864, he immediately reenlisted as a captain in the Twentieth Pennsylvania Cavalry and was mustered out in January 1865. Berry was awarded a brevet of captain, U.S. Army, for gallant and meritorious service at the battle of Antietam in September 1862. In July 1866 he received a regular army commission as first lieutenant in the Seventh Cavalry and was promoted to captain in December 1868. He was honorably discharged on December 31, 1870, at his own request. At the battle of the Washita, he commanded C Company, assigned to Captain West's squadron.

Brewster, Charles. See the introduction to chapter 10.

Cooke, William Winer. Born in Canada in 1846, Cooke enlisted in the Twenty-Fourth New York Cavalry in 1863 and was appointed a second lieutenant in January 1864. Promoted to first lieutenant in December 1864, he was honorably mustered out in June 1865. Cooke earned brevets up to lieutenant colonel, U.S. Army, in recognition of his gallant and meritorious service at the siege of Petersburg in 1864 and the battles of Dinwiddie Court House and Saylor's Creek in 1865. In July 1867 he received a regular army commission as a first lieutenant in the Seventh Cavalry. He participated in the Washita campaign of 1868, the Yellowstone expedition of 1873, the Black Hills expedition of 1874, and the Sioux campaign of 1876. Cooke was serving as regimental adjutant when he was killed on June 25, 1876, in action against Sioux and Cheyenne Indians at the Little Bighorn in Montana. His remains are buried in Hamilton, Ontario. Cooke was described as an able and energetic officer and was one of Custer's favorites. At the battle of the Washita, he commanded the detail of sharpshooters.

Custer, George Armstrong. See the introduction to chapter 6.

Custer, Thomas Ward. This younger brother of General Custer was born in Ohio in 1845. Tom entered the Civil War in September 1861 as a private in the Twenty-First Ohio Infantry. In November 1864 he obtained a commission as a second lieutenant in the Sixth Michigan Cavalry and served on his brother's staff in the Shenandoah Valley. In April 1865 he captured a Confederate battle flag at Namozine Church, Virginia, for which he received a Medal of Honor. Repeating this feat a few days later at Saylor's Creek, Tom was severely wounded by a gunshot to the face, fired by the Confederate color bearer. In recognition of his gallant conduct, he was awarded his second Medal of Honor, the only soldier to earn that distinction during the Civil War. He was mustered out in November 1865 with three volunteer brevets up to major. After the war he served briefly in Texas, then in February 1866 was appointed a second lieutenant in the First Cavalry. He resigned in July 1866 to accept a commission as first lieutenant in the Seventh Cavalry. In March 1867 he was awarded three brevets, though lieutenant colonel, U.S. Army, for his Civil War services, and he was promoted to the regular rank of captain in December 1875. He participated in the Washita campaign of 1868, the Yellowstone expedition of 1873, the Black Hills expedition of 1874, and the Sioux campaign in 1876. Tom Custer was killed on June 25, 1876, in action against Sioux and Cheyenne Indians at the Little Bighorn in Montana. His remains are buried in Fort Leavenworth National Cemetery. He was known in the regiment as a prankster and was well liked by the enlisted men. At the battle of the Washita, he was the junior officer in A Company and assumed command of the unit upon Captain Hamilton's death.

Elliott, Joel H. Born in Indiana in 1840, Elliott entered the Civil War in September 1861 as a private in the Second Indiana Cavalry. He saw action at Pittsburgh Landing, Chaplin Hill, and Stones River. In June 1863 he was appointed a second lieutenant in the Seventh Indiana Cavalry, then promoted to captain in October. He was severely wounded in the shoulder and both lungs during fighting at Guntown, Mississippi, in June 1864 and was left for dead on the field. He returned to active duty in December 1864, and despite partial paralysis of the left arm, he commanded two hundred picked men during Grierson's great raid through Mississippi. After his discharge in February 1866, Elliott pursued a career in the regular army, becoming major of the Seventh Cavalry in March 1867. At the battle of the Washita, he commanded a column of three companies. While in pursuit of fleeing Cheyennes, he and a small detachment of seventeen soldiers were cut off by Indian reinforcements and killed to the last man. His remains are buried in Fort Gibson National Cemetery. Fort Elliott, established in 1875 in Wheeler County, Texas, was named in his honor. Both Sheridan and Custer pronounced him an officer of great enterprise and judgment. The circumstances surrounding Elliott's death, and Custer's failure to recover the remains, resulted in a long-lasting rift between the officers of the Seventh Cavalry.

Gibson, Francis Marion. See the introduction to chapter 9.

Godfrey, Edward Settle. See the introduction to chapter 8.

Hale, Owen. Born in New York in 1843, Hale entered the Civil War in October 1861 as sergeant major of the Seventh New York Cavalry. He was appointed a second lieutenant in May 1863 and promoted to first lieutenant in October 1864. Honorably mustered out in November 1865 with a brevet of captain of volunteers, the following July Hale obtained a regular army commission as a first lieutenant in the Seventh Cavalry, with promotion to captain coming in March 1869. He participated in the Washita campaign in 1868, the Yellowstone expedition in 1873 and the Nez Perce campaign in 1877. Hale was killed on September 30, 1877, while leading his squadron against Chief Joseph's band of Nez Perce in the battle of the Bear Paw Mountains. His remains are buried in Troy, New York. Fort Hale, established in 1879 at the Lower Brule Agency in South Dakota, was named in his honor. Nicknamed "Holy Owen" by his fellow officers, Hale's bearing and conduct personified the image of the ideal cavalry officer. His descent from patriot Nathan Hale contributed to that impression. At the battle of the Washita, he commanded M Company, assigned to Captain Benteen's squadron.

Hamilton, Louis McLane. Born in New York in 1844, the grandson of the eminent statesman Alexander Hamilton, Louis Hamilton entered the Civil War in July 1862 as a private in the state militia and joined the Fourteenth U.S. Infantry a few months later. In September 1862 he was appointed a second lieutenant in the Third U.S. Infantry and promoted to first lieutenant in May 1864. He distinguished himself at Fredericksburg in December 1862, Chancellorsville in May 1863, and Gettysburg in July. Hamilton received a commission as a captain in the Seventh Cavalry in July 1866, becoming the youngest such officer in the regular army. At the battle of the Washita, he commanded a squadron in Custer's column and was killed instantly by a bullet, which ruptured his heart. He was awarded a posthumous brevet to major for gallant and meritorious services. His remains are buried in Poughkeepsie, New York. Hamilton was praised as a soldier of considerable ability and was well liked by his fellow officers.

Johnson, John Mitchell. Born in Iowa, Johnson entered the Civil War in August 1862 as a private in the Twentieth Iowa Infantry. In November 1863 he received appointment to West Point, and upon graduation in June 1867 he was commissioned as a second lieutenant in the Seventh Cavalry. He was promoted to first lieutenant in November 1867 and was honorably discharged on December 31, 1870, at his own request. At the battle of the Washita, he was the junior officer in E Company and assumed command of the unit after snow blindness impaired Captain Myers's vision.

Law, Edward. Law was born in Philadelphia in 1847. After graduation from the University of Pennsylvania in 1867, he obtained a commission as a second lieutenant in the Seventh Cavalry. He was promoted to first lieutenant in March 1869 but resigned the following year to pursue a legal career. Law drowned on October 5, 1881, in a boating accident on the Schuylkill River. At the battle of the Washita, he was the junior officer in K Company, assigned to Captain West's squadron.

Lippincott, Henry. Born in Nova Scotia in 1839, Lippincott entered the medical branch of the army in May 1865 as an assistant surgeon. That same month he was assigned to the Sixth California Infantry and served at Forts Humboldt and Grant. He was honorably mustered out in October 1865. In February 1866 he was appointed assistant surgeon, U.S. Army, with the rank of first lieutenant and was promoted to surgeon and major, U.S. Army, in August 1884. Appointed lieutenant colonel in the Department of the Surgeon General in April 1898, he retired with the rank of colonel and position of assistant surgeon general in April 1901. Lippincott died in New York on January 24, 1908. He was assigned as regimental surgeon to the Seventh Cavalry in October 1868 and was present at the battle of the Washita.

March, Thomas Jefferson. Born in Pennsylvania, March gained an appointment to West Point in July 1864 and graduated in June 1868. He was commissioned a second lieutenant in the Seventh Cavalry but resigned on March 10, 1872. At the battle of the Washita, he was the junior officer in G Company and assumed command of the unit after Captain Barnitz sustained a severe gunshot wound. His superior described him as a young man of good habits and common sense, instilled with a zealous devotion to his profession.

Mathey, Edward Gustave. Born in France in 1837, Mathey entered the Civil War in May 1861 as a first sergeant in the Seventeenth Indiana Infantry. He was appointed second lieutenant in May 1862 but resigned the following August. In September he enlisted as second lieutenant in the Eighty-First Indiana Infantry and was promoted to first lieutenant in March 1863, to captain in November, and to major in September 1864. He was honorably mustered out in June 1865. In September 1867 Mathey obtained a

regular army commission as a second lieutenant in the Seventh
Cavalry. He was promoted to first lieutenant in May 1870 and
to captain in September 1877. He participated in the Washita
campaign in 1868, the Black Hills expedition in 1874, the Sioux
campaign in 1876, and the Nez Perce campaign in 1877. He retired
as a major in December 1896 and was promoted to colonel,
retired, in April 1904. Mathey died in Denver, Colorado, on July
17, 1915. He was not present on the field at the battle of Washita
because of snow blindness, which forced him to remain behind
with the wagon train.

Moylan, Myles. Moylan was born in Ireland in 1838. He served in
the Second Dragoons from June 1857 to March 1863 and rose in the
ranks from private to first sergeant. In February 1863 he gained a
commission as second lieutenant in the Fifth Cavalry but was dismissed the following October for a petty offense. He immediately
enlisted in the Fourth Massachusetts Cavalry under an alias and by
December 1864 had achieved a commission as captain. He was honorably mustered out in November 1865 with a brevet to major of volunteers for gallant and distinctive service in Virginia. In January
1866 he enlisted as a private in the regular army, assigned to the Seventh Cavalry in August 1866, and appointed sergeant major the following September. In December 1866 he was awarded a
commission as first lieutenant. Moylan served as the regimental
adjutant from February 1867 to December 1870 and was promoted
to captain in March 1872. He was the recipient of a Medal of Honor
and a brevet to major, U.S. Army, for gallant service against the Nez
Perce Indians on September 30, 1877, in the Bear Paw Mountains,
during which he was severely wounded. He participated in the
Washita campaign in 1868, the Yellowstone expedition in 1873, the
Black Hills expedition in 1874, the Sioux campaign of 1876, the Nez
Perce campaign in 1877, and the battle of Wounded Knee in 1890.
Appointed major in the Tenth Cavalry in April 1892 but retiring the
following year, Moylan died in San Diego, California, on December
11, 1909. At the battle of the Washita, he was the regimental adjutant
and rode with Custer at the head of the center column.

Myers, Edward. Born in Germany in 1830, Meyers served in the
First Dragoons from August 1857 to July 1862, rising in rank from

private to first sergeant. In July 1862 he gained a commission as second lieutenant and was promoted to first lieutenant in September 1863. Mustered out of the volunteer service in June 1865, he obtained a commission of captain in the Seventh Cavalry in July 1866. In recognition of his gallant and meritorious services in Virginia, he was awarded three brevets, including lieutenant colonel, U.S. Army. Myers died at Spartanburg, South Carolina, on July 11, 1871. He was known for an explosive temper, which nearly led to his discharge in December 1867. At the battle of the Washita, he suffered from snow blindness while commanding a squadron composed of E and I Companies.

Robbins, Samuel Marshall. Robbins was born in New York in 1832. In November 1861 he was appointed captain in the First Colorado Volunteers and served until October 1865, when he was honorably mustered out as chief of cavalry for the District of Colorado. In July 1866 he gained a commission as a first lieutenant in the Seventh Cavalry. He was promoted to captain in November 1868 to fill the vacancy created by the death of Louis Hamilton but was forced to resign on March 1, 1872, for conduct unbecoming an officer. Robbins died on September 25, 1878. During the winter campaign against the Cheyennes, he served on Custer's staff as acting engineer officer but resumed his regular duties as junior officer in D Company during the Washita battle. As engineer officer, Robbins was responsible for assigning names to the major tributaries of the Washita during the march to Fort Cobb in December 1868.

Smith, Algernon Emory. Born in New York in 1842, Algernon Smith was appointed as a second lieutenant in the 117th New York Infantry in August 1862. He received a commission as first lieutenant in April 1864 and was promoted to captain that October. Smith was severely wounded in the shoulder during the assault on Fort Fisher, North Carolina, in January 1865 and was awarded a brevet to major of volunteers. He was mustered out in May 1865. In August 1867 he obtained a regular army commission as a second lieutenant in the Seventh Cavalry, receiving brevets of first lieutenant and captain, U.S. Army, for gallant services at the battles of Drewry's Bluff and Fort Fisher, and earned promotion to first lieutenant in December 1868. He participated in the

Washita campaign in 1868, the Yellowstone expedition in 1873, the Black Hills expedition in 1874, and the Sioux campaign in 1876. Smith was killed on June 25, 1876, in action against Sioux and Cheyenne Indians at the Little Bighorn in Montana. His remains are buried in Fort Leavenworth National Cemetery. At the battle of the Washita, he served as acting commissary and rode with Custer at the head of the center column.

Smith, Henry Walworth. Henry Smith was born in Connecticut in 1827. He enlisted as a second lieutenant in the Fourth Massachusetts Cavalry in January 1864 and earned promotions to first lieutenant in December 1864 and captain in June 1865. He was honorably mustered out in November 1865. Smith received a regular army commission as a second lieutenant in August 1867 and was promoted to first lieutenant in September 1869. He was dropped from the army rolls on January 9, 1871, before charges of embezzlement and desertion could be filed against him. At the battle of the Washita, he was the junior officer in M Company, assigned to Captain Benteen's squadron.

Thompson, William. Born in Pennsylvania in 1813, Thompson entered the Civil War in July 1861 as a captain in the First Iowa Cavalry. He was appointed major in May 1863 and promoted to colonel in June 1864. He was awarded a brevet to brigadier general of volunteers in March 1865 for gallant and meritorious service during the war and was honorably mustered out in March 1866. The following July he obtained a regular army commission of captain in the Seventh Cavalry. He was awarded brevets of major and lieutenant colonel, U.S. Army, in March 1867 for gallant and meritorious services in action at Prairie Grove and Bayou Meto, Arkansas. Thompson retired from the army on December 15, 1875. Prior to his military service, he had practiced law, held a seat in Congress, was a surveyor of public lands, and edited a daily newspaper. Thompson died in Tacoma, Washington, on October 6, 1897. At the battle of the Washita, he commanded a squadron composed of B and F Companies.

Wallingford, David W. Born in Vermont in 1837, Wallingford enlisted as a corporal in the Second Kansas Infantry in June 1861.

He was appointed as a second lieutenant in the Fifteenth Kansas Cavalry in August 1863 and was honorably discharged in April 1865. In July 1866 Wallingford obtained a regular army commission as a second lieutenant in the Seventh Cavalry and was promoted to first lieutenant in June 1867. He was dismissed from the army on May 10, 1870, for conduct unbecoming an officer. Wallingford died in the Kansas Penitentiary on July 11, 1883, while serving a sentence for horse stealing. At the battle of the Washita, he was the junior officer in B Company, assigned to Captain Thompson's squadron.

Weir, Thomas Benton. Weir was born in Ohio in 1838. Upon graduation from the University of Michigan in 1861, he enlisted in the Third Michigan Cavalry with a commission as second lieutenant. By November 1865 he had risen to the rank of lieutenant colonel and was honorably mustered out the following February. In July 1866 Weir obtained a regular army commission as a first lieutenant in the Seventh Cavalry and was promoted to captain in July 1867. That same month he received brevets to major and lieutenant colonel, U.S. Army, for gallant and meritorious services in action at Farmington, Tennessee, and near Ripley, Mississippi. He participated in the Washita campaign in 1868 and the Sioux campaign in 1876. Weir died on December 9, 1876, at Governors Island, New York, while on recruiting service. His remains are buried in Cypress Hills National Cemetery. At the battle of the Washita, he commanded D Company, assigned to Captain Hamilton's squadron.

West, Robert Mathew. Born in New Jersey in 1834, West enlisted as a private in the Mounted Riflemen in April 1856 and was mustered out in February 1861. The following July he received a commission as a captain in the First Pennsylvania Light Artillery. He was appointed major in September 1861 and colonel in July 1862. West transferred to the Fifth Pennsylvania Cavalry in April 1864 and was awarded a brevet of brigadier general of volunteers in April 1865 for gallant and meritorious service at the battle of Five Forks, Virginia. He was honorably mustered out in August 1865. In July 1866 he received a regular army commission as a captain in the Seventh Cavalry. His gallant and meritorious service during the Civil War was acknowledged in March 1867 with three brevets, including that of colonel, U.S. Army. West resigned his commission on March 1, 1869, and died near Fort Arbuckle on September 3, 1869. He strongly disliked Custer for his abusive treatment of enlisted men. West was considered one of the ablest officers in the regiment despite his addiction to alcohol, which was a common problem among frontier officers. At the battle of the Washita, he commanded a squadron composed of C and K Companies, assigned to the center column.

Yates, George Wilhelmus. Born in New York in 1843, Yates enlisted in the Fourth Michigan Infantry in June 1861 and was appointed quartermaster sergeant the following November. He was promoted to first lieutenant in September 1862 and was honorably mustered out in June 1864. Yates reenlisted in August 1864 as a first lieutenant in the Forty-Fifth Missouri Infantry. He was appointed captain in the Thirteenth Missouri Cavalry in September 1864 and was honorably mustered out in January 1866. Yates received brevets to major and lieutenant colonel of volunteers for conspicuous gallantry at Fredericksburg and Beverly Ford, Virginia, and Gettysburg, Pennsylvania. In March 1866 he received a regular army commission as a second lieutenant in the Second Cavalry. He was promoted to captain in June 1867 and was assigned to the Seventh Cavalry. He participated in the Washita campaign in 1868, the Black Hills expedition in 1874, and the Sioux campaign in 1876. Yates was killed on June 25, 1876, in action against Sioux and Cheyenne Indians at the Little Bighorn in Montana. His remains are buried in Fort Leavenworth National Cemetery. At the battle of the Washita, he commanded F Company, assigned to Captain Thompson's squadron.

Appendix B

Squadron Formations of the Seventh Cavalry Regiment at the Washita

Center Column (A, C, D, and K Cos.)

Commanding: Lt. Col. George A. Custer (Bvt. Maj. Gen.)

Strength: 284 military
9 civilians
12 Indian scouts

Staff: 1st Lt. Myles Moylan (Bvt. Maj.), Regt. Adjutant
2nd Lt. Algernon E. Smith (Bvt. Capt.), Actg. Commissary
Assist. Surgeon Henry Lippincott
Actg. Assist. Surgeon William C. Rennick
Sgt. Maj. Walter Kennedy
Sgt. J. Bales, Standard Bearer
Gessau Chouteau, Osage Interpreter
Rafael Romero, Cheyenne Interpreter

Scouts: Ben Clark, Chief of Scouts
Jack Corbin
Jack Fitzpatrick
Joseph Milner
John Poisal Jr.
William Schmalsle

Sharpshooters: 1st Lt. William W. Cooke (Bvt. Lt. Col.)
Enlisted men: 28

Band: Sgt. Albert Piedfort (Chief Trumpeter and Bandmaster)
Musicians: 14

Osage Guides: Little Beaver, Second Chief of Nation
Hard Rope, War Chief
young men: 10

383

Left Wing: Capt. Louis M. Hamilton, Cmdg.
Company A: Capt. Louis M. Hamilton
1st Lt. Thomas W. Custer (Bvt. Lt. Col.)
Enlisted men: 46
Company D: Capt. Thomas B. Weir (Bvt. Lt. Col.)
1st Lt. Samuel M. Robbins (Actg. Engineer Officer)
Enlisted men: 50

Right Wing: Capt. Robert M. West (Bvt. Lt. Col.), Cmdg.
Company K: Capt. Robert M. West
1st Lt. Edward S. Godfrey
2nd Lt. Edward Law
Enlisted men: 55
Company C: 1st Lt. Matthew Berry (Bvt. Capt.)
Enlisted men: 54

East Column (G, H, and M Cos.)

Commanding: Maj. Joel H. Elliott
Strength: 161 military
Initial Orders: Move around the hills north of the Washita; cross the
valley floor and reach the Washita below the village;
move upstream and take position just east of the village.

Left Wing: Capt. Albert Barnitz (Bvt. Lt. Col.), Cmdg.
Company G: Capt. Albert Barnitz
2nd Lt. Thomas J. March
Enlisted men: 52

Right Wing: Capt. Frederick. W. Benteen (Bvt. Lt. Col.), Cmdg.
Company H: Capt. Fredrick W. Benteen
Enlisted men: 51
Company M: 1st Lt. Owen Hale
2nd Lt. H. Walworth Smith
Enlisted men: 50

West Column (E and I Cos.)

Commanding: Capt. Edward Myers (Bvt. Lt. Col.; affected by snow
blindness)
Strength: 108 military
Initial Orders: Move directly to the south bank of the Washita; move
downriver through the skirting timber; take position
within view of the village.

Company E: Capt. Edward Myers
1st Lt. John M. Johnson
Enlisted men: 48
Company I: 1st Lt. Charles Brewster (Bvt. Capt.)
Enlisted men: 57

South Column (B and F Cos.)

Commanding: Capt. William B. Thompson (Bvt. Lt. Col.)
Strength: 115 military
Initial Orders: Countermarch and cross Washita where forded; skirt the
south bank under cover of the bluffs to a point opposite
the village; cooperate with Elliott's column.
Company B: Capt. William B. Thompson
1st Lt. David W. Wallingford
Enlisted men: 56
Company F: Capt. George W. Yates
2nd Lt. Francis M. Gibson
Enlisted men: 55

Ambulance Train (4 ambulances, 2 wagons)

Commanding: 1st Lt. James M. Bell (Bvt. Maj.), Regt. Quartermaster
Strength: 41 military
6 teamsters
1 blacksmith
Initial Orders: To remain halted one mile in the rear of the center
column; move forward as soon as firing is heard.
Guard: Camp Police, sick men, deserters, officers' orderlies.

Wagon Train (25 wagons and 3 ambulances)

Commanding: 2nd Lt. Edward G. Mathey (affected by snow blindness)
Strength: 83 military
1 wagon master
28 teamsters
1 blacksmith
Initial Orders: To follow the regiment from the Canadian River as rapidly
as the terrain permits.
Guard: Men with inferior horses.

Strength of Expeditionary Force

Commissioned Officers:

Strike Force	26
Ambulance Train	1
Wagon Train	1
Total Officers	28

Enlisted Men:

Field and Staff	2
On Duty with Companies	580
Detailed as Sharpshooters	28
Detailed as Musicians	15
Assigned to Headquarters	10
Assigned to Medical Services	2
Baggage Guard	5
Assigned to Wagon Train	82
Assigned to Bell's Train:	
Camp Police	5
Officers' Orderlies	28
Sick	5
Deserters	2
Total Ambulance Train	40
Total Enlisted Men	764

Civilians:

Contract surgeon	1
Scouts	6
Interpreters	2
Teamsters	35
Blacksmiths	2
Total Civilians	46
Indians Scouts:	12
Aggregate Total	**850**

Summary

Strike Force	689
Wagon Train	113
Ambulance Train	48
Aggregate Total	850

Appendix C

Roster of the Seventh Cavalry Sharpshooters at the Washita

Strength: 1 officer
28 enlisted men

		Name	Company
Commanding:		Lt. William W. Cooke	H
Enlisted men:	Sgts.	J. DeLaney	M
		Jno. Fay	A
	Cpls.	P. Harrison	H
		Wm. Taylor	A
	Pvts.:	Wm. Andrews	A
		C. Bacon	M
		Charles Gauion	A
		J. Haney	I
		J. Hick	C
		P. Joyce	K
		J. Lennon	H
		W. Linden	G
		J. Malhoris	F
		M. Mason	M
		J. Milton	F
		C. Mooney	M
		J. O'Leary	H
		D. Penderly	K
		G. Rodgers	E
		W. Schnabler	M
		Jno. Schuller	H
		E. Smith	E
		F. Snisait	G
		J. Sootell	I

B. Tooney	C
James Walker	A
H. Wetzel	M
Daniel Williams	A

Summary

A Co. 6	G Co. 2	
B Co. none	H Co. 4	
C Co. 2	I Co. 2	
D Co. none	K Co. 2	
E Co. 2	M Co. 6	
F Co. 2		

Note: The names of the twenty-eight sharpshooters are taken from "Enlisted Men on Extra or Daily Duty" as reported on the monthly return for November 1868 (U.S. Army 1868). Since the company of sharpshooters consisted of forty enlisted men, some of these marksmen may not have been listed as "sharpshooter" on the duty report. According to Captain Benteen, ten served on headquarters staff as Custer's bodyguard. Perhaps these marksmen are listed among the fifteen soldiers assigned to Custer as orderlies (eight), clerks (two), cooks (one), and fatigue personnel (four).

Appendix D

Roster of the Seventh Cavalry Band at the Washita

Strength: 15 musicians
1 orderly

Position	Name	Company
Bandmaster:	Sgt. Albert Piedfort, Chief Bugler	D
Orderly:	Cpl. A. Gosby	C
Musicians:	Pvts. W. Calfes	M
	H. Huber	G
	A. Kosser	D
	J. McCormick	A
	M. McGaffrey	D
	J. Murphy	G
	F. Newby	F
	W. Piedfort	D
	F. Pierce	M
	H. Seafferman	H
	E. Slurmielke	A
	D. J. Sprague	E
	H. Swielk	E
	J. Wright	I

Summary

A	Co. 2		G	Co. 2
B	Co. none		H	Co. 1
C	Co. 1		I	Co. 1
D	Co. 4		K	Co. none
E	Co. 2		L	Co. none
F	Co. 1		M	Co. 2

Note: The names of the musicians are taken from "Enlisted Men on Extra or Daily Duty" as reported on the monthly return for November 1868 (U.S. Army 1868).

Appendix E

Roster of the Osage Scouts at the Washita

Strength: 12 guides
1 interpreter

Osage Name	Translation
Gessau Chouteau, Interpreter	
Sha-Pa-Shin-Ka, Head Chief	Little Beaver
aka Cha-pa-jen-kan (Keim 1885)	
aka Shaba Shinka (Mathews 1961)	
Wah-Sa-Ke, War Chief	Hard Rope
aka Wen-tsi-kee (Keim 1885)	
aka We-He-Sa-Ki (Mathews 1961)	
Com-Bla-Mosha	I Don't Want It
aka Koom la-manche	Trotter (Keim 1885)
aka ce-ce-M'n-l'n	[Buffalo] Trots as He Travels
(Mathews 1961)	
Che-Pah-Shin	Little Buffalo Head
Wah-Lah-Who-Ah	Draw Them Up
Ce-Wah-Ka-Ka	Sharp Hair
We-Sah-Pah-Sha	Patient Man
Opah-Tink-Ah	Big Elk
Wahsha-Pa-Skunk-Ah	Little Black Bear
Wah-Hunk-Ah	Lightning Bug
Sah-To-Kah-Shin-Ka	Little Buffalo
O-Pah-La-La	Straight Line

Note: The names of the Osage scouts are taken from Capt. A. S. Kimball (assistant quartermaster, Fort Hays), *Report of Persons and Articles Employed and Hired;* Keim 1885; and Mathews 1961. Keim identifies Little Beaver, Hard Rope, and Trotter; Matthews identifies Little Beaver, Hard Rope, Trotter, Big Lynx, Eagle Feather, and Wolf. See also Arthur Shoemaker (1992), who lists the same individuals as Matthews and names two more, Tally and Little [Black] Bear. The Osages enlisted on October 20, 1868; mustered in at Fort Hays on October 29; and were discharged the following March. They received the following monthly payment for their services: the interpreter, one hundred dollars; the two leaders, seventy-five dollars each; and the young men, fifty dollars each. On March 29, 1869, Custer issued a letter of commendation to Hard Rope, stating that "the bearer is head war-chief of the Osages. He was with me on all my marches and campaigns since Nov. 1, 1868, participating in the battle of the Washita, and particularly distinguishing himself by his skill in discovering and following trails. He is a man of excellent judgment, and is a true friend of the white man."

Appendix F

Casualties of the Seventh Cavalry at the Washita

Killed

Elliott's Detachment

Staff:	Joel H. Elliott	Major	Remains taken to Fort Arbuckle.
	Walter Kennedy	Sgt. Maj.	
E Co.:	Harry Mercer	Cpl.	
	Thomas Christie	Pvt.	
	*John McClernan	Pvt.	
H Co.:	William Garrick	Cpl.	
	Eugene Clover	Pvt.	
	*John George	Pvt.	
	William Milligan	Pvt.	
I Co.:	James M. Williams	Cpl.	
	Thomas Downey	Pvt.	
M Co.:	*Erwin Vanousky	Sgt.	
	Thomas Fitzpatrick	Farrier	
	Ferdinand Lineback	Pvt.	
	Carson D. J. Myers	Pvt.	
	John Myers	Pvt.	
	Cal Sharpe	Pvt.	
	*Frederick Slobaccus	Pvt.	

The entire command was killed on November 27, 1868. The remains of only sixteen of the seventeen enlisted men were interred in a mass grave in the big bend of the Washita on December 11, 1868. One man's body was never recovered.

*Remains were not identified.

Village Site

A Co.:	Louis M. Hamilton	Capt.	Died Nov. 27, 1868.
B Co.:	Charles Cuddy	Pvt.	Died Nov. 27, 1868.
	Augustus DeLaney	Pvt.	Died Nov. 27, 1868.
H Co.:	Benjamin McCasey	Pvt.	Died Dec. 1, 1868.

All four men were buried at Camp Supply on December 3, 1868.

Wounded

A Co.:	Thomas W. Custer	1st Lt.	Slight bullet wound in right hand. Treated at field hosp and released.
	William Eastwood	Cpl.	Severe bullet wound in right elbow. Admitted to Camp Supply hospital.
	Martin Gale	Pvt.	Slight bullet wound in right arm. Treated at field hospital and released.
B Co.:	Augustus DeLaney	Pvt.	Severe bullet wound in chest. Died Nov. 27 (see under "Killed").
D Co.:	George Zimmer	Pvt.	Severe bullet wound in left arm. Admitted to Camp Supply hospital.
E Co.:	Frederick Kluik	Pvt.	Slight bullet wound in left arm. Treated at field hospital and released.
F Co.:	William Brown	Pvt.	Slight bullet wound in left arm. Treated at field hospital and released.
G Co.:	Albert Barnitz	Capt.	Severe bullet wound in stomach. Discharged from Camp Supply hospital, Jan. 21, 1869. Retired, Dec. 15, 1870.
	Thomas J. March	2nd Lt.	Slight arrow wound in right hand. Treated at field hosp and released.
	August Martin	Sadler	Severe bullet wound right forearm. Admitted to Fort Dodge hospital, Dec. 14, 1868; discharged, Jan. 12, 1869.

	Daniel Morrison	Pvt.	Slight arrow wound in right temple. Admitted to Fort Dodge hospital, Dec. 14, 1868; discharged, Jan. 12, 1869.
H Co.:	Benjamin McCasey	Pvt.	Severe arrow wound in chest. Died Dec. 1 (see under "Killed").
I Co.:	Conrad Strahle	Pvt.	Slight bullet wound in left ankle. Admitted to Fort Dodge hospital, Dec. 14, 1868; discharged, Jan. 23, 1869.
	Hugh Morgan	Pvt.	Severe bullet wound in right arm. Admitted to Fort Dodge hospital, Dec. 14, 1868; discharged, Feb. 8, 1869.
M Co.:	John Murphy	Bugler	Severe arrow wound in right side of chest. Admitted to Fort Dodge hospital, Dec.14, 1868; discharged, Sept. 3, 1869.

Note: The names listed under "Killed" are taken from "Alterations Enlisted Men," as reported on the monthly return for November 1868 (U.S. Army 1868). The names listed under "Wounded" are taken from "Record of Events," as recorded on the monthly returns for November and December 1868 (ibid.) and the "Register of the Sick and Wounded, Post Hospital Fort Dodge, Kansas, 1868, and 1869" (U.S. Army, 1868–69). The "Record of Events" for November states that the loss to the regiment was two officers and nineteen enlisted men killed and three officers and twelve enlisted men wounded. Private McCasey died on December 1, raising the death toll to twenty enlisted men.

Appendix G

The Indian Casualties

The Keim Listing: Extract of Newspaper Dispatch, December 1, 1868

The decisive character of the victory and the severe blow sustained by the Cheyennes may be judged from the number of "big" chiefs, war chiefs and headmen killed in the "Battle of the Washita." I learn from the squaws, by means of Mr. Curtis, the interpreter, that the following were killed:

Cheyennes:	Black Kettle, chief of the band
	Little Rock, second chief
	Buffalo Tongue
	Tall White Man
	Tall Owl
	Poor Black Elk
	Big Horse
	White Beaver
	Bear Tail
	Running Water
	Wolf Ear
	The Man that Hears the Wolf
	Medicine Walker
Sioux:	Heap Timber
	Tall Hat
Arapahos:	Lame Man

. . . .

Indians wounded and brought in:

One squaw, in the left knee.
One squaw, in the right hip.

One squaw, in the right breast and ranging upwards through the lower jaw.
One boy, in the left thigh.
One girl, in the right side.
One girl, in the left forearm.
All gunshot wounds.

The . . . wounded Indian squaws and children have been placed in the general field hospital in charge of J. J. Marston, Acting Assistant Surgeon, United States Army, and are receiving all the attention the circumstances can afford.

Note: Keim's dispatch containing the Indian casualties was published in the *New York Herald,* December 24, 1868.

The Bent/Hyde Letter

Colony Okla
Aug 28th 1913

George Hyde

My Dear Friend
    I received your letter yesterday, and will give you the names.

Men	Women	Children
Black Kettle, chief		
Little Rock		
Bear Tongue		
Tall Bear		
Blind Bear		
White Bear		
Crazy		
Blue Horse		
Red Teeth		
Little Heart		
Red Bird		

This was all the men killed on Washita River by Custer. Twelve women and six children, girls and boys, was all that was killed.

Lots of Indians [that] are now living were in this fight. Three of them are [here] in [the] office, giving me these names that were [killed] in this fight.

Your Friend,
[Signed:] George Bent

Note: Bent's letter to George Hyde, dated August 28, 1913, is housed in the George Bent Letters, William Robertson Coe Collection, Yale University Library, New Haven, Connecticut; it is reproduced by special permission.

The Grinnell Letter

238 East 15th Street, New York
October 3d, 1916.

Mr. W. M. Camp,
7740 Union Avenue,
Chicago, Illinois.

Dear Mr. Camp:
We were talking only the other night about the Indians killed in the battle of the Washita, and I remembered a footnote in "The Fighting Cheyennes" on the subject, but could not then look it up. I see now that it says that four men who in 1869 talked with General Grierson, at Camp Wichita, stated that the Cheyenne loss was 13 men, 16 women, and 9 children. Hazen says that the Arapahoes had 2 men killed, and the Comanches 1.

I find in a letter from George Bent, written two or three years ago, the names of 14 men killed in that fight, of which 2 are Arapahoes. This same letter says that there were 12 women and 5 children. I think another letter says 6 girls and boys. Bent gives the names of the men as Black Kettle, Little Rock, Bear Tongue, Bad Man, Tall Bear, Blind Bear, White Bear, Crazy, Blue Horse, Little Heart, Lame Arapaho, Tobacco, Red Bird, [and] Red Teeth. The last two he says were Arapahoes. White Bear was a Mexican captive, purchased by William Bent. The women killed were 10 Cheyennes and two Sioux, and five girls and boys.

This agrees pretty well with the footnote on page 289 of "The Fighting Cheyennes." The men talking with Gen. Grierson might perhaps have included people who were wounded, and died later, while Bent's letter may refer simply to people killed on the battleground. At all events, I thought the note would interest you, and it is worth keeping for comparison with other information that you may have.

Yours sincerely,
[Signed:]Geo. Bird Grinnell

Note: This letter is housed in Folder 2, Box 2, Walter Camp Collection, Brigham Young University Library, Provo, Utah; it is reproduced by special permission.

The Bent/Camp Letter

W. M. Camp	Colony, Oklahoma
	Dec 4th 1916

My Dear Mr. Camp

I have just got the list of the Indians killed on [the] Washita River in 1868. I got these names from Packer, [a] Cheyenne Indian who was with Little Rock when he was killed. They were making for the hills when Little Rock was killed. When he fell, Packer picked some of his arrows. Packer says there were three in the party: Little Rock, Packer, and [a] Kiowa Indian that stopped in Black Kettle's village on his way home. He was returning from [a] war party that had been out west hunting Utes who they were at war with [at] that time.

Standing Out or Sun Bear, Cheyennes believe he was the one that killed Capt. Hamilton, as Sun Bear was killed near where Hamilton fell, and Sun Bear had [a] rifle in his hands when last seen by Bear Feathers, now dead. He was standing in front of his tent or lodge when troops were charging the village.

Tobacco, Arapaho Indian [who] I have in the list, ran right in among Maj. Elliott's men and fell among them. He was shot in [the] head as he was stooping down to strike [a] soldier to count coup on him.

Black Kettle, Chief
Little Rock, Sub-Chief
Bitter Man
Fool Man
Standing Out or Sun Bear
Pilan (Mexican)
Red Bird, son of Chief Whirlwind
Blue Horse
Bear Tongue
Sharp Belly
Tall Bear
Tobacco, Arapaho
Lame Man, Arapaho

This was all the men killed. Red Bird, son of Whirlwind, was the one that [the] officer (probably Barnitz—[W. M. Camp]) shot. He was shot through the hand and in [the] breast.

Yours Truly,
[Signed:] George Bent

I will be glad to hear from you any time.

Geo.

Note: This letter is housed in Folder 2, Box 2, Walter Camp Collection, Brigham Young University Library, Provo, Utah; it and is reproduced by special permission. The Red Bird listed in this letter was not Whirlwind's son.

Composite List of Names

DeB. Randolph Keim's List Obtained from Captive Squaws by Interpreter Dick Curtis at Camp Supply on *Dec. 1, 1868*	George Bent's List Obtained for George Hyde from 3 Cheyenne Vets at Colony on *Aug. 28, 1913*	George Bent's List Obtained for George Grinnell from Cheyennes [at Colony] in *1913 or 1914* [not in *Fighting Cheyennes*]	George Bent's List Obtained for William Camp from Packer [at Colony] on *Dec. 4, 1916*
Cheyenne:			
1. Black Kettle	1. Black Kettle	1. Black Kettle	1. Black Kettle
2. Little Rock	2. Little Rock	2. Little Rock	2. Little Rock
3. Bear Tail	3. Tall Bear	3. Tall Bear	3. Tall Bear
4. Buffalo Tongue	4. Bear Tongue [confirmed by Moving Robe]	4. Bear Tongue	4. Bear Tongue
5. Big Horse	5. Blue Horse	5. Blue Horse	5. Blue Horse
6. Hears the Wolf	6. Red Teeth	6. Red Teeth	6. Sharp Belly
7. Medicine Walker	7. Crazy [confirmed by Magpie]	7. Crazy [not in *Life of G. Bent*]	7. Fool Man
8. Poor Black Elk	8. Little Heart	8. Little Heart	8. Sun Bear/Stand Out
9. Running Water	9. Blind Bear [confirmed by Magpie]	9. Blind Bear	
10. Tall Owl	10. Red Bird [confirmed by J. Sipes]	10. Red Bird	9. Red Bird
11. Tall White Man	11. White Bear [Mexican per B. Clark]	11. White Bear	10. Pilan
12. White Beaver		12. Bad Man	11. Bitter Man/ Cranky Man
13. Wolf Ear			
Sioux:			
1. Heap Timber/Bad Bank[?]			
2. Tall Hat/Black War Bonnet[?]			
Arapaho:			
1. Lame Man		1. Lame Arapaho	1. Lame Arapaho
		2. Tobacco	2. Tobacco

Note: Not included in these lists are Double Wolf, Statue, a young man named Hawk, and an Arapaho known as Lone Coyote. Some of the dead may have been identified by their birth name by one informant and by their nickname by another. Variations in the translation of personal names add to the confusion in the identification (*Crazy/Fool* Man and *Bad/Bitter/Cranky* Man).

Aggregate Totals

Indian Authorities

DATE	SOURCE	MEN	WOMEN	CHILDREN	TOTALS
Dec. 1, 1868	Women captives [via Curtis/Keim]	13 + 2 Sioux + 1 Arap.	n/a	n/a	16
Dec. 3, 1868	Black Eagle [Kiowa] [via McCusker]	11 + 3 Arap.	many	many	14+
Dec. 14, 1868	Poisal/Fitzpatrick [via Morrison]	20	40 women & children		60
Apr. 6, 1869	Unidentified Cheyennes [via Grierson]	18	n/a	n/a	18
Apr. 9, 1869	Red Moon, Minimic, Gray Eyes, Little Robe	13	16	9	38
1913	Med Elk Pipe, Red Shin [?] [via Bent/Hyde]	11	12	6	29
1914	Crow Neck [?] [via Bent/Grinnell]	12 + 2 Arap.	10 + 2 Sioux	5	31
1916	Packer [via Bent]	11 + 2 Arap.	n/a	n/a	13
1930	Magpie/Little Beaver [via Brill]	15	n/a	n/a	15

Military Authorities

DATE	SOURCE	MEN	WOMEN	CHILDREN	TOTALS
Nov. 28, 1868	Custer	103	some	few	103+
Dec. 22, 1868	Custer	140	some	few	140+
Dec. 3, 1868	Sheridan	13 + 2 Sioux + 1 Arap.	n/a	n/a	16
1868	Alford	80 + 1 Com. also 1 Kiowa	n/a	n/a	81
1874	Alford				
1899	Ben Clark	75	75 women & children		150
1909	Dennis Lynch, 7th Cav.	106	some	n/a	106+

Appendix H

Exhumations and Reburials of Indian Remains

Excerpt from the *Cheyenne Star*
September 25, 1930
Identification of Indian Remains
Discovered North of Cheyenne in 1917

Mr. [Charles J.] Brill and Mr. [Frank] Rush came to Cheyenne last week [September 19, 1930] and spent considerable time here in an effort to locate the exact site of the scene of the last Indian Battle in Oklahoma and to gather fragments of history concerning the battle. These gentlemen brought with them Chief Magpie, now one of the leading chiefs of the Cheyenne Indians, and who was wounded in the battle of the Washita; Little Beaver who was also in the battle; and John Otterby, Indian Interpreter. They, with these Indians, and some of the early settlers of Cheyenne went to the scene of the battle and located the site where Black Kettle's tepee stood and other scenes of the Battle. The Indians recalled the story of hurriedly burying some Indian comrades as they made their hurried escape during the Battle of the Washita, and they were positive that the spot where the bones of the skeleton which had been kept in Cheyenne through the years, was the site where the hasty interment was made years ago. It was the request of Chief Magpie and Little Beaver that the bones be placed to rest in the local cemetery, and so arrangements were made to place them there with an Indian ceremonial on November 27, 1930. Chief Magpie and other famous Indians will be present and participate in the ceremonial. At this time folks from all parts of the Cheyenne and Arapaho country and historians from all parts of the state are expected to witness the burial.

405

A dollar campaign was started to raise funds to erect a monument to the Unknown Indian Soldier who died in the Battle of the Washita. In this campaign, which is headed by Judson Cunningham, Cheyenne, Oklahoma, no person is allowed to give more or less than a dollar.

It was Judson Cunningham, now Court Clerk of Roger Mills county, who found the skeleton more than fifteen [thirteen] years ago. He was coming to town from his father's farm north and east of Cheyenne when he noticed some human bones that had been brought to surface by some excavating being done along the railroad. It was just after the transfer of the Cheyenne Short Line to the C.& O. W. Railway Company [in 1917] and the roadbed was being repaired. The bones were found about 3/8 mile from the northeast corner of the town site of Cheyenne on the C. G. Miller farm. Judson came on to town and he in company with others went back to the spot and dug up the remains of an entire skeleton which has since been kept in the office of the Cheyenne Star. During the years some of the bones have been lost but most of them still remain. Much speculation was made regarding the bones, but nothing definite was known until last Saturday when Chief Magpie and Little Beaver claimed them as the bones of an unknown Indian soldier.

Excerpt from the *Cheyenne Star*
December 4, 1930
Burial of Indian Remains
Discovered in 1917

It is estimated that 5,000 people assembled on the site of the Battle of the Washita last Thursday, on the anniversary of the battle, to pay tribute to the Unknown Indian Soldier who lost his life in the Battle 62 years ago.

At 2:00 o'clock the vast crowd was called to order by Senator Alvin Moore of Cheyenne, master of the ceremonies. The immense throng crowd[ed] in a circle about the grave as the casket containing the bones was lowered into the grave as the ceremony began.

Frank Rush of Craterville, Oklahoma, styled the Indian's best living friend[,] was the first on the program. Rush paid tribute to the Plains Indians, reviewing events leading to the Battle of the Washita in 1868, concluding with the thought that it was a fitting tribute to the Indians of Oklahoma that the remains of the Unknown Indian Soldier who died in that battle be buried with great ceremony on the site of the battle.

Hon. J. B. Thoburn, noted historian of Oklahoma, whose historical knowledge is recognized by all, spoke on the Cheyenne Indian, reviewing the characteristics of this tribe of Indians.

Mrs. J. E. Standifer of Elk City, vice president of the Federated Clubs of Oklahoma spoke, taking as her subject, "The Pioneer Woman."

Lee I. Seward of Arnett spoke in behalf of the American Legion and paid tribute to the Indian for his part in the World War and pledged the allegiance of the American Legion in memorializing the site of the Battle of the Washita.

The great crowd stood with perfect attention as Chief Magpie, chief of the Cheyennes, with a blanket about him, spoke through his interpreter, John Otterby. Chief Magpie expressed joy that the people were paying tribute to the Unknown Indian. He told the crowd that he forgave General Custer and that he asked God to forgive Custer for the part he had in the Battle of the Washita. He begged the white man to look [with] charity on the Indian of the past and to deal now with justice. The heart of the Indian chief was moved as he recalled the events of the battle and the tears stood in his eyes. Chief Magpie carries a wound received in the battle.

The American Legion fired taps which were echoed by the Indians. Chief Magpie stood at the grave and offered a prayer to the Creator in his native tongue which concluded the ceremony.

The Indians came to Cheyenne on the day before the ceremony and camped on the site where in 1868 the famous battle was fought. They invited the people from Cheyenne to the camp and were communicative. A number of our citizens sat with them in their teepees and enjoyed hearing them tell of earlier days.

Just before the ceremony the Indians killed and butchered beeves given them by Cheyenne. The immense crowd enjoyed seeing them parcel out the beef in the same manner, as was the early day custom.

The spot chosen to bury the Unknown Indian Soldier was on the knoll where the rock on which was engraved the date of the battle was found in an early day. The rock is now in the Court House in Cheyenne.

It is the purpose of those interested to erect a monument to the Unknown Indian Soldier.

***

Excerpt from the *Cheyenne Star*
May 25, 1933
Discovery of Indian Remains
West of Cheyenne

The story published in last week's Cheyenne Star relative to the finding of a skeleton by Ives Finch one-half mile from J. H. Warren's home [nine miles] west from Cheyenne, created considerable interest.[1] More interest was shown when the skeleton was placed on display in the office of the Cheyenne Star Saturday where the bones are now. Some theorized that it was the skeleton of an Indian because of the position in which it was found. Evidently it was the remains of an old man because of the teeth; a man of small stature; a man of intelligence because of the shape of the skull. J. H. Warren, who resided here for forty years, says that in the early days he saw numerous bones of humans near this same spot.

***

Excerpt from the *Cheyenne Star*
April 10, 1952
Discovery of Indian Remains
Near Washita River Bridge
July 13, 1934

Sixty-six years after the famous Indian Chief, Black Kettle, was killed in the battle of the Washita his skeleton was found and every bone intact. These bones are now on display in the window of the Cheyenne Star office building, where the Indians want it to remain until a time when the United States Government sees fit to erect a Memorial on the site of the Battle of the Washita.

---

[1]The burial site also contained an arrowhead, a number of flint chips, and a mortar.

The Jim Bruton Maps

Mr. Jim Bruton of Shamrock, Texas, first visited the Washita Battlefield in 1956. Being an avid student of the historic battle, he befriended John Wesner, owner of the historic site, and through the years became acquainted with many other landowners in the area. Mr. Bruton was also an amateur archeologist who was skilled in the use of metal detecting equipment. With permission from the landowners he began to survey the battlefield and adjacent lands. From 1968 through 1975 he discovered some 150 battle-related artifacts. He recorded his finds on rough-drawn field maps that identify the location and the type of artifact. His inventory of recovered artifacts includes spent ammunition from the Model 1865 Spencer carbine, the Springfield Model 1866 rifle, and the Henry Model 1860 rifle, misfired and unfired cartridges, rivets, military buttons, muzzle-loading balls, steel arrowheads and a spearhead, a broken cast-iron kettle and other items. The original field maps were drawn on lined, legal-size paper. With the passage of time they became worn and faded and are no longer suitable for photographic reproduction. The four maps that follow are copied from the originals and are reproduced hereafter through the courtesy of the owner. The publication of this important material will enhance our knowledge of troop positions and combat activities, and may lead to new scholarly theories as to how the battle was fought.

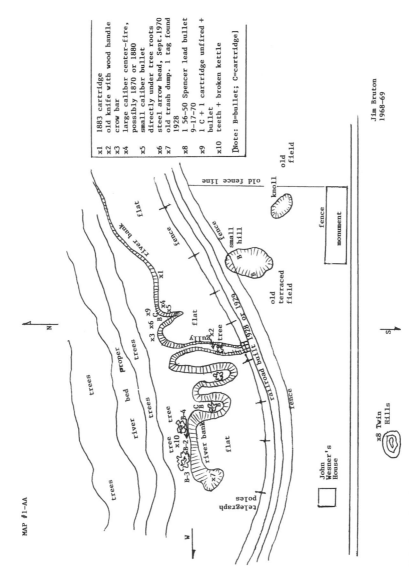

MAP #1-AA

x1　1883 cartridge
x2　old knife with wood handle
x3　crow bar
x4　large caliber center-fire,
　　possibly 1870 or 1880
x5　small caliber bullet
x6　directly under tree roots
　　steel arrow head, Sept.1970
x7　old trash dump. 1 tag found
　　1928
x8　1 56-50 Spencer lead bullet
x9　9-17-70
　　1 C + 1 cartridge unfired +
　　bullet
x10　teeth + broken kettle

[Note: B=bullet; C=cartridge]

Washita Artifact Locations, after a map drawn by Jim Bruton. Map #1-AA.

410

The survey area covers part of the NE Quarter of Section 12, which, along with the NW Quarter, was purchased by John Wesner in 1945. Wesner's house was torn down and only the foundation exists today. It stood near the center of the south section line, on the north side of Highway 47A, which is shown by a double line near the bottom of the drawing. The monument stands along the same highway, but near the southeast corner of the battlefield. North of the railroad right-of-way the land drops down to the floodplain where an old river channel runs parallel with the terrace wall. Near the west end of this slough, north of John Wesner's house, Bruton recovered sixteen impacted .56/50-caliber bullets (only nine were recorded), one Spencer case, and one .39-caliber ball. The artifacts "were imbedded about 8" in the top 12" to 14" of the bank, on riverside." The rounds might have been fired at fleeing villagers who sought shelter in the brush along the frozen slough. Bruton also found a broken kettle containing some bison teeth, which may provide us with a clue about the location and the perimeter of the village. The kettle was discovered "directly beneath this area [of embedded bullets], about 15 feet out from the bottom of the 15[-]feet[-]high banks. One steel arrow was about 50 feet down river and 15 to 20 feet from the bottom of the banks, 1 foot deep." Bruton discovered a second cluster of artifacts along the slough near the center of the map. They included two Spencer cases, one unfired Spencer cartridge, two .56/50-caliber bullets, and one iron arrowhead. These artifacts might be associated with the Pony Kill Site.

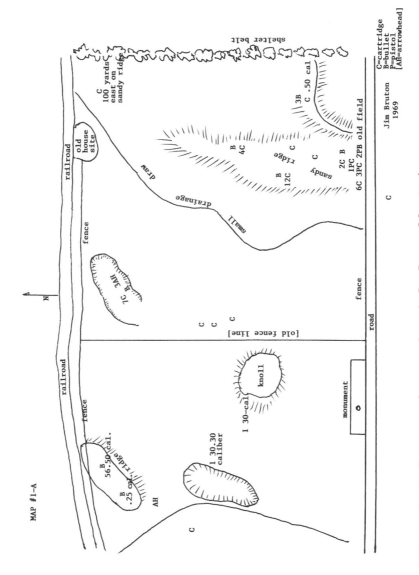

MAP #1-A

N

railroad

railroad

fence

old
house
site

draw

56. .50 cal.
ridge
B
B
.25 cal

AH

C

1 30.30
caliber

monument

1 30-cal
knoll

C

C
C

[old fence line]

7C 3AH
B

fence

small drainage

12C
B

4C
B

sandy ridge

C

C

2C B
1PC
6C 3PC 2PB old field

3B

C .50 cal

C

100 yards
east on
sandy ridge

shelter belt

road

Jim Bruton
1969

C=cartridge
B=bullet
P=pistol
[AH=arrowhead]

Washita Artifact Locations, after a map drawn by Jim Bruton. Map #1-A.

412

The survey was done in 1968 and 1969 and covers the eastern half of the NPS property. The area is bordered by the railroad on the north and Highway 47A on the south. The drawing shows the prominent elevations north of the monument and the artifacts found at these locations. Bruton discovered a cluster of battle-related artifacts on an elevation overlooking the abandoned railroad, northeast of the monument. This location, sometimes identified as Command Knoll or Headquarters Knoll, yielded seven Spencer cases, one .56/50-caliber bullet, and three arrowheads. Over the years Bruton found as many as twenty-five Spencer cases in the same area that are not recorded on this map. The "old house site" was the homestead of J. A. Butler, who settled on this claim during the Land Rush in 1892. Butler sold his property in 1900 to W. T. Bonner, who then owned the western half of the battlefield.

The highest elevation on the NPS property is found in the southeast corner of the site. A son of the Wesner family once lived at this location, which provides a sweeping view of the surrounding area and appears to have been used as a defensive position by Custer's troops. From this point a sandy ridge slopes down along the eastern boundary line. For reference purposes we have named this elevation "Wesner Ridge." Along Wesner Ridge and an eastern spur, Bruton found four positions that yielded a total of thirty-seven battle-related artifacts. The first position was in an old field on the north side of Highway 47A. At this location he discovered eight Spencer cases, one .56/50-caliber bullet, four .44-caliber Henry rim-fire cases, and two .44-caliber bullets. The second position was about one hundred yards further down (north) and contained a cluster of twelve Spencer cases and one .56/50-caliber bullet. The third position, about one hundred yards further down from the second position, yielded four Spencer cases and one .56/50-caliber bullet. The fourth position was along a little spur on the east side of Wesner Ridge, just north of the highway and near the eastern boundary line. The location yielded three .56/50-caliber bullets and one .50/70-caliber center-fire case fired from a Springfield Model 1866 rifle. Three additional .50/70 cartridges found at this location in 1971 are not recorded on the map. Bruton discovered two additional Spencer cases just southeast of the second position and a single Spencer case on the south side of Highway 47A. The highway was constructed in the mid-1960s. It is quite possible that a number of artifacts were displaced or destroyed in the southeast corner during the grading process of the road. The loss of additional in-situ artifacts may have occurred in 1980 when excavation work began on the construction of a dwelling in the southeast corner of the property.

The presence of combat artifacts on Wesner Ridge near the southeast boundary lines provides new evidence about the movements of Custer's troops and the changing flow of the battle. Thompson, Myers, and Benteen led units through this sector at different times during the day. Thompson's squadron crossed the area shortly after daybreak, but was then too far from the village to have been engaged. More likely the spent ammunition came from Myers's squadron when they fought the Indian reinforcements on the high ground late in the morning. Or, perhaps, the firing refuse came from Benteen's troops when he led Myers's squadron early in the afternoon to clear the Indians from his front.

413

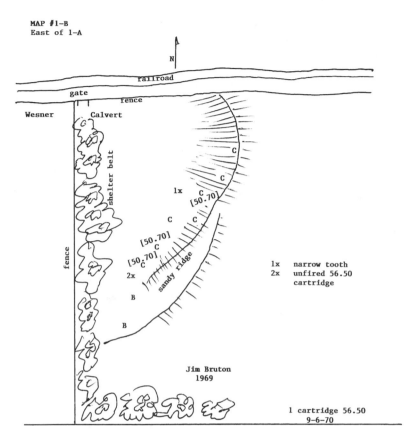

The survey covers the private land along the eastern boundary of the NPS property, identified as the NW Quarter of Section 7, Township 13N, Range 23 WIM. In the upper left corner of the drawing are the names "Wesner" and "Calvert," which stand for John Wesner and D. L. Calvert. Both men were landowners with adjoining properties when Bruton conducted his survey in 1968 and 1970. At some time in the past, the land was sold to the W. Kirk family, and it is now the property of G. Kirk. The shelterbelt bordered a narrow dirt road that divided the two properties. The homestead of the first owner of the east half of the historic site, J. A. Butler, once stood near the west side of this road. The map details the artifact dispersion along a low rise near the west section of the Kirk property, south of the abandoned railroad. For reference purposes, the author has named this sandy elevation "Kirk Slope." Along the east side of Kirk Slope, Bruton discovered three .50/70-caliber center-fire cases, four Spencer cases, one unfired Spencer cartridge, two .56/50-caliber bullets, and one narrow tooth. The .50/70-caliber ammunition may have been fired by the Osage guides who, according to Custer, were "well armed with the improved Springfield breech loading guns." Some Spencer ammunition found at this location was not recorded on the map.

The evidence of combat artifacts on the land east of the NPS site provides new evidence about the movements of Custer's troops. Elliott, Barnitz, Thompson, and Myers led units through this sector at different times during the day. The combat refuge on Kirk Slope might have been left behind by Elliott's detachment while in pursuit of Little Rock's party early in the morning. Barnitz and a detail also pursued Indians in this area. Barnitz was shot down in the vicinity of Kirk Slope and was later rescued by Thompson's company. And late in the morning Myers's troops fought Indian reinforcements in this same sector.

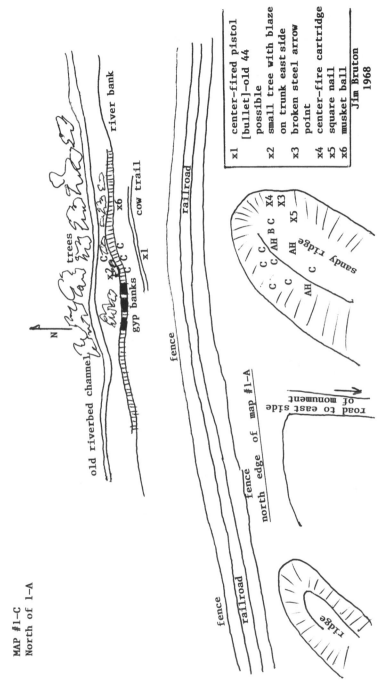

MAP #1-C
North of 1-A

N

trees

old riverbed channel

river bank

x2 x3 x4 x5
C C C
C C
x6

cow trail

gyp banks

x1

fence

railroad

fence
north edge of map #1-A

road to east side
of monument

fence
railroad

ridge

sandy ridge

x4 x3
AH B C x5
AH
C C C
C
AH C

x1 center-fired pistol
    [bullet]-old 44
    possible
x2 small tree with blaze
    on trunk east side
x3 broken steel arrow
    point
x4 center-fire cartridge
x5 square nail
x6 musket ball
          Jim Bruton
             1968

Washita Artifact Locations, after a map drawn by Jim Bruton. Map #1-C.

416

The survey was conducted by Bruton in 1968 and covers the area near the railroad in the SE Quadrant of the Historic Site. The location includes Headquarters Knoll, the terrace directly north of the railroad, and the floodplain below. The artifacts found on Headquarters Knoll include seven Spencer cases, one .50/70-caliber center-fire case, one .56/50-caliber bullet, four iron arrowheads, and one square nail. The terrace north of the railroad yielded one .44-caliber bullet on the south side of a cattle trail. Near the steep edge of the terrace, Bruton found three Spencer cases, and one musket ball a short distance to the east. The floodplain below the steep edge yielded one Spencer case. The presence of arrowheads imbedded among the cartridge cases suggests that the Indian combatants were within close proximity of Headquarters Knoll and may have fired at the soldiers while fleeing east along the wooded slough.

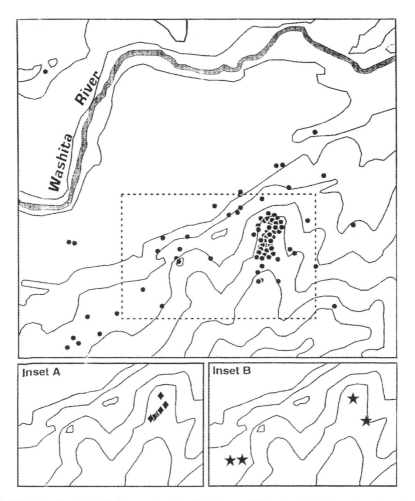

A Washita Battlefield Survey by the Oklahoma Historical Society, showing the
dispersion of Spencer cartridge cases. Inset A shows the dispersion of Henry cartridge cases. Inset B shows the dispersion of .50/70 cartridge cases. Map copyright 2001, reprinted from William B. Lees, "History Underfoot: The Search for
Physical Evidence of the 1868 Attack on Black Kettle's Village," The Chronicles
of Oklahoma (Oklahoma City: Oklahoma Historical Society, 2001).

In 1995 and 1997 personnel from the Oklahoma Historical Society and the National Park Service conducted an archaeological survey on the Washita battlefield with permission from the owner, Betty Wesner. The two surveys recovered a total of 190 artifacts, of which 155 are .50-caliber ammunition for the Spencer carbine carried by the Seventh Cavalry. The Spencer artifacts consisted of 117 cartridge cases, twenty-seven unfired cartridges, and eleven bullets. The archaeologists also found seven Henry and four Springfield cases, presumed to have been fired by the Seventh Cavalry. All but two of the cases were found along a terrace in the southeastern quadrant of the battlefield, now a National Historic Site. The precise location of each of the 126 Spencer, Henry, and Springfield cases were recorded on a topographical map with contour intervals of ten feet. A microscopic analysis of the firing pin and extractor marks revealed that all seven Henry cases were fired from the same weapon, which also proved to be the case with the four Springfield hulls. In regards to the Spencer cases, the signatures revealed that a total of thirty-seven troopers fired 104 rounds. All but five of these troopers took position on a prominent ridge where most of the rounds were fired. The in-situ artifacts reveal *where* the cases were ejected, but not *when*; in other words, the artifact pattern is silent as to whether the troopers congregated on this ridge from a wider area, or whether they fanned out from the ridge afterwards. However, an eyewitness revealed that after Custer entered the west side of the village, he "rode straight to a little knoll that overlooks the village on the south, and from that point issued many of his orders." The artifact pattern on the map seems to bear out this statement. The Spencer cases in the lower left of the map mark the location where Custer's staff ascended the terrace. Riding northeast along the bank, they fired occasionally at targets on the floodplain. The "little knoll" is the elevation containing the dense cluster of Spencer cases. Custer's staff included four officers, three non-commissioned officers, two interpreters, six white scouts, trumpeter orderlies, officers' strikers and cooks, and Custer's bodyguard of ten sharpshooters. Headquarters staff had therefore sufficient strength to account for the artifacts left behind by thirty-seven Spencers, one Henry, and one Springfield.

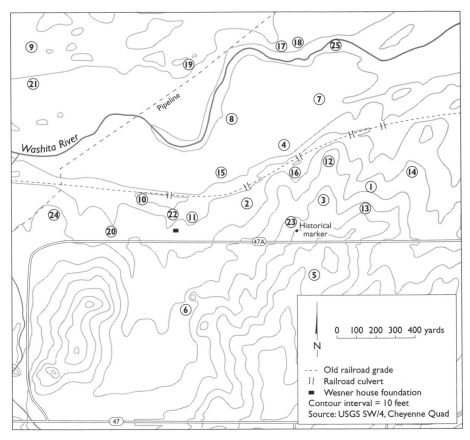

Summary Map of Artifact Discoveries on the Washita Battlefield.

1. Butler field where many shells were plowed up. (Source: Fred Barde)
2. Ravine where many shells were plowed up. (Source: Fred Barde)
3. Big mound where many bullets have been found. (Source: Fred Barde)
4. Location where many ponies were killed. (Source: Fred Barde)
5. Field where Salyer plowed up many bullets. (Source: Fred Barde)
6. North elevation of the Twin Knolls where a Spencer .56/50 bullet was found twenty-five feet up the north slope in 1970. (Source: Jim Bruton)
7. Bottom where an Indian pipe, sword, rifle, canteen, and many bullets have been found. (Source: Alvin Moore)
8. Location where four rusty Indian rifles were plowed up in 1930. Three of these muskets were originally exhibited in the front window of the *Cheyenne Star* and were later displayed at the Black Kettle Museum from 1959 until 1997. Their whereabouts are now unknown. One of these muskets was owned by the father of Irvy Porter. (Source: Irvy Porter to Jim Bruton; Mary Sue Bright to Gary Scott)
9. Field on Eula Cross land where a bent iron arrowhead was found in a sand blow in the 1980s. The location was a few hundred yards north of the Washita River, near the abandoned bridge over the Williams Channel. (Source: Gary Scott)
10. Terrace where an iron arrowhead was found in the 1980s. (Source: Gary Scott)
11. Service road to former Wesner farm complex, alongside which a large brass saddle-brad—the size of a half-dollar coin—with "US" embossed on it was found in 1984. (Source: Gary Scott)
12. Headquarters Hill, where more than seventy artifacts have been found. (Source: OKHS, NPS, and Jim Bruton)
13. Wesner Ridge, where more than forty artifacts have been found. (Source: Jim Bruton) Just SW of this location, Lee Roark (1921–1983), nephew of landowner James Williams, plowed up a leather cap-and-ball pouch with molded .44-caliber pistol bullets, which lay scattered nearby. In all, Mr. Roark collected two boxes of arrowheads, buckles, bullets, and casings on the battle field. Lee's brother, Claude Roark, donated one box with artifacts to the No Man's Land Museum in Goodwell, Oklahoma, around 1940. However, a current listing of the museum's accessions identifies only two unfired Spencer cartridges and nine casings. (Source: Gary Scott, Jim Bruton, Sue Weissinger) This is also the probable location where a Remington 1861 .44-caliber cap-and-ball pistol was dug up. The pistol was originally exhibited in the front window of the *Cheyenne Star* and is now on display at the Pioneer Museum in Cheyenne, Oklahoma. (Source: Judy Tracy, Gary Scott, Jim Bruton)
14. Kirk Slope, where more than ten artifacts have been found. (Source: Jim Bruton)
15. The terrace wall where some sixteen impacted Spencer bullets were recovered. (Source: Jim Bruton)
16. A gully; horse bones were scattered from here all the way south to the present historical marker. (Source: Lloyd Martin [ca. 1917–1997] to Gary Scott. Martin was a Cheyenne merchant.)
17. Location north of the river where horse bones were scattered. (Source: Lloyd Martin to Gary Scott)
18. Sand dune area where .50/70 cases, balls, and buttons have been found. Also location where an Army kettle was found. (Source: Jim Bruton)
19. Spencer case. (Source: OKHS, NPS)
20. Wheat field north of Highway 47A, west of former Wesner house, where one Henry case, two Spencer cases, and three bullets have been found. (Source: Gary Scott)
21. Burial site of an Indian female, a Washita victim. The skeleton was exhumed in 1934 and re-interred near the Black Kettle Museum in 1968.
22. Indian burial site near former Williams House, possibly a Washita victim. The remains were probably transferred in 1928 and re-interred at an undisclosed location in 1987.
23. Burial site of an Indian male, a Washita victim. The skeleton was exhumed along the railroad bed NE of Cheyenne in 1917 and re-interred on Overlook in 1930.
24. Prehistoric burial site. The remains were transferred and re-interred at an undisclosed location by Pat Jarvis in 1972.
25. The approximate burial site of two Indian females, both Washita victims.

It was on July 11 [13], 1934 that workmen while excavating preparatory to rebuilding a bridge across the Washita river west and a little north of Cheyenne discovered a skeleton.

Among the workmen present was George Parker, an old-timer, who directed the men to exercise great care in digging up the bones in order that none of them be destroyed. He and another workman by the name of Jeff Lacy brought the bones to town. They also brought a large number of beads, conchos, rings and other ornaments found with the bones.[2]

Those familiar with the Battle of the Washita felt positive that the bones were the remains of Black Kettle, as they were discovered at almost the identical spot where the Indian Chief was said to have been shot from his horse, and later buried by his children.

A simple announcement [by George Parker] of the discovery of the skeleton was carried in the local paper and almost immediately after the publication Stacy Riggs, a grandson of Chief Black Kettle, came to Cheyenne and positively identified the bones as being those of his grandfather. The identification was made by ornaments found with the skeleton, the age, as shown by the teeth, and the backbones showing that he had been wounded in the back.

Excerpt from the *Cheyenne Star*
December 5, 1968
Burial of Indian Remains
Discovered in 1934

Concluding the Centennial Observance was the symbolic Indian burial ceremony in the flag pole circle of the Black Kettle Museum. This interment ceremony was conducted by Lawrence Hart, a Cheyenne Indian, and a member of the Oklahoma Indian Affairs Commission. Hart is also a minister.

---

[2]The artifacts discovered with the remains consisted of a pipe, a section of a breast plate made of deer bones, a conch shell, and a bead shaped like a disk. These items were displayed in the *Star* window for many years before being donated to the Black Kettle Museum in 1959.

Cheyenne Indians chanted the tribes' funeral cry as they bore the blanket-covered bronze casket containing bones of an unknown Indian [discovered on July 11, 1934], to its resting-place. The grave marker bears the inscription: "The Unknown who lies here is in commemoration of Chief Black Kettle and the Cheyenne [and Arapaho] tribal members who lost their lives in the Battle of the Washita."[3]

Excerpt from the *Cheyenne Star*
May 18, 1972
Discovery of Prehistoric Burial Site

An Indian burial site was located on [the] John Wesner farm west of Cheyenne by Dale Wesner and J. Pat Jarvis. A human skull was plowed up in the course of working the land.

This area covers a five-foot circle about 10 inches deep. Mr. Jarvis estimates that it is a skeleton of an Indian woman who was between 30 and 40 years old at the time of death. It was a custom to include their worldly possessions in the grave with all articles broken so they would be of no useful value to the living. Included in the grave are the following articles: hide scraper; stone abrader, used in some manner as [a] sharpening stone; stone celt; prehistoric ax; smoking pipe, made of pipestone found only in Minnesota; mussel-shell digging tool, used to dig burial pit; bone needle, used for making small holes in leather; bone rasp and shaft straightener; quarts crystal, used for money at that time; turtle shell and small rodent bones [which] indicate that the burial pit also was used as a trash pit. The body was doubled up and probably was lying on its side to conserve space.[4]

---

[3]A few days before the reburial of "Black Kettle's remains," Dr. Clyde Snow of the State Medical Office examined the bones at the request of the Oklahoma Historical Society. His forensic examination revealed that the remains were those of an Indian woman, about eighteen to twenty-two years old, who had been shot in the back.

[4]The remains were reinterred on the Wesner property in 1972.

Excerpt from the *Cheyenne Star*
June 16, 1988
Discovery of Indian Remains
in the Cheyenne Star Basement,
June 15, 1987

On June 15, 1987, a basement which had been sealed by concrete for many years, was discovered in the back of the Cheyenne Star building. After a great deal of work, a hole was chiseled through the floor that allowed someone to enter and explore. The "usual" sealed basement articles were discovered: numerous pieces of antique type, parts of an old printing press, a few pieces of an old whiskey still, roaches 7 feet long, writing on the walls, etc. But something out of the ordinary was also found . . . BONES. Lots and lots of bones. Deputy Sheriff Hay assisted with collecting them and sending them away [to Dr. Clyde Snow of the Oklahoma Medical Office] for study.[5]

Excerpt from the *Cheyenne Star*
June 16, 1988
Reburial of Basement Remains
Discovered on June 15, 1987

In a phone interview, Dr. Snow states that the pieces [of bones found in the Star basement in 1987] fit together into two persons. One had been buried at the edge of the battle area and the other had been buried near the water. This was determined by the condition and coloration of the bones.

---

[5]During his life, John Casady came into possession of four sets of Indian remains. One set, exhumed on the C. G. Miller farm north of Cheyenne in 1917, was reinterred on the present National Park Service overlook in 1930. A second set, discovered near the Washita River Bridge in 1934, was reinterred near the Black Kettle Museum in 1968. A third set was exhumed on the Warren homestead west of Cheyenne in 1933. The fourth and final set was discovered by James Williams while excavating the foundation for a new home west of the present overlook in 1928. Presumably, the last two sets were found in the *Star* basement in 1987.

Victim #1 (buried towards edge of the area) was a middle age male. When pieces of the skull were put together it revealed at least two bullet holes to the temple area. Because of the location of the wound and the fact the holes were so close together it is possible the victim had been wounded earlier in the battle and the head wounds were to make death quicker.

Victim #2 (buried near the water) was found to be a female, age 20–30. No evidence of trauma was found on the bones to give exact evidence of how she died.

Study of the bones was hampered somewhat by the fact that many of the bones were fragmented and had to be assembled. A number of teeth found with the bones did make identification and age of the victims easier.[6]

It took four months to complete the study of the bones before they were turned over to the Cheyenne Tribe for burial. Tribal members, chiefs and even government officials were involved in the preparation. Red tape was in abundance as permission was being sought for a proper place to bury the remains [near the Washita battlefield].

Finally all things were complete and a date set for the traditional burial ceremony. The date chosen was November 27, 1987, the anniversary of the Custer attack on Black Kettle's camp.

---

[6]Dr. Snow's pathology report reveals that the bones of the male showed no signs of disease at the time of death. The robustness of the long bone shafts indicate that the victim was a muscular and physically active individual. Death was caused by two large-caliber bullets that exited on the right side of the skull. A metal fragment embedded in the sacral promontory led to Snow's speculation that this individual was initially incapacitated by a gunshot to his lower torso. The presence of the closely spaced exit wounds suggest that the victim had been dispatched by two gunshots at close range while lying immobile on the ground. The bullets entered the left cranium vault and traveled transversely to exit on the right. The reddish discoloration of the victim's bones indicate a burial in an upland soil, such as a hilltop.

In the case of the female, Snow's report reveals that the gender was determined by the small, thin-walled cranium vault and gracile long bone shafts with slight muscle attachments. The absence of osteoarthritic disease, the lack of any signs of involutional changes, and the fact that the cranial vault sutures were apparently patent at the time of death, indicate an age range of from twenty-five to forty-five years at the time of death. The cause of death could not be determined from the bone fragments, which represented only 15 percent of an adult skeleton. The ash gray discoloration of the remains indicate a burial in dark bottomland soil.

Alfrich Heap of Birds, keeper of the Sacred Arrows, made sure that the traditional Cheyenne burial custom was observed. This included the honoring of the Warrior Society of the deceased. Since the particulars of the two individuals were not know, honor was paid to all societies, including the Kit Fox, Dog Soldiers, Bow Strings, [and] Elk Scrapers.

Appendix I

A Genealogical Outline of Black Kettle

Black Kettle was born in a Sutai camp near the Black Hills about 1797, the oldest of four children born to Black Hawk and Little Brown-Back Hawk Woman (or Sparrow Hawk Woman). The record shows that Black Kettle's father was also known as Swift Hawk Laying Down and Hawk Stretched Out, which convey the same meaning and suggest that Black Hawk may have been an abbreviated name. Upon Black Hawk's death at a young age, his family was cared for by Bear on the Ridge, who was a brother of Sparrow Hawk Woman.[1]

Black Kettle had four wives, with whom he had seventeen children. Some of these children were murdered at Sand Creek in 1864. Two of his wives and several of his remaining offspring were killed at the Washita. His first marriage was with an Arapaho who was known among the Cheyennes as Arapaho Woman. His second marriage was with a Cheyenne named Little Sage Woman. His third wife was a Ponca captive named Medicine Woman Later (or Medicine Woman Hereafter). His fourth and final wife was a Sioux, who was known simply as Sioux Woman.[2]

Very little genealogical information has come to light about Black Kettle's children. Based on statements by a grandson, Stacy Riggs, we assume that the chief's marriage with Arapaho Woman took place about 1830 and resulted in the births of one son, known

---

[1]Grinnell n.d.; Powell 1981, 1:638; Field Notes on Southern Cheyennes, 1902, George B. Grinnell Collection, Braun Research Library, Southwest Museum, Los Angeles; Hyde 1968, 322–23.

[2]White Buffalo Woman to Truman Michelson, in J. H. Moore 1987, 272; Hyde 1968, 316, 323; A. Heap of Birds 1999; Halaas and Masich 2004, 109; Cometsevah 1999.

as Black Kettle Jr., and four daughters: Pipe Woman, White Buffalo Woman, Red Feather Woman, and a fourth girl whose name was not given.[3]

We know little about these four daughters. The unidentified daughter was the mother of Stacy Riggs (known also as Lone Wolf), who was born in 1860 (he died in 1947). Riggs's father was killed by Ute Indians near Bent's Stockade in March 1864 after an unsuccessful raid on Ute horses. Lone Wolf had a younger sister, whose name is not known. She was born about 1862 and was raised by relatives among the Northern Cheyennes in Montana. Otherwise, according to Arapaho oral history, one of these four daughters exhumed Black Kettle's bones at the Washita and reinterred the remains at the North Canadian near Cantonment sometime after 1880.[4]

Black Kettle Jr. was the only son of Black Kettle and Arapaho Woman. Records suggest that he was born in 1831 and died in 1902. He may have had a son named Star, also known as Star Black Kettle. Agency employees Anglicized his name and listed him on the agency rolls as Star Black. He married Flora Red Eye, and they had a daughter named Flora Black. Born in 1907, Flora was better known as Jennie Black. She married Frank Pendleton, who was the son of David "Oakerhater" Pendleton, a Fort Marion prisoner who later became a deacon in the Episcopal Church.[5]

Little Sage Woman, Black Kettle's second wife, was described as a rather attractive young woman of whom the chief was very fond. She accompanied Black Kettle on a war journey against the Utes in the autumn of 1854. During a hasty retreat from a village in the Rockies, Little Sage Woman was thrown from her horse and captured. Despite continued efforts to locate her through Mexican traders, Black Kettle never heard of her again. We do not know if any children were born from this marriage.[6]

Black Kettle's third marriage took place in 1855, when he took Medicine Woman Later as his wife. She was severely wounded at

---

[3]Riggs 1936.
[4]Ibid.; Lone Bear 1999; Berthrong 1963, 175–76; Grinnell 1972, 1:84; Briscoe 1987, 3; A. Heap of Birds 1999.
[5]Mann 1997, 138.
[6]Hyde 1968, 323; Halaas and Masich 2004, 109.

Sand Creek in 1864 but survived the trauma of her nine wounds. On November 27, 1868, she died alongside her husband on the banks of the Washita during Custer's dawn attack. No children were born from this marriage, according to George Bent.[7]

Black Kettle's fourth wife was a Moiseyu woman from the Wutapiu band known as Sioux Woman. This marriage was consummated about 1859 and produced two daughters and a son. Sioux Woman was shot in the back near Black Kettle's campsite on November 27, 1868, and died on the riverbank while leading her three young children to safety. The children miraculously survived. The oldest daughter, Walking Woman, was born about 1860. The other two children were born in 1862 and 1866; their names are not known.[8]

In addition to the offspring mentioned above, Black Kettle is said to have been the father of several children whose maternal ancestor is not known. One of these was a daughter named Yellow Woman. She later married Reuben Black Horse, a Northern Cheyenne who stayed with the Southerners. Yellow Woman survived the attack at the Washita, though a half-sister did not. This other unidentified daughter of Black Kettle was shot down in cold blood despite the fact that she had raised her hands in surrender. The possibility exists that she was not a daughter but instead was Black Kettle's young wife, Sioux Woman.[9]

Another descendent of Black Kettle was a young man known as Blue Horse. He was born about 1847 and was slain by Capt. Frederick Benteen during the attack on the Washita village. Blue Horse was survived by a sister named Magpie Woman, a younger brother, and his mother, Corn Tassel Woman. Magpie Woman married George Bent in 1867. According to Bent, these children were nephews and nieces of Black Kettle. Yet he also states that Magpie Woman was Black Kettle's stepdaughter. Some Cheyenne genealogists are convinced that Black Kettle fathered these three children.[10]

---

[7]Hyde 1968, 316; Halaas and Masich 2004, 109; A. Heap of Birds 1999; Magpie 1930; Moving Behind Woman ca. 1937.

[8]Cometsevah 1999.

[9]Viola 1993, 127; Godfrey 1917.

[10]Hyde 1968, 315, 317–18; Halaas and Masich 2004, 259; Bent [1906].

Jennie Black was yet another daughter of Black Kettle. Although her mother's name is not known, Jennie was born about 1866 and attended Darlington and Carlisle Institute. She graduated in 1885 and married Leonard Tyler in 1889. Tyler's Cheyenne name was Little Magpie. He was born about 1866 and was educated at Carlisle, Haskell Institute, and Indiana College at Fort Wayne. An agency clerk and interpreter, Tyler was one of the signatories who approved the allotment of the reservation and the sale of surplus lands in 1890.[11]

In addition to Black Kettle, three more children were born to Black Hawk and Sparrow Hawk Woman. The second child was a son named Gentle Horse. During most of his life, he lived with the shame of killing his brother-in-law, the husband of his sister, Wind Woman. In later years he assumed the name White Shield to honor the memory of a deceased relative. One of Gentle Horse's sons was named Little Hawk, born about 1840. Another son was enrolled at Carlisle Institute in 1879. Gentle Horse died in 1896.[12]

The third child was a daughter named Wind Woman. She married a Lakota and gave birth to a son named Young Black Bird, or Little Magpie. Her husband was an abusive man and was killed about 1850 near the Platte River in Colorado during a violent confrontation with Gentle Horse. After her husband's death, Wind Woman settled among the Northern Cheyennes and married Spotted Wolf. She died on the Tongue River Indian Reservation in 1915. Little Magpie gained a reputation as a brave man in battles with Crook's soldiers at the Rosebud and Custer's Seventh Cavalry at the Little Bighorn in June 1876. He later assumed the name White Shield and served as a member of the Indian Police at Lame Deer, Montana, attaining the rank of captain in 1886. White Shield died at Lame Deer in 1918.[13]

The fourth and last child was a son named Wolf. His nickname may have been "Iron Teeth," and he was also known as Black Dog.

[11]Berthrong 1976, 145, 316; Ediger 1940, 301.

[12]Grinnell n.d.; and 1972, 1:356; Hodge 1907, 2:975; Grinnell 1956, 330; Mann 1997, 51; Riggs 1936.

[13]Grinnell, Field Notes on Southern Cheyennes, 1902; and 1972, 1:196; Powell 1981, 2:1001; Grinnell 1956, 335; Stands in Timber and Liberty 1967, 272.

Wolf was wounded at Sand Creek in 1864. He assumed the name Black Kettle upon his brother's death in 1868. One of his four sons, born in 1881 from his marriage with Ghost Woman, became known as Jay Black Kettle. This son later assumed the name Gentle Horse to honor the memory of his uncle. His agency name was shortened to Jay Black in a zealous attempt by government employees to Anglicize Indian names. Jay Black Kettle was a highly respected traditionalist who served as the Sacred Arrows Keeper from 1957 through 1962. He died in 1969.[14]

---

[14]Hyde 1968, 322–23; Powell 1981, 1:xxxii, 638; Thetford 1969a.

Bibliography

Afton, Jean. 1977. Techniques for Determining Dates Derived from a Cheyenne Indian Sketchbook. *Southwestern Lore* (June): 11–31.

Afton, Jean, David Fridtjof Halaas, and Andrew E. Masich (with Richard N. Ellis). 1997. *The Cheyenne Dog Soldiers*. Denver: Colorado Historical Society and University of Colorado Press.

Alvord, Henry E. 1868. Summary of Information, December 7. In U.S. Senate, *Indian Battle on the Washita River*, 40th Cong., 3rd sess., S. Exec. Doc. 18.

———. 1874. Letter to Col. W. B. Hazen, April 4. In Some Corrections of "Life on the Plains," *Chronicles of Oklahoma* 3 (4): 295–318.

Armes, George A. 1900. *Ups and Downs of an Army Officer*. Washington, D.C.: privately printed.

Bailey, Mahlon [surgeon, Nineteenth Kansas Cavalry]. 1937. Medical Sketch of the Nineteenth Regiment of Kansas Cavalry Volunteers. *Kansas Historical Quarterly* 6 (4): 378–86.

Baldwin, Alice Blackwood. 1929. *Memoirs of the Late Frank D. Baldwin, Major General, U.S.A.* Los Angeles: Wetzel.

Barde, Fred S. [1899]. Map of Washita Battlefield. Frederick S. Barde Collection, Archives Division, Oklahoma Historical Society, Oklahoma City.

———. 1904. Custer's Oklahoma Fight. *Kansas City Star*, December 4.

———. 1909. Untitled typescript. Partially dated Fort Reno, November 23. Frederick S. Barde Collection, Archives Division, Oklahoma Historical Society, Oklahoma City.

———. 1914. *Life and Adventures of Billy Dixon of Adobe Walls, Texas Panhandle*. Guthrie, Okla.: Co-Operative.

———. 1969. Edmund Gasseau Choteau Guerrier: French Trader. *Chronicles of Oklahoma* 47 (4): 360–76.

Barker, Carolyn. 1996. *Burials in the Fort Reno Cemetery, 1874–1948*. N.p.: privately printed.

Barnard, Sandy. 1996. *Custer's First Sergeant John Ryan.* Terre Haute: AST Press.

———. 2000. Custer and Elliott: Comrades in Controversy. *Fourteenth Annual Symposium Custer Battlefield Historical & Museum Association* (June 26): 18–28.

Barnitz, Albert [captain, Seventh Cavalry]. 1868a. Journal, November 23–27. Albert Barnitz Papers, Beinicke Library, Yale University, New Haven, Conn.

———. 1868b. Letter to Jenny Barnitz, December 5. Albert Barnitz Papers, Beinicke Library, Yale University, New Haven, Conn.

———. 1889. Narrative. Albert Barnitz Papers, Beinicke Library, Yale University, New Haven, Conn.

———. 1910a. Letter to W. M. Camp, January 12. Folder 11, Box 1, Walter Mason Camp Collection, Harold B. Lee Library, Brigham Young University, Provo, Utah.

———. 1910b. Interview by Walter Camp, May 7. Unclassified Envelope 130, Walter Camp Manuscripts, Lilly Library, Indiana University, Bloomington.

———. 1910c. Letter to W. M. Camp, November 18. Folder 14, Box 1, Walter Mason Camp Collection, Harold B. Lee Library, Brigham Young University, Provo, Utah.

———. 1910d. Letter to Joseph B. Thoburn, November 28. Joseph B. Thoburn Collection, Archives Division, Oklahoma Historical Soc., Oklahoma City.

———. 1910e. Letter to W. M. Camp, November 29. Folder 14, Box 1, Walter Mason Camp Collection, Harold B. Lee Library, Brigham Young University, Provo, Utah.

Barrett, Stephen M. 1936. *Hoistah, an Indian Girl.* Oklahoma City: Harlow.

Barry, Louise. 1972. *The Beginnings of the West.* Topeka: Kansas State Historical Society.

Bates, Col. Charles Francis. 1936. *Custer's Indian Battles.* Bronxville, N.Y.: privately printed.

Battey, Thomas C. 1875. *Life and Adventures of a Quaker among the Indians.* Boston: Lee and Shepard.

Bell, James M. [1st lieutenant, Seventh Cavalry]. 1897. Reminiscences. *Journal of the United States Cavalry Association* 10 (39): 343–445.

———. [1910]. Interview by Walter Camp. Folder 1, Box 2, Walter Camp Manuscripts, Lilly Library, Indiana University, Bloomington.

———. 1911. Letter to Walter M. Camp, July 28. Folder 19, Box 1, Walter Camp Collection, Harold B. Lee Library, Brigham Young University, Provo, Utah.

Belous, Russell E., and Robert A. Weinstein. 1969. *Will Soule: Indian Photographer at Fort Sill, Oklahoma, 1869–74.* Los Angeles: Ward Ritchie.

Bent, George. 1869. Letter to Col. S. F. Tappan, September 27. Ms 617, Tappan Collection, Colorado Historical Society, Denver.

————. 1905. Letter to George Hyde, September. George Bent Collection, Colorado Historical Society, Denver.

————. 1905–1906. Forty Years with the Cheyennes. *The Frontier: A Magazine of the West* 4 (4): 3–7; 4 (5): 3–5; 4 (6): 3–7; 4 (7): 3–6; 4 (8): 3–7; 4 (9): 3–8.

————. [1906]. Letter to Robert M. Peck. *Kansas Historical Collections* 10 (1907–1908): 441–42.

————. 1911. Letter to Joseph B. Thoburn, December 27. Joseph B. Thoburn Collection, Archives Division, Oklahoma Historical Society, Oklahoma City.

————. 1912. Letters to Joseph B. Thoburn, January 9, 19. Joseph B. Thoburn Collection, Archives Division, Oklahoma Historical Society, Oklahoma City.

————. 1913. Letter to George Hyde, August 28. Bent-Hyde Correspondence, William Robertson Coe Collection, Beinicke Library, Yale University, New Haven, Conn.

————. 1916. Letter to W. M. Camp, December 4. Folder 2, Box 2, Walter Camp Collection, Harold B. Lee Library, Brigham Young University, Provo, Utah.

Benteen, Frederick W. [captain, Seventh Cavalry]. 1869. The Battle of the Washita. *New York Times,* February 14.

————. 1895. Letters to David F. Barry, August 29, September 28. David F. Barry Correspondence, Little Bighorn Battlefield National Monument Library, Crow Agency, Mont.

————. 1896. Letters to Theodore W. Goldin, February 12, 17, 22. In *The Benteen-Goldin Letters on Custer's Last Battle,* by John M. Carroll.

————. n.d.(a). Hunting the Southern Cheyennes in the Spring of 1869 from Medicine Bluff Creek to El Llano Estacado. In *Cavalry Scraps: The Writings of Frederick W. Benteen,* by John M. Carroll.

————. n.d.(b). Annotations in his personal copy of W. L. Holloway, *Wild Life on the Plains and Horrors of Indian Warfare.*

Berthrong, Donald J. 1963. *The Southern Cheyennes.* Norman: University of Oklahoma Press.

————. 1976. *The Cheyenne and Arapaho Ordeal.* Norman: University of Oklahoma Press.

————. 1989. From Buffalo Days to Classrooms: The Southern Cheyennes and Arapahos and Kansas. *Kansas History* 12 (2): 101–13.

Bingaman, Josephus [private, Nineteenth Kansas Cavalry]. n.d. Interview by Eli S. Ricker. Folder 3, Box 6, Eli S. Ricker Collection, Battle of the Washita, Nebraska State Historical Society, Lincoln.

Black, Steve (National Park Service, Washita Battlefield Site). 2002. Letters to author, April 23, May 7. In author's files.

Blinn, Richard F. Various dates. Collection. Folder 12, Box 1, Harrington Family Files, Western History Collections, University of Oklahoma, Norman.

Blinn, Mrs. R. F. 1868. Letter [to William Griffinstein], November 7. In U.S. Senate, *Indian Battle on the Washita River*, 40th Cong., 3rd sess., S. Exec. Doc. 18.

Bradshaw, Larry [landowner west of Washita Battlefield]. 2002. Letters to the author, September 15, November 15. In author's files.

Brady, Cyrus Townsend. 1904. The Battle of the Washita. *Pearson's Magazine* 12 (July—December): 85–96.

Brewster, Charles [1st lieutenant, Seventh Cavalry]. 1899. Battle of the Washita. *National Tribune*, May 18.

Brill, Charles J. 1930. The End of the Cheyenne Trail. *Daily Oklahoman*, November 23.

———. 1935a. The Battle of the Washita. *Daily Oklahoman*, November 10.

———. 1935b. Clearing the Washita. *Daily Oklahoman*, November 17.

———. 1938. *Conquest of the Southern Plains*. Oklahoma City: Golden Saga.

Brininstool, E. A. 1953. *Fighting Indian Warriors*. Harrisburg, Pa.: Stackpole.

Briscoe, James. 1987. *Archeological Reconnaissance of the Cheyenne Tribe Reburial Project on the Black Kettle National Grasslands, Roger Mills County, Okla.* Copy of report in author's files.

Briscoe, James, and Joe Watkins. 1990. Historical and Archeological Evaluation of the Battle of the Washita. Appendix I of *Archeological Survey Report on the Shell Western Seismic Line 6112, Roger Mills County, Oklahoma*, April 4. Copy of report in author's files.

Brooks, E. O. [Sarah White]. 1933. Reminiscences of the Life of Mrs. E. O. Brooks—Telling of Her Capture by Indians in Early Days. *The Kansas Optimist*, January 26.

Brown, William E. 1964. *Special Report on Washita Battlefield, Oklahoma*. Cultural Landscape Inventory Files. Santa Fe: National Park Service, Southwest Region.

———. 1966. *Historical Justification for Proposed Boundaries at Washita Battlefield*. National Register Files. Santa Fe: National Park Service, Southwest Region.

Bruton, Jim. 1968–69. Sketch maps of metal-detecting surveys at Washita Battlefield. Cultural Landscape Inventory Files, National Park Service, Southwest Region, Santa Fe. Copies in author's files.

———. 2002–04. Correspondence with the author. In author's files.

———. 2003. Photocopies of artifacts found on and around Washita Battlefield. In author's files.

———. 2003–2004. Topographical map and sketch maps of artifact locations on and around Washita Battlefield. In author's files.

Bull Coming, Kathryn [Cheyenne]. 1999. Interview by Mary Jane Warde. Cheyenne/Washita Oral History Project, Oklahoma Historical Society, Oklahoma City.

Burchardt, Bill. 1961. Battle of the Washita. *Oklahoma Today* 11 (Summer): 10–13.

Burgess, Henderson Lafayette. 1929. The 18th Kansas Volunteer Cavalry and Some Incidents Connected with Its Service on the Plains. *Winners of the West* (August 30): 6.

Burkey, Blaine. 1976. *Custer Come at Once!* Hays, Kans.: Thomas More Prep.

Burns, Louis F. 1989. *A History of the Osage People.* Fallbrook: Ciga.

Cahill, Luke. 1927. An Indian Campaign and Buffalo Hunting with Buffalo Bill. *Colorado Magazine* 4 (4): 125–35.

Camp, W. M. 1910. Letter to Albert Barnitz, November 6. Walter Camp Collection, Little Bighorn Battlefield National Monument Library, Crow Agency, Mont., copy.

———. 1911. Letter to J. M. Bell, May 12. Folder 17, Box 1, Walter Camp Collection, Brigham Young University, Provo, Utah.

———. 1919. Letter to Elizabeth B. Custer, November 3. Reel 3, Elizabeth B. Custer Collection, Little Bighorn Battlefield National Monument Library, Crow Agency, Mont., microfilm.

———. n.d.(a). Field Notes. Folder 3 (Edward S. Godfrey), Box 5, Walter Camp Collection, Harold B. Lee Library, Brigham Young University, Provo, Utah.

———. n.d.(b). Field Notes. Unclassified Envelope 50, Walter Camp Manuscripts, Lilly Library, Indiana University, Bloomington.

Carriker, Robert C. 1970. *Fort Supply, Indian Territory.* Norman: University of Oklahoma Press.

Carroll, John M. 1974. *The Benteen-Goldin Letters on Custer and His Last Battle.* Mattituck, N.Y.: J. M. Carroll.

———. 1978a. *General Custer and the Battle of the Washita: The Federal View.* Bryan, Tex.: Guidon Press.

———. 1978b. *Washita!* Bryan, Tex.: privately printed.

———. 1979. *Cavalry Scraps: The Writings of Frederick W. Benteen.* Bryan, Tex.: Guidon Press.

———. 1981. *Custer: From the Civil War to the Little Big Horn.* Bryan, Tex.: Guidon Press.

———. 1983. *Camp Talk: The Very Private Letters of Frederick W. Benteen of the 7th U.S. Cavalry to his Wife, 1871 to 1888.* Mattituck: J. M. Carroll and Co.

Casady, John C. n.d. Inventory of John C. Casady Collection. Copy in author's files.

Casady, Klina E. 1974. *Once Every Five Years: A History of Cheyenne, Oklahoma.* Oklahoma City: Metro.

Chalfant, Billy [landowner north of Washita Battlefield]. 2003. Phone conversations with the author, February 2, 9, March 2.

Chalfant, William Y. 1997. *Cheyennes at Dark Water Creek.* Norman: University of Oklahoma Press.

Chandler, Melbourne C. 1960. *Of Gary Owen in Glory: The History of the Seventh United States Cavalry Regiment.* Annandale, Va.: Turnpike.

Cheyenne Star. 1914. An Old Scout [Ben Clark] Commits Suicide. August 6.

———. 1930a. Ceremonial by Noted Indians. September 25.

———. 1930b. Chief Magpie Addresses Crowd. December 4.

———. 1932a. Early History of Cheyenne and Many Things Interesting to Note. April 14.

———. 1932b. History of the Cheyenne Short Line Railroad and How We Got It. April 14.

———. 1932c. Battlefield Is to Have Marker. July 21.

———. 1933a. Washita Battlefield Is Marked. January 19.

———. 1933b. Survivor [Edward S. Godfrey] Tells Story of the "Battle of Washita." August 10, 17, 24 (serialized).

———. 1934. Identify Remains as Indian Chief. July 26.

———. 2000. Celebrating the Nation's First Upstream Flood Control Rehabilitation Project. April 14 (spec. ed.).

Cheyenne Transporter. 1884. Jack Stillwell. August 30.

Chief of National Cemetery. 1970. *Fort Smith National Cemetery.* Washington, D.C.: GPO.

Clark, Ben [chief of scouts, Seventh Cavalry]. 1887. Ethnography and Philology of the Cheyennes. George B. Grinnell Collection, Southwest Museum Library, Los Angeles, manuscript.

———. 1899. Custer's Washita Fight. *New York Sun,* May 14.

———. 1903. Letter to Fred S. Barde, May 1. Frederick S. Barde Collection, Archives Division, Oklahoma Historical Society, Oklahoma City.

———. 1904. Custer's Oklahoma Fight. *Kansas City Star,* December 4.

———. 1910a. Revised *Kansas City Star* article. Box 3 (Battle of the Washita), Walter Camp Manuscripts, Lilly Library, Indiana University, Bloomington.

———. 1910b. Interview by Walter Camp, October 22. Box 3 (Battle of the Washita), Walter Camp Manuscripts, Lilly Library, Indiana University, Bloomington.

———. 1910c. Field Notes. Folder 4, Box 2, Walter Camp Manuscripts, Ben Clark, Lilly Library, Indiana University, Bloomington.

Coel, Margaret. 1981. *Chief Left Hand, Southern Arapaho.* Norman: University of Oklahoma Press.

Cohoe, William [Cheyenne]. 1964. *A Cheyenne Sketchbook by Cohoe.* Commentary by E. Adamson Hoebel and Karen Daniels Petersen. Norman: University of Oklahoma Press.

Collins, Hubert E. 1928. *Warpath and Cattle Trail.* New York: William Morrow.

———. 1932. Ben Williams, Frontier Peace Officer. *Chronicles of Oklahoma* 10 (4): 520–39.

Colyer, Vincent. 1869. Inspection Report to Felix B. Brunot, Commissioner, April 9 entry. In *Report of the Secretary of the Interior,* 41st Cong., 2nd sess., Exec. Doc.

Cometsevah, Colleen [Cheyenne]. 1999. Interviews by Mary Jane Warde, August 20, September 10. Cheyenne/Washita Oral History Project, Oklahoma Historical Society, Oklahoma City.

Connelley, William E. 1928. John McBee's Account of the Expedition of the Nineteenth Kansas. *Collections of the Kansas State Historical Society* 17 (1926–28): 361–74.

Conover, George W. 1927. *Sixty Years in Southwest Oklahoma.* Anadarko, Okla.: N. T. Plummer, Printer.

Cowley, Jill. 1999. *Cultural Landscape Inventory, Level Two, Washita Battlefield National Historic Site.* Santa Fe: National Park Service, Intermountain Region.

Craig, Reginald S. 1965. Custer on the Washita. *Brand Book of the Denver Westerners* 20 (1964): 183–200.

Craig, Stephen C. 1998. Medicine for the Military: Dr. George M. Sternberg on the Kansas Plains, 1866–1870. *Kansas History* 21 (3): 188–206.

Crawford, Samuel J. [colonel, Nineteenth Kansas Cavalry]. 1911. *Kansas in the Sixties.* Chicago: A. G. McClurg.

Creel, Heber M. n.d. Field Notes. Notebook D (Marriages), File 8, Lt. Heber M. Creel Papers, Gilcrease Museum Library, Tulsa, Okla.

Criqui, Orvel A. 1985. A Northern Cheyenne Called Roman Nose. *Kansas History* 8 (3): 176–85.

———. 1986. *Fifty Fearless Men: The Forsyth Scouts and Beecher Island.* Marceline, Miss.: Walsworth.

Curtis, Edward S. 1923. *The Southern Cheyenne.* Vol. 19 of *The North American Indian.* Cambridge: The University Press.

Custer, Brice C. 1999. *The Sacrificial Lion: George Armstrong Custer.* El Segundo, Calif.: Upton and Sons.

Custer, Elizabeth B. 1966. *Following the Guidon.* Norman: University of Oklahoma Press.

———. 1967. *Tenting on the Plains.* Norman: University of Oklahoma Press.

———. Various. Collection. Little Bighorn Battlefield National Monument Library, Crow Agency, Mont., microfilm.

Custer, George Armstrong [lieutenant colonel, Seventh Cavalry]. 1868a. Letter
    to K. C. Barker, November 8. Merrington Papers, New York Public Library.
———. 1868b. Report to P. H. Sheridan, November 28. In U.S. Senate, *Indian
    Battle on the Washita River,* 40th Cong., 3rd sess., S. Exec. Doc. 18.
———. 1868c. Report to P. H. Sheridan, December 22. In U.S. Senate, *Indian
    Affairs in the Military Division of the Missouri,* 40th Cong., 3rd sess., S. Exec.
    Doc. 40.
———. 1869a. Report to P. H. Sheridan, March 21. Sheridan Papers, Library of
    Congress, Washington, D.C.
———. 1869b. Letter to K. C. Barker, May 26. Detroit Scientific Papers, Bur-
    ton Historical Collection, Detroit Public Library.
———. 1869c. Letter to Mrs. Philip Hamilton, August 29. In Memoriam:
    Louis McLane Hamilton, Captain 7th U.S. Cavalry. *Chronicles of Oklahoma*
    46 (4): 362–74.
———. 1873. The Battle of Washita. *Army and Navy Journal* (June 21): 719–20.
———. 1874. *My Life on the Plains, or, Personal Experiences with Indians.* New
    York: Sheldon.
———. 1966. *My Life on the Plains.* Edited with introduction by Milo Milton
    Quaife. Lincoln: University of Nebraska Press.
Davis, Theodore R. 1867. The Indian War. *Harper's Weekly,* May 11.
———. 1868. A Summer on the Plains. *Harper's New Monthly Magazine* 36
    (February): 292–307.
De Smet, Rev. P. J. 1881. *Western Missions and Missionaries: A Series of Letters.*
    New York: Excelsior Catholic Publishing.
DeBarth, Joseph. 1958. *Life and Adventures of Frank Grouard.* Norman: Univer-
    sity of Oklahoma Press.
Despain, S. Matthew. 1999. Captain Albert Barnitz and the Battle of the
    Washita: New Documents, New Insights. *Journal of the Indian Wars* 1 (2):
    135–44.
Dixon, David. 1980. Edmund Guerrier: A Scout with Custer. *Research Review*
    14 (12): 3–8.
———. 1981. A Scout with Custer: Edmund Guerrier on the Hancock Expedi-
    tion of 1867. *Kansas History* 4 (3): 155–65.
———. 1987. Custer and the Sweetwater Hostages. In *Custer and His Times,
    Book Three.* Conway: University of Central Arkansas Press.
Dixon, James W. 1886. Across the Plains with General Hancock. *Journal of the
    Military Service Institute* (June): 195–98.
Dunn, Dorothy. 1969. *1877 Plains Indian Sketch Books of Zo-Tom and Howling
    Wolf.* Flagstaff, Ariz.: Northland.
Dyer, Mrs. D. B. 1896. *Fort Reno.* New York: G. W. Dillingham.

Ediger, Theodore A. 1940. Chief Kias. *Chronicles of Oklahoma* 18 (3): 293–301.

Ediger, Theodore A., and Vinnie Hoffman [Cheyenne]. 1955. Some Reminiscences of the Battle of the Washita. *Chronicles of Oklahoma* 33 (2): 137–41.

Elliott, Joel H. [major, Seventh Cavalry]. 1868. Letter to Theodore R. Davis, October 31. *Chronicles of Oklahoma* 5 (10): 57–58.

Enfield, W. H. 1868. Details of Gen. Sheridan's Recent Movements. *New York Times*, December 27.

Epple, Jess C. 1968. *Black Kettle Museum, Cheyenne, Oklahoma.* Muskogee, Okla.: Hoffman Printing.

———. 1970. *Custer's Battle of the Washita and a History of the Plains Indian Tribes.* New York: Exposition.

Finney, Frank F. 1955. Reminiscences of a Trader in the Osage Country. *Chronicles of Oklahoma* 33 (2): 145–58.

Foley, James R. 1996. Walter Camp and Ben Clark. *Research Review: The Journal of the Little Big Horn Associates* 10 (January): 17–27.

Forrest, Earle R., and Joe E. Milner. 1935. *California Joe, Noted Scout and Indian Fighter.* Caldwell, Idaho: Caxton Printers.

Fougera, Katherine Gibson. 1940. *With Custer's Cavalry.* Caldwell, Idaho: Caxton Printers.

Franks, Kenny A. 1974. The Plains Tribes with Frederic Remington. *Chronicles of Oklahoma* 52 (4): 419–38.

Frost, Lawrence A. 1968. *The Court-Martial of General George Armstrong Custer.* Norman: University of Oklahoma Press.

Gage, Duane 1967. Black Kettle: A Noble Savage? *Chronicles of Oklahoma* 45 (3): 244–51.

Galvin, Kevin E. 2003. *"Such Signal Success"? Confrontation along the Washita: A Collection of Essays.* The British Custeriana Series, vol. 3. London: Westerners Publications Limited.

Garfield, Marvin H. 1931. The Military Post as a Factor in the Frontier Defense of Kansas, 1865–1869. *Kansas Historical Quarterly* 1 (1): 50–62.

———. 1932a. Defense of the Kansas Frontier, 1864–1865. *Kansas Historical Quarterly* 1 (2): 140–52.

———. 1932b. Defense of the Kansas Frontier, 1866–1867. *Kansas Historical Quarterly* 1 (4): 326–44.

———. 1932c. Defense of the Kansas Frontier, 1868–1869. *Kansas Historical Quarterly* 1 (5): 451–73.

Garland, Hamlin 1900. Notes on the Southern Cheyennes. Hamlin Garland Collection, Doheny Memorial Library, University of Southern California, Los Angeles.

———. 1957. *A Daughter of the Middle Border.* New York: Sagamore.

Gibson, Francis M. [2nd lieutenant, Seventh Cavalry]. Our Washita Battle. 1907. Gibson-Fougera Collection, Little Bighorn Battlefield National Monument Library, Crow Agency, Mont., manuscript.

Godfrey, Edward S. [1st lieutenant, Seventh Cavalry]. 1868. Letter to Jennie Barnitz, December 5. Albert Barnitz Papers, Beinicke Library, Yale University, New Haven, Conn.

———. 1896. Cavalry Fire Discipline. *Journal of the Military Service Institution* 19 (83): 252–59.

———. 1913. Letter to J. B. Thoburn, August 31. Joseph B. Thoburn Collection, Archives Division, Oklahoma Historical Society, Oklahoma City.

———. 1917. Interview by Walter Camp, March 3. Box 3, Walter Mason Camp Collection, Harold B. Lee Library, Brigham Young University, Provo, Utah.

———. 1918. Letter to Elizabeth B. Custer, December 15. Reel 3, Elizabeth B. Custer Collection, Little Bighorn Battlefield National Monument Library, Crow Agency, Mont., microfilm.

———. 1926. Critique on Homer W. Wheeler, *Buffalo Days.* Reel 9, Elizabeth B. Custer Collection, Little Bighorn Battlefield National Monument Library, Crow Agency, Mont., microfilm.

———. 1927. Some Reminiscences, Including an Account of General Sully's Expedition against the Southern Plains Indians, 1868. *The Cavalry Journal* 36 (148): 417–25.

———. 1928. Some Reminiscences, Including the Washita Battle. *The Cavalry Journal* 37 (153): 481–500.

———. 1929. Medicine Lodge Treaty Sixty Years Ago. *Winners of the West* (March 30): 8.

Graham, William A. 1926. *The Story of the Little Big Horn.* New York: Century.

———. 1953. *The Custer Myth.* New York: Bonanza Books.

Graves, W. W. 1986. *History of Neosho County.* Reprint, 2 vols. in 1. St. Paul, Kans.: Osage Mission Historical Society.

Greene, Candace S. 1992. Artists in Blue: The Indian Scouts of Fort Reno and Fort Supply. *American Indian Art Magazine* 18 (1): 50–57.

Greene, Jerome A. 2004. Washita: The U.S. Army and the Southern Cheyennes, 1867–1869. Norman: University of Oklahoma Press.

Grierson, Benjamin H. 1869. Letter to Father Kirk, April 6. Edward E. Ayer Collection, Grierson Papers, Newberry Library, Chicago, Ill.

Griffis, Joseph K. [Tahan] 1915. *Tahan, Out of Savagery into Civilization: An Autobiography.* New York: George H. Doran.

———. 1930. The Battle of the Washita. *Chronicles of Oklahoma* 3 (3): 272–81.

Grinnell, George B. 1900. *The Indians of To-day.* Chicago: Herbert S. Stone.

———. 1913. *Beyond the Old Frontier.* New York: Charles Scribner's Sons.

———. 1916. Letter to W. M. Camp, October 3. Folder 2, Box 2, Walter Camp Collection, Harold B. Lee Library, Brigham Young University, Provo, Utah.

———. 1928. *Two Great Scouts and Their Pawnee Battalion.* Cleveland. Arthur H. Clark.

———. 1956. *The Fighting Cheyennes.* Norman: University of Oklahoma Press.

———. 1971. *By Cheyenne Campfires.* Lincoln: University of Nebraska Press.

———. 1972. *The Cheyenne Indians.* 2 vols. Lincoln: University of Nebraska Press.

———. n.d. Names of Noted Cheyennes and the Approximate Dates of Birth and Death. Folder 119, George B. Grinnell Collection, Braun Research Library, Southwest Museum, Los Angeles.

Guerrier, Edmund. 1869. Affidavit in Reference to the Hostility of the Cheyennes, February 9. In U.S. House, *Difficulties with Indian Tribes.* 41st Cong., 2nd sess., H. Exec. Doc. 240.

Hackbusch, H. C. F. 1873. Report of the U.S. Survey of Western Indian Territory. GLO Plat Book, Roger Mills County Courthouse, Cheyenne, Okla.

Hadley, James A. [1st sergeant, Nineteenth Kansas Cavalry]. 1908. The Nineteenth Kansas Cavalry and the Conquest of the Plains Indians. *Transactions of the Kansas State Historical Society* 10 (1907–1908): 428–56.

Hafen, LeRoy R. 1931. *The Life of Thomas Fitzpatrick.* Denver: Old West Publishing.

Haines, Joe D., Jr. 1999. For Our Sake Do All You Can. *Chronicles of Oklahoma* 77 (2): 171–83.

Halaas, David Fridtjof 1995. All the Camp Was Weeping. *Colorado Heritage* (Summer): 2–17.

Halaas, David F., and Andrew E. Masich. 1998. George Bent: Caught between Two Worlds. *Colorado History Now* (July): 3.

———. 2004. Halfbreed: The Remarkable True Story of George Bent— Caught between the Worlds of the Indian and the White Man. Cambridge, Mass.: Da Capo.

Hammer, Kenneth. 1995. *Men with Custer: Biographies of the 7th Cavalry.* Hardin, Mont.: Custer Battlefield Historical and Museum Association.

Hammond, Al. 1975. Battle of the Washita Aftermath. *(Los Angeles Westerners Corral) Branding Iron* (March): 14–16.

Hardorff, Richard G. 1990. Some Recollections of Custer and His Last Battle. *(Little Big Horn Associates) Research Review* 4 (2): 15–21, 30–31.

———. 1993. *Hokahey! A Good Day to Die. The Indian Casualties of the Custer Fight.* Spokane: Arthur H. Clark.

Harrison, Emily Haines. 1908. Reminiscences of Early Days in Ottawa County. *Collections of the Kansas State Historical Society* 10 (1907–1908): 622–31.

Harrison, Peter. 1998. *The Eyes of the Sleepers: Cheyenne Accounts of the Washita Attack.* Reprint, The (English Westerners) Brand Book.

———. 2000–2003. Correspondence with the author. In author's files.

Hart, Lawrence H. [Cheyenne]. 1999. Legacies of the Massacre and Battle at the Washita. *Oklahoma Today* (May—June): 59–63.

Hatch, Thom. 2004. *Black Kettle: The Cheyenne Chief Who Sought Peace but Found War.* Hoboken, N.J.: Wiley and Sons.

Haywood, Robert C. 1998. *The Merchant Prince of Dodge City: The Life and Times of Robert M. Wright.* Norman: University of Oklahoma Press.

Hazen, W. B. 1868. Record of a Conversation Held between Colonel and Brevet Major General W. B. Hazen, U. S. Army, on Special Service, and Chiefs of the Cheyenne and Arapaho Tribes of Indians, at Fort Cobb, I.T., November 20. In U.S. Senate, *Indian Battle on the Washita River,* 40th Cong., 3rd sess., S. Exec. Doc. 18.

———. 1869a. Letter to James A. Garfield, January 18. *New York Times,* February 21.

———. 1869b. Report to Gen. W. T. Sherman, June 30. In *Report of the Secretary of the Interior.* 41st Cong., 2nd sess., Exec. Doc.

———. 1925. Some Corrections of "Life on the Plains." *Chronicles of Oklahoma* 3 (4): 295–318.

Heitman, Francis B. 1903. *Historical Register and Dictionary of the United States Army, 1789–1903.* 2 vols. Washington, D.C.: GPO.

Heap of Birds, Alfrich [Cheyenne]. 1999. Interview by Mary Jane Warde, July 23. Cheyenne/Washita Oral History Project, Oklahoma Historical Society, Oklahoma City.

Heap of Birds, Homer [Cheyenne]. 1930. Interview by Alvin Rucker. *Daily Oklahoman,* July 27.

Heap of Crows [Cheyenne]. 1967. General George Armstrong Custer. *Prairie Lore* 3 (4): 244–46.

Hensley, Claude E. 1940. Letter to Mr. Neifert, August 18. Section 10, Cheyenne and Arapaho Indians, History, Archives Division, Oklahoma Historical Society, Oklahoma City.

Hodge, Frederick W., ed. 1907. *Handbook of American Indians North of Mexico.* 2 vols. Bureau of American Ethnology Bulletin 30. Washington, D.C.: GPO.

Hoig, Stan. 1961. *The Peace Chiefs of the Cheyenne.* Norman: University of Oklahoma Press.

———. 1974. *The Western Odyssey of John Simpson Smith.* Glendale, Calif.: Arthur H. Clark.

———. 1979. *The Battle of the Washita.* Lincoln: University of Nebraska Press.

———. 1992. *People of the Sacred Arrows: The Southern Cheyenne Today.* New York: Cobblehill Books.

————. 1993. *Tribal Wars of the Southern Plains.* Norman: University of Oklahoma Press.

Holloway, W. L. 1891. *Wild Life on the Plains and Horrors of Indian Warfare.* St. Louis: Continental Publishing.

Hornbeck, Lewis N. 1908. The Battle of the Washita. *Sturm's Oklahoma Magazine* 5 (5): 30–34.

Hunt, Fred A. 1979. The Subjugation of Black Kettle. Reprinted in *A Seventh Cavalry Scrapbook* 5. Edited by John M. Carroll. Bryan, Tex.: privately printed.

Hunt, George [Kiowa]. n.d. Eone-ah-pah: The Only Kiowa Indian Who Participated in the Battle of the Washita. Folder 1, Box 38, William Garey Brown Collection, Norlin Library, University of Colorado, Boulder, manuscript.

Hutton, Paul Andrew. 1985. *Phil Sheridan and His Army.* Lincoln: University of Nebraska Press.

Hyde, George E. 1968. *Life of George Bent.* Edited by Savoie Lottinville. Norman: University of Oklahoma Press.

Inman, Henry. 1898a. *The Old Santa Fe Trail.* New York: Macmillan.

————. 1898b. *Tales of the Trail.* Topeka: Crane.

Jaastad, Ben. 1956. *Man of the West: Reminiscences of George Washington Oaks, 1840–1917.* Edited by Arthur Woodward. Tucson: Arizona Pioneer Historical Society.

Jacob, Richard T. 1924. Military Reminiscences of Captain Richard T. Jacob. *Chronicles of Oklahoma* 2 (1): 8–36.

Jakes, John. 1987. *Heaven and Hell.* New York: Harcourt Brace Jovanovich.

James, Louise Boyd. 1982. Mysterious Death at the Washita. *True West* (June): 20–23.

Jenness, George B. [captain, Nineteenth Kansas Cavalry]. 1869. History of the 19th Kansas Cavalry, Indian War of 1868–69. Kansas State Historical Society, Topeka, manuscript.

————. 1907. Lost in the Snow at Old Camp Supply. *Sturm's Oklahoma Magazine* 5 (4): 52–57.

Justus, Judith P. 2000. The Saga of Clara H. Blinn at the Battle of the Washita. *Research Review* 14 (1): 11–20.

Kan, Michael, and William Wierzbowski. 1979. Notes on an Important Southern Cheyenne Shield. *Bulletin of the Detroit Institute of Arts* 57 (3): 124–33.

Kansas Daily Tribune. 1868. A Page of Indian Cruelty. December 30.

————. 1869a. Particulars of the Saline Massacre. June 22.

————. 1869b. Scalped at the Washita. June 25.

Katz, D. Mark. 1985. *Custer in Photographs.* New York: Bonanza Books.

Keim, DeB. Randolph. 1868. The Indian War. *New York Herald,* December 8, 24, 26.

———. 1869. The Indian War. *New York Herald,* January 4.

———. 1885. *Sheridan's Troopers on the Border.* Philadelphia: David McKay.

King, Charles. [1925]. Introduction to *The Story of the Little Big Horn,* by W. A. Graham.

King, James T. 1963. *War Eagle: A Life of General Eugene A. Carr.* Lincoln: University of Nebraska Press.

Kinsley, D. A. 1968. *Favor the Bold: Custer the Indian Fighter.* New York: Promontory.

Knight, Oliver. 1960. *Following the Indian Wars.* Norman: University of Oklahoma Press.

Kraft, Louis. 1995. *Custer and the Cheyenne.* El Segundo, Calif.: Upton and Sons.

Kurtz, Henry I. 1968. Custer and the Indian Massacre, 1868. *History Today* (November): 769–78.

Langley, H. [private, Seventh Cavalry]. 1925. Another Survivor of the Black Kettle Fight [letter to the editor]. *Winners of the West* (December 15): 7.

Lavender, David. 1972. *Bent's Fort.* Lincoln: University of Nebraska Press.

Leckie, William H. 1963. *The Military Conquest of the Southern Plains.* Norman: University of Oklahoma Press.

Leckie, William H., and Shirley A. Leckie. 1984. *Unlikely Warriors: General Benjamin H. Grierson and His Family.* Norman: University of Oklahoma Press.

Lecompte, Janet. 1957. Charles Autebees. *Colorado Magazine* 34 (3): 163–79.

———. 1968. John Poisal. In *The Mountain Men and the Fur Trade of the Far West,* ed. LeRoy R. Hafen, 353–58. Glendale, Calif.: Arthur H. Clark.

Lees, William B. 1996. Synopsis of Archeological Findings, Washita Battlefield National Historic Landmark. Oklahoma Historical Society, Oklahoma City, research paper.

———. 1999. Archaeological Evidence: The Attack on Black Kettle's Village on the Washita River. *Journal of the Indian Wars* 1 (1): 33–41.

Lees, William B., Douglas D. Scott, and C. Vance Haynes. 2001. History Underfoot: The Search for Physical Evidence of the 1868 Attack on Black Kettle's Village. *Chronicles of Oklahoma* 79 (2): 158–81.

Llewellyn, Karl N., and E. Adamson Hoebel. 1941. *The Cheyenne Way.* Norman: University of Oklahoma Press.

Liddic, Bruce. 1999–2004. Correspondence with the author. In author's files.

Liddic, Bruce R., and Paul H. Harbaugh. 1995. *Camp on Custer.* Spokane: Arthur H. Clark.

Lippincott, Henry. 1868a. Special Report of Recovery and Condition of the Body of an Officer [Joel H. Elliott] Killed at the Battle of the Washita,

Indian Territory, on the 27th Day of November, 1868. File F, Record Group 94, Records of the Adjutant General's Office, National Archives, Washington, D.C. In *The Battle of the Washita,* by Stan Hoig.

————. 1868b. Special Report of Recovery and Condition of Bodies of Enlisted Men Killed at the Battle of the Washita, Indian Territory, on the 27th Day of November, 1868. File F, Record Group 94, Records of the Adjutant General's Office, National Archives, Washington, D.C. In *The Battle of the Washita,* by Stan Hoig.

Little Beaver [Cheyenne]. 1933. Interview by Howard F. Van Zandt. *Chronicles of Oklahoma* 62 (1): 67–69.

Litton, Gaston. 1957. *History of Oklahoma.* Vol. 1. New York: Lewis Historical Publishing.

Lockard, Frank M. 1924. *Black Kettle.* Goodland, Kans.: R. G. Wolfe.

————. 1927. A Version of a Famous Battle. *Chronicles of Oklahoma* 5 (3): 297–310.

Lone Bear, Mary Belle Curtis [Cheyenne]. 1999. Interview by Mary Jane Warde and Jim Anquoe, July 30. Cheyenne/ Washita Oral History Project, Oklahoma Historical Society, Oklahoma City.

Lone Wolf, Mrs. [Cheyenne]. 1905. Interview by J. L. Puckett. In *History of Oklahoma and Indian Territory,* by J. L. and Ellen Puckett.

Lynch, Dennis [private, Seventh Cavalry]. 1909. Interview by Walter Camp, February 8. Box 2, Interview Notes, Walter Camp Collection, Harold B. Lee Library, Brigham Young University, Provo, Utah.

Magpie [Cheyenne]. 1930. Interview by Charles J. Brill et al., September 17. *Daily Oklahoman,* November 23.

Males, Mrs. L. L. 1967. General Custer Forgets to Mention Scout Following Battle of the Washita. *Elk City (Okla.) Daily News,* November 5. Clipping in Betty Wesner Battle of the Washita Scrapbooks. Copies in author's files.

————. 1968. Custer's Battle of Washita against Black Kettle Traced. Unidentified Woodward (Okla.) newspaper, November 13. Clipping in Betty Wesner Battle of the Washita Scrapbooks. Copies in author's files.

Mann, Henrietta [Cheyenne]. 1997. *Cheyenne–Arapaho Education, 1871–1982.* Niwot: University Press of Colorado.

Marcot, Roy M. 1983. *Spencer Repeating Firearms.* Irvine, Calif.: Northwood Heritage Press.

Marquis, Thomas B. 1967. *Custer on the Little Bighorn.* Lodi, Calif.: Marquis Custer Publishers.

Masters, Joseph G. 1935a. Interview by Sarah Brooks, July 27. Folder 19 (The Southwest, 1935), Box 2, Joseph Gailio Masters Collection, Kansas State Historical Society, Topeka.

———. 1935b. Interview by Judson Cunningham, July 29. Folder 19 (The Southwest, 1935), Box 2, Joseph Gailio Masters Collection, Kansas State Historical Society, Topeka.

Mathews, Joseph. 1961. *The Osages*. Norman: University of Oklahoma Press.

Mathey, Edward G. [2nd lieutenant, Seventh Cavalry]. n.d. The Washita Campaign and Battle of the Washita. Special Collections and Manuscripts, Harold B. Lee Library, Brigham Young University, Provo, Utah.

Maurer, Evan M. 1977a. Indians at the Art Institute. *The (Chicago) Westerners Brand Book* 34 (5): 33–34.

———. 1977b. *The Native American Heritage*. Lincoln: University of Nebraska Press.

Mayhall, Mildred P. 1962. *The Kiowas*. Norman: University of Oklahoma Press.

McChristian, Douglas C. 2000. Plainsman—or Showman? George A. Custer's Buckskins. *Military Collector and Historian* 52 (1): 2–13.

McCusker, Philip. 1868. Report to Thomas Murphy, December 3. In U.S. Senate, *Indian Battle on the Washita River*, 40th Cong., 3rd sess., S. Exec. Doc. 18.

McGillycuddy, Julia B. 1941. *McGillycuddy, Agent*. Stanford, Calif.: Stanford University Press.

McKay, R. H. 1918. *Little Pills: An Army Story*. Pittsburgh, Kans.: Pittsburgh Headlight.

McLaughlin, Louis A. n.d. Letter to *Kansas City Star* [clipping bearing the heading "From an Old Indian Scout"]. Folder 12, Box 1034.69, Harrington Family Files, Richard F. Blinn Collection, Western History Collections, University of Oklahoma, Norman.

McMechen, Edgar Carlisle. 1924. *Life of Governor Evans, Second Territorial Governor of Colorado*. Denver: Wahlgreen Publishing.

Mead, James R. 1986. *Hunting and Trading on the Great Plains, 1859–1875*. Norman: University of Oklahoma Press.

Meredith, Grace A. 1927. *Girl Captives of the Cheyennes*. Los Angeles: Gem.

Merrington, Marguerite. 1950. *The Custer Story*. New York: Devin-Adair.

Methvin, Rev. J. J. 1899. *Andele, or The Mexican-Kiowa Captive, a Story of Real Life among the Indians*. Anadarko, Okla.: Plummer Printing.

———. n.d. *In the Limelight, or, History of Anadarko (Caddo County) and Vicinity from the Earliest Days*. Oklahoma City: privately printed.

Michelson, Truman. 1932. The Narrative of a Southern Cheyenne Woman. *Smithsonian Miscellaneous Collections* 87 (5): 1–13.

Miles, Nelson A. 1897. *Personal Recollections and Observations*. Chicago: Werner.

Mills, Charles K. 1985. *Harvest of Barren Regrets: The Army Career of Frederick William Benteen, 1834–1898*. Glendale, Calif.: Arthur H. Clark.

Monnett, John H. 1992. *The Battle of Beecher Island and the Indian War of 1867–1869*. Niwot: University Press of Colorado.

Mooney, James. 1907a. *The Cheyenne Indians*. Memoir 1. Washington, D.C.: American Anthropological Society.

———. 1907b. A Cheyenne Tree Burial. *The Southern Workman* 36: 95–97.

Moore, Alvin. 1968. Letter to Bernard S. Heeney, October 20. Unidentified Woodward (Okla.) newspaper, November 13. Clipping in Betty Wesner Battle of the Washita Scrapbooks. Copies in author's files.

Moore, Horace L. [colonel, Nineteenth Kansas Cavalry]. 1900. The Nineteenth Kansas Cavalry. *Collections of the Kansas State Historical Society* 6 (1897–1900): 34–52.

Moore, John H. 1984. Cheyenne Names and Cosmology. *American Ethnologist* 11 (2): 291–311.

———. 1987. *The Cheyenne Nation*. Lincoln: University of Nebraska Press.

———. 1996. *The Cheyenne*. Cambridge, Mass.: Blackwell.

Morris, John W., Charles R. Goins, and Edwin C. McReynolds. 1976. *Historical Atlas of Oklahoma*. Norman: University of Oklahoma Press.

Morrison, James S. 1868. Letter to E. W. Wynkoop, December 14. In U.S. House, *Difficulties with Indian Tribes*. 41st Cong., 2nd sess., H. Exec. Doc. 240.

Morrison, William Brown. 1936. *Military Posts and Camps in Oklahoma*. Oklahoma City: Harlow Publishing.

Moving Behind Woman [Cheyenne]. ca. 1937. Interview by Theodore A. Ediger and Vinnie Hoffman. *Chronicles of Oklahoma* 33 (2): 137–41.

Munhall, C. S. 1924. The Seventh U.S. Cavalry at the Battle of the Washita. *Nebraska History* 7 (4): 123–24.

Murphy, John. 1923. Reminiscences of the Washita Campaign and of the Darlington Indian Agency. *Chronicles of Oklahoma* 1 (1): 259–78.

Murphy, Thomas. 1868. Letter to N. G. Taylor, December 4. In U.S. House, *Difficulties with Indian Tribes*. 41st Cong., 2nd sess., H. Exec. Doc. 240.

National Park Service. 2000. *Washita Battlefield National Historic Site Trail Guide*. N.p.: Southwest Parks and Monuments Association.

———. 2001. *Washita Symposium: Past, Present, and Future*. N.p.: privately printed.

Nesbitt, Paul 1925. Battle of the Washita. *Chronicles of Oklahoma* 3 (1): 2 32.

New York Daily Tribune. 1868. Gen. Custar's [*sic*] Battle. December 29.

Nicholson, William. 1934. A Tour of Indian Agencies in Kansas and the Indian Territory in 1870. *Kansas Historical Quarterly* 3 (3): 289–326; (4): 343–84.

North, Luther. 1961. *Man of the Plains*. Lincoln: University of Nebraska Press.

Noyes, C. Lee. 1999. A Tale of Two Battles: George Armstrong Custer and the Attacks at the Washita and the Little Bighorn. *Journal of the Indian Wars* 1 (1): 5–31.

Nye, W. S. 1962. *Bad Medicine and Good.* Norman: University of Oklahoma Press.

———. 1969. *Carbine and Lance: The Story of Old Fort Sill.* Norman: University of Oklahoma Press.

O'Leary, John. 1973. Black Kettle: A Brief Profile. *American Indian Crafts and Culture* 7: 8–11.

Page, Elizabeth M. 1915. *In Camp and Tepee.* New York: Reformed Church in America.

Page, John H. ca. 1895. Reminiscences of Indian Wars in Kansas and Indian Territory, 1866 and 1871. Manuscript in two installments, Collections, Old Guard Museum, Fort Myer, Va.

Painter, C. C. 1893. *Cheyennes and Arapahoes Revisited.* Philadelphia: Indian Rights Association.

Paxson, Frederic Logan. 1915. *The Last American Frontier.* New York: Macmillan.

Pearson, Henry [private, Nineteenth Kansas Cavalry]. 1926. Campaign against Indians in Oklahoma, Kansas, Colorado and New Mexico, [and] Indian Territory, '68–69. *Winners of the West* (December 30): 5.

Peck, Robert Morris. 1904. Recollections of Early Times in Kansas Territory. *Transactions of the Kansas State Historical Society* (1903–1904): 484–507.

Peery, Dan W. 1935. The Kiowa's Defiance. *Chronicles of Oklahoma* 13 (1): 30–36.

Penney, David W. 1999. Letter to author, July 22. In author's files.

Perez, Martha Koomsa [Kiowa]. 1999. Interview by Mary Jane Warde. Cheyenne/Washita Oral History Project, Oklahoma Historical Society, Oklahoma City.

Petersen, Karen Daniels. 1968. *Howling Wolf: A Cheyenne Warrior's Graphic Interpretation of His People.* Palo Alto, Calif.: American West Publishing.

———. 1971. *Plains Indian Art from Fort Marion.* Norman: University of Oklahoma Press.

Petter, Rodolphe. [1936]. *Some Reminiscences of Past Years in My Mission Service among the Cheyenne.* N.p.: privately printed.

Pickens, J. C. [private, Seventh Cavalry]. 1920. Letter to Jas. H. Wooley, April 13. Folder 8, Box 2, Walter Camp Collection, Harold B. Lee Library, Brigham Young University, Provo, Utah.

———. 1921. Letter to Elizabeth B. Custer, January 29. Reel 3, Elizabeth B. Custer Collection, Little Bighorn Battlefield National Monument Library, Crow Agency, Mont., microfilm.

Porter, Millie Jones. 1945. *Memory Cups of Panhandle Pioneers.* Clarendon, Tex.: Clarendon Press.

Powell, Peter J. 1969. *Sacred Medicine: The Continuing Role of the Sacred Arrows, the Sun Dance, and the Sacred Buffalo Hat in Northern Cheyenne History.* Norman. University of Oklahoma Press.

———. 1981. *People of the Sacred Mountain: A History of Northern Cheyenne Chiefs and Warrior Societies, 1830–1879.* 2 vols. New York: Harper and Row.

Pratt, Richard Henry. 1905. Some Indian Experiences. *Cavalry Journal* 16 (July): 200–217.

———. 1964. *Battlefield and Classroom.* Ed. with introduction by Robert M. Utley. New Haven, Conn.: Yale University Press.

Prosser, Arthur. 1979. Custer at Washita, 1868. *War Monthly* (December): 24–29.

Puckett, J. L., and Ellen Puckett. 1906. *History of Oklahoma and Indian Territory and Homeseekekers' [sic] Guide.* Vinita, Okla.: Chieftain Publishing.

Purcell, Joe [Cheyenne]. 1937. Interview, August 16. Indian-Pioneer History Collection, vol. 41, Grant Foreman Papers, Oklahoma Historical Society, Oklahoma City.

Rallya, A. C. [private, Seventh Cavalry]. 1927. General Sully's Campaign; or, Fighting Indians from an Ambulance. *Winners of the West* (May 30): 5.

Rath, Ida Ellen. 1961. *The Rath Trail.* Wichita: McCormick-Armstrong.

Rea, Bob. 1996a. Battle of the Washita: An Estimate of the Combat Strength, Seventh Cavalry Regiment, November 27, 1868. Unpublished report. Copy in author's files.

———. 1996b. Battle of the Washita: An Estimate of the Number of Persons [in] Black Kettle's Village, November 27, 1868. Unpublished report. Copy in author's files.

———. 1998. The Washita Trail: The Seventh U.S. Cavalry's Route of March to and from the Battle of the Washita. *Chronicles of Oklahoma* 76 (3): 245–61.

———. 2002–2003. Letters to the author. In author's files.

Record of Engagements with Hostile Indians within the Military Division of the Missouri from 1868 to 1882. 1882. Washington, D.C.: GPO.

Reed, Joseph M. 2000. Washita Connection: The Shell Jacket of Louis McLane Hamilton in the State Museum of History. *Chronicles of Oklahoma* 78 (2): 234–39.

Red Bird Black [Cheyenne]. n.d. Statement. In *Death on the Prairie,* by Paul I. Wellman.

Riggs, Stacy [Cheyenne]. 1934. Letter to George Parker. In *Cheyenne Star,* undated clipping, Indian Files, Washita Battle Collections, Washita Battlefield Historical Site, Cheyenne, Okla.

———. 1936. Interview by Thomas Benton Williams, November 18. In *The Soul of the Red Man,* by Thomas Benton Williams.

Rister, Carl Coke. 1940. *Border Captives: The Traffic in Prisoners by Southern Plains Indians, 1834–1875.* Norman: University of Oklahoma Press.

————. 1944. *Border Command.* Norman: University of Oklahoma Press.

Roberts, Gary L., and David Fridtjof Halaas. 2001. Written in Blood: The Soule-Cramer Sand Creek Massacre Letters. *Colorado Heritage* (Winter): 22–32.

Rock, Marion Tuttle. 1890. *Illustrated History of Oklahoma.* Topeka: C. B. Hamilton and Son.

Rodgers, Joseph Phelps [private, Nineteenth Kansas Cavalry]. n.d. A Few Years of Experiences on the Western Frontier. Miscellaneous Collections, Manuscript Division, Kansas State Historical Society, Topeka, manuscript.

Roenigk, Adolph. 1933. *Pioneer History of Kansas.* N.p.: privately printed.

Roman Nose Thunder [Cheyenne]. 1913. Interview by Walter Campbell. In *Warpath and Council Fire,* by Stanley Vestal.

Rosenblatt, Jean. 1992. "Ledger Art" Reveals Life and Rituals of American Indians. *Chronicle of Higher Education* (April 29): B5.

Ross, Danita. 1988. The Indian Captivity of Clara Blinn. *American West* 25 (June): 45–47.

Rucker, Alvin. 1925. The Battle of the Washita—After Fifty Years. *Daily Oklahoman,* August 2.

————. 1930. A Playground on Indian Battlefield. *Daily Oklahoman,* July 27.

Runyon, A. L. [private, Nineteenth Kansas Cavalry]. 1940. A. L. Runyon's Letters from the Nineteenth Kansas Regiment. *Kansas Historical Quarterly* 9 (1): 59–75.

Rush, Frank. 1930. What Indian Tongues Could Tell: The Red Man's Story of the Conquest of the Western Plains. (Chapter 7: The Washita Massacre.) *Wilds and Waters* 2 (12): 11–13, 27, 34.

————. 1931. What Indian Tongues Could Tell: The Red Man's Story of the Conquest of the Western Plains. (Chapter 8: The Men Whom Custer Forgot.) *Wilds and Waters* 3 (1): 11–13.

Ryan, John [corporal, Seventh Cavalry]. 1908. The Battle of the Washita. *Cheyenne Star,* June 4. Clipping in the Betty Wesner Battle of the Washita Scrapbooks. Copies in author's files.

————. 1909. Ten Years with General Custer among the American Indians. *Newton (Mass.) Circuit,* April 2, 9.

Sanders, J. G. 1928. *Who's Who among Oklahoma Indians.* Oklahoma City: Trave.

Schwarck, Don. 1992. Campaigning in Kansas with Maida and Blucher, General Custer's Staghounds. *(Little Big Horn Associates) Research Review* 6 (2): 15–21.

————. 1994. Black Kettle's Ring. *(Little Big Horn Associates) Newsletter* 28 (10): 4–5.

Schukies, Renate. 1993. *Red Hat, Cheyenne Blue Sky Maker and Keeper of Sacred Arrows.* Hamburg, Germany: Hamburg University Press.

Scott, Douglas D. (National Park Service, Great Plains Region). 2002–2004. Letters to the author. In author's files.

Scott, Gary [Betty Wesner's son-in-law]. 2004a. Phone conversations with the author, January 22, 27, 31, February 21, March 15, 16.

———. 2004b. Topographical map showing artifact finds on Washita Battlefield. In authors files.

———. 2004c. Photos of collection of Washita artifacts, March 10. In author's files.

———. 2004d. Artifact locations and historic landmarks on and around the Washita Battlefield, March 10. DVD. In author's files.

———. 2004e. Sheridan's campsite in the Big Bend of the Washita and other historic landmarks near the battlefield, April 5. DVD. In author's files.

Scott, Hugh Lennox. 1910. Letter to Walter Camp, December 4. Folder 15, Box 1, Walter Camp Collection, Harold B. Lee Library, Brigham Young University, Provo, Utah.

———. 1914. Letter to the Editor [Ben Clark's obituary]. *New York Times*, July 31.

———. 1928. *Some Memories of a Soldier.* New York: Century.

———. 1931. Letter to E. S. Godfrey, July 2. Edward Settle Godfrey Collection, Library of Congress, Washington, D.C.

———. n.d. Interview Notes. Unclassified Envelope 8 (Hugh L. Scott), Walter Camp Manuscripts, Lilly Library, Indiana University, Bloomington.

Seger, John H. 1956. *Early Days among the Cheyenne and Arapaho Indians.* Norman: University of Oklahoma Press.

Seventh U.S. Cavalry. 1868. Regimental Muster Rolls, November. Robert M. Utley Collection, private accessions, microfilm.

Sherman, Caroline B. 1935. A Young Army Officer's Experiences in Indian Territory. *Chronicles of Oklahoma* 13 (2): 146–53.

Sheridan, P. H. 1868a. Report to W. A. Nichols, December 3. In U.S. Senate, *Indian Battle on the Washita River,* 40th Cong., 3rd sess., S. Exec. Doc. 18.

———. 1868b. Report to W. A. Nichols, December 19. In U.S. Senate, *Indian Battle on the Washita River,* 40th Cong., 3rd sess., S. Exec. Doc. 18.

———. 1869. Report to W. A. Nichols, January 1. In U.S. Senate, *Indian Battle on the Washita River,* 40th Cong., 3rd sess., S. Exec. Doc. 18.

———. 1888. *Personal Memoirs.* 2 vols. New York: Charles L. Webster.

Shirk, George H. 1958a. The Case of the Plagiarized Journal. *Chronicles of Oklahoma* 36 (4): 371–410.

———. 1958b. The Battle of the Washita: An Indian Agent's View. *Chronicles of Oklahoma* 36 (4): 474–75.

———. 1959. Campaigning with Sheridan: A Farrier's Diary. *Chronicles of Oklahoma* 37 (1): 68–105.

———. 1969. Military Duty on the Western Frontier. *Chronicles of Oklahoma* 47 (2): 118–25.

———. 1971. Journal of Private Johnson. *Chronicles of Oklahoma* 49 (4): 437–50.

Shoemaker, Arthur. 1992. Osage Scouts Helped George Armstrong Custer Track Down Cheyenne Raiders on the Washita. *Wild West* 5 (June): 10, 12, 71–72, 74.

Sipes, John L. [Cheyenne]. 1997. Young Warrior Red Bird Died Bravely at Washita. *Watonga Republican,* June 18.

———. Various. Letters to the author, dated July 30, 2002; March 13, April 10, 2003. In author's files.

Smith, William R. [private, Nineteenth Kansas Cavalry]. 1926. Camp Starvation. *Winners of the West* (March 30): 7.

Sneed, R. A. 1936. Reminiscences of an Indian Trader. *Chronicles of Oklahoma* 14 (2): 135–55.

Snow, Dr. Clyde. [1987]. History and Pathology of Human Remains from Cheyenne, Oklahoma. Copy of report in author's file.

Spotts, David L. [private, Nineteenth Kansas Cavalry]. 1925. Reminiscences of an Old 19th Kansas Cavalry Man. *Winners of the West* (September): 6.

———. 1933. Letter to Emmett Searcy, February 7. Box 5–21, Emmett Searcy Collection, Western History Collections, University of Oklahoma, Norman.

———. 1988. *Campaigning with Custer.* Lincoln: University of Nebraska Press.

Stands in Timber, John, and Margot Liberty. 1967. *Cheyenne Memories.* Lincoln: University of Nebraska Press.

Stanley, Henry Morton. 1867. Dispatches, *Daily Missouri Democrat,* October 19, 21, 23, 25, 28, 31, November 2.

Stewart, Edgar I. 1955. *Custer's Luck.* Norman: University of Oklahoma Press.

Stewart, Milton [major, Nineteenth Kansas Cavalry]. 1869. From the 19th Regiment [letters]. *Kansas City Weekly Union,* February 6, 27, March 13, April 10.

Stone, Larry. 1982. Moses Milner. *Research Review* 16 (6): 11–12.

Strate, David Kay. 1970. *Sentinel to the Cimarron: The Frontier Experience of Fort Dodge, Kansas.* Dodge City: Cultural Heritage and Arts Center.

Stratton, Joanna L. 1981. *Pioneer Women: Voices from the Kansas Frontier.* New York: Simon and Schuster.

Strong, William E. 1960. *Canadian River Hunt.* Intro. by Fred P. Schonwald. Norman: University of Oklahoma Press.

Sutton, Lawson A. 1929. Landmarks of Custer's Fight Disappearing. Undated clipping from *Sayre Record.* In author's files.

Swett, Morris. 1935. Sergeant I-See-O, Kiowa Indian Scout. *Chronicles of Oklahoma* 13 (3): 340–54.

Szabo, Joyce M. 1992. *Howling Wolf: An Autobiography of a Plains Warrior Artist.* Oberlin: Allen Memorial Art Museum.

————. 1994. *Howling Wolf and the History of Ledger Art*. Albuquerque: University of New Mexico Press.

Tappan, S. F. 1869. The Indian Question. *New York Tribune*, December 17.

Tatum, Lawrie. 1970. *Our Red Brothers and the Peace Policy of President Ulysses S. Grant*. Lincoln: University of Nebraska Press.

Taylor, Nat M. 1968. Custer Led Thanksgiving Day Charge. *Kansas City Times*, November 27.

Thetford, Francis. 1969a. Black Kettle's Line Revealed. *Daily Oklahoman*, January 12.

————. 1969b. Battle of the Washita Centennial, 1968. *Chronicles of Oklahoma* 46 (4): 358–61.

Thoburn, Joseph B., and Muriel H. Wright. 1929. *Oklahoma, a History of the State and Its People*. New York: Lewis Historical Publishing.

Thomas, Kevin. 1980. Ben Clark, the Scout Who Defied Custer. *The Oldtimers Wild West* (February): 22–29, 48–50.

Thrapp, Dan L. 1988. *Encyclopedia of Frontier Biography*. 3 vols. Glendale, Calif.: Arthur H. Clark.

Thrasher, Luther A. 1908. Diary. *Transactions of the State Historical Society* 10 (1907–1908): 660–64.

Tracy, Judy [landowner near Washita Battlefield]. 2001. E-mails to Bruce Liddic. Copies in author's files.

————. 2002–2004. Correspondence with the author. In author's files.

Trails the Enemy [Kiowa]. n.d. Interview by George Hunt. Folder 1, Box 38, William Carey Brown Collection, Norlin Library, University of Colorado at Boulder.

Trenholm, Virginia C. 1970. *The Arapahoes, Our People*. Norman: University of Oklahoma Press.

Turner, Alvin O. 1992. Journey to Sainthood: David Pendleton Oakerhater's Better Way. *Chronicles of Oklahoma* 70 (2): 116–43.

Turner, Don. 1968. *Custer's First Massacre: The Battle of the Washita*. Amarillo: Humbug Gulch.

Underhill, Lonnie E., and Daniel F. Littlefield Jr. 1976. *Hamlin Garland's Observations on the American Indian, 1895–1905*. Tucson: University of Arizona Press.

U.S. Army. 1868. Monthly Returns of the Seventh Regiment of Cavalry. Post Returns, Record Group 393, Records of Army Continental Commands, 1821–1920, National Archives, Washington, D.C., microfilm.

————. 1868–69. Fort Dodge, Kans., Weekly Reports of Post Hospital, and Register of Patients. Record Group 393, Records of Army Continental Commands, 1821–1920, National Archives, Washington D.C., microfilm.

Unrau, William E. 1964. Investigation or Probity?—Kiowa-Comanche Agency. *Chronicles of Oklahoma* 42 (3): 300–319.

Utley, Robert M. 1949. Major Elliott Again. *The (Chicago) Westerners Brand Book* 6 (4): 27.

———. 1977. *Life in Custer's Cavalry.* New Haven, Conn.: Yale University Press.

———. 2001. *Cavalier in Buckskin: George Armstrong Custer and the Western Military Frontier.* Rev. ed. Norman: University of Oklahoma Press.

Van De Water, Frederic F. 1934. *Glory-Hunter: A Life of General Custer.* Indianapolis: Bobbs-Merrill.

Van Zandt, Howard F. 1984. The Battle of the Washita Revisited: A Journey to a Historic Site in 1933. *Chronicles of Oklahoma* 62 (1): 56–69.

Vestal, Stanley. 1948. *Warpath and Council Fire: The Plains Indians' Struggle for Survival in War and in Diplomacy, 1851–1891.* New York: Random House.

Viola, Herman J. 1993. *Ben Nighthorse Campbell: An American Warrior.* New York: Orion Books.

Wagner, Karen. 1999. Letter to author, July 6. In author's files.

Warde, Mary Lane. 1999. Field Interviews of Cheyennes. Cheyenne/Washita Oral History Project, Oklahoma Historical Society, Oklahoma City.

———. 2000. Letter to author, March 15. In author's file.

Watson, Elmo Scott, and Don Russell. 1948a. The Battle of the Washita, or Custer's Massacre? *The (Chicago) Westerners Brand Book* 5 (9): 49–56.

———. 1948b. Sidelights on the Washita Fight. *The (Chicago) Westerners Brand Book* 5 (10): 57–60.

Wellman, Paul I. 1934. *Death on the Prairie: The Thirty Years' Struggle for the Western Plains.* New York: Macmillan.

Welty, Raymond L. 1927a. The Indian Policy of the Army, 1860–1870. *The Cavalry Journal* 36 (148): 367–81.

———. 1927b. The Daily Life of the Frontier Soldier. *The Cavalry Journal* 36 (149): 584–94.

Wesner, Betty J. [former owner of the Washita Battlefield]. Various. Battle of the Washita Scrapbooks. Copies in author's files.

———. 2001–2002. Various E-mails to Bruce Liddic. Copies in author's files.

———. 2002–2003. Correspondence with the author. In author's files.

Wesner, Brian [Betty Wesner's son]. 2004. Letter to the author, postmarked January 24. In author's files.

West, Robert M. [captain, Seventh Cavalry]. 1869. Captain L. M. Hamilton. *Army Navy Journal,* January 2. Reprinted in *Chronicles of Oklahoma* 46 (4): 374–79.

Westbrook, Henriette Johnson. 1933. The Chouteaus and Their Commercial Enterprises. *Chronicles of Oklahoma* 11 (2): 786–97 (part 1); 11 (3): 942–66 (part 2).

Wheeler, Homer W. 1923. *The Frontier Trail.* Los Angeles: Times-Mirror Press.

White, Lonnie J. 1967. Winter Campaigning with Sheridan and Custer: The Expedition of the Nineteenth Kansas Volunteer Cavalry. *Journal of the West* 6 (1): 68–98.

———. 1969. White Women Captives of the Southern Plains Indians, 1866–1875. *Journal of the West* 8 (3): 327–54.

Wilder, D. W. 1886. *The Annals of Kansas.* Topeka: Kansas Publishing House.

Williams, Thomas Benton. 1937. *The Soul of the Red Man.* N.p.: privately printed.

Wilson, Hill P. 1904. Black Kettle's Last Raid, 1868. *Collections of the Kansas State Historical Society* 8 (1903–1904): 1–8.

Wilson, Terry P. 1985. *The Underground Reservation: Osage Oil.* Lincoln: University of Nebraska Press.

Wolf Belly Woman. 1939. Interview by Theodore E. Ediger. *Chronicles of Oklahoma* 33 (2): 141.

Wright, Muriel H. 1958. A Cheyenne Peace Pipe Smoked and Betrayed by Custer. *Chronicles of Oklahoma* 36 (1): 89–92.

———. 1959. In Memory of Captain Louis McLane Hamilton. *Chronicles of Oklahoma* 37 (3): 355–59.

Wright, Robert M. 1906. Reminiscences of Dodge. *Collections of the Kansas State Historical Society* 9 (1905–1906): 66–72.

———. 1913. *Dodge City: The Cowboy Capital and the Great South West.* Wichita: Wichita Eagle Press.

Wynkoop, E. W. 1868a. Report of an Interview between Colonel E. W. Wynkoop, United States Indian Agent, and Little Rock, a Cheyenne Chief, Held at Fort Larned, August 19. In U.S. Senate, *Indian Battle on the Washita River,* 40th Cong., 3rd sess., S. Exec. Doc. 18.

———. 1868b. Report to the U. S. Indian Commission, December 23. *New York Times,* December 24.

Young, Delia Iona Cann. 1929. The Battle of the Washita. *Cheyenne Star,* May 23.

Young Bird, Mrs. B. K. [Cheyenne]. 1937. Interview, June 22. Indian-Pioneer History Collection, vol. 52, Grant Foreman Papers, Oklahoma Historical Society, Oklahoma City.

Index

Afraid of Beavers, 301, 327 & n9, 328
Ah-toh-nah (Trails the Enemy's wife), 345
Alights on a Cloud, 329, 358n9
Alvord, Henry A., 57, 368; background of, 267–68; statements of, 268–69
Andrews, William, 387
Antelope Hills, Ind. Terr., 10, 56, 134, 165, 186, 211, 212, 221, 276
Arapaho Woman (Black Kettle's wife), 427, 428
Arapaho Woman (Stacy Riggs's wife), 317. *See also* Poisal, Mary Ella
Arikaree Fork, Colo. Terr., 9, 37
Arkansas River, 3, 6, 8, 9, 38, 41, 53, 181, 286, 289
Asahabet, 280
Asch, Morris, 103 & n, 238, 255
Asher Creek, Kans., 38
Auchiah, James, 63n3
Autobees, Charles, 302n3

Bacon, C., 387
Bad Bank (High Bank), 269n2, 310n16, 311 & n18, 324n3
Bad Man (Cranky Man), 15, 399
Baggage Site, location of, 23
Bailey, Mahlon, 71n8

Baird, Mrs., 120n19
Bald Eagle (Eagle Head), 369. *See also* Minimic
Balenti, Mike, 362n16
Bales, J., 383
Barde, Frederick S., 235, 292n2
Barker, Kirkland C., 80; background of, 80n17
Barnhill, Mr., 362n16
Barnitz, Albert, 12, 18, 23, 130, 145, 152, 163, 173, 177n3, 191, 214, 219 & n24, 384, 394; background of, 96–97; duel of, 16–17, 115–16, 117, 155, 308n12; role of, in attack, 16, 103, 113–14, 117, 122–23, 200n2, 218, 222, 256n14; statements of, 98–128; wound of and condition of, 65, 89, 102, 115, 131, 141, 142, 161, 182, 244, 394
Barnitz, Jennie, 98, 102, 145
Barnitz Creek, Ind. Terr., 121, 124, 125 & n22
Barnitz Hill, 12, 25, 120, 122, 226, 234
Bassett, Mr., 38
Bassett, Mrs., 38
Bates, Charles F., 166n10
Bear Bow, Walter, 295, 297
Bear Feathers, 54, 321, 400
Bear on the Ridge, 427
Bear Shield, 106n10

Bear That Goes Ahead, 48

Bear Tongue, 324 & n1, 398, 399, 401

Bear Trail, 397

Beaver Creek, Ind. Terr., 66, 164

Beaver Creek, Kans., 39, 146

Beebe, William M., Jr., 146, 249; background of, 146n13

Beecher, Frederick H., 38

Beecher Island, Colo. Terr., 52n1

Bell, Emily H., 150 & n20

Bell, James M., 11,14, 26, 130, 135 & n8, 138, 150, 150n21, 165–66, 167, 211, 228, 243, 385; background of, 162–63; and baggage site skirmish, 22–23, 90, 131, 139, 154, 156, 166 & n10; statements of, 163–70

Bell, Joseph, 366n25

Bell Children, 47n8

Bent, Charles, 3

Bent, George, 47n7, 50, 53, 85n21, 258n19, 260n22, 328, 330n2, 365n23, 399, 429; background of, 353–56; letters from, 356–66

Bent, Julia, 50

Bent, William, 50, 302n3, 365n23, 399

Benteen, Frederick W., 11, 12, 16, 25, 33, 91, 84n20, 106, 113, 130, 138, 152, 158n2, 163, 165–66, 191, 192n6, 195n9, 199, 243, 384; animosity of, toward Custer, 177n3, 178, 179n4, 213, 227, 231n45; background of, 174–75; and duel with Blue Horse, 16, 65, 84, 187, 245; letter from, 175–79

Bent's Fort, 5, 34, 35, 37

Bent's Stockade, 3, 317

Berry, Matthew, 25, 153, 223, 226, 243, 373, 384; background of, 373

Big Bow, 276n1

Big Head, 47, 363n18; background of, 47n7

Big Horse, 397

Big Jake (Little Wolf), 53; background of, 53n3

Big Jake's Crossing, 53n3

Big Lynx, 391

Big Man, 229n43, 301, 306, 308n10

Big Mouth, 142n12, 276n1, 282

Big Red White Man, 357n6

Big Sandy, Colo. Terr., 37

Big Shield Woman, 331n3

Big Springs, Kans., 34

Bingaman, Joseph, 190n2

Bird Chief, 330, 331n3

Bitter Man, 15, 401. See also Bad Man (Cranky Man)

Bittle, Isidore, 229–30, 229n44

Black, Flora, 428. See also Black, Jennie

Black, Jay (Jay Black Kettle) (Black Kettle, Jr.'s son), 318n3

Black, Jay (Jay Black Kettle) (Wolf's son), 431

Black, Jennie, 430

Black, Nettie (Nettie Black Kettle), 318n3

Black, Star (Star Black Kettle), 428

Black Beaver, 31

Black Coyote, 229n43

Black Dog, 430. See also Wolf (Iron Teeth)

Black Eagle, 72 & n9, 74, 75, 350

"Blackfoot Smith" (John S. Smith), 45n3

Black Hairy Dog, 362n16

Black Hawk (Hawk Stretched Out), 54. See also Black Hawk Lying Down

Black Hawk, Mrs., 323

Black Hawk Lying Down, 318n5, 427, 430

Black Horse, Reuben, 429

Black Kettle, 52, 71, 80, 182, 195 & n10, 207, 243, 255, 273, 276, 283, 307, 314 & n2, 319, 332, 335, 352–, 360, 366, 397, 398, 399, 401, 408, 427, 428, 429; background of, 54–55; and burial of remains, 309,

322 & n12, 328; death of, 15, 160,
239–40, 309, 321, 328; and failure to
heed danger warnings, 290, 319 &
n6, 324–25, 325n6; family and
relatives of, 15, 20, 54, 321, 427–31;
statement of, 55–57
Black Kettle, Jr., 318 & n3, 428
Black Kettle (Wolf), 431
Black Kettle Museum, 121n20, 292n2,
422
Black Kettle's Tree, 293 & n4, 305 &
n7
Black Kettle's Village: attacked, 14,
16, 17–18, 82, 98–99, 114, 130, 139,
154, 160, 178, 182, 186–87, 191–92,
208, 218–19, 221–22, 225, 243, 268,
307, 319, 321, 325, 333, 335, 346; and
burning of lodges, 24, 90, 100, 143,
167, 172, 194, 196, 211–12, 320;
location of, 14, 63, 119, 215, 218n18,
234, 235, 276 & n1, 296, 297,
304–305, 306; and slaughter of
ponies, 26–27, 91–92, 100, 143–44,
167, 178, 182, 187, 197, 211, 247, 258,
310–11, 319–20, 327, 336
Black War Bonnet, 255 & n11
Blind Bear, 310n16, 398, 399
Blinn, Clara, 38, 160 & n4, 213–14 &
n14, 277 & n4; background of,
41–42; burial and exhumation of,
236n51, 236n52; message of, 42–43;
remains of, discovered, 71n8,
76n14, 227, 235 & n50, 262 & n26;
wounds of, described, 213–14, 265,
278 & n6
Blinn, Richard F., 41, 42n2, 227 &
n39, 236n51
Blinn, Willie, 41, 43, 71n8, 235n50,
262–63 & n26, 265–66, 278 & n6
Blucher (Custer's dog), 93, 190n2
Blue Horse, 16, 34–85, 245, 398, 399,
401, 429; background of, 85n21
Bluff Creek, Kans., 165n6, 253, 254
Bob (dog), 190

Bobtail Bear, 358
Boggs Ranch, Kans., 41
Bonner, Mrs. W. T., 120n19
Bonner, Ms., 120n19
Bonner, William T., 119, 224 & n, 227
& n38, 234, 299
Boone, Albert G., 365 & n23
Borden, George P., 254 & n10
Bosley, Harriet, 41
Botzer, Edward, 104 & n6
Bradley, Henry, 371
Breaks Marrow Bones, 46n6
Brewster, Charles, 17, 153, 168, 255,
385; background of, 157; narrative
of 158–61
Brewster, Daniel A., 227n39
Bridger, Jim, 229
Brill, Charles J., 258n19, 302 & n1,
308n12, 314n2, 405
Broken Leg Creek, Okla., 17, 225, 227
& n38
Brooks, H. C., 343
Brooks, Sarah C. (Sarah C. White),
background of, 343; statement of,
343–44
Brown, William, 394
Brown's Creek, Kans., 39
Buckner's Fork, Kans., 52
Buffalo Tongue, 397
Buffalo Trots as He Travels (Trotter),
391
Bull Bear, 34, 52; background of, 52n1
Bull Bear, Jock (Thunder Cloud), 52n1
Bull Horn (Little Woman), 203. See
also Moka
Butler, Capt., 34
Butler, Jonathon A., 220n25
Butterfield, David A., 51
Buttless, John F., 41

C. & O. W. Railway, 406
Calfes, W., 389
"California Joe" (Moses Milner), 25,
87, 187, 192 & n6, 134, 145, 185, 188,

"California Joe" (*continued*) 192n11, 225, 227; background of, 134n6, 240

Camp, Walter M., 30, 116n15, 122, 149, 292n2, 399, 400

Campbell, Q., 40

Camp Sandy Forsyth, Kans., 177n3

Camp Supply, Ind. Terr., 9, 26, 27, 28, 44, 102, 106, 125, 126, 145, 164, 165, 180, 181, 183, 212, 221, 227, 236, 278, 320

Camp Wichita, Ind. Terr., 229n43, 286

Canadian River, 9, 10, 107, 108, 122, 125, 134, 165, 167, 181, 182, 186, 241, 264, 268, 325n6

Canton, Okla., 369n1

Cantonment, Ind. Terr., 322n12, 369n1

Capron, Allyn K., 292n2

Captive River, Tex., (Sweetwater Creek), 320n10

Carlisle Indian School, 321

Carr, Eugene A., 39, 51

Carrick, William, 69

Carrying Quiver Woman, 342

Casady, John C., 292n2, 300, 314n3, 424n5

Ce-Wah-Ka-Ka (Sharp Hair), 391

Che-Pah-Shin (Little Buffalo Head), 391

Cherokee Nation, 236n52

Cherry Creek, Col. Terr., 5, 283n1

Cheyenne, Okla., 18, 19, 20, 119, 215, 220, 234, 296, 300, 303, 315

Cheyenne-Arapaho Land Run, 305n6

Cheyenne Belle, 362n16

Cheyenne Jack, 41, 42n1

Cheyenne Jennie (William Griffinstein's wife), 210n9, 289; background of, 289n1

Cheyenne Platonic Club, 120, 312n1

Cheyenne Short Line Railway, 406

Cheyenne Wells, Colo. Terr., 34

Cheyenne Wells Station, Colo. Terr., 35

Chicken Hawk (Edmund Guerrier), 50

Chivington, John M., 7, 45n1, 271

Chouteau, Auguste L., 228n42

Chouteau, Gessau, 136n9, 228, 383, 391; background of, 228n42

Chouteau, Louis P., 228n42

Christie, Thomas, 69, 399

Cimarron Crossing, Kans., 33, 36, 163

Cimarron River, Kans.-Ind. Terr., 8, 33, 53, 205

Clair, E. F. (Elihu Clear), 131

Clancy, Thomas, 292n2

Clark, Ben, 23, 27, 119, 120, 121, 158n2, 163n3, 168, 196n11, 215, 225, 227, 292n2, 308n11, 359n11, 360, 363n18; background of, 202–204; discloses the killing of women and children, 27, 220, 226, 229–30; statements of, 204–36

Clark, Emily (daughter), 203

Clark, Emily (wife), 202–203

Clark, Jennie, 203

Clarke & Company, 37

Clear, Elihu, 20, 131 & n2

Clover, Eugene, 69, 393

Clown, 324, 328

Cody, William F., 185n3

Colfax, Schuyler, 36

Colony, Okla., 356n3

Colorado City, Colo. Terr., 36

Colyer, Vincent, background of, 367, report of, 367–71

Comanche (horse), 163 & n4

Com-Bla-Mosha (I Don't Want It), 391. *See also* Trotter (Trots as He Travels)

Coming In Sight Woman, 142n12

Commission Creek, Ind. Terr., 10

Comstock, William, 34

Conrad, Sgt., 140

Cooke, William W., 13, 138, 145, 146, 153, 184n1, 191 & n3, 199, 207, 208, 209, 218, 222, 228, 243, 249, 255, 383, 387; background of, 158n3, 373–74

Coon Creek, Kans., 39

Corbin, Jack, 135, 145, 185, 206, 227, 383; background of, 135n7

Corbin, Joe, 206

Corn Stalk Woman, 324

Corn Tassel Woman, 85n21, 429

Courtenay, Mrs., 22, 166 & n11, 186n6, 231 & n45

Courtenay, Sgt., 166n11

Crane, 327

Cranky Man, 15. *See also* Bad Man (Cranky Man)

Cranny Creek, Kans., 33

Crawford, Mr., 135n7

Crawford, Samuel J., 9, 66, 277; background of, 66n5

Crazy (Fool Man), 310n16, 398, 399

Crocker, Jennie Lund, 283n3

Crocker, Lt., 283n3

Crocker, Mrs., 283 & n3

Crooked Nose Woman (Miriam Mann), 357n6

Crooked Wrist, 328

Crosby, John S., 53, 66, 146, 238, 249, 255; background of, 53n5

Crow Neck, 109n12, 325n6

Cuddy, Charles, 183n9, 394

Cunningham, Judson, 406, background of, 312; interview of, 312–16

Curly Hair, 321, 363n18

Curran, Louis, 164 & n5

Curry, Jim, 185; background of, 185n6

Curtis, Dick, 252, 276, 397; background of, 252n8

Custer, Elizabeth, B., 59, 149, 150n21, 190n1, 199, 231n45

Custer, George A., 9, 23 120, 121, 124, 125, 126, 131, 145, 146, 155, 158, 161, 165, 175, 186, 194, 199, 205 & n4, 215, 234, 237, 240, 244, 249, 250, 255, 256, 258, 261, 262, 264, 271, 277, 293, 294, 300, 306, 315, 320, 330, 332, 333, 359, 362, 363 & n18, 368, 383, 407; abuse of female captives, 230–31, 231n45; attacks village, 15, 17, 25, 114, 122, 123, 153-54, 160, 172, 184, 208, 209, 218–19, 220, 222–23, 225, 230, 243–44, 257, 321, 343; background of, 58–60; destroys village, 24, 26–27, 167, 187, 196, 197, 211, 229, 253; discovers village, 11, 110, 137, 151–53, 159, 165–66, 190, 205–206, 242; and Elliott controversy, 23–24, 102, 148, 350 & n11; evaluations of the attack of, 29–31; failure to recover bodies of Elliott's command, 27–28, 167, 177, 178, 213, 227; Indian casualty count inflated, 78 & n15, 261n24, 283, 287 & n2, 309–10; march of, to Washita, 9, 10, 11, 106, 107, 108, 109 & n12, 133, 134, 158, 241; and plan of attack, 12–13, 111, 113, 137–38, 159–60, 165, 168, 170, 190, 206, 207, 218, 225, 228, 242–43; reports and writings of, 60–95; rift in regiment, 28–29, 179n4; and Sweet Water confrontation, 361–64, 362n17, 369, 370–71; withdraws command, 132, 144, 198, 336

Custer, Thomas W., 65, 146, 153, 158, 161, 182, 186, 199, 205, 214, 223n30, 243, 249, 256, 261n24, 383, 394; background of, 374–75; and involvement with Meotzi, 231n45

Custer Bend, Ind. Terr. (Strong City, Okla.), 225n35

Custer Hill (Headquarters Hill), 27

Custer Knoll, 18, 219n22, 222, 292n2

Custer's Crossing, 11, 206n5, 219n22, 305n7, 328 & n10

Cut Arm, 330n1
Cut Lip Bear, 85n21

Darlington, Brinton, 334
Darlington Agency, 229n43, 282, 283,
    302n3, 334 & n2, 369n1
Davis, Bill, 40, 254 & n9
Davis, Richard A., 52n1
DeGresse, William J., 175 & n1
DeLaney, Augustus, 183n9, 394
DeLaney, J., 387
Deming, E. W., 52n1
Denton, Mr., 117, 118 & n17, 122
Denver City, Colo. Terr., 5, 6, 45n 1,
    271, 283n1
Dittoe, Sgt., 36
Double, 330
Double Wolf, 335, 337
Downey, Thomas, 69, 393
Draw Them Up, 391
Dull Knife, 363n18

Eagan, Pvt., 195
Eagle Feather, 391
Eagle Head, 369n2
Earp, Wyatt, 185n3
Ear Ring, 358n9
Eastwood, William, 394
Eayre, George S., 6
Ediger, Theodore A., 324, 341, 556n3
Elliott, Joel H., 27, 28, 65, 117, 120,
    122, 130, 136, 145, 155, 173, 182, 201,
    212, 214, 227, 236n52, 243, 249, 256,
    358, 384, 393; background of, 3–115;
    burial of, and his men, 68, 121,
    236n52, 262, 266; and Canadian
    River scout detail, 10, 107–108,
    134, 135, 165, 131, 200, 241; last
    stand of, 20, 23, 27, 68, 132, 148,
    161, 176, 177, 220, 223, 235 & n48,
    244, 259–61, 265, 278n5, 294,
    315–16, 358–59, 359n10, 364; and
    pursuit of fleeing Indians, 18–19,
    140, 147, 186, 192, 210, 220, 226, 231

& n46, 234, 244, 258–59, 278,
    313–14, 315, 336, 356–58, 359 & n11;
    role of, in attack, 12, 17–18, 61, 89,
    103, 111–14, 117–18, 137–38, 139, 152,
    207; search for and discovery of,
    68, 69, 93–94, 144, 167, 175, 212–13
    & n13, 255
Ellis Station, Kans., 37
Ellsworth, Kans., 38
El Reno, Okla., 282, 303
Enid, Okla, 322
Eonah-pah (Trails the Enemy), 345
Eubanks, Isabella, 271n2
Evans, John, 6, 7

Fanny (Custer's dog), 190n2
Fargo, Okla., 9
Fat Bear, 321, 363. See also Little Bear
Fay, Jonathon, 387
Finch, Ives, 408
Fish, 229n43
Fisher Creek, Kans., 39
Fitzpatrick, Jack, 78n15, 227, 283, 365,
    383; background of, 283n2
Fitzpatrick, Thomas, 69, 193, 197, 283,
    393
Fitzpatrick, Thomas J., 365 & n22
Fitzpatrick, Virginia T., 283n2
Fletcher, Mary, 361n15
Flying Woman, 333–34
Fool Man, 401. See also Crazy (Fool
    Man)
Forsyth, George A., 9, 37, 238n1, 271;
    background of, 271n1
Forsyth, James M., 238, 255;
    background of, 238n1
Fort Arbuckle, Ind. Terr., 236n51,
    279
Fort Arbuckle Cemetery, 42n2
Fort Bascom, N. Mex. Terr., 9, 37
Fort Cobb, Ind, Terr., 30, 41, 72, 74,
    126, 148, 262, 263, 264, 266, 273,
    276, 277, 278, 279, 281, 284, 306,
    307, 311

Fort Dodge, Kans., 8, 33, 34, 35, 38, 40, 41, 101, 126, 163, 199, 253, 276, 281
Fort Elliott, Tex., 321
Fort Elliott Trail, 229n43, 297
Fort Gibson National Cemetery, 236n52
Fort Harker, Kans., 32, 39, 40, 41, 101, 126
Fort Hays, Kans., 40, 361, 363
Fort Laramie, Dak. Terr., 302n3
Fort Larned, Kans., 8, 38, 44, 48, 143, 272, 276, 277
Fort Lincoln, Dak. Terr., 163n4
Fort Lyon, Colo. Terr., 4, 6, 9, 35, 38, 42, 263, 266
Fort Reno, Ind. Terr., 297
Fort Riley, Kans., 107, 283
Fort Sill, Ind. Terr., 222, 361
Fort Wallace, Kans., 34, 36, 281
Fort Wise, Colo. Terr., 4
Fort Zarah, Kans., 33, 38, 39, 273
Forwood, William H., 284; background of, 284n5
Fox Tail, 362n16

Gale, Martin, 394
Garfield, James A., 289
Garrick, William, 393
Gauion, Charles, 387
Geary, Okla., 214
General (Barnitz's horse), 141, 148
Gentle Horse (Black Kettle's brother), 318n5, 325n6, 326n7, 430
Gentle Horse (Jay Black Kettle), 431. See also Black, Jay (Jay Black Kettle) (Wolf's son)
George, John, 393
German, John, 329
Ghost Woman, 431
Gibson, Francis M., 150 & n19, 150n21, 152, 243, 385; background of, 151; narrative of, 151–56
Gibson, Katherine F., 150n19
Gibson, Katherine G., 150n19

Glorieta Pass, N.Mex. Terr., 45n1
Godfrey, Edward S., 15, 20, 21, 23, 25, 27, 78n15, 102, 131, 132, 150n21, 153, 158n2, 243, 384; background of, 129–30; statements of, 130–50
Goombi, Lillian, 345
Gosby, A., 389
Graham, Capt., 37
Granite City, Okla., 120n19
Gray, Mrs. A. G., 120n19
Gray Eyes, 369
Greer, Ms., 120n19
Gregoire, Mrs., 120n19
Grierson, Benjamin H., 363n18, 367, 370; background of, 285; letter from, 286–87
Griffinstein, William, 41, 42n1, 210n9, 276n2, 289 & n1, 307n9
Grinnell, George B., 258n19, 357n7
Grinnell Station, Kans., 39
Grover, Sharp, 34
Guerrier, Edmund, 552, 254n9; affidavit of, 52–53; background of, 50–51
Guerrier, Rosa, 51
Guerrier, William (father), 50
Guerrier, William (son), 51

Hackberry Creek, Ind. Terr., 165
Hale, Owen, 18, 140, 146, 147, 152, 190, 193, 199, 201, 243, 249, 256, 258, 262 & n25, 384; background of, 375–87
Half Leg (Peg Leg), 324n2
Hall, Frank, 34, 35
Hamilton, Alexander, 136, 161, 219, 251
Hamilton, Louis M., 13, 14, 122, 123, 130, 136, 138, 153, 163, 164, 165, 173, 250, 360, 364, 384, 394, 400; background of, 376; burial of, 146, 183, 249, 376; death of, 65, 89, -117, 147, 155, 161, 182, 192, 208, 214, 219 & n23, 222, 243–44; role of, in attack, 15, 162 & n16, 122–23, 218, 243

Hammon, Okla., 229n43, 299
Hammon Flood, 235n48, 299, 305n7
Hancock, Winfield S., 7, 8, 51, 271
Haney, J., 387
Hard Rope, 383, 391, 392
Harrington, William T., 41, 42
Harris, Pvt., 106
Harrison, P., 387
Harvey, Winfield S., 236n52;
    background of, 180; diary of,
    180–83
Hawk, 310n16
Hawk Stretched Out, 54, 427
Hazen, William B., 41, 44, 55, 72, 74,
    75, 269, 276 & n2, 279, 280, 306,
    307 & n9, 324n5, 325n6;
    background of, 288–89; letter
    from, 289–90
Headquarters Hill, 219n22, 225, 234,
    257n17, 359n11
Heap of Birds, 295, 323
Heap of Birds, Alfrich, 295
Heap of Birds, Homer, 295n1, 296,
    297, 300, 305n7; background of,
    295; statement of, 295–300
Heap Timber, 397
Hennessey, Patrick, 329
Hensley, Claude E., 362n16
Hick, J., 387
High Bank, 15, 269n2, 311n18, 324n3
High Forehead (Shingled Hair),
    348n5
High Singer (Ann Little Raven),
    46n5
Hoarse Voice (Charles Autobees),
    302n3
Ho-eh-a-mo-a-ha (Breaks Marrow
    Bones), 52
Hoffman, Vinnie, 323
Hooxeeche (Lodge Pole Creek),
    185n2. See also Washita River
Horseshoe Hills, 11, 12, 15
Howling Wolf, 369n2
Huber, H., 389

Hughes, Sgt., 140
Hugo Springs, Colo, Terr., 36
Hunt, George, 345
Hyde, George, 258n19, 361, 398

I Don't Want It (Com-Bla-Mosha),
    391
Inman, Henry, 101, 146n15, 236n52,
    253, 254 & n9; background of,
    101n2
Iron Teeth (Wolf), 430
Island, 321, 363n18
Issenon, 369n1

Jackson, Henry, 126; background of,
    126n24
Jarvis, Pat, 423
Jenness, George B., 262n26
Johnson, John M., 13, 153, 243, 385;
    background of, 376
Jones, H. P., 368
Joyce, P. 387

Keim, DeB. Randolph: background
    of, 237; dispatches of, 237–63
Kennedy, John, 164 & n5
Kennedy, Walter, 18, 69, 121, 161, 182,
    193, 226, 244, 258n18, 359n11, 383, 393
Keogh, Myles, 163 & n4, 199
Kicking Bird (Striking Eagle), 75;
    background of, 75n12
Kiowa Creek, Ind. Terr., 204–205
Kiowa Creek, Kans., 35
Kiowa Station, Kans., 35
Kirk, Alice, 286n1
Kirk, John, 286 & n1
Kirtley, Mr. (Kirkley, James A.), 218
    & n19
Kluik, Frederick, 394
Kosser, A., 389
Kruger, Charles, 165n6

Lacy, Jeff, 314 & n2, 422
Lake Station, Colo. Terr., 34, 35, 37

Lame Arapaho (Lame Man), 399
Lame Man, 352n4, 397, 401
Law, Edward, 15, 20, 140, 147, 153, 159, 243, 384; background of, 376–77
Lays on Top of Hill, 332
Lean Bear, 6
Lean Face (Slim Face), 363n18
Leavenworth, Henry, 365n24
Leavenworth, Jesse H., 50, 365 & n24
Lee & Reynolds, 51
Left Hand, 207, 214, 220, 223, 226, 283n1, 317
Lennon, J., 387
Lester, Jim M., 121n20, 292n2, 300
Lightning Bug, 391
Linden, W., 387
Lineback, Ferdinand, 69, 197, 393
Lippincott, Henry, 69, 70, 99, 103 & n5, 131, 141, 153, 262, 278n6, 383; background of, 377
Little Arkansas River, Kans., 7, 277
Little Bear, 363n18
Little Beaver (Osage), 136, 137, 239, 244, 383, 391; background of, 136n9
Little Beaver (son of Wolf Looking Back), 258n19, 303 & n4, 306, 310n16, 357n7, 405, 406
Little Big Jake (Little Medicine), 53n3
Little Black Bear, 392
Little Brown Back Woman (Sparrow Hawk Woman), 54, 427
Little Buffalo, 391
Little Buffalo Head, 391
Little Chief, 358n8
Little Coon Creek, Kans., 36, 40
Little Hand, 295
Little Hawk, 430
Little Heart, 398, 399
Little Magpie (Leonard Tyler), 430
Little Magpie (White Shield) (Wind Woman's son), 430
Little Man, 362n16
Little Medicine, 53n3

Little Mountain, 63n3, 70n7, 276n1
Little Raven, 46, 63, 70, 207, 272, 276n1, 281, 368; background of, 46n5
Little Raven, Anna, 46n5
Little Robe, 276n1, 290n3, 368; background of, 369n1
Little Rock, 14, 19, 31, 45, 52, 260n20, 261n24, 310n16, 347n4, 397, 398, 399, 400, 401; background of, 44; death of, 260, 310n16, 347 & n3, 357 & n4, 397, 398, 399, 400, 401; family of, 44, 63, 149n17, 231n45, 248n7, 310n17, 357n6, 357n7; interview of, 45–49; protects fleeing women and children, 19, 347 & n2, 356–57, 360; shield and scalp of, in Custer's possession, 80 & n18, 261n24
Little Sage Woman, 427, 428
Little Sioux Woman, 229n43
Little Wolf (Big Jake), 53n3
Little Wolf (Kiowa), 72, 279; background of, 70n7
Little Woman (Red Fern) (Ben Clark's wife), 203
Little Woman (Homer Heap of Bird's wife), 295n1
Little Woman (Red Bird's sister), 330n1, 331
Llano Estacado (Staked Plains), Tex., 286
Lodge Pole Creek (Washita River), 330
Lone Coyote, 214n15, 261 & n23, 352n4
"Lone Soldier," death of, 258n19
Lone Wolf (Kiowa), 70, 72, 73, 76, 279; background of, 70n7
Lone Wolf, Mrs.: background of, 335; narrative of, 335–37
Lone Wolf (Stacy Riggs), 317, 329n10. See also Riggs, Stacy
Lottinville, Savoie, 258n19

Lyman, Wyllys, 227n41
Lynch, Dennis: background of, 184 &
    n1; interview of, 184–88
Lyon, T. P., 196n11

Magpie, 258n19, 303, 305 & n7, 308 &
    n10, 310n16, 312, 313, 315, 327n9,
    405, 406, 407; background of, 301;
    narrative of, 302–11
Magpie Woman (Big Man's wife),
    301, 306
Magpie Woman (George Bent's
    wife), 360 & n12, 366, 429
Magpie Woman (Mahwissa's
    mother), 75n13, 85n21
Mahwissa (Red Hair Woman), 75n13,
    248 & n7, 279
Malhoris, J., 387
Man Above, 53n3
Man on a Cloud, 329
Manes, William M., 146n15
Man that Hears the Wolf, 397
Mann, Fred (Spotted Horse), 357n6
Mann, Miriam, 357n6
Man Who Breaks Marrow Bones, 52
Many Magpies (Clyde Standing
    Bull), 296n1
Marble, Daniel, 271n2
March, Thomas J., 65, 103, 110, 152,
    161, 182n6, 192, 214, 384, 394;
    background of, 377
Marsh, Elias J., 103 & n5
Marshall, Nate, 40, 254 & n9
Marston, J. J., 398
Martin, August, 394
Mason, M., 387
Masters, Joseph G., background of,
    312
Mathey, Edward G., 103, 136, 151n1,
    155, 165, 241, 385; background of,
    377–78
Ma-wota (Red Feather), 318
McCarty, William, 34
McCasey, Benjamin, 183n9, 394, 395

McClernan, John, 393
McCorbet, Cyrus W., 165n6
McCormick, J., 389
McCusker, Philip, 75; background of,
    349–50; report of, 350–52
McDermott, Sgt., 16, 17, 113, 114
McGaffrey, M., 389
McGinnis, John, 163n3
McGonigle, Andrew J., 238, 255;
    background of, 238n2
McKinney, Mrs., 120n19
McKinney, Ms., 120n19
McLaren, R. W., 255
Mead, James R., 21on9
Measure Woman, 331 & n3
Medicine Arrow (Medicine Arrows),
    52, 276n1, 301, 362 & n16, 370. See
    also Rock Forehead (Stone
    Forehead)
Medicine Bluff, Kans., 368
Medicine Lodge Creek, Kans., 272,
    360
Medicine Walker, 397
Medicine Water, 329, 331n3
Medicine Woman Hereafter
    (Medicine Woman Later), 309n13
Medicine Woman Later, 15, 309 &
    n13, 321, 327n9, 328, 427, 428
Mennonite Mission, 229n43
Mennonite Mission School, 252
Meotzi, 44, 149n17, 248n7, 357n6;
    relationship of, with officers,
    231n45
Mercer, Harry, 69, 393
Meyers, Carsten D. J. (Carson D. J.
    Myers), 70
Meyers, John, 70, 197
Mier, Pvt., 197
Miles, John D., 369n1
Miles, Nelson A., 227, 282, 294
Miller, C. G., 406, 424n5
Milligan, William, 69, 393
Milner, Moses, 227, 383
Milton, J., 387

Minimic, 368

Mitchell, Mrs., 120n19

Moka, 203

Monahsetah (Meotzi), 231n45

Monument to the Unknown Indian,
312n1, 406

Mooney, C., 387

Moore, Alvin, 292n2, 296n2, 311, 406

Moore, John H., 38

Moore, Thomas W. C., 238;
background of, 238n3

Morgan, Anna Belle, 227n39, 277 &
n4

Morgan, Hugh, 395

Morrison, Daniel, 245n6, 395

Morrison, Emma, 282

Morrison, Jennie, 282

Morrison, James S. (Jesse S.), 45;
background of, 282; letter from,
283–84

Morrison, Ned, 282

Morrison, Nellie, 282

Motovata (Black Kettle, Jr.), 318

Mountain, 348n5

Mouse Road, Paul, 330n2

Moving Behind Woman:
background of, 323; narrative of,
323–28

Moylan, Myles M., 109, 153, 155,
158n3, 240, 243, 256, 383;
background of, 378

Mulberry Creek, Kans., 40, 253, 254

Mullen, Pat, 104

Murphy, John, 196, 245n6, 389, 395

Murphy, Thomas, 75, 350;
background of, 270; report of,
270–73

Myers, Carson, D. J., 200n1, 393

Myers, Edward, 13, 20, 144, 168,
177n3, 199, 385; background of,
378–79; and killing of women and
children, 18, 208, 220, 222–23,
225–26, 230; role of, in attack,
17–18, 23, 24, 25, 61, 91, 130, 132, 138,

139, 142, 148, 152–53, 195n9, 207 &
n6, 209–10, 218, 221, 228, 243

Myers, John, 200n1, 258n19, 393

Namay-Day-Te (Young Lone Wolf),
70n7

Na-to-mah (John S. Smith's wife),
45n3, 284 & n4

Ne-sou-hoe (Mrs. Crocker), 283n3

Newby, F., 389

Nichols, W. A., 275, 278, 231

Nineteenth Kansas Volunteer
Cavalry, 9, 66, 104, 262n26, 264,
277, 278, 280

North Canadian River, Ind. Terr., 4,
9, 278, 322

Nowlan, Henry J., 104 & n7

Oh-e-ah-mohe-a (Breaks Marrow
Bones), 46

Oh-has-tee (Little Raven), 367

Oklahoma State Indian Fair, 302n2

Old Medicine Water, 329

Old Stands in Timber, 363n18

Old Whirlwind, 341

O'Leary, J., 387

O-Pah-La-La (Straight Line), 391

Opah-Tink-Ah (Big Elk), 391

Osage Indian Scouts, 11, 14, 26, 63,
67, 72, 106, 107, 134, 145, 153, 158,
171, 183, 205, 208, 226, 228, 229, 239,
242, 244, 246, 248, 256, 261n24, 268,
278, 326n8, 352 & n5

Osage Knoll, 12, 13, 17; location of, 11

Osage Mission, Kans., 228n42

Otterby, John, 302n3, 341

Otterby, John, Jr., 341; background of,
302n3

Packer (She Wolf), 260n20, 400

Page, John H., 163n3

Panhandle Short Line Railway, 299

Parker, George, 314 & n2, 320n9, 422

Path Woman, 229n43

Patient Man, 391
Pawnee Fork, Kans., 8, 33
Peck, Robert M., 356; background of, 356n1
Peg Leg, 31, 324n2
Peller Brothers, 120n19, 312n1
Penderly, D., 387
Pendleton, David ("Oakerhater"), 428
Pendleton, Frank, 428
Penrose, William H., 37
Pepoon, Silas, 66; background, 66n5
Petter, Rodolpho, 361n15
Pickens, J. C., background, 199; letter from, 199–201
Picking Bones Woman, 302n3
Piedfort, Albert, 12, 13, 383, 389
Piedfort, W., 389
Pierce, F., 389
Pilan (White Bear), 187 & n10, 209–10, 226, 229–30; 360n13, 401; background of, 210n9
Pipe Woman (Black Kettle's daughter), 318, 428
Pipe Woman (White Antelope's wife), 46n6
Platte River, 7, 271 & n2
Plum Creek, Ind. Terr., 15, 18, 206n5, 218n20, 299, 308n10
Plunkett, John, 300
Poisal, John, Jr., 78n15, 283, 383; background of, 283n1
Poisal, John, Sr., 227, 283n1, 217
Poisal, Margaret, 283n1, 283n2
Poisal, Mary, 283n1
Poisal, Mary Ella, 317
Poisal, Matilda, 283n1
Poisal, Robert, 283n1
Pond Creek, Colo. Terr., 34
Plony Kill Site, 257–58 & n18
Poor Black Elk, 397
Porcupine Bear, 47n7, 48
Powder Face, 207
Prairie Dog Creek, Kans., 39

Pratt, Capt., 142n12
Pueblo, Colo. Terr., 3
Purgatory River, Colo. Terr., 3, 6, 37, 52
Pushing Bear, 308n10

Quartermaster Creek, Ind. Terr., 121, 124

Rath, Charlie, 362n16
Red Bird (Cut Arm's son), 329, 330 & n1, 330n2, 331 & n3, 398, 399, 401
Red Bird (Stacy Riggs), 317
Red Black Bird, background of, 338; statement of, 338
Red Dress, 303n4
Red Eye, Flora, 428
Red Feather Woman, 318, 428
Red Fern, 203
Red Hair, 75n13, 248n7, 361
Red Moon (Red Sun), 229, 284n4, 369; background of, 229n43
Red Moon School, 229n43
Red Nose (Cheyenne), 46, 16, 52
Red Nose (George A. Custer), 234
Red River, Tex., 72, 3.61
Red Springs, Colo. Terr., 35
Red Sun, 229n43
Red Teeth, 398, 399
Remington, Frederick, 52n1
Rennick, William C., 99, 103 & n5, 153, 231n45, 360, 383
Republican River, Kans., 33, 37
Riggs, Evert, 322
Riggs, Stacy, 314n2, 318 & n2, 320 & n9, 320n10, 422, 427, 428; background of, 317–18; statements of, 318–22
Road Maker, 362n16
Robbins, Samuel M., 45, 121, 126, 153, 199, 240, 243, 256; background of, 379, 384

Rock Forehead (Stone Forehead), 362n16, 362n17
Rodgers, G., 387
Rodgers, Joseph P., 262n26
Roll Down, 324, 328
Roman Nose Thunder, 319, 358, 359n10, 364
"Romeo" (Rafael Romero), 87, 88, 142, 148, 185, 192
Romero, Ella, 142n12
Romero, Rafael, 21, 142, 227, 231, 363n18, 383; background of, 142n12
Roper, Laura, 271n2
Running Water, 397
Rush, Frank, 302 & n2, 303, 405, 406–407
Ryan, John, 200n1, 201n4, 231n45, 245n6; background of, 189–90; narrative of, 190–98

Sacred Arrows, 54, 362 & n16
Sage Woman, 46n6
Sah-To-Kah-Shin-Ka (Little Buffalo), 391
Saline River, Kans., 8, 32, 37, 46, 47, 48, 52, 163n2, 271, 281
"Sallie Ann" (Meotzi), 231n45
Sand Creek, Colo. Terr., 5, 6, 31, 41, 227, 229n43
Sand Hill, 361 & n15, 362
Sand Hill, Robert, 361n15
Sand Hill Woman, 142n12
Santa Fe Trail, 4, 8
Sappa Creek, Kans., 361n15
Satanta (White Bear), 63, 70, 71, 72, 73, 76, 81, 263, 273, 279, 345; background of, 63n3
Satanta, Mark, 63n3
Sayre, Okla., 120
Scabby Man, 324, 327
Schmalsle, William, 227 & n41, 383
Schnabler, W., 387
Schuller, Jonathon, 387

Scott, Hugh L., 121, 175, 219, 222, 292n2, 294; background of, 291–92; statements of, 292–94
Seafferman, H., 389
Sebrowski, Pvt., 106
Seger Colony, Ind. Terr., 53n3
Sergeant Major Creek, Ind. Terr., 20, 25, 121, 214, 220, 235, 235n48, 259, 313, 315, 316
Set-Maunte (Bear Paw), background of, 345
Seventh Cavalry, 9, 39, 66, 71, 104, 120, 176, 255, 256, 264, 278, 280; weapons of, 225n36
Seventh Cavalry Creek, 121, 124, 146
Seward, Lee I., 407
Sha-Pa-Shin-Ka (Little Bear), 391
Sharp Belly, 401
Sharpe, Cal, 70, 197, 393
Sharp Hair, 391
Sharp's Creek, Kans., 38
Shattuck, Okla., 10
Sheridan, Andrew, 146n15
Sheridan, Kans., 34, 36
Sheridan, Philip H., 8, 28, 30, 56, 76n14, 100, 104, 120, 126, 145, 146, 165, 175, 183, 212, 221, 234, 236, 238, 249, 254, 255, 257n17, 258, 261, 264, 266, 270, 283, 286, 287, 368; background of, 274–75; reports of, 275–81
Sherman, William, 7, 187, 252, 278, 281
She Wolf, 19, 44, 347n2, 356 & n3, 359 & n10, 358, 360
Shingled Hair, 348n5
Short, Oliver F., 329
Sioux Woman, 15, 427, 429
Sipes, John, account of, 330–31
Sitting Medicine (Young Little Robe), 369
Sitting With, 229n43
Skunk Creek, Ind. Terr., 182
Skunk Woman, 44, 149n17

Sky Walker, 75
Slim Face, 363 & n18
Slobaccus, Frederick, 393
Slurmielke, E., 389
Smith, Algernon E., 153, 240, 383; background of, 379–80
Smith, Andrew C., 224 & n33, 234
Smith, E., 387
Smith, H. Walworth, 152, 243, 245 & n6, 384; background of, 380
Smith, Jack, 45n3, 284n4
Smith, John S., 45, 283, 234n4; background of, 45n3
Smoke (Smoky), 214n15, 292 & n3, 351n2, 352n4. *See also* Tobacco
Smoky Hill River, Kans., 7, 46
Smoky Hill Road, 8, 35
Smoky Hill Trail, 28
Snake Woman, 283n1, 317
Snisait, F., 387
Snow, Clyde, 314n2, 423n3, 424, 425n6
Solomon Fork, Kans., 5
Solomon River, Kans., 8, 33, 47, 48, 52, 163n2, 271, 281
Solomon Valley, 227n39
Sootell, J, 387
Soule, William S., 363n18
South Canadian River, Ind. Terr., 336
Spanish Fort, Tex., 35
Sparrow Hawk Woman, 54, 318n5, 427, 430
Spirit Woman, 338n1
Spotted Horse, 357n6
Spotted Wolf, 276n1, 430
Sprague, D. J., 389
Spring Grass (Meotzi), 44, 231n45
Stair, William C., 186n6
Standifer, Mrs. J. E., 407
Standing Bird, 330, 331n3
Standing Bull, Clyde, 295 & n1, 296
Standing Out (Sun Bear), 324n4, 400, 401
Standing Water, Sam, 299

Stands in Timber, John, 363n18
Star, 428
Statue, 324 & n4, 326
Sternberg, George M., 103 & n25
Stewart, Milton, background of, 264; letter from, 264–66
Stilwell, Frank C., 185n3
Stilwell, Simpson E. ("Jack"), 185; background of, 185n3
Stobias, Pvt., 197
Stone Calf, 301, 369n1
Stone Forehead, 320n10, 321
Strahle, Conrad, 395
Straight Line, 391
Striking Eagle, 75n12
Strong City, Okla., 225n35, 332n1
Sturgis, Samuel D., 157
Sully, Alfred, 8, 33, 37, 101, 126, 164, 165, 168; background of, 101n3
Sumner, Edwin V., 5, 54
Sun Bear, 324n4, 400, 401
Sweetwater Creek, Tex., 31, 185
Swielk, H., 389
Swift Hawk Laying Down, 427

Tahnea (Measure Woman), 331n3
Tah-tah-tois-neh (William Guerrier, Sr.'s wife), 50
Tall Bear, 398, 399, 401
Tall Bull, 362n16
Tall Hat (Tall War Bonnet), 397
Tall Owl, 397
Tall White Man, 397
Tall Wolf, 48, 362n16
Tally, 392
Taylor, William, 387
Thoburn, Joseph, 29, 124, 365, 366, 407; background, of, 124n21
Thompson, William B., 12, 17, 20, 61, 94, 111, 114, 117, 130, 138, 139, 152, 207, 208, 225, 228, 243, 385; background of, 380
Thompson & McGee, 37

Thunder Cloud, 52n1
Tobacco, 214n15, 261 & n23, 310n16, 319, 399, 400, 401
Toch-E-Me-Ah (Emily Clark), 202
Tooney, B., 388
Topeka, Kans., 9
Touching the Sky, 358n9
Trails the Enemy, 19, 44, 63n3, 260n20, 356 & n2, 357 & n5, 400; background of, 345; narrative of, 346–48
Trotter (Trots as He Travels), 239, 391
Turkey Creek, Kans., 36
Turner, G. Frank, 215 & n17
Turner, H. Frank, 224 & n34, 234, 305 & n6, 311
Turner, Mrs., 120n19
Turner, William E., 305n6
Turtle Woman, 303n4
Twin Butte Creek, Kans., 34
Twin Knolls, 18, 220, 222, 226, 308 & n12
Tyler, Leonard, 430

Usher, Ambrose, 271n2

Vanousky, Erwin, 193, 197, 201n4, 393

Wah-Hunk-Ah (Lightning Bug), 391
Wah-Lah-Who-Ah (Draw Them Up), 391
Wah-Sa-Ke (Hard Rope), 391
Wahsha-Pa-Skunk-Ah (Little Back Bear), 391
Walker, James, 388
Walking Woman (Afraid of Beaver's daughter), 301, 327n9
Walking Woman (Black Kettle's daughter), 326n8, 429
Walks Different (Cut Arm), 330n1
Walks with His Toes Turned Out (Medicine Arrow), 362n16

Wallingford, David W., 36, 152, 243, 385; background of, 380–81
Walnut Creek, Kans., 46
Ward, Seth, 50
Warren, Henry, 63n3
Warren, J. H., 408
Washita Battlefield Monument, 292 & n2, 306 & n8, 314 & n3
Washita Battlefield National Historic Site, 11, 12, 31, 206n5, 357n4
Washita River, 9, 10, 11, 12, 17, 21, 27, 31, 40, 57, 67, 70, 72, 98, 102, 109, 110, 119, 120, 121, 124, 139, 156, 158, 166, 168, 182, 185n2, 190, 191, 208, 212, 215, 220, 222, 224, 225, 227, 228, 235, 261, 264, 276, 279, 281, 299, 303, 314, 315, 324, 325n6, 328, 332, 333, 350, 359
Washita River Bridge (at Custees Crossing), 299, 305n7, 314 & n2, 408, 424n5
Weir, Thomas B., 25, 91, 153, 163, 243, 246, 249, 384; background of, 381
We-Sah-Pa-Sha (Patient Man), 391
Wesner, Betty, 18, 224
Wesner, Dale, 299
Wesner, John, 206n5, 220n25, 224n34, 299, 423
West, Robert M., 13, 15, 24, 25, 26, 130, 138, 139, 153, 168, 192, 243, 384; background of, 381–82
Weston, J. F., 256
Wetzel, H., 388
Wheeler, Homer W., 147 & n16, 302n3, 331n3
Whirlwind, 276n1, 290n3, 302n3, 318 & n4, 319, 332n1
White, Sarah C., 277 & n4, 343
White Antelope, 46; background of, 46n6
White Bear (Cheyenne), 362n16

White Bear (Pilan), 210n9, 398, 399
White Bear (Satanta), 63n3
White Beaver, 397
White Bird, 369n1
White Buffalo Woman (Black Kettle's daughter), 317, 318n2, 428
White Buffalo Woman (Little Rock's sister), 19, 20, 44, 258n19, 310n17, 357, 357n7, 358; background of, 357n6
White Buffalo Woman (Red Bird's sister), 330, 331
White Shield (Gentle Horse), 318 & n5, 319, 430
White Shield (Red Moon's son-in-law), 229n43, 369n1
White Shield (Wind Woman's son), 430
Wichita Mountains, Ind. Terr., 73, 98
Williams, Daniel, 388
Williams, James H., 292n2, 297n3, 299, 305n7, 424n5
Williams, James M., 69, 393
Williams, Thomas Benton, 318n1, 320n10
Williams Channel, 299
Willow Creek, Ind. Terr., 10
Willow Springs Station, Colo. Terr., 36
Wilson, Sgt., 40
Wind Woman, 430
Wolf (Iron Teeth), 430, 431
Wolf (Osage), 391
Wolf Belly Woman, 302n3; background of, 341; statement of, 341–42

Wolf Creek, Ind. Terr., 9, 133, 134, 145, 164, 165, 181n3
Wolf Ear, 397
Wolf Looking Back, 303n4, 306
Wood, 75n13
Wooden Legs, 321
Woodworth, J. H., 35
Wright, J., 389
Wright, Robert M., 33, 135
Wynkoop, Edward W., 44, 45, 55, 163, 252, 282, 361n15, 366, 368; background of, 45n1

Yates, George W., 26, 67, 151, 163, 164n5, 186, 243, 256, 385; background of, 339, 382; statement of, 339–40
Yellow Bear, 41, 76n14, 235n50, 276n1
Yellow Calf, 46n6
Yellow Haired Woman, 329
Yellow Hair Woman, 362n18
Yellow Horse, 361n15
Yellow Wolf, 45n3, 229n43, 284n4
Yellow Woman, 429
Yocucy Creek, Kans., 39
Yoo-nap (Trails the Enemy), 345
Young, Mrs., 120n19
Young Bear, 334
Young Bird, Mrs., background, 332; narrative, 332–34
Young Black Bird, 430
Young Black Kettle, 313 & n3
Young Little Beaver, 303n4
Young Lone Wolf, 70n7

Zimmer, George, 394